Georges de La Tour

Jacques Thuillier

Georges de La Tour

Translated from the French by Fabia Claris

Flammarion

In affectionate homage to
Victoria Cabanel,
from her most admiring protégé

About the author
Jacques Thuillier (1928–2011) was an internationally renowned specialist on seventeenth-century art. He was a professor at the Sorbonne University in Paris and the University of Dijon, and an honorary professor of the Collège de France, and was a member of several cultural committees and commissions. He also organized a number of exhibitions on French painting. A prolific author, his many works include *History of Art: Architecture, Sculpture, Painting* (Flammarion, 2003), which earned the Grand Prix d'Histoire Chateaubriand. He received numerous distinctions during his illustrious career, including the Legion of Honor and the Order of Arts and Letters.

Design by Pascale Ogée
Copyediting by Miriam Rosen
Typesetting by P.F.C., Dole, France; additional typesetting by Nord Compo and by IGS, France
Digitized by IGS, France
Color Separation by Bussière Arts Graphiques, Paris
Printed in China by C&C Offset Printing Co., Ltd.

Originally published in French as *Georges de la Tour*

Previous English-language editions

This English-language edition

editions.flammarion.com

12 13 14 3 2 1

ISBN: 978-2-08-020145-4
Dépôt légal: 11/2012

CONTENTS

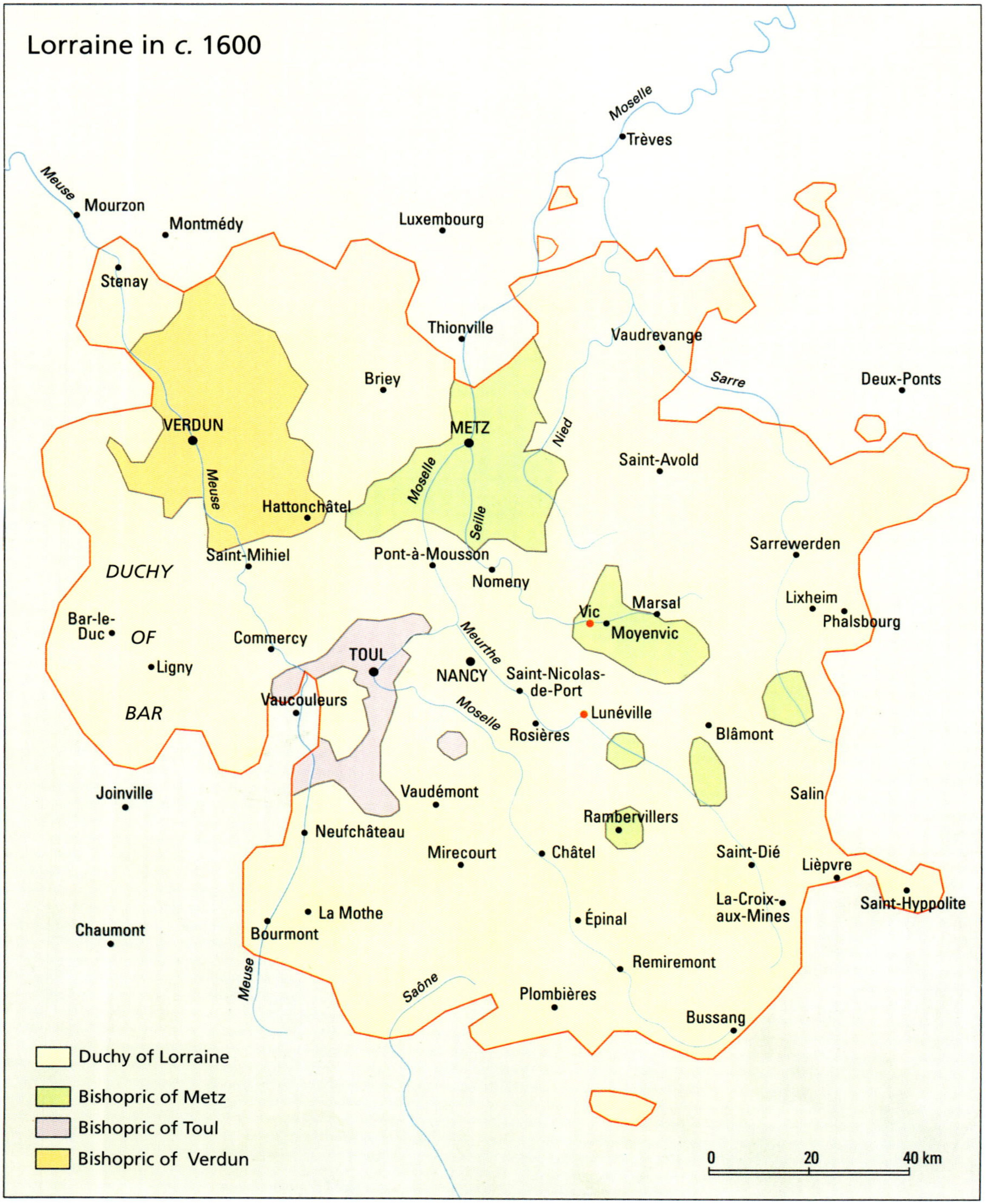

Lorraine in c. 1600
Moselle
Trèves
Meuse
Mourzon
Montmédy
Luxembourg
Stenay
Thionville
Vaudrevange
Sarre
Deux-Ponts
Briey
VERDUN
METZ
Nied
Saint-Avold
Meuse
Moselle
Hattonchâtel
Seille
Sarrewerden
Saint-Mihiel
Pont-à-Mousson
Nomeny
DUCHY
Lixheim
Phalsbourg
Marsal
Vic
Moyenvic
Bar-le-Duc
OF
Commercy
Meurthe
TOUL
Ligny
NANCY
Saint-Nicolas-de-Port
Vaucouleurs
Moselle
Lunéville
BAR
Rosières
Blâmont
Joinville
Vaudémont
Salin
Rambervillers
Neufchâteau
Mirecourt
Châtel
Saint-Dié
Lièpvre
La-Croix-aux-Mines
Saint-Hyppolite
La Mothe
Épinal
Chaumont
Bourmont
Remiremont
Meuse
Saône
Plombières
Bussang
Duchy of Lorraine
Bishopric of Metz
Bishopric of Toul
Bishopric of Verdun
0
20
40 km

INTRODUCTION

Georges de La Tour, though a seventeenth-century painter, is almost our contemporary. He did not enter history until 1863, on the day that Alexandre Joly, a scholar from Nancy, published a brief study of him in the *Journal de la Société d'Archéologie Lorraine* based on the local archives. He slipped unobtrusively into art history in 1915, when Hermann Voss tentatively attributed two paintings in the Nantes museum to him in the *Archiv für Kunstgeschichte.* In 1934 Paul Jamot and Charles Sterling included a number of his paintings in the exhibition entitled "Peintres de la Réalité" at the Orangerie in the Tuileries, which brought him to the attention of a public that was immediately captivated. He became one of the grand masters of French painting in 1948, when François-Georges Pariset defended his major thesis at the Sorbonne. It was not until 1972, when virtually all his surviving works were brought together in a monographic exhibition, once again at the Orangerie, that his true genius became fully apparent. Although 1993 marks the quadricentennial of La Tour's birth, it is barely in the last sixty years that he has had any real existence—that he has had a place in books, in people's minds, and in the ranks of the great masters.

He is now assured of immortality, returning to life after more than two centuries of almost total neglect. History may be able to do a great deal, but it cannot make up for the silence of several centuries.

"Master Georges La Tour, painter, renders himself odious to the people by the number of dogs he keeps, both greyhounds and spaniels, as if he were the local lord, hunting hares through the cultivated fields, trampling and spoiling them. . . ." So runs the only surviving contemporary description of La Tour (in a document dated 1646). It conjures up something of the man but has nothing to do with the artist. Other than this, virtually nothing has come down to us. We do not have a single letter, nothing more than the odd line penned at the bottom of a legal document or certificate. Not a single house where he once lived is still standing—such was the devastation war brought to Lorraine—not a single object which once belonged to him remains, nor a single likeness of him that is sure. None of his works has been found in its original location. There are no references to him in any letters or memoirs of the period. Only by going back to the French "primitives" do we find a similar dearth of information—and even then we have a known self-portrait of Jean Fouquet. What a contrast with the likes of Simon Vouet and Nicolas Poussin, not to mention the great names in Italian painting of the same generation!

Suffice it to say that we cannot talk about La Tour in the same way that we can of any other artist of the seventeenth century. It is absurd to suppose, as some critics would have us do, that there is a single art-historical method (theirs, of course) that we can apply, regardless of the subject, to reveal the secret of an individual artist's work. The subject must dictate the method. We cannot possibly approach a fifteenth-century master in the same way we do a painter who has left us a diary and sketchbooks; we cannot analyze the work of an artist like Masaccio in the same way we do that of Delacroix or Matisse. Even though La Tour was a contemporary of Poussin and Guercino, we cannot treat him as we treat them. Barring miracles, we will never have for La Tour the equivalent of Poussin's letters, which seem to summon up his very tone of voice, or that of Guercino's record book, which gives us a comprehensive list of his works, complete with dates and prices. In the case of La Tour, assertion and explanation have to give way more often than not to doubts, questions, and admissions of ignorance. If we are to avoid distorting a truth that is still vague and fragile about this artist only so recently restored to us, we must proceed with extreme caution, by the most roundabout means, and employ, so to speak, all the delicate subterfuge of devotion.

When an artist has disappeared in this way, almost without a trace, only through scholarship—and scholarship of the most rigorous kind—can we hope to salvage any vestige of truth. With La Tour, the process began only in 1863; it is just in the last half-century that it has really taken off, and it is not yet over. François-Georges Pariset led the way with his pioneering research, but new generations of

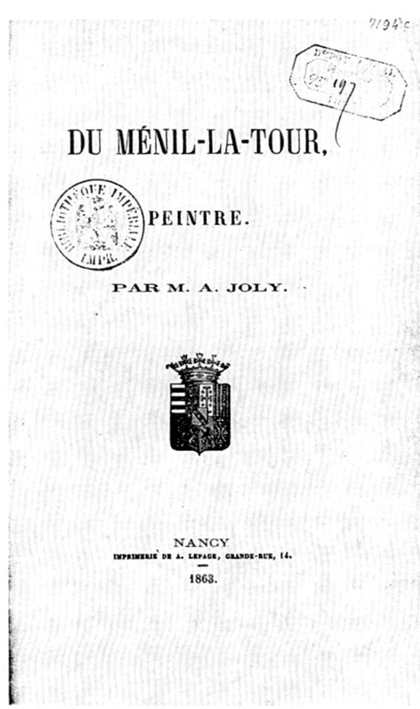
DU MÉNIL-LA-TOUR,

PEINTRE.

PAR M. A. JOLY.

NANCY
IMPRIMERIE DE A. LEPAGE, GRANDE-RUE, 14.
1863.

THE FIRST PUBLISHED STUDY OF LA TOUR: The article by architect Alexandre Joly published in the *Journal de la Société d'Archéologie Lorraine,* 1863 (Offprint).
Bibliothèque Nationale, Paris

scholars—Henri Tribout de Morembert, Michel Antoine, Michel Sylvestre, Anne Reinbold, Paulette Choné—showed that there were still major discoveries to be made. No one wanting to get a true picture of La Tour can avoid this irksome task: those who have tried to take shortcuts now appear to have been building castles in the sand. Brilliant and profound though their theories may have seemed, they have ultimately been refuted by the facts, and sometimes made to look utterly ridiculous.

Unsound reasoning always leads to unsound conclusions, but the reverse is not automatically true: it is perfectly possible to reason clearly and still go astray if the facts are unreliable. We must start, therefore, by establishing the facts as solidly as we can. I hope I may be forgiven for stressing them in this book, and even for assembling at the end the basic known facts, however trivial, which allow us to piece together a picture of La Tour. The reader is not expected to plow through these documents; they are included primarily for reference and as supporting evidence. I hope they may also help future La Tour scholars.

We have to be similarly cautious in that other fundamental, and all-too-often overlooked area of research, which might be called the scholarship of the eye. A group of pictures has gradually come to be accepted as constituting La Tour's oeuvre. However, it is clear that the composition of this corpus has changed considerably in the space of the last few decades, and paintings that we now regard as key were long ignored or dismissed in favor of others which we currently reject. The famous Chancelade *Christ*, for instance, was unanimously accepted immediately after the Second World War, as were several works painted by Trophime Bigot or in his style. A number of visitors to the Orangerie in 1972 complained of not finding the *St. Jerome* from the Church of Saint-Séverin included in the exhibition. By the same token, we received a number of letters rebuking us for having tastelessly if not criminally exhibited under the name of La Tour such daylight pictures as the Nantes *Hurdy-Gurdy Player* and the Grenoble and Stockholm versions of *St. Jerome* when the master of "night" scenes could not possibly have painted works of such extraordinary light and draftsmanship. Again, until the 1972 exhibition, the first version of *The Cheat*, although reproduced by François-Georges Pariset, was not recognized as one of La Tour's major works; only its subsequent purchase by the Kimbell Museum fully resolved the question. It was also in the seventies that a certain English historian, not devoid of humor, had a field day in the newspapers and on television claiming that he could name the forger who had sat down sometime in the 1930s and painted *The Fortune Teller* acquired by the Metropolitan Museum. There were enough people ready to believe his story for the illustrious museum to deem it necessary to make a public protest, and for Pierre Rosenberg to point out in *The Burlington Magazine* that the painting's history could be traced back as far as 1879.

There has been broad consensus since 1972 on at least thirty canvases, some of which, moreover, are signed. The discussion is far from closed, however. La Tour almost certainly painted between four and five hundred works, many of which became immediately famous. Only four of the lost compositions were engraved, but a great many were copied. To understand La Tour, we have to examine this hinterland, piece together the facts, try to establish dates, and in so doing, begin, tentatively at least, to fill in some of the glaring gaps that remain in his oeuvre. This is a complex process, as will be obvious later. It may well be that in the case of an artist like La Tour, art history has to resort to techniques more akin to those we normally think of as reserved for archaeology.

What of La Tour the man? Should we try to discover what he was like? There are no known portraits of him, as I have said, and a single portrait would have told us more than any amount of extrapolating from the scanty information we do have about his life. These are almost exclusively of an adminstrative order, and though invaluable when it comes to establishing points of chronology, they tell us nothing about his character. Benedict Nicolson used to say that the only discernible trace left behind by his long study of La Tour and his many voyages to Lorraine was a stack of parking tickets. We should not delude ourselves: all too often the traces of La Tour that have come down to us are not much better. Even when we come across a document that seems more explicit, we should beware. Especially because Georges de La Tour was an artist, and the artist is often not the same as, and is indeed sometimes even diametrically opposed to the man, subject as he is to social constraints. And

ARCHIV FÜR KUNSTGESCHICHTE

HERAUSGEBER: DETLEV V. HADELN, HERMANN VOSS, MORTON BERNATH

VERLAG VON E. A. SEEMANN IN LEIPZIG. — II. JAHRGANG, LIEFERUNG 3–4: TAFEL 121–160

121–122. **GEORGES DU MESNIL DE LA TOUR. Der Engel erscheint dem hl. Joseph. – Petrus und die Magd.**

Leinwand, hoch 93 cm, breit 81 cm und hoch 120 cm, breit 160 cm.
Nantes, Museum.

123. **DERSELBE. Geburt Christi.**

Leinwand, hoch 76 cm., breit 91 cm.
Rennes, Museum.

Die beiden aus der Sammlung Cacault (1810) stammenden Nachtstücke in Nantes tragen rechts oben bzw. unten die Signatur G. de La Tour, auf Tafel 122 mit dem Zusatz: in. et fec. und dem Datum 1650. Als der Urheber wurde im Katalog von 1854 der Pastellmaler Maurice Quentin de La Tour (geb. 1704!) genannt, während der Katalog von 1913 einen Künstler G. de La Tour als nicht nachweisbar ansieht. – Über Georges de La Tour (fälschlich öfter als Claude d. L. T. aufgeführt) lassen sich aus den Urkunden von Lunéville folgende Notizen zusammenstellen: Heirat vor dem Jahre 1621, demgemäß sind als Zeit der Geburt die letzten Jahre des 16. Jahrhunderts anzusehen; Tod 30. Januar 1652. Eine Geburt Christi ist von 1644 datiert, ein hl. Alexis 1648 für den Gouverneur von Nancy gemalt; von mehreren Darstellungen des hl. Sebastian eine im Jahre 1649 entstanden. Auch eine Verleugnung Petri wird erwähnt; und durchweg findet sich als stilistisches Kennzeichen die Nachtbeleuchtung hervorgehoben („Dans une nuit" oder „dans un clair-obscur"). Seine Meisterschaft in dieser Darstellungsweise verschaffte ihm Aufträge von seiten des Herzogs Karl IV. von Lothringen und Ludwigs XIII.

Die Übereinstimmung dieser Angaben mit den Gegenständen, der Signatur, dem Datum und der Kunstweise der Bilder in Nantes erlaubt uns, den Lunéviller La Tour als ihren Urheber zu bestimmen. Wir lernen in ihm einen Künstler kennen, der die Tradition der Helldunkelstücke des Caravaggio-Kreises, besonders des Gerard Honthorst und seiner Schule, in etwas provinzieller, aber eigenartiger und persönlicher Weise fortführt. Die starre Behandlung der Linie und die harte Zeichnung der Glieder seiner Figuren findet ihren Ausgleich in einem ganz wundervollen, obgleich ebenfalls herben und eigenwilligen Kolorit, in dem ein Zinnober und Lila dominieren. An die Bilder von Nantes schließt sich die Geburt Christi in Rennes als in allen Stücken stilverwandt an. Sie war 1793 Schalcken zugeschrieben und trägt seit 1854 den Namen Le Nain. Trotz kleiner Ähnlichkeiten mit manchen Arbeiten der 3 Brüder weicht sie doch in den entscheidenden Stilmerkmalen von diesen ab, was L. Gonse, der an Le Nains Autorschaft festhält, durch Annahme verschiedener Stilphasen im Schaffen dieses Künstlers erklären möchte. Um so schlagender ist in jedem Punkte die Verwandtschaft mit den Arbeiten La Tours, von dem überdies überliefert ist, daß er die „Nativité" öfter als Helldunkelstück dargestellt hat. Eine verwandte Kompo-

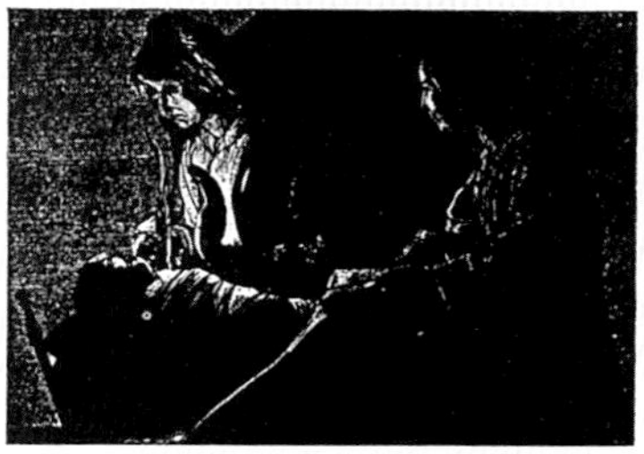

sition, die zweifellos ebenfalls auf ein Bild La Tours zurückgeht, ist mir durch einen Stich bekannt geworden, der den Namen des Jacques Callot, allerdings fälschlich, trug, aber der ganzen Behandlung nach doch aus seinem Kreise herrühren muß. (Siehe Textabbildung.) Der am Herzogshofe in Nancy tätige Stecher und unser Lunéviller Maler waren als Lothringer engere Landsleute und zudem Zeitgenossen. Auch bei Callot finden wir hier und da Versuche, Nachtstimmungen zu geben (M. 65 und 666), deren Zusammenhang mit Italien von mir im Repert. für Kunstwissenschaft XXIII, S. 217 dargelegt worden ist. Es ist denkbar und selbst wahrscheinlich, daß La Tour von dieser Seite Anregungen erhalten hat, oder daß Wechselwirkungen bestanden haben.

Literatur: Réunion des Sociétés des Beaux-Arts, Vol. IX, 126, XXIII, 493, XXVII, 680. – M. A. Joly, Dumesnil-La-Tour, peintre. Nancy 1863. – Kataloge

THE DECISIVE ARTICLE IN THE REDISCOVERY OF LA TOUR:
Hermann Voss's analysis of three panels in the *Archiv für Kunstgeschichte*, 1915.
Bibliothèque d'Art et d'archéologie Jacques Doucet, Paris

these were troubled times. I quoted earlier the only surviving contemporary description of La Tour. It comes from a petition addressed to the duke of Lorraine, then in exile and in open war with the king of France, by the people of Lunéville, at a time when La Tour, flattered by Louis XIII, had almost certainly thrown in his lot with the French. There would probably have been a parallel petition to the king of France, and if ever it turns up, it may well paint him in a very different light. Accounts like this have their limitations and cannot be taken at face value.

All of these considerations have led me to focus great attention on the environment, especially because of the very particular one in which La Tour lived.

It cannot be stressed enough that La Tour was not a French artist. He was a Lorrainese artist, a Lorrainese artist at a time when the course of Lorraine's history was not entirely the same as that of the kingdom of France. La Tour was born in the bishopric of Metz, where, it is true, the French king's influence had been predominant for several decades. In Rome, however, where he seems almost certainly to have gone, he would have been part of the "Lorrainese nation," although this did of course have very close ties, notably through language, with the "French nation." He worked as a painter in Lunéville, which belonged to the duke of Lorraine, and he witnessed the ruling prince's attempts to gain the support of the German emperor in order to escape from the clutches of the French. Most important, he lived through the terrible tragedies that beset Lorraine, plunged by the duke's reckless political gambles into the very heart of the Thirty Years' War. In this respect his experience was entirely different from that of Vouet or Poussin, for example, who were his exact contemporaries but had only indirect knowledge of these disastrous events that tested the country to the limits of human endurance. In a sense, as a friend and indeed a relative of Alphonse de Rambervillers, and as someone who had lived in both Rome and Paris, La Tour belonged to that great republic of letters and the arts then existing in Europe that transended national borders. His roots, however, were in this ancient land wedged between the Holy Roman Empire and the kingdom of France, a land proud of its long history but whose great turmoil he was soon to witness, sometimes benefiting from it, but undoubtedly suffering as well.

These circumstances help to explain the peculiar resonance of his painting and its tension, unmatched even by the penetrating genius of Poussin in Rome or the gravity of Tournier in Toulouse. There can be few artists whose work springs more directly from a particular time and place. Some people may feel that I dwell excessively on the international situation or on the special nature of Lorraine and of its institutions, customs, and ways of thinking. With La Tour, however, such insights are vital. I have no doubt that our understanding of La Tour has been enhanced by René Taveneaux's study of religious life in Lorraine, by Guy Cabourdin's study of everyday life and attitudes, and by the various pieces of information, often trivial in appearance, but in fact crucial in helping to piece together the creative context of La Tour's work, similarly provided by François-Georges Pariset, Henri Tribout de Morembert, Michel Sylvestre, the canon Jacques Choux, Marie-Thérèse Aubry, Hubert Collin, Anne Reinbold, and Paulette Choné. We are deeply indebted to them all.

Anyone who engages in the long and arduous task of research sooner or later has to confront the limits of interpretation. Just where do you draw the line? How far do you go with the bold and uncompromising methods that art historians are so often and sometimes so peremptorily urged to adopt?

Not so very long ago, we were being told that the key to the mystery of all artistic creation lay in what is often called psychoanalysis but which is generally no more than Freudian psychology. The imposing and very artificial Freudian edifice has since collapsed of its own weight, in the manner of the Berlin Wall, and the few survivors of the old school are too busy clearing away the rubble to worry about artistic exegesis just yet. Besides, the idea of taking a phantom like La Tour, whose face, voice, and life were all utterly unknown, and laying him down on a couch frankly defied belief. No one has ever taken seriously the revelations that Freud managed to wring from Leonardo or the American rearguard from poor Cézanne. Trying to get La Tour to confess his libido was worse than absurd.

The same applies to attempts to interpret the painter in the light of various simplistic economic and sociological theories. La Tour does not appear to have been a conspicuously ordinary or easy character when alive. Dead and laid out for dissection, he continues to prove intractable. On the strength of his uncompromisingly realist paintings of peasants and beggars, some people would have promoted this baker's son to a

Left:
Claude Deruet. *The Rape of the Sabine Women.*
Alte Pinakothek, Munich

Right:
Jean le Clerc. *Group of Musicians by Night.*
Alte Pinakothek, Munich

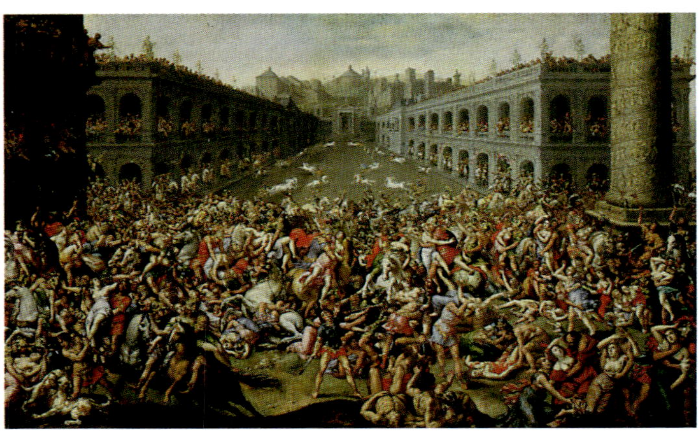

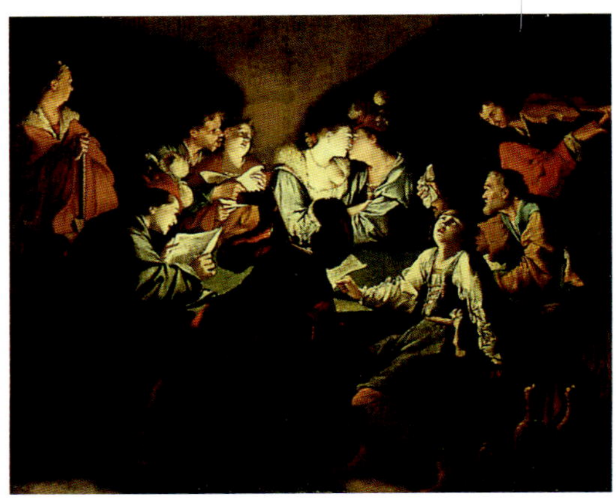

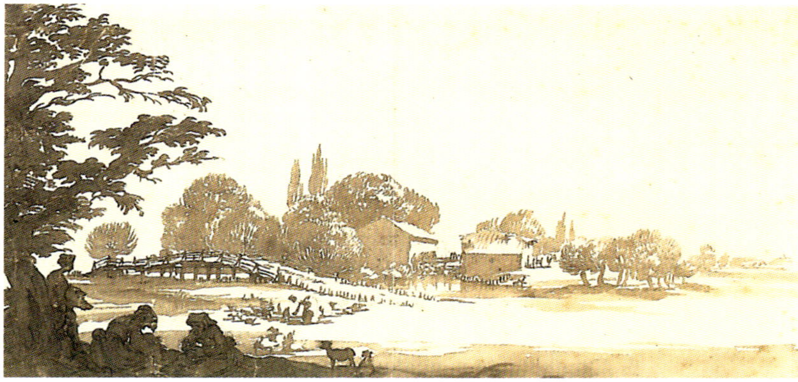

Jacques Callot. *Landscape.*
Black chalk and bistre wash.
Teyler Museum, Haarlem

champion of the peasant proletariat; it was the fashion at the time to take the periodic little upheavals that occurred in the provinces, magnify them, and set them against the oppression of the "aristocracy" and the selfishness of the "middle classes." The discovery of the 1646 document quoted above soon discredited such attempts: the would-be champion of the proletariat played at being a lord. Any lingering idea of La Tour as a socialist painter was put to rest once and for all by the discovery of another document that showed him giving a local peasant a rain of blows with his stick. Another great idea was to present him as a defender of Lorrainese culture resisting its annexation by the French monarchy, and therefore deliberately eschewing Parisian styles of painting. Unfortunately, Dom Calmet had already mentioned that La Tour, with regrettable opportunism, had presented one *St. Sebastian* to the duke and another to Louis XIII.

Even with less primitive theories, critics ran up against problems. Here was an artist whose inspiration seemed to spring from his environment. From there, it was only one step further to explain his style of painting and choice of subjects in terms of the social and economic conditions in Lorraine. Those who tried to do so had to abandon the idea. There were three other important artists in Lorraine in La Tour's day: Callot, Le Clerc, and Deruet. All four artists came from very similar backgrounds, all four went to Italy, and all four shared the same patrons and clients and had broadly parallel careers. It would be hard, however, to imagine four more different worlds than those they conjure up, four styles of expression more disparate in every way, be it line, color, or representation of space. Once again La Tour defies categorization. He makes a mockery of our long-cherished pigeonholing of "baroque" painting with the monarchy and Catholicism, and of "classical" painting with the middle classes and their often Protestant or Jansenist leanings. No one could possibly term the very Catholic Lorraine of the dukes "classical" or "middle class." By the same token, *The Newborn Child* could not be more removed from baroque lyricism or *St. Sebastian* from the pathos of a Bernini.

For my part, I am not going to propound one of those wonderful theories that neatly reduces a body of work to a formula and makes an artist into a symbol. Art history should have nothing to do with such arid simplifications, even when it aspires to a history of thought. The case of Georges de La Tour recalls art history to its true purpose and its only valid method: to concentrate on the artist's work, accepting it for the irreducible entity it is, while diversifying the approaches, none of them capable of elucidating the mystery of his art, but all nevertheless useful in shedding some light on it, and steering clear of causal explanations, which at best serve only to break the work down into a series of influences or mechanical factors.

My hope is that by the end of this book the reader will be more interested in La Tour than at the start, but will find him more difficult to understand. Through all this documentary evidence, hopefully as accurate and reliable as possible, and this range of different approaches, intended to be both prudent and varied, I have sought to make La Tour's genius more obvious and less explicable than before. I will be satisfied if at the end of it all, after so many pages and so many facts, the mystery of Georges de La Tour, like that of all great masters, appears more fascinating and more impenetrable than ever.

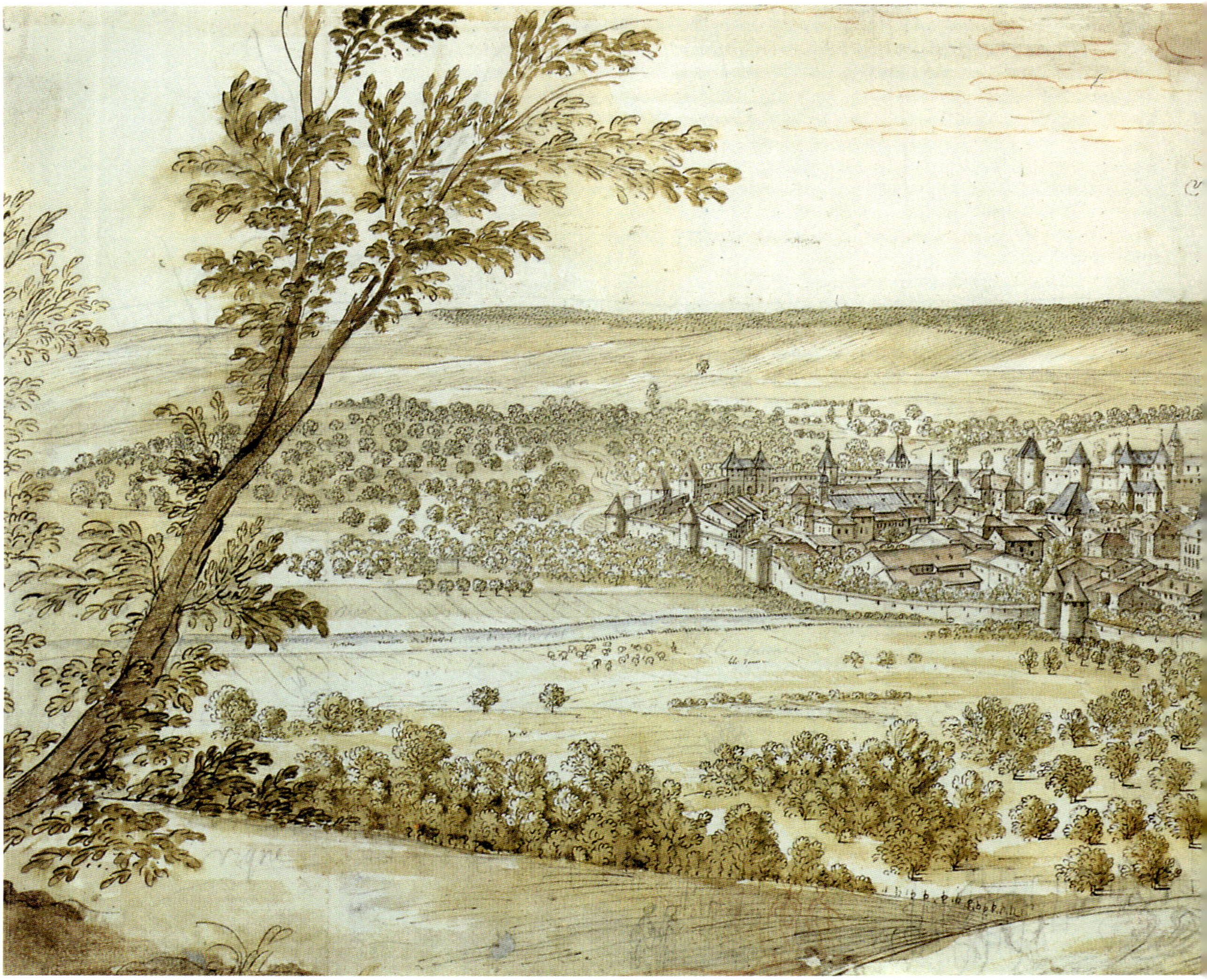

A YOUNG PAINTER FROM VIC

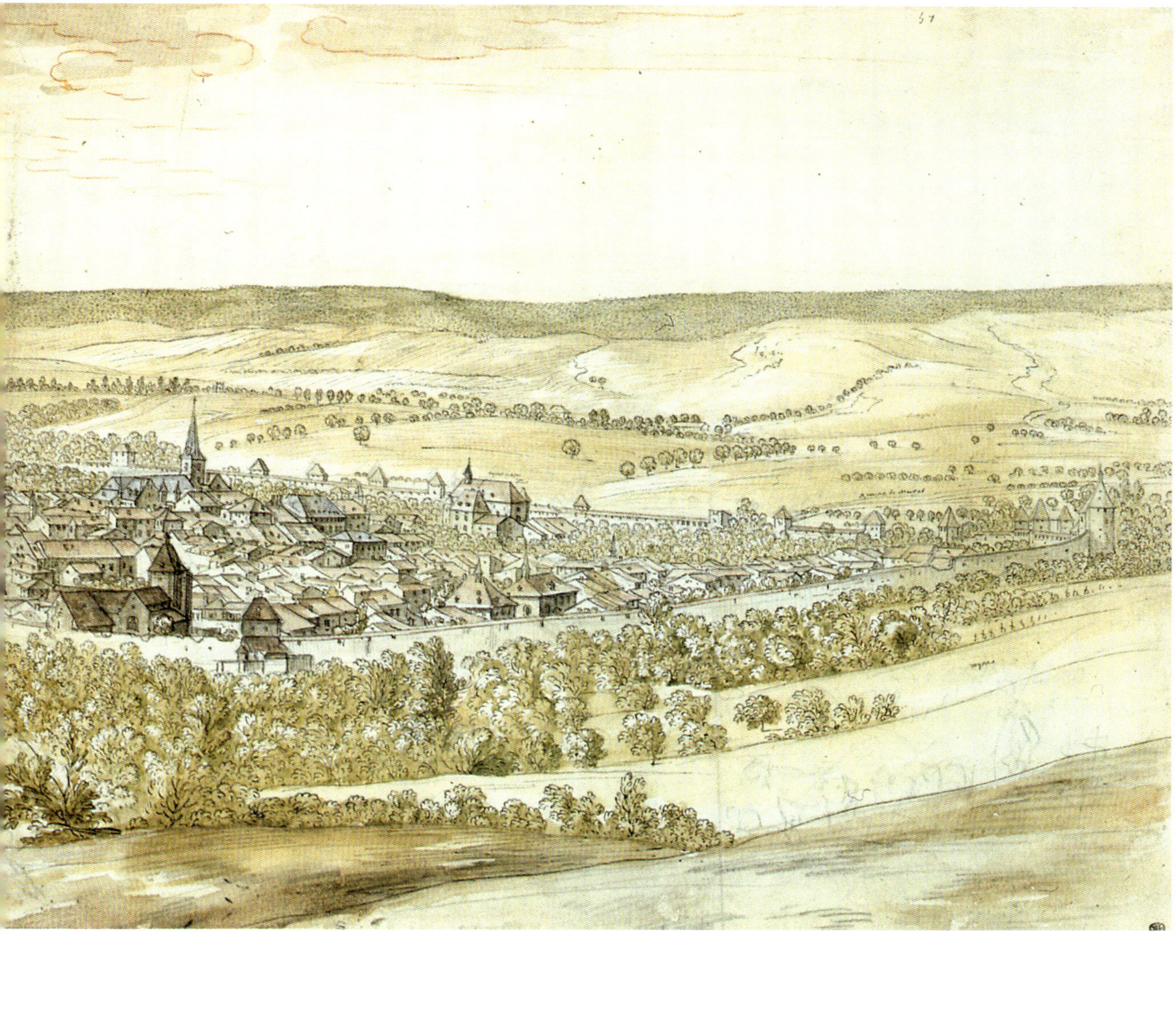

Georges de La Tour was born in Vic-sur-Seille in Lorraine in 1593. This is one of the few facts that art history has been able to establish with certainty, though belatedly and not without a certain amount of difficulty. None of the very meager early sources specifies a date. Dom Calmet speaks in his *Bibliothèque Lorraine,* written in 1751, of a "Claude du Ménil de La Tour," born in Lunéville. For the first study devoted to the artist, published in 1863, Alexandre Joly chose the title "Du Mesnil-La-Tour, Painter." Hermann Voss, tentatively attributing two paintings to him for the first time in 1915, refers to him as "George Du Mesnil de La Tour." Even as late as 1934, when the painter from Lorraine stole the show at the great "Peintres de la Réalité" exhibition, Charles Sterling opened his introductory essay to the catalogue with the words: "The place and date of this artist's birth are unknown." In fact, his baptism was recorded not at Lunéville but at Vic, and the entry in the register for 1593 reads: "George, son of Jean de La Tour baker and Sybille his wife, was baptized on March 14. Godfather Jean Desboeufs haberdasher. Godmother Pentecoste wife of Nicolas Le Meusnier, all from Vic." We know, then, that the painter was called simply Georges de La Tour, that he was the son of a baker in Vic, and that if indeed he was baptized on 14 March 1593, he may well have been born on the thirteenth.

So much for an initial certainty. But what did it mean to be born in Lorraine at the beginning of 1593, four centuries ago? What would a small town like Vic have been like to look at and live in at that time? Can we draw on recent memory and long-held attitudes that still link us with that time in order to understand it? We can, by sketching out some important features, provide a picture of the Lorraine region where the baker's son grew up and the artist subsequently practiced. We no longer believe, as was sometimes naively maintained in the nineteenth century, that genius is the product of a particular race, place, and time. Nevertheless, a knowledge of the place and circumstances in which an artist's work was produced can, if not explain it, at least throw some light on it. A tragedy was soon to be played out in this theater, one of the most violent tragedies of the century, which was to sweep a whole population along with it and have a direct bearing on the course of La Tour's life.

THE WORLD OF LORRAINE

Maurice Barrès, who was born in Lorraine, writes in his *Cahiers* in 1901: "I say to the compilers of dictionaries: 'I forbid you to call Claude Gellée a French painter, Callot a French printmaker, etc.' " Had he known of Georges de La Tour, he would undoubtedly have included his name in the list. Lorraine at the end of the sixteenth century was not yet a part of France, and the course of Georges de La Tour's career was not exactly that of a French painter.

To understand this situation and to avoid oversimplification, we have to go a long way back to Lorraine's origins, for Lorraine is a product of history. It has no natural boundaries, or even the kind of geographical unity inherent in other regions. It owes its character to a long succession of trials and dangers. The region first began to take shape under Roman rule when the far-flung "province" of Reims, Belgian Gaul, was divided into two parts, and the "First Belgium" came into being with Trèves as its capital, and Metz, Verdun, and Toul as major cities. After centuries of prosperity and catastrophes, the heirs of Clovis incorporated the area into the newly formed region of Austrasia, which extended as far as Thuringia and Vienna, and from that time on, Lorraine was to gravitate naturally toward the Holy Roman Empire. Another fateful step was taken in 843 with the Treaty of Verdun, which gave Lothair both Italy and the lands traversed by the Meuse and the Rhine, and which revived this ancient Gallo-Roman's attraction region to the south and in particular to Rome. This newly created kingdom of Lotharingia was already something of a buffer state between Germania and Frankish Gaul. The bitter conflict that was to manifest itself with such dire consequences in La Tour's day was inherent in Lorraine's very beginnings.

Lotharingia originally extended from Brabant to Basel, but a series of territorial divisions soon began to reduce it to "Haute Lorraine," a multiplicity of feudal states more or less affiliated with the Holy Roman Empire occupying the area of the Meuse and Moselle rivers between Franche-Comté and the bishopric of Liège. It was only with

Preceding double page:
Israël Sylvestre. *A View of Vic in the 17th Century.* Watercolor.
Cabinet des Dessins, Musée du Louvre, Paris

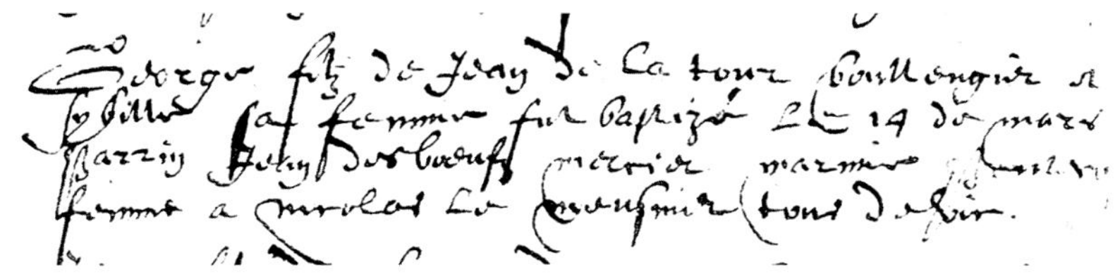

Record of Georges de La Tour's baptism in Vic, 14 March 1593.
Parish records, Municipal Archives, Vic

the union of the territories of the dukes of Lorraine and Bar during the fifteenth century that a single state of any power reemerged, enabling René II to resist the covetous ambitions of both Charles the Bold and Louis XI. From then on, anyone in Europe would have to reckon with the duke of Lorraine, who was simultaneously beginning to distance himself from the Holy Roman Empire. As the duchy began to assert itself, however, it became clear that Lorraine's future as an independent state would depend on maintaining a shrewd policy of neutrality, or at least of balance, between its powerful neighbors whose battle for supremacy was soon to dominate the European stage.

René II never succeeded in winning over the cathedral cities of Metz, Toul, and Verdun, which were firmly entrenched in their ancient traditions. His failure was costly: in 1552, while Charles V was preoccupied with troubles of his own, the king of France, Henri II, seized his chance and, backed by the Protestant princes of Germany, marched into all three cities. Charles V rushed to Metz with sixty thousand men but had to abandon the siege three months later. France now had a foothold in the heart of Lorraine and was in position not only to prevent the emperor's armies from marching to Paris but also to keep an eye on the duke. Just when Lorraine was assuming the form of a modern state, the duchy was already doomed.

In a sense the ruling family was aware of this fact. The duke of Lorraine, a reigning duke like those of Tuscany and Savoy, coveted a crown. He realized, however, that his neighbors would always be too powerful for him to be able to seize any of their land to expand his duchy and wield the influence he needed in Europe. He used his strategic position instead to negociate a series of advantageous marriages, and his family was soon represented in almost every Catholic court. The assumption seemed to be that a crown was more likely to come their way by inheritance than by turning the duchy into a kingdom. They were right: by 1580 the duke of Lorraine was in a position to claim the title to the French throne. Had it not been for the future Henri IV's recantation of the Protestant faith, he might well have been successful. Later years were to see the Lorraine dynasty foresake Nancy in favor first of the grand duchy of Tuscany, and then of the Austro-Hungarian Empire. That day had not yet dawned, however, and the duchy's future was impossible to imagine. In 1593, when La Tour was born, Charles III had been duke of Lorraine since 1545, ruling with equal measures of caution and ambition. He was soon forced to abandon all hope of becoming king of France, however, and a succession of bad harvests from 1592 to 1595 made for a number of difficult years. Things quickly picked up after that, and Lorraine entered the most glorious period in its history.

The vicissitudes of history had gradually provided the region with the identity that nature had denied it. The people of Lorraine had a strong sense of being a "nation," and this sense was even more powerful than their deep-rooted attachment to the ducal family. In foreign eyes as well, whether in Madrid or Rome, Florence or Vienna, although most of its population spoke French, it was most definitely not to be confused with France. In Lorraine itself, however, the problem was more complicated.

As a result of its checkered history and the lack of a strong unifying force, Lorraine had become a collection of disparate feudal entities that were virtually impossible for the duke to alter, each with its own constitution, obligations, and prerogatives, both material and spiritual. On a political level, what we call Lorraine then included the duchy itself, with Nancy as its capital, the duchy of Bar, half of which was subinfeudated (the "Barrois mouvant") and the other not, and the Trois-Evêchés, or "Three Bishoprics" (Verdun, Toul, Metz), each with its own ruling bishop empowered to mint coins and administer justice, not to mention a host of little enclaves, principalities, and domains that were all more or less independent. The duke had sovereign power in his own duchy and in the duchy of Bar but was himself answerable to the imperial Diet and had to pay tribute to the king of France for the half that was subinfeudated. The king also had a firm footing in the Three Bishoprics, although, in theory at least, this did not undermine the bishops' power. The towns constituted another important force: many were fortified, and their aldermen were very attached to their traditional privileges. To make matters worse, Nancy did not not have a bishop. The dukes had failed to persuade the Pope to grant them an episcopal see for their capital city, which, would have profoundly altered the ancient and almost hallowed territorial repartition. In terms of religion, therefore, the duke's subjects came under the authority of the three ruling bishops. The religious and political maps were far from the same, even in the Three Bishoprics, and a village belonging to the bishopric of Toul, could quite easily come under the religious authority of the bishop of Metz. All the various courts, taxes, rights, and rents were the product of time-honored traditions and often changed from one town to the next, and even within a single town from one side of the street to the other.

This dispersal of power increased the importance of the bureaucracy and provided the people with an invaluable safeguard against tyranny. At the same time, however, it hampered enterprise and progress. There were no great landed estates in Lorraine, nor any of the expansion of industry and commerce found in Flanders and the wealthy cities of Germany in the fifteenth century. Except in Saint-Nicolas-de-Port and especially Metz, Lorraine had none of that enterprising middle class that elsewhere was already dreaming of business operations on an international scale. At the close of the sixteenth century, however, this may have been more of an advantage than a handicap. Because the land was parceled up and given over to such a variety of uses—pasture, wheat fields, vineyards, forests, and salt, copper, and tin mines—Lorraine could more than supply all its own needs, despite the sharp rise in population. Since there was such a small privileged class, Protestantism never really made much impact, and the threat of religious strife that emerged in the towns, most notably in Metz, Toul, and Saint-Mihiel, was quickly laid to rest. As a result, Lorraine escaped the civil wars that devastated other parts of the empire and almost the whole of France. This in itself made the duchy seem a haven of prosperity and happiness during La Tour's childhood.

According to Charles de Lespine's famous account, written on a voyage to Frankfurt in 1612, "Lorraine is a very beautiful place, rich in all the necessities of life, for it lacks nothing. Indeed it can be said to have no need of its neighbors, having plentiful supplies of all manner of human comforts: copious stores of fine, beautiful wheat, vines that produce excellent wine, fruit of all kinds. It also has very beautiful ponds full of good fish, salt mines that yield His Highness a fine income, and silver, copper, tin, lead, and iron mines. . . . There is not a country in the world where one could be better received." The picture Lespine paints is one of a lush garden on France's doorstep. This Lorraine may have been at that time, but only through the skillful management of the duke they were to call Charles the Great: Charles III astutely kept Lorraine out of all the conflicts and balanced intelligence with efficiency in his running of the duchy. He was not able to expand the actual territory, but he did triple the size of the capital by adding the Ville-Neuve, or "New Town," with its wide streets, possibly designed by the Italian Jeronimo Citoni. He created a strong army and built what were reputed to be the most modern fortifications in Europe. He developed salt production, which provided him with half his personal income, opened new copper mines, managed to attract metalworkers from Liège, and tried to set up luxury-goods industries in Nancy—the manufacture of silk sheets and gold and silver thread. Everything everywhere was whirring, and the arts were no exception. Lorraine had a strong architectural tradition, as was evident in its cathedrals and churches. Lorrainese sculpture was at its height with Ligier Richier in Saint-Mihiel, and Pierre Woeiriot ranks as one of the major engravers of the sixteenth century. Eager to do as other princes of the time did and surround himself with painters, Charles III had called Claude Henriet to his court. Henriet seems to have been highly regarded in his day, and although none of his own work survived, he may have been the true founder of the great "Lorraine school," setting an example for both Bellange and Lallemant, and responsible for turning the duke's court into an artistic center at a time when the civil wars had destroyed most of the existing studios in France.

This prosperity was not confined to the ducal states. Vic, La Tour's birthplace, is an excellent example. It was a small town compared to Metz, which had some nineteen thousand inhabitants around 1610, or Nancy, whose population would reach sixteen thousand, we are told, around 1628, or even Verdun and Bar-le-Duc where the popula-

GOOD TIMES IN LORRAINE

Top:
Jacques Callot. *The Fair at Gondreville, or May Day in Xeuilley*. c. 1625. Etching.

Bottom:
Jacques Callot. *The Gardens of the Ducal Palace in Nancy*. c. 1625. Etching.
Cabinet des Estampes, Bibliothèque Nationale, Paris

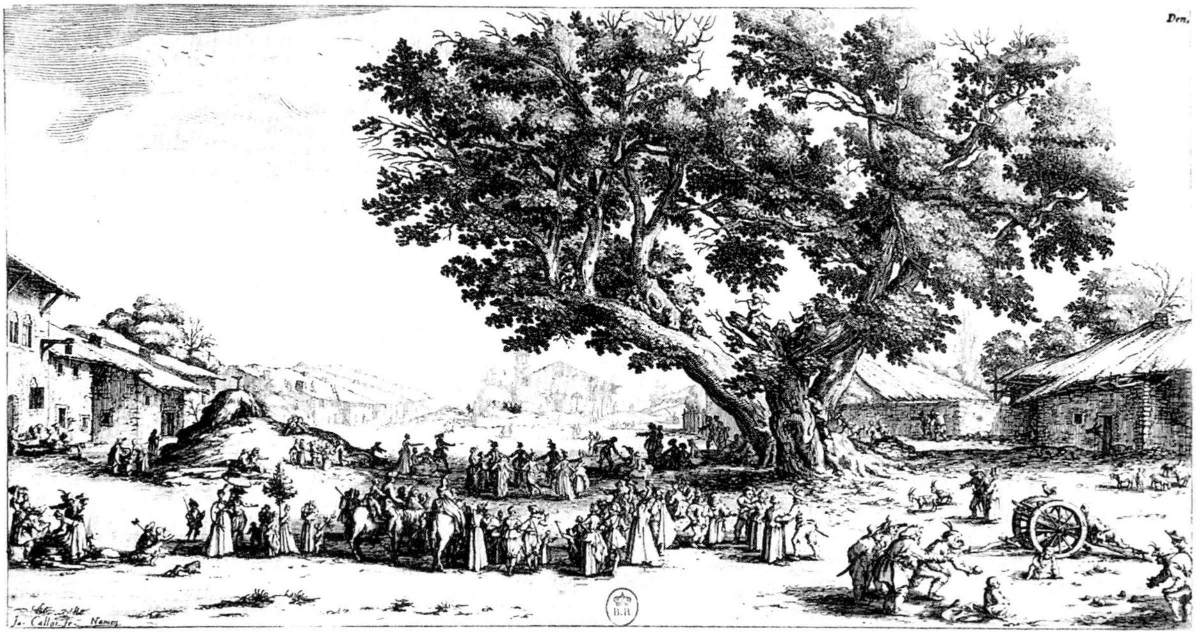

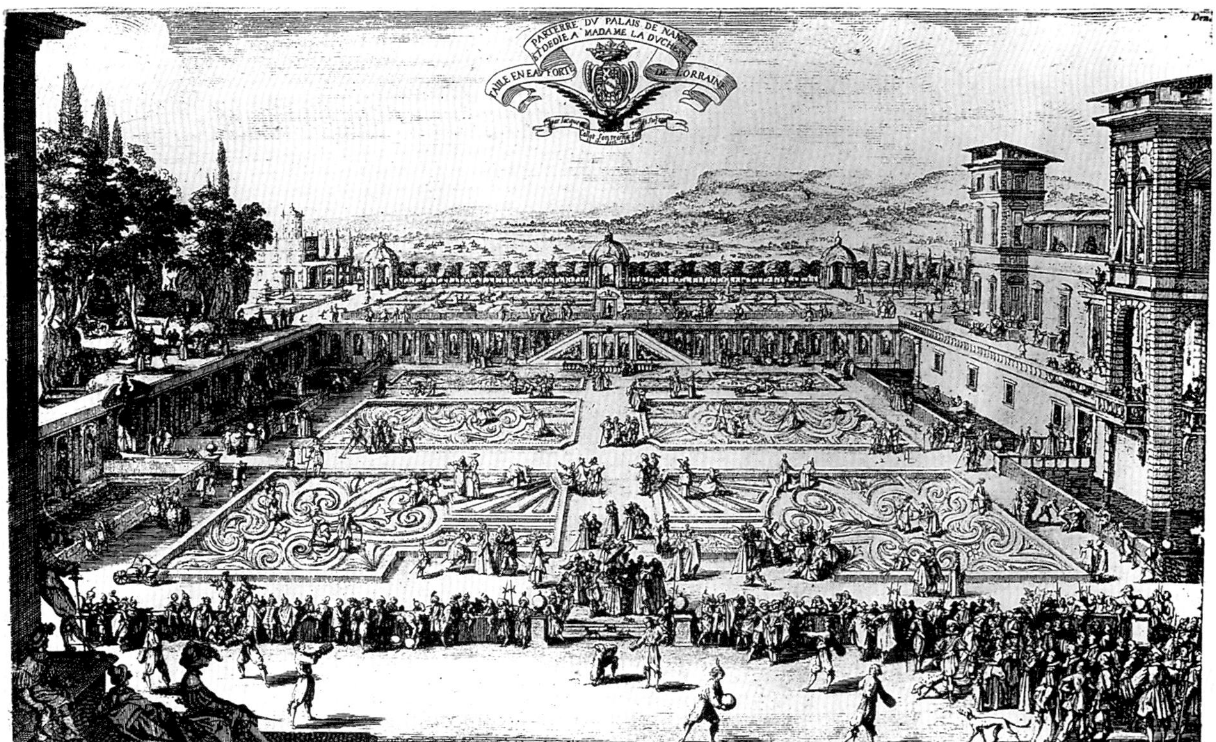
PARTERRE DV PALAIS DE NANC
ET DEDIE A MADAME LA DVCHE
TAILLE EN EAV FORTE
DE LORRAINE
façonné des honneurs des printemps,
d'obiectz de diuers passetemps;
C'est uostre aage, Madame douceurs encloses
Nous sont autant de fleurs, ou Rosiers precieux
Qui pousseront sans fin des doux-flairantes roses
Dont l'odeur aggréra aux hommes et aux Cieux

tion cannot have been more than six or eight thousand. It was a capital in its own way, however, with the pride of a capital and an intellectual and artistic life of its own. Close though it was to Nancy, Vic did not belong to the duke of Lorraine, but came under the authority of the bishop of Metz. When the French installed a governor and a garrison in the episcopal city in 1552, the bishop deemed it prudent to move the seat of his temporal power. Vic therefore became his administrative capital. It was there that his lieutenant general lived, he himself had a château where he frequently stayed.

The town was well fortified, and as attractive as it was secure. There had been a settlement here, on the verdant banks of the river Seille, since time immemorial. The town was large, and the walls ran down to the river's edge. The river itself split into many little channels ideally suited for mills and tanneries. Vineyards celebrated for their wines stretched all along the near-by hillsides, which were crowned with beautiful forests. Excavations have proven that the layers of salt in the subsoil were being intensively worked even earlier than the Gallo-Roman period. By the sixteenth century, the salt marshes had shifted closer to Marsal, but Vic remained an important trading center for the surrounding area. The Counter-Reformation had yet to bring its new religious communities to the town, but Vic had its quota of traditional monasteries, as well as its own particular cults, some long established, and others, like that of the blessed Bernard de Bade, of more recent date. Because of the presence of magistrates and senior officials of the bailiwick, and the regular visits the bishop and his court made, Vic became a center open to French, Italian, and Germanic cultures and had several printer-booksellers. We will have more to say about Alphonse de Rambervillers, the lieutenant general who was also a poet, scholar, and collector, and about the other painters and sculptors of varying fame who were firmly established there. Vic was a far cry from the little village of Chamagne which, seven years after Georges de La Tour's birth, welcomed Claude Gellée into this world. It was one of those modest but lively little places that abounded in the old Europe and which all at some point or another had their hour of glory and produced an illustrious son of whom they could be justly proud.

LA TOUR'S CALLING

It was certainly possible to have a career as an artist in Vic, but propitious circumstances alone cannot create an event. Vic may have allowed a Georges de La Tour to happen, but it does not explain him. Indeed, is it ever really possible to fathom why someone chooses a certain vocation? The process depends on a succession of choices made and obstacles avoided, first as a child, then as an adolescent, when one is more or less unconscious of the path taken. No one can account for such a process—not even the mature artist, and certainly not an historian four hundred years later.

A number of critics have nevertheless attempted to do so. Some have talked vaguely of predestination, but this amounts to avoiding the issue rather than clarifying it. Others have been rather more daring and have advanced specific motivations for the "baker's son" turned painter. Letting their imaginations run wild, they have conjured up pictures of the boy watching his father and the assistants at work before a gaping bread oven, one moment no more than silhouettes against the scarlet flames, the next towering red giants in the still of the night. They see him entranced by the moving shadows on the wall, the rims of light around the quiet faces, and they argue that it was to recapture these images of his youth, to rekindle that lost world with all its stillness and glow, that La Tour painted pictures like *The Newborn Child,* now in Rennes, the *Flea Catcher,* in Nancy, or *Job Mocked by His Wife,* in Épinal.

This is a poetic extrapolation, but utterly specious. La Tour, may well have retained very vivid impressions from his childhood, and it could be argued that his early experience gave him a particular and almost instinctive ability to conjure up glowing red light amid a shadowy gloom. It is worth remembering, however, that this was a time when candles and fires were the only form of light available, in both town and country, and that such "night" effects were familiar to everyone, indeed commonplace, and so hardly likely to make a great impression on a child. It was painting that coaxed the poetry out of these nocturnal lights, and not the other way around.

The hypothesis put forward by Henri Tribout de Morembert in 1974 demands closer consideration. He discovered from Jean the baker's marriage contract that his wife's maiden name was *Sibille de Cropsaux*. The first name has an unusual, noble ring that has always excited critics. It is worth pointing out here, however, that far from having its origins in antiquity, Sibille (like Sybille and Sébille) is in fact one of many Lorrainese variants of the common names Isabelle or Elisabeth, and, along with Sibillon and Babillon, a form then very popular throughout the country. It is on the "de Cropsaux," however, that the argument hinges. Sibille's mother was named Marguerite Trompette. Her first husband was called François Mélian or Milian, a messenger by trade, and her second was a baker by the name of Demange Henry: there seems to be no Crospaux connection there. Her daughter was first married to one Nicolas Bizet, and in the marriage contract of 9 January 1583 the lawyer duly gives her name as Sibille and describes her as the daughter of the late Milian. The signing of the contract was witnessed by one Jacquemin de Cropsal (or Cropsaulx or Cropsaux), who was described as a close relative. He does not appear in Sibille's second marriage contract, this time with Jean de La Tour (dated 31 December 1590), but her name, however, is given as "Sibille de Cropsaulx," and, following standard practice in the case of widows, there is no mention of her father's name. It is tempting to infer from this that Georges de La Tour's mother was in fact none other than the rather belatedly acknowledged illegitimate daughter of Jacquemin de Cropsaux. This is what Tribout de Morembert appears to believe. If so, Georges de La Tour had noble blood in his veins, illegitimate blood, it is true, but during this period, less importance was attached to illegitimacy than during the nineteenth century. Aware of his noble heritage, La Tour, without rejecting his family, would have disdained his father's trade and aspired all his life to attain the noble status of his maternal ancestors. Above all, having heard that artists mix with princes, he would have been attracted to painting as a means of achieving this deep-seated ambition.

Once again, we must not let ourselves be too readily swayed. We need to be sure that the "sieur de Cropsaux" was, in fact, a member of the nobility. What grounds do we actually have for supposing that this was the same Jacquemin de Cropsaux who was then keeper of Count Jean de Heemstatt's castle and agent for his estate at Château-Voué? No rank or title is associated with his name in the 1583 contract. Morembert himself notes that there was also a furrier by the name of Jean de Cropsaux in Vic about 1570. Although he was clearly connected with the family in some way, there is no reason why this Cropsaux, whoever he was, could not simply have been a friend rather than the girl's father. It is not unheard of, after all, for lawyers to make mistakes about their clients' relationships to one another. We can only await the discovery of other deeds in which Sibille is actually referred to by the name "de Cropsaux," but until then Morembert's theory must remain pure conjecture.

On the other hand, the pursuit of nobility may well have its origins in La Tour's family background without any history of illegitimacy. Georges's branch of the La Tour family was an intricate one, possibly originating from Moyenvic or Marsal but long established in Vic, and, in spite of everything, difficult to pin down. "Claudon le Vieil" ("the Elder") was long assumed to be Georges's grandfather and founder of the family line. In fact he was only Georges's great-uncle, and even then there was already more than one branch to the family. The next generation saw a whole panoply of first cousins settled in Vic, all engaged in a variety of respectable trades. "Claudon le Jeune" ("the Younger"), son of Claudon le Vieil, was a cobbler, for instance, his cousin Mérian, son of François, a tailor, and Jean, whose father has yet to be traced, a baker. There was another La Tour clan, however, divided between Moyenvic and Marsal; this included among others Nicolas de La Tour, a canon from Marsal, and his four brothers: Adam de La Tour, lord of Affléville, who lived in Moyenvic around 1610-1618; Jacques and Philippe, both residents of Marsal, and Jean, about whom little is known except that he could hardly have been Georges's father. Not far away, in Dieuze, was a third contingent made up of Paul de La Tour, the governor of Puxe, and his children. To date, there is no concrete evidence that the three lines were related in any way, but they were far from being unaware of each other's existence; Canon Nicolas, for instance, was godfather to one of Claude le Vieil's grandsons. They might well have shared a common ancestry in some more or less distant past. The La Tours of Vic could have been a junior branch of a large noble family that lacked the means to provide all its offspring with the necessary land or living and had therefore resorted to a variety of plebeian occupations, all preferable, however, to the life of a soldier. Or, it may have been the other way round: one member of the family could have struck it rich and contrived to acquire a fief and a title. The archives are not particularly enlightening on such issues and are distinctly lean for the sixteenth century. In any case, similar instances abound for this period, in Lorraine and throughout France. The sheer fact that there were noble La Tours in the area, moreover, whether they were distant relatives or simply happened to share the same name, would have been enough to inspire emulation in a young child.

Ultimately, all of that is irrelevant. It would have been enough for La Tour to have sensed the particular direction he wanted to follow early on. We should not imagine that Jean de La Tour's station in life was too humble for any of his children to be drawn to a career as an artist. Jean the baker was not a member of the nobility, it is true, and Georges himself, clearly driven by a desire to attain noble status, died too soon, in times too troubled, to acquire the desired patent. Bakers were not without rank, however, and to be a baker in Vic was to be a local notable. We have to forget our nineteenth-century notions. This was the end of the sixteenth century, and food supplies were still a problem everywhere. Bread was central to the daily diet and was a source of concern for government and local authorities alike. The baker, who bought the flour and sometimes even the grain, and who produced this essential food, was a key figure in the city. There were price scales and controls to put a stop to monopolies and speculation and to allow the confiscations of batches of loaves that failed to respect the legal weight. Such measures did not prevent the irreplaceable baker from often becoming a rich man, however, and it was not uncommon for a baker to be appointed town alderman. Jean de La Tour appears to have been very well off. It is difficult to estimate his wealth from the documentary evidence we have to date. There are, however, records of him paying out five hundred francs' worth of wheat to a confectioner in Moyenvic in 1592, for instance, and again, in 1596, spending over 750 francs on a single purchase. These were very considerable sums, which implies that he must have had solid capital behind him. For one of his children to decide to become an artist would not necessarily have indicated a desire to break with his family.

It is clear from the archives, moreover, that La Tour was not the only artist that Vic produced during this period. Like the majority of French artists, they were the product of the same general world of comfortably well-off craftsmen and minor officials. A certain Pierre Georges, for example, who was born some time between 1592 and 1597, and of the same generation as La Tour, was the son of a tanner, Nicolas Georges. He became a painter and went to Rome to improve his skills, then returned to Vic in 1616-1617. Unfortunately, he died shortly after his return, so we will never know how talented he might have been. In 1612, Jean Saint Paul, who was then very highly regarded in Nancy, came to Vic to hire an apprentice called Claude de Hey. We do not know what happened to him. La Tour scholars seem all too often to forget, moreover, that in 1591, two years before La Tour was born, Vic was also the birthplace of François Derand, later the great architect of the Jesuits and rival to Martellange. He designed the present Church of Saint-Paul-Saint-Louis in Paris, which was consecrated in 1641, at just the time when La Tour was beginning to enjoy success in the capital. It is hardly surprising that Vic should have generated such accomplished artists, for it was able to offer them the kind of encounter with art at a very early age that dictates the course of an entire life. Vic could boast beautiful examples of fine architecture, such as what is known today as the Hôtel de la Monnaie, along with sculptures and paintings in the churches, but there was something far more influential: an avid collector, who was also the most prominent person in the vicinity, the lieutenant general of the bailiwick, Alphonse de Rambervillers.

Sooner or later everyone who makes a study of La Tour comes across this interesting figure, who was to become a close relative of the painter by marriage. Vic was too small and Rambervillers too important for La Tour not to have known of him as a child, not to have heard of his collection of curios and works of art, and indeed, not to have visited it. It has sometimes been suggested that Rambervillers had a particular fondness for the baker's son and encouraged him in his studies, helped foster his career, and even taught him the rudiments of painting. There is no proof of this, but various letters do reflect his interest in a number of young apprentice painters, and it would not be unreasonable for us to suppose that Georges was one of them.

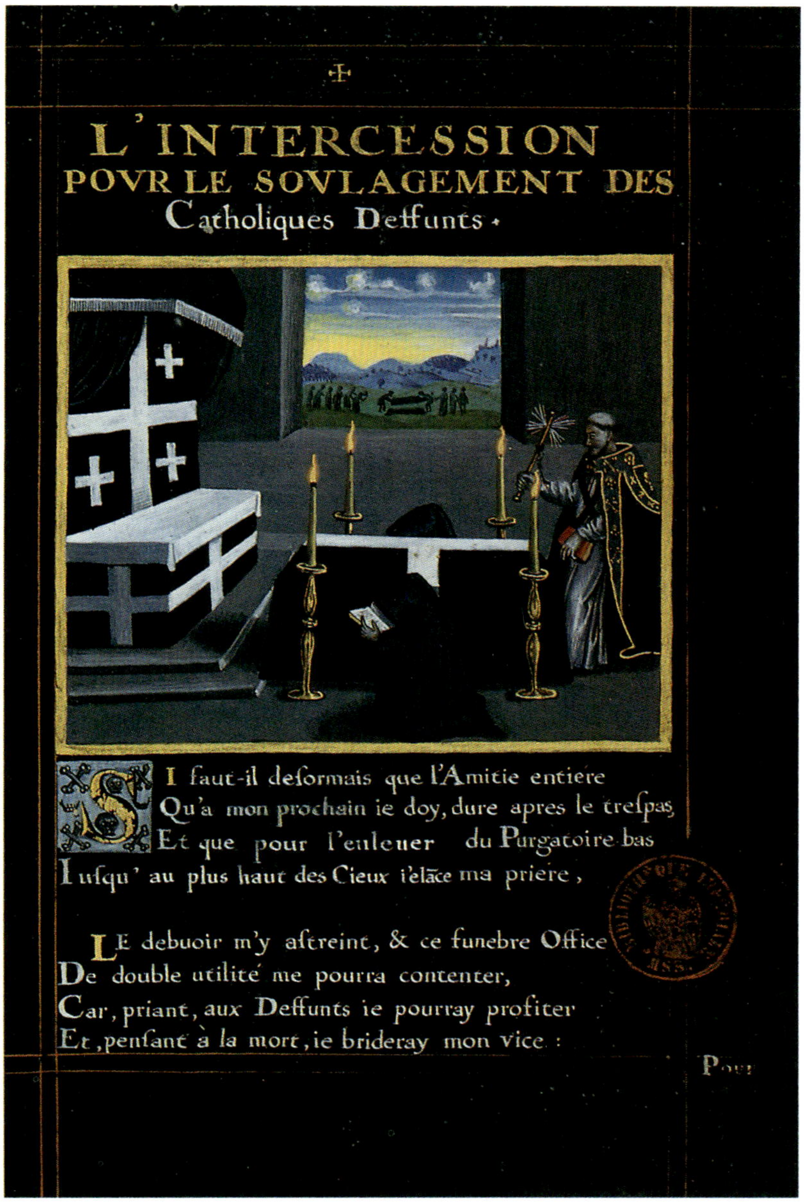
L'INTERCESSION
POVR LE SOVLAGEMENT DES
Catholiques Deffunts.

SI faut-il desormais que l'Amitie entiere
Qu'a mon prochain ie doy, dure apres le trespas,
Et que pour l'enleuer du Purgatoire bas
Iusqu'au plus haut des Cieux i'elãce ma priere,

LE debuoir m'y astreint, & ce funebre Office
De double utilité me pourra contenter,
Car, priant, aux Deffunts ie pourray profiter
Et, pensant à la mort, ie brideray mon vice :

Pour

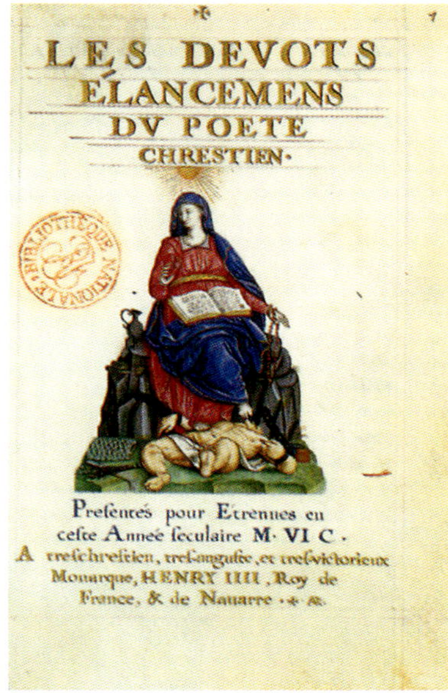
LES DEVOTS
ELANCEMENS
DV POETE
CHRESTIEN.

Presentés pour Etrennes en
ceste Annee seculaire M. VI C.
A treschrestien, tres-auguste, et tresvictorieux
Monarque, HENRY IIII, Roy de
France, & de Nauarre.

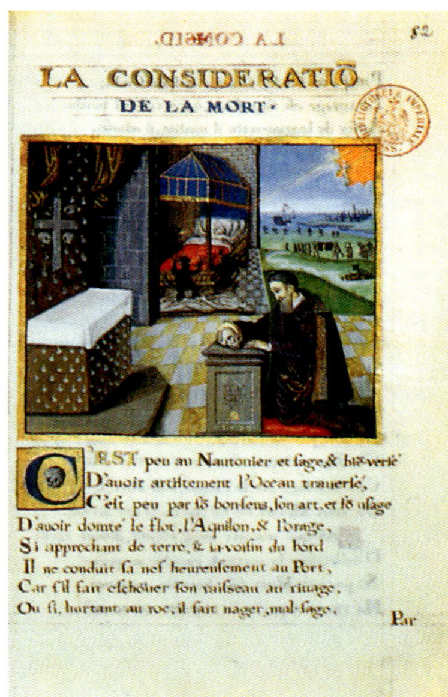
LA CONSIDERATIO
DE LA MORT.

The Pious Learnings of the Christian Poet. Manuscript written and illustrated by Alphonse de Rambervillers and presented to Henri IV in 1600.
Département des Manuscrits, (FR. 25423).
Bibliothèque Nationale, Paris
Left: *Intercession for the Consolation of Deceased Catholics* (fol. 94).
Above right: Title page (fol. 1).
Below right: *The Contemplation of Death* (fol. 82).

Rambervillers was a descendant of a noble family that can be traced to the end of the twelfth century. He was the son of a public prosecutor and city councilman in Toul, and nephew of the lieutenant general of the bailiwick of the bishopric of Metz in Vic. After studying law in Toulouse, he went on to become prosecutor to the bailiwick of Vic in 1587. He succeeded his uncle as lieutenant general on 24 July 1593, the year La Tour was born, and thus became one of the leading figures in the town. He was a scholar in the sixteenth-century mold with a truly inquisitive mind, interested in everything from geometry to theology, from ancient medals to the study of local legal customs, from fortifications to glass engraving. He was friends with Du Vair and corresponded with Peiresc. He did not simply admire and collect art: painting was one of his hobbies. A manuscript that he presented to Henri IV for the jubilee of 1600, the *Pious Learnings of the Christian Poet*, is preserved in Paris. Not only are the verses his own, but he is also the painter of the miniatures, which rank with the best of the period and reveal a true artistic sentiment. In his will Rambervillers touches on his artistic leanings with a certain amount of melancholy when he describes how he has "made a point of buying and otherwise acquiring various paintings, some of which are by my own hand, some by friends, and with which my rooms are furnished." He was a true collector and wanted his walls to be kept just as he had hung them: "I wish, intend, and order that the said pictures remain exactly as they are in my house and solemnly forbid my heirs to dispose of any of them, but command them rather to preserve them as decoration of my house and as a token of my love for the art of painting, which has so often served to relax my tired mind." He had no illusions, however: "Nothing is certain in human affairs," he adds, followed by the wish that "if necessity compels them to be moved," some of them should go to the chapel that he had built in the Church of the Observant Friars. La Tour must have penetrated those "rooms" at a fairly early age and feasted his eyes on the lieutenant general's beautiful lute "of ivory and ebony," the volume of prayers on fine vellum "written and illuminated by [his] hand," his ancient medals, his other "rarities," and all his paintings, and if he did not see them with his own eyes, he would have heard enough about them to make an indelible impression.

In Rambervillers's day, amateur painters were no less talented or skilled in their craft than their nineteenth-century counterparts such as Moreau-Nélaton and Caillebotte. They were more than capable of providing excellent teaching to a young child with a bent for art, and this may have been how La Tour first learned his art. But this was not necessarily the case: Vic was home to a number of painters, of whom we know unfortunately very little. They may have been no more than craftsmen who spent their days painting walls, beams, and ceilings and never attempted anything more difficult than decorative motifs, but this was certainly not the case for all of them. More often than not they would have earned their living painting altarpieces for churches, little religious and comic "Flemish" pictures to sell at fairs, and wedding portraits. There were probably some talented masters among them. One, Barthélémy Braun, a German from Cologne, could pride himself on being named *peintre ordinaire* by Duke Charles III and given noble status. As Barthélémy Le Brun he turns up in Nancy around 1583, but also in Vic and Metz at the turn of the century, doubtless drawn there by the bishop. More frequent mention is made of Claude Dogoz or Dogue, who was born in Romont in Switzerland and moved to Vic when he was still young, around 1605. He took on an apprentice there in May 1607 and another in 1610 and married into a fairly rich family in 1611. In 1632 he painted an altarpiece for Vic's collegiate church of Saint-Étienne, for which he was paid the considerable sum of three hundred livres, which indicates that he was already an artist of some standing. The young Georges de La Tour may well have been impressed by the reputation of these artists and may have been drawn to their studios. He may even have received his first training from one of them. This brings us to the difficult but crucial question of how La Tour learned his trade.

APPRENTICESHIP

As with other "trades," there were two ways to become a painter in the sixteenth and seventeenth centuries. The first, and obviously the easiest, was to be born into the craft. A painter's son could begin in his father's studio as soon as he was out of the cradle, but would generally complete his training away from home with a master painter or gaining experience abroad. He would then have the facilities to take over from his father or set up on his own. This was the case for Vouet and Le Brun in Paris and Tassell in the provinces. Then, as now, however, vocation was unpredictable. A young street urchin on the run could, like Michel Serre, become the most sought-after artist in Marseilles. More often, the artistic calling would manifest itself among the children of craftsmen and merchants, or indeed, much to their parents' chagrin, young men of means whose sound education destined them to a brillant career. Poussin and Du Fresnoy are only two such examples. Du Fresnoy's mother is known to have never understood how a boy so good at Greek and Latin could possibly have let himself be lured into wielding a paintbrush. In such instances, before Vouet opened his studio and the Academy was founded in 1648, the only way to learn the craft was as an apprentice to a master painter.

Such apprenticeships were not just local arrangements, but social and legal institutions, and were almost always sanctioned by a contract drawn up by a lawyer. They generally began after primary school, between the ages of eleven and thirteen, but sometimes not until much later, and they lasted between three and five years. The apprentice began by grinding colors and preparing the master's canvases, practicing first drawing and then painting, and through experience slowly getting to know the tricks of the trade. This almost always meant boarding with the artist in question. Board and lodging did not come cheaply. Even if he were treated as a sort of servant boy in the master's house and given all sorts of chores to do, an apprentice not only received no wages but was actually required by the contract to pay a carefully fixed sum in compensation for the master's expenditures on his behalf—"victuals, food, drink, heat, bed, room, and light," as well as—"showing and teaching his art to the best of his ability." This amount varied considerably. It depended not only on the master's reputation, but also on his lifestyle, and on the degree of comfort desired by the apprentice's parents and afforded by the artist's domestic circumstances—a mattress in the attic or a room to himself?—and on the quality of his table. An apprenticeship entailed a certain financial sacrifice that not everyone could afford.

It would be very surprising if La Tour, as a baker's son, did not follow this route and duly undertake an apprenticeship with a "master painter" in the accepted fashion around 1605-1611. Poussin appears to be practically the only one of his contemporaries to have escaped this norm, and even this is not certain. Research has so far failed to turn up a contract in Georges de La Tour's case, so we are left with hypotheses. Did he stay in Vic? Did he move on to a more important center such as Metz or Nancy? Or might he not even have gone to the kingdom of France?

The most natural assumption is that he was apprenticed to a painter in Vic. Most scholars propose the name of Dogoz, who lived in Vic and later had dealings with La Tour. Indeed, Master Claude Dogoz, who established himself in Vic around 1605, when he was about twenty, appears to have always commanded a considerable reputation in the city. We have already seen that in May 1607 he took on as a first apprentice François Pierson, the abbot's nephew, followed in 1610 by the son of a lawyer to the bishopric's bailiwick. In reality, however, this would mean that unless Dogoz had two apprentices at once (which seldom happened unless an artist had a major project underway), La Tour's apprenticeship could not have started until after 1611 at the earliest, which would surely have been too late. It is not very likely, therefore, that La Tour was apprenticed to the young Dogoz, who seems to have been only ten or fifteen years his senior. At most, Dogoz may have inspired La Tour by his example and influenced his taste at the outset of his career. Barthélémy Braun is another possibility, and his title of *peintre ordinaire* to Duke Charles III would have been a point in his favor. He appears to have been living in Metz in the period around 1605-1611 but maintained links with Vic. His wife, whom he married in Vic, is known to have been there in 1605. The fact that he lived in Metz would not have ruled out an apprenticeship, which often occured much farther from home.

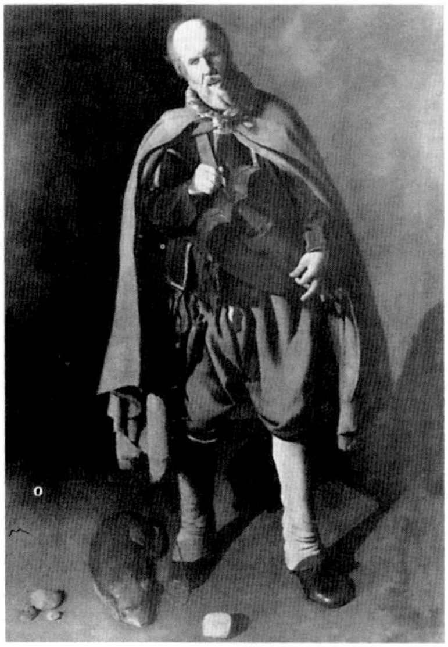

Hurdy-Gurdy Player with a Dog.
Musée Municipal, Bergues

Jacques de Bellange. *Blind Hurdy-Gurdy Player.* Etching.
Cabinet des Estampes, Bibliothèque Nationale, Paris

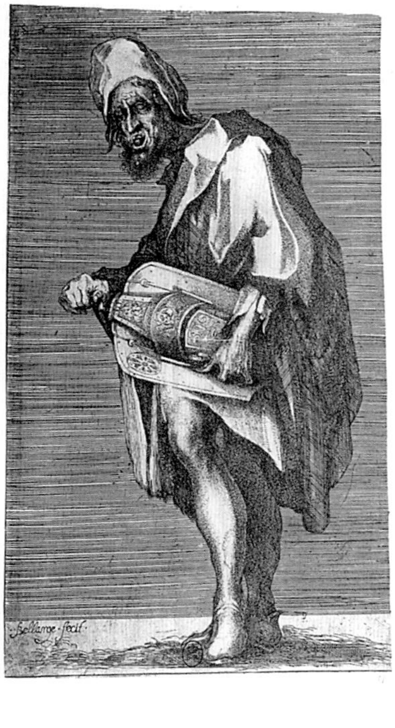

This was, after all, a period that recognized the value of learning from a great artist. La Tour's family was relatively affluent and his parents would have wanted to entrust their son to the best master available. If he had been born thirty or fifty years later, La Tour would surely have gone to Paris for part or all of his apprenticeship. This would have been even more likely given the fact that one of Jean de La Tour's first cousins, Martin de La Tour, son of his uncle François, according to a deed dated June 1607, was working as a tailor in Paris. During the period in question, however, the French capital was still recovering, and it is less certain that anyone would have contemplated sending a child that far away. Nevertheless, it is not impossible that La Tour learned or at least perfected his craft under some Parisian master, which would also help to explain the ease with which he later negotiated the capital. Indeed, the daily registers in which the Parisian guilds recorded the names of those who were admitted as "masters" contains a rather intriguing entry for 12 December 1613 (Paris, Archives Nationales, Y 9313, fol. 28v), which no one seems to have bothered much about. It is highlighted by a note in the margin that reads, "Master painter and sculptor in the Faubourgs Saint Honoré: Lhomme," and runs as follows: "Today by virtue of a royal warrant granted by the King on the occasion of the birth of his Grace the duke of Anjou, delivered in Paris on the twelfth day of December in the year one thousand six hundred and three, signed Phelippeaux, the honorable Jean Lhomme was received as master painter, sculptor and illuminator in the Faubourgs Saint Honoré, in the presence of Georges La Tour and Nicolas Duchesne, master of this craft in this town . . . before M. Lefebvre, deputy."

People were often accepted into the guilds on the strength of such letters of patent, and they were particularly prized by those from the provinces who would otherwise have found it impossible to penetrate the guilds. The clerk's handwriting is atrocious, but there can be no doubt about the name of Jean Lhomme. Could this be the painter from Troyes who was later to appear in Rome, first in Vouet's circle, then in Valentin's? He was said to be about forty on his death in January 1633, which would mean that he was born around 1593. It certainly would not be surprising to find him seeking to worm his way into one of the Parisian guilds at the age of twenty. The name of Nicolas Duchesne is also quite clear. This can have been none other than the painter who later directed the interior decorations of the Luxembourg Palace, where he employed the youthful Champaigne and Poussin. There does not seem to be much question either about the reading of "Georges La Tour." Is this our man? If so, he must already have ranked as a master himself, probably in the guild of the Faubourg Saint-Honoré, unless he was present at the occasion simply as Lhomme's friend. Both interpretations are possible since he would have been twenty years old. And if he had been in Paris by then, it would be quite tempting to conclude that he probably did his apprenticeship there.

A historian cannot construct a biography, however tentative, on such a slender and isolated piece of evidence. Let us just keep this in mind as a possibility. Others spring to mind as well. There were painters much closer, and even in Nancy, who were highly regarded, and whom La Tour's parents would certainly have considered.

The most famous at the time was without doubt Claude Henriet, who seems to have been one of the leading artists at the court of Charles III and was in fact related by marriage to Rambervillers. He died sometime around the end of 1606, however. Also highly regarded at the court of Lorraine was Jean Saint-Paul, who, as we have said, took on an apprentice by the name of Jean de Hey in Vic at the end of July 1612. The most gifted artist in Lorraine around 1605, however, was undoubtedly Jacques de Bellange. His first recorded apprentice was the son of a quartermaster for the cardinal of Lorraine, a boy named Louis Loys, who began working for him in February 1595. The very comfortable Deruet family similarly chose to send him young Claude (born around 1588) in April 1605. Deruet was apprenticed to Bellange for four years and was to be influenced by this artist of genius all his life, although he never displayed anything like his talent. It is surely not impossible that La Tour's family chose, with or without the advice of Rambervillers, to do likewise with Georges, who was four or five years Deruet's junior.

La Tour's parents probably sent him to one of the little schools that Vic offered. He seems to have known Latin, and it is likely that he was educated to a high level, which would have delayed the start of his apprenticeship until he was fourteen or even sixteen. Bellange would then have been at the height of his career.

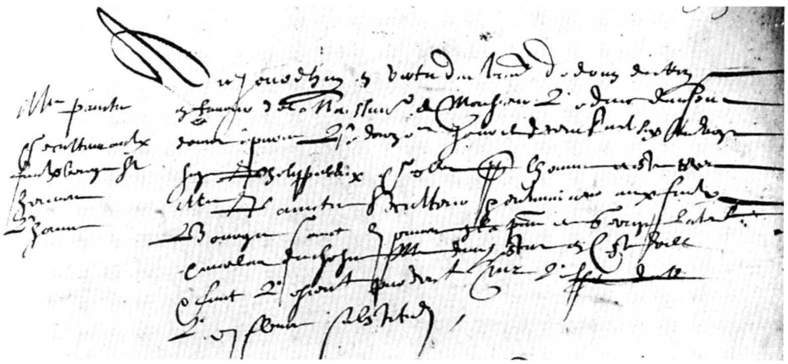

LA TOUR IN PARIS IN 1613?
Record of Jean Lhomme's admission to a Parisian artists' guild on 12 December 1613 (?).
Register of Admissions to Parisian Guilds (Y 9313, fol. 28v). Archives Nationales, Paris

Deruet seems to have left him in April 1609. La Tour could easily have taken his place, whether he had just completed his schooling or had learned the rudiments of his art in Vic before embarking on an apprenticeship with the famous painter.

This would be no more than a convenient hypothesis, and one that might sound too plausible not to be suspect, were there not convincing arguments in its favor. There are distinct links between Bellange's art and La Tour's. These could simply reflect the influence of Bellange's works, which La Tour could have seen in and around Nancy or known through engravings that would have been easy for him to obtain and study at his leisure. Or, these could indicate a master-pupil relationship between the two artists. In his early paintings, La Tour uses a technique that was very uncommon in Europe at the time, and quite different from any being taught in Italy or even in Paris. The composition is powerful and the volumes firm, while details such as hair, beards, and wrinkles are handled with a very fine brush, so that the broadly applied colors are masterfully overlaid with line. Such fluidity, elegance, and expressive force reveal the sensibility of a draftsman. The only place we find anything like it at the time is in Bellange's drawings and engravings. However profound the differences between them, it seems clear that La Tour felt this influence early on and never wholly lost it regardless of the various experiments that followed. Could this have been the case if La Tour had known the Nancy master only through his works? Moreover, although these early paintings, which are generally presumed to date from the time when La Tour settled in Lunéville, are very much in the spirit of Italian painting of the day, their subject matter is quite unlike anything one would expect to find in Italy around 1610-1616. La Tour did not paint tavern scenes, like Valentin or Régnier, but rather peasants or beggars, either in full-length, single-figure compositions or in groups of half-length figures. Interestingly, Bellange's engravings reveal him to have been a far more varied artist than may at first appear, and it is clear that he too had a penchant for such realist scenes. More particularly, it was Bellange who seems to have set the trend for the full-length portraits of hurdy-gurdy players that became a favorite subject for La Tour.

We shall come back to these issues, but one last detail must be mentioned. La Tour was the only artist in Lorraine, to our knowledge, to sign his paintings with much the same handwriting and presentation as Bellange. This is a very small point, and one that only emerges somewhat later, but it is precisely such a recurring detail that betrays an artist's past connection with a particular studio.

Once again, this represents nothing more than a hypothesis. Let us even admit that it is surprising to find a pupil of Bellange displaying so little interest in court art and decorative cycles. Even more surprising is his complete abandonment of techniques such as black chalk, wash, and etching. Was La Tour, like many painters of his generation, so heavily influenced by the commanding example of Caravaggio that he rejected any means of expression associated with Mannerism? Was he thus prompted to transpose the taste for drawing Bellange had given him into painterly terms? The reactions of an artist are as unpredictable as his motivations are uncertain. The final decision about La Tour's apprenticeship will have to await further documentary evidence, and there are still a good many archives to explore.

A COMPARISON OF SIGNATURES: BELLANGE AND LA TOUR
From top to bottom:
Bellange: *The Virgin with a Spindle*; *Three Saints*; *The Resurrection of Lazarus*. Etchings.
La Tour: *St. Thomas* (Louvre).

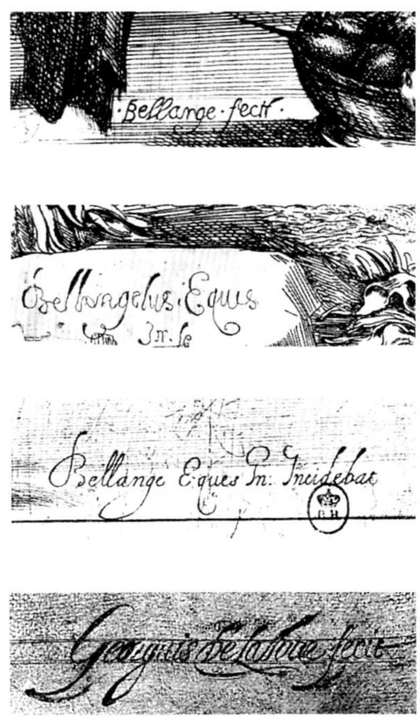

THE VOYAGE TO ITALY

Perhaps these same archives will reveal what La Tour did after his apprenticeship. We have no records for this period, but we are virtually certain about one thing: he spent at least part of it in Italy, although we do not know exactly when he went, for how long, or what pictures he would have painted there.

The idea of such a stay in Italy has long been a subject of debate. Some critics would prefer to think of La Tour as a "pure" Lorrainese painter, or at least as a "pure" French painter. Benedict Nicolson, for his part, dwelt particularly on the links La Tour may have had with the Northern European followers of Caravaggio and believed that he must have spent time in either Utrecht or Amsterdam. Lorraine, as we have said, was very much a thoroughfare: it was possible to meet people of all origins, and there were frequent comings and goings. One thing is clear, however: every Lorraine-born artist of La Tour's generation went to Rome. Le Clerc, for instance, born around 1587-1588, set off in 1602 or thereabouts, while Callot, born in 1592, made two youthful escapades there, one around 1602, and another around 1606, before finally settling in Rome in 1608. Deruet, born around 1588, was there by about 1613. Didier Barra and François de Nomé, born in Metz in about 1590 and 1593 respectively, both went to Italy when they were young, not to mention Pierre Georges, of whom we have already spoken, who was born in Vic around 1592-1597, and was probably still in Rome around 1614-1616. The next generation seems to have felt the pull of Italy just as strongly—Charles Mellin, Claude Gellée, and Nicolas de la Fleur all went there in their turn. It would be extraordinary if La Tour alone had resisted this fascination, which was in fact shared by painters from Paris, Liège, or Utrecht. Moreover, there is not the slightest sign of La Tour's presence either in Vic or elsewhere in Lorraine before October 1616, when the traces start to multiply. By that time he would have been twenty-three. His apprenticeship could not possibly have lasted until then. Where could he have been from 1613, at the latest, to 1616, if not in Italy?

Rome was then in its artistic heyday. Caravaggio had just died, and all the young painters were fascinated by his dashing life, bold inspiration, and highly individual technique. He had created a veritable wave of followers: the "Caravaggesque" movement was aptly named. His was not the only contemporary influence, however. Annibale Carracci's work, notably in the famous Galleria Farnese, reflected a different but equally new approach, while Cavaliere d'Arpino proposed a revived version of Mannerism that was more brillant and alluring than before. Old Masters such as Raphael, Michelangelo, Daniele da Volterra, Salviati, and Polydorus were as revered as ever. Rome itself had something to teach at every turn: its façades, many of which were painted, the churches and palaces bursting with famous pictures. Along with these attractions, there were distinct practical advantages as well. The many artists' colonies of all nationalities, allowed newcomers to overcome solitude and language barriers alike. No travel was free from the dangers of penury and disease, but in Rome these twin terrors, which turned every journey into an adventure, lost their sting: the presence of compatriots and associations ready to help meant that no one would be left to struggle alone. Lodging and work were easy to come by in Rome: there were no guilds to contend with, there was no shortage of rooms to rent, and the inhabitants were used to foreigners in their city. The art trade was already highly organized, so artists could always manage to sell their early work and thus survive until they received a commission. At a time when much of Europe had been destroyed by the religious wars, Rome had developed into a veritable international center, comparable only to Paris in the first half of the twentieth century.

All the young painters of the day—Vouet, Vignon, Valentin, Poussin, Blanchard, Brébiette, to name only the most famous—flocked to Rome from Paris as soon as they could find the money for the trip. There were artists fresh from the provinces too: Guy François from Puy, Jacques Stella from Lyons, Richard Tassel from Langres, Nicolas Tournier from Montbéliard. It was a time when Lorraine, moreover, had a very special relationship with Rome.

Since the return of the popes from Avignon, the Eternal City had seen countless natives of Lorraine pass through its gates and in many cases settle there permanently. The records of the papal chancery and the tombstones in the churches of

Trinità dei Monte and San Luigi dei Francesi are full of the names of both ecclesiastical and lay dignitaries from the dioceses of Metz, Toul, and Verdun. In a letter to St. Pierre Fourier, Father Guinet estimated that there were six thousand Lorraine natives in Rome—roughly two-thirds of the population of Nancy. They included papal residents and their households, members of the Curia, various monks, a great many merchants, and cooks, who were highly valued in the papal administration.

As a result, there seems to have been a constant flow of voyagers between Rome and Nancy. Travel was never a safe business in those days, and people tended to travel in groups: pilgrims accompanied merchants, and ordinary travelers joined the retinues of ecclesiastics and dignitaries. Félibien tells of the young Callot, who, "having heard tell of the beautiful sights to be seen in Italy," had "such a powerful desire to go there that, although he was no more than eleven or twelve years of age, he resolved to leave his father's house" and "joined a group of Gypsies who were also bound for Italy; without a care for the company he was keeping, or for the rigors of the journey, or for the disgraceful life he was leading, he went with them as far as Florence," and from there finally reached Rome, but "had no sooner arrived when he met with a group of merchants from Nancy who recognized him . . . and took him back to his parents." Although Félibien's accounts are normally based on information drawn directly from contemporary sources and are generally reliable, this story was viewed by Callot's biographers as no more than pure fantasy. Upon reflection, however, it is not so implausible. Such an escapade was perfectly conceivable where Rome was concerned. The "passion to see Italy" was common in Lorraine and the journey there no longer intimidating. Thus, in 1623, we find François de Nomé declaring, in the presence of a lawyer this time, and without the slightest hint of any ulterior motive, that he left Metz, his home, and his mother at the tender age of nine, to go to Rome "with other persons."

It was not as if these young travelers left Lorraine completely behind when they reached Rome. Mail came once a week from Nancy via Venice. Money did not present a problem, thanks to the various bankers with representatives in Rome, such as the Machon family of Nancy whose correspondent was Canon Jennel, an important prelate in the Curia. It was very rare for a new arrival not to have some relative, or at least an acquaintance, already in Rome, and in any case, there were always compatriots ready to help out. The natural meeting place for these expatriates was the Church of San Luigi dei Francesi. Lorrainers would not have a true church of their own until 1662, when the pope granted them San-Nicola-in-Agone, but they did have the chapel of St. Nicolas in San Luigi dei Francesi. Charles III was anxious to contribute to the building and decoration of the French church because, to quote his order of 3 March 1582, "a number of our subjects, prompted by extreme devotion and piety to see the holy places of the city [of Rome] or engaged in particular business of their own, together with other persons eager to travel and driven by an instinctive and laudable desire to see and know with their own eyes all the antiquities and vestiges of the former greatness of this erstwhile famous republic of which they have heard tell, transport themselves to the said city [of Rome]," and "given the difference of the Italian language and the close affinity our subjects have to the French nation and the understanding and command they have of its language, they could not hope to find a better place to perform their devotions and discharge their duties to God than the church of Saint-Louis . . . and have long been welcomed there . . . and poor pilgrims and other indigent of our subjects are treated no differently from native Frenchmen, but given alms and shelter in the hospital in just the same way, at the cost and expense of the said church. . . ." Indeed, of the twenty-four members of the congregation of Saint-Louis, twelve were French, six were from Savoy, and six were from Lorraine, and the chapel of St. Nicolas became home to the Order of the Faithful of both sexes from Lorraine and the duchy of Bar. In addition, the prelates from Lorraine, who were very active and in good standing with the pope, were quick to defend and promote the interests of their compatriots, even when these conflicted with those of the French king's subjects.

Included in this number were the artists, many of whom managed to set themselves up and carve out the beginnings of an excellent career in Rome. Jean Leclerc worked with Saraceni, one of the best-known artists in Rome around 1617-1620, and would certainly have continued doing so if a large commission had not taken them both off to Venice, where Saraceni died unexpectedly. Claude Deruet found such favor with the pope that he was awarded the cross of Knight of Christ by the pontiff in 1618. Charles Mellin, who was younger but in Rome even before 1618, quickly acquired such a reputation that he was nicknamed "le Lorrain," *il Lorenese*, a sobriquet that passed to Claude Gellée on Mellin's death in 1649. By then Claude was at the height of his career: as early as 1640 we find Mazarin's secretary in Rome observing that "he has no compunction about demanding three hundred écus for one of his largest canvases and taking eight months to deliver it. . . ."

In recounting the story of Callot, Félibien describes the young Lorrainer as being seized by "a passion to see Italy and a love of painting." Georges de La Tour was almost certainly inspired by the same combination of emotions. He appears to have been rather more prudent, however, and thus would have waited until his apprenticeship was over before setting off for Rome. As Tribout de Morembert has suggested, he may well have made the journey with Pierre Georges, who was born in Vic, was more or less the same age as La Tour, and could have been a friend.

What finally convinces us that La Tour must have gone to Rome is quite simply the fact that the painter we find in Lorraine in 1616 is deeply imbued with the spirit of Caravaggio that had prevailed in Rome since 1610 and which he could only have encountered there. The Albi paintings, for instance, are marked by a brand of realism akin to that of Valentin, and what distinguishes La Tour's paintings of hurdy-gurdy players from those of Bellange is the Caravaggesque approach. The very subjects La Tour chooses, from cardplayers to Christ with St. Joseph in the carpenter's shop, are related to this period and style of Roman painting. It seems almost inconceivable that La Tour should have learned about this style of painting indirectly rather than experiencing it in person as a young man of twenty actually in Rome.

There remains one objection to the hypothesis: no trace of La Tour has been found in Rome, whereas almost all the other artists from Lorraine have turned up in the archives sooner or later. We know absolutely nothing about his life in Italy, his travels, his connections or adventures. One reason for this is perhaps that the Easter census records, the *stati d'anime*, which are by far the best source, show many gaps for this period and have not yet been thoroughly studied. Another is that young artists were often referred to by their first name alone: our earliest precise document on Leclerc dates from when he was in his thirties, and that on Deruet, when he was twenty-five. At that age, George La Tour was already back in his native Lorraine. On the other hand, it may be that La Tour was already fortunate enough to have solid recommendations. If he came to Rome under the patronage of some diplomat or ecclesiatical dignitary, or if he was lodged in a monastery, it would be understandable that his name does not appear in any of the contemporary parish records.

LA TOUR BEFORE LA TOUR?

In my view, the silence of the Roman archives is not enough to rule out an Italian voyage. It is hardly rash to think that La Tour was in Rome until about 1616, and that his stay there was a relatively long one. He is unlikely to have run across Callot, who probably left Rome for Florence as early as 1611. He is very likely, however, to have come across Jean Le Clerc, who, if Félibien is to be believed, arrived in Rome when he was about fifteen and did not leave until 1619. The same would be true for Claude Deruet, who was there between 1613 and 1619, and Israël Henriet, Claude Henriet's son, who stayed there at about the same time. He would not have taken any notice of Claude Gellée, who was still too young to be anything more than a *garzone* in Tassi's studio, and he could not have encountered Charles Mellin or Nicolas de la Fleur, both of whom belonged to a different generation.

Far more interesting to him than these artists from Lorraine would have been the group of French painters who were eagerly taking up Caravaggism, from which they derived personal forms of expression: Vignon, Vouet (who arrived there in 1613), Valentin, Tournier, and Régnier. He may have come across Terbrugghen, who was born in 1588 but already back in Utrecht by 1614, and possibly knew Honthorst, born in 1590 and apparently in Rome by 1612, and Baburen, who was born in about

The "Serrone Master." *Christ and the Virgin with Saint Joseph in his Workshop.*
Church of Santa Maria Assunta, Serrone (Foligno)

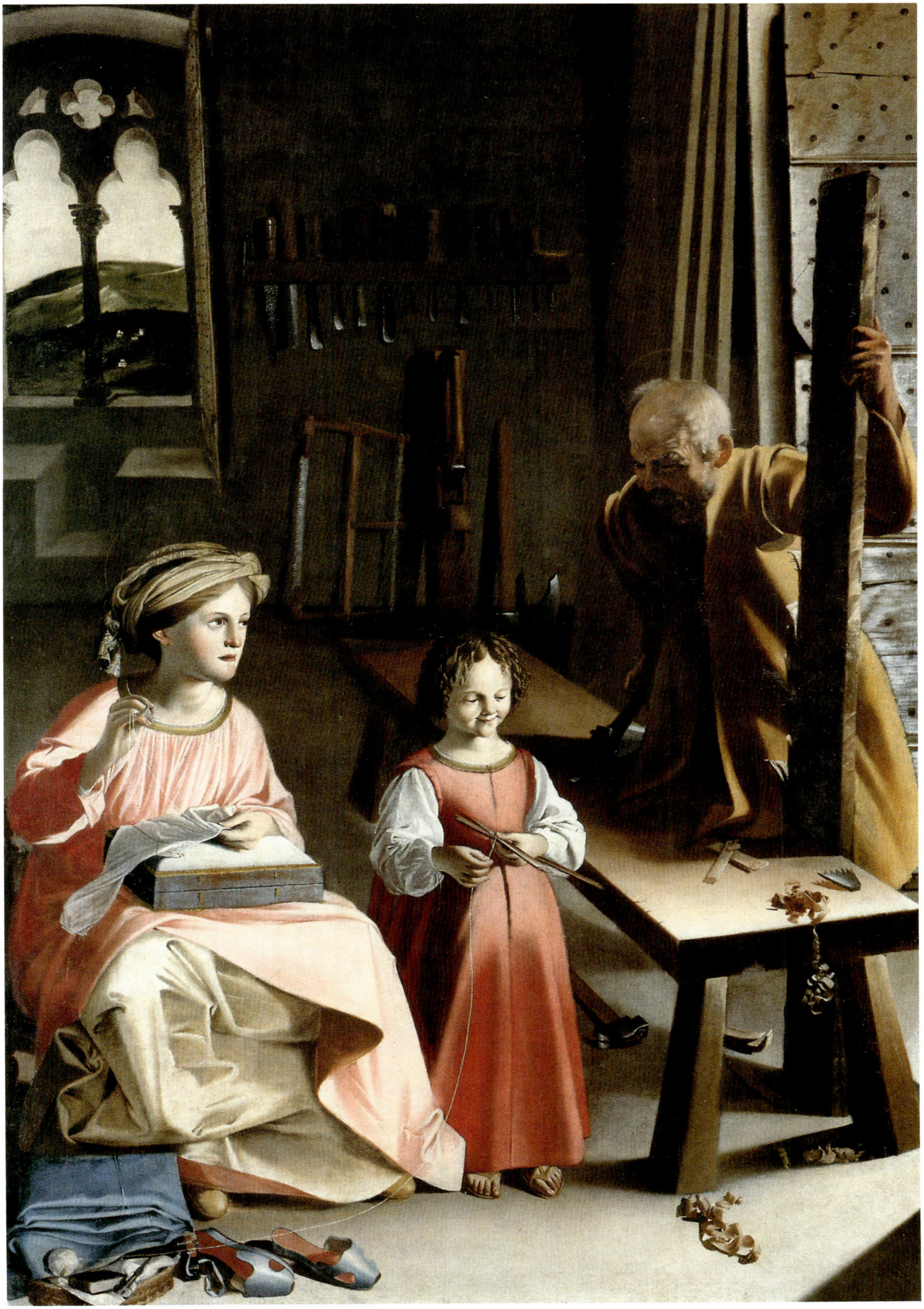

1587 and probably also in Rome by the same year. He must have known Ribera, who was born in 1591 and was in Rome in 1613, and especially Manfredi, who was born in 1582 and died after 1622. This list is intended simply to indicate the vast range of contacts La Tour could have made. Amid such a wealth of choices, chance alone dictates encounters, and whether or not something will develop depends on personal affinities that we can never fully understand. People do not become friends simply because they are the same age. On the other hand, the work of a distant painter can often play a more decisive role than a friendship close at hand, and contact with a disciple can often prove more formative than learning from the master himself.

Only La Tour's paintings could enlighten us on this score, but these are virtually impossible to identify. In a matter of weeks, young hopefuls freshly arrived in Rome and open to every influence would be painting in the style of the current artist in favor, and their work would become indistinguishable from the rest. It took time for them to develop a character of their own. If they were not sufficiently successful or did not stay long enough, in contrast with Vouet or Valentin, the Roman collections, show no trace of their names while giving their works more impressive attributions.

Mention must be made here of a recently discovered painting. We would be rash to leap to any conclusions about it, but equally wrong simply to pass over it. As a result of the systematic research carried out over the last few years in Umbria under the direction of Bruno Toscano, a painting that had hitherto escaped the notice of art historians was discovered in the old parish church of Serrone, an out-of-the-way village on the road from Rome to Loretta and Ancona. It is a fairly large altarpiece (263 x 183 cm) showing the infant Christ with Joseph in the carpenter's shop, and it hung above one of the altars in the transept. Unfortunately, it is unsigned; the parish records seem to have been destroyed, and it would require an exceptional stroke of luck for the original commission to reappear. Recognized as the early work of an obviously great artist, the painting was published in the second volume of *Ricerche in Umbria* in 1980, but for lack of a satisfactory attribution, it was finally credited to an unidentified Caravaggesque painter of Flemish or French origin. For the 1989 exhibition, "Pitture del Seicento: ricerche in Umbria" held at the Rocca Alborzia in Spoleto—one of the most remarkable shows in Italy in recent years—the painting was stripped of all its old varnish and reemerged in excellent condition. Because of its high quality, the work was placed at the center of the exhibition, even though it was competing with many famous names and fine works. Its strange poetry, refined use of color, and the original treatment of the subject made it instantly compelling. This was clearly the work of a remarkable individual. For want of anything better, the artist was given the conventional title of *il Maestro di Serrone*, the Serrone Master.

The authors of the exhibition catalogue admitted their surprise. Nothing, in the painting of Umbria, the Marches, or Rome could explain this style. In terms of character, it was unlike anything art historians could recall. Not a single name sprang to mind, even for the sake of comparison—except that of Georges de La Tour.

It was a fairly audacious idea, and Bruno Toscano was wary in advancing it. To someone who knew the painting only in reproduction, it might seem more specious than serious. At the time of the 1980 publication, I had immediately thought of La Tour but quickly dismissed the idea as being too convenient, since it so neatly bore out the supposition that La Tour had spent time in Italy. The opportunity to see the work with my own eyes after it had been cleaned and to examine it afresh convinced me, however, that the hypothesis cannot be dismissed so lightly.

In terms of style and in overall conception, the painting seems to belong to the period around 1612-1620. The subject fits perfectly with the religious mood of the day, which highlighted the infancy of Jesus: different versions of the same theme turn up in the Roman works of Honthorst and Trophime Bigot. At the same time, in its overall spirit and in many details, this work is quite unlike any other of the period. It bears the stamp of a young painter of genius who has absorbed everything around him but has already developed a personality of his own, and even at the risk of seeming awkward, wants to say something different in a different way.

The work certainly is startling. At the center stands the Christ child, still in an infant's dress. He is looking down with a strange smile fixed on his lips. He has taken two scraps of wood from his father's workbench and is tying them together in the shape of a cross with a piece of thread from his mother's sewing basket in what

The "Serrone Master." *Christ and the Virgin with Saint Joseph in his Workshop*, detail: The Child Christ.

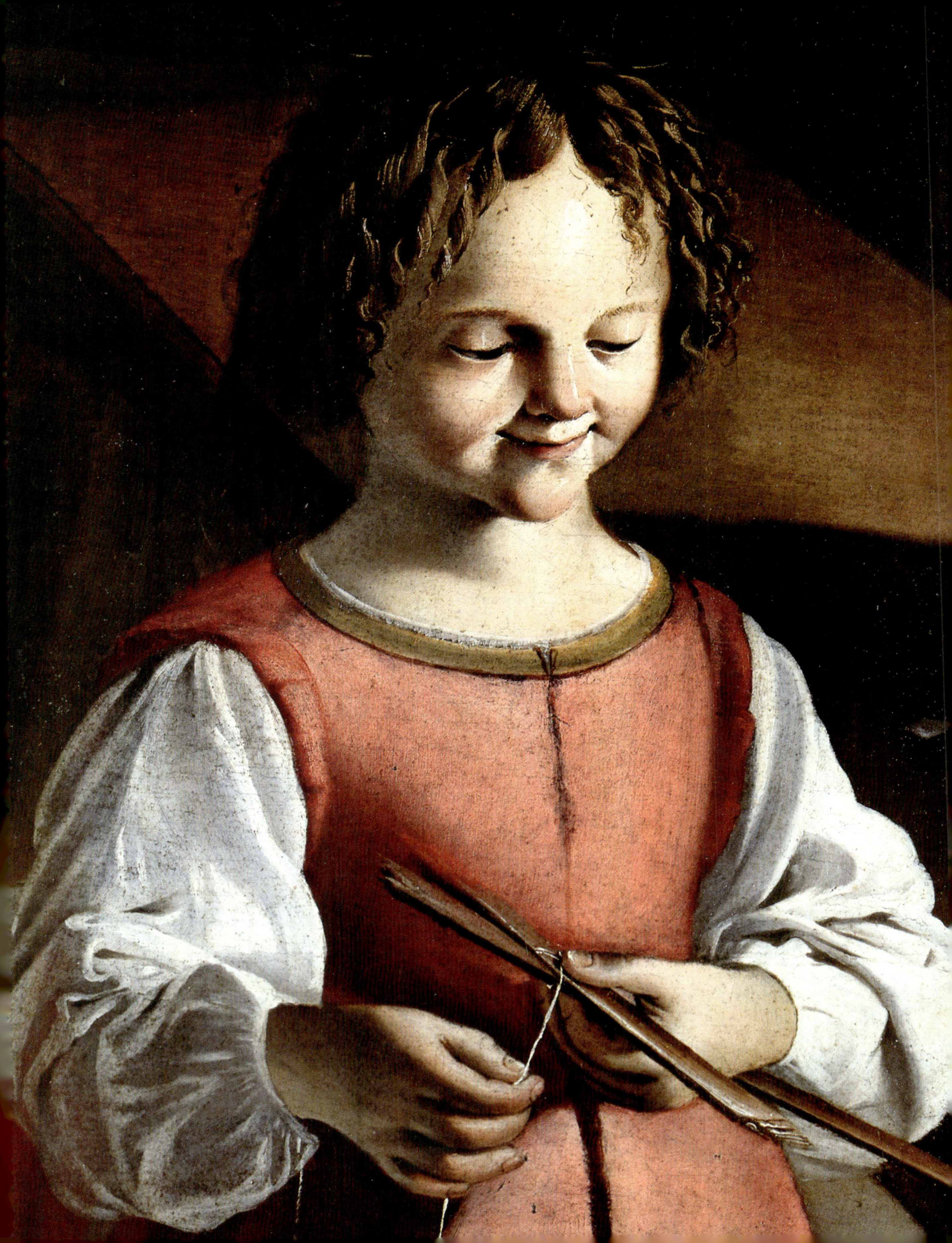

is clearly a prefiguration of the Passion. His parents have stopped their work to watch him. This could have been little more than a clever anecdote, anticipating the intellectual subtleties of the Pre-Raphaelites. Instead, it is both solemn and powerful. The Virgin is shown sitting and embroidering, dressed in a pink smock, with a curious kind of yellow turban on her head. Her expression is rapt, as if she were contemplating an invisible but henceforward certain future. The Sacrifice has just entered into this everyday scene, and time has stopped. Nonetheless, a beautiful light filters in through the half-open door of the workshop, and falling on the hoary, bald-headed figure of Joseph, it brings out the back of the old man's neck and his ear as he begins to guess at what is to come without yet understanding it. The Albi *Apostles*, which we shall discuss in due course, spring immediately to mind: hardy, concerned, but ready to stand any test of devotion.

The color scheme is distinctive: predominantly light, with grays and ochres livened up here and there with reds and a clever touch of blue for contrast. The technique is meticulous throughout, with certain impressive passages where the artist has clearly made a special effort, such as the rough-planed plank of wood shown in section, the wood shavings, the work basket that, in combination with the two clogs, becomes a carefully composed still life, and the old door with studded panels treated almost in trompe-l'oeil. The drawing is deliberately crisp in places, but fluid and light in the details. The pronounced realism that expresses itself in the rendering of materials and the quasi-ethnological presentation of the carpenter's tools is, paradoxically, combined with an obvious economy: the floor is stripped bare, the workbench clear, the Infant's hair represented by stylized locks, the Virgin's face reduced to a few simple planes. But there are still more startling aspects. A gothic window appears in the background, as surprising to find in Umbria as François de Nomé's whimsical reminiscences of Metz were in Naples. No other Caravaggesque painting has anything like it, and the same is true for the little Italian landscape visible beyond it, deliberately designed to draw the eye out of the picture. The disordered folds of the Virgin's golden, red-lined skirt, are quite unlike any drapery in Italian art, and recall the sculptures of Burgundy and Konrad Witz's paintings of saints. Why such throwbacks to the fifteenth century in a work painted around 1615? Most surprising of all, these disparate elements—the archaic, the Caravaggesque, and the deliberately singular—all combine to render the painting a poem. The painting arrests the eye, and the poem has something of the calm, the grandeur, the blend of truth and nobility of La Tour.

There were plenty of art lovers in Rome, but there were even more artists, and commissions from outside the city were certainly not spurned, particularly by younger painters. There were works in the Spoleto exhibition by other French painters such as Noël Quillerier, who received various commissions for churches in Bervia, Serpete and Belfiore in 1625, and Jean Lhomme himself who painted a large *Pardon of Assisi* for the church in Notoria in 1631. Could it be that after a certain amount of time in Rome, La Tour hastened to accept a commission for an altarpiece? There is certainly nothing to say that this was not the case. Should we therefore see this as his first masterpiece? Such a conclusion would be precipitous.

It is hard to understand why a young painter, still reeling from his first exposure to Rome and by all accounts quite converted to Caravaggio, should have gone in the opposite direction with clearly defined volumes and a light palette. It is equally hard to explain gothic elements in the work of a painting coming from Nancy, where no one else seems to have had any particular interest in the Middle Ages. On the other hand, this painting exists, and we have to ask ourselves whether such a curious amalgam would be more explicable if a young Bavarian, Czech, or Portuguese artist were to turn up in the role of the "Serrone Master."

There are cases when art history has to admit its uncertainties and accept doubt as the only honest position. Let us prudently retain the "Master of Serrone" attribution. But let us keep in mind that such a canvas might have been painted at the time La Tour is likely to have been in Rome. Let us remember, too, that in this great melting pot it was not unknown for the stronger personalities to preserve an independent character of their own.

The "Serrone Master." *Christ and the Virgin with Saint Joseph in his Workshop*, detail: Saint Joseph.

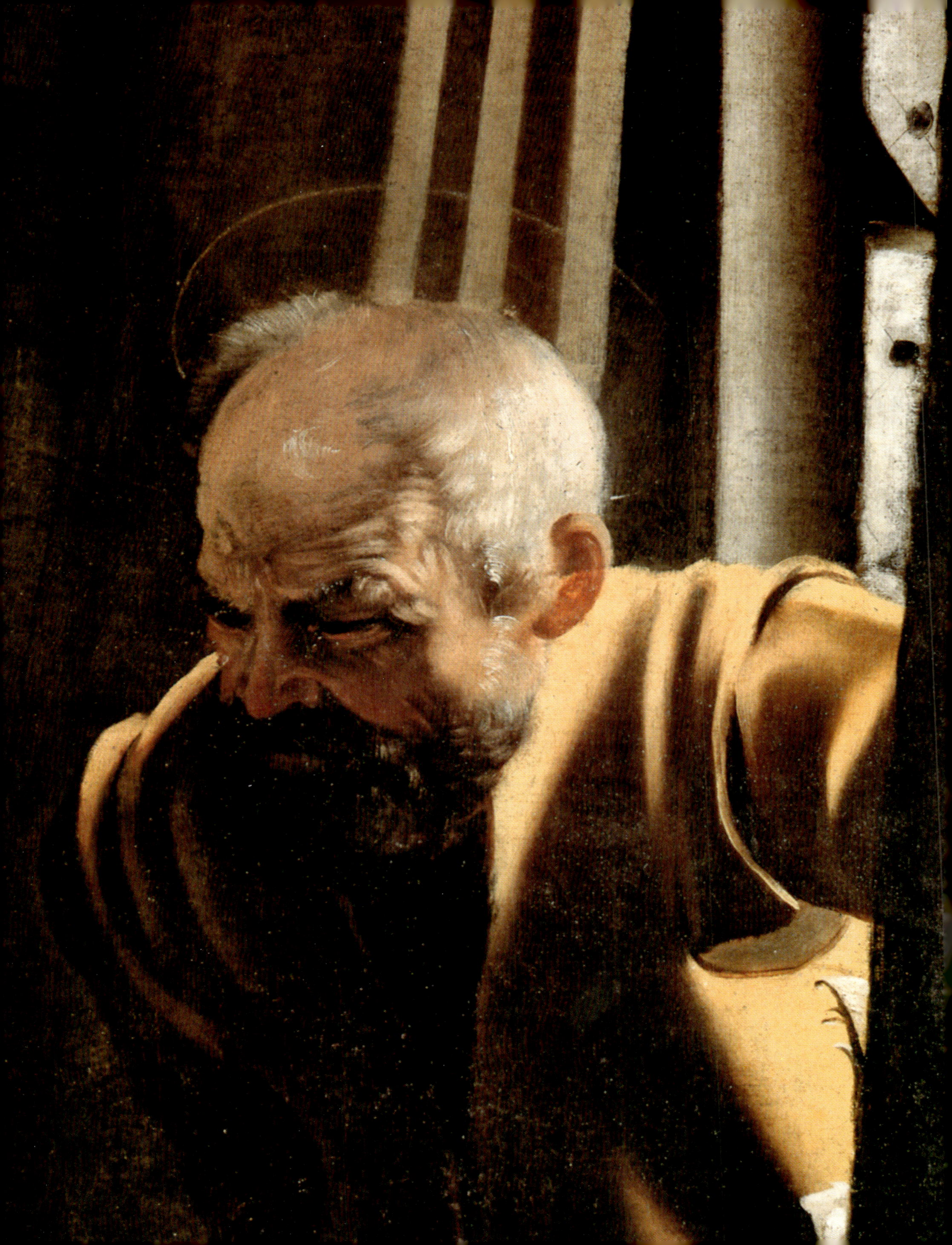

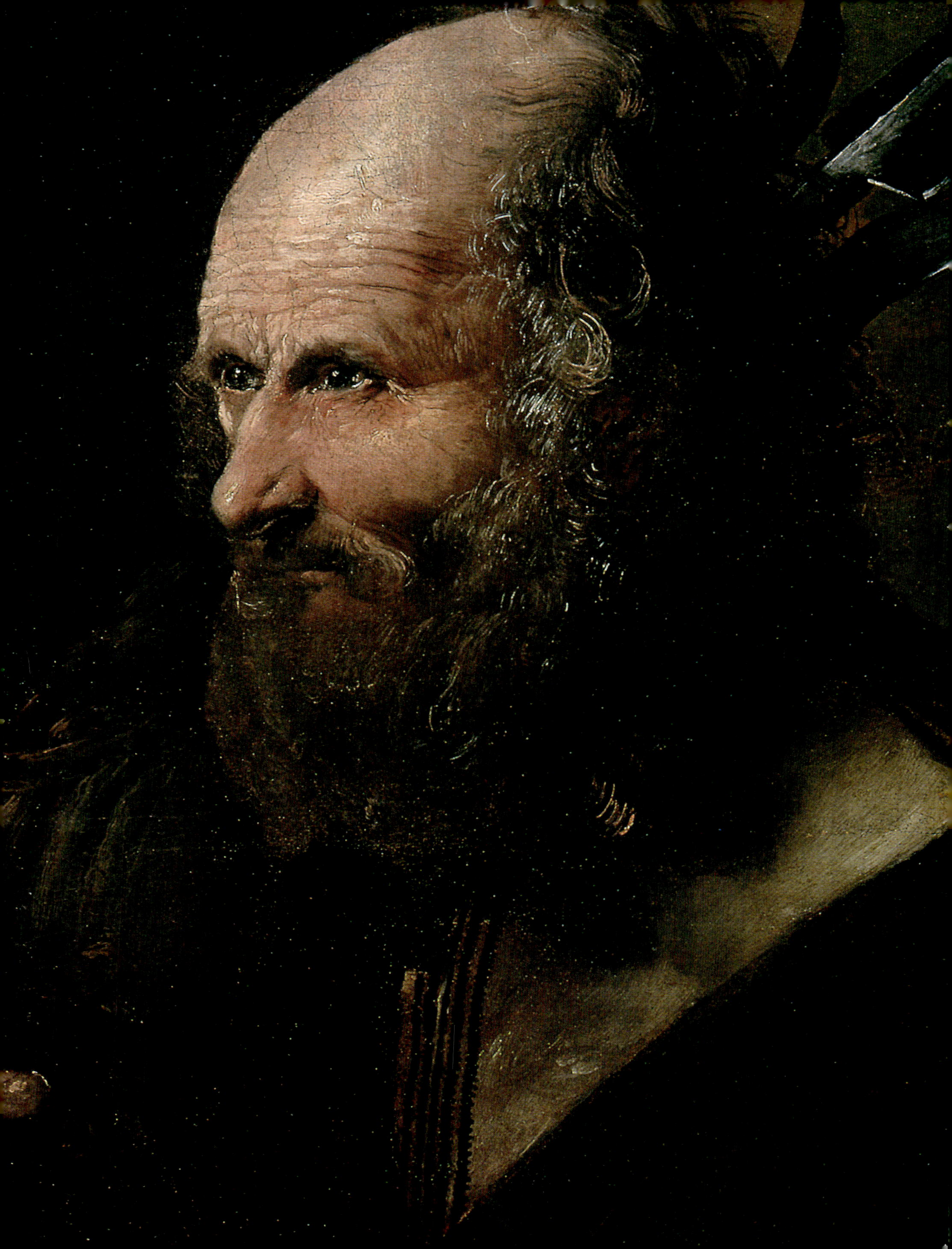

THE CERTAINTIES OF REALISM

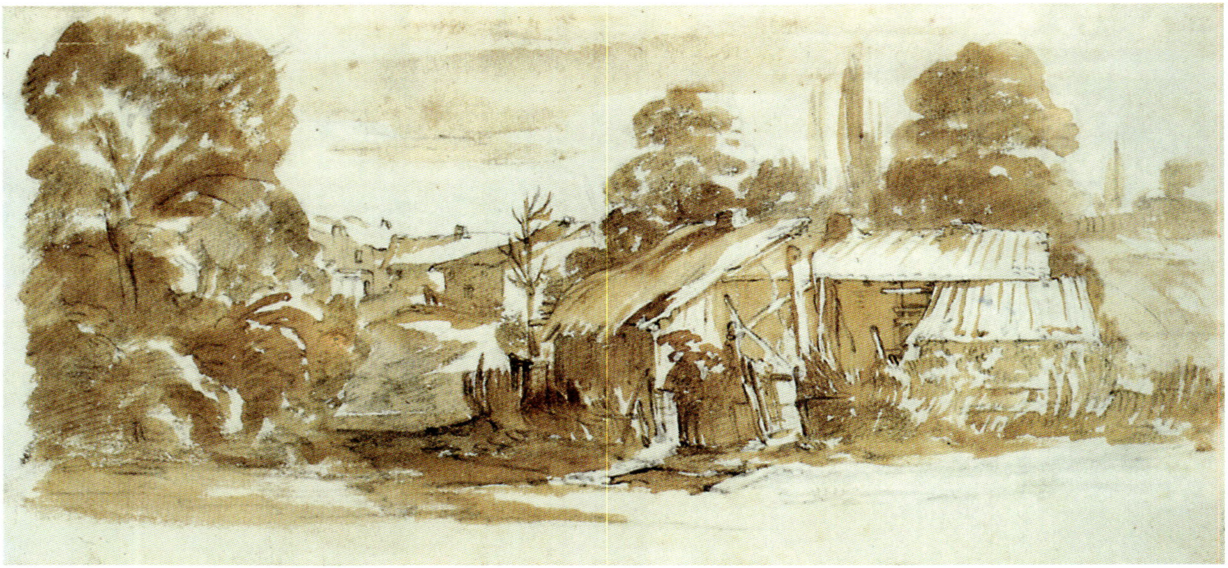

THE RETURN TO LORRAINE

On 20 October 1616, in Vic, Georges de La Tour became godfather to a girl named Marguerite, the daughter of one Claude Fontaine. The record of the event, discovered in the municipal archives, is of little interest in itself, but of major importance for the history of the painter. La Tour was in Vic by that date; he had returned to Lorraine. At twenty-three, it was time for him to settle down and choose a career.

It is possible that La Tour had left Italy quite recently. He may well have spent a number of years there, either in Rome itself or in one of the provinces, and then come straight back to Lorraine. Or, he may, relying on a patron or possible commissions, have made various stops along the way home. He may have been in no hurry to abandon the carefree life of a wanderer. We can readily imagine him at this stage, for instance, being drawn to Albi to paint the series of Apostles discussed later.

There is even an odd coincidence in the timing of La Tour's reappearance in Vic. Jacques Bellange, the celebrated painter to the duke of Lorraine, is known to have died some time between 10 August 1616 and the end of the same year. La Tour reappeared in Lorraine on 20 October. This could have been no more than a fluke. On the other hand, the ambitious young painter may have heard about Bellange's demise and decided that there was an opportunity waiting for him in Lorraine.

A document that has resurfaced recently from the archives may provide another clue. Michel Sylvestre has rediscovered an acknowledgment of two large debts, of 9,170 and 1,000 Barrois francs, to a merchant in Nancy. It is in the name of Claude de Lisseras, captain of Châtel-sur-Moselle, lord of Anderny, and gentleman of the duke of Lorraine's chamber. Claude de Lisseras was young but of considerable rank. He was descended from one of the oldest noble families in the district, and in 1610 he married a member of another, Claire de Choiseul. In 1616 his father was made seneschal of Lorraine and the Barrois, one of the highest honors in the duchy. One of the two witnesses to the document, apparently on the merchant's side, was a tailor from Nancy. The other was "sir George de la Thoure, attendant of the said sir of Anderni." The text is dated 21 February 1617.

Could this have been our Georges de La Tour? It seems more than likely. True, he is not referred to as a painter, and we must always remember that there were noble branches of the La Tour family. Anne Reinbold has pointed out that there was another La Tour at the time, also called Georges, but a gentleman by rank and easier to picture in the retinue of the seneschal's son. But he would have been nearly fifty at the time the document was signed, while the lawyer who drafted it refers simply to "sir Georges de la Tour" and not "nobleman Georges de La Tour," and he gives his name second, which would not be unusual if the witness were still a minor, as the painter would have been at the time. In fact, there is nothing surprising about the idea of young Georges de La Tour, painter, attending a young lord in Nancy.

Preceding page:
St. Judas Thaddeus, detail.
Musée Toulouse-Lautrec, Albi

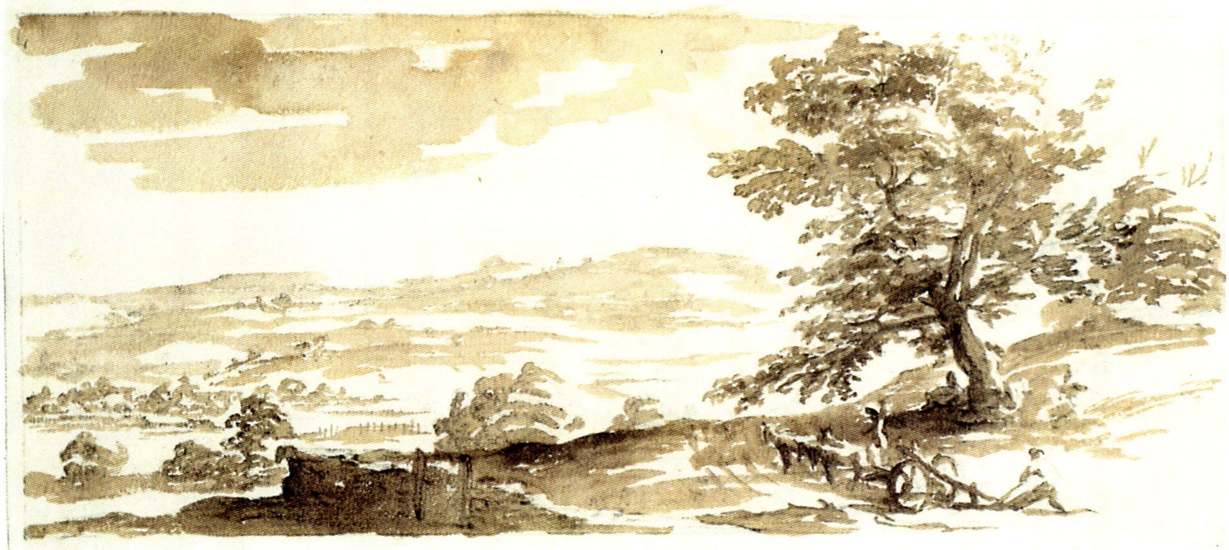

The court of Lorraine welcomed newcomers and was more attentive to talent than titles. A man was judged on his looks, his swordsmanship, his dress, his knowledge of the outside world, his ability to hold a literary conversation, his wit, and his gallantry. La Tour was probably competent in several of these domains, as well as having his talents as a painter and his experience of Italy to recommend him. A young man of twenty-three could quite happily make his way in the very best of Nancy society on a good deal less, even without a title. François-Georges Pariset relates how three young adventurers managed to worm their way into the duke's circle in 1614. One of the three, Jean-Baptiste de Montureux, who was about twenty-one, was a gentleman by birth, from Franche-Comté. The second, who was twenty-five or twenty-six and came from a respectable Cambrésis family, was named Choisnin and claimed to be of noble stock; in fact, he had led a debauched life with a band of strolling players and had decided to lie low in Lorraine while the dust settled on a number of scandals in which he was implicated in France. The third, Ogier Mollinary, was twenty-one and came from the Ville Basse area of Carcassonne, where he had already been sentenced to prison in absentia. He called himself Baron de La Roque Saint-Martin and lived by swindling, but he swept the Lorrainers away with his perfume, his curled hair, and the golden sword at his side, and his elegant appearance gained him access all the way to the duchess's bedroom. These three had a literary talent of a sort and penned little verses, epigrams, and anagrams that made them the darlings of the ladies at court. Their scribbling was to be their undoing: they became cocky and went too far, circulating a scandalous lampoon entitled *In Praise of the Heroic and Veneric Ladies of the Court of Nancy*. This time they were hunted down, exposed, interrogated, sentenced to make amends, dressed in nothing but their shirts, beaten with birch rods, and then banished from the duchy for life. All things considered, the punishment was a light one. What is truly surprising is the readiness with which the court of Lorraine had accepted these strangers on their word alone. It was this same attitude, however, that allowed the talented young Abraham Racinot, who came from a common but reasonably well-to-do Lorraine family, to flourish as he did. With no more than a background in art and literature acquired in Italy, good looks, and an exceptional skill in fencing, Racinot managed to get into the court of Charles III and went on to become the nobleman André Des Bordes, first lord-in-waiting to Henri II, lord of Gibeaumeix and Loupvent, and member of both State and Privy Council as of October 1617, in other words, one of the most powerful political figures in the duchy, and one of the wealthiest.

Georges de La Tour was obviously nothing like the bogus baron de La Roque, nor could he rival Henri II's famous favorite, who was then at the height of his success. But it is easy to imagine that, coming back from Rome, probably with money earned from his painting and accustomed to his liberty, having neither studio nor apprentice and doubtless full of ambition, he would not have rushed to settle down.

LORRAINE IN GEORGES DE LA TOUR'S TIME
Left: Jacques Callot. *Landscape with Peasant Cottages*. Above: *Landscape with Laborer*. Black chalk and bistre wash.
Album Silvestre (Nos. 391 and 389), Chatsworth

There is no reason to suppose, if this were the case, that La Tour fell into the sort of youthful debauchery that he was to treat in later masterpieces: women, gambling, tobacco, and wine were probably not an issue. Returning from abroad, La Tour would have had little to gain from living quietly with his mother and father in Vic. True talent does not get anywhere by burying itself away. The best way to obtain favors from the duke and to rise to rapid fame was to make himself known in Nancy, to mix with the lords at court, and to win their esteem, or better, their friendship.

We should be wary of reading too much into a fragment from a legal document. Yet it could well reflect a faithful picture of the kind of person La Tour really was at the time. He returned from Italy not as some small provincial craftsman coming back to his home territory, but as a painter whose Italian experience had made him fully aware of the importance of his art and of his own worth, who was convinced that his travels and talent put him on a par with noble society, and who was intent on achieving well-deserved recognition. At all events, a friendship with Claude de Lisseras and his circle would help to explain how La Tour came so quickly to profit from the strokes of good fortune, not normally within reach of a young unknown from Vic, that have hitherto surprised historians: a brillant marriage with a nobleman's daughter and letters of exemption from the duke of Lorraine himself.

MARRIAGE TO DIANE

It was very rare for painters from Lorraine or France to marry while they were in Italy, unless they became rich and famous: getting married meant setting up house and having children, and thus almost inevitably having to make a career there. When they came back, however, it was normally a top priority and as a rule they married within a year, sometimes even six months. At home, the sort of easy relationships that were perfectly acceptable in Rome, where foreign visitors were part and parcel of life, were frowned upon not only in the provinces, but also in Paris. Outside of the Church, therefore, bachelor life had little to recommend it. Moreover, a wife often brought a dowry with her and almost always had useful connections for getting established and building up a clientele. La Tour was no exception. On 2 July 1617 he drew up a marriage contract with Diane Le Nerf, a native of Lunéville. The church service was probably held shortly afterward, but the parish register is now lost.

It was a very good match, and one that must have caused quite a stir in Vic. On the La Tour side, the marriage contract was witnessed by the mayor, Jean Martiny, and on the Le Nerf side, by the lieutenant general Alphonse de Rambervillers himself and Jean Du Halt, treasurer general of the bishopric of Metz. It may have also been a marriage of love. Diane must feature in a number of La Tour's paintings, but we have no way of identifying her among the painter's female models. What about the oval-faced courtesan in *The Cheat*, with her full lips, her finely chiseled Roman nose, sleek hair, and wide, shallow-set eyes? She reappears in the guise of the woman with the book in the engraved version of *The Newborn Child*, in the Fabius *Magdalen*, and in an older-looking version as St. Anne in *The Education of the Virgin*. Be that as it may, we have no reason to suppose that Diane was ugly, and a year and half's difference in age (she was born in October 1591, Georges not until March 1593) hardly made for an incongruous match. From the time they married until their deaths (within a few days of each other), there is not the slightest hint of anything but complete harmony between them.

One thing is certain: La Tour did not marry Diane Le Nerf for her dowry alone. The marriage contract stipulated a communal estate settlement, and Diane stood to inherit a not inconsiderable fortune from her side of the family. For the time being, however, the dowry was relatively modest: five hundred francs contributed by her aunt, who seems to have been particularly fond of her; two cows and a heifer, some clothes, and a few pieces of furniture. It is true that Georges did not bring much to the match either: his father paid for the wedding and provided clothes for his son, the basic household furniture, and a small annual allowance until the inheritance came through. It seems that the young La Tour had already demonstrated his ability to make money from his painting and that his talent was respected.

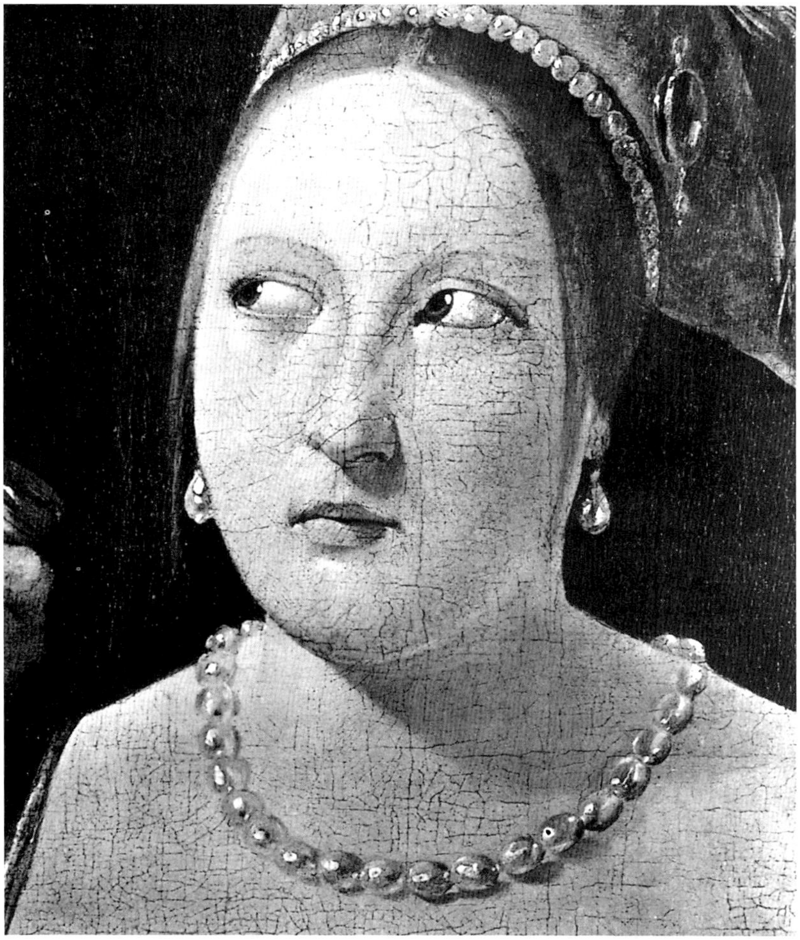

THE FACE OF DIANE,
GEORGES DE LA TOUR'S MODEL?
Left:
The Cheat with the Ace of Diamonds, detail.
Musée du Louvre, Paris

Below left:
The Repentant Magdalen, detail.
National Gallery of Art, Washington, D.C.

Below right:
The Education of the Virgin, detail.
Frick Collection, New York

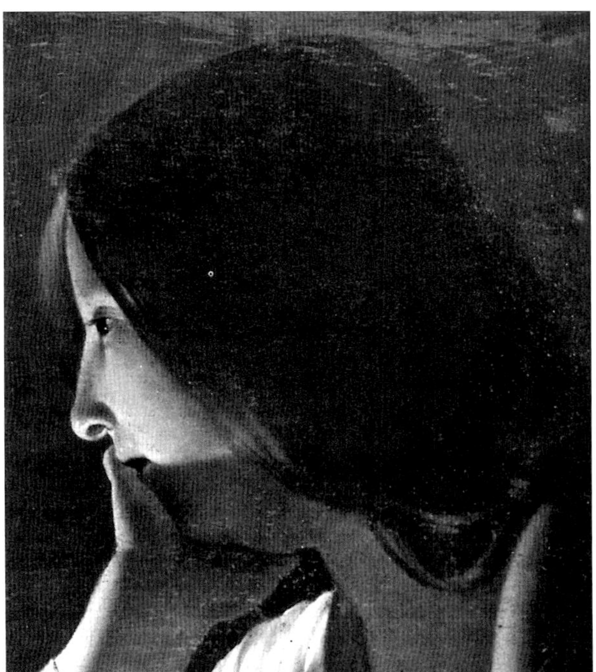

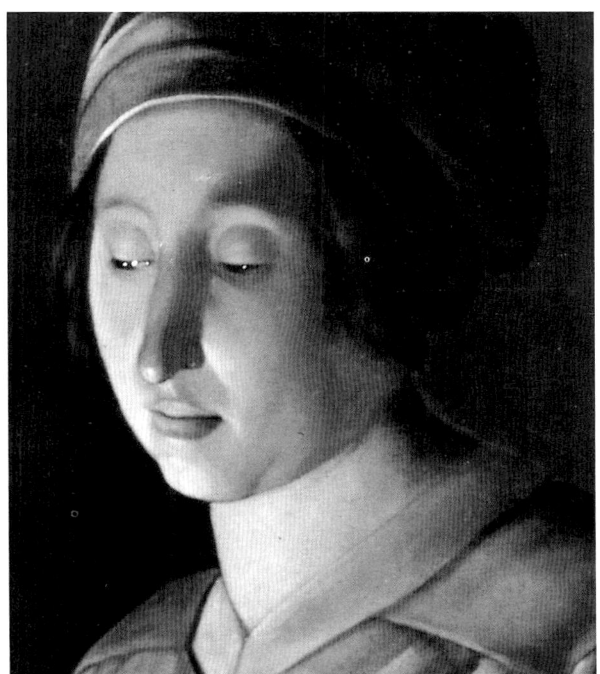

Diane's dowry may have been meager, but her family was rich and noble. They were minor nobles, admittedly, and not of long standing: Diane's grandfather, Lucas Le Nerf, was a rich wool merchant who had been elevated to the nobility in 1555. Her father, Jean Le Nerf, however, was the duke's Surperintendent of Finance and well established in Lunéville; in 1595 he was credited as being one of the richest and most important men in the city. The rest of her family ranged from minor lords down to parish priests, notary publics, and master apothecaries. All twelve of Jean Le Nerf's known children married well: Marie, for instance, married the lord of Dieuze, and Claude, the captain of Romy-à-la-Gaillarde. Jean's niece, Anne Raoul, married Alphonse de Rambervillers. La Tour was thus first cousin by marriage to the lieutenant general of the bailiwick, with direct connections to the local nobility.

It is difficult to imagine a marriage more likely to lead to a highly successful painting career and a rapid rise in social status while not in any way offending convention. As already indicated, there was no real barrier separating the world into which Georges was born and the one into which he married. The only appreciable difference was the question of noble status, to which La Tour had no official title, unlike Diane, who is always appropriately referred to in documents as *dame* or *demoiselle*. This was no trifling detail, but it did not imply any real difference in culture or wealth. As soon as he had a house, land, and money to his name, La Tour would be entirely accepted by his wife's family.

It was often the case, and even a term of the marriage contract, that newlyweds lived with the groom's parents for a year or two after they were married. This is probably what happened to Georges and Diane. Indeed, when Georges's only surviving brother, François, who was seven years his junior (Jean and Sibille saw five of their children die), married in 1622, his mother, by then a widow, declared that she wanted to give him "the same advantages that her said late husband and she had given to the said Georges de La Tour," promising namely to "accommodate the said couple in her own house, for a period of two entire consecutive years, starting from the day of their marriage." Georges lived in Vic, then, after his marriage, and it was there that his first known child, Philippe, was baptized on 5 August 1619. The boy's godfather was a nobleman, Jean Philippe Demion, lord of Gombervaux and a person of some standing, and his godmother was Diane de Beaufort, lady of Saulcerotte, namely Diane's aunt and benefactress, to whom she owed her dowry: the young painter clearly valued his newly acquired connections.

THE MOVE TO LUNÉVILLE

La Tour would hardly have remained idle in Vic. Perhaps he continued cultivating his lofty connections at the court in Nancy, but he must have jumped at every chance of work that came his way. He may have secured big commissions in the area, or even farther afield. If the Albi series were not painted on La Tour's way back from Italy, it could equally well have been done at this point. A great many monasteries were being established or expanded in Lorraine at the time: he may well have managed to paint some altarpieces. On the other hand, he may have sought to build up a private clientele by producing smaller paintings of both religious and other subjects. He may have tried to carve out a niche for himself in Vic, where, however, Dogoz was already well established and liable to fight off competition all the more fiercely because he appears to have had a number of outstanding debts at the time. Alternatively, he may still have had his sights set on Bellange's empty place at the duke's court. We have no record of Henri II buying anything from him at this point, however. Nor is there any documentary evidence of work done for churches or monasteries in Lorraine, although it is true that this was often done by private agreement rather than formal contract. In the absence of hard facts, we can do no more than speculate.

We do know, though, that two key events took place within the family during the second half of 1618: the death of Diane's father, Jean Le Nerf, in Lunéville, where he was buried on 30 July, and that of Georges's father, Jean de La Tour, in Vic at an unknown date, although certainly before the end of May. We know nothing of the psychological effects of these events. We do not know much more about how the estates were divided, but whatever the details of La Tour's inheritance, it clearly made setting up on his own a realistic proposition. Georges and Diane were due to leave his father's house anyway in the summer of 1619. The birth of Philippe at the beginning of August must have delayed events somewhat, but the decision on where to go was becoming urgent. They opted for Lunéville. By July 1620 the young couple and their baby were settled there.

We should not be surprised at their choice. Diane was from Lunéville, and she was living there when she got married. In France at that time it was not unusual for a husband to settle in his wife's hometown, especially if she had, or hoped to come into, property there. Moreover, there was no competition from other painters in Lunéville, which was no longer the case in Nancy.

In 1619 Claude Deruet returned home from Rome. He was born in Nancy, and his father was known to the duke. He was dapper, sported the cross of the Order of Christ of Portugal, and boasted that he was a favorite of the pope; he could also claim to have been Bellange's pupil and liked to think of himself as his successor. Although he had none of Bellange's inspiration, he charmed the world with his portraits, his romantic scenes, and the pious style of his religious subjects, and was quite at home with large-scale decoration. Duke Henri II seems to have wasted no time in adopting him as his painter: by October 1619 he had granted Deruet a house to keep him in his service. La Tour was ill equipped to compete with him. The realist tradition of Caravaggio jarred with court art and did not accommodate decoration of any sort, yet La Tour was too much under its sway to change direction abruptly. When Le Clerc in turn reappeared in Nancy in 1620, bearing the title of Knight of St. Mark and fresh from painting a vast composition for the council hall in the Doge's Palace in Venice, he did attempt to set his grand Italian style side by side with Deruet's sweet nothings, and he succeeded. La Tour did not take the risk.

Once Nancy was excluded, Lunéville seemed a convenient alternative. It had great advantages for La Tour, both materially and socially. The Le Nerfs were of considerable standing in the town and had large holdings there. Diane de Saulcerotte was connected to all the most important families. Diane Le Nerf had grown up there, and her noble status was known to all. It was easy for La Tour to become a part of the tiny local aristocracy that, through its extensive land holdings and its jealously guarded privileges, solidly controlled the town.

Contrary to what one might expect, La Tour was not cut off there. Lunéville, a mere ducal town, may not have had the grandeur of Vic, which was the administrative capital of the bishops of Metz, but it was a prosperous market town at the crossroads between Burgundy, Metz, and Nancy. It was also one of Lorraine's fortified towns, with a long-established military tradition. Surrounded by ramparts, it gave direct protection to Nancy on the eastern side. The duke had the old medieval castle altered, or rather rebuilt, according to the design of his favorite architect, La Hière, and liked to stay there with his court. Given his taste for the arts, he must surely have been delighted at the idea of a brillant young painter just back from Italy settling there.

La Tour and his in-laws most likely thought to exploit this situation to its fullest potential. There would have been a certain amount of negotiating before La Tour settled in Lunéville. In leaving Vic for his wife's birthplace, La Tour was also leaving the temporal jurisdiction of the bishop of Metz and the French protectorate to become a subject of the duke of Lorraine. Henri II had just presented Deruet with a house in Nancy to keep him there. The duke could have made a similar gesture to entice a skillful painter like La Tour to one of his states. At the very least, friends must have brought La Tour to his attention. It was certainly not a sudden whim that prompted La Tour to address him the now-famous petition where he requested, in compensation for the move to Lunéville, "letters of franchise" exempting him from taxes, services, and other obligations. It is worth studying the text closely. Every word seems to have been carefully weighed:

To His Highness

In all humility, Georges de La Tour, painter born in Vic, where he now lives, remonstrates that, having married a young woman of noble rank in Lunéville, he wishes to retire thither, to render there most humble service to Your Highness, there being no other person engaged in the art and profession of the Remonstrant there nor in the vicinity. And though this art be noble in itself, he dares not hope, however, to live under your sovereignty exempt from the customary taxes and other constraints, if he does not receive letters of exemption from Your Highness, whom he very humbly beseeches to be willing to grant him this by special grace, that he may not be subject to worry or annoyance on this head, and that he may enjoy all the franchises afforded to the other freemen under your sovereignty. And he shall beseech Our Lord that Your Highness may know greatness and prosperity.

La Tour's message is clear, and it is cleverly conveyed with elegance and restraint: both the condition he lays down for settling in the ducal states and the extent to which it was in Henri's interest to settle a painter in an area that had none. There is more than a hint of pride in the request, and it is presented almost as a question of form, since painting is "noble in itself," and La Tour had married into a noble family. This was an argument that would not have carried much weight in many parts of France at the time, including the capital, when the foundation of the Académie Royale in Paris was still twenty-eight years off. It did with Henri II and his court, however. The request was sent from Vic; the reply came from Nancy dated 10 July 1620:

In view of the present request
We,
in consideration of the profession of our dear and beloved petitioner Georges de la Tour, and of his expressed wish to take up residence in our town of Lunéville,
Do by special grace and sovereign authority hereby exempt the said petitioner from all duties, fees, taxes and personal obligations due to us and our estate, along with all aids and subsidies both general and personal, ordinary and extraordinary, to be levied now or in time to come. . . .

This decree of exemption for life gave La Tour virtually all the benefits of nobility without the title—and was the first step toward actually granting him noble rank. It was no small favor. The reference to "dear and beloved George de la Tour" indicates that the duke knew the painter personally, or at least that the latter had been very thoroughly recommended to him; it was not a term the duke's secretary would have used by chance. In fact, La Tour must have presented a painting to the duke before being granted this privilege. A nobleman such as Claude de Lisseras would have been rather well placed to arrange a meeting between them.

Indeed, everything must have been carefully planned because hardly a month later, on 19 August, we find La Tour already settled in Lunéville and taking on a tailor's son by the name of Claude Baccarat as his apprentice. The contract was for four years, and the sum paid by the boy's father to his master was two hundred francs. This was relatively little, and La Tour's lifestyle must also have remained rather modest and his quarters cramped. The young man was from Lunéville and undoubtedly went back to his parents' house to sleep every night: the contract specifies that the master "should feed and keep him with victuals only." To take on an apprentice at all, however, implied having a studio and a regular turnover of work. La Tour was thus established; his career had begun.

LA TOUR, THE PROVINCIAL PAINTER

The 1620s were a prosperous decade in Lorraine, despite the apprehension that arose following Henri II's death on 31 July 1624 and Charles IV's accession to power. It was also a positive time for Georges de La Tour, during which he secured his position in Lunéville society, made his name as a painter, and explored his pictorial language to the full. It would be interesting to know what part his wife played here. But the administrative documents, the only records we have, are not particularly informative. Diane often appears alongside her husband, acting in conjunction with him. The register of births, marriages, and deaths, meanwhile, tells us that the marriage was fruitful, as was the custom of the day. Between 1619 and 1636 there were ten births—half boys and half girls—spaced out at regular intervals of between fifteen to seventeen months. Guy Cabourdin's research has shown that this pattern was typical

The petition submitted by La Tour to the duke of Lorraine in 1620.
Archives de Meurthe-et-Moselle (3 F 320, fol. 36)

A Son Altesse

Remonstre en toute humilité Georges de La Tour Peintre natif
de Vic, où il demeure, qu'ayant espousé une fille de qualité noble à
Luneville, il désireroit s'y retirer pour y rendre ses treshumbles
services à V.A. n'y ayant là ny aux environs personne de l'art et profession
du Remonstrant. Et bien que cet art soit noble de soy, si n'oseroit il esperer
de demeurer en vostre Souveraineté exempt des tailles ordinaires et autres
subjections, s'il n'a lettres d'exemption de V.A. laquelle il supplie tres
humblement luy vouloir accorder de grace specialle afin qu'il ne soit
inquieté ny molesté pour cet esgard, et qu'il jouisse de toutes les franchises
dont usent les autres francs de vostre Souveraineté. Et il suppliera nre Seigneur
pour la grandeur et prosperité de V.A.

Veue la presente requeste, nous certiorés de la profession et noble art de peinture dudit
George de La Tour suppliant [illegible]
de Luneville, Avons de grace specialle et authorité souveraine affranchy et affranchissons
par ces presentes ledit suppliant de tous traits, tailles, redevances et prestations personnelles
appartenantes à nous et à nostre dommaine ensemble de tous aydes et subsides generaulx
personnels ord^res et extraord^res imposés et à imposer. Mandons à nos treschers et feaux
les Srs Commis et deputés à la direction de nos aydes generaulx, President et gens des
Comptes de Lorraine, Procureur general de nostredit duché, ou ses substituts, receveur et
Controlleur dudit Luneville, et à tous autres nos officiers et justiciers qu'il
appartiendra de faire et souffrir jouyr ledit suppliant de l'effet de nostre presente
grace d'affranchissement sa vie naturelle durante sans luy mettre ou donner ny
souffrir luy estre mis ou donné aucun trouble ou empeschement au contraire. Et ils
rapportant et representant par nosdits receveur et controlleur copie d'icelles collationnée
en [illegible] nostre [illegible] où il appartiendra, elle leur servira de descharge des cottes dudit
suppliant. Car ainsy nous plaist. Expedié à Nancy le dixième jour de
juillet mil six cent vingt [illegible] Comte de Tornielle Grand Maistre de l'Hostel et
Surintendant des finances et [illegible] de Lorraine presents. Ainsi signé Henry
[illegible] secretaire [illegible]

Copie extraicte et deuement collationnée à l'original par le Tabellion soubsigné
[illegible]

[illegible]

in Lorraine at the time and that women generally stopped bearing children in their forties. It is not altogether impossible that there was another birth after 1636, but it is highly unlikely. Diane was forty-five by then, and with the onset of the troubles in Lunéville, La Tour was often separated from his family. By the time life returned to normal in 1642, Diane would have been fifty-one. Of the ten children, only three of the first five survived their parents. With one exception, we do not know when the others died; it may be that they perished in the great epidemics of the 1630s. To begin with, though, the painter of *The Newborn Child* gave every appearance of being surrounded by what was, for that era, a beautiful, healthy family.

We do not know where La Tour lived when he first came to Lunéville. It is unlikely to have been in the *meix* that he bought on the last day of August 1620 from the Sisters of St. Francis for 224 francs. A *meix* is a small parcel of land with a rudimentary farmer's dwelling. La Tour's *meix*, known as that of the "sheepfolds" and situated along the rampart, cannot have amounted to anything much, judging by the price. The painter was far more likely to have settled temporarily in a house belonging to the Le Nerf family or even to have moved in with his mother-in-law. In 1623, however, she decided to rejoin her son François, who was by then the parish priest of Tonnois. La Tour bought a house from her for the not inconsiderable sum of 2,500 francs. It had outhouses in the front and back, a barn, a *meix* to the rear, and a meadow, and in the front it looked onto the street leading to the Church of St. Jacques. It would seem to have been a very fine property, and one that was altogether worthy of a "notable." It was there that La Tour must have set up the studio where he was to paint the masterpieces that followed. Over the years, his standard of living improved. In 1626, for instance, he took on a new apprentice, Charles Roynet, from Remiremont, agreeing this time to provide lodging as well as board. His fee for three years was five hundred francs: every bit as high as in Paris.

La Tour clearly had the support of his relatives in Lunéville, for there are many instances where family members performed services for each other. La Tour frequently acted as a witness to legal documents, especially when they involved his immediate family or more distant relations, such as Étienne Gérard and his wife Marie Le Nerf (24 May 1621, 21 February 1623), Claude Berman (16 April 1624), Jean Berman and Claude Chamant (27 October 1625), Louis de Rambervillers, the lieutenant general's son and La Tour's cousin by marriage, who also settled in Lunéville (7 November 1629), or Nicolas Gérard (25 December 1629). People often asked him to be godfather to their children, not only local notables such as Chrétien George (6 February 1624) and the public prosecutor Demenge Mougenot (11 January 1628), but artisans including the stonemason Claude Ely and the builder Gaspard Billery. When it came to choosing godparents for their own children, Georges and Diane always opted for people of standing, and these were frequently relatives to boot. Thus for Étienne, christened on 2 August 1621, it was grandmother Catherine Le Nerf and the lawyer Étienne Gérard, a first cousin; for Claude, a baby girl baptized on 13 October 1623, the parish priest of Tonnois, who was a brother-in-law, and the damsel Claude Berman; and for Louis, christened on 7 October 1628, Louis de Rambervillers and Lucie Le Nerf, La Tour's sister-in-law. La Tour also chose people who could prove to be useful allies: Marie, for instance, born in January 1625, was given the chief magistrate Didier Clément; Christine, in June 1626, Chrétien de Nogent, a nobleman in the duke's service, together with Anne Le Nerf, another one of La Tour's sisters-in-law; and Nicolas-George, born on 4 August 1630, Nicolas Boullion, Duke François's quartermaster, and Étienne Gérard's daughter. La Tour was clearly mindful of the importance of good connections.

He seems to have managed his financial affairs with equal care. To be able to buy a house for 2,500 francs as he did as early as 1623, La Tour must have been more than secure financially, despite the fact that he applied for and was granted a loan of 100 francs shortly afterward. He would have come into a certain amount of capital on the deaths of his father and father-in-law in 1618, followed by that of his mother in 1624. La Tour seems to have owned some livestock in Lunéville and a reasonable area of farmland, however, and it is more than likely that there was a steady flow of highly profitable corn into his granary. The information we have on this score is scanty, sometimes even contradictory, and it is hard to determine his holdings and the income they brought him. That he was a shrewd farmer who never lost

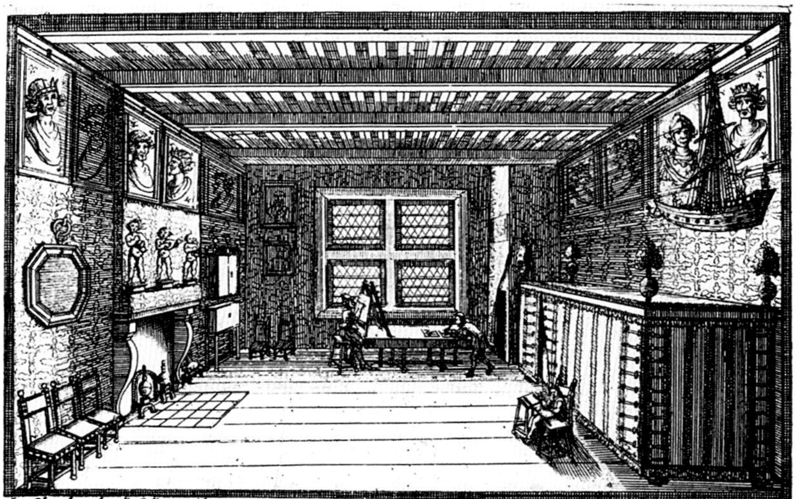

AN ARTIST'S STUDIO IN LA TOUR'S DAY
Jacques Callot's studio in his house in Nancy. Drawing and engraving by his apprentice, François Collignon, 1630.
Private collection, Paris

sight of his own interests, however, there can be no doubt, as we shall see in due course. The bulk of La Tour's income, nevertheless, probably came from his painting.

Once again there is a dearth of information, and we know virtually nothing about who bought La Tour's work during this period or what they paid for it. We know only from the official account books that Duke Henri II acquired two of La Tour's paintings, one for 123 francs, paid on 12 July 1623, and the other, referred to as an "image St. Peter," for 150 francs, paid before July 1624. These were hefty prices, particularly if the second, as seems the case, was the *Penitent St. Peter* and consisted of a single figure, rather than a complex scene featuring several figures, such as a *Denial of St. Peter* with servant and guards. They may reflect the duke's patronage, or were simply inflated to ensure high price quotations for the artist's work. Alternatively, they may express La Tour's gratitude toward his patron. In any case, they cannot be regarded as a standard for the rest of his work.

The period immediately following the return from Italy and the subsequent move to Lunéville must in fact have been extraordinarily productive. La Tour was young. He needed money and was eager to make his name. He would surely have seized every opportunity that came his way and turned out paintings of all sizes one after the other. Like every budding artist he probably set himself huge canvases to paint, great masterpieces that would show off his talent, but was not above painting smaller pictures that were both lucrative and easy to sell.

This was a time when there was a growing fashion for large painted altarpieces. No monastery, old or new, could bear to be without one, and there was not a single parish priest for whom they were not an absolute necessity worth great financial sacrifice. In Bourges, for example, a painter such as Jean Boucher made a specialty out of them and charged between three and five hundred livres apiece. La Tour is unlikely to have turned his back on this source of income, even if he must have had competition from Deruet and Leclerc in Nancy. So far, however, the archives have failed to yield any commission of this kind.

La Tour would surely also have gone in for portrait painting, a handy means of making money and useful acquaintances. All that we know of his work shows that he was quite competent in this field, but the texts of his day make no mention of his having pursued it. He seems to have been most alive to the substantial demand among both middle-class and noble clients seeking paintings for their homes, not only the religious themes that one might expect, but also, and above all, secular subjects, or indeed a subtle blend of the two. This was a safe field, highly profitable and a good deal less restricting for the artist than church painting or portraiture. La Tour seems to have been quick to realize this and to direct his talents accordingly, rather than seeking to compete with his rivals in Nancy. In this sense, he was very much a modern artist, diametrically opposed to the traditional ideal, shunning commissions for large-scale works for churches or palaces, and preferring to make a living from the dictates of his imagination. We know this is how Poussin worked in Rome from 1630 onward. La Tour appears to have done the same thing in Lunéville, perhaps less systematically, but as early as 1620.

He seems to have been successful as well. La Tour was a wealthy man, which means that he must have earned a great deal of money from his painting, and to do so he must have painted a great deal. He painted everything himself, moreover. His only assistants were simple apprentices who were young and inexperienced. At this stage, there is absolutely no question of studio works: everything that we have is either an original or a copy. Unfortunately, we have very little.

CARAVAGGESQUE REALISM: THE ALBI *APOSTLES*

So few works have come down to us from the period between 1616 and 1630 that there must be a particular reason. We do not have to look very far to find it: as we shall see, the fire that gutted Lunéville in 1638 and the looting of the city and surrounding countryside that followed more than account for the disappearance of works executed before then. The few paintings we do have would appear to have survived because they happened to be nowhere near Lunéville at the time—in Nancy or in one of the odd parts of Lorraine to have escaped ruin, or already in France.

As we have said, La Tour must have painted portraits, but none survives. We have gone as far afield as Munich and Florence on the chance that some princely likeness received as a diplomatic offering might be hidden away somewhere and attributable to him, but nothing has turned up. Living as he did in Lunéville, La Tour would have had less access to the duke's family than other painters. His sitters would have come from the nobility or the middle class. Here again, such works would have been destroyed in the looting, and any altarpieces La Tour might have painted for local churches would have met a similar fate. All that we have of this early period is a handful of smallish religious pictures and a few genre paintings.

These do not amount to much: even including compositions that have come down to us through copies, there are no more than twenty-six or twenty-seven known works for the period. Indeed, it would be more accurate to say fifteen, for half the works make up a single series of thirteen figures representing Christ and the twelve Apostles. They are separate paintings, but the format is the same, and they were clearly conceived as a set. Quite surprisingly, the series was discovered in the south of France, which may explain how it came to survive at all.

None of the paintings is signed, but since they were first discovered, no one, among experts at least, has expressed the slightest doubt about their attribution to La Tour. The series now hangs in the Musée Toulouse-Lautrec in Albi, but it came from the cathedral, where the Revolutionary inventory of 1795 specifies "twelve little paintings, the size of portraits, depicting the twelve Apostles, in the strong, dark manner of Michelangelo da Caravaggio." As of now, their prior history can be traced back only to a March 1698 account of the bishop's visit. In the sixth chapel, dedicated to St. John, is indicated "a painted and gilded rood-screen, a crucifix, and four candlesticks of gilded wood donated for the said chapel by the late sire Nualard, canon, with thirteen paintings depicting Our Lord and the twelve apostles in gilded frames, to maintain them around the said chapel as they are." Nothing is known about this Canon Nualard. The "with" is ambiguous: does it mean that he donated the paintings as well as the crucifix and the candlesticks? According to the 1795 inventory, the person responsible for placing the paintings in the chapel was "an Italian canon and art lover by the name of Bandinelli." Unfortunately, beyond the fact that he was a syndic in the chapter, that he died in April 1671 at the age of seventy, and that he was buried in the next chapel, we know nothing about Jerome Bandinelli either.

Comparable series of apostles had been engraved in France, and even Callot had executed one. No other painted series is known from this time, however, either

THE ALBI APOSTLES
Christ and the Apostles (the following sequence is arbitrary; it is probable that the series was originally displayed along a single line in the wood panelling of the chapel).

From top to bottom and from left to right:
Salvator Mundi, copy (Albi)

St. Peter, *St. Paul*, copies (Albi)
St. John (lost)

St. James the Great, copy (Albi)
St. Andrew, original (private collection)
St. James the Less, original (Albi)

St. Thomas, original (private collection)
St. Philip, original (Chrysler Museum)
St. Judas Thaddeus, original (Albi)

St. Matthias, copy (Albi)
St. Simon, copy (Albi)
St. Bartholomew or *St. Matthew* (lost)

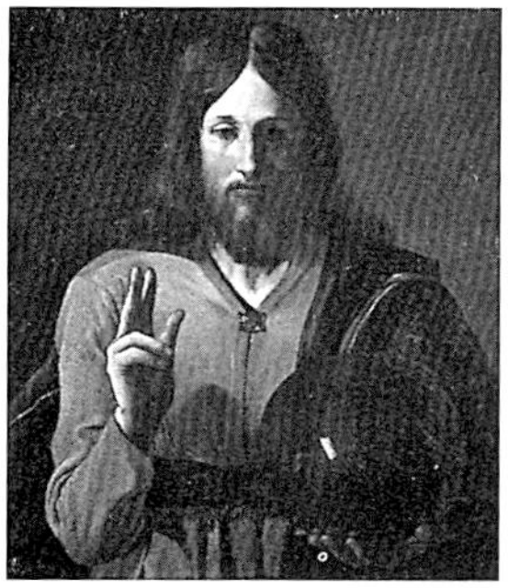
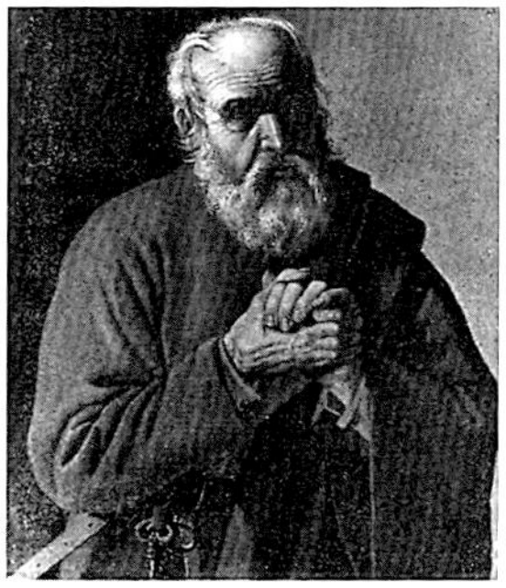
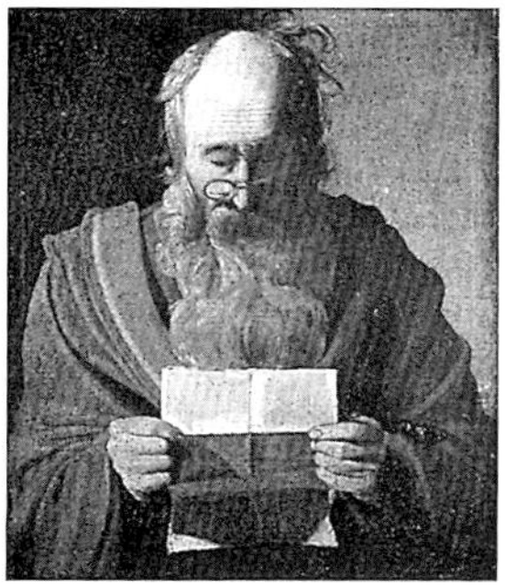
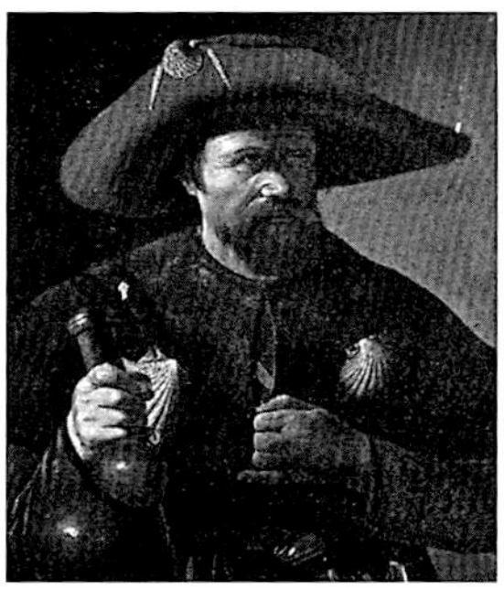
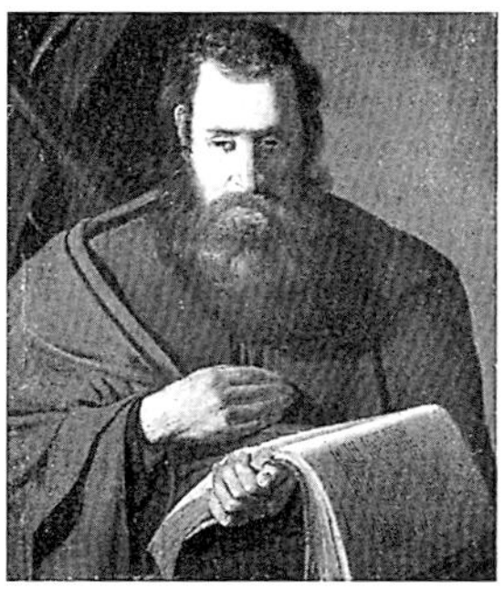
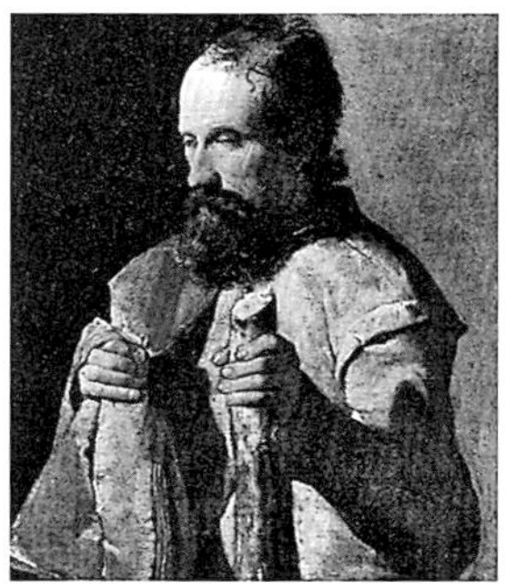
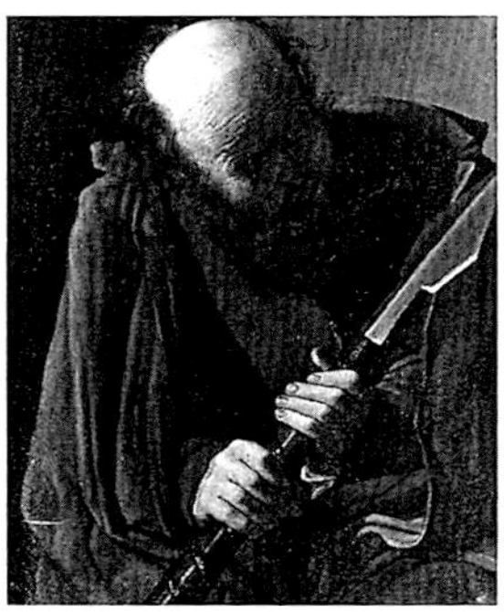
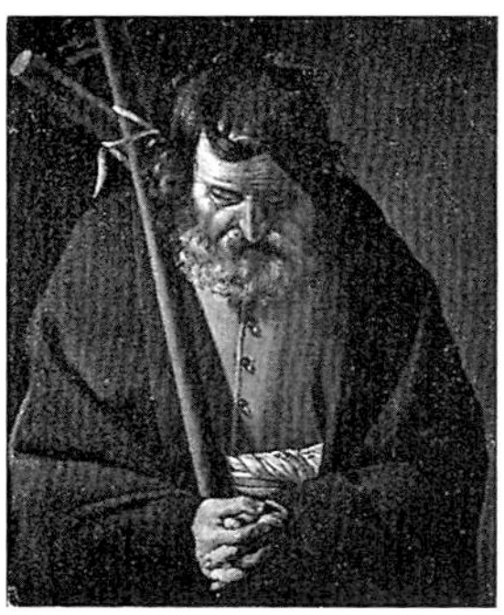
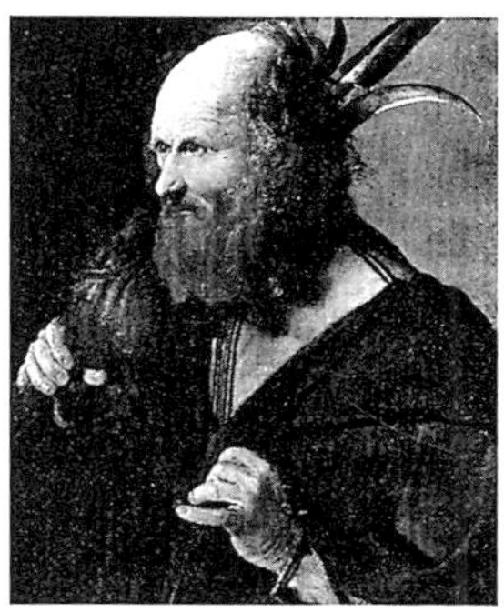
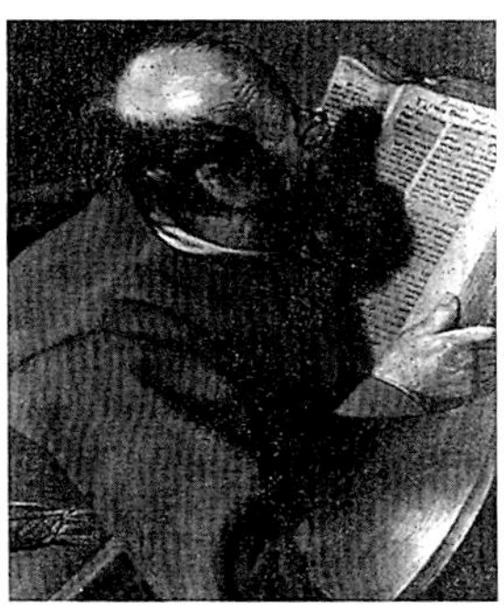
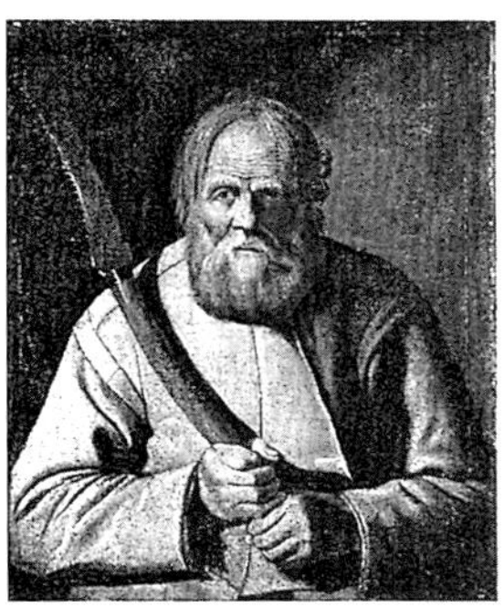

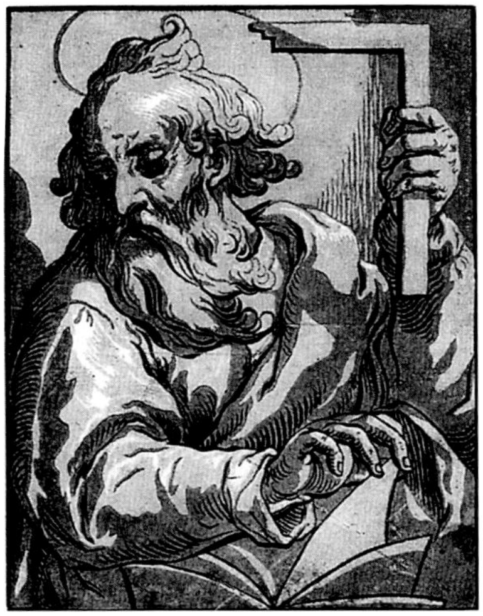

After Georges Lallemant. *The Apostles: St. Thomas.* Engraving by Ludwig Büsinck
Private collection, Paris

Jacques Callot. *St. Matthew.* From the series known as the *"Grands Apôtres."*
Cabinet des Estampes, Musée des Beaux-Arts, Nancy

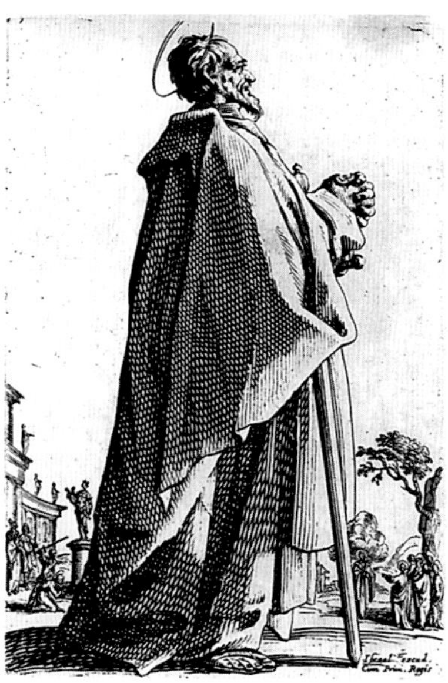

in Lorraine or in Paris. This kind of chapel decoration seems to have been more common in southern painting. Could this have been a commission for Albi from the very beginning? If so, why call on a young and virtually unknown painter living in Vic or Lunéville? Perhaps some religious order was responsible, or an unknown patron, passing through Lorraine. If it was a canon at the Albi cathedral, Italian or otherwise, who arranged the commission, it could be imagined that he initially met and possibly even commissioned La Tour in Rome, and that, rather than returning to France through Venice, the painter made a detour through the south of France.

Other hypotheses remain plausible. One that cannot be ruled out entirely is that the series was originally designed for a church in Lorraine and moved to the other side of France sometime around the middle of the century. Such transfers are not unknown. The troubles in Lorraine (of which more later) brought not only tremendous levels of destruction but looting too, and some soldiers were astute enough not to destroy the paintings they seized. In addition, these were times of great hardship for the churches. La Tour was to become very famous in the 1640s, and a parish priest in need of cash might well have made a deal with an art-loving canon to sell a set of paintings that had been commissioned from the young painter in better times. There were a great many southerners among the French troops stationed in Lorraine, and around 1650 La Tour even had a manservant by the name of "Montauban." One other strange coincidence is worth mentioning. The museum in Albi also owns a copy of *The Adoration of the Shepherds* now in the Louvre. It is very mediocre, but it is old and does give us an idea of the original size and shape of the picture, which has since been cut along the bottom. It is hard to explain why there should be yet another La Tour in Albi, particularly since *The Adoration of the Shepherds* belongs to the very end of La Tour's career and has no connection with the series of Apostles—unless, of course, they go back to the same admirer.

The series is obviously of key importance for any study of La Tour's earliest work. It must be kept in mind, however, that we know it today in a cruelly mutilated form. Of the thirteen paintings recorded in 1698, the two remaining in Albi have been well-preserved, but the other three surviving originals are not in equally good condition. Of the remaining eight, two are no longer known, and six exist only in mediocre copies.

The scientific analysis made in 1972 amply confirms what was obvious to the naked eye: of the eleven paintings that now make up the series in the Albi museum, only *St. James the Less* and *St. Judas Thaddeus*, both of excellent quality, are by La Tour. The others were replaced at the end of the eighteenth century or the very beginning of the nineteenth with relatively faithful but somewhat heavy-handed copies, either because the originals were thought to be in too bad condition or because they had caught the eye of some art lover. The copy of the *Salvator Mundi* is even painted on an old canvas showing a nobleman in seventeenth-century dress and a kneeling monk, and the *St. Thomas* on a piece taken from a larger composition. The originals do not appear to have been destroyed once the copies were made, however. One of them reappeared in 1941 and is now in the Chrysler Museum in Norfolk. This could have seemed no more than a chance survival had two other originals—*St. Thomas* and *St. Andrew*—not similarly reappeared and gone up for sale in 1991. Perhaps the remaining six originals corresponding to the Albi copies will eventually turn up, or indeed the two others that have disappeared without a trace. In any case, there is enough at hand to give us a good idea of the quality of the original series, and so it is here that the study of La Tour's art must begin.

There is no sense in trying to pin a precise date onto these paintings: as I have endeavored to show, there are all sorts of plausible hypotheses and it would be rash to opt for one rather than another without further evidence. Let us simply say that they are among La Tour's earliest surviving works and try to look at them without preconceptions, although we should obviously pay particular attention to *St. James the Less* and *St. Judas Thaddeus* in the Musée Toulouse-Lautrec. We are confronted with the most realist of painters. La Tour was not content to render Christ's first disciples as a collection of venerable pontiffs distinguishable only by their attributes. He interpreted the Gospels literally, and since most of the apostles were supposed to be simple, common men, he had peasants model for him. Indeed, it would not be out of place to speak of portraits. La Tour observes hands and faces minutely, describing every gnarled finger and grimy nail, faithfully reproducing lined foreheads and small eyes with their lashless lids squinting against the light. He meticulously recreates the thinning hair and the patches of weathered scalp, the wayward locks, and the rough old necks. There is no cruelty, but no indulgence either.

This precision should not be confused with the taste for the picturesque. Realism can often turn into expressionism, but there is no hint of that in this series. The truthfulness of these portraits may come close to verism, but it stops in time. The figures are calm, forever fixed in their set poses. Out of the ten apostles known to us, four are shown head on and immobile, and four in three-quarter view. Only St. Thomas and St. Matthias suggest any movement. Painters of such *apostolados* often sought to break the monotony of twelve otherwise static and similar half-length portraits and use looks and gestures to link one canvas to another; nothing of the sort seems to have been considered here. Nor is there any attempt to make the faces say more than they do in themselves. There are no contortions or grimaces: these old men seem quite silent, and some even cast their eyes downward. There is nothing in the way of setting; just neutral backgrounds like blank walls, livened up at the most by a quiet shift from light to shade.

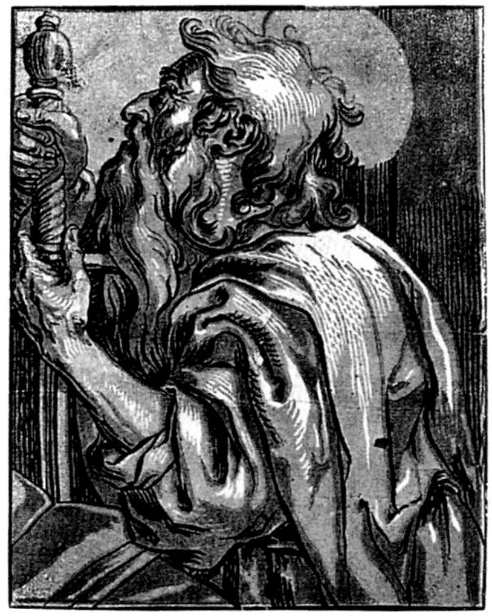

After Georges Lallemant. *The Apostles: St. Paul.* Engraving by Ludwig Büsinck.

The colors are kept to a limited range, subtly blended and graded. We get a foretaste of the red that was to dominate La Tour's palette, as a great splash lights up the canvas, but it is still too dull to disturb the harmony of the image or to attract undue attention. Everything centers, in fact, around the face and hands. They impose the presence of beings charged with experience and endowed with particular qualities and failings, with a past and a mind, individuals not to be confused with any others. Far from becoming symbolic figures, these apostles appear as the meager human beings they are. The general idea gives way to the specific. The description is so incisive, however, that we are left wholly convinced that, in art as in life, this petty reality is all there is, and that through it alone can we apprehend spiritual truth.

This was the fundamental lesson of Caravaggio's art and the powerful spiritual motor behind its success. This lesson was clearly not lost on La Tour. It was a veritable revelation to him, and like so many other artists at the time, he took it back to Lorraine as a great a revolution in art, which indeed it was.

All art since Raphael had been preoccupied with achieving quite the opposite, seeking to get away from the specific and extricate essential form from the trappings of everyday reality, in order to be able to give direct expression to ideas. Painting seemed gloriously suited to the purpose: it could refashion the visible forms of the real world at will to fit with an idea. If the term "Mannerism" means anything at all, it is surely the pursuit of this ambition to the point where the idea takes over as an end in itself and, through a series of intellectual breaks with reality, finally eliminates all references to it. Bellange's figures, including his Apostles, epitomized this tendency. Bellange had just died when the Albi *Apostles* were painted, and his art had by no means ceased to inspire the duke's court. Figures like those of Albi propose a negation of Bellange; they represent an art that was not merely different from the prevailing trend in Lorraine at the time, but ran fundamentally counter to it. Neither Deruet, whose faltering style was unaffected by Caravaggio, nor Callot, who became very much a Florentine artist, nor even Le Clerc, who worked as assistant to Saraceni (not exactly of Caravaggesque persuasion, whatever may have been written of him in the past) and was quite influenced by Venetian art, brought such an innovation to their art.

Jacques Callot. *St. Paul.* From the series known as the *"Grand Apôtres."*
Cabinet des Estampes, Musée des Beaux-Arts, Nancy

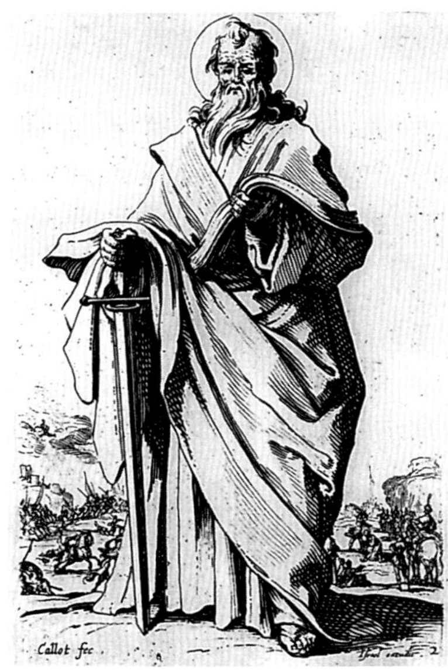

What complicates the problem a bit is the fact that La Tour was no mere exponent of Roman Caravaggism. Certainly an image like the *St. Judas Thaddeus* could not have been produced by anyone who had not fully absorbed the new spirituality Caravaggio and his followers were aiming for and understood the complete change of direction they advocated—in poetic terms even more than pictorial ones—but it reflects a very personal solution. Nowhere in Roman painting do we find such quiet analysis of human psychology; and nowhere in Caravaggesque painting such handling of detail, which seems to recall the refinements of the fifteenth century.

The Italian Caravaggesque painters were too concerned with the powerful effects of chiaroscuro to get involved in minute description. La Tour's desire to capture character in all its specific detail led him to retain a clear light enveloping rather than destroying the forms and bringing out the tactile quality of substances. In other words, the opposite of Caravaggio or Manfredi. Far from sweeping away all detail in strong contrasts of light and shade, this light allows La Tour to draw every line of hair, beard, and wrinkle with the precision of Dürer or Grünewald. It is difficult to say what produced La Tour's particular brand of Caravaggism. It seems unlikely to have resulted from any contact with Gentileschi, or the examples of Baburen or Terbrugghen, with whom La Tour has only a superficial affinity. A more likely explanation is that La Tour deliberately turned to the great masters of the past. Once again, we are left wondering if the key to the mystery is not to be found in a painting like the one in Serrone, at once so modern in its realism and yet so strangely full of archaisms.

At any rate, it is clear that whatever anyone else made of Roman Caravaggism—and everyone had a different view—La Tour was not drawn to its powerful sense of tragedy that so impressed the likes of Valentin and Tournier and stirred the characters in their paintings. There are no hauntingly wide-eyed Judiths in La Tour, no melancholy and elegant ruffians. He was far more detached from his models. La Tour's whole object was to describe: in a way, he did not want to show anything but the outer skin of people or things, and thus sought to reveal inner character through outward appearance alone. He studies the pattern of lines on faces and the twist of hands, because details like these create a sense of presence. He pays careful attention to the material that clothes are made of—leather, wool, or coarse sackcloth. He delights in reproducing every hint of light that St. Philip's clear glass buttons throw on his purple tunic. St. James's staff is a real branch, straight and rough, complete with badly planed edges, splintering, and knots, captured in all its tactile detail with a brush that does not hide its traces.

This was a far cry from the lofty ideas that Caravaggio propounded in *The Martyrdom of St. Matthew* in San Luigi dei Francesi. His Ambrosiana *Still Life* probably comes closer. But La Tour's need to come to grips with the world through its external appearance, even if this meant using all manner of illusionism and virtuosity, was not something he inherited from any artistic tradition. It signified a conception of painting, an approach as a painter, that could only stem from a spiritual choice.

La Tour was by no means the only artist to be driven by an urge to capture the real world. What is extraordinary is that in his case this impulse was coupled not with any sense of exhilaration from within, but with a gravity, a severity stemming from a reflective cast of mind more than from the sheer pleasure of painting. It is surprising, and in a way indicative of an internal contradiction, that even at this early stage La Tour seems to have set the strictest limits on the universe he was seeking to capture. Man was the focus of his interest, and it was on man's outward appearance, from his face to his clothes, that he concentrated his attentions, insofar as this is our only clue to his inner being. From this time on, nature seems to have been proscribed in its entirety: sky, water, greenery, fruit, flowers, distant horizons, everything that painters have always cherished as their own and proclaimed to be their privileged domain, relative to the sculptor. As we shall see in looking through La Tour's paintings, there is never the slightest indication that the people in them are surrounded by nature. Now and again we come across an object carefully singled out for its physical state: the roughness of wood or iron, or the fragility of glass or paper. Sometimes there is a staff, a stone, or very exceptionally an animal. La Tour's universe is pared down to the absolute limit. It is reduced to a rudimentary form of creation, not as in Caravaggio's later work, by any half-light obscuring things that are in fact there, but by a light that isolates them, brings them out, yet sets them apart. This is a curious paradox, but given La Tour's commitment to painting what he saw, one that reflects as well the dictates of an ascetic impulse.

CHRIST AND THE APOSTLES

p. 51: *St. Thomas.*
Private collection

p.52: *St. James the Less.*
Musée Toulouse-Lautrec, Albi

p. 53: *St. Judas Thaddeus.*
Musée Toulouse-Lautrec, Albi

p. 54: *St. Andrew.*
Private collection, Switzerland

p. 55: *St. Philip.*
Chrysler Museum, Norfolk, Virginia

pp. 56 and 57: *St. James the Less,*
enlarged details

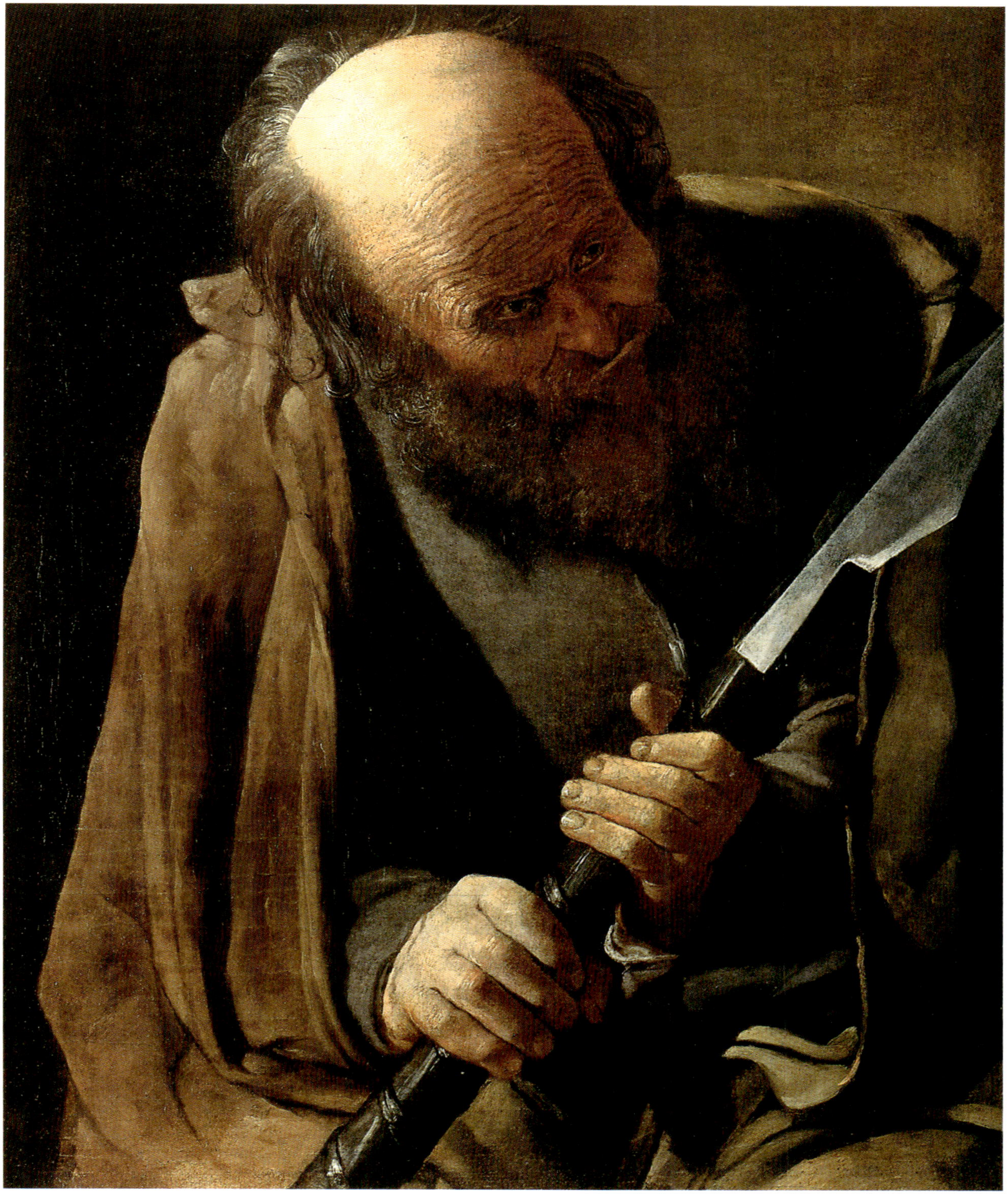

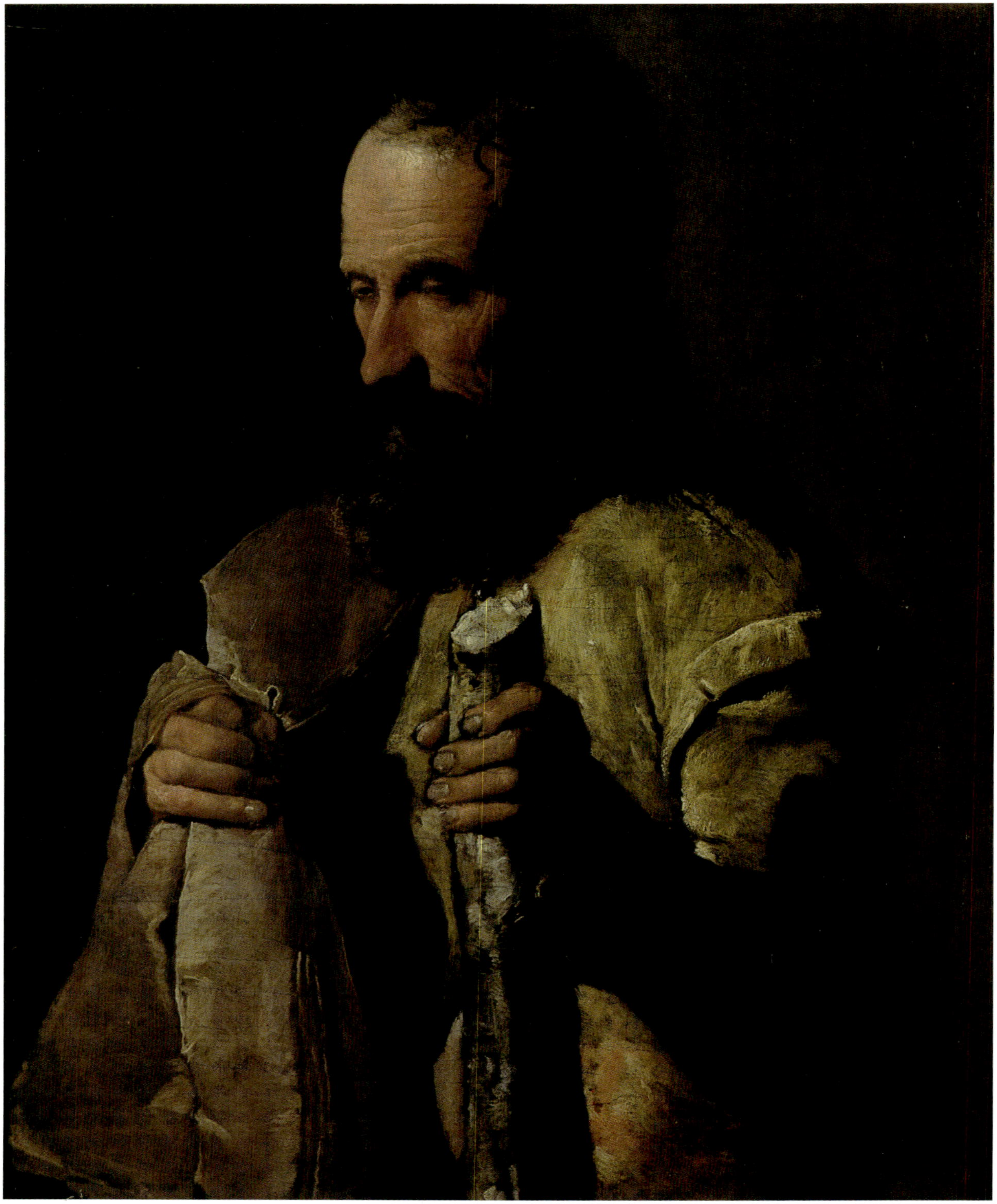

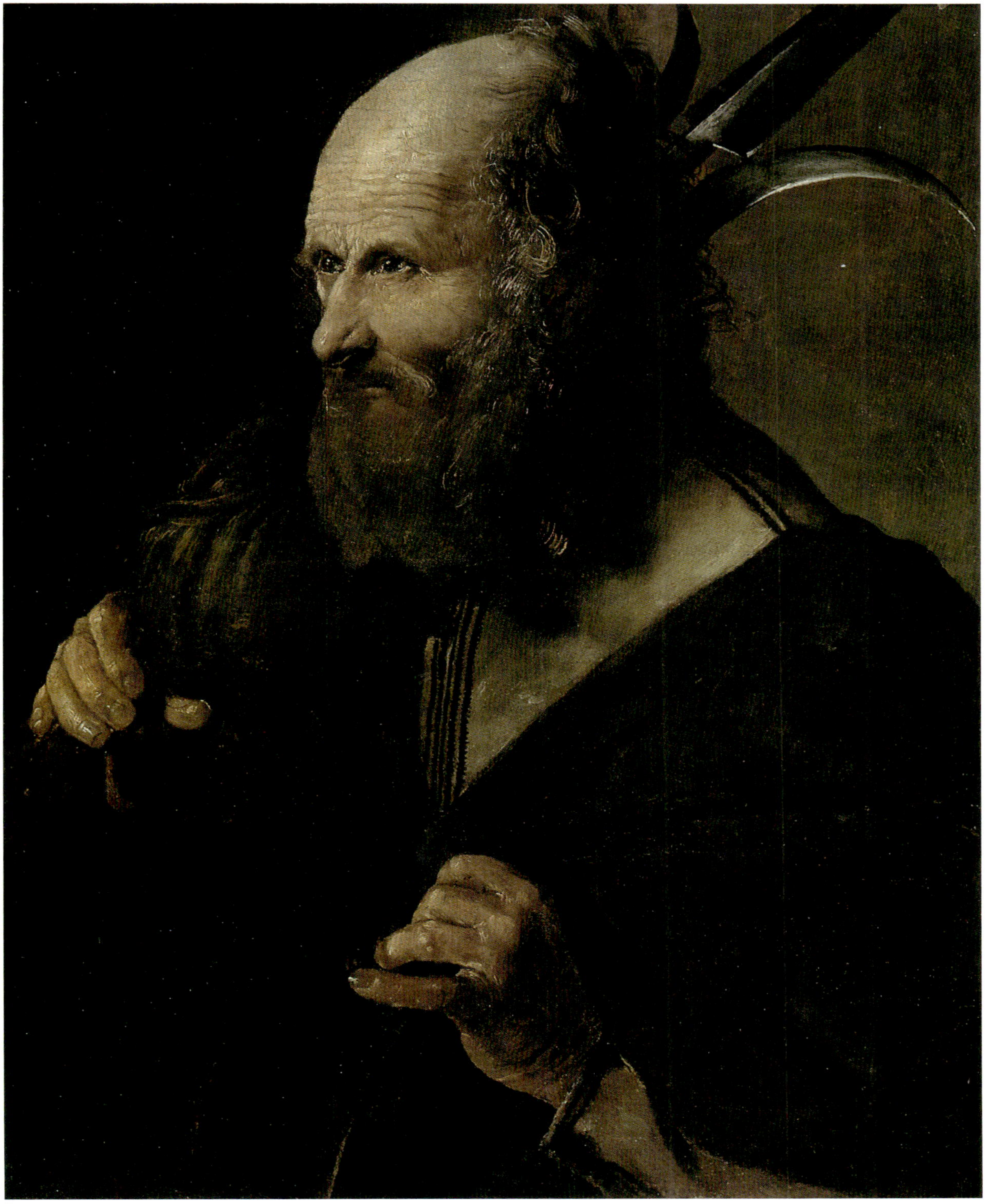

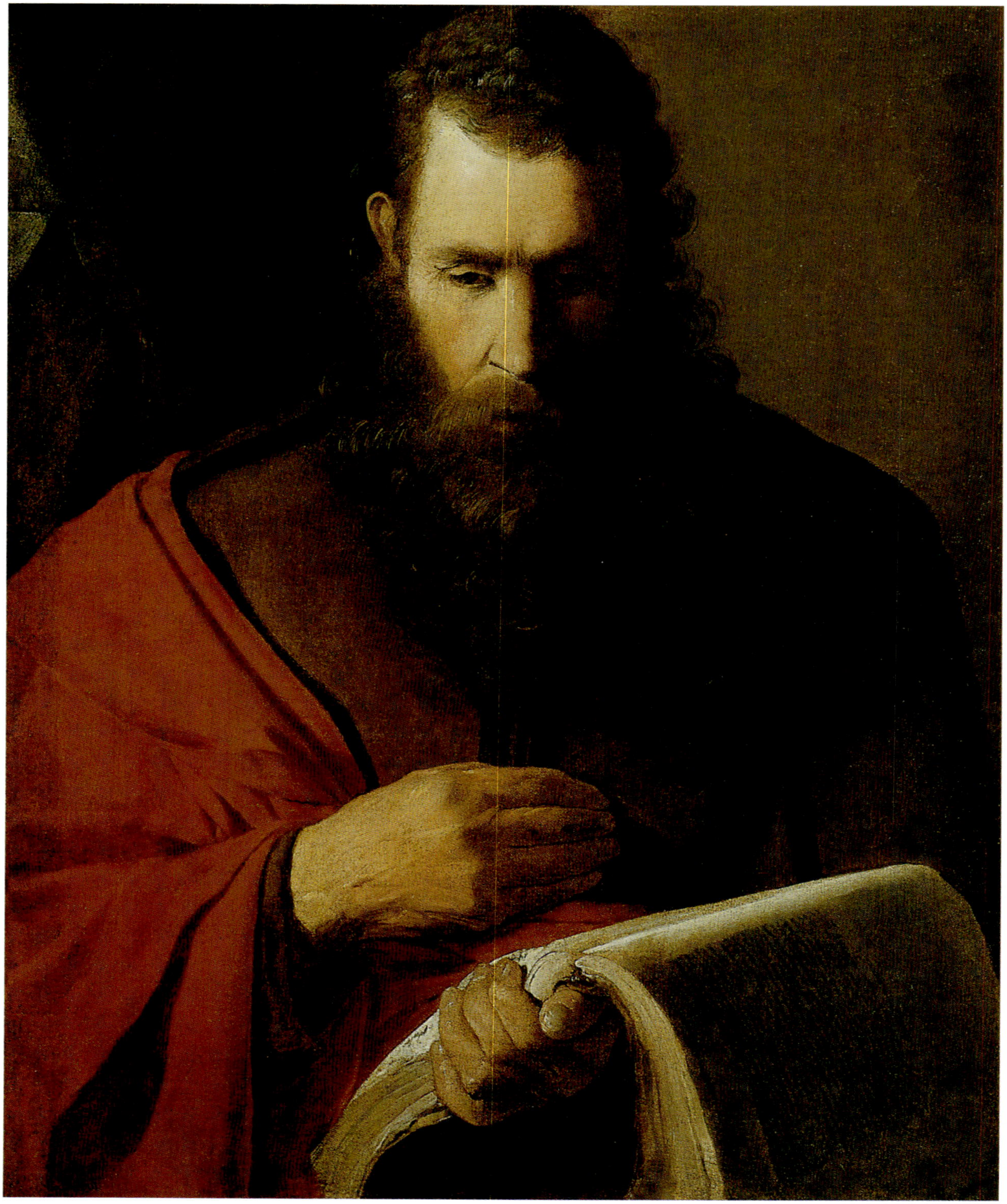

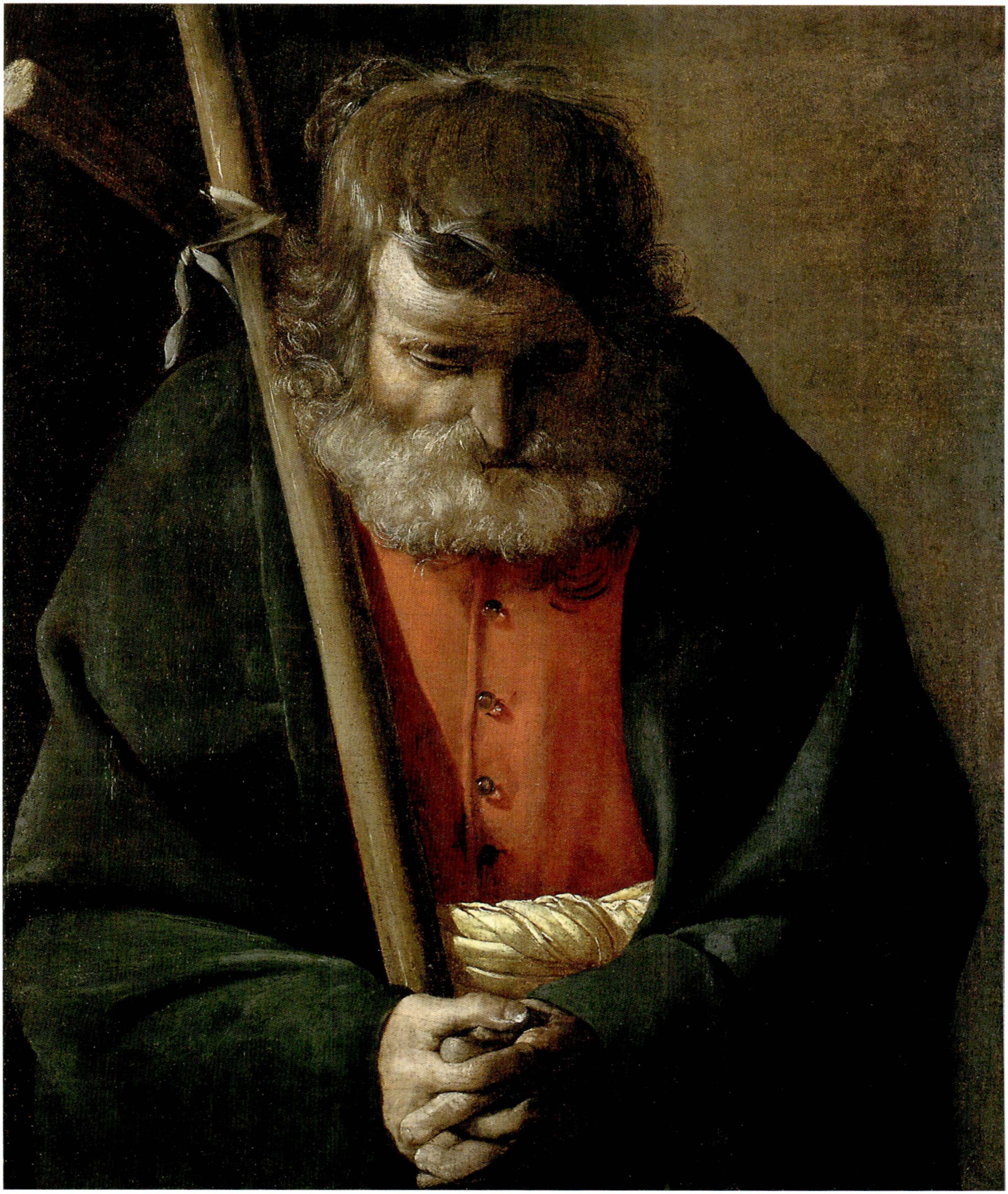

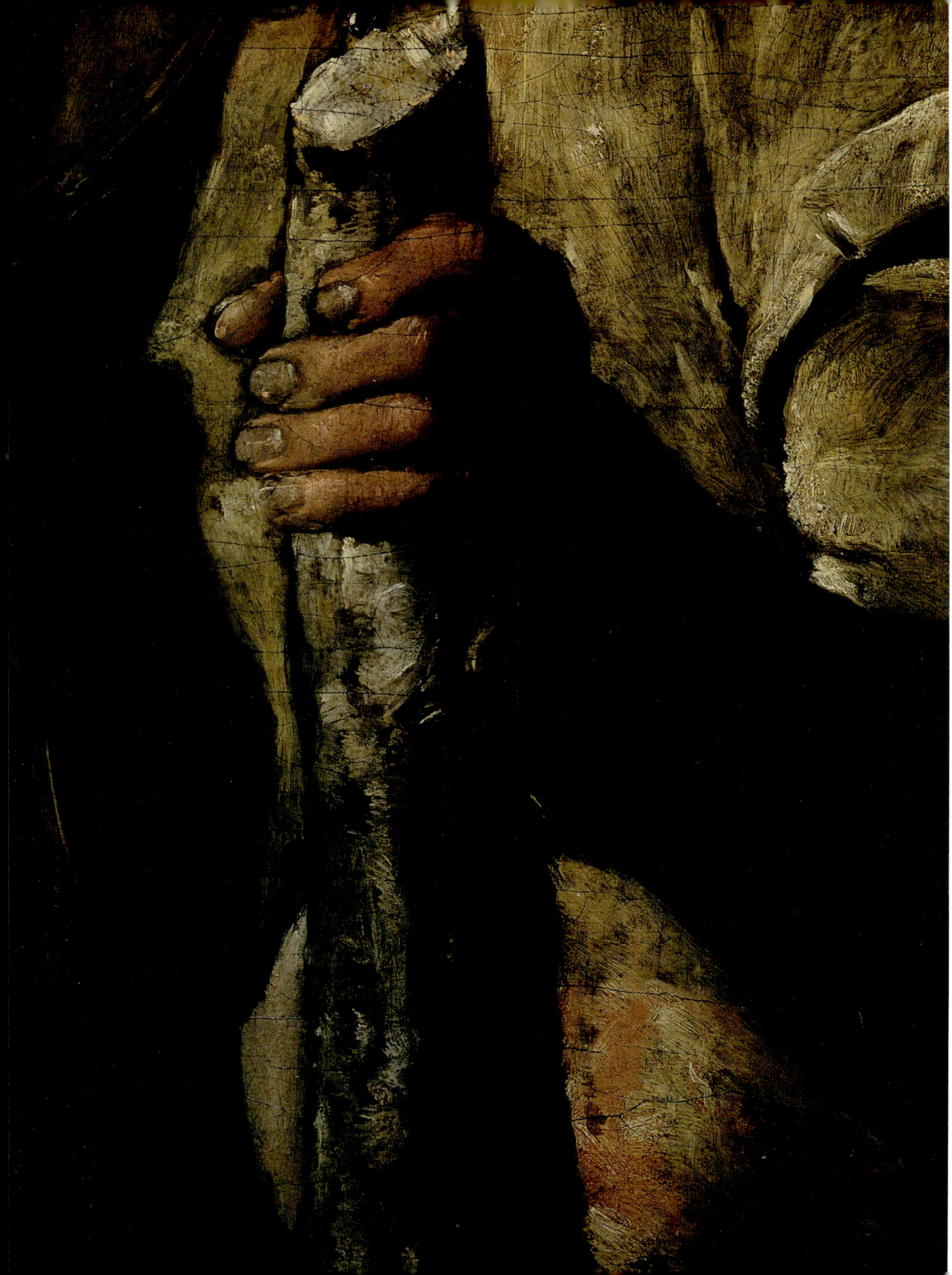

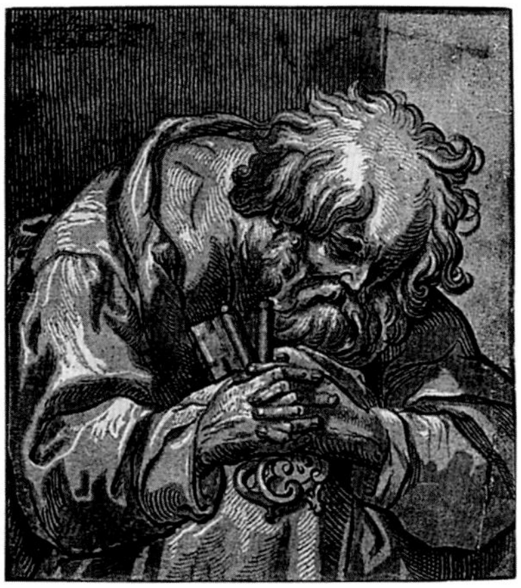

After Georges Lallemant. *The Penitent St. Peter.* Wood engraving by Ludwig Büsinck.

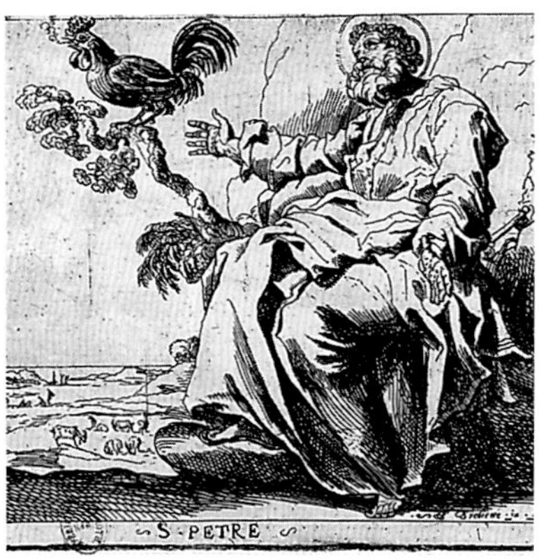

Pierre Brébiette. *The Penitent St. Peter,* detail. Etching.
Cabinet des Estampes, Bibliothèque Nationale, Paris

St. Jerome Reading.
Royal Collection, Hampton Court Palace

THE FIRST "SERIES": *ST. PETER* AND *ST. JEROME*

This ascetic realism is not the only feature that distinguishes La Tour so strikingly from his contemporaries. He displayed yet another atypical tendency that was also to become increasingly marked as time went on, to the point of constituting a very personal way of working. La Tour did not go in for a great deal of invention, as we have seen, or, more precisely, he did not feel the need to invent. He rejected the gratuitously free hand the Mannerists allowed themselves and deliberately confined himself to a few objects, a few subjects, a few themes. At the same time, however, he took these up over and over again, repeating them, modifying them, and perfecting them in painting after painting. La Tour was the painter of series par excellence.

Thus, there are several distinct groups of pictures clearly associated with the *Apostles* series: these include a few religious paintings, all showing half-length saints, and two sets of genre pictures, the first consisting of half-length figures combined in narrative compositions, and the second, paintings of individual full-length figures.

The Albi *St. Peter,* unfortunately known to us only through the copy, seems to have been the first of a long series devoted to the repentance of St. Peter that spanned La Tour's entire career. The subject encapsulates sin and contrition, issues at the heart of religious life, and was particularly dear to the Catholic Counter-Reformation because it addressed the role of the Church and confession, both of which Protestantism rejected. It was treated by Caravaggesque painters, as well as the poets of the day, most notably Malherbe in *The Tears of St. Peter.* Malherbe, like Tanzillo before him, invoked the stars, the woods, the sea, the whole universe, and turned the saint's lament into the most Mannerist of French poems for the gratification of Henri IV and his court. Georges de La Tour, by contrast, chose to depict the saint as starkly as possible, but this does not seem to have lost him any admirers.

As we have indicated, Duke Henri II, who granted La Tour his letters of franchise, bought at least two paintings from him. We do not know the subject of the first of these, paid for in July 1623. The second, bought for 150 francs shortly before the duke's death in July 1624, was an "image St. Peter." This would seem to suggest a single figure, in all probability a penitent St. Peter. In 1875, the Nancy archivist Lepage wrote that the painting was presented by the duke to the church of the Minim order of Lunéville, but he does not give a source, and no documentary evidence for such a donation has yet been found. If he were correct, however, the painting could well have disappeared in the great fire of 1638. Alternatively, it could have been carried off in the looting that followed and sold as lawful war booty. A number of scholars have identified it with the *Penitent St. Peter,* also known as *The Tears of St. Peter,* recorded in the seventeenth century under La Tour's name in the collection of the archduke Leopold Wilhelm, an avid collector of paintings. This work, which has now disappeared without a trace—though it may not have been destroyed—was well known, and in 1973 François-Georges Pariset discovered a miniature by an unknown hand in the Kunsthistorisches Museum in Vienna that is directly inspired by it. It was also reproduced in the *Theatrum artis pictoriae* published in 1731, this time as the work of Guido Reni. The engraving is mediocre and probably not particularly accurate; it allows us nevertheless to be quite certain that the painting was not by Reni but rather, as first thought, by La Tour.

The composition almost certainly dates from the 1620s. It appears to have been a reworking of the Albi version of *St. Peter,* on a larger scale (approximately 135 x 160 cm) and in a horizontal format, but otherwise essentially the same in treatment. La Tour gives his saint an unusual gesture that is the very incarnation of anguish and contrition: his hands are clasped, with one inside the other, but he is twisting them in a gesture of confession rather than prayer. Throughout his career this was to be the way he portrayed the penitent St. Peter. With the change in format, he has made the drapery more intricate and placed an old book with a broken binding in the background—the same book that was later to reappear in the

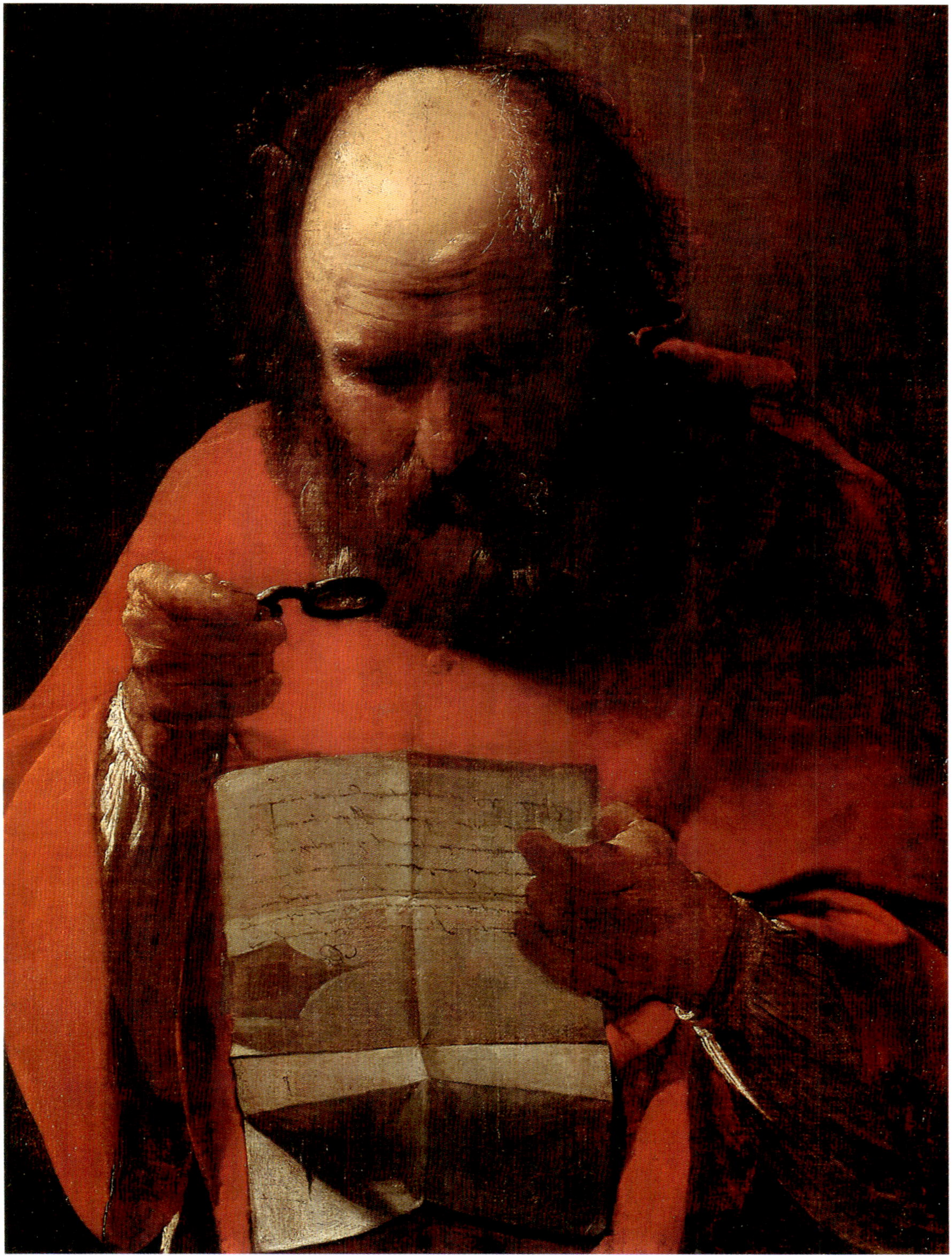

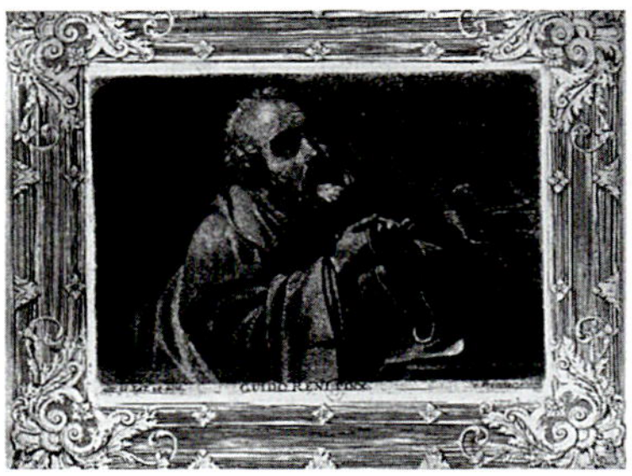

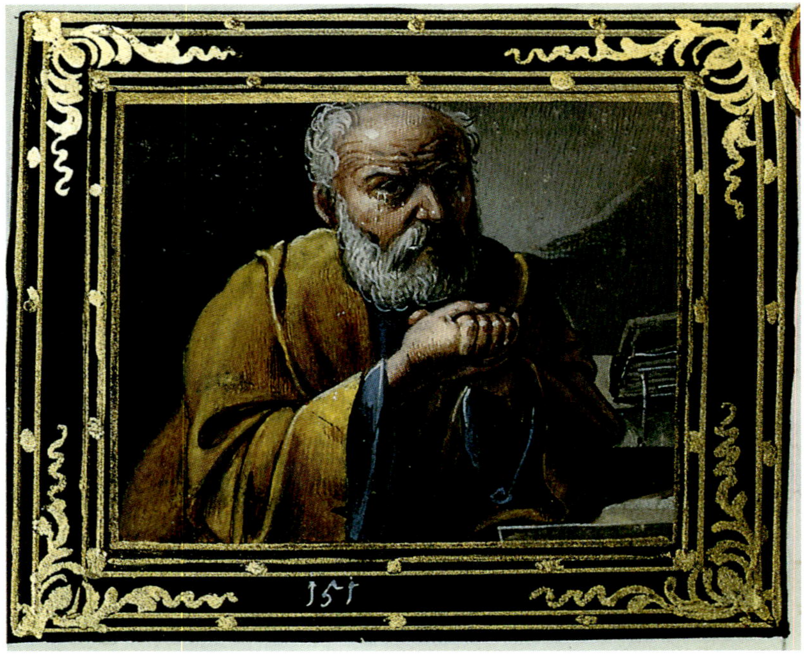

After Georges de La Tour.
The Penitent St. Peter.
Formerly collection Archduke Leopold Wilhelm

Above: Reproduction in mezzotint (16 x 22 cm). by Anton Joseph Prenner (1683-1761) in the *Theatrum Artis Pictoriae* vol. III, 1731 (attributed to Guido Reni).
Cabinet des Estampes, Bibliothèque Nationale, Paris

Right: A reproduction in miniature by an anonymous artist.
Kunsthistorisches Museum, Vienna

St. Thomas now in the Louvre. We should beware, however, of making too much of the differences between a copy and a poor engraving. The most we may conclude is that for the engraved version to have been attributed to Guido Reni, La Tour must have refined and lightened the rather summary color scheme of the Albi painting.

The Albi *St. Paul* would similarly seem to be related to several St. Jeromes, where the same venerable, bald-headed old man is again shown frontally, reading a letter, but the costume has now been modified—to the obligatory scarlet—and the realistic motif of the reading glasses added to signal the church father's erudition. Here, too, there must have been a whole series of variations on this theme, including some that were quite late. One of the earliest, probably painted in the 1620s, was the *St. Jerome Reading* now at Hampton Court, and acquired after 1662 by Charles II with the identification "manner of Dürer." The work has suffered, but in a way that reveals it to be more akin to the rediscovered originals of the Albi series than to the copies. There are only traces of the fine brushwork on the hair and lines of the face that, together with the light, even color, prompted the reference to Dürer. The painting's realism, subtle lighting, and powerful use of red, however, preserve its poetic quality.

La Tour was to continue working on the theme until it took on a monumentality entirely missing from the Windsor painting. This process led, among others, to the version of *St. Jerome Reading* now in the Louvre, which is unfortunately no more than a rather stiff, albeit faithful, copy of a lost original. There is a second copy of the composition that is missing the still life in the foreground. I am convinced, however, that this still life was La Tour's invention, and that what we see is no chance scattering of objects by an incompetent painter, but a very deliberate arrangement. The scene is viewed from above in an exaggerated way typical of La Tour's early years, but the simplified volumes and harsh lighting point to the 1630s, and without the original it is really impossible to fix a date. The task is made all the more difficult because another *St. Jerome Reading*, which will be discussed later, proves that Georges de La Tour continued to produce variation after variation of this theme all his life.

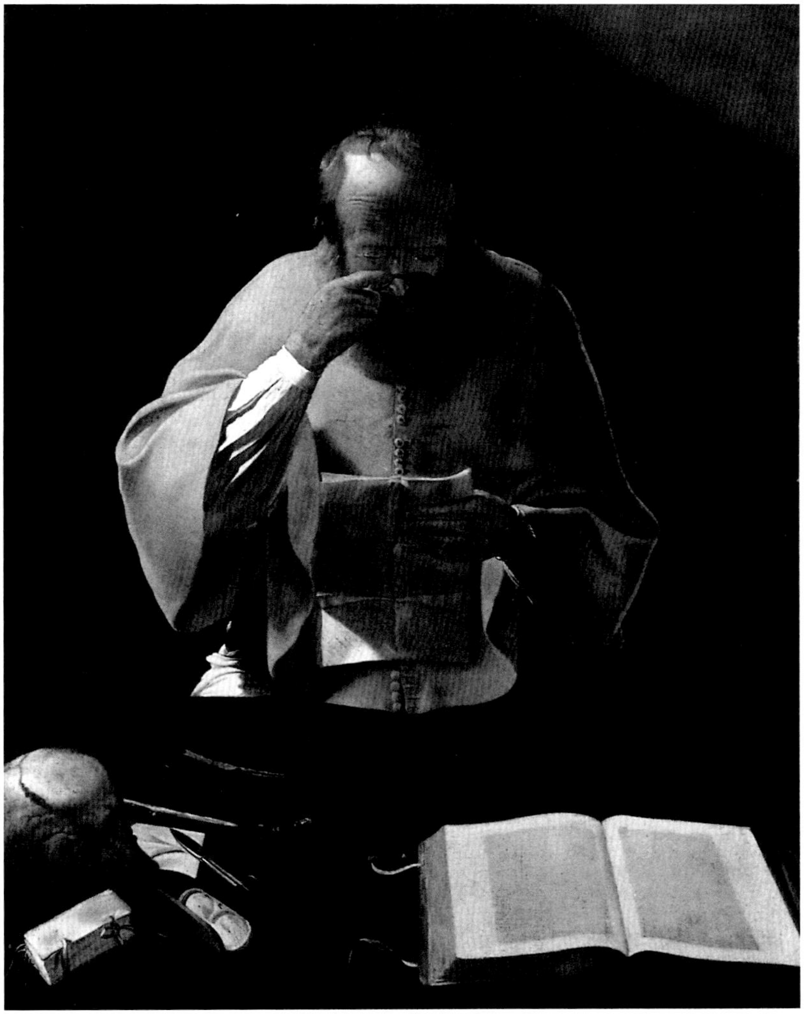

After Georges de La Tour. *St. Jerome Reading*, also called *St. Jerome in His Study*
Musée du Louvre, Paris

Pierre Brébiette. *St. Jerome Meditating.* Etching.

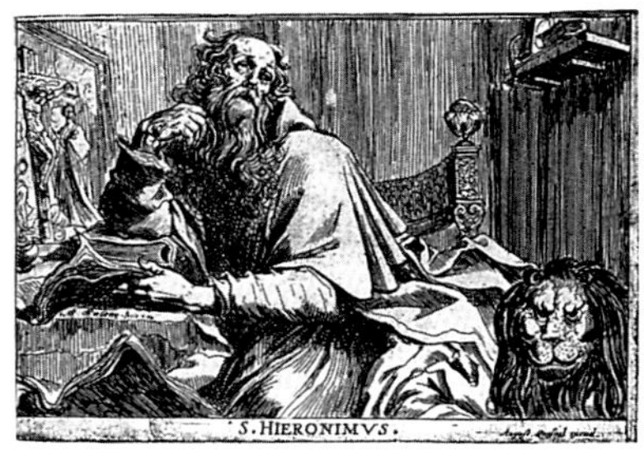

Anonymous. *St. Jerome Writing.*
Galleria Doria-Pamphili, Rome

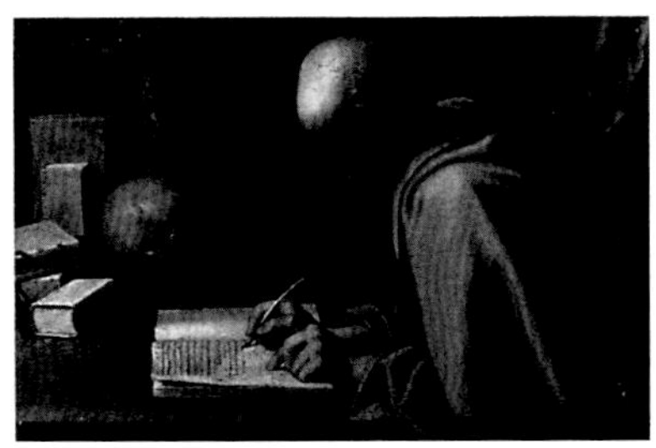

THE HALF-FIGURE GENRE SCENES

La Tour's genre paintings, which afforded his realism an even freer rein, must have met with great success. They may well have traveled rather far, which would explain why a number of them have survived. La Tour seems to have been drawn to two kinds of paintings, which involved him in rather different kinds of problems and gave rise to two major series.

The first is very much in the Caravaggesque mold of horizontal compositions featuring groups of half-length figures. The formula goes back much farther, however. It was very popular with painters of the Venetian school, and Giorgione in particular produced a number of widely imitated models. By the sixteenth century it was also current in France, and even in Lorraine. Although we do not have any paintings of this type by Bellange, we know from the series of six engravings after him by Crispin de Passe, entitled *Mimicarum aliquot Facetiarum icones ad habitum italicum expressi*, that Bellange did in fact draw and probably paint several genre scenes of this kind, inspired more or less directly by Italian theater. The importance of this evidence has been too often overlooked. With a great deal of ease, Bellange linked two

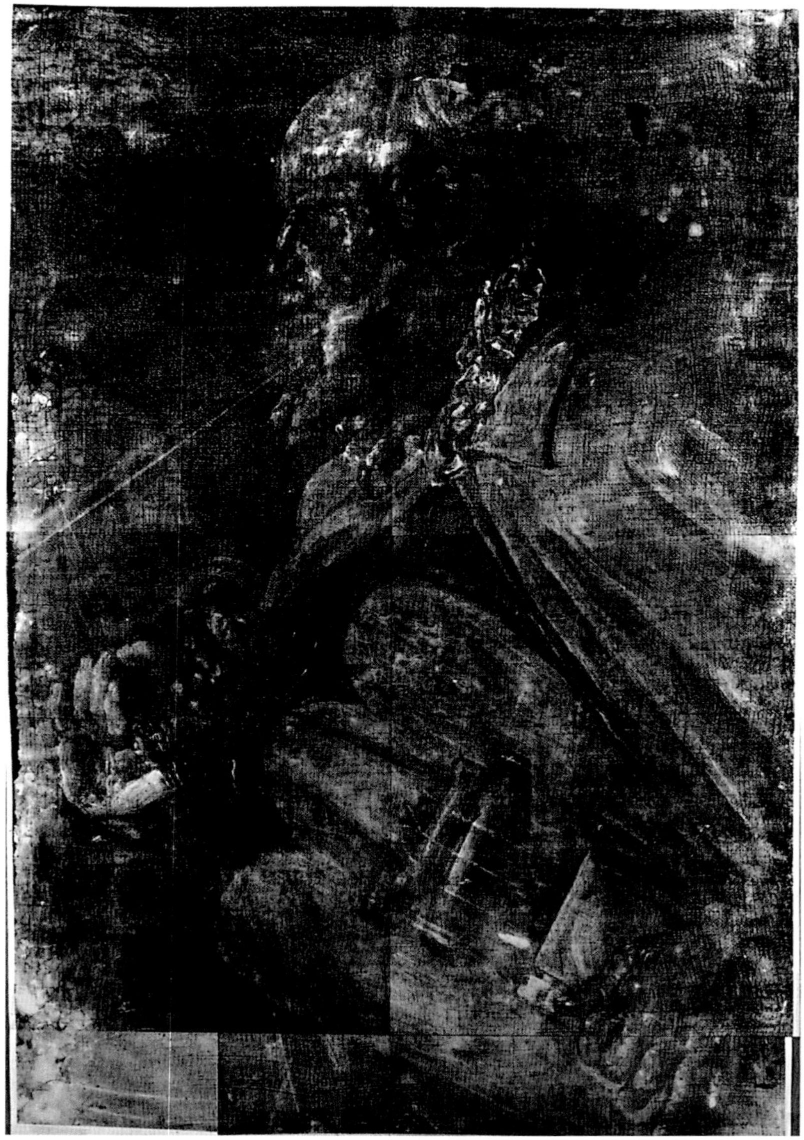

The Hurdy-Gurdy Player, fragment.
X-ray photograph.

or three half-length figures together in an action animated by expressive hands and eyes, and brought a rhythm to his compositions with a tight but unobtrusive geometric structure. He knew how to avoid the monotony that threatened such half-length compositions by deliberately introducing an element of asymmetry and suggesting a background without actually carving one out (except in the first scene, the *Jeannette*, which is a theme story set out of doors). La Tour had certainly seen these engravings, which must have been produced at the very beginning of the century, around 1600, or possibly even the paintings corresponding to them. They would have had a strong impact on him. La Tour's exposure to Roman Caravaggism made him alter the spirit somewhat, but it only strengthened his attachment to the formula. The *Cheat* paintings and *The Fortune Teller* were to be faithful and glorious sequels to it. But in fact, La Tour adopted this kind of composition from the very start of his career.

He made use of it in two series showing musicians either giving concerts or fighting with each other. Evidence of the first kind of composition came to light when a heavily overpainted portrait bust of a hurdy-gurdy player in the Musée des Beaux-Arts in Brussels was X-rayed, revealing it to be a fragment of a larger canvas that depicted at the least one other figure: a violinist's hand and bow are clearly visible at his side. More likely, however, there was a concert with four to six musicians and singers. The subject was well suited to a half-length format, and Georges de La

The Hurdy-Gurdy Player, fragment.
Musée des Beaux-Arts, Brussels

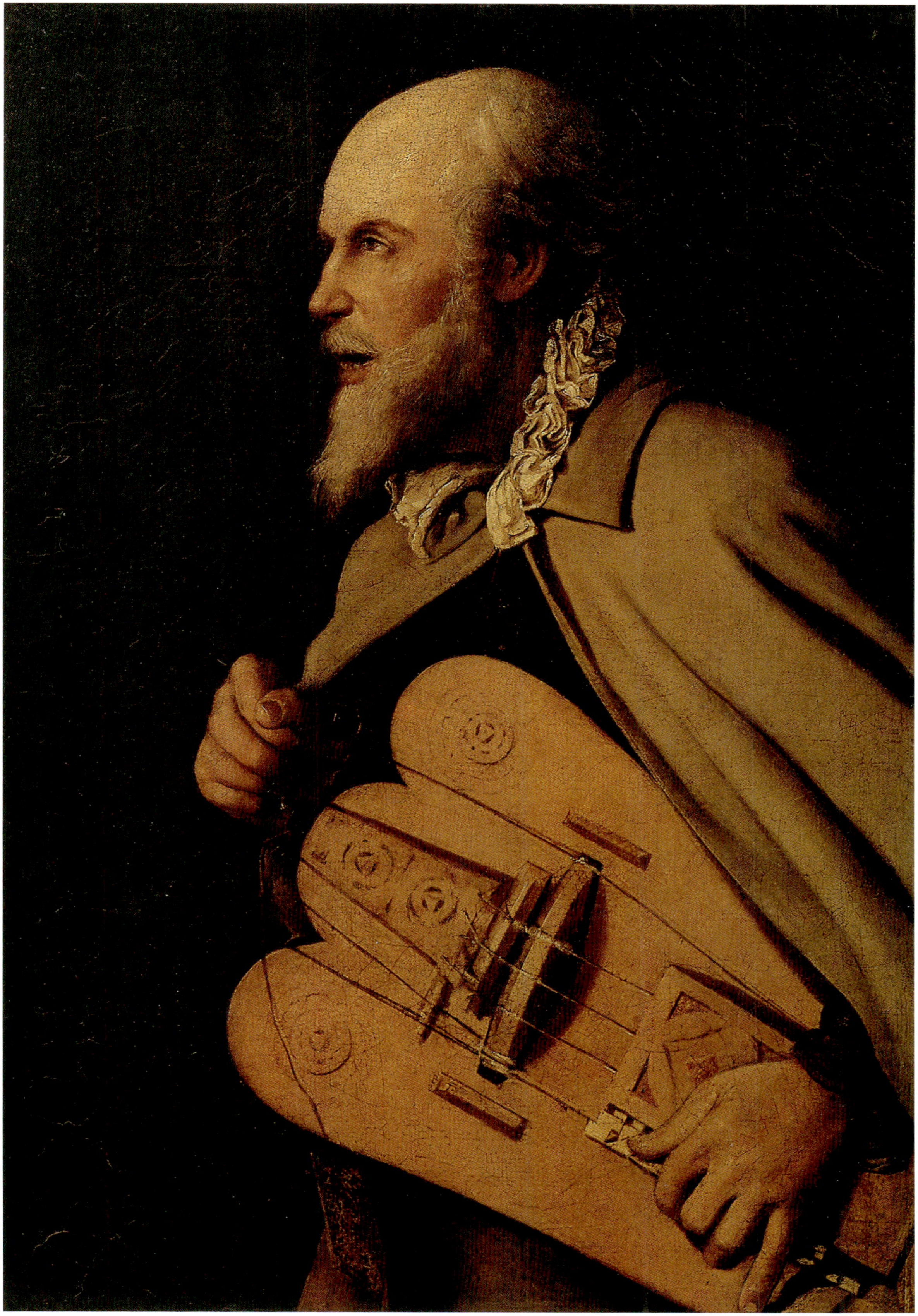

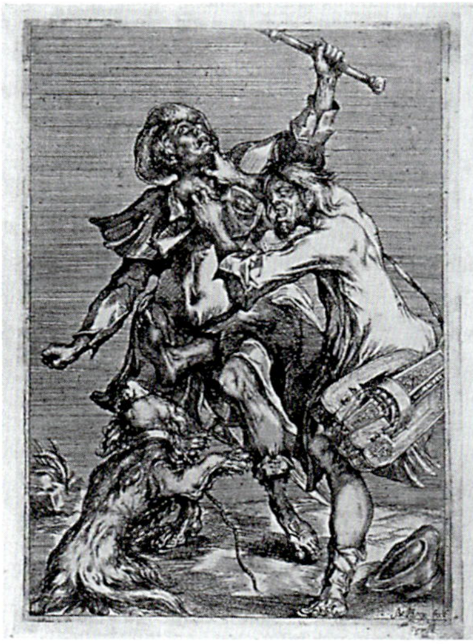

Jacques de Bellange. *Brawl Between A Beggar and a Pilgrim.* Etching.

Tour probably tackled it repeatedly, as did many other artists. It was common in Italy, and a painting in the Wawel Castle in Kracow points to its also being favored in Lorraine. We shall see later how La Tour was to use it in a number of major night pictures, and he would certainly have explored the theme with a series of daytime concerts first. But nothing at all apart from this fragment has yet surfaced.

By contrast, a rather different and surprising composition has come down to us intact in *The Beggars' Brawl.* For a long time the composition was known only through a good copy in the Chambéry museum. The original, which had long been hidden behind a convenient attribution to Caravaggio, eventually came to light in England around 1957. First mentioned in 1958, published in 1971, and exhibited in Paris in 1972, it was finally purchased at auction by the Paul Getty Foundation.

The scene shows five half-length figures in a frieze-like composition. In the center are the two fighting musicians, seen in profile. They are framed by two lesser characters, both shown frontally—a crying woman on the left, and an amused piper on the right. At the extreme right, a violinist in three-quarter position disrupts what would otherwise be a relentlessly rigid composition with its deliberate isocephaly and strictly symmetrical distribution of lines, gestures, and even masses of color. For all of the extreme violence, the clenched fists, and the gleaming blade, the scene is oddly static, the action frozen in a way that concentrates all the expressive force in the faces. These are minutely observed in all their detail—warts, crumbling teeth, streaks of gray hair. They are very similar in appearance to those of the Apostles but have none of the nobility of spirit that so distinguishes the old men of Albi.

Critics have been troubled by the subject, yet it relates to a popular theme of the day, the beggar musician. The figure on the left, brandishing a knife in one hand and the iron handle to his hurdy-gurdy in the other, is clearly blind, and the woman wailing behind him is probably his guide. Blind men commonly sought to make a living as itinerant musicians at the time. Here he is attacking a fellow musician, who attempts to fend him off with his flute, and who inspires little confidence as well. The musette player and the fiddler chuckling on the right belong to the same sinister world. It has often been studied, and Jean-Yves Ribault has shown that in Bourges during this same period there was a genuine organization of blind men who earned a living for themselves and their guides, normally a woman or child, by playing some instrument or other, especially a hurdy-gurdy. The archives even contain records of similar brawls. Artists were quick to latch onto the subject of the beggar with a hurdy-gurdy. It turns up in the work of painters as diverse as Teniers and Rembrandt, and Callot produced a famous engraving on the theme. The scene portrayed in the Malibu painting, however, is altogether more complex and uncompromisingly realist in character.

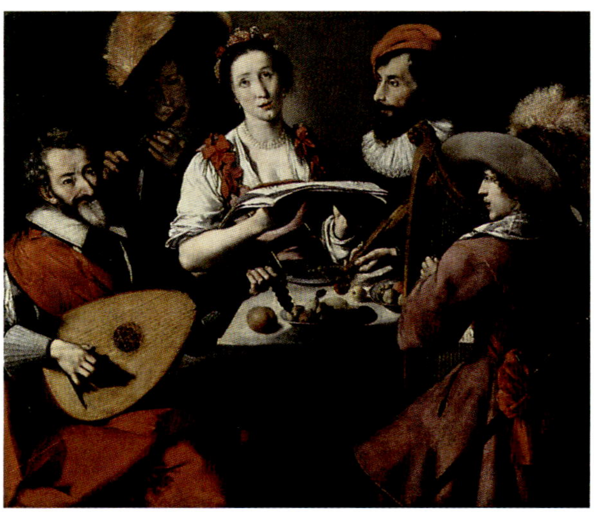

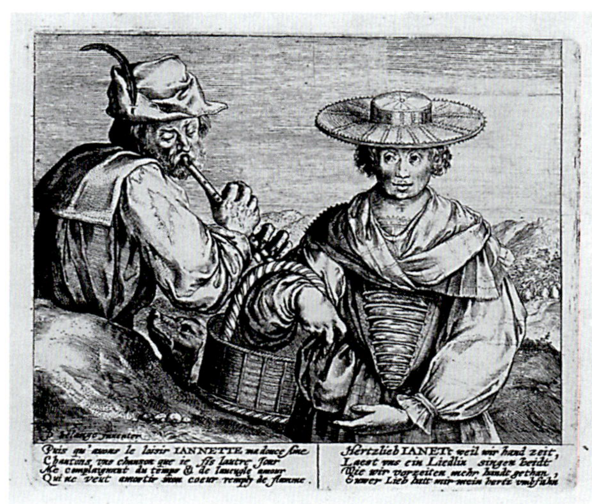

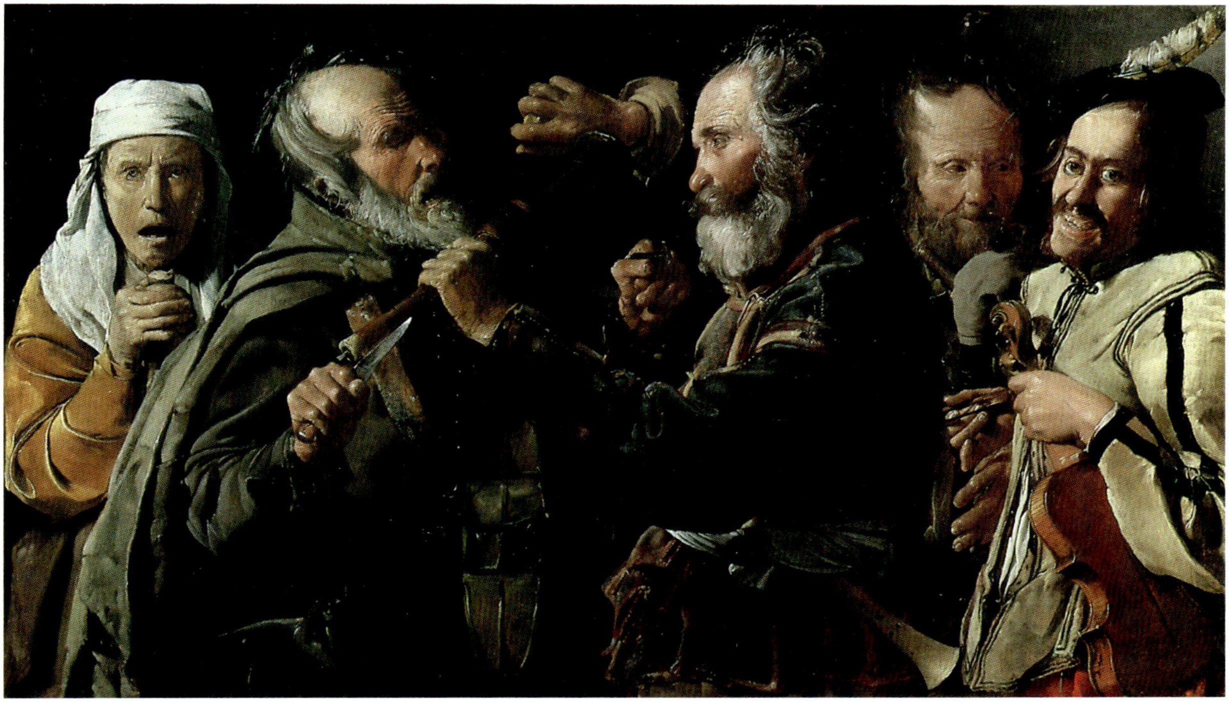

In fact, La Tour did have a direct predecessor: once again, Bellange. This most sophisticated and theatrical of painters engraved two beggar scenes: a solitary hurdy-gurdy player, and, more to the point, a brawl between a pilgrim and an itinerant musician. Signed *Bellange fecit*, this second engraving was well known and widely circulated. The Musée Lorrain in Nancy has a print of it dated 1615. The plate was subsequently distributed in Paris by the publisher Le Blond, and a copy of it by Matthieu Mérian was published in Strasbourg. The scene, shown in full-length, is strikingly violent. Gestures and facial expressions are contorted in the extreme, as one would expect from Bellange, and with their rags and ugliness and yapping dog, these people no longer seem human. La Tour's debt to Bellange is obvious as soon as one puts their work side by side, but so too is the distance separating him not only from Bellange, but from the Mannerist tradition as a whole. La Tour deliberately makes the situation static, neutralizes the violence, and freezes the cries in order to recapture the human content and to get away from purely dramatic effects and back to a precise description of reality.

The Beggars' Brawl.
John P. Getty Museum, Malibu

From left to right:
Anonymous Lorrainese artist (?).
The Concert.
Wawel Museum, Krakow

After Jacques de Bellange. From the *Mimicarum aliquot Facetiarum icones ad habitum italicum expressi.* Engravings by Crispin de Passe.
Kupferstichkabinett, Öffentliche Kunstammlung, Basel

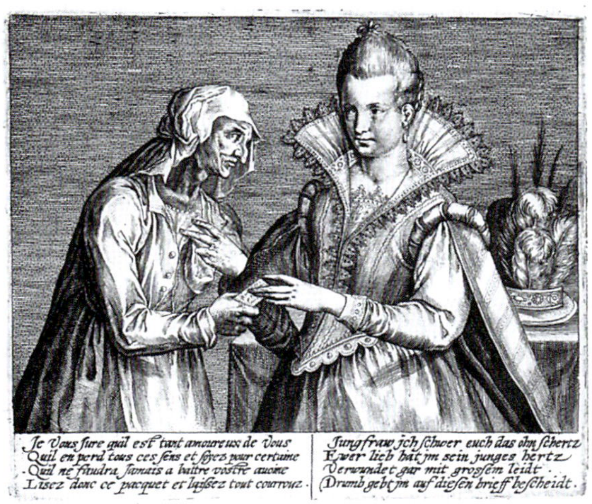

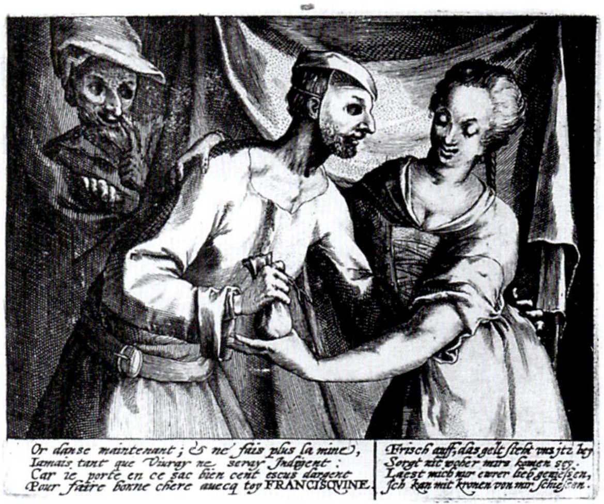

Is there another meaning to the scene? In the past I have pointed out that Matthieu Mérian's copy of the Bellange engraving bears the Latin title *Mendicus mendico invidet*: the beggar envies the beggar, or in other words, no matter how wretched you are, there is always someone more wretched to envy you. That seems to be what the mocking onlooker, the fiddler on the right, is thinking. The maxim may well have prompted the painting, but in fact what is portrayed is the poverty of this underworld, and portrayed for what it is, as misery and as part of the spectacle of life. La Tour seems no more interested in preaching to us than he is in treating us to an entertaining tidbit. He observes every scar of the beggars' faces, but his study of their heavy clothes, the cracked violin, the gleaming blade of the little knife, the hurdy-gurdy player's worn and grimy leather strap, and the old woman's meager head shawl is no less minute. He wants to grasp every element of this pitiful little world that is devoid of wisdom but, after all, part of the human universe.

This need to master a subject in all its detail is evident in a painting that reappeared only in 1975 and is still little known: *Old Peasant Couple Eating*. First published by Ferdinando Bologna, it was acquired shortly afterward by the museum in Berlin. A small and rather bad copy in the Musée Lorrain confirms that the canvas has not been trimmed and that the figures were never full-length. On the other hand, the man and woman had been separated, and they were discovered hanging as pendants. Now that they have been reunited, the painting has recovered not only its balance but also its rawness.

Could this work represent Taste in a hypothetical series depicting the five senses? That seems highly unlikely. It is difficult to imagine five paintings constructed on these lines, and there is no mention of any set of this kind conceived in this format and spirit. On the other hand, a painting entitled *A Pea-Eater and His Wife* was listed in the collection of the Nancy merchant César Mirgodin in 1643. It appears alone and does not seem to have warranted any literary explanation. Historians have surely too often resorted to this kind of symbolism, in fact very superficial, which mainly served as a convenient pretext for small Flemish paintings. It is often considered to underlie the work of various Caravaggesque artists, even though this means bending the interpretation somewhat, and though the texts of the period give no indication that this is what a given artist actually intended or what his contemporaries would have seen in it. No one has yet been able to find any convincing symbolism to explain Annibale Carracci's famous *Bean-Eater* in the Galleria Colonna. It is not entirely absurd to suppose that La Tour may have known this painting; in any event, he had no more need of a symbolic theme to demonstrate his particular realism than did Annibale Carracci several decades earlier.

This is what Caravaggesque realism was all about—painting a peasant and his wife eating chickpeas, and not representing the sense of taste. In this period of the 1620s, it seems La Tour could quite happily go about painting subjects like this for their own sake and have them admired by his buying public in Lorraine—just as fellow Lorrainer Bastien-Lepage's paintings *Haymaking* and *The Potato Harvest* were to be admired some 250 years later by rich Parisian society. Once again, La Tour is uncompromising in his presentation of the ravages wrought by old age and work—wrinkles, flaccid folds of skin, gnarled hands. The attitudes are deliberately simple and exclude any anecdotal explanation. There are no added details to distract the eye, and even the color is kept to a minimum: the brick red of the man's coat is the only warm tone in an otherwise neutral palette of whites and grayish-browns. All this combines to give the canvas a gravity rarely found in paintings of the same type of subject at this time, but which forcefully anticipates the peasant pictures of the Le Nain brothers.

Perhaps it is due to the condition of the canvas that the brushwork and surface modeling are rather different from those of the *Apostles* and *The Beggars' Brawl*. Should we therefore assume that it is earlier in date? This has already been the case, especially since the painting was discovered too late to be included in the 1972 exhibition and thus we have never had a chance to see how it fits with the rest of La Tour's oeuvre. It must be acknowledged, however, that it does seem to be more removed in technique and style from the influence of Roman Caravaggism. Should we therefore date it around the time—probably the late 1620s—when La Tour first showed signs of moving toward simpler forms and began to make far greater use of white, a practice that was to culminate many years later in the Stockholm version of *St. Jerome*? For the moment, the painting is too isolated to permit a reply.

pp. 67-71: *The Beggars' Brawl*, details.

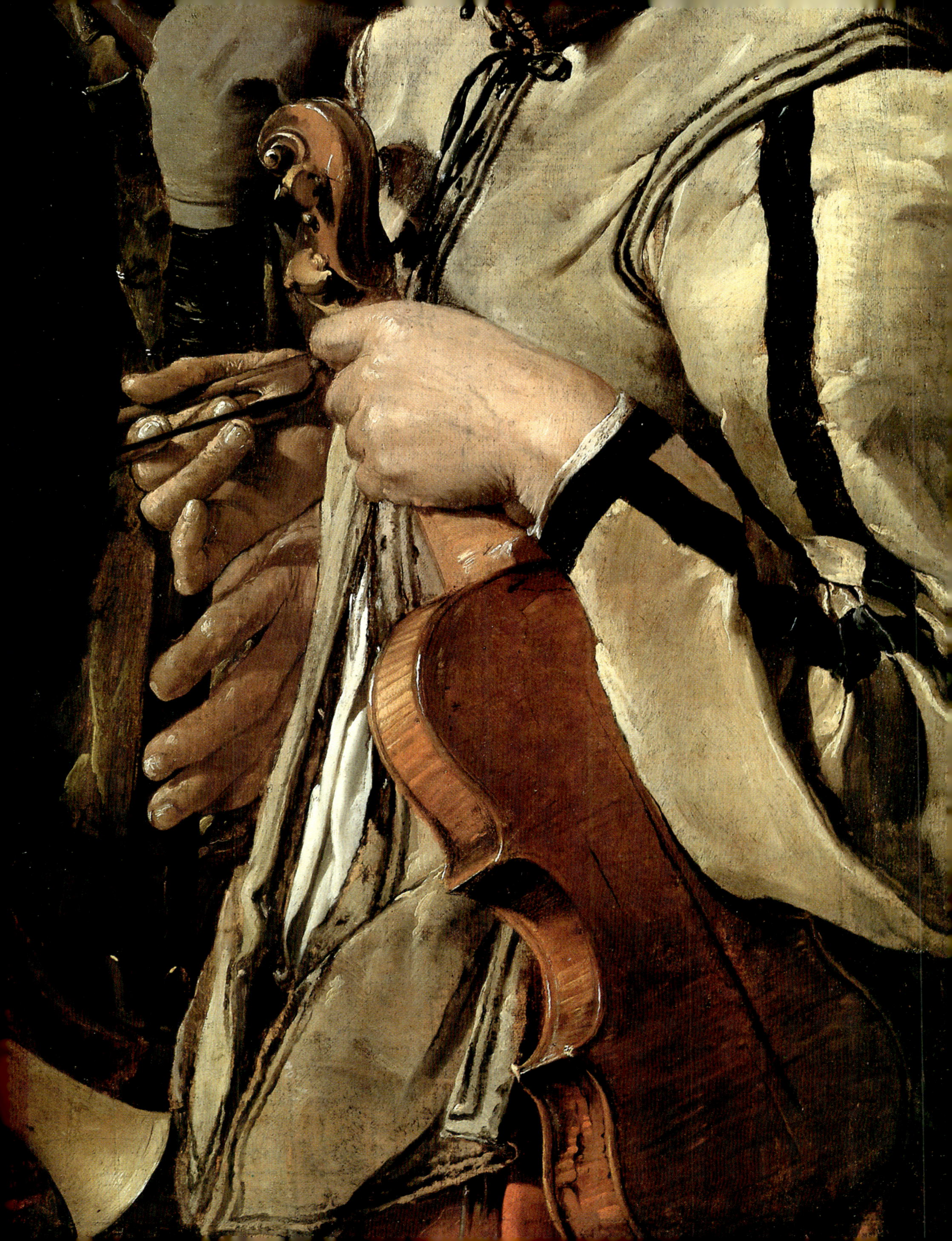

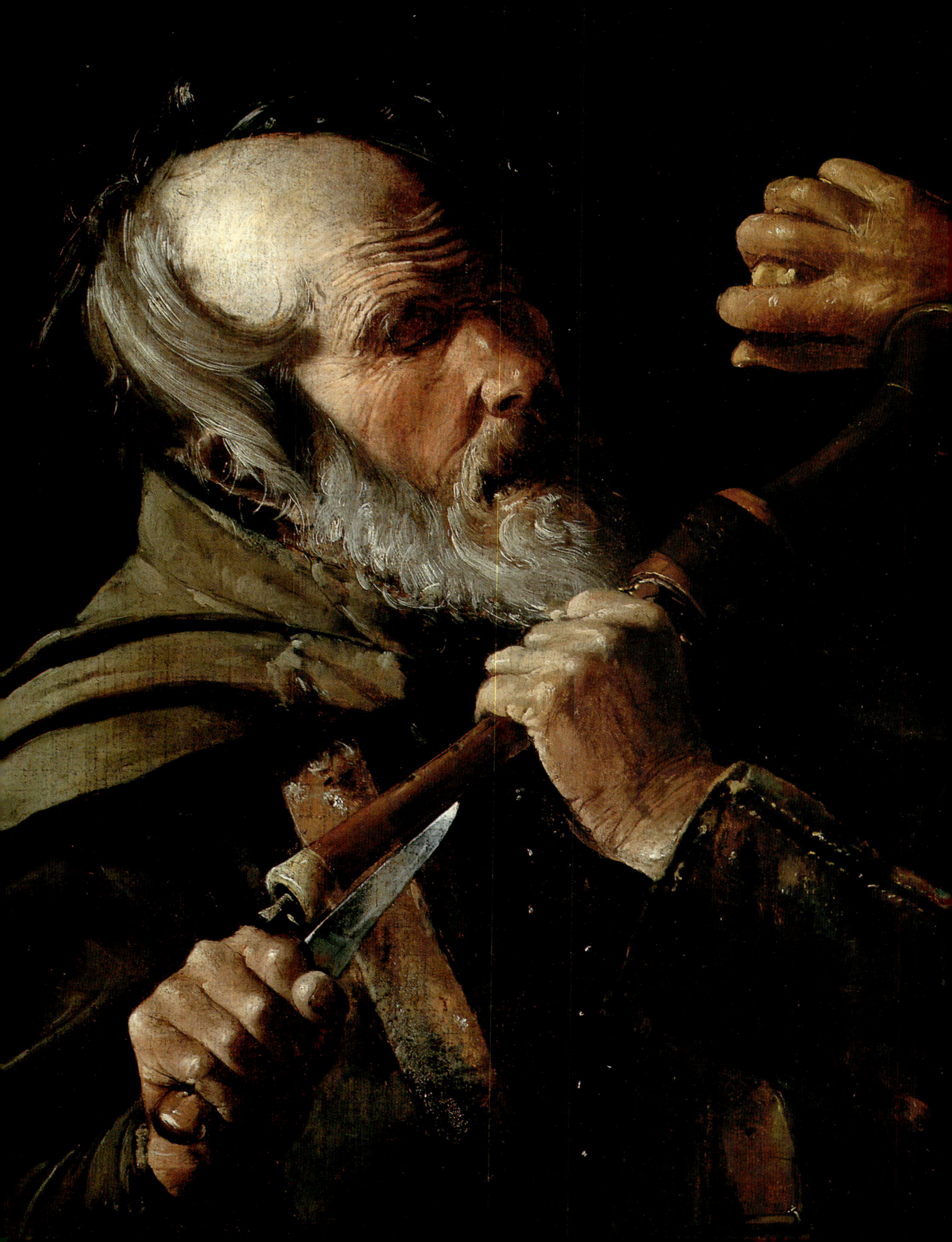

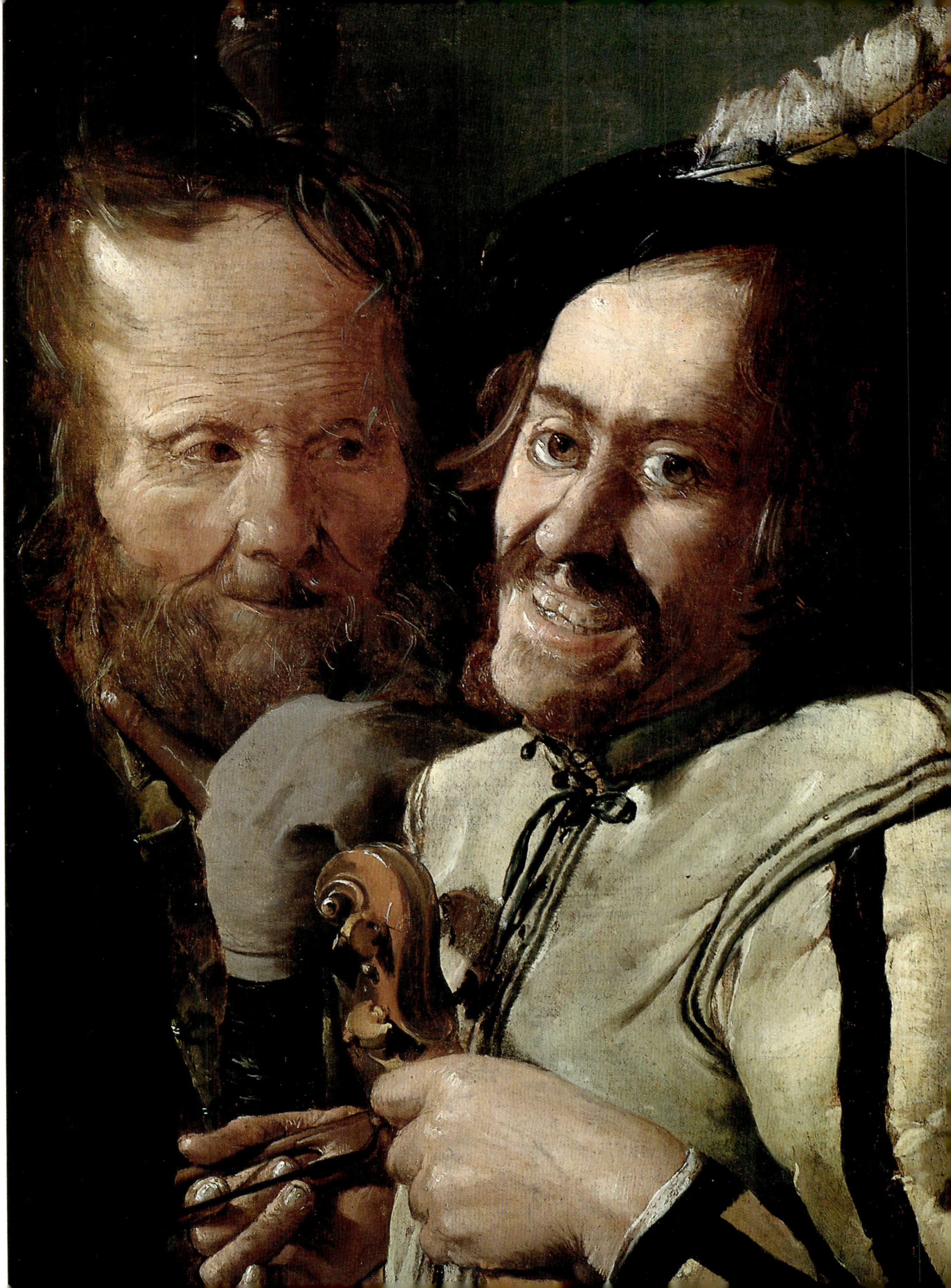

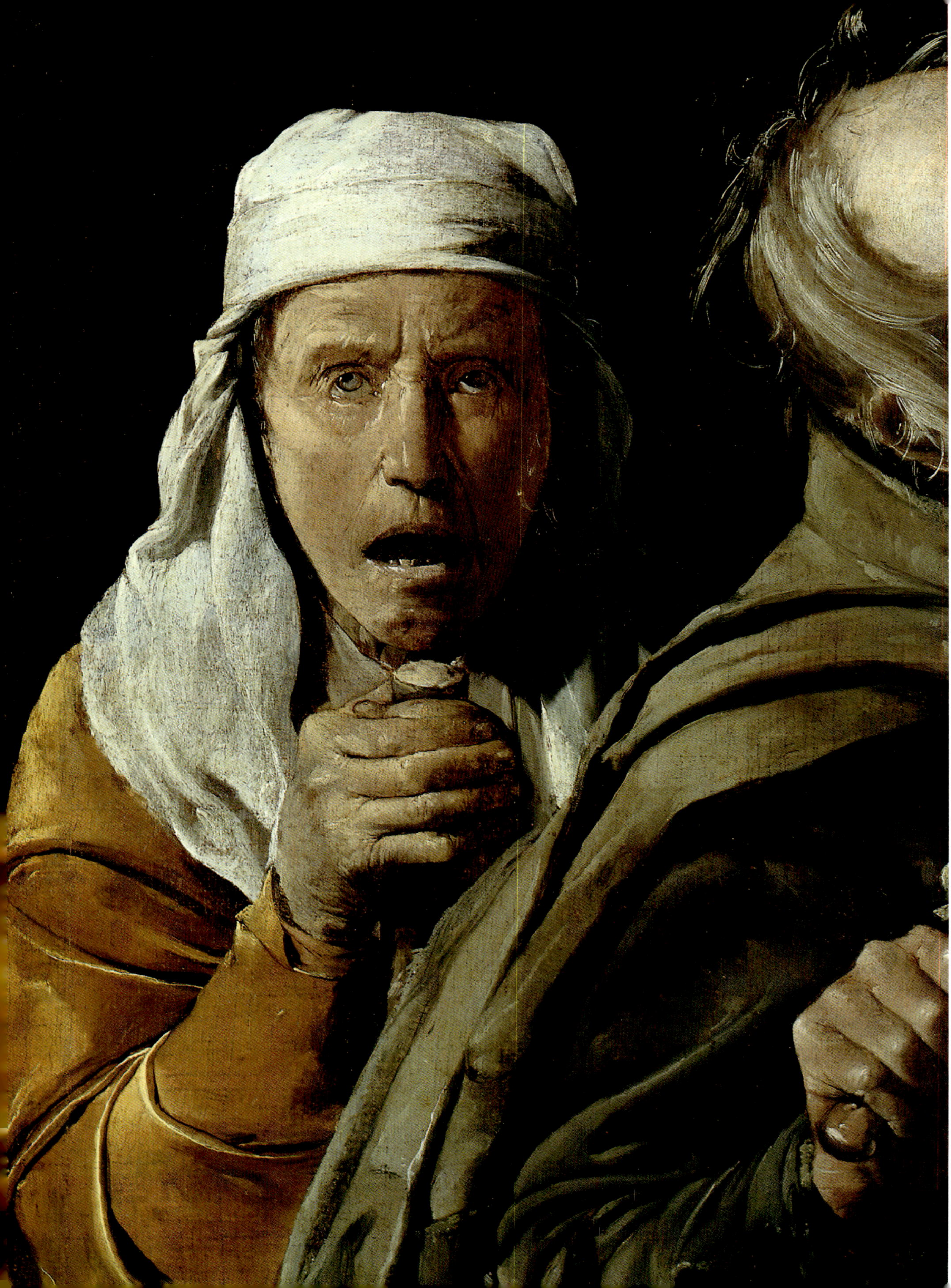

7
7

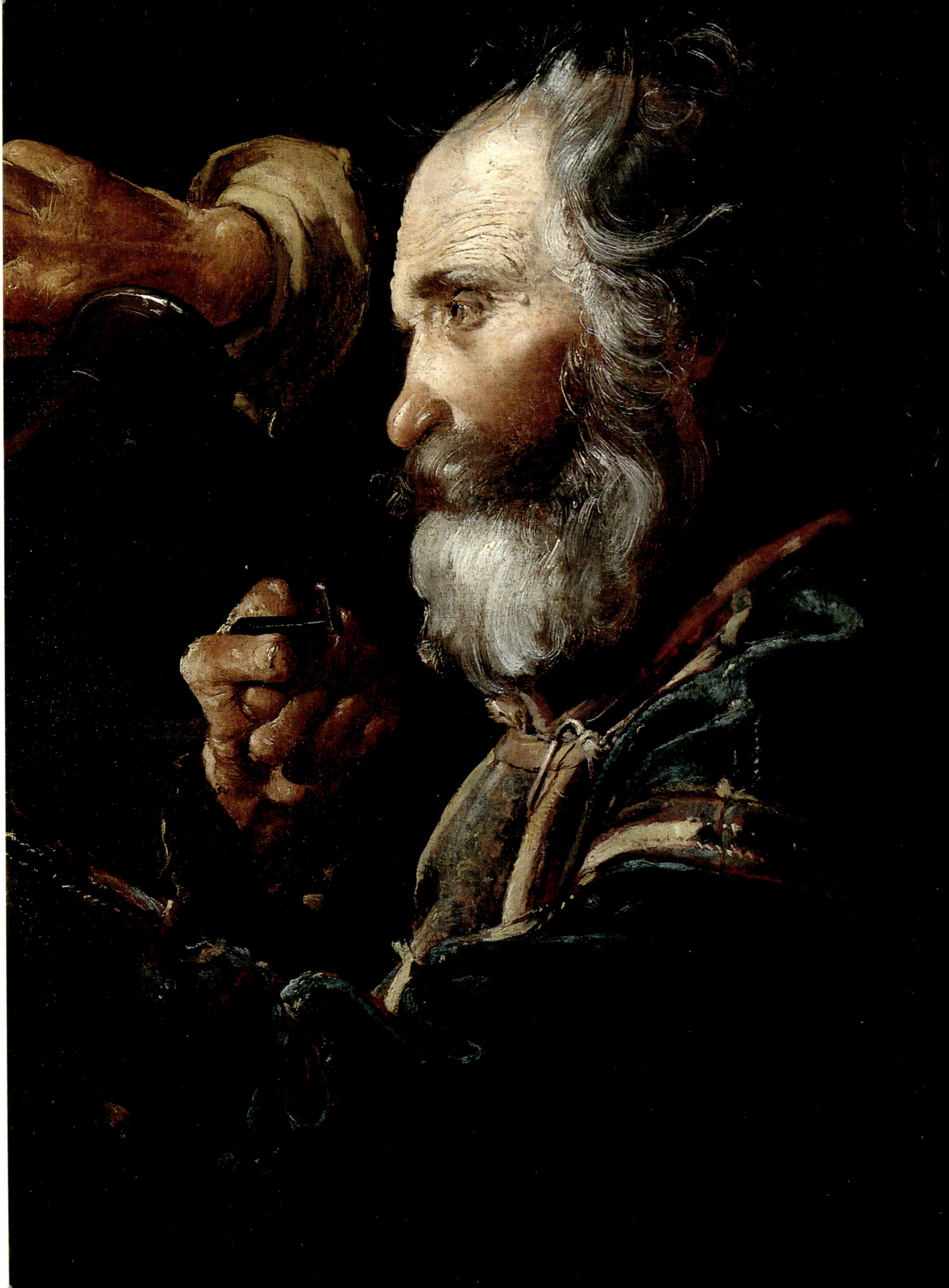

After Georges de La Tour.
Woman Playing a Triangle.
Private collection, Antwerp

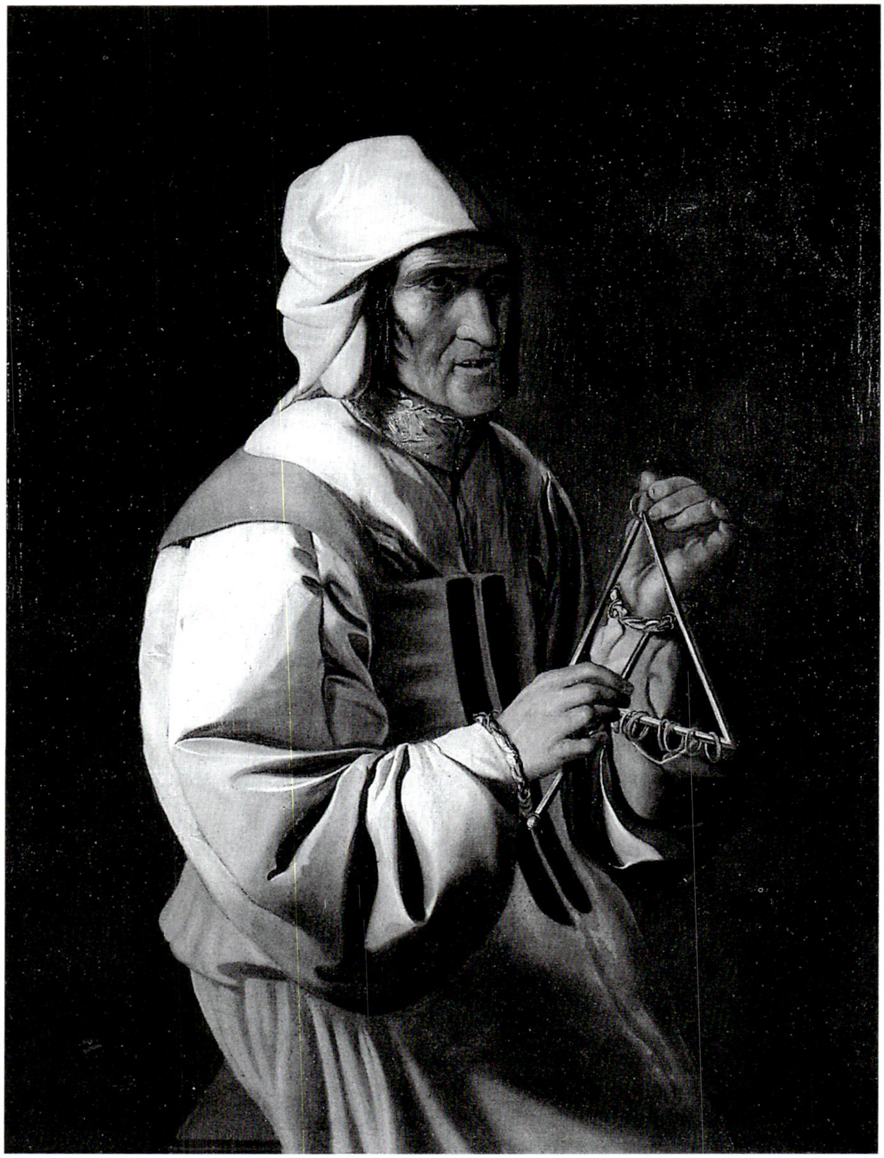

Annibale Carracci. *A Bean-Eater.*
Galleria Colonna, Rome

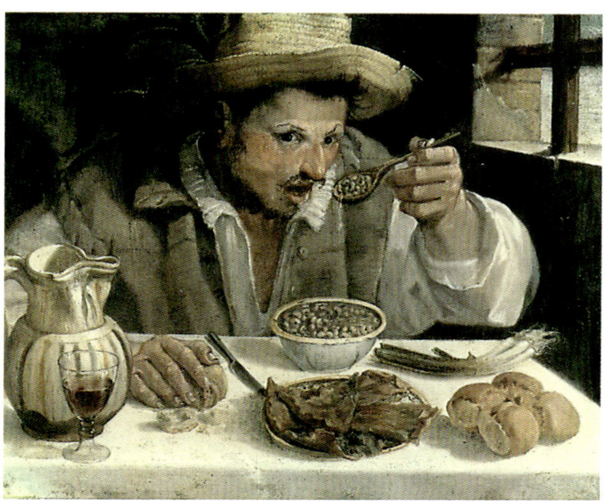

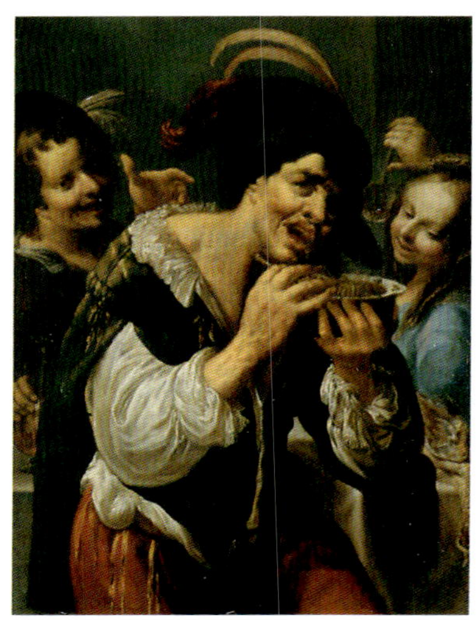

Georges Lallemant.
George and the Bowl of Broth.
National Museum, Warsaw

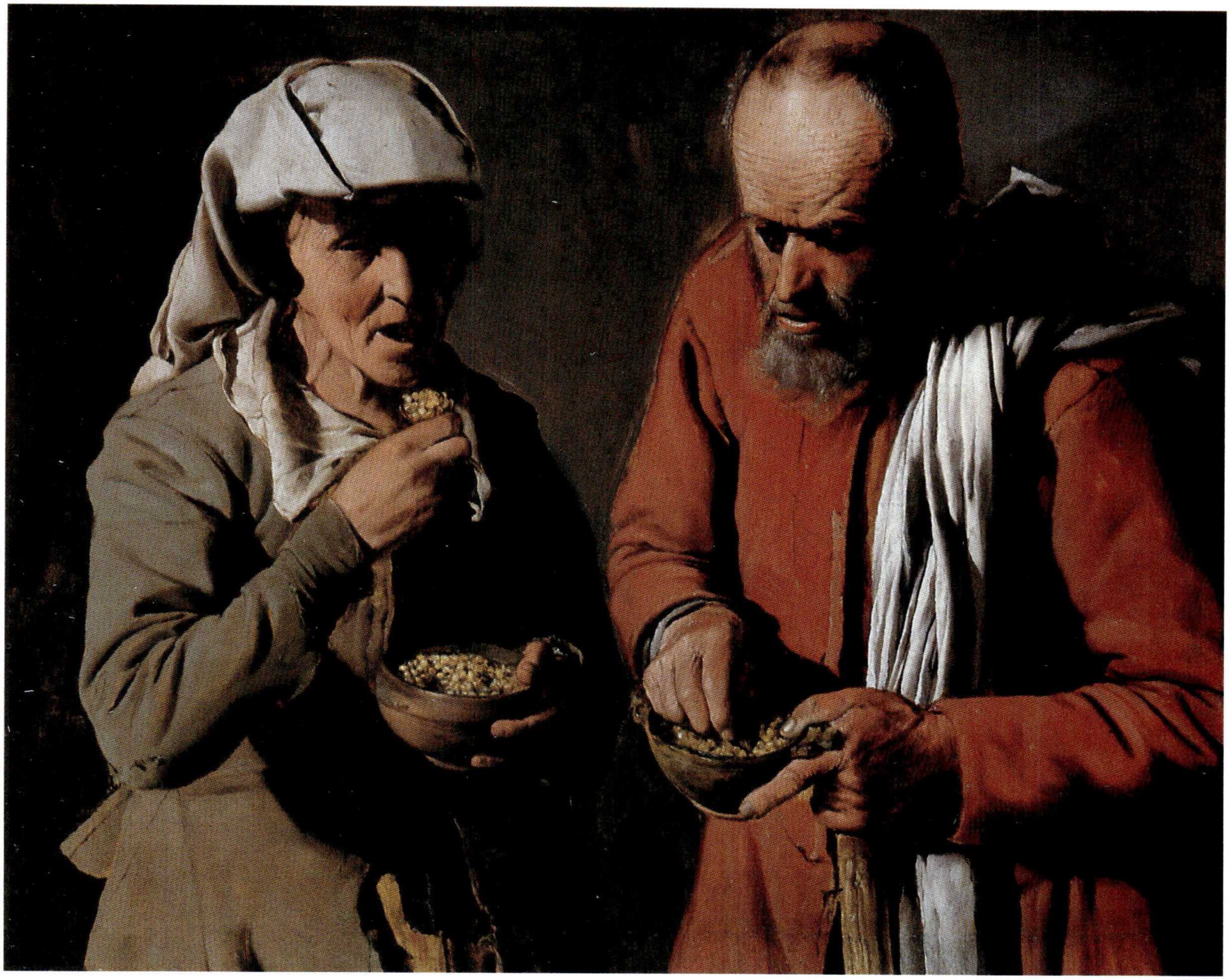

Old Peasant Couple Eating.
Staatliche Museen, Berlin-Dahlem

GEORGES DE LA TOUR AND THE "POPULAR" TRADITION

As I have said, contrary to an idea that is too widespread, especially among specialists in iconography, traditional painting does not always have a religious, mythological, or historical subject, or a more or less latent symbolic meaning. From the fifteenth century on, artists began to look at the real world and to reproduce it for its own sake, and they found buyers for their work who did not look for anything more than what they saw. This was certainly the case with the majority of still lifes. It was similarly true of paintings of popular figure types, which very soon gave way to straightforward, honest representations. The most famous example of this kind is undoubtedly Annibale Carracci's *Bean-Eater* (*c.* 1584).

During La Tour's lifetime, *Pea-Eater* is the simple title that inventories in Lorraine gave to paintings akin to the one in Berlin, if not the Berlin work itself. The *Woman Playing a Triangle*, recently identified in a good copy by Pierre Rosenberg, similarly depicts a woman of the common people, perhaps one of those who went around with blind hurdy-gurdy players, acting as guides and sometimes accompanying their playing (engravings of the day often show a hurdy-gurdy player with a triangle player at his side). Very probably the original version served as a pendant to a now lost *Hurdy-Gurdy Player*.

Sometimes these popular subjects verged on the "burlesque": Lallemant's *George and the Bowl of Broth* was probably inspired by some farce mounted by the players of the Pont-Neuf in Paris. It highlights the dignity that La Tour's figures preserve even in the depths of poverty and decrepitude.

pp. 74 and 75: *Old Peasant Couple Eating*, details.

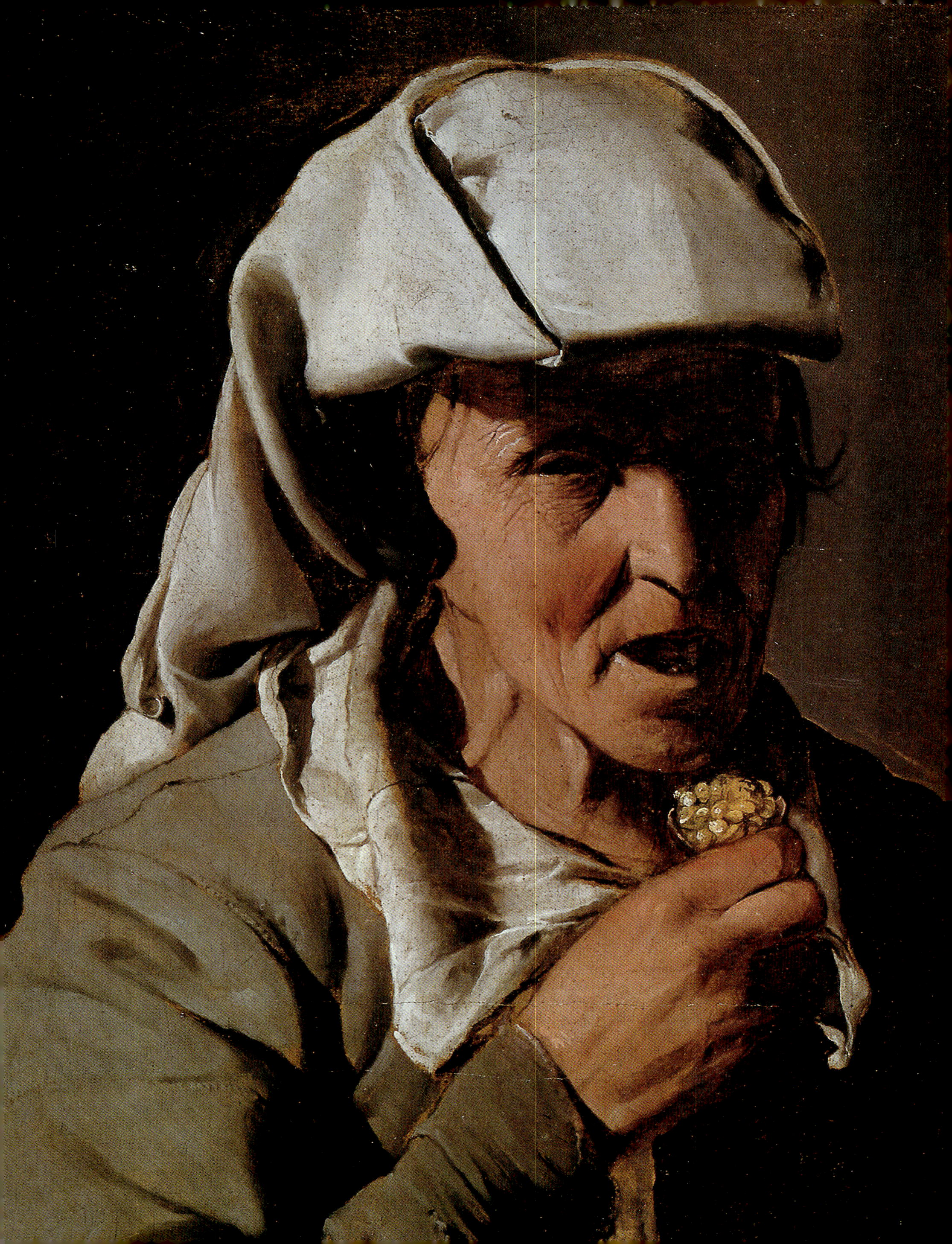

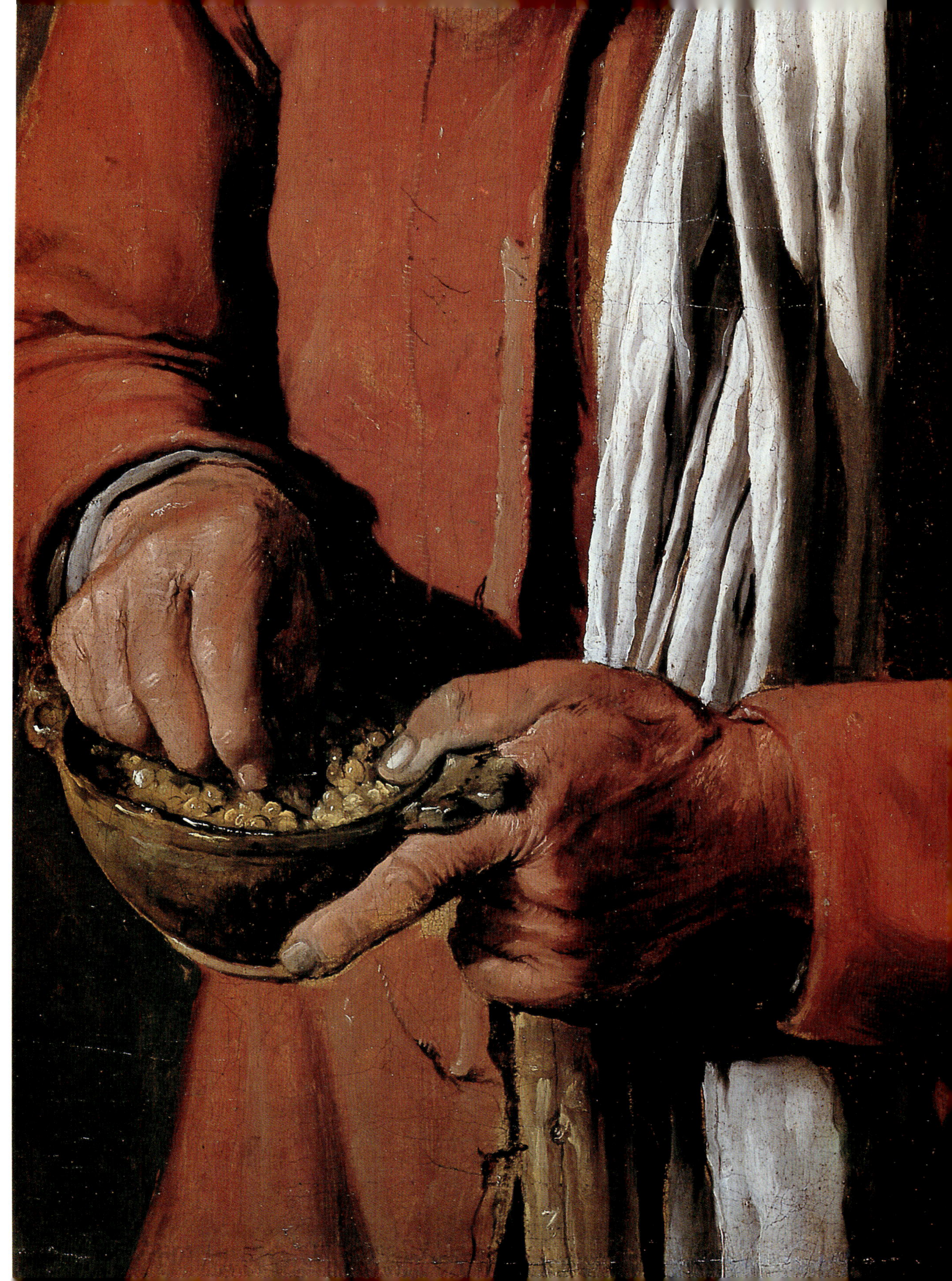

4

5

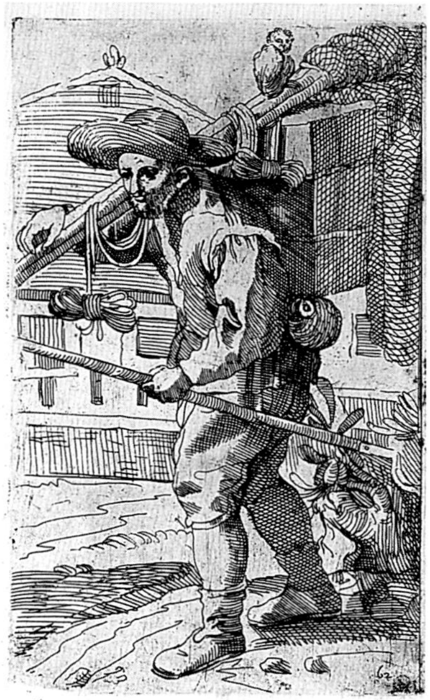

After Annibale Carracci. *Bird-caller with an Owl.* From the series *The Cries of Boulogne* (Plate 62). Engraving by Simon Guillain.

THE LARGE SINGLE-FIGURE PAINTINGS

We should beware of leaping to conclusions and placing the *Old Peasant Couple Eating* at the very beginning of La Tour's oeuvre on the grounds that the composition, with its two figures set virtually side by side, is far less skillful than *The Beggars' Brawl.* La Tour was more than capable of arranging a group of figures in two and three dimensions, and he went on producing five- and six-figure compositions until the end of his career. Paintings of this kind were in demand, and the greater the number of figures the picture included, the higher the price they could command. La Tour consistently tended to avoid complex arrangements, however, seeking instead to focus on single figures and to capture them in immobility. In this respect, he went even further than Caravaggio himself, not to mention Manfredi and Valentin, in his rejection of Mannerism, which sought to occupy every spatial direction and include as many figures as possible. In contrast to Cavaliere d'Arpino and Fréminet, but also to Callot, who triumphantly packed whole universes into engravings such as *The Fair at Gondreville* and *The Martyrdom of St. Sebastian*, and to Deruet, whose masterpiece was to be the Munich *Rape of the Sabine Women*, with its hundreds of figures, La Tour preferred to paint single full-length figures, seated or standing, against a neutral background or one that simply ranged from light to dark, and without any accessories to distract the eye. Indeed, this was to be his favorite form, particularly in the early phase of his career. It was not a question of convenience, however, but one of choice. In this sense, La Tour's *Hurdy-Gurdy Player* was to the Lorraine of his day, still under the influence of Bellange's *Stag Hunt* and captivated by Le Clerc, Deruet, and Callot, what Manet's *Fifer* was to nineteenth-century Paris, with its taste for imperial decoration and Salon paintings. It was something different, painted in a different way, in another spirit and for a new clientele.

This type of composition also gave rise to variations and series. To date, his paintings of the *Peasant* and *Peasant's Wife* now in San Francisco seem to be in a class of their own, but it would not be surprising if related figures were to turn up. The Bergues *Hurdy-Gurdy Player with His Dog*, the Remiremont *Hurdy-Gurdy Player in Profile* (of which the Musée Lorrain has an old copy), the *Hurdy-Gurdy Player with Pink Ribbon* that came onto the London art market recently and made its way to Japan before finally being acquired by the Prado (and which shows only the upper half of the figure, but was almost certainly cut from a larger canvas very similar in design to the Remiremont painting), and, best preserved of all, the Nantes *Hurdy-Gurdy Player*, are effectively variations on a single theme. We must also add a *Hurdy-Gurdy Player* recorded as hanging in the king's bedroom in the duke's castle in Commercy in 1764: this was certainly the version La Tour painted for the duke, which could have been one of the four works just mentioned but is still more likely to have been a fifth. Even leaving this aside, however, we know of at least six surviving figures of this kind.

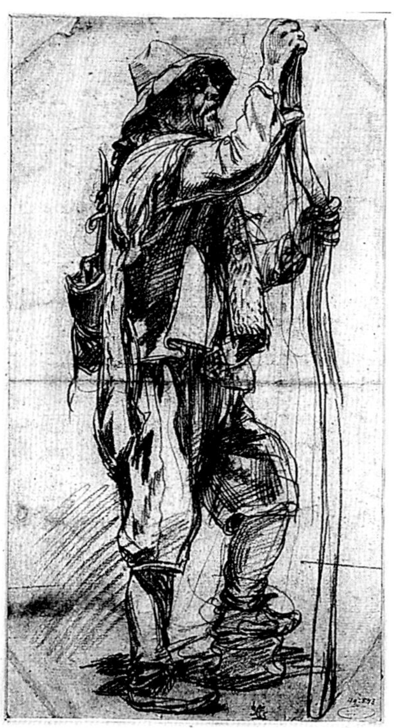

Pierre Brébiette. *Man with a Staff.* Preparatory drawing in red chalk for the engraving *Spring Festival.*
Rijksprentenkabinet, Rijksmuseum, Amsterdam

Peasant.
De Young Memorial Museum, San Francisco

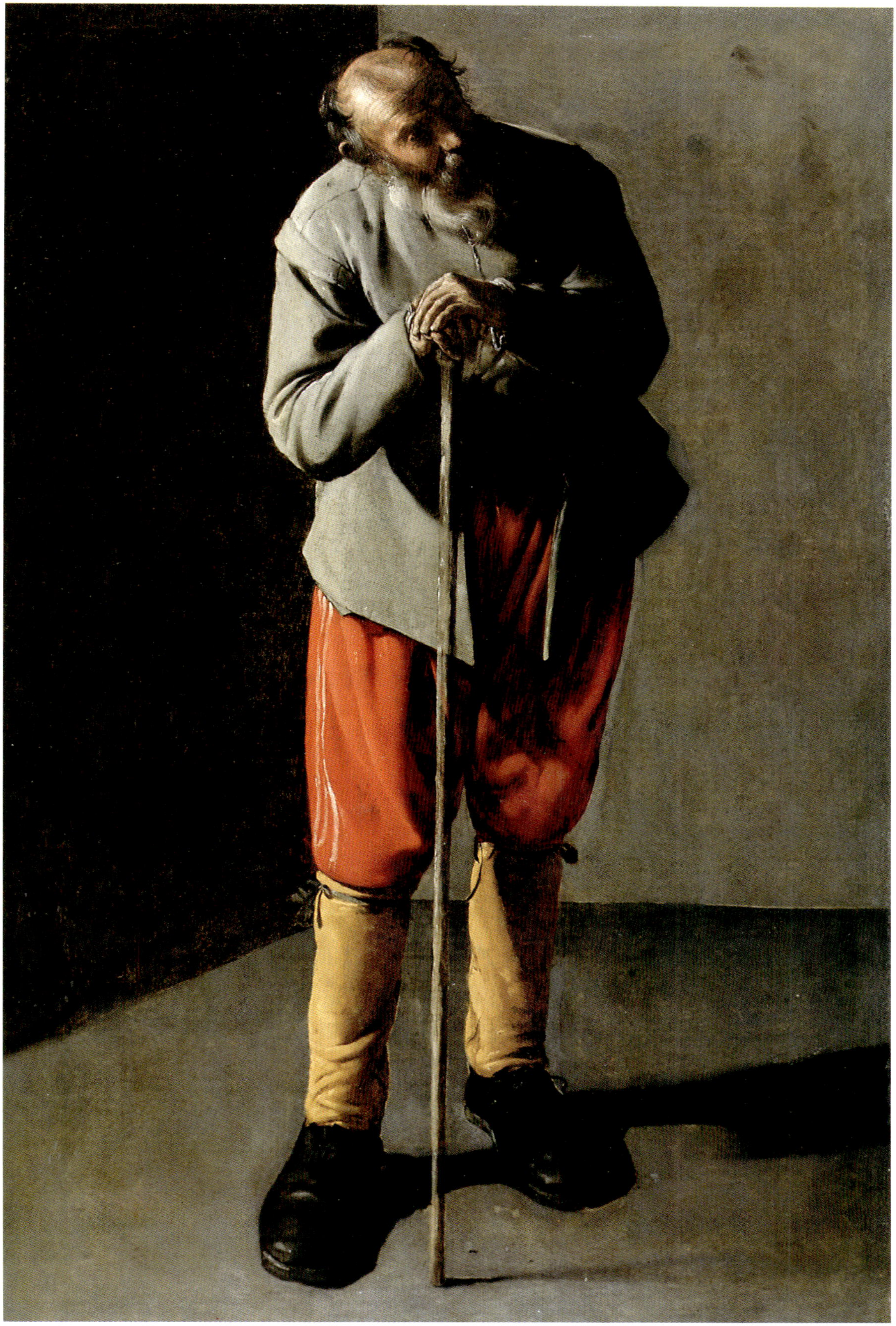

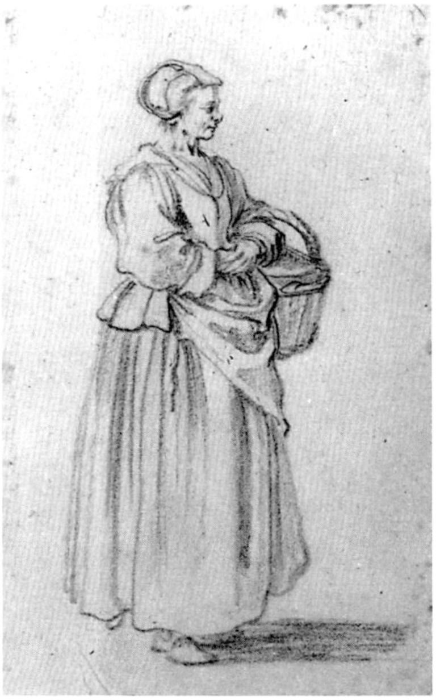

Jacques Callot. *Woman with a Basket.*
Black chalk. Album Sylvestre (No. 299), Chatsworth

Below: Jacques Callot. *Young Woman.*
Black chalk. Album Sylvestre (No. 304), Chatsworth

The two in San Francisco are the most surprising. Before the exhibition in 1972, doubts were raised about the attribution itself, even though their quality, style, and palette rule out any hesitation. What shocked was the absence of any pretext. Here were two ordinary people, an old man and an old woman, with no accessories, no particular expression on their faces, seen in a typical stance, but not doing anything other than looking toward each other, as was fitting for pendants. There had to be some reason for them. They were compared to theatrical characters, but this argument was unconvincing. The costumes suggest people of comfortably modest means. They are even a bit dressed up, particularly the old woman, who has put on a freshly pressed apron with a pretty border of braid. We have to take these two figure paintings for what they are: straightforward representations of reality and no more, with no hidden meaning or extraneous purpose. There is no invention here: these good people have simply posed in front of La Tour, who has not bothered to add any accessories but has painted them as subjects in their own right, as one would a landscape or still life.

La Tour would certainly have heard the story of Caravaggio and the Gypsy woman that was the talk of all the studios in Rome. Bellori relates how, "When Merisi was shown the most famous statues of Phidias and Glicon to study, his reply was to point to the crowd, saying that nature had provided him with masters enough. And to prove his point he called out to a Gypsy woman who happened to be passing in the street, took her with him to the inn, and painted her telling fortunes as these Gypsy women do. He added a young man with his left hand on his sword, the other open in the woman's as she studies it. And Michelangelo [Caravaggio] captured the true aspect of these two figures so perfectly that he quite substantiated his claim."

For, as Bellori goes on to say, "Caravaggio was more interested in reproducing reality than conjuring up beauty." All the same he does transform his raw model into a subject, and the impression one has when looking at the painting, which is in the Louvre, is that he gives the Gypsy woman and her young client rather more than their rightful share of youthful charm. La Tour, on the contrary, once again takes the theory to its logical conclusion: there is no theme, no action to these pictures, and no particular appeal to these old people, except as impressive examples of painting from "real life."

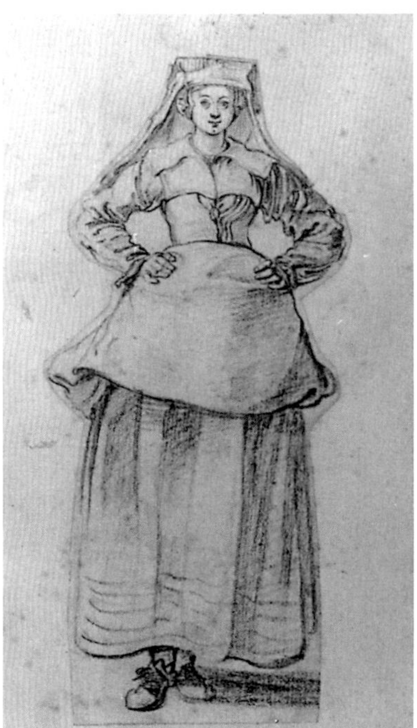

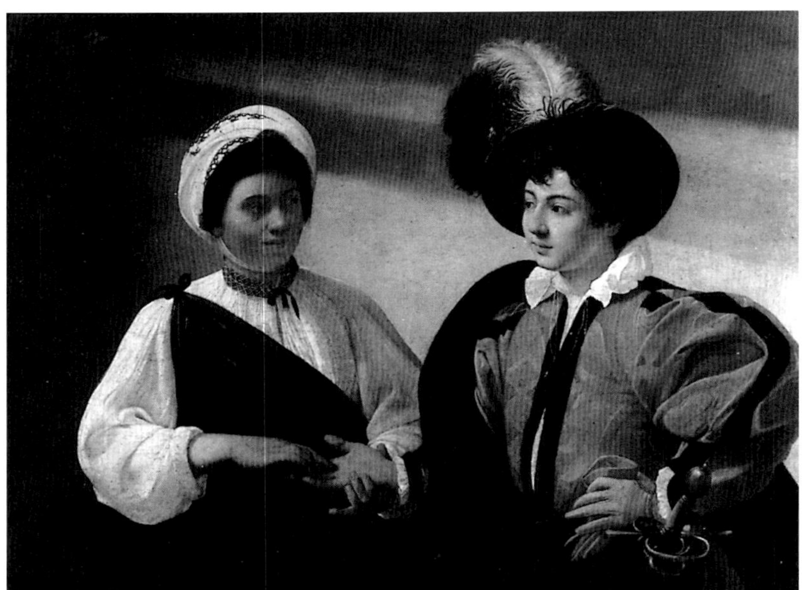

Michelangelo Caravaggio.
The Fortune Teller.
Musée du Louvre, Paris

p. 79: *Peasant's Wife.*
p. 80: *Peasant.* p. 81: *Peasant's Wife*, enlarged details
De Young Memorial Museum, San Francisco

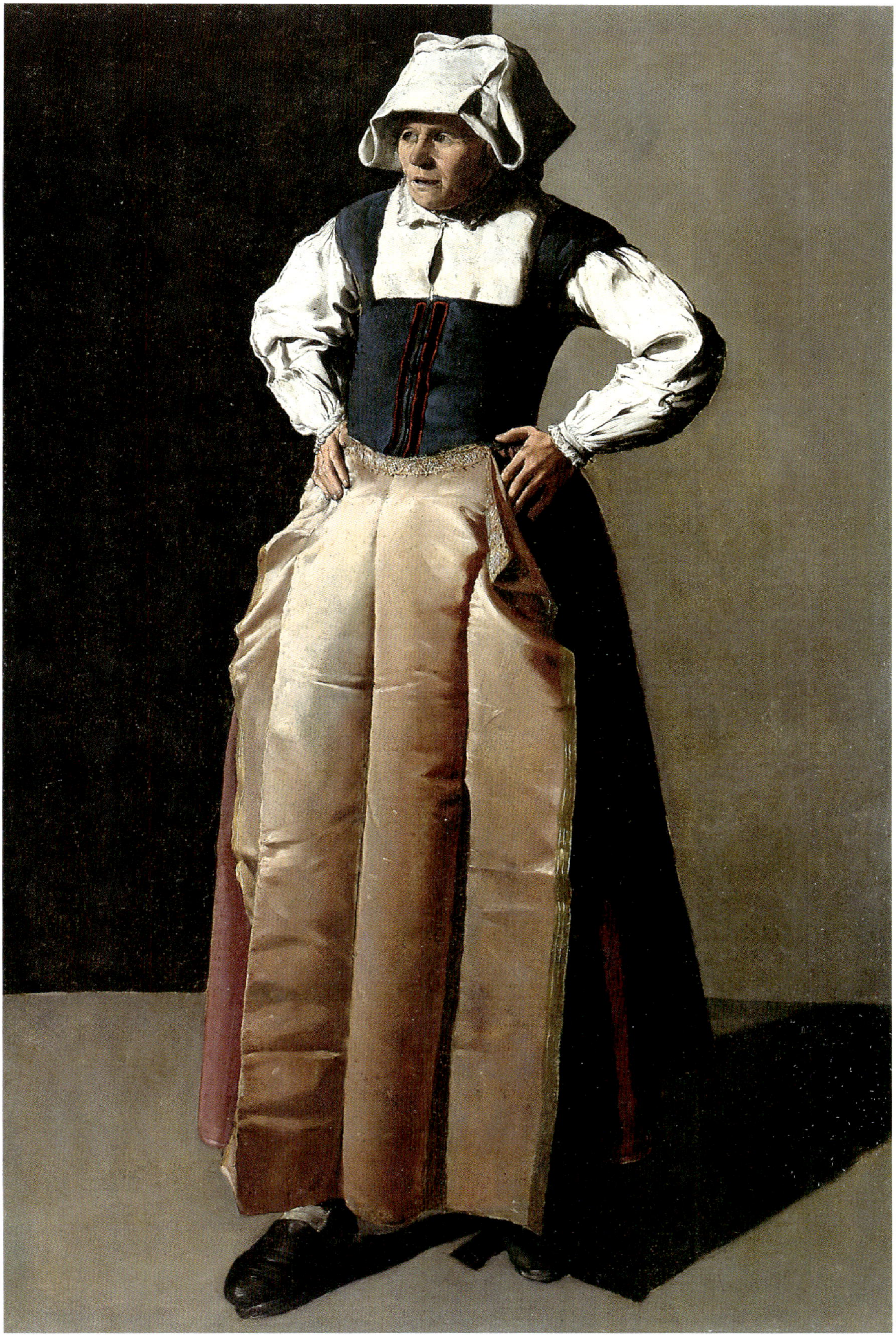

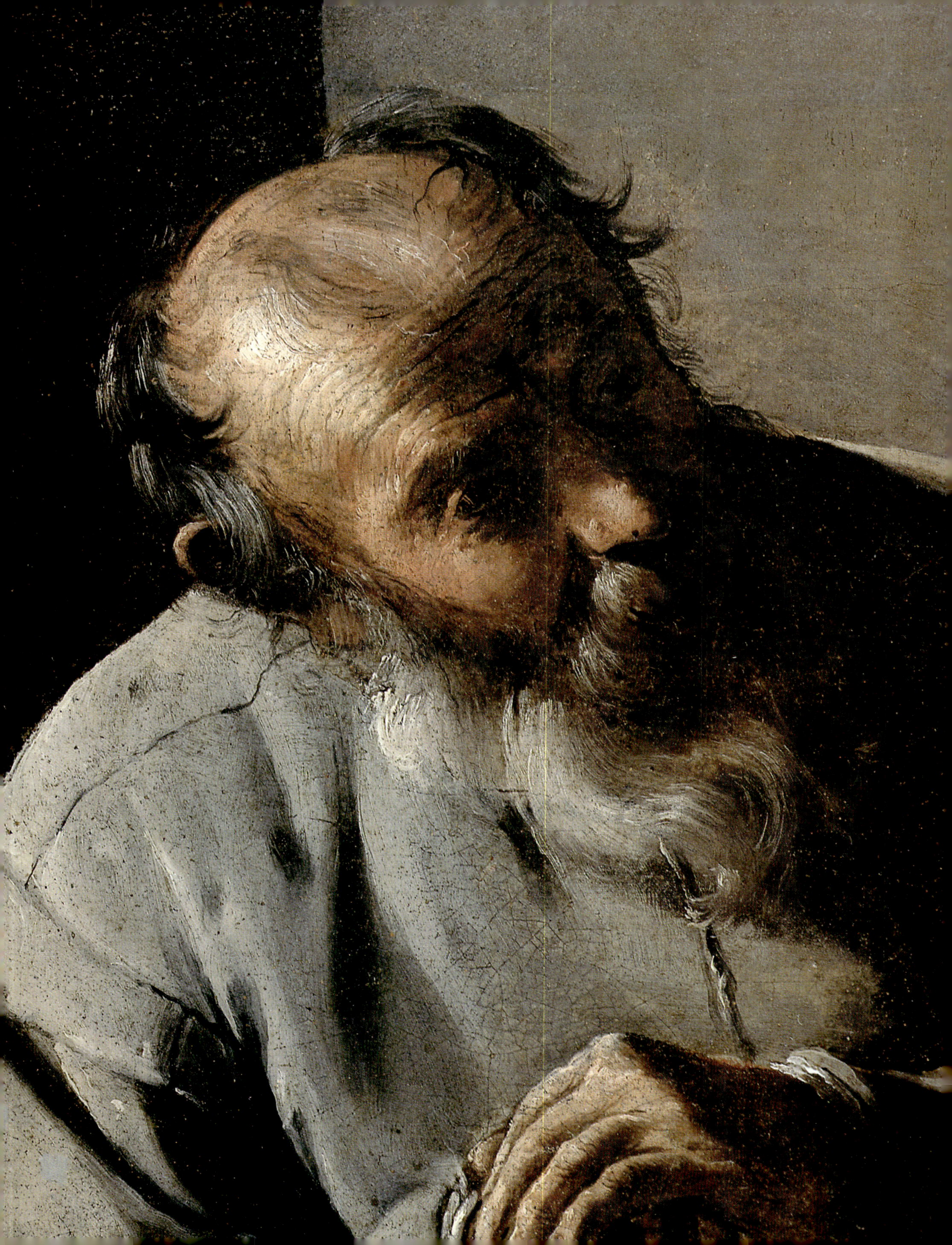

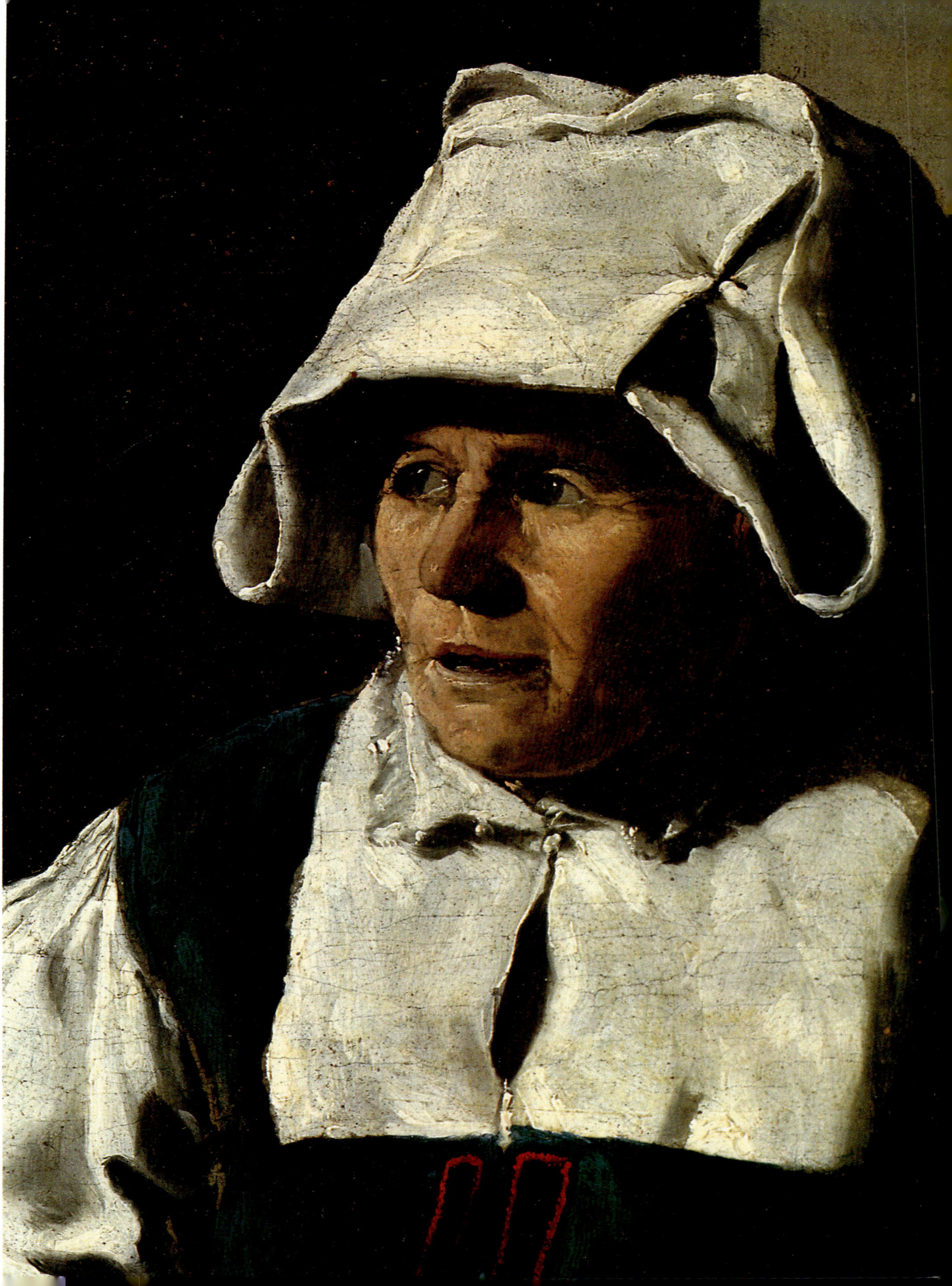

A Hurdy-Gurdy Player with a Ribbon.
The Prado, Madrid

There is hardly more of a theme when La Tour takes a blind musician as his model for the different versions of a *Hurdy-Gurdy Player,* now in Bergues, Remiremont, and Nantes. Each time, he alters the pose a little—standing, seated in profile, seated in a three-quarter view. He changes a detail of the man's dress or the rosettes on the hurdy-gurdy. He places a different object in the foreground: a guide-dog, a satchel, a plumed hat. Each time, the painting is new and the approach is different, but the spirit is the same. More than ever, we see how the series works. Mastering the subject by mere description is no longer enough for him: by going back over the same ground, and playing on the similarities and differences, he achieved a more thorough understanding—as Monet, among others, was to discover.

With this method came greater and greater technical dexterity. Through repetition, La Tour lived his subject so intensely, as it were, that he knew instinctively where to put each stroke for maximum effect, which detail to alter for the specific character of each painting. Like all true Caravaggist painters, La Tour did not make preparatory drawings. Where other artists slowly developed their ideas on paper, producing sheet after sheet of studies in black chalk or wash, La Tour attained the same progressive maturity with brush in hand, creating one version after another of the same subject. There is nothing more certain or more forceful than this kind of painting. Volumes are modeled in a clear light with shadows often expressed in half-tones so that a light outline, or more precisely, a network of lines filled in, can be superimposed to define the features of a face, pick out fingers, nails, and folds of skin, and rapidly sketch in hair and beard, while objects and fabrics are painted with a stiff brush, well suited to producing a wide range of strokes that render texture along with color. Consider the hands of the Nantes hurdy-gurdy player: with the juxtaposition of two similar tones, the simple addition of a precise outline, and a few strokes of highlighting, La Tour conjures up a sense of volume. His style lends itself to the maximum economy of means, but this kind of simplicity borders on virtuosity.

Hendrick Terbrugghen.
A Bagpipe Player. 1624.
Ashmolean Museum, Oxford

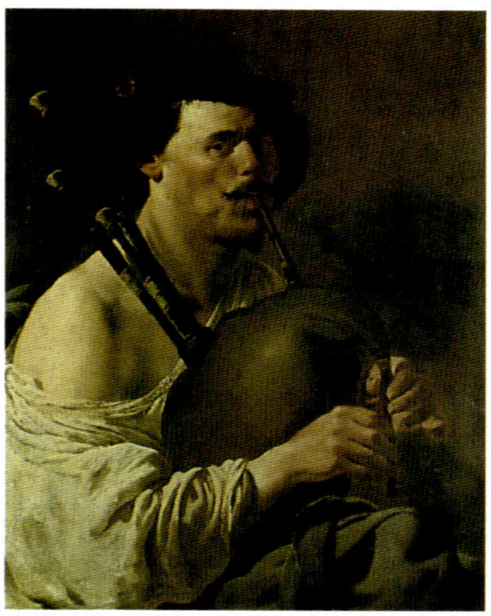

Clearly, La Tour delighted in this. He is by no means the only artist to have evolved a highly contrived style to accommodate a realist vision. Making something look real often involves tricking the eye. Why else should we find a fly resting on the hurdy-gurdy of the Nantes version, in the most conspicuous place possible? It is so skillfully painted, moreover, that we cannot immediately tell whether it is part of the picture or not, and our first instinct is to brush it aside with our hand. This was precisely the sort of detail the Flemish painters added to their little still lifes to complete the illusion and demonstrate their technical skill. It is the very opposite of Italian Caravaggism, which was only concerned with projecting inner psychology. With this masterpiece—which perhaps dates from the 1630s, but is in fact the culmination of a series of the previous decade—La Tour reached a limit. The pursuit of reality was in danger of leading to the opposite, of becoming an imitation of the outside world, with technique reduced to an end in itself. In a sense, the *Hurdy-Gurdy Player* in Nantes was not so far removed from that of Bellange.

Events in Lorraine were already pulling La Tour away, however, and leading him in other directions.

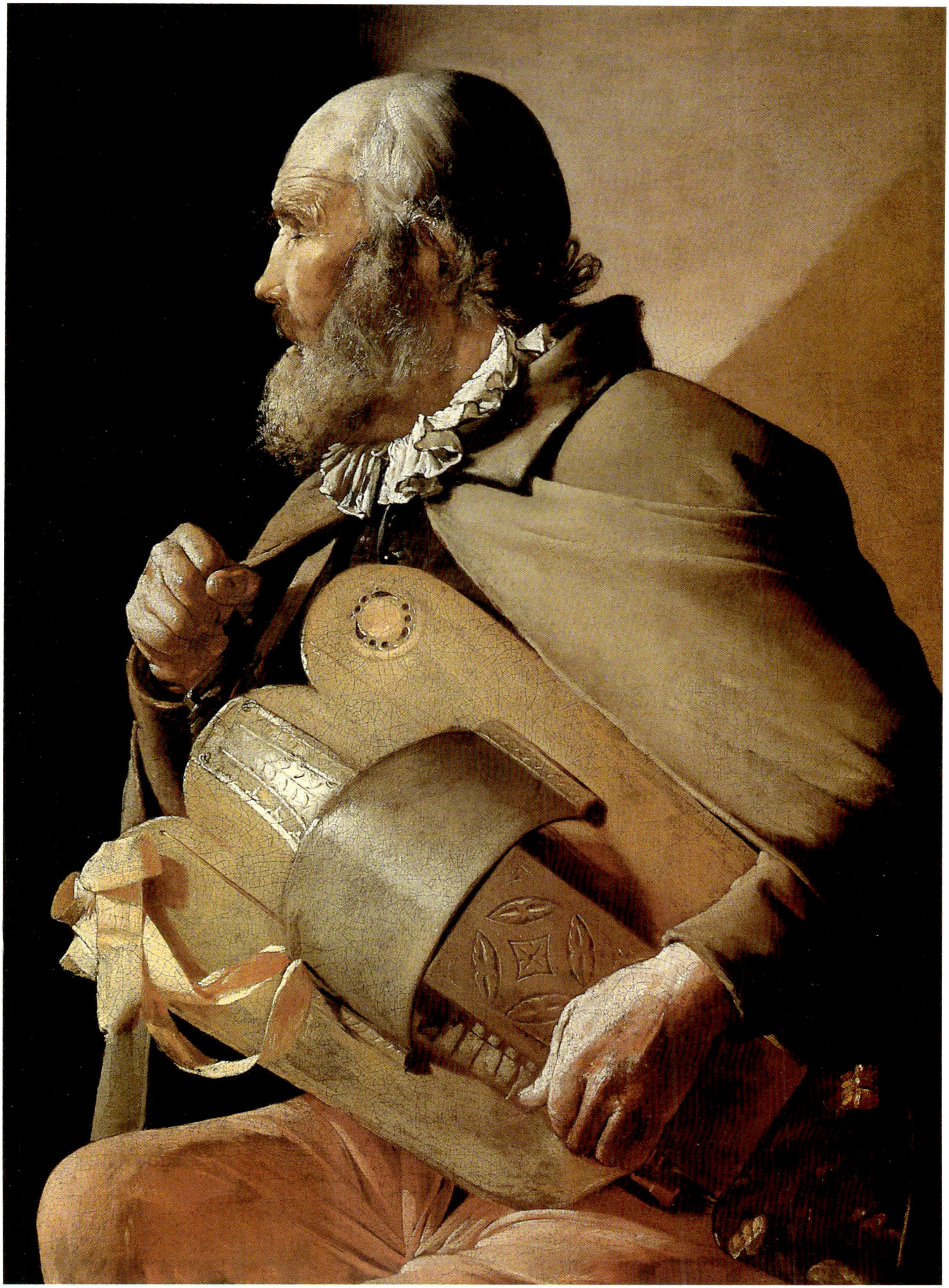

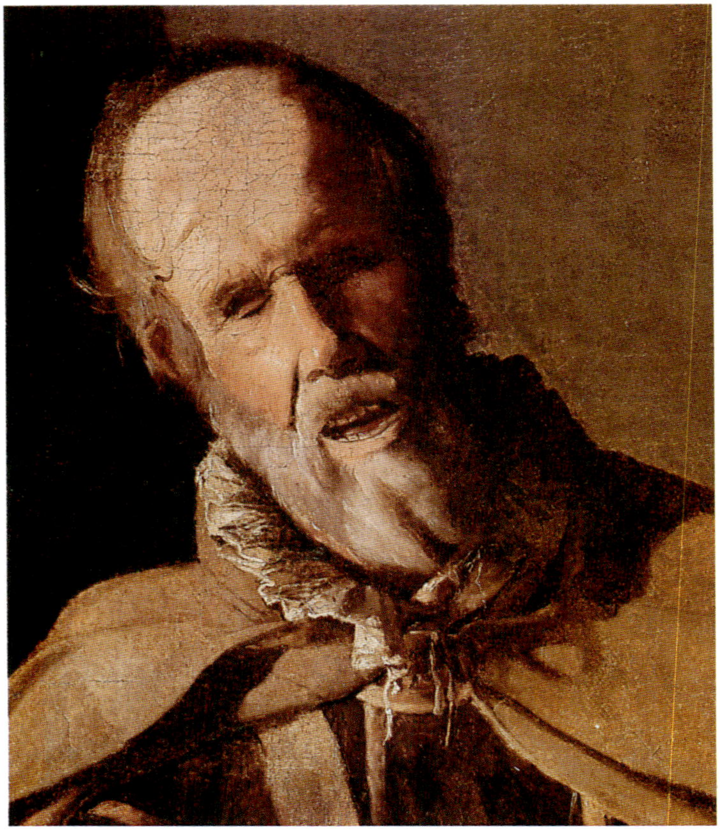

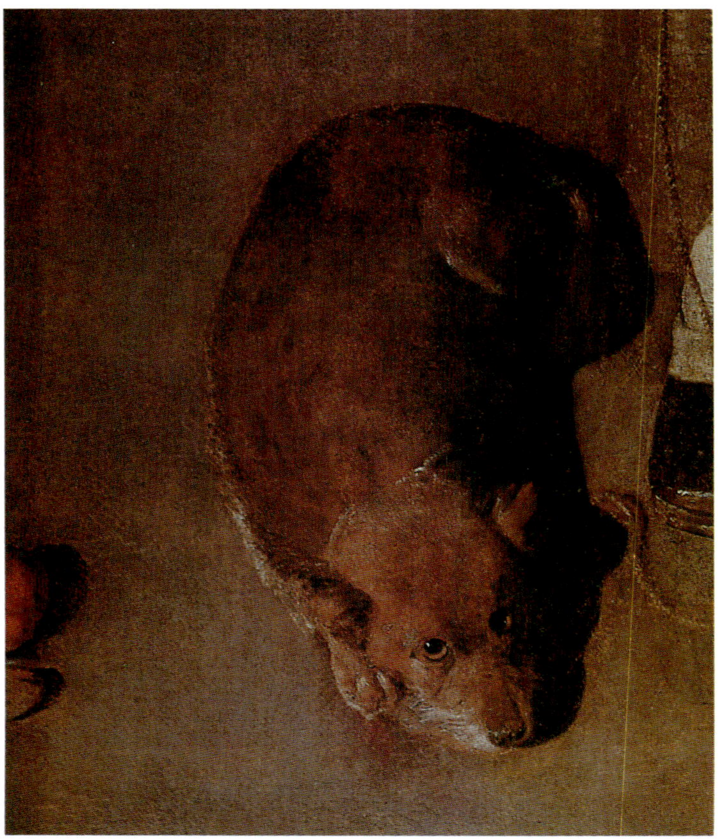

A Hurdy-Gurdy Player with his Dog.
Complete work and details.
Musée Municipal, Bergues

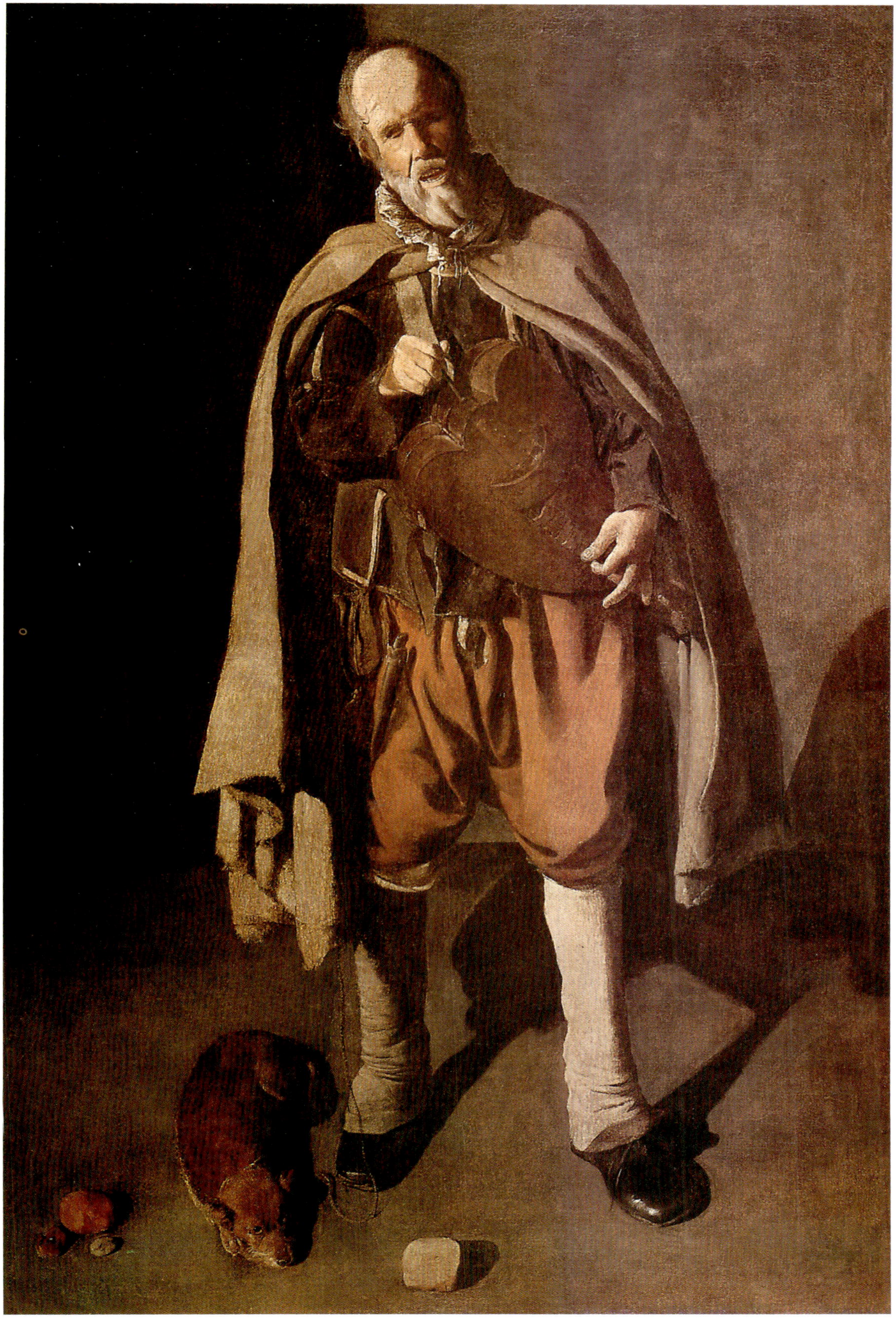

Charles Friry (1802-1884). Etching after *A Hurdy-Gurdy Player in Profile*, at that time in his collection (*c*. 1850).

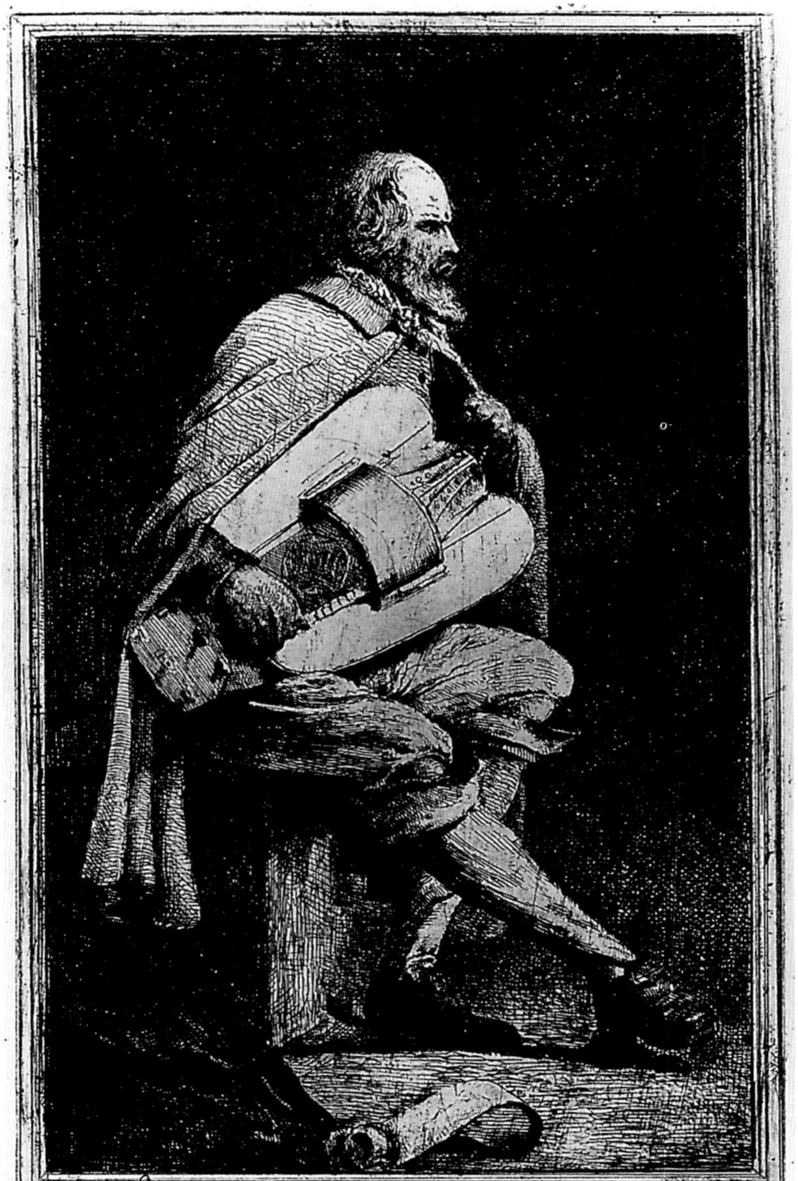

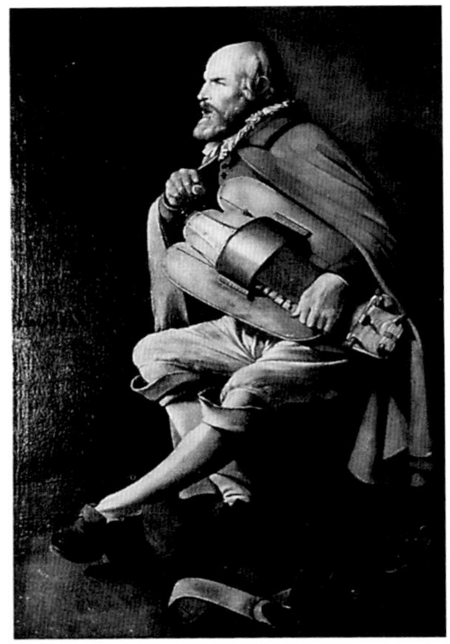

A Hurdy-Gurdy Player in Profile, copy.
Musée Lorrain, Nancy

A Hurdy-Gurdy Player in Profile.
Musée Charles Friry, Remiremont

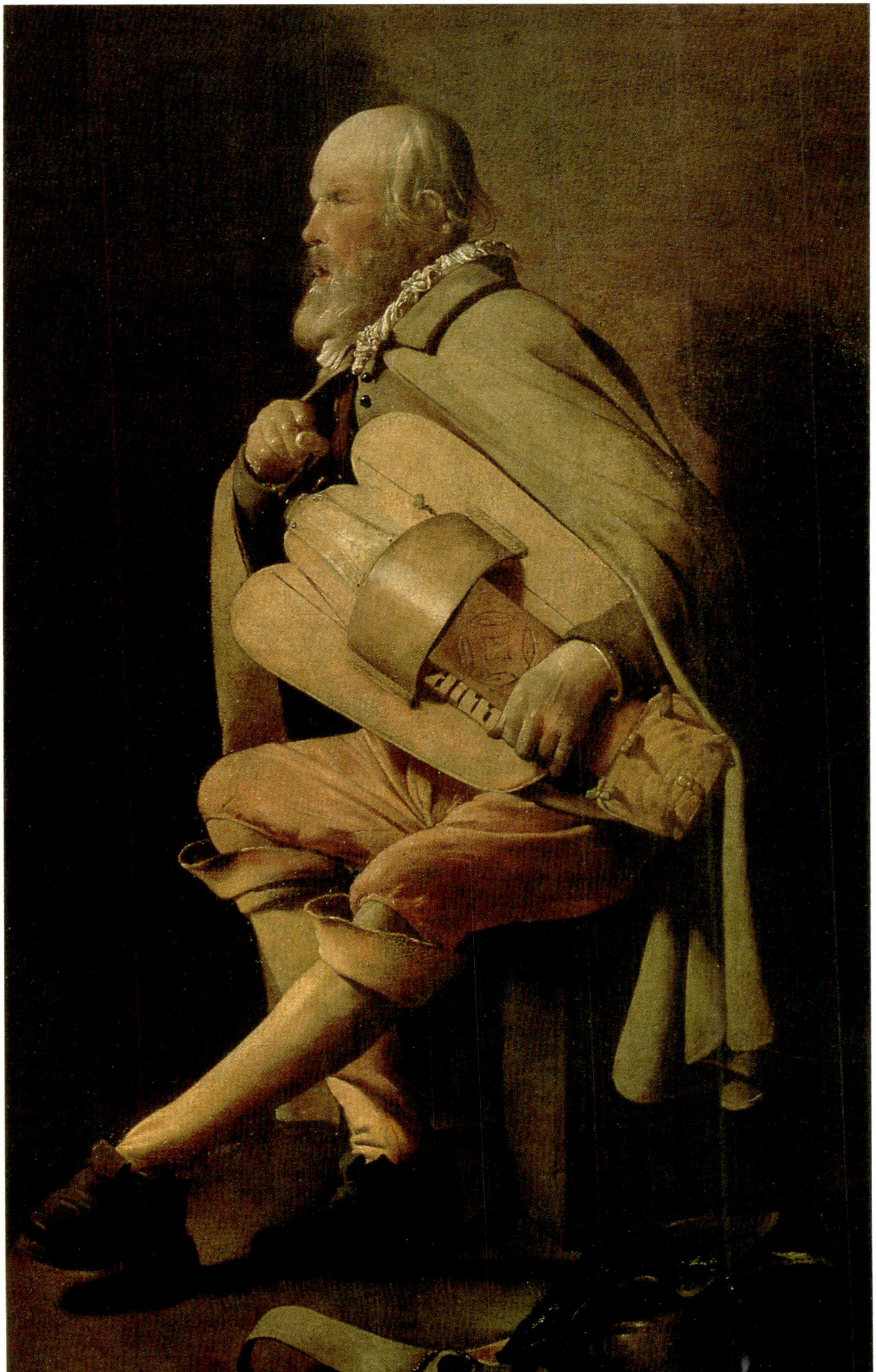

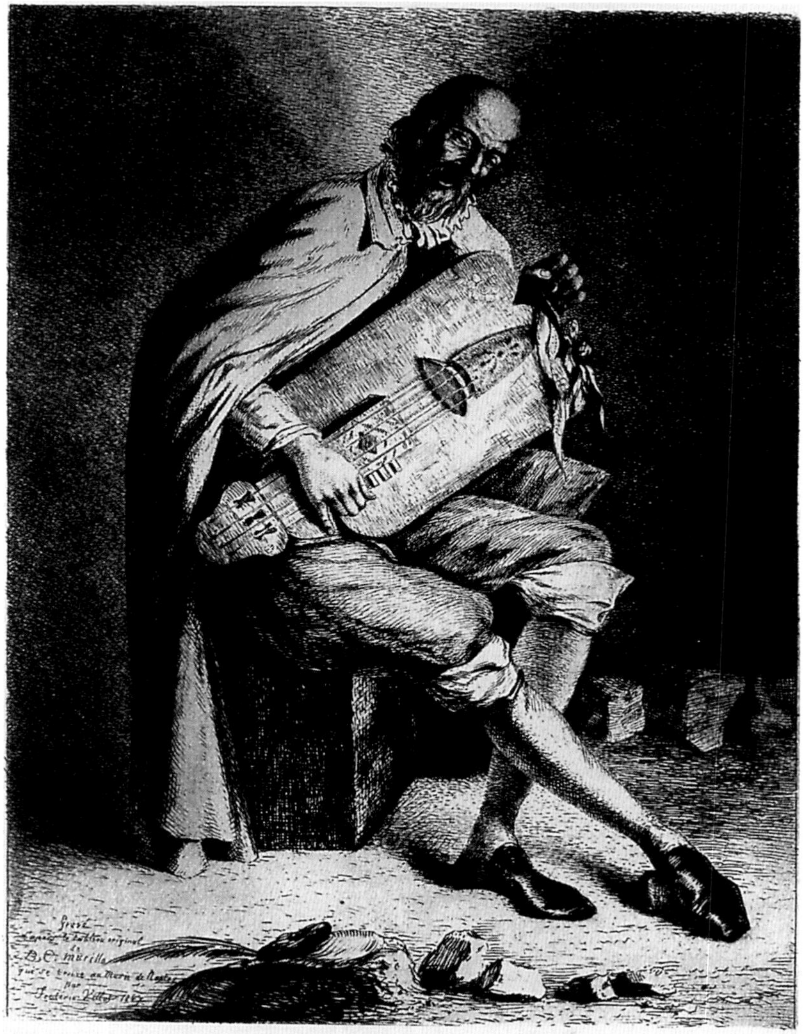

Frédéric Villot (1809-1875, a friend of Delacroix and later Chief Curator of the Louvre). Etching after the *Hurdy-Gurdy Player* now in the Musée des Beaux-Arts in Nantes, 1847.
Private collection

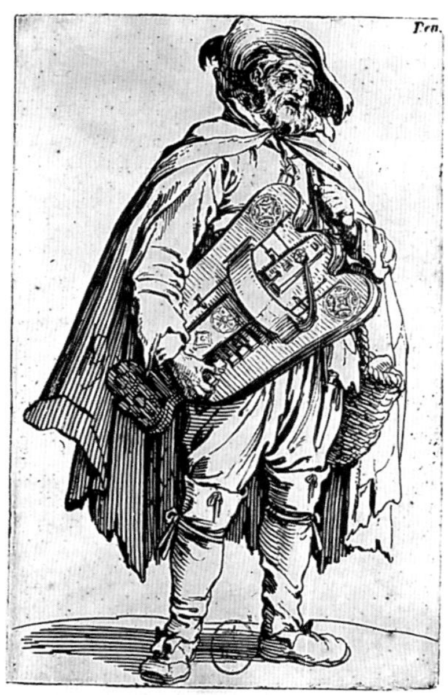

Jacques Callot. *Standing Hurdy-Gurdy Player.* Etching.
Cabinet des Estampes, Bibliothèque Nationale, Paris

A Hurdy-Gurdy Player.
Musée des Beaux-Arts, Nantes. Formerly the François Cacault Collection

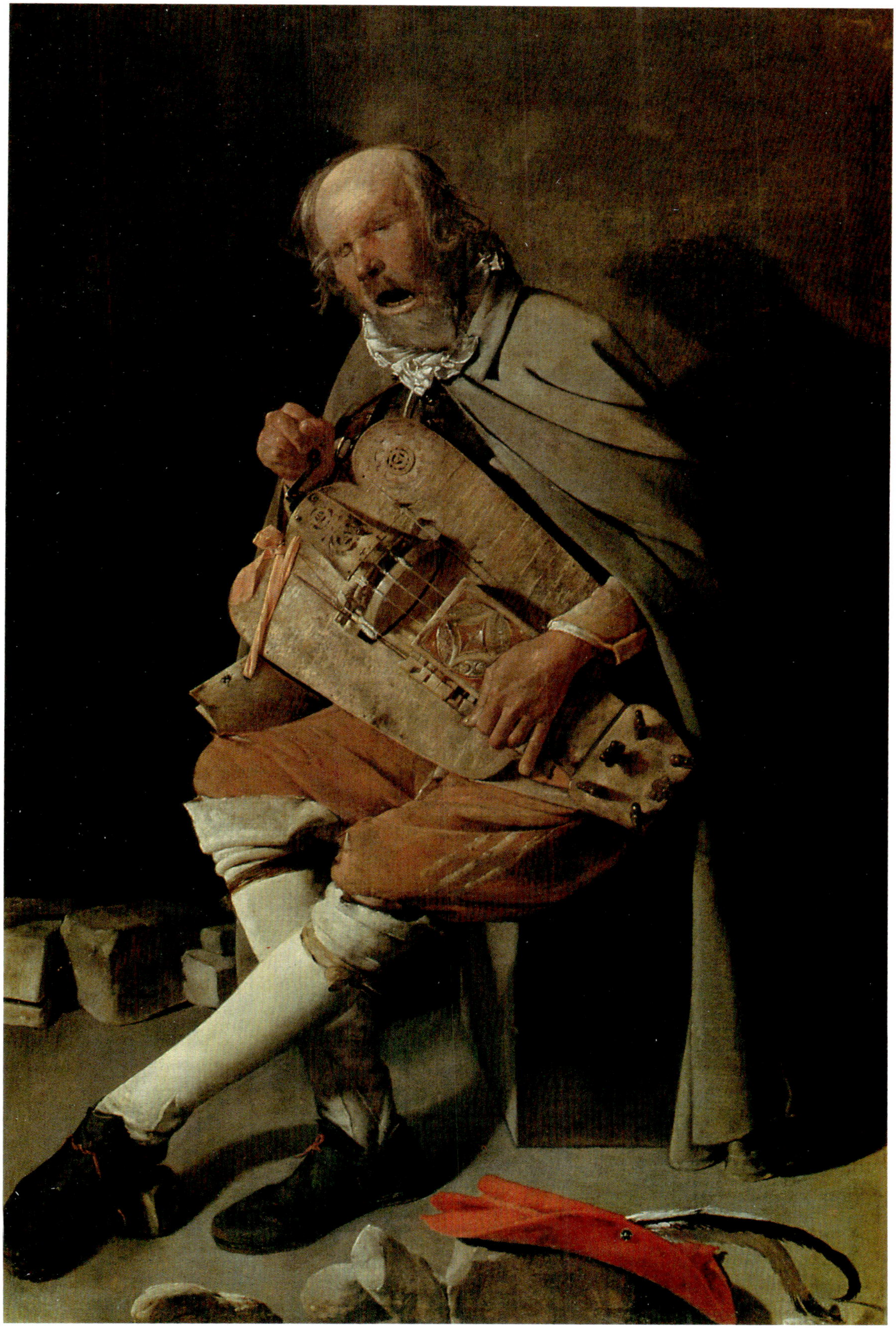

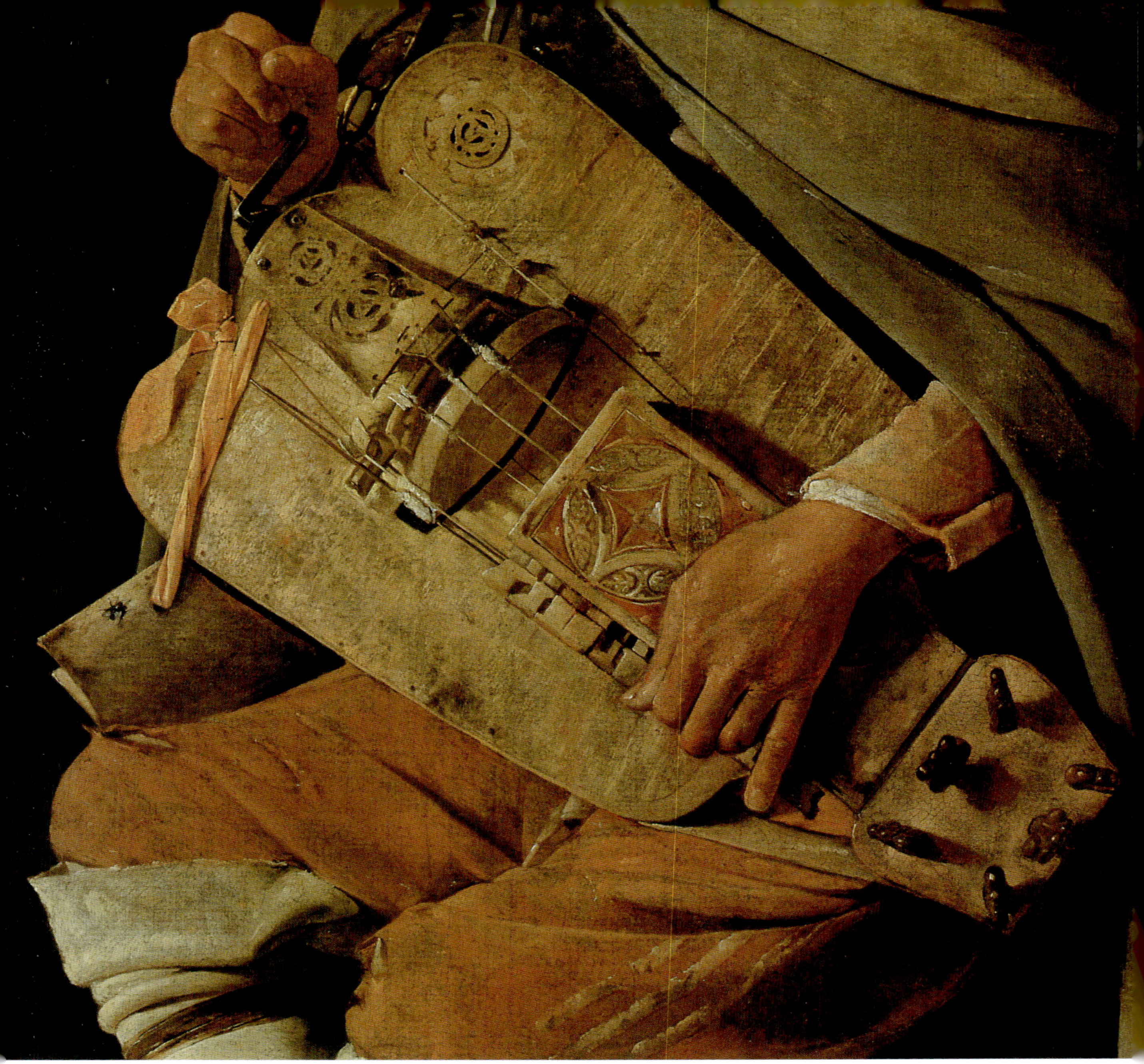

pp. 90-93:
A Hurdy-Gurdy Player, details.
Musée des Beaux-Arts, Nantes. Formerly the François Cacault Collection.

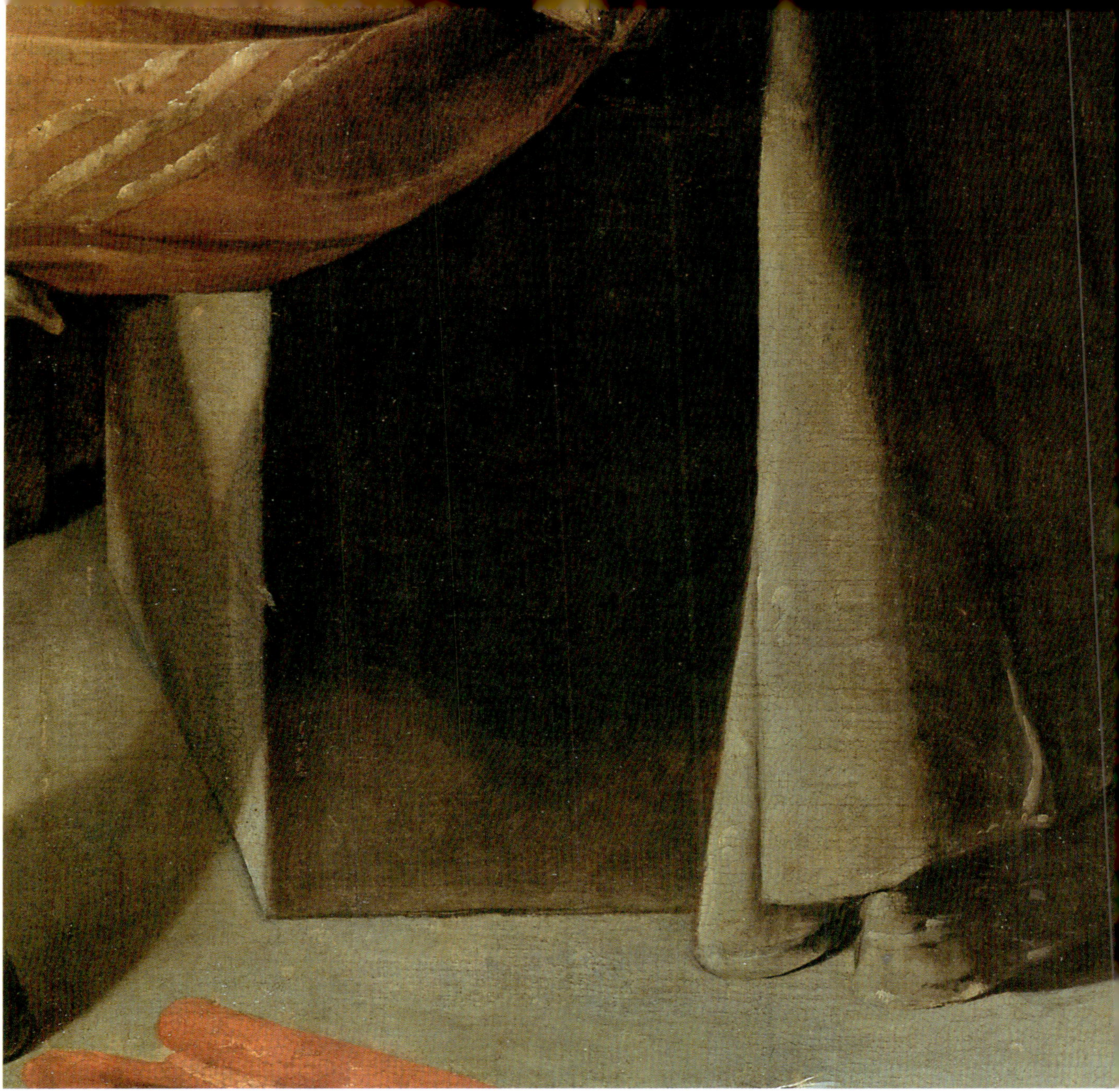

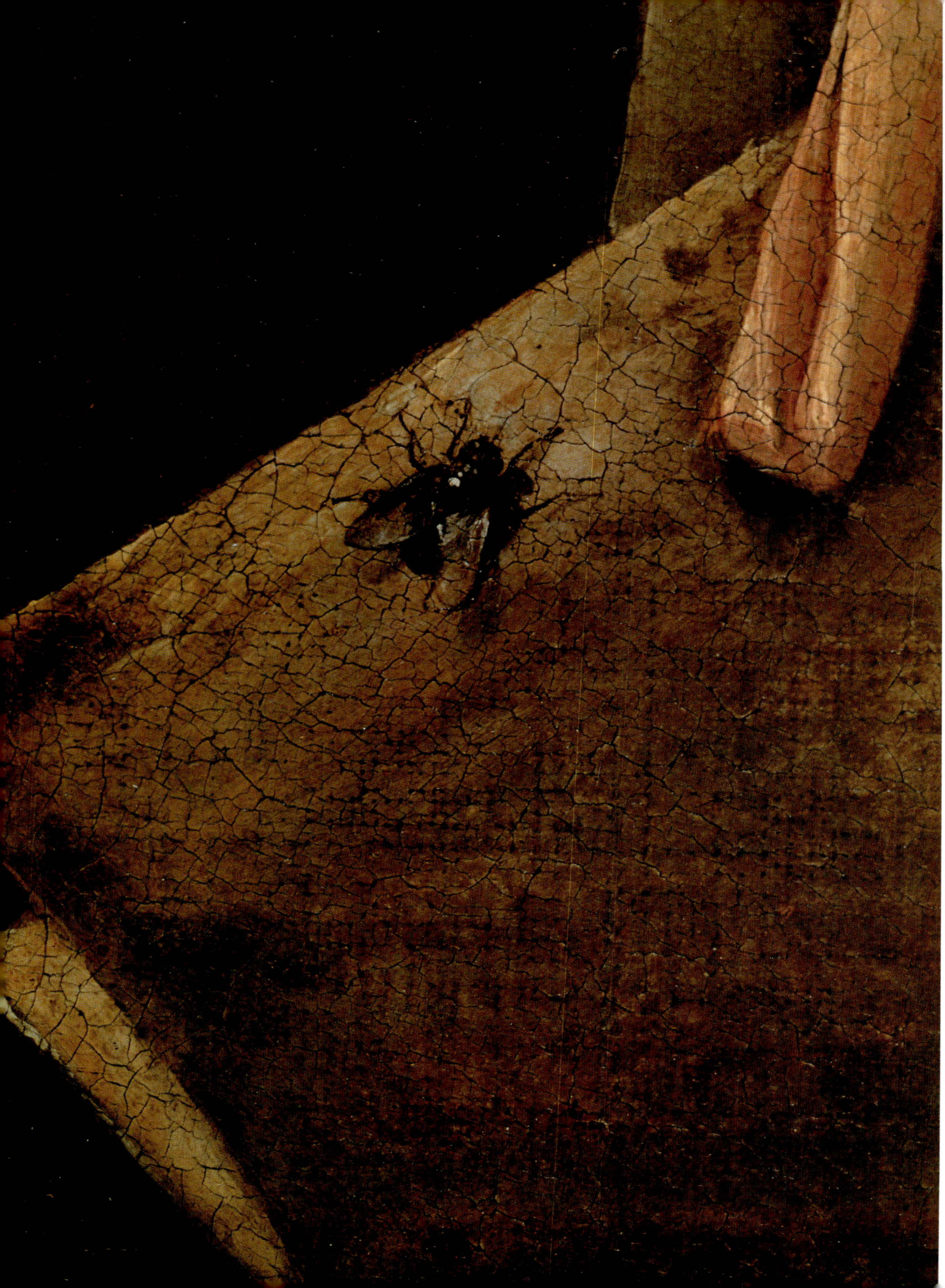

92

93

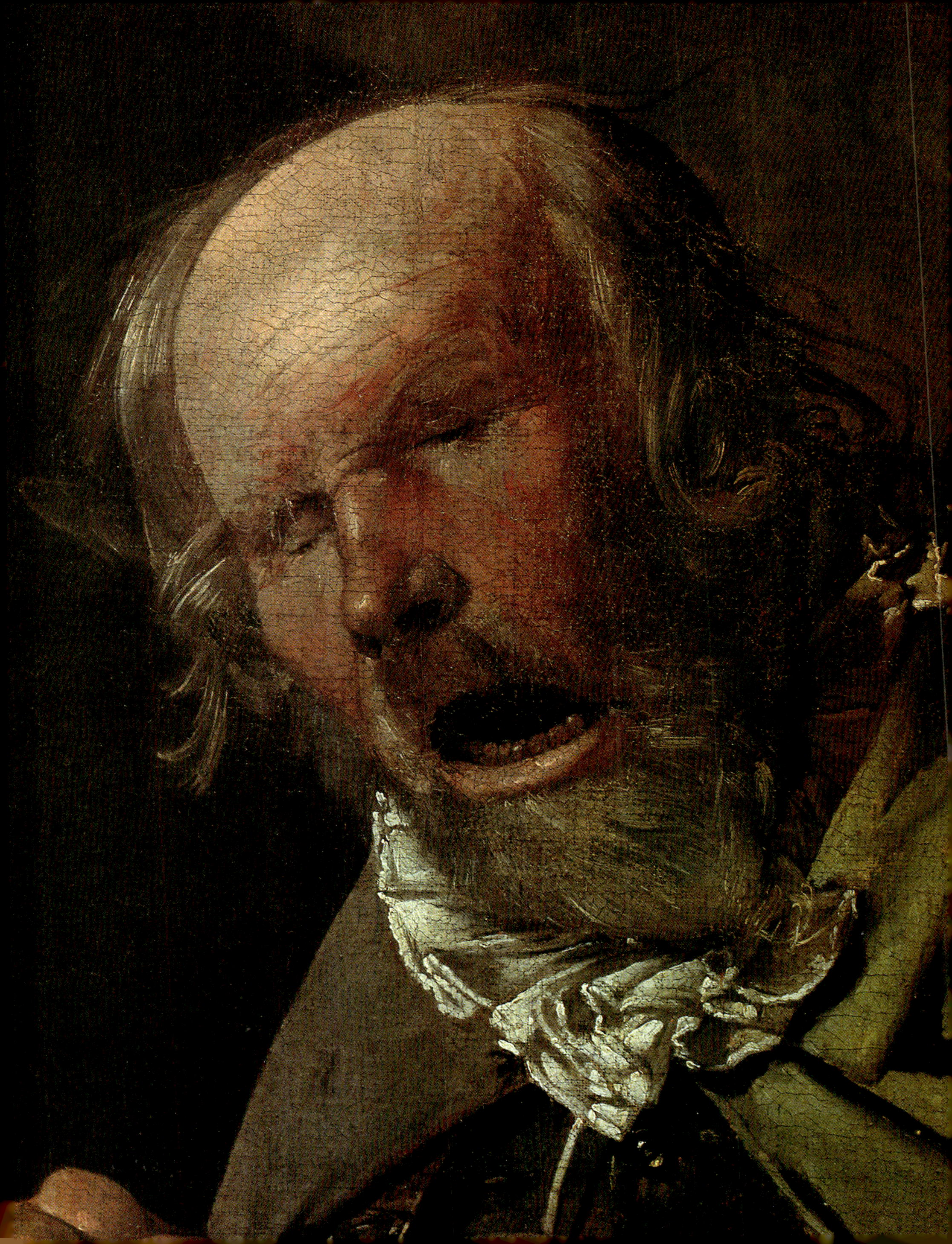

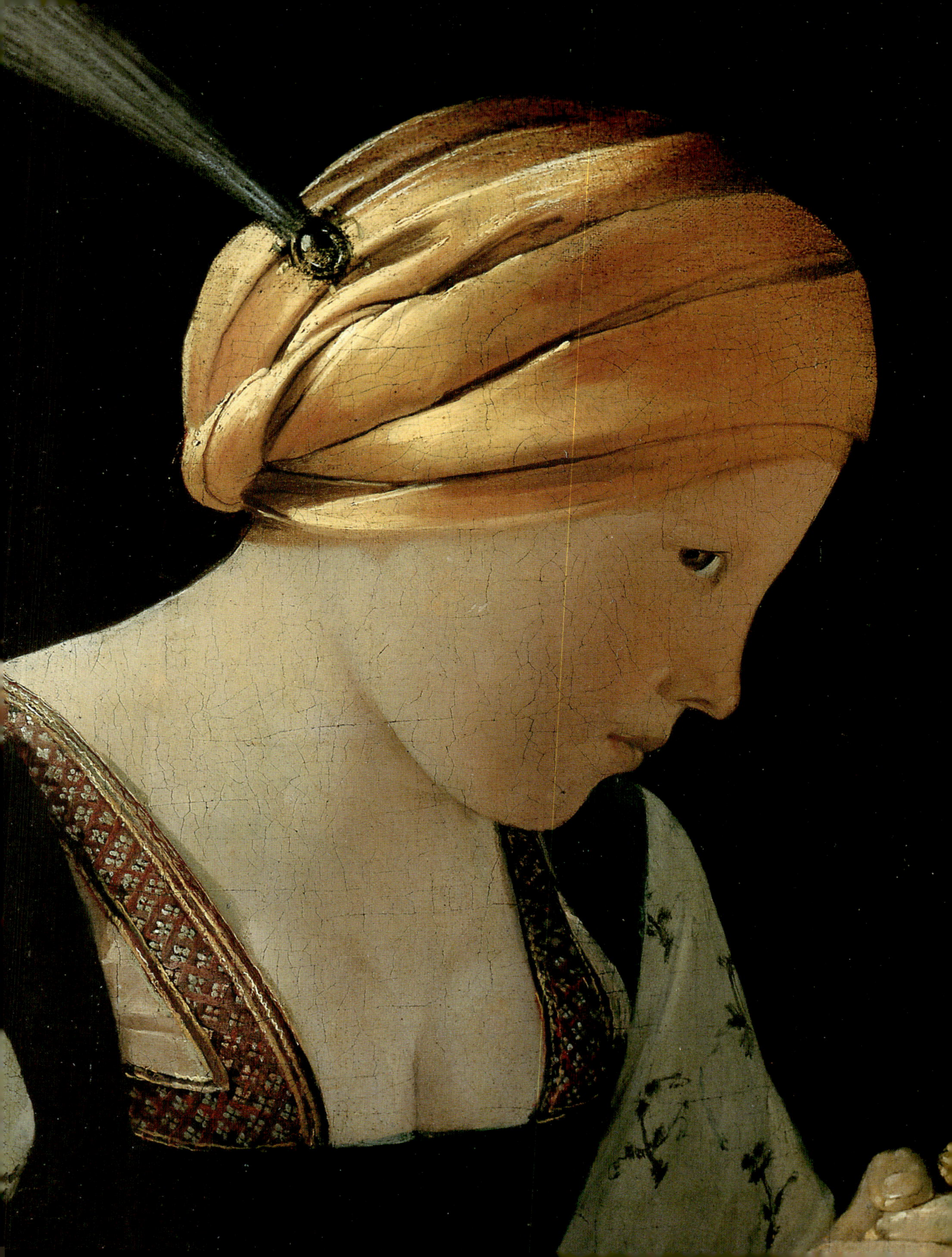

PAINTING, TRIUMPH, AND TRAGEDY

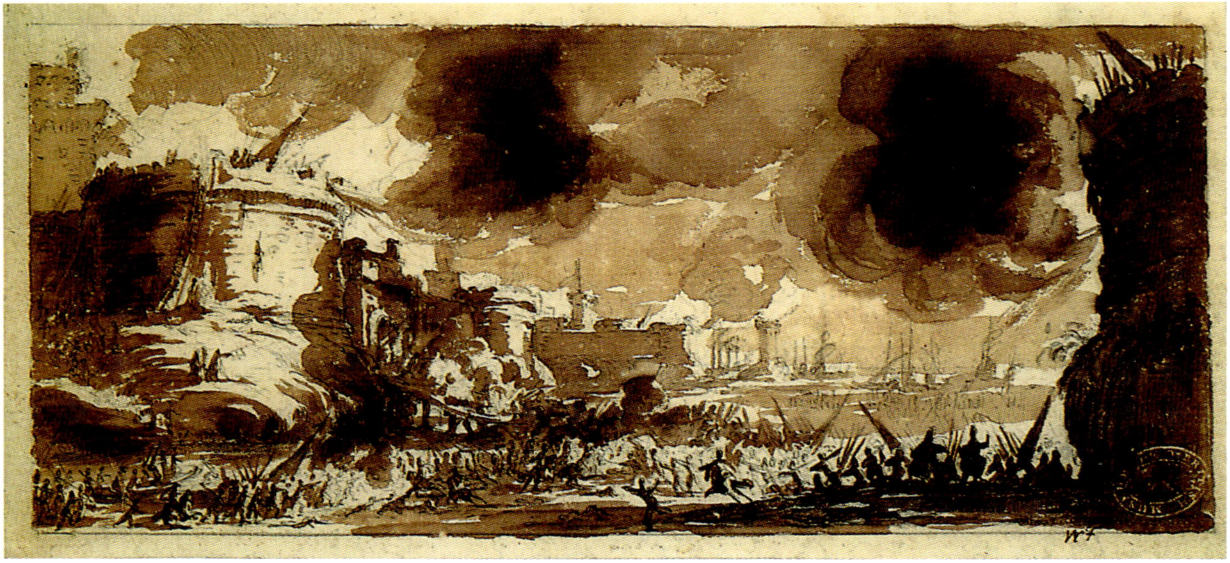

THE ERRORS AND MISFORTUNES OF DUCAL POLICY

Duke Henri II died in July 1624, and from then on Lorraine's future was to become increasingly bleak. Henri himself is said to have foreseen the worst. When accused of extravagance, he apparently retorted, "After me will come others of a different order, and it will then be clear who has governed well." His only heirs were his daughters, the princesses Nicole and Claude. There were two rivals for the elder's hand: Louis, baron of Ancerville and later prince of Phalsbourg, an illegitimate son of the cardinal de Guise whom Henri would have welcomed as his successor, and Charles de Vaudémont, Henri's nephew, a brave young man bent on glory, but scheming and secretive by nature, quick to strike a bargain and even quicker to break it. Henri II was hesitant and the court divided. Charles pressed his suit so hard, however, that the duke finally agreed to give him Nicole's hand. The new duke was to involve Lorraine in a series of intrigues that rapidly escaped his control and led to tragedy.

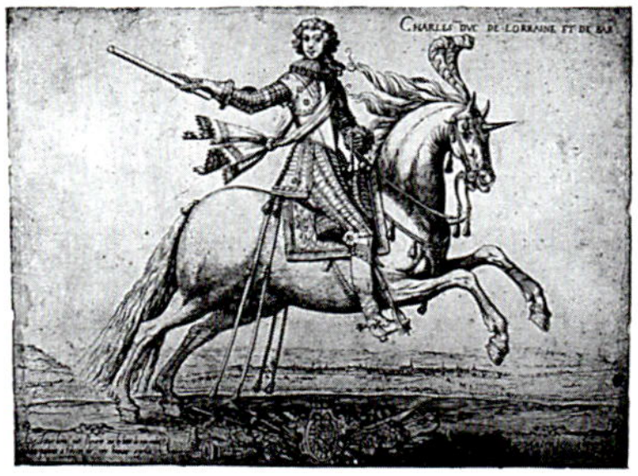

Claude Deruet. *Charles IV, duke of Lorraine. c.* 1625. Engraving.
Cabinet des Estampes, Bibliothèque Nationale, Paris

No sooner was Henri II dead than Charles de Vaudémont, now Charles IV, began to show his true colors. He started by taking revenge on those who had opposed his marriage, most notably Henri II's favorite, André des Bordes, whom he tried for witchcraft. Des Bordes was found guilty and sentenced to be strangled and publicly burned. Since Charles had no affection for Nicole and did not want to depend on her for the crown, he suddenly decided that Salic law, which excluded women from succession and governed the French monarchy, applied to Lorraine, and that the duchess and he therefore had no right to the throne. In November 1625, in a charade that fooled no one, the States-General in Nancy deposed the duchess, and Charles ceded the crown to his father, François, brother of the late duke and his successor according to Salic law. François assumed the title of duke, dispensed a few titles of nobility to his friends, helped himesIf liberally to public funds to pay off his debts, and abdicated the same month in his son's favor. Charles could now claim the dukedom in his own right, by inheritance. He then set about having his marriage dissolved. To get his way, he contrived another witchcraft trial. This time the accused was Henri II's personal chaplain, Canon Melchior de La Vallée, who was duly condemned to death and burned at the stake. With La Vallée thus shown to have been a sorcerer, Charles could challenge the validity of Duchess Nicole's baptism and that of his marriage at the same time.

Charles, meanwhile, had begun to side openly with the Holy Roman Empire and to defy Louis XIII. The court of Lorraine became a sanctuary for French exiles.

Preceding page: *The Cheat with the Ace of Diamonds*, detail.
Musée du Louvre, Paris

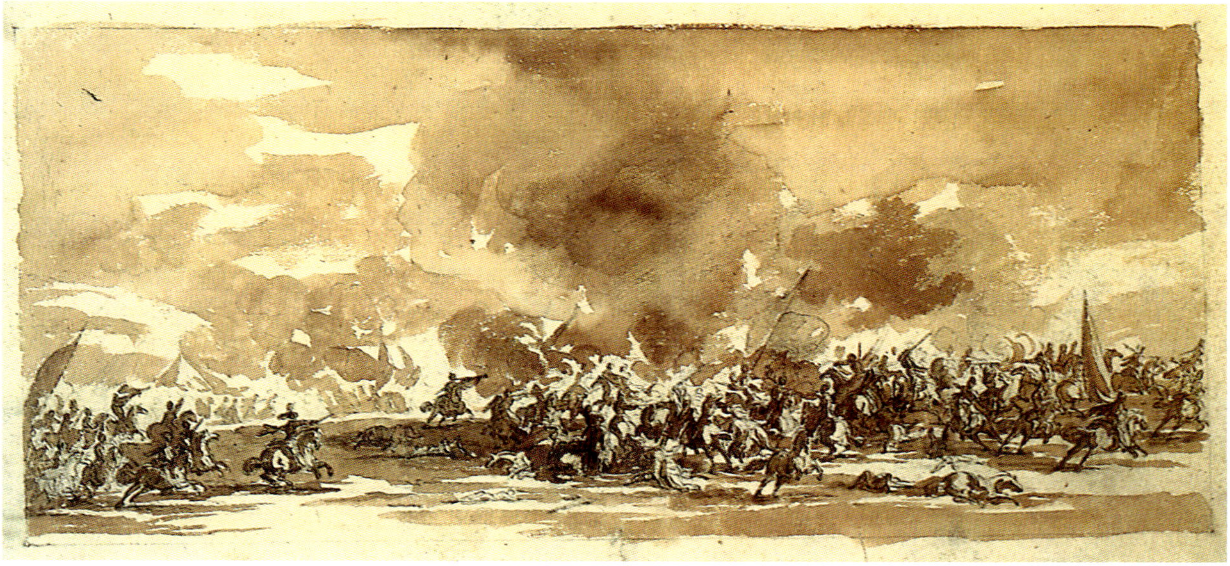

TRAGEDY IN LORRAINE:
Left:
Jacques Callot. *Attack of a Fort.* Black chalk and bistre wash.
Right:
Jacques Callot. *Battle Scene.* Black chalk and bistre wash.
British Museum (Add. 32 and 30), London

The duchess of Chevreuse, for instance, who was implicated in the notorious Chalais conspiracy, met with a lavish reception there in 1626, and appears to have been more than ready to test her charms on the duke, who was an inveterate philanderer. She was followed in September 1629 by Gaston of Orléans, Louis XIII's brother, after the discovery of the plot against the king. On top of this, Charles had been getting an allowance of 24,000 écus from Philip IV of Spain since the end of 1627 and was now fighting a campaign in the Palatinate against Louis XIII's allies, the Swedes. There was no longer any doubt as to where Lorraine stood. Charles IV's gamble could have paid off. In supporting the emperor, with whom, as count of Vaudémont, he had fought at the Montaigne Blanche in 1620, he may well have believed that there was no real risk to Lorraine's independence, and possibly a great deal to be gained. However, Louis XIII had no children and was known to be ill, and Gaston could be called to take his place on the French throne at any moment. Fate was to upset all of his plans. Louis XIII lived until 1643, and his queen finally produced two healthy children, thus ruining all the hopes pinned on Gaston. Above all, from 1630 onward Charles IV had to contend with the eagle-eyed and indefatigable Richelieu, against whom he stood little chance with his endless and often crude scheming. He had underestimated Louis XIII, who, like his father, loved battle and did not care to be deceived. Charles's posturing could not go on for long. The situation with regard to the Holy Roman Empire, always complex, was becoming too dangerous for France to give an unreliable prince like Charles free rein, when he could let the imperial troops in at any moment at the eastern gate of the kingdom, and thereby open the way to Paris. With the surrender of La Rochelle, Louis XIII was free to take the duke of Lorraine in hand.

In the spring of 1630 the imperial troops occupied Vic and Moyenvic, which depended on the bishopric of Metz. By late 1631 Maréchal de La Force arrived with a large army, retook Moyenvic, and occupied Château-Salins and Vic. The king himself appeared, and on 3 January 1632 he was in Vic. Charles IV could not hope to hold out against this great army massed on the frontier of his duchy. He sought out the king and on 6 January signed the treaty of Vic, which gave France the fortified town of Marsal and a promise of loyalty from the duke. Three days earlier, however, against Louis XIII's express wishes, Gaston of Orléan had secretly married Marguerite of Lorraine, the sister of Charles IV, with the latter's complicity. Such a union at this time put the Lorrainese princess in direct line for the throne of France and made the duke of Lorraine the brother-in-law of the king of France.

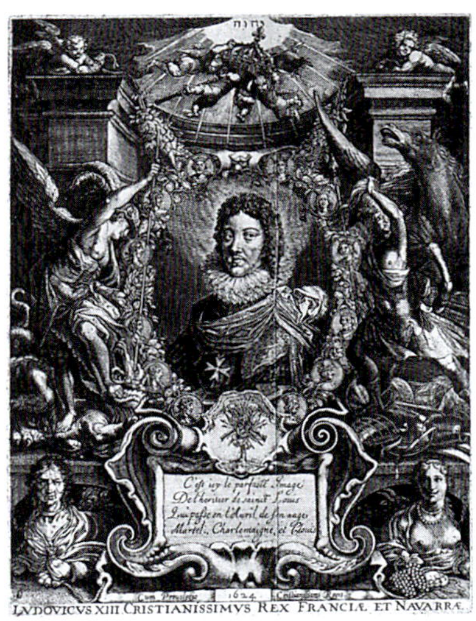

Crispin de Passe. *Louis XIII, king of France.* 1624. Engraving.

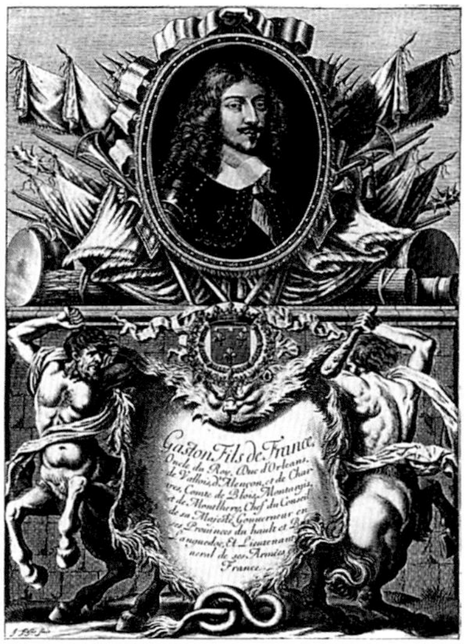

Jean Frosne. *Gaston of Orléans, brother of Louis XIII:* Engraving.

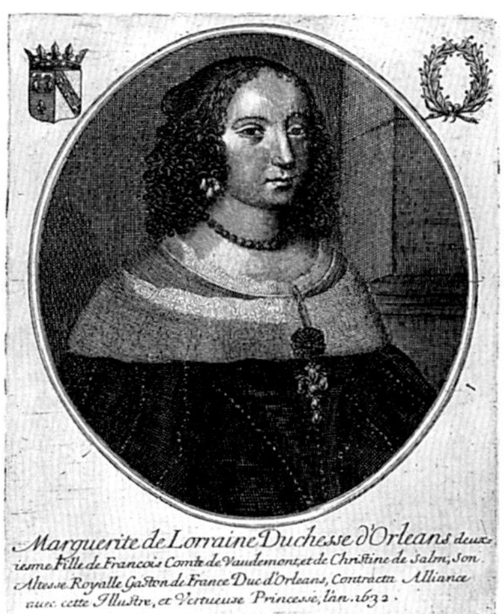

Anonymous. *Marguerite of Lorraine, sister of Charles IV.*

This was the last straw. The French troops arrived and occupied Noméný and Pont-à-Mousson. The king, who had gone back to Champagne, returned and seized Bar. There was a new round of negotiations at Liverdun, and another treaty was signed, which was tougher on Charles IV. Even so, the following year the duke took on the Swedes in Alsace and attempted to lift the blockade of Hagueneau but was soundly defeated. The inhabitants of Lorraine were terrified that this time the Swedes would invade the duchy: they were the soldiers most feared throughout Europe for their cruelty. To everyone's relief, it was the French who marched in. In August 1633 the king came in person to lay siege to Nancy. Maréchal de Sourdis entered Lunéville on 1 September. Charles IV gave up Nancy without a fight, and Louis XIII, accompanied by the queen, took formal possession of it on the twenty-fifth. Lorraine was placed under the temporary authority of a French governor. Following the commonly-held view that Salic law did not apply to the duchy, and rejecting the 1625 coup d'état, Louis XIII declared Nicole to be sole heir to the duchy, with her sister Claude next in line.

Charles IV had withdrawn to the safety of imperial soil. As was his wont, he decided to retreat into the wings for a time and abdicated in January 1634 in favor of his brother, Cardinal Nicolas-François, thus casting the question of the ducal crown in an entirely new light. At this point a romantic incident occured that was to set all of Europe buzzing and, interestingly enough, took place at Lunéville Castle. Cardinal Nicolas-François was staying there with his cousins Nicole and Claude when Charles IV abdicated. Louis XIII dispatched Maréchal de La Force with orders to get the two princesses into safe custody and bring them to Paris, where the idea was to marry Claude off to some French prince. The cardinal, however, after brief consultation with a few local theologians, granted himself the necessary dispensations to get married, and Father Maretz, the parish priest of Saint-Jacques, was called upon to marry him to Claude in the chapel of the castle. La Force and his regiment arrived too late to stop him and could do nothing more than separate the newlyweds and take them off to Nancy as prisoners. Nicolas-François and Claude escaped from the duke's palace, however, and managed to get away disguised as common people:

> With baskets on their backs, with dung o'erlied,
> As real peasants they slipped out unespied.

They made it to Besançon where the duke was waiting to greet them with open arms.

Richelieu and Louis XIII were furious and began to take an even harder line. A governor and administrator were appointed to rule the duchy, a supreme council brought in to replace the local bodies, and commissioners named to elicit oaths of allegiance from all the inhabitants. From his retreat, Charles IV, who had taken back the title of duke from his brother, publicly told people to refuse to take the oath while privately advising them to take it, but with moral reserve. In Lorraine itself, the Capuchins were entirely behind the Catholic emperor and against Richelieu, the friend and ally of the Protestants, and openly pressed for revolt; many were expelled by force. The people of Lorraine were loyal to the dukes and generally accepted the French presence as the lesser of two evils. The duchy's neutrality was compromised by these sorry events, and Lorraine was drawn into the heart of the decisive conflict between France and Spain that divided Europe. There was no longer a choice: if it was not the French army they had to endure, it was the Swedes, who were their allies but who struck terror wherever they went, or the imperial troops, who were barely any better. Charles IV's own troops, who were allied with those of the emperor, showed themselves to be so rapacious and brutal that the people eventually rose up against them. Lorraine had long been spared the horrors of war. Now it was to be exposed to them. They would be atrocious.

DISASTROUS TIMES

Even if we think of recent events in Lebanon or Yugoslavia, it is hard to imagine what Lorraine went through in the seventeenth century. The troops lived off the population, and every so often they had to be given a castle or a town to plunder. Remonviller is a case in point. Five or six hundred peasants were living in the castle there, which was once again functioning, as in former times, as a place of refuge.

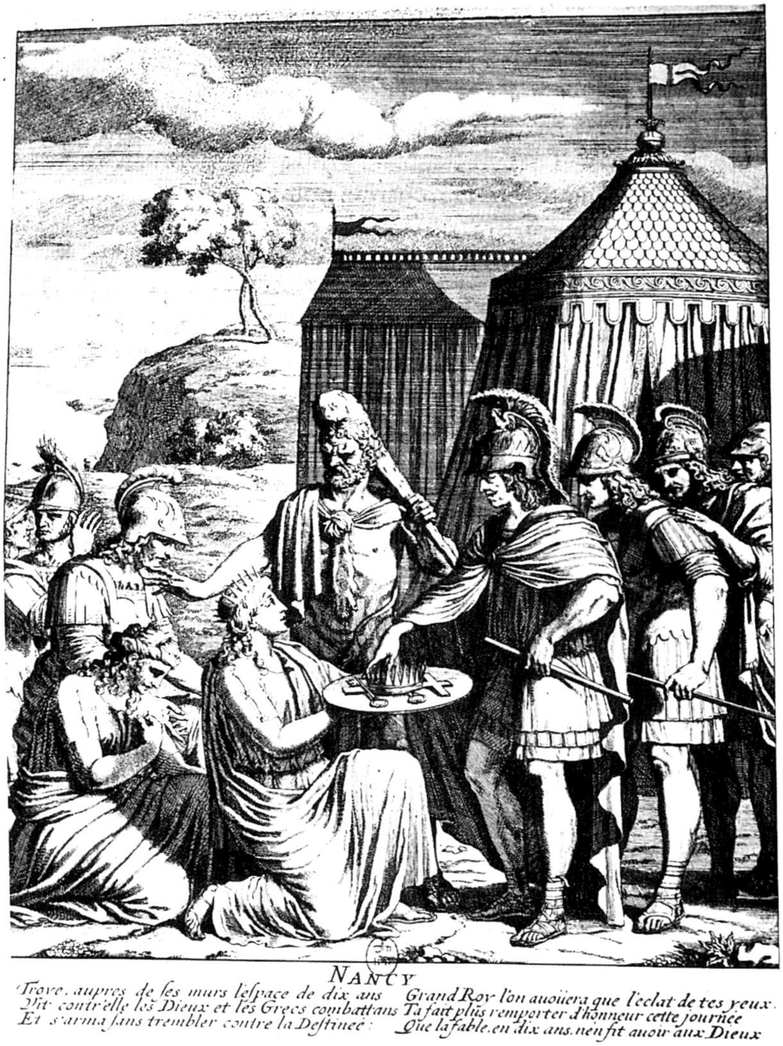

The Surrender of Nancy, allegorical engraving (after a drawing by Bertholet Flémalle?) for the *Triumphs of Louis the Just* published by Jean Valdor, Paris, 1649.
Cabinet des Estampes, Bibliothèque Nationale, Paris

The surrender of Nancy, boasting as it did the most modern of fortifications and reputed to be impregnable, caused a sensation throughout Europe. Indeed, the propaganda coup was carefully orchestrated by Richelieu. Félibien tells us that Louis XIII personally asked Callot to commemorate the event with a large engraving, like those he had produced to mark the captures of Ré and La Rochelle (Callot refused, not wanting to do anything against his homeland or his duke). Even though it only cost Louis XIII a military excursion, the occupation of Nancy was thought to be one of the great feats of his reign. After the king's death, when Jean Valdor assembled the sumptuous volume entitled *The Triumphs of Louis the Just, thirteenth of that name, king of France and Navarre, containing the greatest battles at which His late Majesty was present in person,* he made a point of including along with the illustrations of Pas-de-Suze, La Rochelle, and the recapture of Corbie, one of the surrender of Nancy, which cut off the imperial armies' eastern approach.

In fact, the engraving, very probably taken from a drawing by the Liège painter Bertholet Flémalle, remains firmly allegorical. Valdor, the ruling bishop of Liège's representative in Paris, was keenly conscious that Gaston of Orléans's wife Marguerite of Lorraine was the duke's sister, that France had never considered Lorraine enemy territory, and that at any moment a reconciliation could occur and past divisions be forgotten. His own father, moreover, had himself been Charles IV's official engraver. By keeping studiously to the most conventional of language, the engraving manages to avoid alluding too directly to the town of Nancy and the treachery of Duke Charles IV. The affairs of Lorraine had long been deemed worthy of the utmost tact.

The duke of Weimar gave it to the troops to pillage, with the result that they killed the men and the older women, raped the younger ones, looted everything they could lay their hands on, and then burned down the castle with the children inside. Saint-Nicolas-du-Port, a holy shrine that was the commercial center of Lorraine, was ravaged in turn by the Hungarians and the Poles on 4 November 1635, Maréchal de La Force's French troops on the next day, and the duke of Weimar's troops on the next. Furious at finding nothing worth taking, the duke's men set about killing the inhabitants and incinerating the town in a blaze that set fire to the famous basilica on 11 November. Saint-Nicolas-du-Port never regained its former prosperity.

Everyone in Lorraine lived in permanent fear of the troops. The Germans and other foreigners, wrote Cassien Bidot, "have brought indescribable devastation to the length and breadth of our land. The town of Saint-Mihiel alone has been divested of more than three million francs for taxation, to say nothing of the revelling, robbery, oppression, or the sheer cruelty inflicted on the poor peasants by these unnatural creatures with their insatiable northern fury [and] whom they clap into irons and bind hand and foot until they find their money; they come equipped for the purpose with wagons laden with manacles, ropes, and other instruments of cruelty with which to torture the poor people. In some places, they strung them up in the air with ropes under their arms and great stones attached to their feet and hit them across the body to get money out of them, and when finally they uttered the words their torturers wanted to hear, these poor souls were left hanging until their friends came and cut them down. . . . The villages are all practically deserted and uninhabited, because most of them have been burned for the most part, and also because, with all this robbery and the unprecedented level of taxation imposed on them, the poor people are left without means of subsistence. . . ."

Not even the churches were spared, particularly by the Swedish troops, who, as Protestants, had no compunction about looting them and vied with each other, according to Jean Héraudel, to see

> . . . who could an altar of its ornament soonest divest,
> Who a chalice, or a ciboriourn before the rest
> Could seize. . . .

Driven from the towns and villages by fire and fear, and seeing that no sanctuary was immune from the troops, people did not know where to turn for shelter, and

> Forced to abandon their erstwhile homes,
> Like vagabonds they roam the country wide,
> . . .
> With no downy bed but the stony ground,
> No cover but the sky, to perils round,
> Malign stars and wicked weather exposed. . . .

It was not just blind men who were beggars now, but people who were once comfortably off, peasants who had seen their crops laid to waste and their beasts stolen:

> If in squares or churches you chance to be,
> Their terrible misfortunes soon shall you conceive,
> From the endless streams of miserable beggars,
> Who shiver, haggard, hideous, tattered, and forlorn. . . .

This was only one aspect of the disaster. With the soldiers came another peril, perhaps more terrible still: the plague. It made its appearance fairly early in Lorraine, brought, it was said, by some of the imperial troops. By 1630, Metz, Moyenvic, and Vic succumbed to a "Hungarian" strain, which would seem to have been a kind of typhus. Stringent sanitary measures were introduced but, in their inevitable inappropriateness, failed to provide an adequate barrier. The epidemic spread and the death toll mounted. Lunéville initially escaped it, and the duke and his family retreated to the castle there in 1630. The summer of 1631 was appalling, however: the plague erupted in June and lasted until the end of October. The town was completely cut off from the outside, and everything ground to a halt. The epidemic returned in 1633 but did not last as long, although Nancy was severely hit. Then it erupted again in April 1636, and with all the more virulence: the real bubonic plague. It took until December to blow over. This time, 160 of those who fell ill recovered, while some 80 did not.

The authorities did all they could to keep the country running, but chaos reigned. As always in situations like these, food started to become scarce. True, a good part of the population had succumbed to ill treatment and disease, and there were therefore fewer mouths to feed, but the troops expected to live off the country, and the requisitions became more and more harsh. In addition, many of the fields lay fallow. Even where there were enough peasants left to work the land, it was far from easy to do so. In many places all the livestock was gone, requisitioned or pillaged by the troops, or stolen by vagabonds. Peasants and even priests took to the plow themselves:

> Yoked together ten or twelve at a time,
> Like horses and oxen, their labours perform,
> Tilling, harrowing, and work of every form. . . .

The harvests were meager, and often stolen before the crops could ripen. Cereals were scarce: speculators moved in. With the winter came famine and its train of woe:

> Hunger is an ill which makes its victims
> Worse than rabid, worse than frenzied:
> The people eat dogs, the people eat cats,

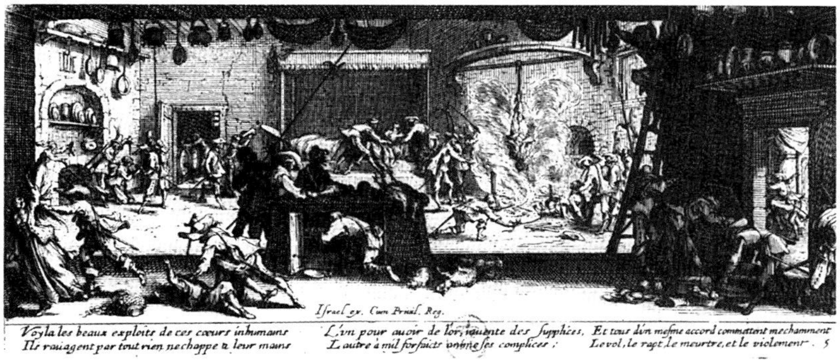

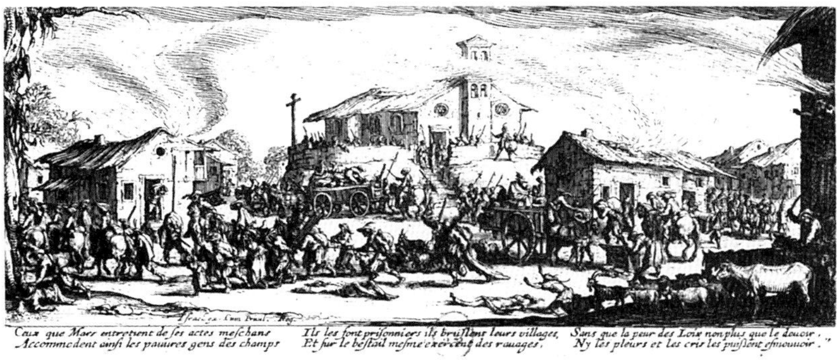

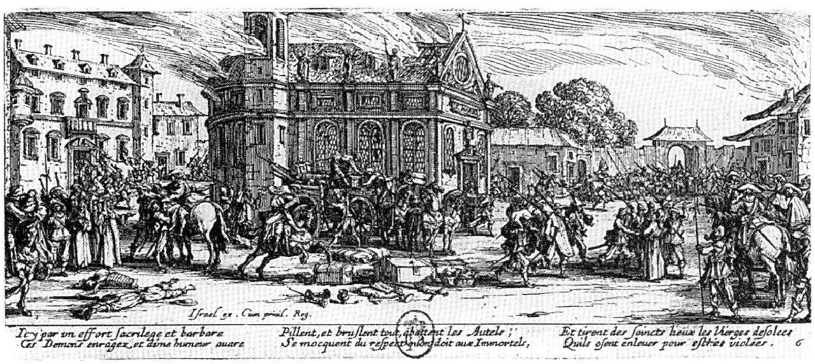

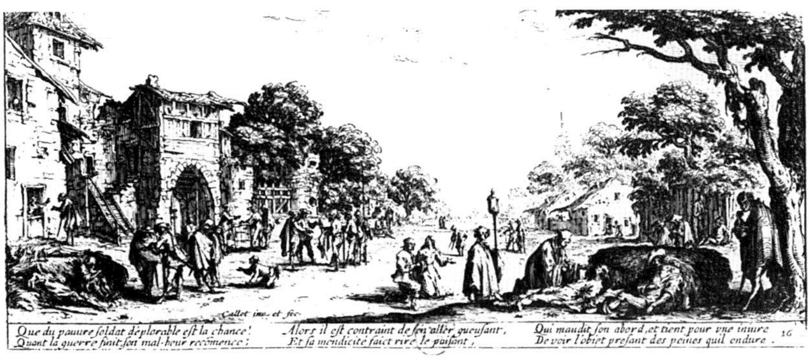

DISASTERS IN LORRAINE
Jacques Callot. *The Misery and Suffering of War (known as Les Grandes Misères de la Guerre).* 1633. Etchings.
From top to bottom:
The Pillaging of a Farm.
The Pillaging and Burning of a Village.
The Destruction of a Monastery.
The Wounded Dying along the Road.
Cabinet des Estampes, Bibliothèque Nationale, Paris

They even do their job for them by eating rats.
Barely is a horse dead and dragged from its stable
Than they rip it apart as soon as they are able
Not stopping to skin it, or let it on the scrapheap
Rot. . . .

Hunger overcame all scruples—the age-old aversion to eating horsemeat was only one:

Strange turn of events, the rotting carcass
Which once even the meanest villager refused,
He now considers it to be a very grand favor,
Beyond all measure the smallest piece to receive. . . .

We know, on more than one good authority, that famine drove people to cannibalism. Heraudel, for one, describes the poor unfortunates of Lorraine at the time:

Cutting each other's throats, and eating each other,
With no show of horror, a son not scorning his
Father's stinking corpse, nor a father his own son's
Flesh, nor a daughter her mother's. . . .

This is no flight of poetic fancy. We know from Cassien Bidot that, "It was confirmed by the magistrate at Vic, who sent a report of the affair to the gentlemen of the Council at Metz, that in a village near Morhange, a son ate his dead father and was in turn eaten by his mother when he died." There is worse to follow:

In another village, near Saint-Avold, the mayor was killed by a rogue and then ripped open and tossed to the townsfolk to assuage the raging hunger consuming them. I have heard from a number of reliable individuals that more than five hundred people died of hunger there; every day about another eight or ten are buried, in such a way that only a third or quarter of the population is left. . . . Future generations will find it hard to believe what I am about to describe. . . . During one of the coldest spells, a young man went to get warm at a friend's in Badonviller. As he stood by the fire, the master of the house killed him, for no other reason than to eat him. The authorities alerted, the man was duly apprehended, and he openly admitted to what he had done, driven to it by rabid hunger. And he had indeed devoured great chunks of the man's flesh.

There are so many accounts like these that they cannot have been exceptional cases. Amid such famine, even the soldiers were reduced to their last crumb. It is difficult to dispute the words of a man like Forjet, Charles IV's physician, who tells us that in 1638, there was such misery and starvation in our army [that of the duke of Lorraine himself] that it would be an understatement simply to say that people ate horsemeat; it was a feast—it was even served at His Highness's table. All those who could gorged themselves on human flesh, and even more impossible to believe, when a musket went off in a soldier's hands, fracturing his left hand, gangrene set in and the surgeon who cut it off asked to be given it for his pains, whereupon he ate it.

It is worth remembering that La Tour was henceforth to paint amid such suffering and horror. Two hundred years later, Géricault was moved by similar tales of shipwrecked mariners abandoned off the coasts of Africa to produce *The Raft of the "Medusa,"* a powerful study of human dereliction and hope. In 1638, it was not a single raft but a whole province that was in distress on the high seas, and the ordeal was to last not only days, but years on end. La Tour's perspective was not that of a man who has read an account by survivors, but of a man in the thick of events, threatened by suffering, and sometimes directly affected by it.

LA TOUR, THE DUKE, AND THE KING

The history of Lorraine is marked by harsh times such as these: no other region, for instance, suffered anything nearly as badly during the First World War. The people of Lorraine are solidly realist and stubborn by nature as a result, and they often present a selfish and forbidding exterior that belies their innate lyricism—the sheer rapture that bursts out at happy moments in Jean Lamour's exuberant wrought-iron gates and the sensuous scrolls of Gallé and Prouvé. Georges de La Tour was very much in this mold. For a time, he may have seemed immune to the tragedy of Lorraine that surrounded him. When at last it caught up with him, he refused to let himself be laid low, which does not necessarily mean that he was cynical or hard-hearted.

La Tour was not directly affected by the vicissitudes of politics. He seems to have been detached from the court of Lorraine, even though he had links with it. He did not throw in his lot, professionally or otherwise, with either of the chief protagonists in this tragedy. Unlike his neighbor Jean Des Fours, the head of a great noble family in Lunéville who decided quite early to support Charles IV and followed him into exile, La Tour sided with no one. He was born a Lorrainer, but also a subject of the bishop of Metz, at a time when there was a strong French influence on the bishopric. The Vic of his childhood was under the authority of Henri de Bourbon-Verneuil, the illegitimate son of Henri IV, who, although still a child, was elected bishop after the death of the cardinal of Lorraine in 1607. From 1618 to 1623, moreover, the town was placed in the hands of the suffragan bishop Antoine Coeffeteau, who was born in the Sarthe and was one of the great Parisian men of letters in his day. To be sure, La Tour settled in the duke's territories and received his letters of exemption from him, but it is not certain that the granting of this favor would have been enough to inspire the artist with the deep-seated sense of loyalty that those families who had been subjects for generation after generation often felt toward the ruling family of Lorraine.

We know virtually nothing about the kind of relations La Tour had with the dukes. A recently discovered document suggests, as we have seen, that La Tour struck up a friendship with Claude de Lisseras on his return from Italy and probably frequented the duke's court. The art-loving Henri II seems to have known him personally and bought at least two paintings from him. Charles IV was far less concerned about patronage, and there is no trace of a commission from him. We need not infer from this, however, that he was completely indifferent. Dom Calmet tells us that La Tour presented Duke Charles IV with a *St. Sebastian* that in his day hung in the castle of Houdemont, near Nancy. Whether it was a commission or a gift, this painting was clearly a token of La Tour's respect for the master of the territory in which he was living. Nonetheless, his deference toward the duke does not seem to have extended to expressing open hostility to the French presence in Lorraine. This was perhaps the course of a man who had read and traveled and knew that it was wisest not to get drawn into the affairs of princes. Indeed, several years later, Poussin, contemplating the disasters befalling Europe from the safety of Rome, was to observe: "Though furthest from our thoughts, the future should give us even more cause for fear than the present; but let us leave it to those it touches the most to consider; let us flee if we can, hidden under the fleece of the ewe, and escape the bloody hands of the wild and raging Cyclops." To us, as modern readers, Poussin's words have a selfish ring. To our seventeenth-century counterpart, conscious of the uncertainty of action and the inherent danger of passion, they would have seemed like Stoic wisdom. This would more than likely have been La Tour's view.

Nor would he have been alone in adopting such a position. The people of Lorraine remained largely loyal to their dukes, who had always been popular, but they were disturbed by the deposition of Duchess Nicole and by Charles IV's incessant turnabouts, and then by the cruelty of his troops, who were no kinder to the population than the "Croats" or the Swedes. They generally recognized French suzerainty without too much difficulty because they were already used to it in the Trois-Évêchés and because it was not in any way intimidating. Later on, they even seem to have appreciated the government's efforts to provide the duchy with necessary supplies and to regenerate its economy. It was not so much the French as such who provoked hostility, but rather Louis XIII's antagonism to the Party of the Devout, which held that Catholic interests and a Spanish victory were necessarily linked. We know very little about La Tour's religion, but it seems unlikely that he was one of the "devout" in this sense, and that, like the Capuchins, he would have considered the French presence a threat to Catholicism in Lorraine.

Conversely, La Tour may well have been attracted by France. We do not know what it meant to him in the early 1630s or whether he went there from time to time. There is no documentary evidence. The road from Nancy to Paris was easy and well traveled, and the trip relatively quick. Surprising though it may seem, Callot and Deruet both made such regular journeys back and forth that it is impossible to make out, if we are not explicitly told, whether a particular month found them in Paris or in Nancy. La Tour was clearly a good horseman. He could very well have gone to Paris before 1638, perhaps as early as the 1620s. In any case, even if he only knew of it secondhand through Callot, Deruet, or one of the many Frenchmen who came to Lorraine from the capital, he could not have been unaware of the brilliant developments in Parisian art, which underwent such a rapid transformation from 1624-27 onward, and particularly in the early 1630s. Our Lunéville artist would have had some inkling of Rubens's Medici Gallery series, of the first great Parisian masterpieces of Vignon and Vouet (whom he certainly would have met in Rome), and of Blanchard and Champaigne. The Holy Roman Empire had nothing comparable to offer.

Moreover, as part of their campaign to win over the Lorrainers by any means they could, Richelieu and Louis XIII used their patronage to the fullest. Even before the military events of 1630, the mere fact of being a Lorrainer was enough to guarantee an artist a good reception at the French court and to secure him favors seldom bestowed on his Parisian counterparts. As early as 1628, it was not a young artist like La Hyre or Lasne or an engraver from Antwerp who was chosen to celebrate the capture of La Rochelle and the Ile de Ré, but Callot, who was brought specially from Nancy for the purpose. He was not reproached for receiving Gaston of Orléans in his studio in 1629 (according to Félibien, the king's brother used to go to Callot's lodgings every day with the count of Maulévrier and spend two hours there drawing), or for refusing in 1633 to produce a *Capture of Nancy* as a pendant to the *Capture of La Rochelle*. "Callot begged His Majesty, with great respect, to be so good as to excuse him, because he was a Lorrainer, and he believed he should not do anything that was against the honor of his prince and against his country." Louis XIII, Félibien adds, "accepted his excuses, saying that the duke of Lorraine was very fortunate to have such loyal and devoted subjects." The renowned engraver was feted in Paris: it was Paris that established his reputation, and from Paris that his work was widely distributed by Israël Henriet. The same was true for Deruet, whom the king came to treat as a friend. When they came to Lorraine in 1633, it was not in the ducal palace that Louis XIII and the queen chose to stay, but in the painter's handsome residence. In June 1634 the king sent Deruet letters of protection from Saint-Germain-en-Laye to safeguard his house at Autrey-sur-Brenon, which was then threatened by the military operations. The king himself executed a portrait of the painter in pastel; sadly reduced to a ruinous condition by three and a half centuries of exposure to the light, this work is now in the Musée Lorrain. The queen asked Deruet for a *Road to Calvary*, and Richelieu, for four paintings for his castle in Poitou. Deruet became as much a Parisian painter as a Lorrainese one, and, according to Félibien once again, lived in Paris in these harsh times "with the train and retinue of a great lord."

La Tour did not live in Nancy, and it is likely that no one would have taken much notice of him at first. When the French troops arrived in Lorraine, however, and Lunéville, as an important military position, acquired a governor, the situation seems to have changed quickly. Among the French there were collectors well enough informed to recognize La Tour's talent. The marquis de Sourdis, for instance, whose regiment took up position in Lunéville in September 1633, was one of the most prominent connoisseurs of his day. "He combines the arts of Mars and Apollo so well that he is celebrated throughout Europe for his accomplishments," Dom Jacob wrote of him in 1644. His art collection was held to be one of the most beautiful in Paris. It would be extraordinary if he had not found the time to visit La Tour's studio.

Also worth noting is the important document recently discovered and published by Claude Mignot: the posthumous inventory, carried out on 25 October 1650, of the effects of Jean-Baptiste de Bretagne, one of the leading Parisian collectors in the first half of the century. There are no fewer than five paintings by La Tour catalogued under his name: a *Nurse and Child* and *The Fortune Tellers,* which are both specifically described as "originals," doubtless because they were clearly signed; a *Sleeping Monk*, a group of *Pipers Playing by Candlelight* (which was the most highly prized of the five along with *The Fortune Tellers*), and *Two Capuchins Meditating by Candlelight*. Jean-Baptiste Bretagne had been superintendent of war. Claude Mignot notes that he was in Nancy in December 1639 and again in September 1645, and that he took part in the assault on the city of Dieuze in 1642. We have not been able to establish whether or not he was in Lorraine from the time that the army first put in an appearance. Be that as it may, he belonged to an old Burgundy family and was probably a close relative of Bretagne, a member of the Dijon parliament whom Richelieu appointed first president of the newly created parliament in Metz in 1633. It is possible that the five La Tours that he owned at his death were acquired in Lorraine, and that they were bought either from soldiers who had looted them or directly from the artist himself. Through people like Bretagne and Sourdis, La Tour could well have been known and admired in Paris by the 1630s.

There is no indication, however, that La Tour had any personal links with France of the kind that Callot and Deruet were so quick to forge. The only thing we know, and that was just recently discovered, is that he welcomed the French unreservedly. We used to believe that he had avoided or refused the oath of allegiance to the king demanded of the Lorrainese in 1634. Anne Reinbold has shown, on the contrary, that he was one of the first to come forward to take it. The royal commissioner designate, Jean de Bullion, brother of the superintendent of finance, Claude de Bullion, and member of the Parliament of Metz, arrived in Lunéville on 7 November. La Tour, described on this occasion as "Georges de La Tour, nobleman," offered his signature alongside those of the leading figures in the town, immediately after the members of the ancient aristocracy, the officers of the bailiwick, and the municipal officials. It has to be said, however, that with the exception of the Capuchins, no one in Lunéville voiced any opposition to the oath.

In La Tour's case, however, this oath does not seem to have been accompanied by the "moral reservation" that Charles IV advocated from over the border. Not long after, at his daughter Marie's baptism on 28 March 1636—a month before the new outbreak of plague—we find La Tour asking a man by the name of Pédamon to act as godfather. This was none other than Sambat de Pédamond or Padamoux, captain of the Picardie regiment, at this moment the French governor of Lunéville. It is clear that La Tour was not worried about openly displaying his sympathy with France.

LA TOUR AND THE TRAGEDY OF LORRAINE

La Tour may not have been particularly worried at first by the troubles besetting Lorraine: he was independent enough to be able to view the political ups and downs with equanimity, and rich enough to envisage riding out the storm without too much difficulty. The tragic events of the day crept up on him little by little, and eventually swept him along with them.

It could even be said that, in a way, the situation was initially advantageous to him. There was hardly any cash around: faced with epidemics and the prospect of being taxed to pay for the maintenance of the troops, of having to lodge the soldiers, and of being endlessly pillaged, people had hidden their money away or dispatched it to safety in France or in the North. They even fled themselves if they could. By the same token, La Tour would have seen many of his regular customers disappear, it is true, but it is likely that he would have replaced at least some of them with the Frenchmen passing through Lorraine. At the same time, exempt from almost all taxes as he was, and with property to his name, he was in a position to make a tidy profit. François-Georges Pariset describes how in 1635 La Tour sold some corn for "629 francs 16 gros 8 deniers, [which was] far above the prices other citizens received or demanded." This has not been possible to verify, but it seems quite plausible.

With money at his disposal at a time when cash was scarce, La Tour was doubtless able to add to his estate. We have, for example, indications of a May 1638 agreement that had the makings of a profitable deal. A widow by the name of Jeanne Aubry decided to leave Lunéville and go to France. She surrendered her house on the rue de la Boucherie to La Tour for a period of two years and sold him all the furniture in it in exchange for the sum of 320 francs and the cancellation of any debts she might have with him. The contract states that the 320 francs she received were to enable her to "make, and defray the cost of, her journey to France": in other words, to take shelter from the storm that was brewing. La Tour could quite simply have been doing a neighbor a good turn—furnishing a woman who lived alone with the means to escape the horrors of war and undertaking to look after her property in her absence. On the other hand, it could be that he saw this as an easy way to get rich. It may well have been a bit of both. What the conclusion of the story was, the records do not say. It may be noted, however, that La Tour, with the pessimism and caution that were the order of the day, had a clause inserted allowing him to return the property not in the state in which he received it, but in whatever state it happened to be at the end of the two-year period.

At that point, any action was a bit of a gamble in Lorraine, where the future could not have looked more bleak. People's possessions, their very lives—as each one of them knew—were mere pawns in an obscure game of chance. For all his privileges, La Tour's life and livelihood were hardly safer than those of the next person.

First of all, there was the plague. La Tour had enough money to retreat to safety during the epidemics. But how could he abandon his house and studio to the pillaging hordes? He seems to have escaped the great plague that broke out in Lunéville in June 1631 and brought everything to a halt. His house was struck, however, in the violent epidemic of 1636. A document dated 16 May states that "La Tour's valet, being deceased at his dwelling, was examined and found to be full of purpura." Yet another, even more coldly factual reference to the episode in the town records makes it clear that the dead man was not a valet but La Tour's young nephew François Nardoyen, whom he had taken on as his apprentice that February: "Master de La Tour, painter, in respect of his nephew dead from the plague, examined by doctor François and taken away by barrow and buried by the corpse-carriers; the aforementioned owes . . . 14 fr. 5 gros 15 deniers. In addition to which, he is liable for one day at a rate of 15 gros spent by young Claude airing his house. . . . 1 fr. 3 gros in all."

Should we thus conclude that La Tour had left the adolescent to look after the house, while he and his family took off to some part of the country where there was less danger of infection? This has certainly been argued, but there is nothing to prove it. There is nothing to indicate that La Tour was guilty in any way. There is also nothing to show that his own children were not among those who perished. The death registers for this period were very badly kept: even the priests succumbed to the epidemic. La Tour is known to have had at least ten children. By about 1650, only four were still alive. Did the other six die in infancy, or did they succumb instead to the plague or the hardships of the times? In March 1636, as we have seen, one of La Tour's daughters was christened Marie. In fact, one of his daughters had already been given this name in January 1625—could it be that she had recently died, at the age of ten or eleven? We know nothing about these deaths, which, in the seventeenth century, sometimes meant very little to the parents and in other instances might be just as painful as they would be today.

An even more devastating calamity was to befall Lunéville, however, and this time no one escaped unscathed. On 30 September 1638 the entire city went up in flames. The little that survived the fire was plundered soon after and the surrounding area ravaged. According to reports, only thirty families remained in the city after the fire. La Tour's was not among them. It is very unlikely that his beautiful house and studio were spared when everything around went up in smoke.

This disastrous event merits detailed examination, for it was undoubtedly the most critical moment in La Tour's life. Lunéville was occupied by the French, and the governor was the same Sembat de Pédamond who had acted as godfather to little Marie. In the course of the military campaigns of 1638, Pédamond learned that the duke of Lorraine's troops (whom Charles IV had gathered together in exile) were advancing. He did not believe he could hold the position, so he ordered his men to set fire to "the town and the castle." Abbot Généval reported that in the dead of night "by the glow and light of the fire it was possible to read on the first little hill that rises up from Lunéville to Finville." The duke of Lorraine's troops marched into the town. Louis XIII, who had intended to secure the fortifications of Lunéville, was furious. Pédamond was tried and condemned in absentia to be stripped of his noble rank and hanged. When the French troops recaptured Lunéville, anything that had escaped the fire was pillaged, even in the surrounding area. The devastation was such that the city walls were deemed to be beyond repair, and the king decided that they should be razed to the ground.

What remained of La Tour's possessions in the aftermath of this turmoil? It is likely that when this voluntary blaze was decided, the inhabitants of Lunéville had enough warning to get all their livestock and the most precious of their possessions out of the way. La Tour could well have been among the first of those to be alerted. What did he manage to salvage? What happened to his studio? We do not know that La Tour ever drew, as Bellange did, but if so—and everything points to the fact that he did, at least until the stay in Rome—we can assume that not one sheet of paper escaped the flames. Similarly, any models he might have kept as references for later

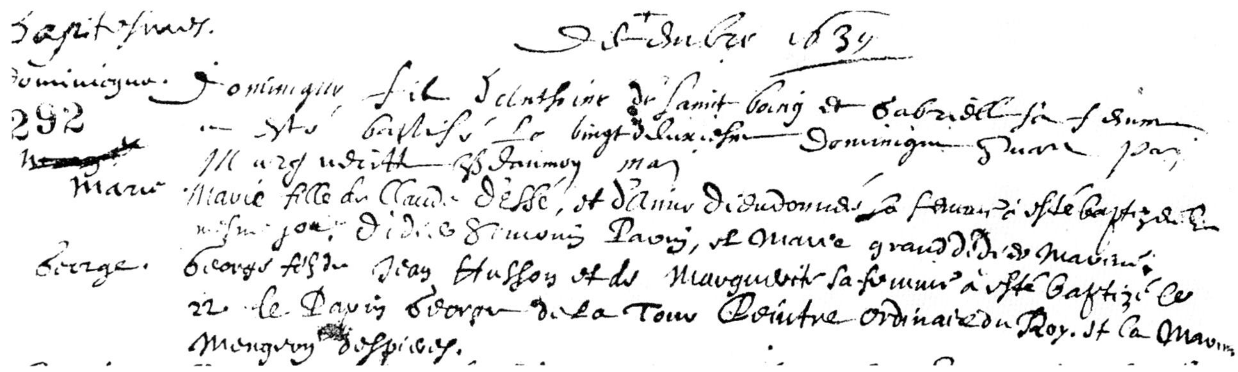

FIRST MENTION OF THE TITLE
"PEINTRE ORDINAIRE DU ROI"
The certificate of Georges Husson's baptism on 22 December 1639 in the parish of Saint-Sébastien in Nancy.
Archives Municipales (GG4), Nancy

"variations" would not have survived. The same would be true of the canvases he might have had in the studio, and there may well even have been a great many, if the studio inventories of other painters of the period are anything to go by. Above all, there were the pictures he had painted for churches, convents, and private patrons in Lunéville: all of these would have been burned or destroyed by army rabble. It seems highly unlikely, given the violence of these events, that anything was salvaged as spoils of war. Most of the work La Tour had produced up to 1638 almost certainly disappeared on that day. Part of it was already gone in the disasters that had befallen the other cities of Lorraine. Most of Tournier's surviving work was found in Toulouse, Jean Boucher's in Bourges, and Tassel's in Langres. La Tour's was found in Albi, Nantes, and Rennes; there is not a trace left in Lunéville or the surrounding area.

La Tour was forty-five, already almost old for the time. This could have been the end of his career. In such a time of collective disaster, however, adversity was a spur. Driven from Lunéville, reduced to reach Nancy, which was already bursting with refugees, the painter looked to Paris.

"REFUGE" IN NANCY AND PARIS

Not surprisingly, La Tour's trail is very difficult to follow after September 1638 in the chaos brought to Lorraine by fighting and pillage and amid the innumerable war refugees streaming to Paris from the east and the north. It is probable that the family sought immediate refuge in Nancy. From 8 February 1639 at the earliest, the family was staying in the new part of the town in a beautiful house belonging to the nobleman Olivier Brossin, first gentleman of the bedchamber to the late François de Lorraine, who was old and had presumably fled the troubles. On 23 March, Diane became godmother, in Nancy, to a son of the painter Jean Capchon. On 13 August, a tax of three thousand francs was levied on the inhabitants of Nancy to pay for the razing of Lunéville's fortifications. Contributions were based on the number of livestock owned, and we find that La Tour, like Deruet, owned one cow, and therefore had to pay three francs, the idea being that the tax should be "paid by people of all classes, privileged and unprivileged alike." In September, Diane once again acted as godmother in Nancy, and the La Tour family cannot have made too bad an impression in the city, because the godfather on this occasion was a former member of the court of Lorraine, a nobleman by the name of François René Dubois, lord of Hincourt, Hoeville, and Semi-Bezange. Georges himself acted as godfather to the son of one Jean Husson on 22 December in the Church of Saint-Sébastien and, interestingly, is described in the records by the high-sounding title of "*peintre ordinaire du roi.*"

In 1640, by contrast, the municipal rolls for various taxes list La Tour as being "away since the month of February." Diane, meanwhile, seems to still have been in Olivier Brossin's house, probably along with the children: the 8 January 1641 record of taxes received for garbage collection shows that "the house of nobleman Olivier Bressy [*sic*], in which the painter La Tour resides, has paid half." By then, however, the family had clearly decided to move back to Lunéville. A petition dated 4 February 1641 describes La Tour as "resident in Lunéville," and on 15 August he was a witness to the marriage contract of his niece Claude de Ronny, who lived close by, at Rosières.

Nothing proves that La Tour, or indeed Diane, was a permanent resident by then, however. There are only records of the children—their son Étienne, then aged twenty, and daughter Claude, then eighteen, serving as godfather and godmother on a number of occasions from May to the end of the year. Could they not have been supervising the rebuilding of the family house, while their parents were elsewhere? In contrast, from 1642 on, we come across an ever-increasing number of documents to suggest that La Tour must have been in Lunéville. In January the bills for the Nardoyen brothers' tuition were finally settled. In April, there was some business relating to the livestock La Tour kept, and on 9 April he embarked on a critical battle with the city. Lunéville faced a heavy burden of taxation at the time. La Tour was in all probability comfortably settled back in by then, and the city authorities wanted to make him pay his share of the taxes, maintaining that his letters of exemption "[did] not apply in times of war damage." No doubt they secretly hoped that La Tour's letters from the duke would not be recognized by the royal authorities. When a livestock tax was levied, the sergeant of the bailiwick was sent to La Tour's house to collect his share. La Tour did not receive him kindly, as is clear from the following account, written by the sergeant himself, whose name was Pierre Manvisse:

". . . I went this ninth day of April 1642, accompanied by Jean Corpey, sergeant in the said town [of Lunéville], to the house of Sire Georges de La Tour, painter in the said place. Speaking to him from the path outside his house, I politely questioned him several times about the payment of the sum of sixteen francs and six gros for which he is liable for his said livestock; to which he replied that he had no intention of paying anything. And after I asked him to pay the sum or force me to seize him, he told me to seize him. And as I was preparing to enter his house to do so, he gave me a sharp kick and shut his door, saying angrily that he would shoot anyone who dared come any nearer, so I could do no more. . . . " Clearly La Tour was not afraid of strong-arm tactics.

He almost certainly foresaw the consequences of such action and played for time. Summoned to appear before the deputy public prosecutor on the strength of the sergeant's report, he deliberately failed to turn up. A decision was made against him in his absence, whereupon he declared that he would appeal and summoned the city before the Parliament of Metz, which then sat at Toul. At the same time he must have carefully manoeuvred the powerful patrons he had in Nancy and Paris to get his letters of exemption endorsed by the king; after various judicial episodes, the city was ultimately forced to drop the case. La Tour had succeeded in winning back his old privileges, even more pronounced than before now that the nobility of Lunéville had been decimated by epidemics and exile. This dispute must have caused lasting bitterness on both sides.

La Tour was not a man to be discouraged by difficulties like these, however. He probably started putting his house and land holdings in order and on 16 September 1643 he took on a new apprentice, Chrétien Georges, son of a Vic family to whom he was related by marriage. Life was finally getting underway again.

Between September 1638 and September 1643, was La Tour simply one of the countless Lorrainese refugees, floating between a house in Nancy that did not belong to him and the ruins of an estate in Lunéville? Did he survive five years in a country ravaged by war and with more pressing things to worry about than painting without a single client or commission? We have long contended that La Tour must have gone to Paris during this time, certainly with the intention of working, and perhaps even with the idea of settling there. Lorrainers, as we have seen, were well received. Deruet's success with Louis XIII might well have encouraged La Tour to follow in his footsteps and convinced him that it would not be difficult to win the king's favor. There was also the example of Callot, who had acquired great renown before his death in 1635, and his engravings were still widely circulated by Israël in Paris, not without considerable financial rewards. Moreover, the political situation around 1638 was still very uncertain; the war showed no signs of coming to an end. A great many Lorrainers could see no future for their country and were turning instead to Paris. Indeed, the title of "*peintre ordinaire du roi*" by which La Tour describes himself in Nancy in December 1639 can mean only one thing: that he wanted to paint and sell his works in Paris. It was undoubtedly a gratifying title to have, but it did not bring with it any automatic rights of exemption, privileges, pensions, or commissions. It simply freed an artist from the tyrannical hold of the Paris guild of painters and sculptors that made sure no provincial or foreign artist could work in the city and take its members' customers. On the other hand, obtaining this royal warrant required considerable support, canvassing, gifts, and often even ready cash, and painters living in the provinces normally did not bother. After the terrible events of 1638 it is hard to imagine La Tour paying a hefty price for a useless title. If he coveted and finally got it, he must have wanted to make use of it.

It always seemed highly unlikely that we would ever have proof of any of this. The Paris records were almost entirely destroyed, first during the Revolution, then during the Commune. Among the manuscripts preserved in the Bibliothèque Nationale (not in the National Archives), however, Michel Antoine came across the following unexpected item in a volume of accounts that by some quirk of fate escaped being burned with most of the others: "To Georges de La Tour, the sum of a thousand livres payable to him in respect of the journey that he made from Nancy to Paris on affairs relating to the service of His Majesty, together with his stay of six weeks and his return journey." This Georges de La Tour traveling from Nancy must be our painter. Even if they do not give the exact date of the journey, the accounts seem to suggest that it took place at the end of 1638 or the beginning of 1639, precisely when La Tour had not yet moved into Olivier Brossin's house.

Why the trip and the reward, surely far too large to be a simple reimbursement of expenses? Perhaps La Tour was assigned some kind of mission that was diplomatic rather than artistic. Perhaps he came to Paris on his own initiative, and was able, with the help of a few well-placed acquaintances, to approach the king or Richelieu and win their favor. Everything seems to suggest that it was during this trip that the famous episode recounted by Dom Calmet took place. The story must have been very well known: at a time when every other detail of La Tour's life, and even his precise name, had been forgotten, it was the only piece of information about him to come down to the historian. Dom Calmet's account reads as follows: "He presented King Louis XIII with a painting by his own hand, a night scene showing a St. Sebastian; the piece was of such perfect taste that the king removed all the other paintings from his chamber, so that this one might hang on its own." This was the gesture of a man who really did appreciate art. It was also a clever form of praise on the king's part, guaranteed to bind an artist to him forever. The word *presented*, as used by Dom Calmet, almost certainly means "given as a present." A thousand livres would have been far more than such a medium-sized painting with three figures was worth, and must rather have been a measure of the king's thanks. The warrant of *peintre ordinaire* would have followed soon after, insofar as La Tour had people to back him up and was able to hurry its delivery. We know that he was only in Paris for six weeks—this was presumably the longest he could afford to leave his family and his activities in Lorraine. He would, however, almost certainly have made more than one trip there and probably had someone in Paris to look after his affairs. Michel Antoine has also unearthed a deed from 25 August 1640 mentioning a certain Baptiste Quarin, who is described as "the agent of Monsieur de La Tour, *peintre ordinaire du roi*, residing in the galleries of the Louvre."

The king granted very few apartments in the galleries of the Louvre, and these were highly sought after; obtaining one usually necessitated waiting a long time and obtaining the highest patronages. This favor, much more appreciable than the first, accorded La Tour the various privileges conferred on the "peers of the Royal Houses." And, above all, it allowed him to store paintings in Paris, well away from the prying eyes of the guild, until his warrant of *peintre ordinaire* was officially registered, for the guild had a right to inspect all paintings brought into Paris but was not allowed into the Louvre. La Tour seems to have set about capitalizing on his success straightaway. The king's gesture might have well sparked off a sudden craze. As we have seen, La Tour was already known to and protected by a number of Parisian art-lovers, and it was perhaps through one of them that he was received by the king. These people also must have helped to spread his name around the capital, although no direct evidence of this has come down to us. What we do know is that from this moment on, La Tour's work began to feature in all the most illustrious collections in Paris.

After the king, the most influential figure in Paris was Cardinal Richelieu, a passionate devotee of art and an avid collector. Richelieu is known to have owned a

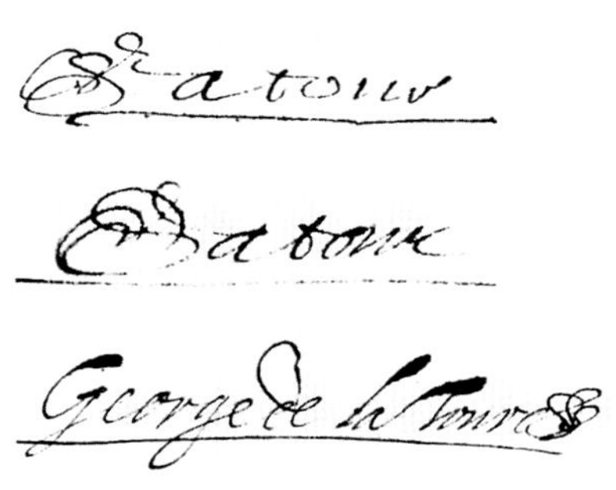

THE TRANSFORMATION OF LA TOUR'S SIGNATURE
From top to bottom:
Act of 1626; act of 1631; act of 1638.

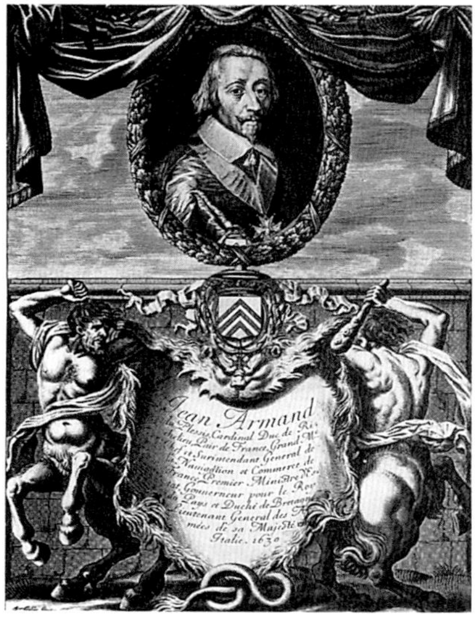

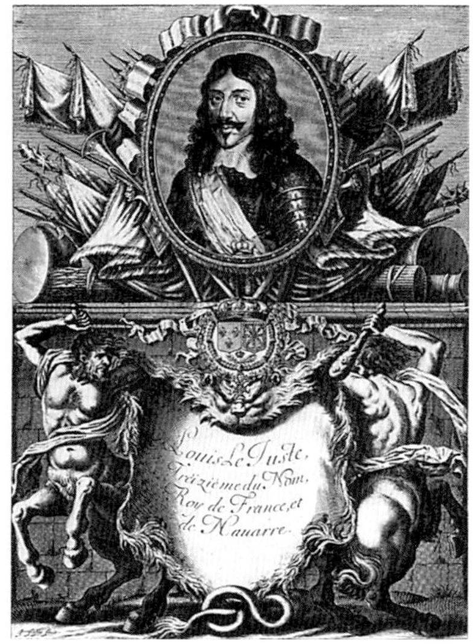

THE OWNERS OF LA TOUR'S PAINTINGS IN PARIS

From left to right:

Jean Frosne. *Cardinal de Richelieu.* Engraving.
Jean Frosne. *King Louis XIII.* Engraving.
Anonymous. *Claude de Bullion, Superintendent of Finance.* Engraving (the so-called Moncornet series).
After Charles Le Brun. *Chancellor Pierre Séguier.* Engraving by Van Schuppen. 1662.

St. Jerome—this must have been the version now in Stockholm in which the prominence given to the cardinal's hat can only be explained as a deliberate piece of flattery. It seems very likely that this painting was presented to Richelieu when the *St. Sebastian* was presented to the king, if not a little before, since this was fairly common practice. In any event, the cardinal seems to have been equally pleased with his painting: on his death in December 1642 it was found hanging in his personal dressing room. Richelieu appears to have owned another work by La Tour as well. Listed in the rather perfunctory inventory of his castle at Rueil is a "Night picture" with musicians, which seems to turn up again in 1675 in Paris, in the inventory of his niece, the duchess of Aiguillon, but detailed in full this time: "A night picture, painted on canvas, by the so-called La Tour, representing a group of musicians." However beautiful the *St. Jerome*, Richelieu clearly had one of his "candlelight" paintings as well.

Next in importance after the cardinal was Séguier, the chancellor of France, a great patron and devoted protector of Simon Vouet and Le Brun. There were no paintings attributed to La Tour in Séguier's collection, at least according to two inventories carried out much later, the first upon his death in 1672, the second upon the death of his wife in 1683. There are, however, intriguing references to a "night picture of Saint Hiérosme, an original by master Rou," a "Night picture with Our Lord holding a light for Saint Joseph, an original by master Rousse," and a "Saint Hiérosme, in the manner of master Rouce." Who was this artist, whose subjects, as Yannick Nexon has pointed out, were so remarkably like La Tour's? We can rule out Rosso Fiorentino: although he was known as Master Roux at the time, it is difficult to imagine him painting a Joseph in the carpenter's shop. It would be quite exceptional, on the other hand, if Séguier owned two or three paintings by an artist who, though well enough known in his day for people to talk of paintings in his "manner," has disappeared without a trace. We can only hope that Le Brun's own 1650 inventory of his patron's paintings will turn up, since the precise attribution should be there. As things stand, I am convinced that this "Rousse" is none other than La Tour, and that the chancellor, future patron of the Academy, bought three paintings from him, including perhaps the *Christ with St. Joseph in the Carpenter's Shop* now in the Louvre.

After the chancellor came the financial secretary, the sumptuous Bullion, who was also a great protector of Vouet and a generous patron. He died at the end of 1640, and the inventory carried after his death indicates that in a little room next to

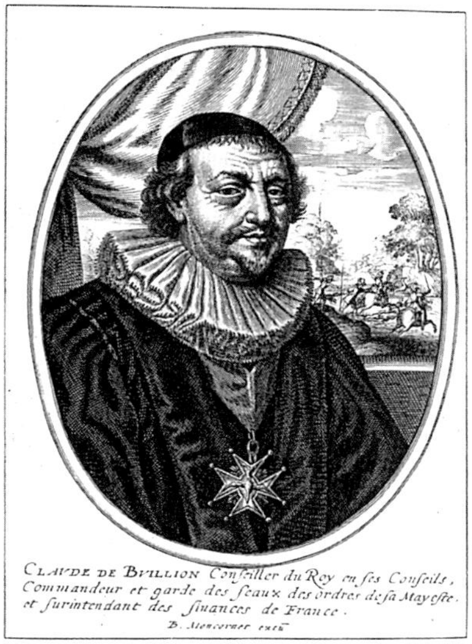

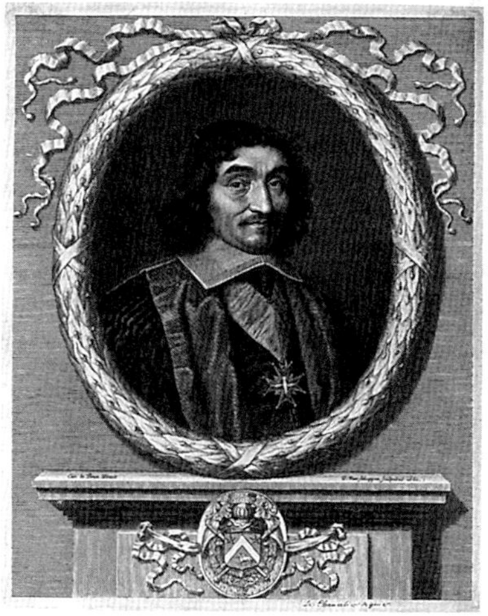

the ambassadors' hall in his Paris residence there was "a painting that depicts a night scene representing Saint Peter denying Our Lord, painted by Latour, complete with its stretcher and burnished gold frame, measuring four foot wide by three foot high or thereabouts." The description and the horizontal format suggest not a *Penitent St. Peter*, but a *Denial* this time, set in a guardroom with a servant girl. This too may have been a present: no one was better placed than the financial superintendent to help La Tour get established in Paris. Indeed, it was Bullion who countersigned the order for payment of the thousand pounds in 1639. This is by no means an exhaustive list, and there are doubtless a good many other surprises waiting to be revealed by future research. Among La Tour's patrons and collectors at this time we should include, as we have said above, Jean-Baptiste de Bretagne, whose inventory dates from 1650 but who might have acquired at least some of his five La Tours before 1639. We should also add to the list a variety of lesser-known collectors and dealers. Richard Beresford, for example, has shown that the Parisian painter Simon Cornu, who was a cousin by marriage of Jacques Blanchard, also owned a La Tour. Listed in his house on rue d'Angoumois in August 1644, with about a hundred originals and copies of all sizes, is "a Saint Hiérosme by Mr. Latour the Lorrainer."

Such success could have tempted La Tour to settle in the capital. The competition was fierce, however. Blanchard may have died at the end of 1638, but Vouet, despondent over his wife's death in October of the same year, soon rallied back and went on to produce masterpiece after masterpiece. His pupils were gradually making a mark; Champaigne was the cardinal's favorite, and La Hyre was beginning to attract attention. In December 1640 the long-awaited and long-reluctant Nicolas Poussin arrived in Paris and received official honors from the superintendent of buildings. La Tour must have quickly realized that artists in Paris made their name by working on great decorative schemes, embellishing halls, chapels, and galleries—in short by engaging in all the kinds of work his early Caravaggist experience and the isolation of Lunéville had turned him away from. Whatever the flattering praise he had received, trying to make a career in Paris would be a hard struggle, and the outcome would be uncertain.

It is curious that Poussin should have had the same experience one year later. Paintings like *The Triumph of Pan* and *The Israelites Gathering Manna* were greatly admired in Paris, and Poussin was lured from Rome to Paris by flattery and money. When he got to Paris, however, he was asked for great church paintings, ceilings, and the decoration of the *Grande Galerie* in the Louvre, everything he had specifically said he did not want to do, and he was left no free time for the meditation that was such a crucial part of his work. It was not that people misunderstood his talent, but this was the nature of life in Paris. Poussin soon grasped this and escaped by the end of 1642. The same probably applied to La Tour. Even more than the well-read Poussin, La Tour needed time to ripen his masterpieces. He may well have found the turmoil of Lorraine less unbearable than the giddy whirl of Paris. Moreover, all his assets were in Lorraine and impossible to transfer for the moment. There may not have been much left in the way of movable goods, but his various properties were still worth a tidy sum. His investments and the various debts owed him, all in the hands of his compatriots, required constant vigilance to avoid having the capital dwindle along with the interest. Abandoning Lorraine would have meant abandoning all that he had inherited and greatly increased, and which he owed his children. The right thing to do was to watch over his estate carefully and build it up again as quickly as possible. It also would have meant losing his letters of exemption, and he would never have been able to obtain anything similar in Paris. After all, his painting was the sort that could be produced at a distance and entrusted to a good dealer. His estate in Lorraine, on the other hand, required him to be there.

One day, no doubt, we will have documents to show that La Tour made several trips to Paris between 1648 and 1653, just like Deruet, who, as we have seen, was such a regular visitor to the capital that it is often difficult to know whether he was in Lorraine or in Paris at a given moment. Once back in Lunéville, La Tour probably continued selling work in Paris through his "agent" or another intermediary. Bullion died in December 1640, however, Richelieu at the end of 1642, and Louis XIII at the beginning of 1643. Before long, ministers began to come and go, and political rivalries stirred up uncertainty in people's minds and chaos in the streets. La Tour seems to have turned away fairly quickly from a court and a city that were beginning to be dominated by the Fronde and to have given up all notion of a career there. In the end, the *"peintre ordinaire du roi"* was never to be a Parisian painter.

THE ARTIST'S RESPONSE

It may seem rather arbitrary to mark a turning point in La Tour's work around 1630. An artist's creation rarely changes according to the the decades of the calendar. In this case, however, there are other factors involved: the outbreak of the plague in Lorraine in 1630, the arrival of the French troops at the end of 1631, followed by that of Louis XIII in Vic in January 1632, the devastation inflicted by the epidemic of 1633 on Lunéville, which suddenly found itself the center of international news, then the full-scale calamity of Lorraine and the destruction of La Tour's personal property. All of these events must have terribly jolted a man already in his forties and profoundly altered his perception and way of thinking, not to mention his art.

La Tour seems to have spent his first ten years in Lunéville pretty much locked into the little world of Lorraine, even though he was somewhat aloof from it. True, as we have said, Nancy was a crossroads, and La Tour would almost certainly have been able to see the works of Paris, Rome, and Utrecht there, in the form of both paintings and engravings. At this time, however, his art often seems to have been shaped by Bellange, then still very much in the fore, and the last sparks of Mannerism, as well as by his Nancy rivals Deruet and Jean Le Clerc. He had sought an entirely different identity, and thus another clientele, but one that must have remained essentially local. During the 1630s, this state of grace disintegrated.

Circumstances could not have been more unfavorable for painting in Lorraine: in these unstable times, with the devastation wreaked by the troops and the ever-increasing special taxes that were crippling the population, people must have been increasingly disinclined to buy paintings. The competition among artists would have been even more fierce as a result, at least until the death of Jean Le Clerc in October 1633. La Tour probably benefited less from his death than did minor artists, such as Raymond Constant, who were based in Nancy and were prepared to adapt to circumstances. Lorraine, on the other hand seemed *volens nolens* to be looking more and more toward Paris, and Georges de La Tour was certainly compelled to take a greater interest in the French capital.

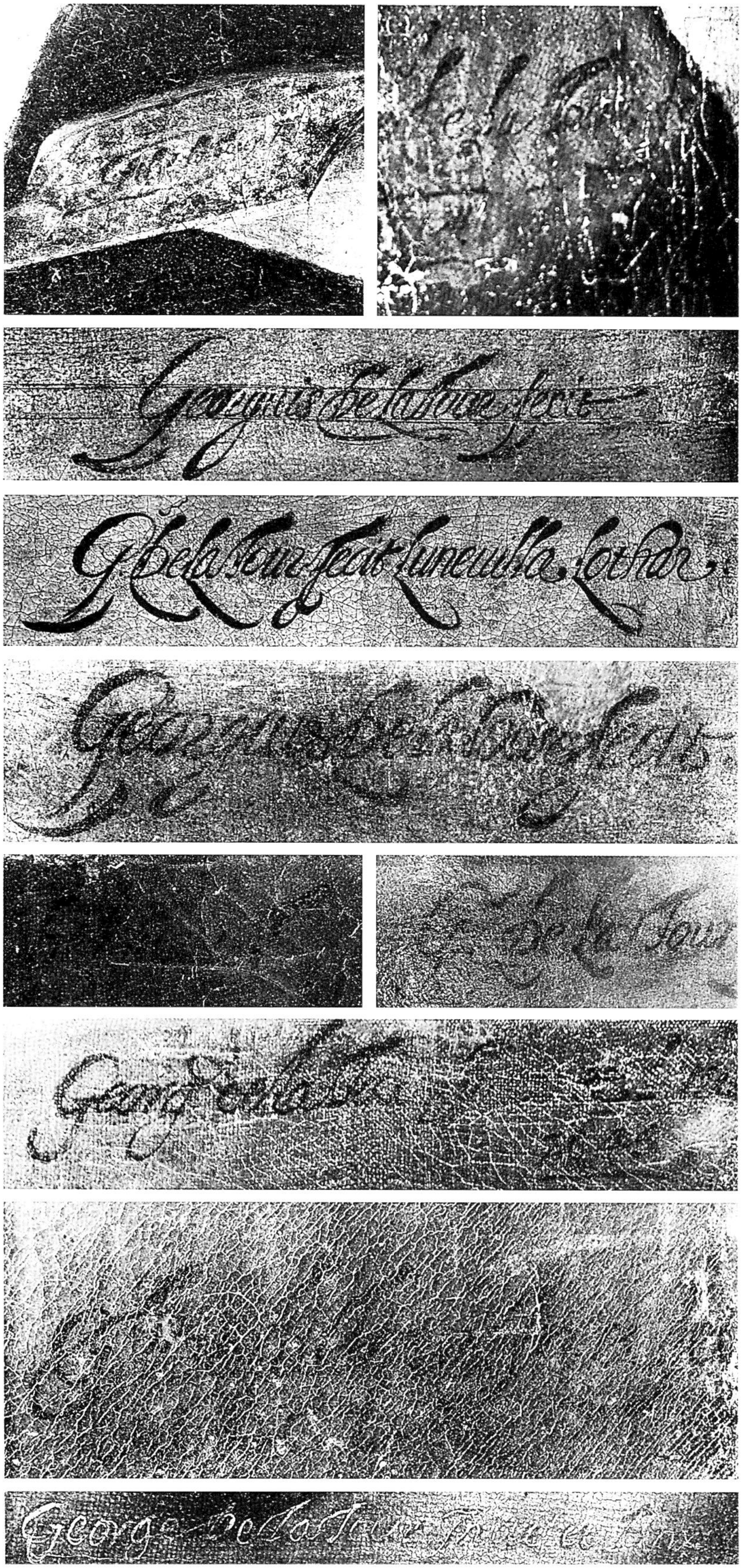

THE APPEARANCE OF SIGNATURES ON
LA TOUR'S PAINTINGS:
From top to bottom and from left to right:
The Hurdy-Gurdy Player, fragment. Brussels (catalogue no. 17).
The Payment of Dues. Lvov (Lemberg) Museum (catalogue no. 23).
St. Thomas. Louvre (catalogue no. 29).
The Fortune Teller. New York (catalogue no. 31).
The Cheat with The Ace of Diamonds. Louvre (catalogue no. 39)
A Boy Blowing on a Charcoal Stick. Dijon (catalogue no. 47).
The Dream of St. Joseph. Nantes (catalogue no. 50).
The Penitent St. Peter. Cleveland (catalogue no. 58).
The Denial of St. Peter. Nantes (catalogue no. 76).
Dice Players (Five Figures). Teeside (catalogue no. 78).

First there were the famous exiles received by the court of Lorraine: the duchess of Chevreuse in 1627, followed in 1629 by none other than Gaston of Orléans, the legitimate heir to the throne, who brought with him a chaotic but cultured train. Then came the French army, and the king himself for a while, and, soon after, the royal administration. Lorrainers were not permitted to forget Paris. In the early 1630s, moreover, on the artistic level, Paris was no longer the city that a young painter just back from Rome could easily dismiss in 1616. This point is worth remembering. Paris now contained a great many art lovers, with marked tastes, fancies, and dislikes of their own, and a great deal of money. Sophisticated engravings gradually took the place of the popular prints of the past, providing widespread distribution of images that were potential models for other artists. Indeed, Paris was now quite likely to undermine all the aesthetic certainties an artist like La Tour might have derived from Rome fifteen years earlier. But how can we measure its impact? How can we chart his development? When did La Tour go to Paris, where we know he had friends and even fairly close relatives? He may have gone there before the end of 1638 and the destruction of Lunéville. Possibly he did not meet Louis XIII before then. We must repeat that these points escape us, and yet they are precisely the ones that would allow us to understand La Tour's development as an artist.

His work clearly underwent a marked change between 1630 and 1643, however. The psychology is profoundly different, as one might expect after all the hardships in Lorraine. Yet his painting did not become stiff and hard on such a tragic diet; on the contrary, La Tour's art became both richer and more complex, his concepts bolder. By virtue of the tragedy itself, La Tour ceased to be the painter of Lunéville. He had to show what he was made of, able to work for the king of France, for Richelieu, Europe's most famous statesman, to compete with Vouet, Champaigne, and Poussin. Suddenly, he was known and courted in high places. He had always believed in himself, but inner certainty is not enough for an artist. If these were testing times for La Tour, they also brought him one supreme gift: public recognition of his talent.

A small detail is worth noting here. No signatures appear on La Tour's early paintings, but from this point on they become frequent. There was no general rule about signatures in the seventeenth century. Some artists, such as La Hyre in Paris and Jean Boucher in Bourges, signed virtually all their works, while others, such as Poussin, signed virtually none. The Caravaggists followed their master's example and traditionally did not sign their work, which often makes it very difficult to decide whether a painting is by Manfredi, Valentin, or Tournier, or even by Trophime Bigot. Often, however, whether a painting was signed or not depended on how it was sold. A painter dealing directly with a collector he knew would feel no need to sign his work. If, on the other hand, he sent his work far away and sold it through dealers, who were usually painters themselves, he would quickly get into the habit of signing it—to acquaint prospective patrons with his name, but also to avoid the risk of annoying confusions or swindles that could lead to disputes over money.

This seems to be what happened in La Tour's case. The magnificent Latin signature on *The Fortune Teller*, finely scripted and deliberately positioned in the lightest part of the painting, would seem to be a piece of self-advertisement addressed to the art-loving public of Paris. The more straightforward signatures that appear as the paintings become more numerous (and often in a dark area of the canvas) may well correspond to a growing business activity. Although he does not seem to have used a dealer as such, La Tour did have an "agent" in Paris, and his paintings were probably left in the galleries of the Louvre, where there were a great many studios. It seems likely that he signed all the canvases that passed through Quarin's hands, but (contrary to what we would expect today) not by and large those that he delivered in person to important people. Presumably, he started signing the smaller compositions early on—Magdalens and smoking or blowing figures—in order to distinguish them from copies and imitations. Such forgeries must have been a source of repeated annoyance to him as they were to Claude when he was similarly plagued by them in Rome. The fact that a Caravaggesque artist like La Tour should start signing his canvases proves that his works, thus far restricted almost exclusively to Lorraine, were finding new outlets and reaching collectors far and wide.

THE ADVENT OF THE NIGHT PICTURES

Everything suggests that this expansion was gradual, as was the development of La Tour's style and thought. Like Poussin, La Tour was not the sort to abruptly change course. He certainly did not hesitate to continue the series that he had developed some time before. We have already observed that the Nantes *Hurdy-Gurdy Player*, the culmination of the series of blind musicians, could well be somewhat later than 1630. Similarly, La Tour continued to develop the half-length figure composition he had used in *The Beggars' Brawl*. Its narrative quality made it particularly appropriate for his new clientele, and it gave rise to his great masterpieces of the 1630s, the two versions of *The Cheat* and *The Fortune Teller*. On the other hand, two major changes are soon apparent. The color is lighter, brighter, and more varied, and conversely, there are more and more night pictures, which come to form the nucleus of his work by about 1638-1642 and, indeed, dominate his very creativity.

The appearance of the "night pictures" is an enigma that has long prompted many theories and hypotheses among art historians. About twenty years ago, however, a painting that suddenly reappeared managed to discredit most of the commentaries and radically alter the givens of the problem. This was *The Payment of Dues* in the Lvov museum, which is generally accepted as La Tour's earliest surviving "night" picture.

The canvas, which was long overlooked, had belonged to Alexander Dombsky (1751-1824) before entering the Lyubomirsky collection, which subsequently became a museum in 1823. Yuri Zolotov has shown that it was given to Dombsky by the Polish wife of Charles-Eugène de Lambesc (1754-1825), who was descended from a great Lorraine family. The late Pierre Moisy said that he was very intrigued by the canvas when he saw it on a visit to the Lyubomirsky Museum in 1939, and that he suspected that it was more Lorrainese rather than northern in origin. The painting was finally associated with the name of Georges de La Tour, and M. I. Cherbatova devoted an article to it in a 1970 Russian publication.

In fact the painting is quite different in style from all the rest of La Tour's known work. Nonetheless, most scholars were immediately convinced that this was a La Tour. Pariset was almost the only person to reject the attribution. The issue was soon resolved, however: careful restoration revealed a signature in the left-hand margin, partly trimmed but incontrovertibly authentic. Alongside it is a date, but unfortunately the last two figures are truncated. Yuri Zolotov proposes a reading of 16(41) or 16(42), but this remains open to question. On the contrary, Pierre Rosenberg and François Macé de Lépinay make the painting the very first entry in their catalogue. My personal inclination would be to set it somewhere between the two.

The scene is a good deal more complex than *The Beggars' Brawl*. There are six figures, and all six are drawn together by a single action. An old man, a craftsman or peasant, is counting out some money that he has taken from his purse. Opposite him, a man seated in front of an open register stares fixedly at the coins being counted, which are clearly destined to join the pile already on the table. A secondary figure moves the candle closer to make it easier to check the money, while another is busy trying to make out a list. None of this gives a very clear idea about the meaning. We had to rule out various religious subjects. This cannot, for instance, be Judas either receiving or returning the thirty pieces of silver for which he betrayed Christ, because the gestures, the secular dress, and the register would hardly be appropriate. Nor can it represent the Calling of St. Matthew, since there is no Christ to give this usury scene its evangelical significance. The absence of any weapons seems to exclude the payment of a ransom to a group of soldiers or brigands. Genre painters did sometimes depict bankers and usurers, but in such cases, it was to show the act of lending and not, as here, the payment of a few coins.

In fact, La Tour seems to have had in mind the money changer's table in Caravaggio's *Calling of St. Matthew* in San Luigi dei Francesi, the church he would almost certainly have attended in Rome. Here he has merely adapted his model to a half-length composition, which, as we have seen, was also widely adopted by Roman Caravaggist painters—but now in order to create a scene borrowed directly from everyday life. From 1631 onward the people of Lorraine were burdened with intolerable tax levies. Special taxes were imposed for various and numerous reasons, but above all to finance the cost of maintaining the troops and rebuilding the defenses. These came on top of the heavy dues and other taxes, and, as already stated, eventually bled the inhabitants dry. In his letters of exemption, La Tour deliberately had it specified that he was not subject to taxes of this kind, and he obstinately refused to submit to them. Such exemptions, which were automatic for the nobility and the clergy, forced the craftsmen to bear the brunt of the levies and were detested as a result. La Tour's was no exception and, as we will see in due course, was very badly received by the people of Lunéville. This is not enough, however, to preclude our interpretation of the painting. The scene is consistent in every detail with a tax levy at that time and in Lorraine. The ledger opened toward the old man, for instance, could be a register of taxpayers, and the paper being read, a list detailing the amount he was taxed (which naturally varied according to some sign of wealth). The elegant man looking away from the viewers to preside over the scene and the grimace on the old man's face as he is forced to hand over his money are just what we would expect to see on such an occasion. To try to identify which tax of all those levied in Lunéville is being collected here, or to see the painting as a protest (when in fact La Tour managed to get out of paying the tax), would be going too far. Had he wanted to, La Tour would have added one detail or another to specify the circumstances. As the painting appears, a viewer in La Tour's day would only have been able to interpret it in a general way. We must see this work like the *Old Peasant Couple Eating*: a realist scene painted for its own sake. The taxpayer's open purse and care-worn face, the collector's hooked nose and intent gaze are enough to set the scene; La Tour refuses any allusion that would reduce the subject to anecdote.

The real enigma lies elsewhere: in the use of only artificial light, here, a candle. This is what was called at the time a "night" picture. La Tour was to explore this formula over a long period and to derive his greatest masterpieces from it. All of his other known "night" pictures, however, reveal a much more personal approach, and this originality becomes increasingly pronounced right up to the last works. *The Payment of Dues* is manifestly the earliest surviving "nocturne" we have from his hand.

Why should he have chosen this path when he was so alert to the virtues of daylight and the subtle shades of color it produced, and when the scene was hardly one that could only take place at night? Where did he get the idea? Whose example did he follow?

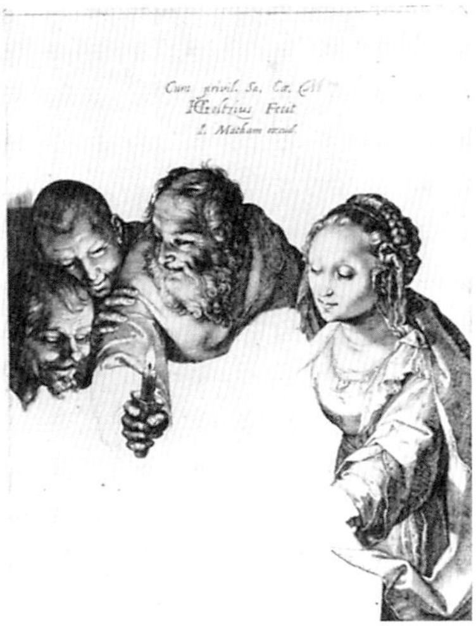

Hendrick Goltzius. *The Adoration of the Shepherds*. 1617. Unfinished etching.
Private collection

Michelangelo Caravaggio. *The Calling of St. Matthew*.
Church of San Luigi dei Francesi, Rome

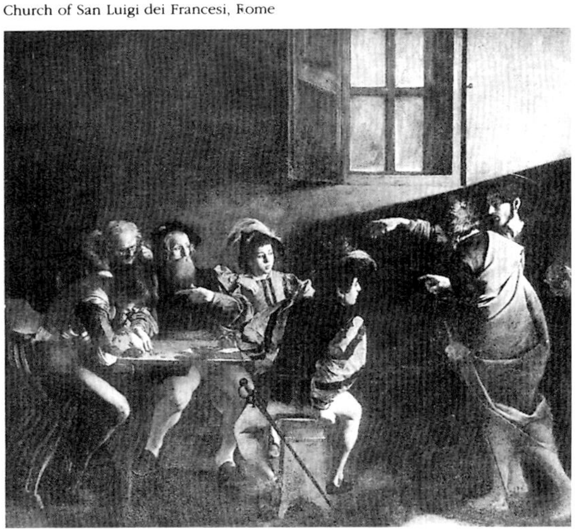

Hendrick Terbrugghen. *The Calling of St. Matthew*. 1621.
Centraal Museum, Utrecht

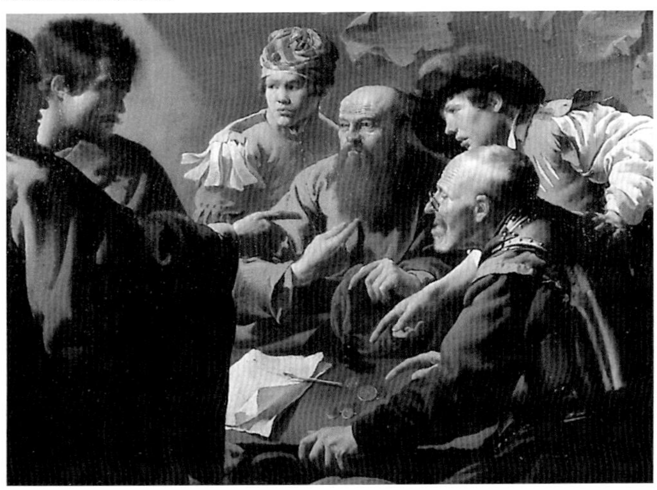

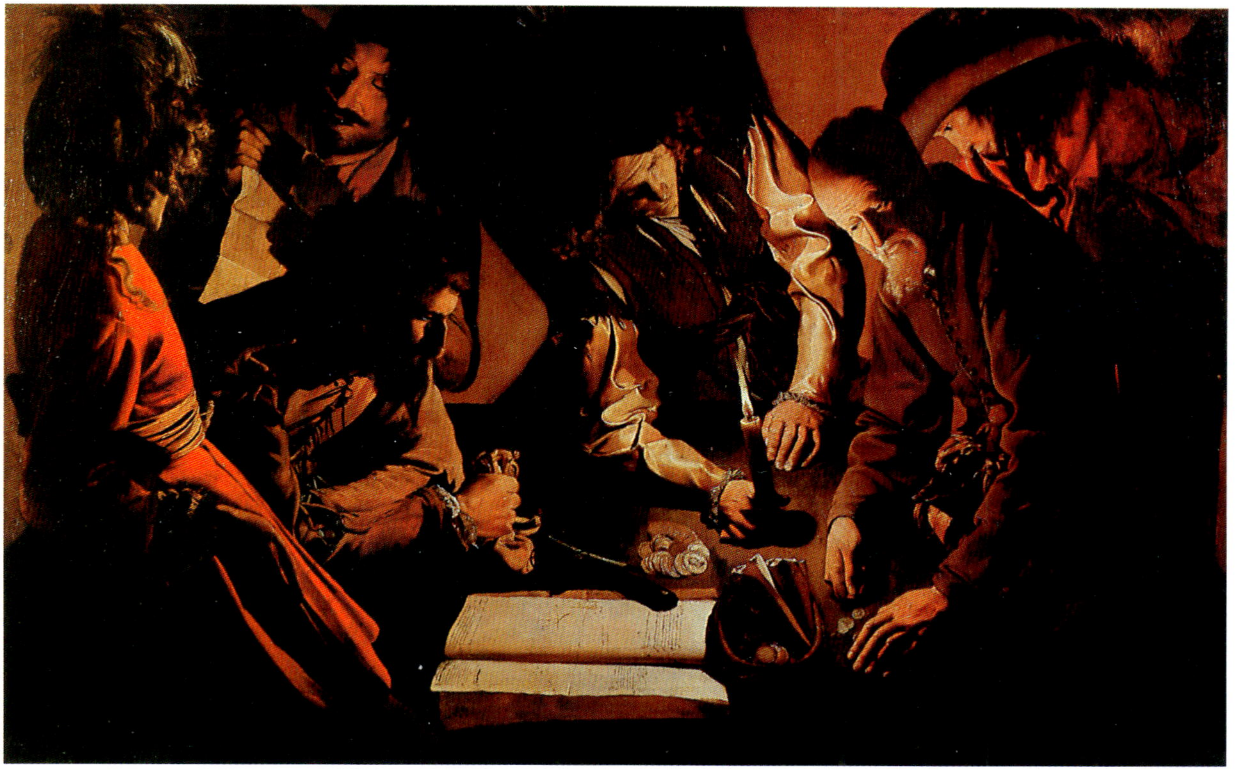

The Payment of Dues.
Lvov (Lemberg) Museum

Night pictures are often wrongly presented as a Caravaggesque art form. At a certain point, Caravaggio did develop a taste for the dramatic effects of chiaroscuro, but he never painted a "night" picture in the true sense of the term, and there is not a single scene with a candle to be found in his work. The closest he comes to one is the burning torch in the *Seven Works of Mercy*. In fact, "night" pictures are as old as western painting, and by the fifteenth century, the "Maître du Cœur d'amour épris" was already capable of using the night scene to produce a masterpiece like the *Delivery of the Heart*. In the sixteenth century a whole tradition arose, from the very well-known *Holy Night* by Correggio to the various nocturnes of the Bassano family. The late Mannerists fell on it with delight, as a convention that would allow their virtuosity full rein and enable them to attract attention by novel effects and studied use of color. The northern painters were particularly taken with it, as we can see in the example of Abraham Blomaert with his 1604 *Adoration of the Shepherds*, now in Göttingen, or that of Wtewael, dated 1607 and owned by the Kunsthistorisches Museum in Vienna. Such compositions were even reproduced as engravings, although this was not an obvious medium for them. The great Goltzius himself etched a "night" scene of *The Adoration of the Shepherds* on copperplate, which, we are told, was left unfinished at his death in 1617 and published, in the reduced form of four figures grouped around a candle, by his pupil Jacob Matham, who refused to finish it out of respect for his master. The engraving is a masterpiece, and La Tour may have known it.

This was a trend that Lorraine certainly would not have ignored, and the inventories of numerous collections contain references to anonymous "night" scenes that scholars have been quick to attribute to La Tour, often on no factual grounds. Moreover, a *Lamentation over the Dead Christ* in the Hermitage is attributed to Bellange. Here again there is no conclusive proof of authenticity, and Bellange's

After Hans von Achen. *The Lamentation.*
Engraving by R. Sadeler.
Private collection

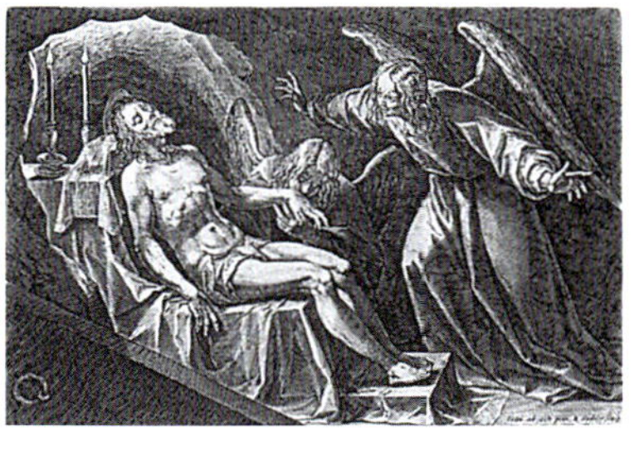

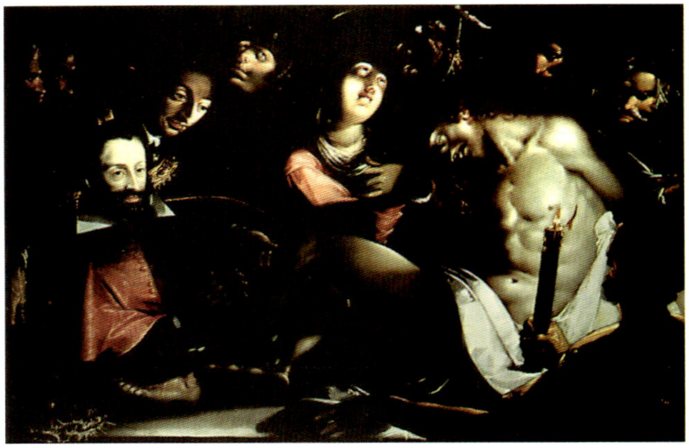

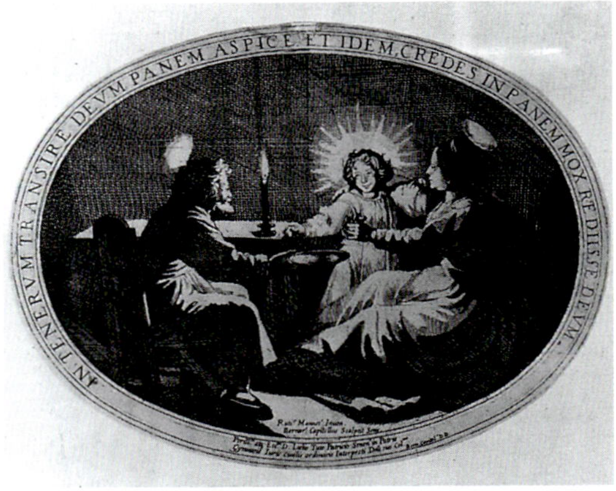

Left:
Jacques de Bellange (copy?).
The Lamentation.
The Hermitage Museum, St. Petersburg

Right:
After Rutilo Manetti. *The Holy Family by Candlelight.* c. 1627. Engraving by Bernardino Capitelli.
Private collection

Gerrit van Honthorst.
Christ Before the High Priest. c. 1617.
National Gallery of Art, London

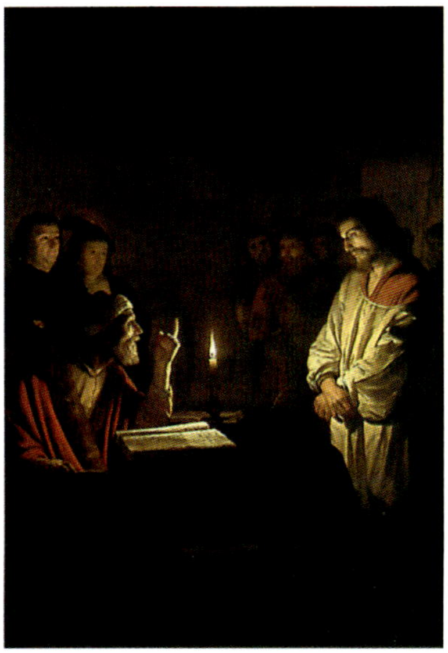

engravings, our chief point of reference, are markedly different in quality, but the original work was probably painted in Lorraine by Bellange himself well before La Tour's "night" scenes.

On the other hand, in Rome, before 1616, La Tour may have seen the Caravaggesque "night" pictures stemming from the great Italian tradition. Once again, however, we have to exercise some caution. The master in this field was Gerardo delle Notte, "Gerard of the Nights," or Gerrit van Honthorst. There is no record of any of these famous "night" scenes, which were to make his name in Italy and internationally, before 1616. The first to have an impact in Rome were *Christ before the High Priest*, now in the National Gallery in London, which appears to date from 1617, the *Infant Christ and St. Joseph* in the monastery of San Silvestro, painted at more or less the same time, and the *Beheading of St. John the Baptist* in Santa Maria della Scala that dates from 1618. Honthorst is said to have been in Rome by 1610 solely on the basis of a reference in the archives to one "Gerardo Fiammingo," a very slender argument given the number of Flemings who passed through Rome and the commonness of the name. Nevertheless, Honthorst, born in 1590, was of the same generation as La Tour. The two painters were probably in Rome together, and La Tour may well have spent time with Honthorst and witnessed the first attempts at "night" scenes that preceded the final successes. Everything is possible; nothing is certain. In terms of style and spirit, we could more readily imagine La Tour consorting and exploring new ideas with the Provençal artist Trophime Bigot, but there is no record of Bigot in Rome before 1620. This means that the Caravaggist "night" tradition proper would have had little to do with the origins of La Tour's "nocturnes." Earlier influences, such as those of the celebrated Correggio and the Bassano family, or conversely, more recent examples not connected with Caravaggism, such as those of Saraceni in Rome and Procaccini in Milan, could have been far more influential. Indeed, it should not be forgotten that La Tour's earliest known works in Lorraine reveal an artist obsessed not with night effects but with exploring daylight to the fullest.

La Tour was, however, to find "night" scenes in Nancy. Saraceni had been interested in the effects of artificial light, and his Lorrainese disciple Jean Le Clerc followed his lead. We know for certain that Le Clerc painted a *Group of Musicians by Night* that met with enough success for the artist himself to engrave it and paint several versions of it. One of these is known in Venice (recently transferred to a collection in Rome) and another in the Munich Pinakothek. Both are clearly originals and show marked variations. According to Pariset, there is a third in Paris. It is not impossible that the engraved version was produced in Rome, that is to say before 1619—there is a *Denial of St. Peter* in the Corsini Gallery in Florence that includes a guardroom scene entirely composed and painted in the same spirit. The Venetian version of the *Group of Musicians* may well date from Le Clerc's stay in Venice, around 1619-1621, and he must have taken up this popular composition again when he was trying to establish himself as an official painter in Nancy around 1622-1625. This painting, and probably several others like it that have since disappeared, seem to have been appreciated and set something of a trend; this is the impression we get from local inventories. We do

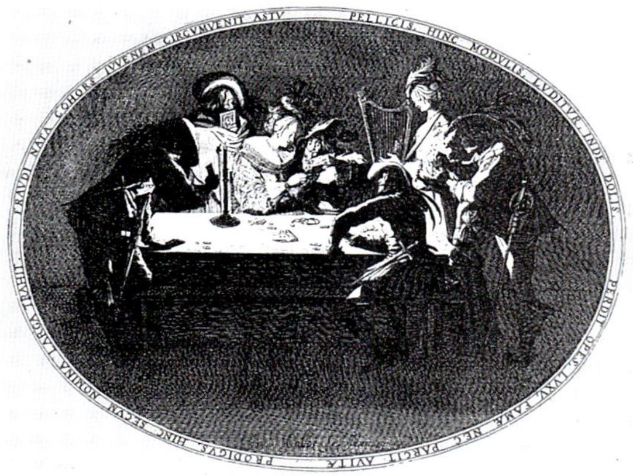

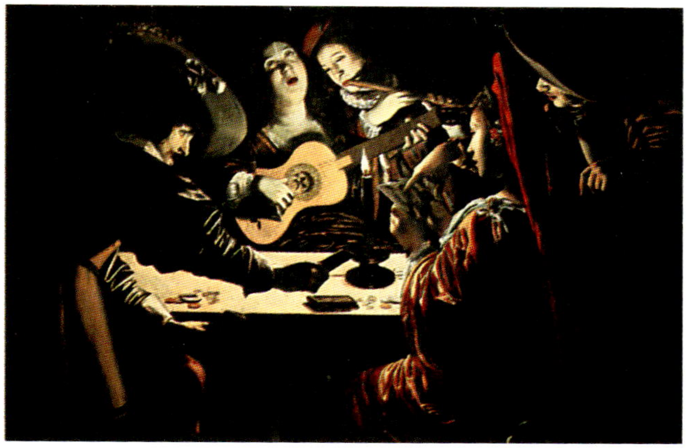

Left:
Jacques Callot, *The Cheat by Candlelight*, also called *Le Brelan*. c. 1628. Etching.
Cabinet des Dessins, Musée des Beaux-Arts, Nancy

Right:
Rutilio Manetti. *Group of Musicians by Candlelight*. c. 1626.
Chigi Saracini Collection, Monte dei Pache di Siena, Sienna

know, moreover, that Callot engraved two "nocturnes," under the credit *fecit* (rather than *Invenit et fecit*), and that the *Brelan* in particular is at least directly inspired by Le Clerc's work and proves a revival of interest in "night" scenes in Lorraine at the time.

There can be no doubt that one way or another La Tour would have known Le Clerc's *Group of Musicians by Night*. Perhaps the success of Le Clerc—the only one of his Nancy rivals whose work La Tour can have respected—prompted him to take up this kind of genre painting. At what point? It could have been around 1625, when Le Clerc was the duke's favorite painter, and northern masters such as Terbrugghen were also beginning to turn out "night" scenes. Alternatively, it might not have been until after Le Clerc's death in 1633, which would make *The Payment of Dues* later. Indeed, the date on the canvas has been read by some as 1634 rather than 1641. Let us simply venture to say that the steep angle of view and the still life formed by the open register, writing case, purse, and pile of gold point to an early work, better situated in the 1620s (Pierre Rosenberg and François Macé de Lepinay, as I have indicated, place the picture at the very head of their catalogue), but are not inconsistent with a date around 1630. We are on shaky ground here, and it is always dangerous to be too specific: what seems likely is not necessarily true.

There are two other points worth noting. The first is that the painting is signed, and, as we have seen, La Tour probably did not start signing his work until about 1630. The second, and to my mind most telling, point is that the Lvov painting has a complex composition in which six figures are distributed over several planes and drawn together in a dramatic scene: this is a far cry from the isolated and static figures that dominated the painter's work throughout the 1620s.

Moreover, this painting cannot have been La Tour's first attempt at the "nocturne": he has clearly mastered most of the inherent problems it poses and displays a style that cannot be confused with any other, be it the great Mannerist tradition, the Utrecht School, or, indeed, Saraceni and Le Clerc. The unity of the composition, clearly centered on the twin patches of light formed by the open register, the subtle atmosphere, and the soberness of the mood are all peculiar to La Tour. There were undoubtedly other "night" scenes before this one. La Tour quite possibly perfected the technique of painting small half-length figures such as the *Boy Blowing on a Charcoal Stick*, the *Smoker*, and the *Girl Blowing on a Brazier* rather early. The versions that have survived all appear to be relatively late, but they are surely the culmination of a whole line of paintings that are now lost. Pariset has pointed out that listed next to a hurdy-gurdy player in the November 1636 posthumous inventory of the collection of Nicolas-François Regnault, first gentleman of the bedchamber to Duke François II, is a "figure blowing on a light," and although there is no mention of any painter's name, he believes this was very probably by La Tour. This would be proof, if proof were needed, that La Tour painted his first "nocturnes" before 1638, before the fire at Lunéville, and before he came into close contact with Paris. All the same, the 1630s seem to have been mainly devoted to the daylight paintings, which reached their height of perfection during this period.

THE GREAT DAYLIGHT MASTERPIECES

The *St. Thomas* acquired by the Louvre in 1988 through a public subscription campaign is a very fine example of La Tour's daylight pictures. The work follows in the line of Apostle figures that started with the Albi series. La Tour opts here for the same half-length presentation as Albi and virtually the same dimensions. This time, however, an impressive Latin signature is prominently placed against the light part of the background: *Georgius de la Tour fecit.* With time, the lines drawn in with a ruler to ensure a perfect script have become visible, thus proving the attention that the artist gave it. The style of the painting has evolved considerably. Much more air circulates around the figure; the heightened contrast between light and shade is pursued in the sharp opposition of warm and cold colors, no longer obtained with splashes of red but through the effect of an almost lemon yellow set against slate blues—a rare combination that only works for great masters like Vermeer or Donato Creti. The composition is more skillful and solid than ever, with the diagonals meeting to form a St. Andrew's cross, and the draftsmanship is increasingly accomplished: the lines on the saint's wrist and the leaves of the old book are picked out with the tip of a brush that gently outlines the forms without imprisoning them.

La Tour's style remains fundamentally realist, however, in the direct line of Caravaggism. St. Thomas is a big, old, timeworn fellow with a hooked nose and missing teeth. Here again La Tour divorces himself from those painters who want the Apostles to partake of Christ's beauty as they partook of his wisdom. He imagines them instead in all their human reality, marked by the scars of age, years of lowly labor, and indulgence in all manner of sins prior to their enlightenment. Nowhere is this more obvious than with Thomas the sceptic, who will only believe what he has seen, but then acknowledges Christ as "my Lord and my God," and goes off to spread the Gospel among peoples across the world, and seek the fatal lance that will end his life in India. La Tour must have seen, in print form at least, a great many St. Thomases touching the wound in the side of the resurrected Christ, most notably the version by Salviati, which was then in Lyon and was reckoned to be one of the most celebrated paintings in France, and that of Caravaggio, in the very famous Giustiniani Collection in Rome. Not one of them, however, depicted the doubting Apostle as La Tour does. He makes him a dry-bearded, bald-headed tough old man who does not let himself be taken in, even by God, and who will only believe in Christ after he has placed "his finger in the wound." Thereafter, his squinting little eyes will see only the truth, even if this leads him to his death. He has a book in one hand, a spear in the other; his unseeing glance knows the right way. Such is the mystery of spiritual certitude.

A similar sense imbues the two versions of *St. Jerome* in Grenoble and Stockholm, which also continue the series of large single figures, but with a very different meaning. This time the subject is no longer St. Jerome in his "study," translating the Bible into Latin and preparing the Vulgate that was to remain the sacred text par excellence for centuries to come, but St. Jerome the penitent. This theme was quite old—both Leonardo da Vinci and Lorenzo Lotto have left impressive renderings of it. The seventeenth century brought an unexpected revival. St. Jerome offered a kind of masculine pendant to the repentant Magdalen, with youthfulness and love now replaced by age and erudition. Jerome is not about to expiate the sins of the flesh, but those of the mind: the angel in his vision has reproached him for being more "Ciceronian" than Christian. The fact that the painters of the seventeenth century often paused to evoke the vision or describe the penitence, showing the man of letters humbling himself with a stone before the crucifix, amply bespeaks the anxiety of a clergy caught between the exercise of the mind and devotion. If La Tour favored the second theme, it is perhaps because it excluded the presence of these angels that, like the overly anecdotal lion, he would not let himself represent. But it may also be that the contrast between the decrepit body and the relentless requirements of will provided him with the most striking image of ascetism.

The Grenoble version, the better preserved and the more brilliant of the two, comes from the famous abbey of Saint-Antoine-en-Viennois. Tribout de Morembert has suggested, though without producing any hard evidence, that it was painted for the Antonite monastery in Pont-à-Mousson, which was dissolved in 1680 with the result that its holdings passed to the mother order in the Viennois. Never was La

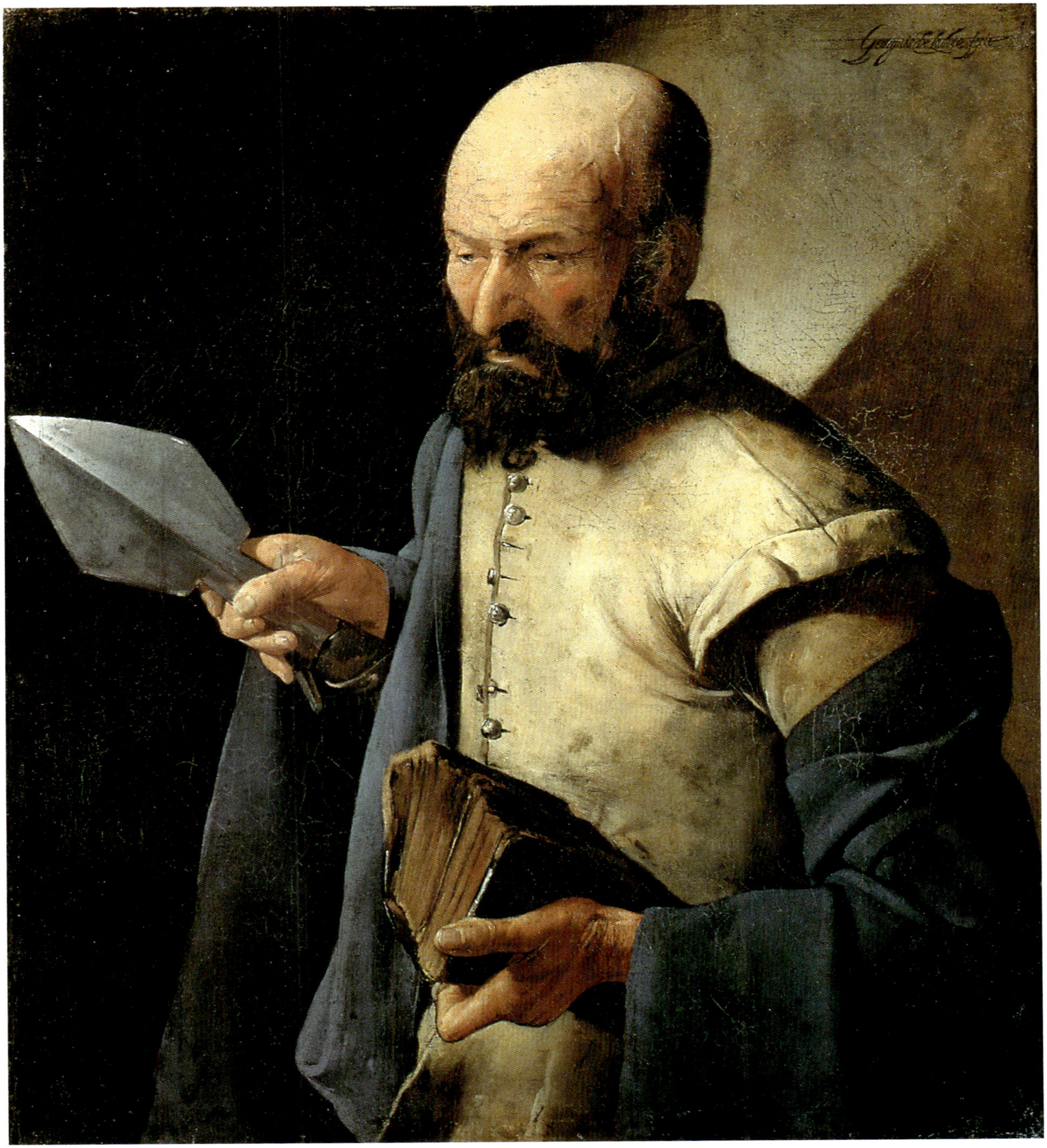

St. Thomas.
Musée du Louvre, Paris

pp. 122-123:
St. Thomas, details.

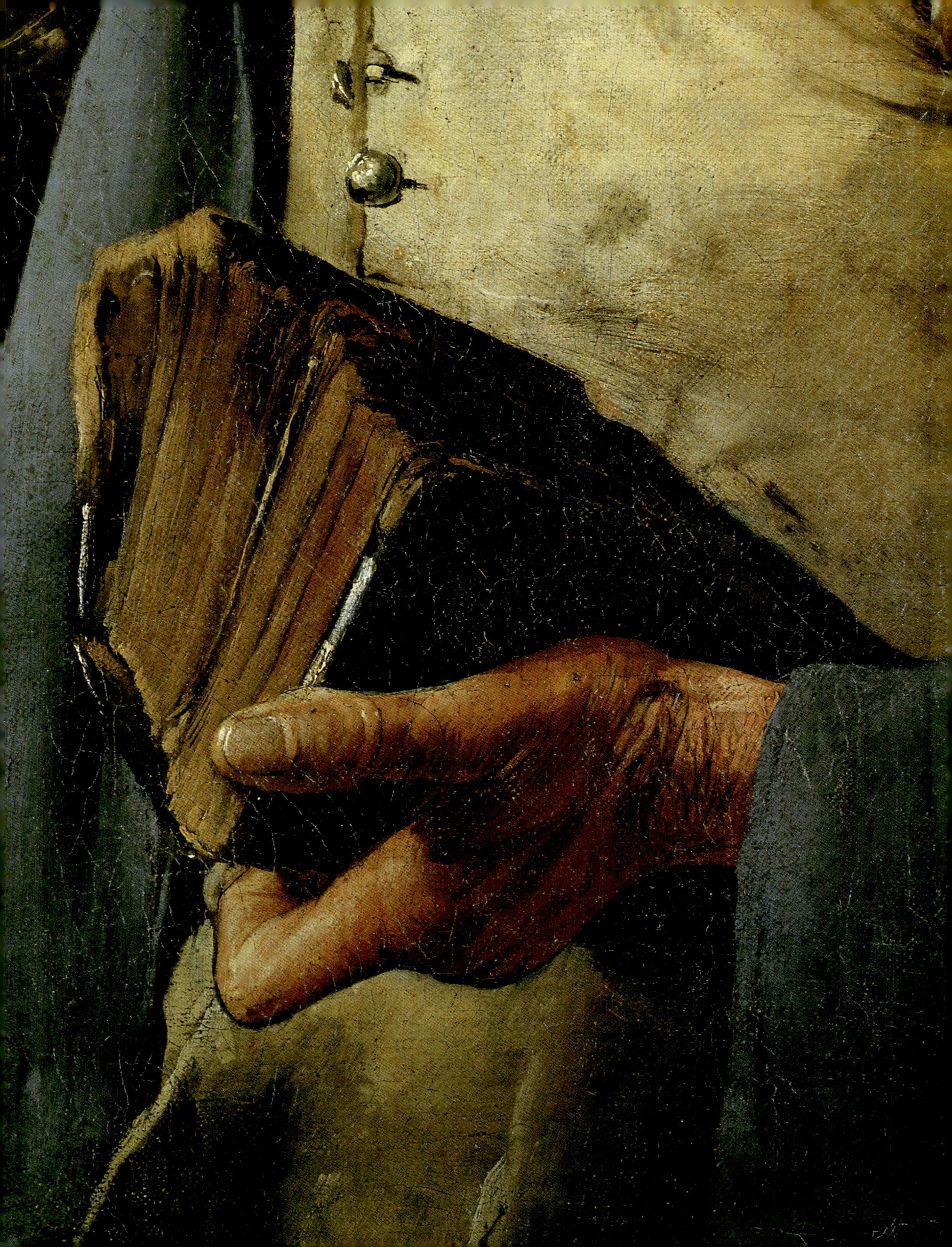

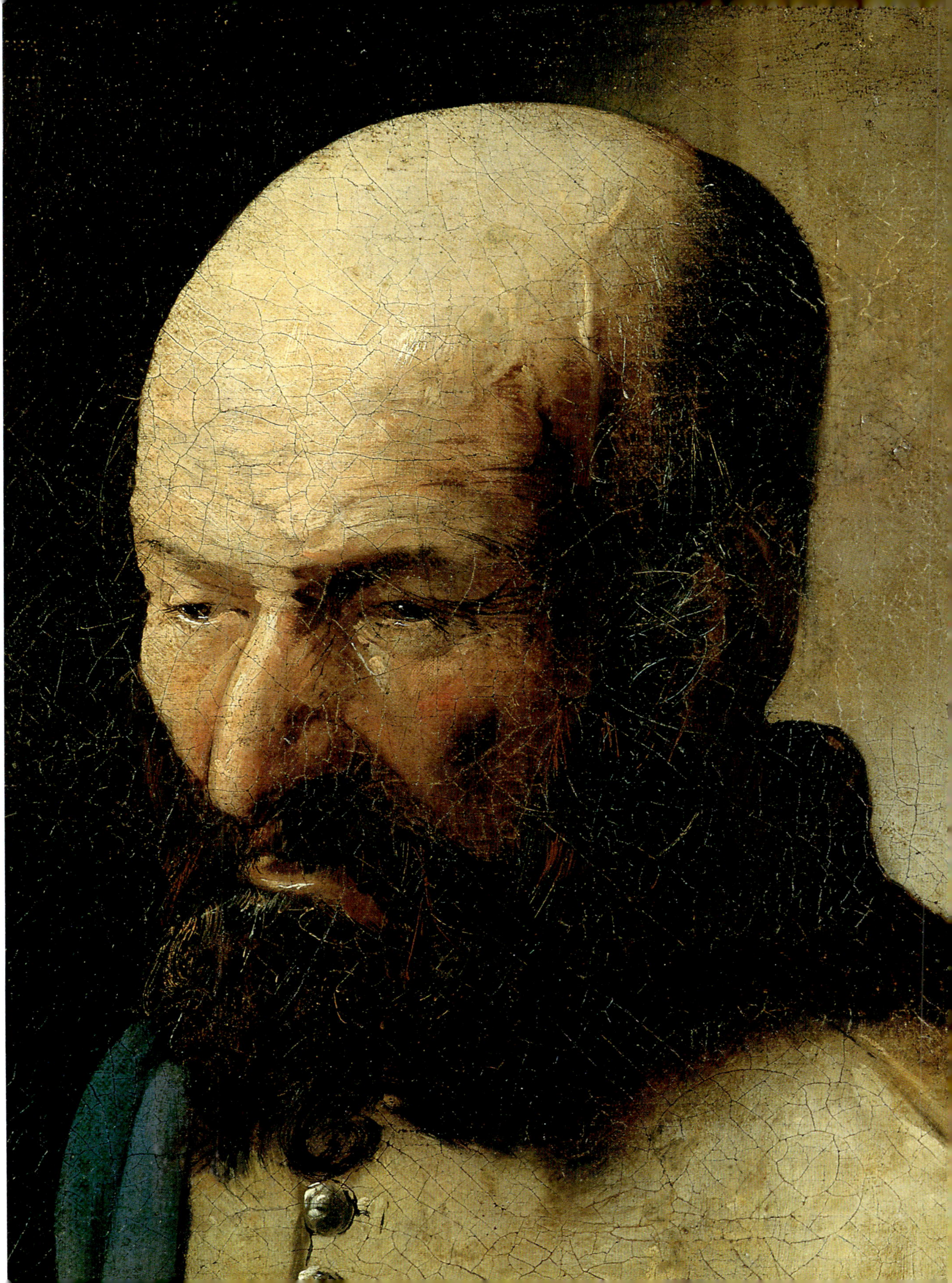

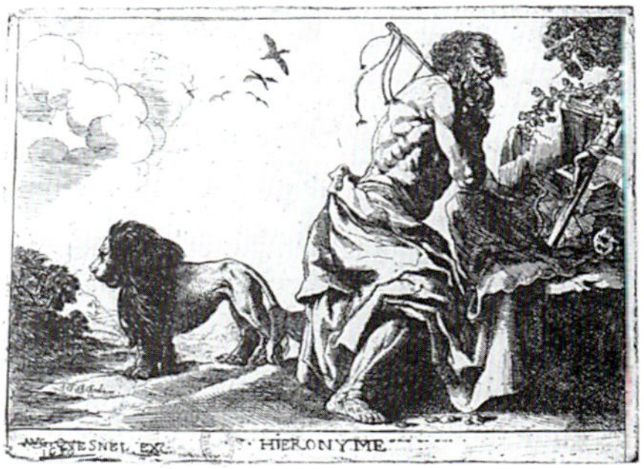

Pierre Brébiette.
St. Jerome. Etching.
Private collection

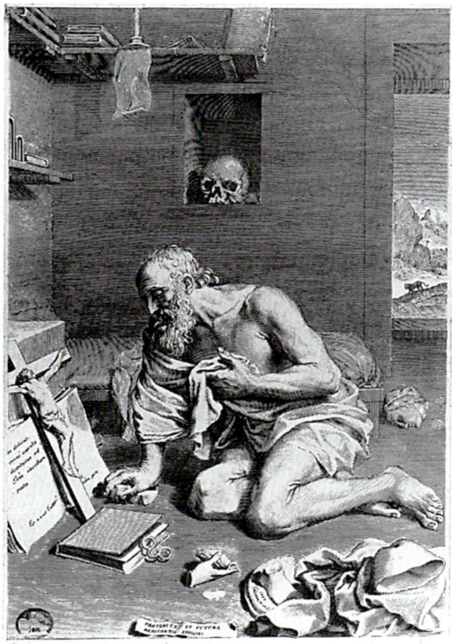

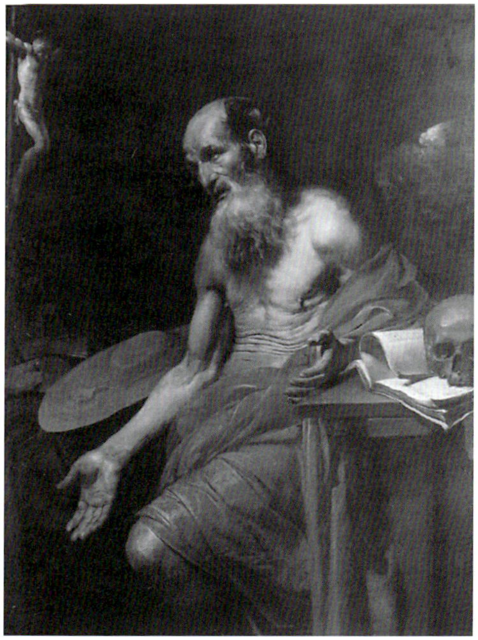

Left:
Claude Mellan.
St. Jerome. Engraving.
Private Collection

Right:
Attributed to Jean Valentin (also called Jean de Boulogne or Moïse Valentin). *St. Jerome.*
Jewett Arts Center, Wellesley, Massachusetts

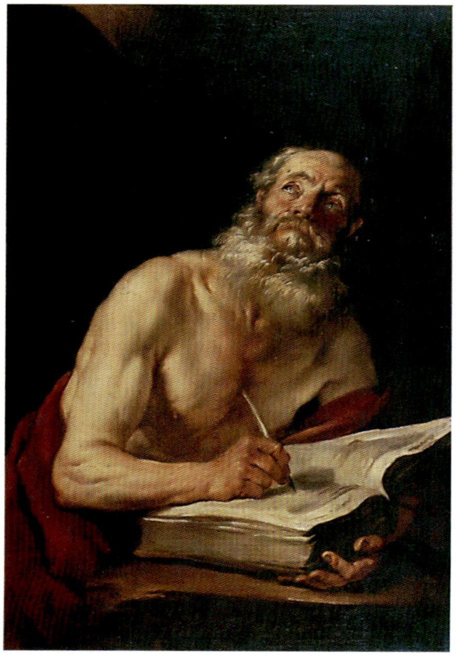

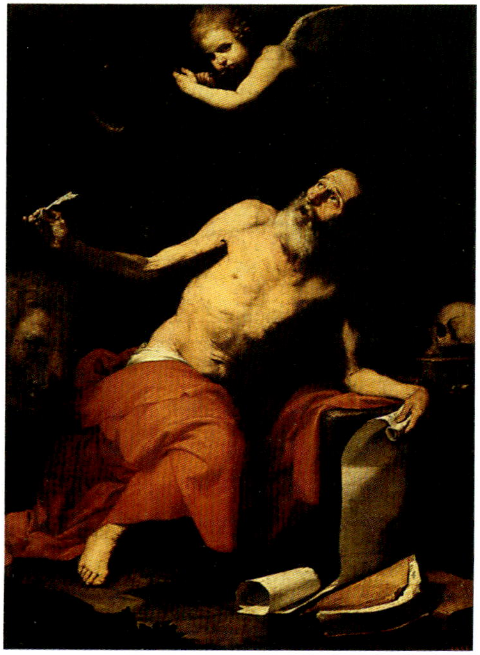

Left:
Jacques Blanchard.
St. Jerome Writing.
Musée des Beaux-Arts, Grenoble

Right:
Giuseppe de Ribera.
St. Jerome and the Angel of Judgement.
The Hermitage Museum, St. Petersburg

Facing page:
St. Jerome.
Musée des Beaux-Arts, Grenoble

pp. 126-127: *St. Jerome,* details.

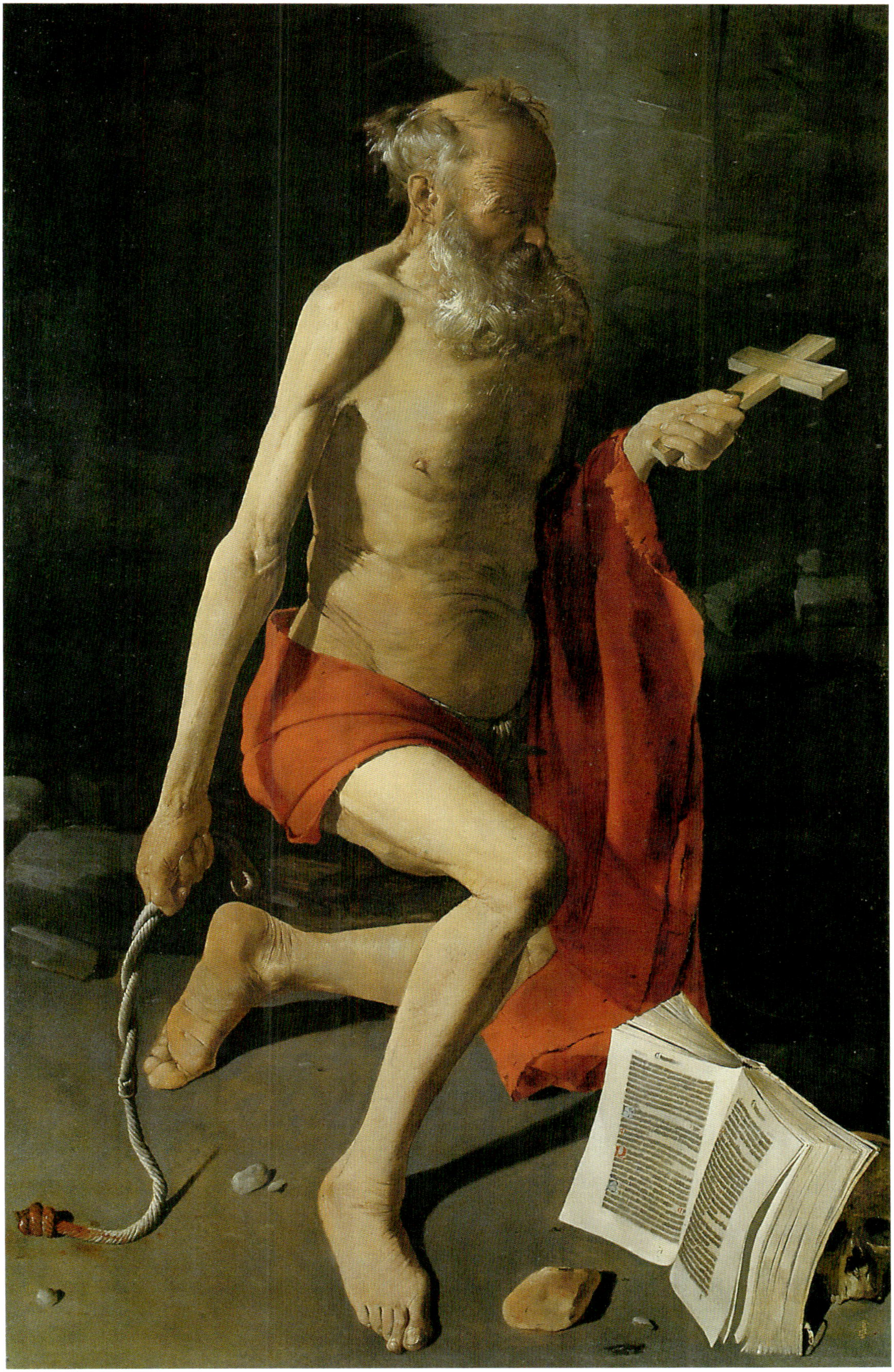

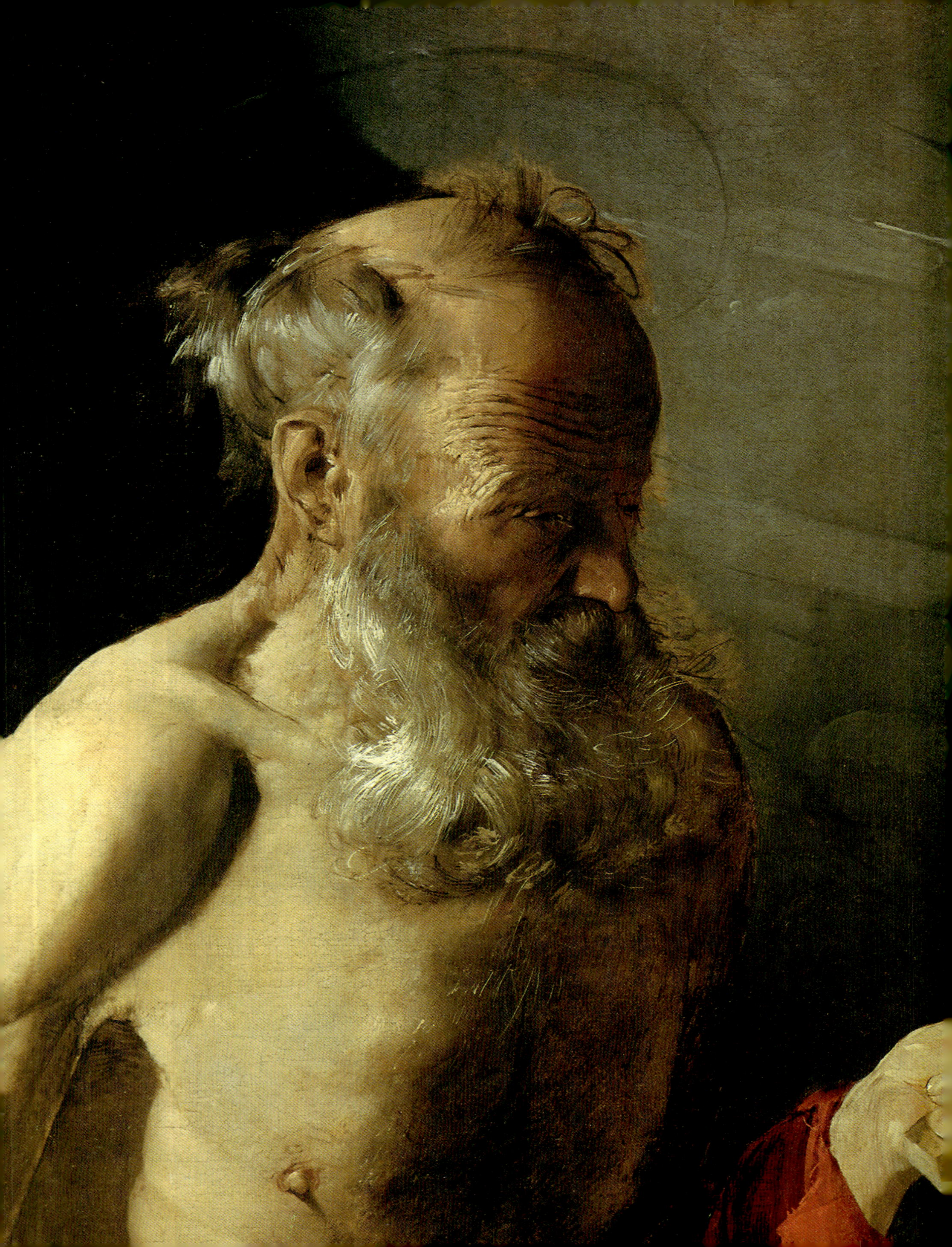

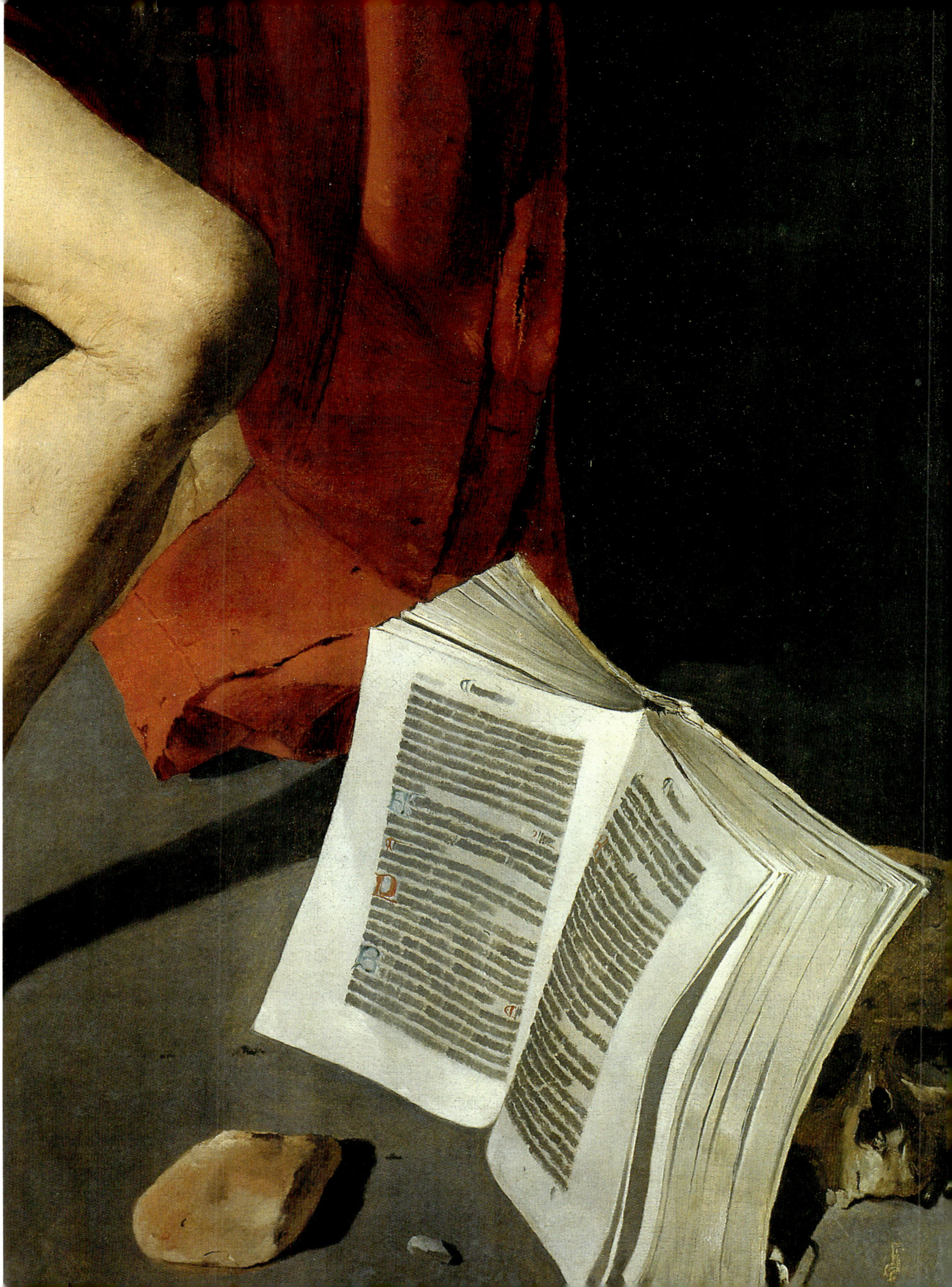

Tour's hand surer, more subtle, and more expressive. The focus of his attention this time is a nude, which he treats with the most remarkable skill. There are only five surviving nudes by La Tour: these two figures of *St. Jerome*, the two of *St. Sebastian*, and the single one of *Job Mocked by His Wife*—in other words, three bodies of old men with bloated flesh and two much younger, nearly adolescents, but plunged into the darkness of night. La Tour was a past master of the nude in his daylight canvases, and what wonders might we not have if only he had painted his St. Sebastians, or a St. Agnes or a Venus, in the same clear light as his *St. Jerome*. In fact, did he ever paint any? Perhaps he ran up against the Church's traditional mistrust of nudes, especially female nudes, and was prevented by the narrow little world of Lunéville, where everything was known and talked about, from doing what he would doubtless have had free rein to do in the capital. Or perhaps it was the prudishness of a later generation that destroyed a whole facet of La Tour's work. It is hard to think that La Tour should have contented himself with celebrating beautiful young faces and never have applied his consummate skill as a daylight painter to a beautiful young body.

La Tour's representation of *St. Jerome* is once again uncompromising in its realism. He may possibly have gone even further in his representation of the ugliness of the old Gypsy woman's face in *The Fortune Teller*. His brush analyzes every detail of an entire body with clinical precision. The old man's distended stomach, the twisted feet, the flaccid thigh, and the coarse, wrinkled skin all expose the decay of the flesh in much the same way that the earlier *transis* effigies of Lorraine sculpture did. Here, however, there is even more force because the decay is living, and the stunning brushwork evokes it right down to the white hairs on the old man's chest and the callus on his big toe. Neither Guido Reni nor Caravaggio ever went so far, and, by comparison, Ribera seems trammeled by studio convention and Blanchard limited by his habitual gentleness. La Tour, on the other hand, seems to take pleasure in this description. With unsurpassed speed and freedom, his brush superimposes a precise pattern on barely defined areas of local color. Hair and beard are suggested by short, sharp strokes that contribute as much to the rhythm of the picture as to the saint's appearance, while the wrinkled skin is conjured up with a wavering line. We may not have a single drawing by La Tour, but here he reveals himself to be a brilliant draftsman.

Nonetheless, by its very nature, this refinement precludes expressionism and even the desire, however moral, to insist on ugliness. Expressionism inevitably makes use of brutal means, while La Tour's brush uplifts everything it touches. St. Jerome invites neither ridicule nor pity. His worn body unashamedly discloses its ruinous state: the ruin is noble, the prelate's dignity and the powerful authority of the church father intact. The movement is concentrated in the two emphatic diagonals of the old man's arm and leg, supported by a great sweep of purple conjuring up an energy that is undiminished, a spiritual force capable of scorning and mortifying the sinful flesh. There is a stoicism in La Tour's St. Jerome that was never before so apparent.

However brutal the subject matter, the painting must have been well received, because we have a second version of it, which the Stockholm museum is lucky enough to own. This second version is less tragic, with the saint's dignity more noble and more conscious, owing to slight changes in the proportions and the introduction of handsome verticals on either side of the figure to frame his body and help slow down its movement. At the same time, it is all the more striking because of the raw white of the flagellant saint's undergarment, juxtaposed with the cloth thrown over one arm and the huge three-tasseled hat that appears on his other side, both of them so compelling in their pure scarlet color and precise geometry that there must be an underlying intent. Such a forceful allusion to St. Jerome's status as prelate can only be to make the contrast with the humility of his flesh. As indicated above, we believe that this version was painted for Cardinal Richelieu, and that it corresponds to the painting of this subject listed in the 1643 inventory of his collection. La Tour could well have given it to him around 1638-1639 at the same time that he presented the *St. Sebastian* to Louis XIII. It was common practice for someone seeking favor with the court to present a gift to the minister and to the king simultaneously, and occasionally even to present the minister with a gift first in order to obtain the permission for the gift to the king. The *St. Jerome* could have made its appearance in the court slightly before the *St. Sebastian*. Poussin was faced with comparable problems around the same time and

Right:
St. Jerome.
Nationalmuseum, Stockholm

pp. 130-131: *St. Jerome*, details.

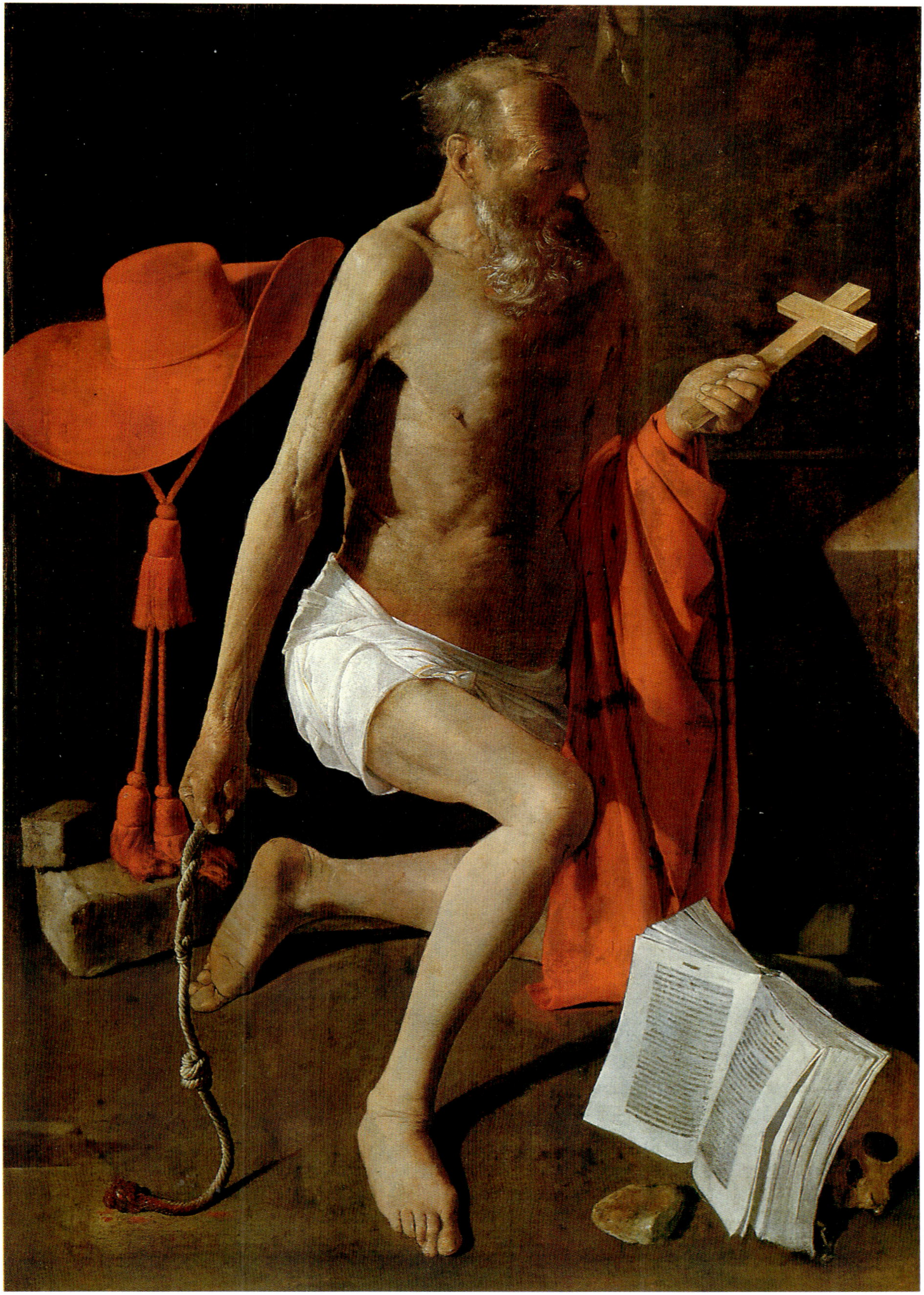

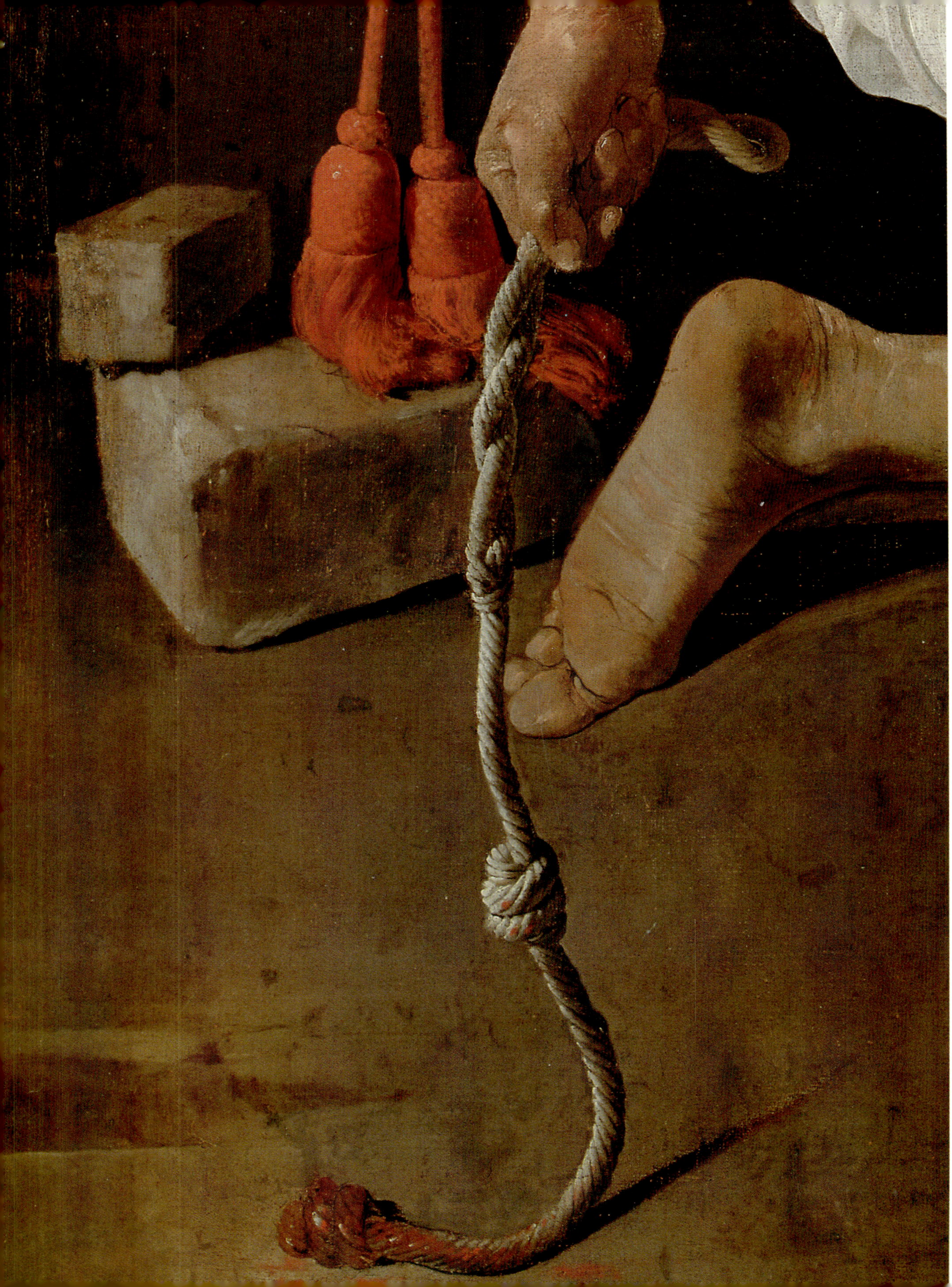

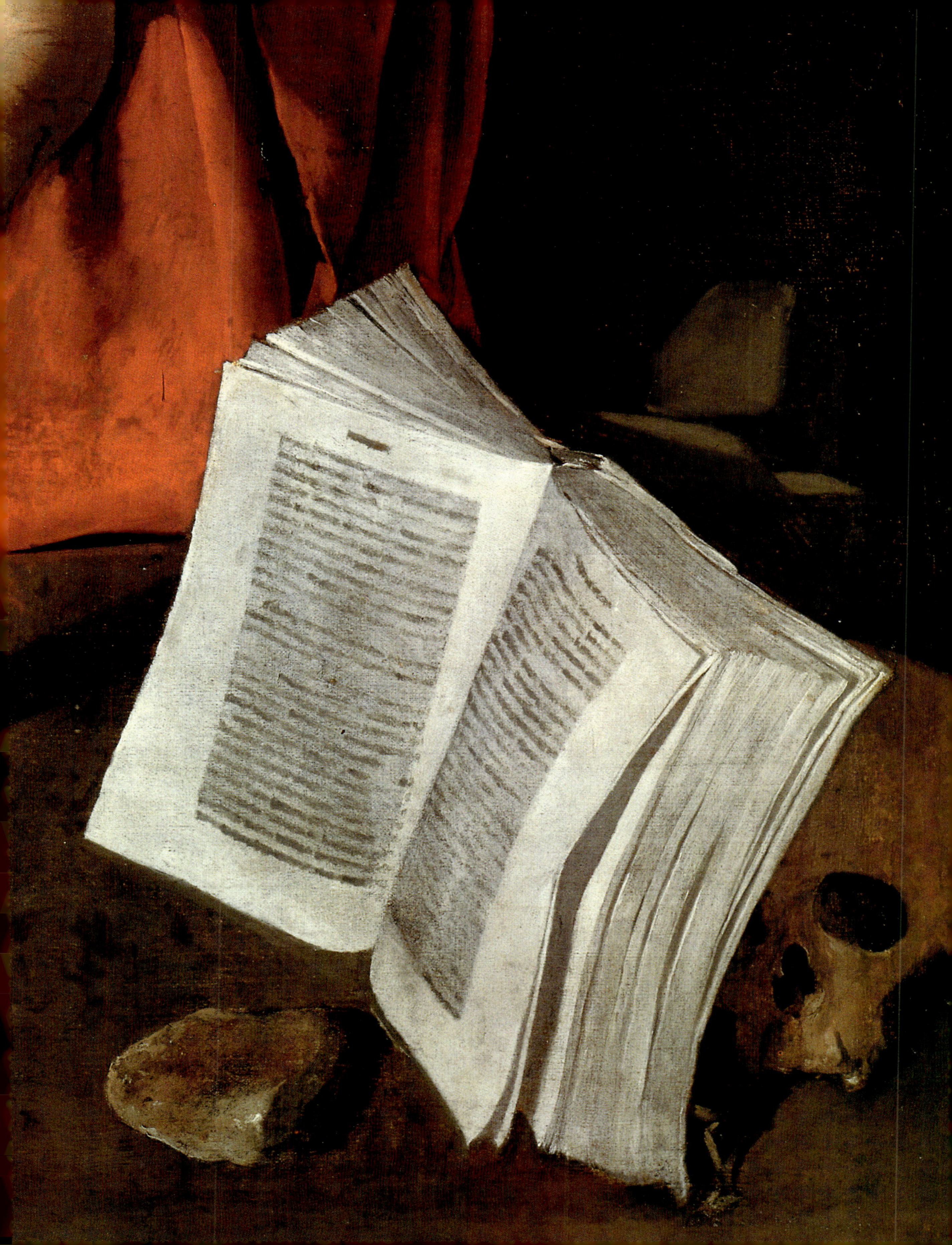

also had to know how to handle the delicate sensibilities of his two great patrons.

La Tour seems to go into a completely different register with *The Cheat*, a genre scene that appears to be completely secular. In fact, although the subject is different and considerably more engaging, the message turns out to be rather similar.

Here again two versions survive, probably the remains of a whole series that may have been begun fairly early. The version now in the Kimbell Art Museum in Fort Worth had until recent years remained virtually unknown in an old Geneva collection, while the version bought by the Louvre in 1972 had been discovered in Paris around 1926 by Pierre Landry. The artist has amused himself in differentiating them, not only by a number of variations but by one decisive detail: in the first version, the card the cheat draws from his belt is an ace of clubs, and in the second it is an ace of diamonds. This can only be a deliberate gesture, and one that illustrates the extent to which La Tour consciously played on the idea of the series.

Card players in general, and cheats in particular, were popular subjects with the Caravaggists; they feature in the work of a number of artists of the time, beginning with the impressive Valentin now in Dresden. Here, however, the subject is subtly interwoven with what to all appearances is the story of the Prodigal Son with the harlot. A frequent theme in priestly sermons at the time, it provided an excellent way of giving moral justification to images that might otherwise seem rather too seductive.

Tobacco, wine, women and gambling,
Our souls with pleasure delight,

runs the caption under an engraving published in Paris by Langlois. Tobacco is not seen here, but the other three perils of youth are clearly in evidence:

Wine, women and gambling,
Our souls destroy,

and the naïveté of the gullible young man in all his finery is made sufficiently obvious that there can be no doubt about the message. It is unlike any of Valentin's brutal and melancholy genre scenes, or the work of the great Roman Caravaggists. We have to look to the northern artists to find the woman in such a central position as the object of desire and instrument of ruin. Closer at hand, in Nancy, even Bellange's Italian scenes and Le Clerc's *Group of Musicians* similarly place the woman in the center of gatherings whose intentions were not always of an exemplary sobriety.

This moralizing painting also has its dangerous charms. There are quite stunning details, such as the three hands surrounding the wicker-bound bottle, the glass of wine, and the silver and enamel bracelet. The cheat himself has a slightly shifty appeal, with his thin mouth half hidden under a fine sandy-colored moustache, and

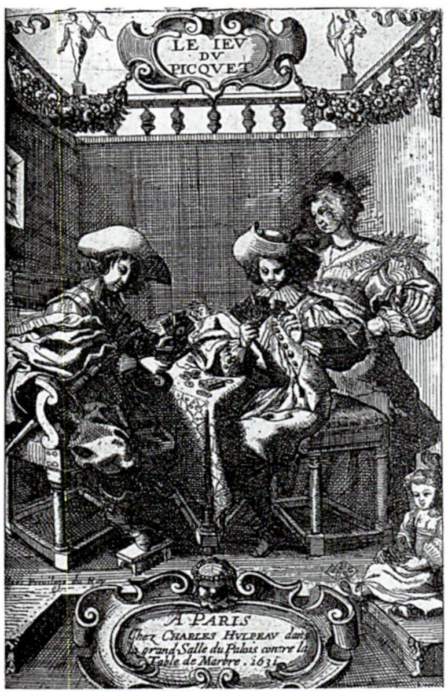

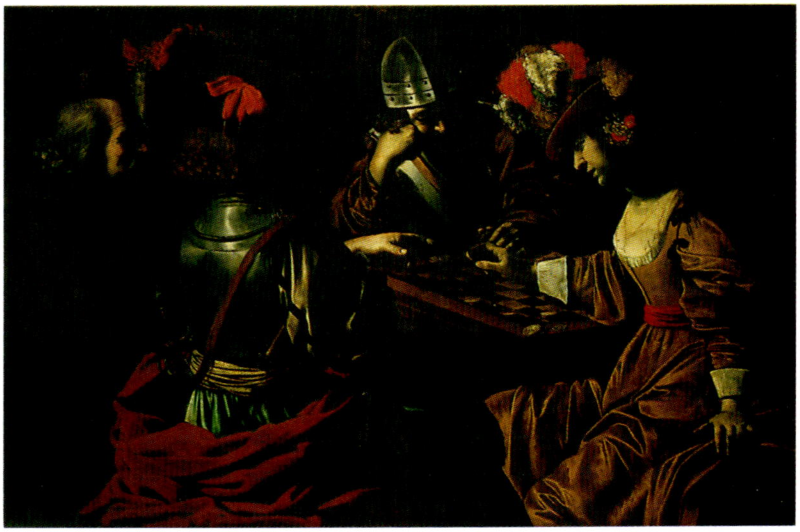

GAMBLING AND WOMEN

Above: Pierre Brébiette.
Frontispiece for *The Game of Piquet*.
Cabinet des Estampes, Bibliothèque Nationale, Paris

Right: Rutilio Manetti.
The Game of Checkers. 1631.
Chigi Saracini Collection, Monte dei Pache di Siena, Sienna

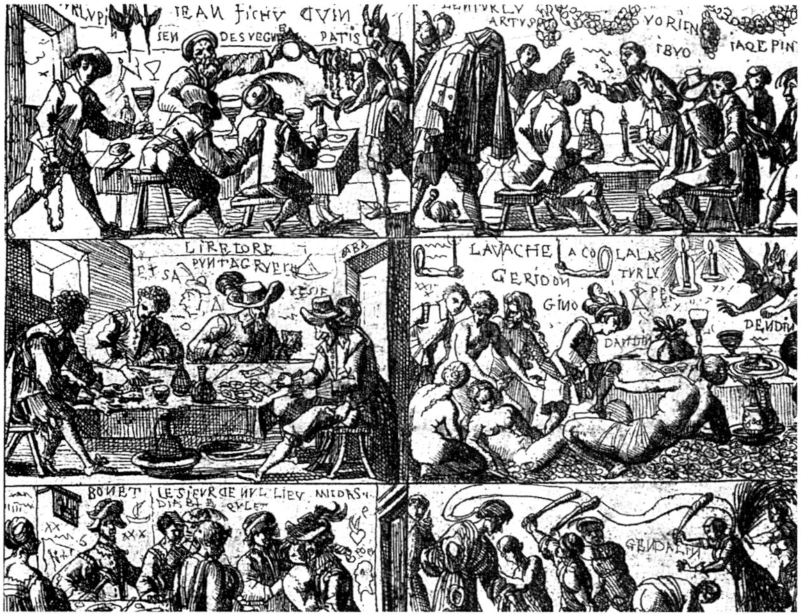

DEBAUCHERY

Left:
Pierre Brébiette. *The Life of Geiton*, detail. Etching.

Below:
Jacques Callot. *The Prodigal Son*. 1635.
From left to right: *Frontispiece; The Prodigal Son Squanders his Fortune; The Prodigal Son is Ruined*. Etchings.
Cabinet des Estampes, Bibliothèque Nationale, Paris

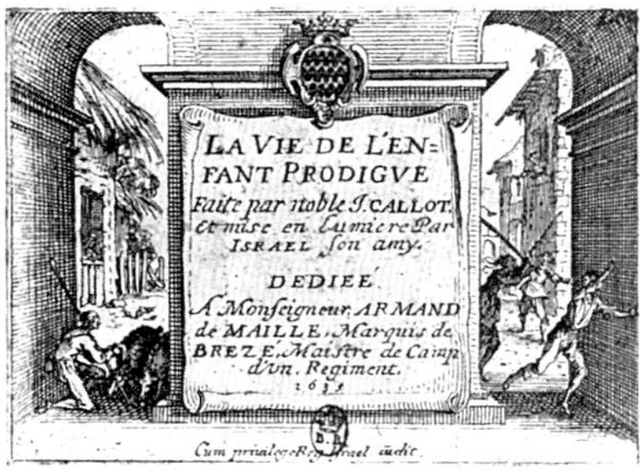

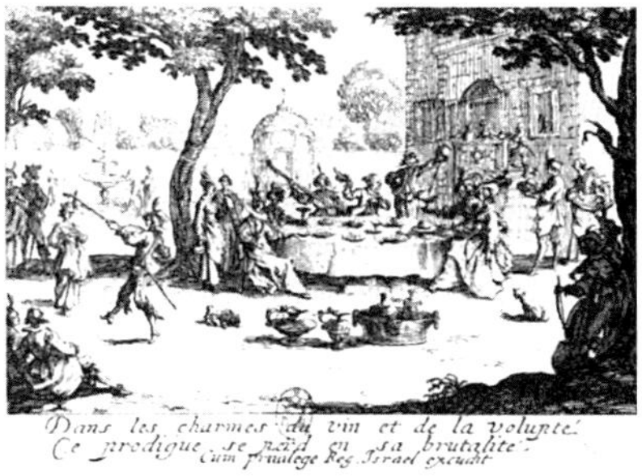

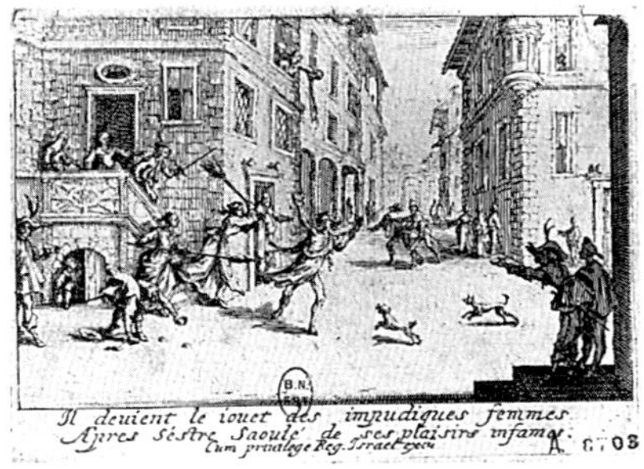

his half-veiled glance to the spectator like a cat waiting for the kill. The whole scene is painted in pinks and reds that stand out against a background of darker tones ranging from mustard yellow to tobacco brown, with brighter patches of pure white spread over the cards, the great batiste sleeve embroidered with black and gold, the pearls, and the reflection on the glass.

The same brilliant light is manifest in *The Fortune Teller* in the Metropolitan Museum, a work that has become almost legendary. First there was its discovery in a castle in the provinces, then the deft manner in which it was spirited out of the country beyond the reach of French museums, and the ensuing scandal and questions it provoked in the French Chamber of Deputies. Then, an expert on antique textiles, whose knowledge proved to be less than perfect, began to cast doubts on its authenticity, followed by a scholar who had earlier co-authored a book with Benedict Nicolson presenting the work as the painter's masterpiece and who now claimed on American television that it was a recent fake. In the space of a few years the canvas has acquired a complex history, quite mediocre and futile in the end, but none of these incidents has been able to undermine its exceptional beauty. By going on so interminably about its authenticity, which is obvious at a glance, and which Pierre Rosenberg has now proven with historical evidence, critics have tended to overlook the painting's one real defect: the narrow strip about six centimeters wide that has been added to the top, and more important, a much broader strip about twenty-five to thirty centimeters wide that must have been destroyed on the left side, upsetting the balance and the skillful geometry that are present in all of La Tour's compositions. This work must have had virtually the same proportions as *The Cheat with the Ace of Clubs* (96 x 155 cm, compared with the 102 x 123 cm it now measures), with the young man almost in the center of the composition. However, the brilliance of the color, the beauty of the figures, and the skill manifest in every detail are such that we forget this mutilation.

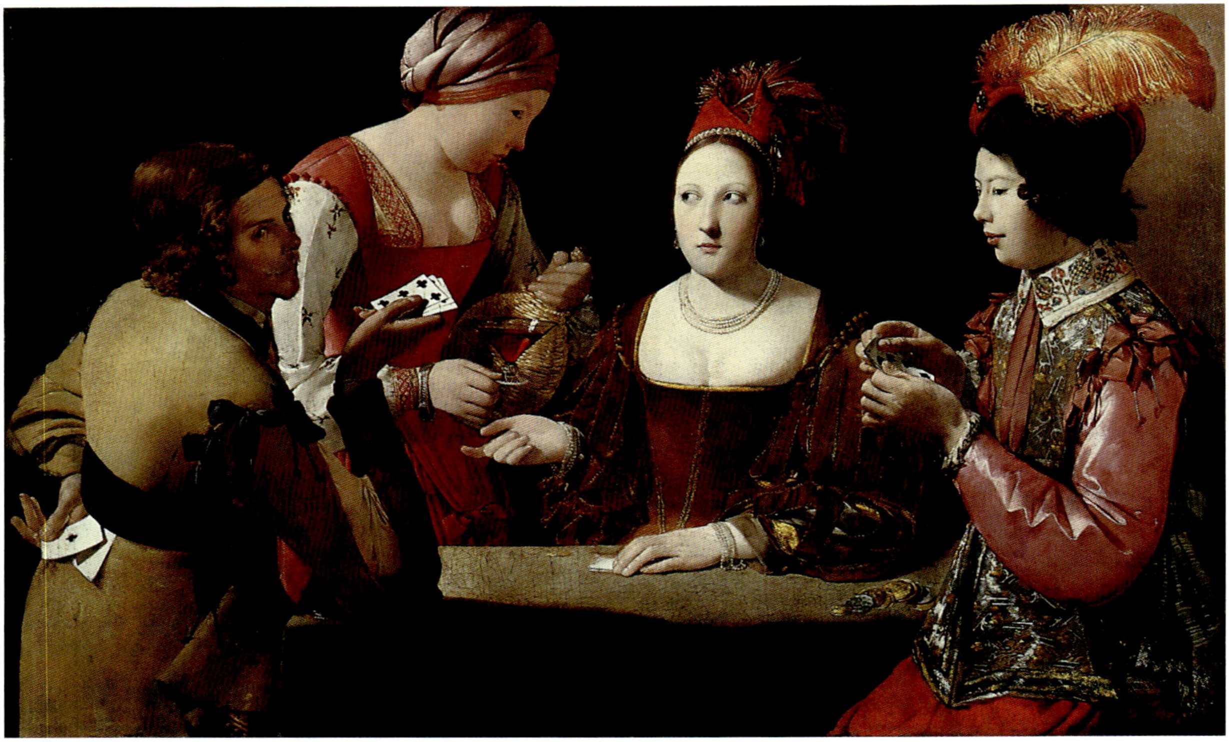

The Cheat with the Ace of Clubs.
Kimbell Art Museum, Fort Worth, Texas

WINE AND TOBACCO

By all accounts La Tour had a taste for good wine. His hometown of Vic boasted vineyards famous throughout Lorraine, and we know that his family had several plantations of their own. The municipal accounts for 1649, the year in which La Ferté asked the town for a work by its famous painter, record the sum of *"four francs paid to sire Joly for the supply of three pots of wine to have a drink at the house of sire La Tour painter when the contract was signed with him for the said picture of Saint Sebastian as a gift for Monsieur the Governor of Nancy. . . .* " Like the brothers Le Nain, who were also from a wine-growing area, La Tour knew how to capture the ruby-colored wine in all its glory. But in this painting, instead of being associated with tranquility and repose or a jovial family occasion, wine becomes a symbol of pleasure, conjuring up taverns, gambling, and every kind of dissipation and debauchery.

Left:
Anonymous. *The Drinker with a Snuffbox* (formerly attributed to Georges de La Tour).
Musée des Beaux-Arts, Besançon

Anonymous German artist. *A Drinker and a Smoker.* Engraving.

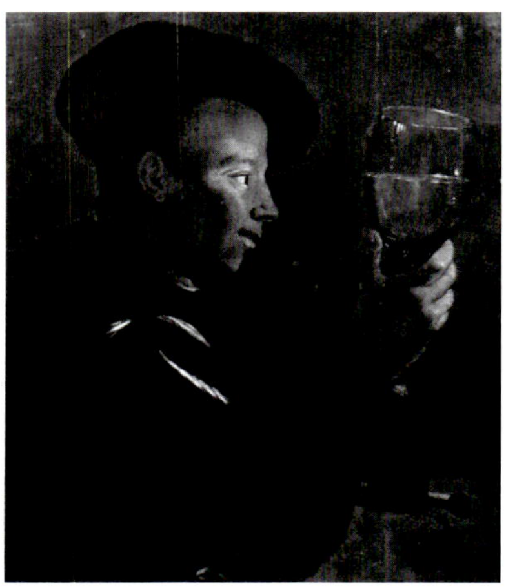

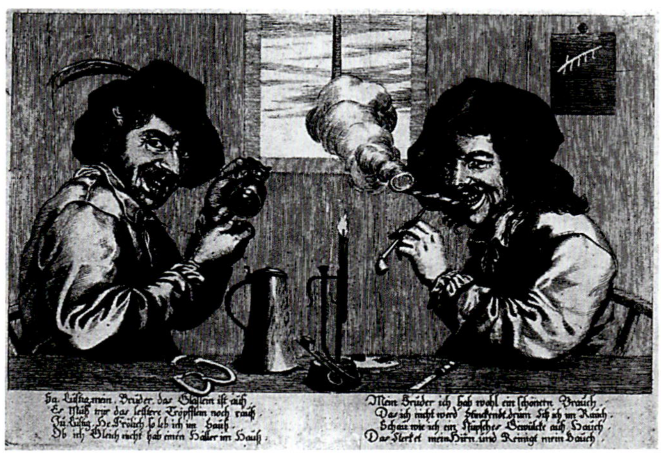

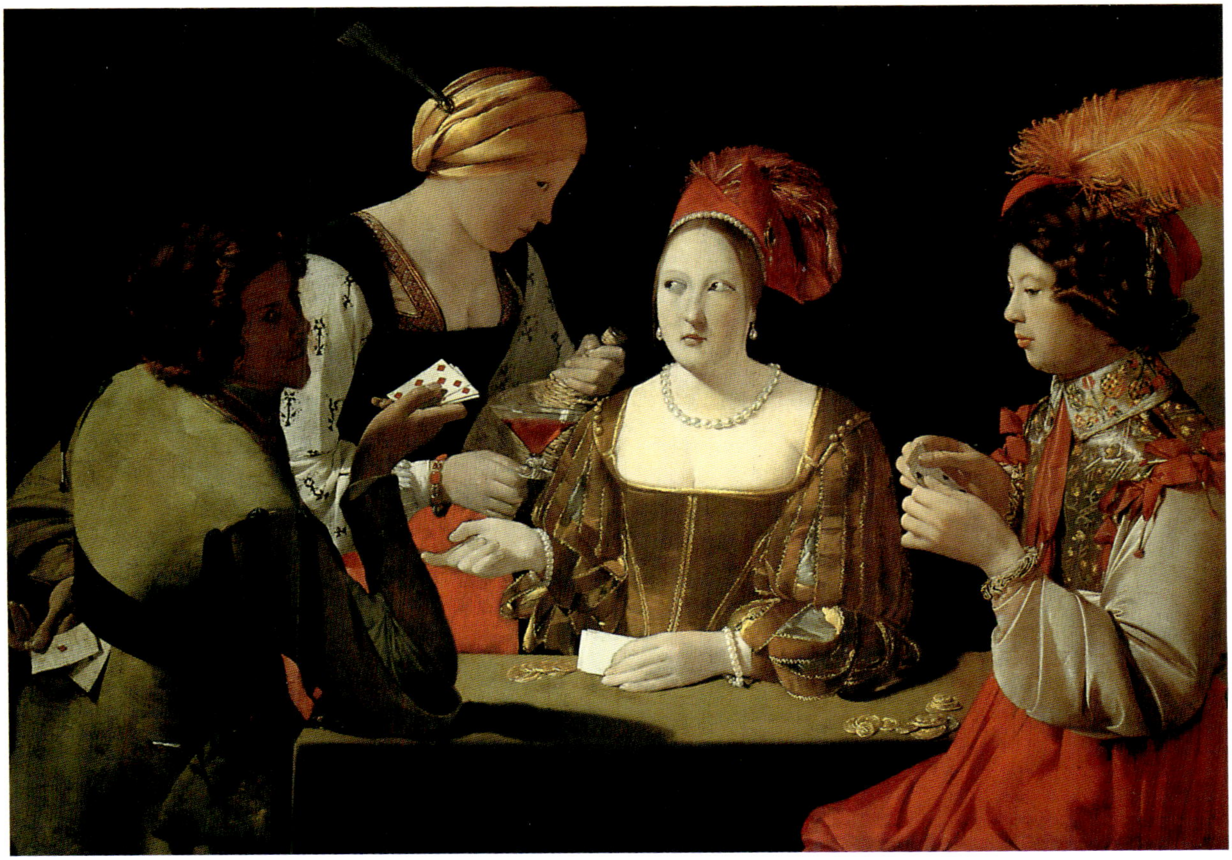

CHEATING AT CARDS

Cards were one of the chief scourges of the seventeenth century. They went hand in hand, of course, with excessive gambling, and led often to ruin and disgrace, and sometimes to crime. They were to be found on every level of society: people played in the very presence of the king as they did in the lowest of taverns. People played and people cheated: even the most eminent figures were not always entirely above suspicion. Some cheated out of desperation; for others, however, it was a way of life. Caravaggio tackled the theme of the cheat, like that of the Fortune Teller, in a famous painting then in the Barberini Collection, which was well known to painters at the time. The theme was taken up around 1615-1625 by the French painters then in Rome, such as Valentin and Régnier, who produced a whole series of paintings around it, each one varying the pattern of looks and hands, as well as the psychological interaction between the characters.

The Cheat with the Ace of Diamonds.
Musée du Louvre, Paris

Left:
Jean Valentin (also called Jean de Boulogne or Moïse Valentin). *The Cheat.*
Gemäldegalerie, Dresden

Right:
Nicolas Régnier (attributed to). *The Cheat.*
Galleria Academia, Venice

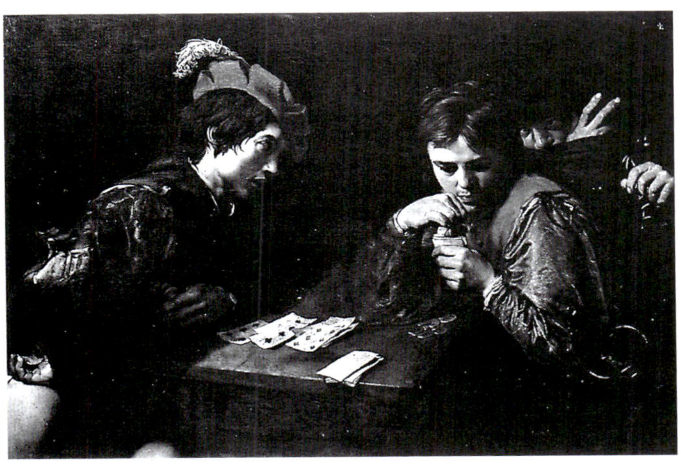

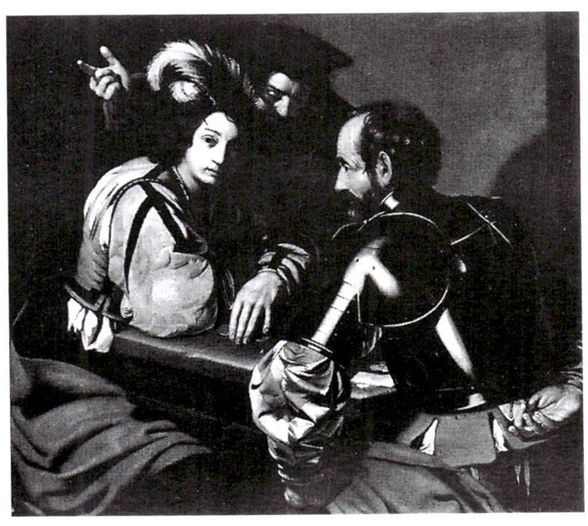

This quality and the magnificent signature, no less prominent and even more complete than the one on the *St. Thomas—G. de La Tour fecit Lunevillae Lhotharfensi]*— have led people to assume that it is a unique, and in some way exceptional, masterpiece. It is true that we have no evidence of any other version, and that the reference to a "Fortune Tellers" in Jean-Baptiste de Bretagne's collection could apply to this painting. Here too, La Tour may have painted an entire series, be it long or short. The subject is common in the paintings and engravings of the time. In a memorable exhibition, Jean-Pierre Cuzin showed that there were many precedents and that with the canvas now in the Louvre Caravaggio had revitalized the subject and brought it back into fashion. Because of the famous circumstances in which it was painted, related above, Caravaggio's *Fortune Teller* was regarded as the supreme example of a realist subject drawn from the simplest everyday life. Caravaggio himself, however, had already overlaid the basic subject of fortune-telling with the suggestion of an amorous dialogue. The Roman Caravaggists were forever trying to outdo each other. By about 1613-1619 in Rome, the theme of the deceiver deceived was treated, with Vouet, Valentin, and Régnier all vying to see who could be most clever. La Tour chooses instead to add in the story of the prodigal son, concentrating on the young dupe as he falls for the old Gypsy woman's illusions, and, above all, for the charms of the three extraordinarily beautiful girls.

After Simon Vouet. *The Fortune Teller.* Anonymous engraving.

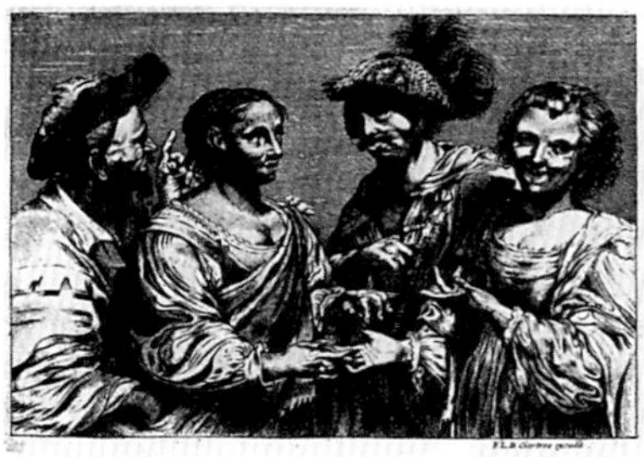

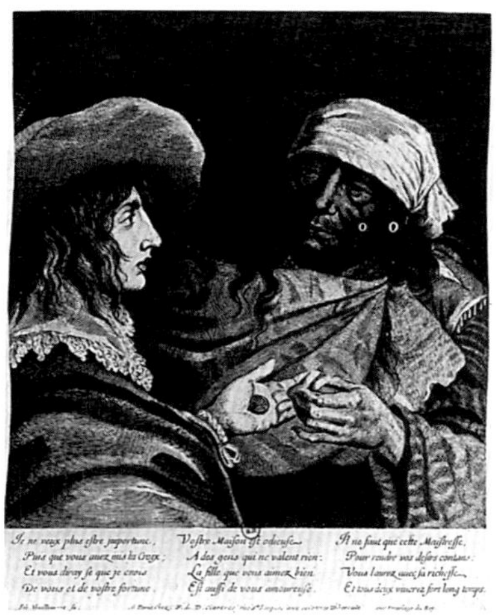

After Sébastien Vouillement. *The Fortune Teller.* Engraving by Michel Lasne. Cabinet des Estampes, Bibliothèque Nationale, Paris

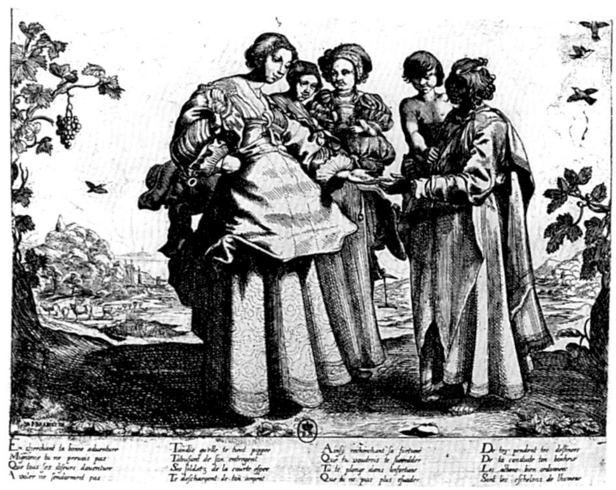

Pierre Brébiette, *The Fortune Teller.* Cabinet des Estampes, Bibliothèque Nationale, Paris

THE FORTUNE TELLER

The subject of the painting now in the Metropolitan Museum has often been misunderstood, but the explanation is to be found in a number of engravings of the period from Rome, Paris, and even Lorraine. In the seventeenth century, fortune tellers were always "Egyptians," which meant Gypsies, usually women, but occasionally old men. There were always scores of Gypsies roaming through wealthy Lorraine. The fortune-telling centered on a coin placed in the palm of the subject's hand, which the Gypsy would hold open toward her. This can be seen clearly in the engraving after Sébastien Vouillemont (above, left), in which the artist vividly renders every detail of the woman's dark complexion, her straggling hair, and the typical cloak, a loose, multicolored drape pinned at one shoulder and concealing that other key accessory, the pouch. The Gypsy is usually shown looking at her client; seldom do we see her pouring over the hand and struggling to interpret the lines etched in it: true palmistry remained the province of learned occultists.

There was no interdiction of fortune-telling by the religious authorities, nor was it deemed morally wrong, either to tell a fortune or to have one told. All too often, however, while the Gypsy woman held her client transfixed with fabulous revelations, her associates would take the opportunity to carry out cunning and distinctly unpleasant thefts. This is what is happening in the charming engraving by Pierre Brébiette (above, right): strolling in the country with her son at her side in his nurse's arms, a young lady of standing is accosted by a Gypsy, and while the two women listen naively to her predictions, two scoundrels are busy ferreting about in the pockets of their skirts. Sometimes the tables were turned, however. In Simon Vouet's version of this subject, painted in Italy but widely known in France through an engraving (top, left), while a courtesan and her ruffian escort are having their fortune told, their accomplice has his greedy hand in the Gypsy's pouch.

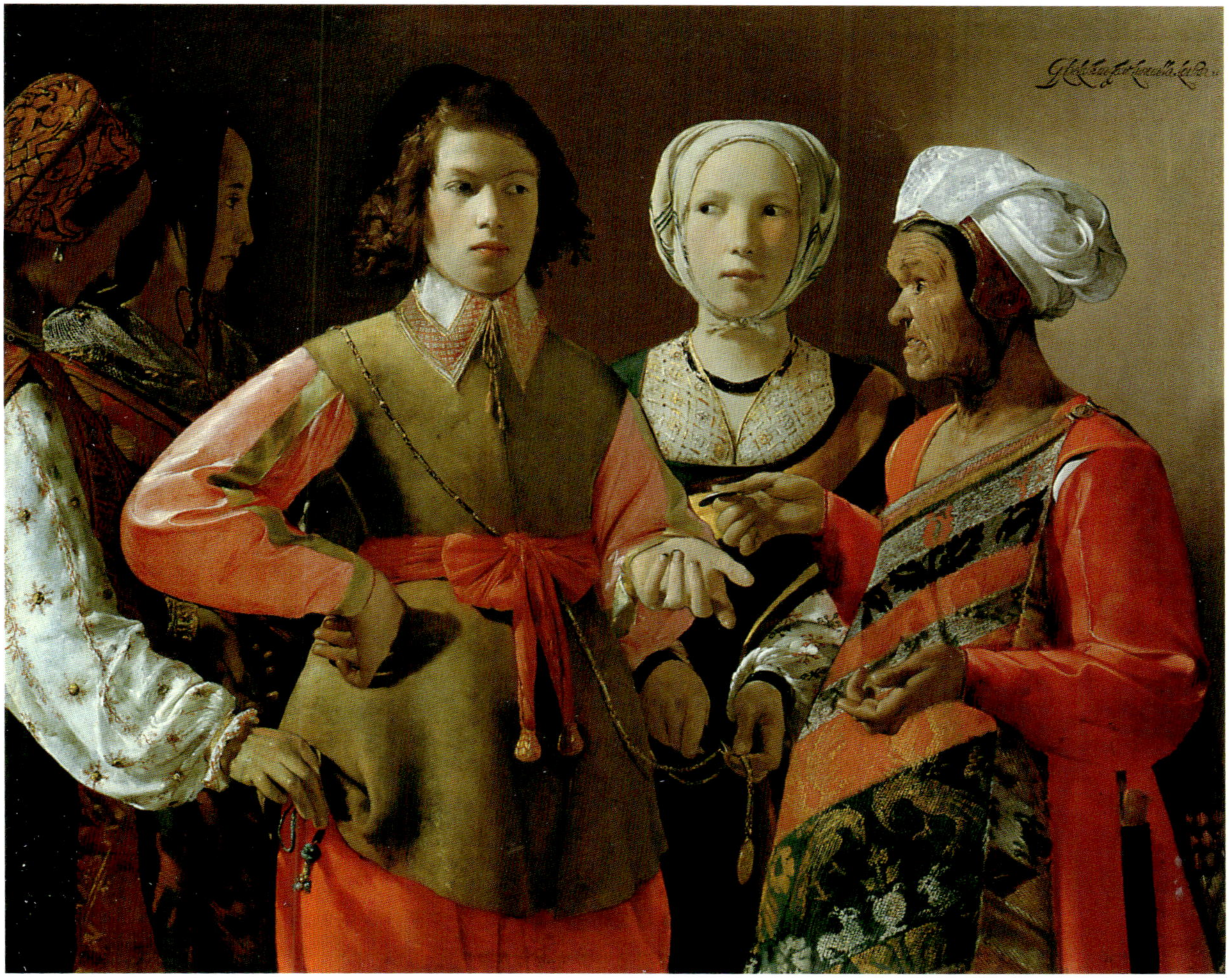

The Fortune Teller.
The Metropolitan Museum of Art, New York

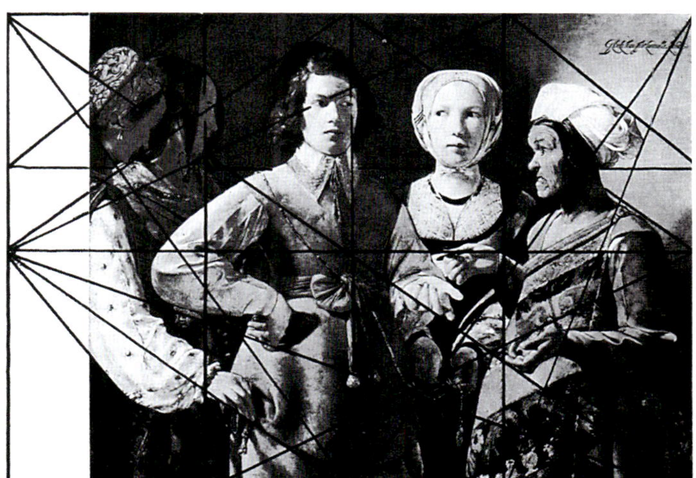

Sketch showing the probable original composition, as reconstructed by Hélène Toussaint.

Once again La Tour uses half-length figures, as he did in *The Beggars' Brawl* and *Old Peasant Couple Eating,* without the table to set them off. Once again he relies on the whites dotted across the canvas, on a harmonious balance of reds and browns, and more than ever on a subtle and skillful play of hands. "Playing hands, thieving hands" runs the old proverb, and it is the hands that tell the story here, from the old woman's hand that places a coin with a cross on it in the open palm, as was the custom, to the pair of hands in the shadows that snip through the gold chain, to the one in the front that is pulling the purse from the man's pocket in order to pass it to the waiting hand of the girl behind her with the pretty, innocent profile. The story builds up from one character to the next, reinforced by the insistent glances that are an even more integral part of the composition than in *The Cheat.* Nimble hands and eyes are, after all, necessities for cheating and theft. At the same time, the scene allows La Tour once again to indulge his penchant for calm poses, slow gestures, and set faces. Few artists since Piero della Francesca have been able to paint a woman's face in an oval as perfect as that of the beautiful Gypsy girl with the jet beads round her neck, using so few colors and so little modeling for so much relief, and all of this to imbue such smooth purity with such an ambiguous smile. In the whole of eastern and western painting, there is little to surpass it in boldness, in sensitivity—or beauty. Here again, La Tour is reaching a limit. This brushwork that evokes gauze, embroidery, and multicolored cloth with such fluidity and ease in fact locks the forms into an increasingly deliberate and constraining geometry. Like the beautiful Gypsy's luminous face, the boy's jerkin, the old woman's sleeve, and the heavy Gypsy mantles become regular curves and simple planes brought to life just in time by clever interruptions, while here and there little ornamental motifs divert the eye. The style can hardly be richer; soon, however, it is to be stripped bare.

This tendancy is already more apparent in *The Cheat with the Ace of Clubs* in the Louvre, which merits comparison with the Fort Worth version. At first sight, especially in reproduction, the two canvases could be confused. They are very different, however, and were manifestly painted some time apart.

In the Louvre version, almost all the details have been altered: the clothes are a different color, the necklaces and bracelets a different size. On a deeper level, however, the very spirit has changed. The composition is more emphatically geometric, the tonal contrasts are stronger. Take the figures of the cheat, for instance. In the Fort Worth painting, he is sharply defined against an even light. In the Louvre version, the shoulder knots on his tunic form three very dark parallel strips that run down to meet the right angle of the table and are echoed in the black motif embroidered on the servant's sleeve and the dark blue line of her bodice. The overall scheme displays a clearer geometry: the woman's face is fuller, her eyes larger, and the servant's profile outlined in light. Gone is the subtle gradation of reds of the Fort Worth version. This gives way in the Louvre version to a single shade maintained throughout, from the young man's voluminous breeches to the cap perched on his head, from the courtesan's turban to the servant's skirt, which lends the painting great plastic unity, but at the cost of its luminous tonal range. Even more than *The Fortune Teller,* this painting relies on unexpected and purely decorative devices to bring it to life, with the virtuoso brushwork serving to conceal the almost cursory sobriety of the composition: the prodigal son's tabard and the servant girl's sleeve, for instance, or the intricate fall of the slashes on the woman's sleeves, trimmed with gold braid and lined with yellow against a gray silk background. La Tour's brush has lost none of its deftness or flavor, but the spirit is now quite remote from that of the Albi *Apostles.* This world is no longer an event captured and reproduced in literal detail, but a world reconstructed piece by piece, on the basis of thoughts rather than models. To be sure, La Tour has copied real costumes and real fabrics. He may have brought a woman in his entourage, possibly even his wife, to pose for the courtesan, and taken the yellow reflection in the corner of her eye or the hint of light defining the crease of her chin from life. It is, however, the artist's imagination that has drawn this disturbing face out of a regular volume, that has plastered this "ostrich egg"—to use Roberto Longhi's image—with flat yellow strands of hair, slightly twisted the nose and corners of the mouth, and from this coarsened face fashioned the selfish and richly ornamented image of the world's falseness. It is now his own thinking that La Tour seeks to capture in his canvases.

pp. 139-141: *The Cheat with the Ace of Clubs*, details.

pp. 142-147: *The Fortune Teller*, details.

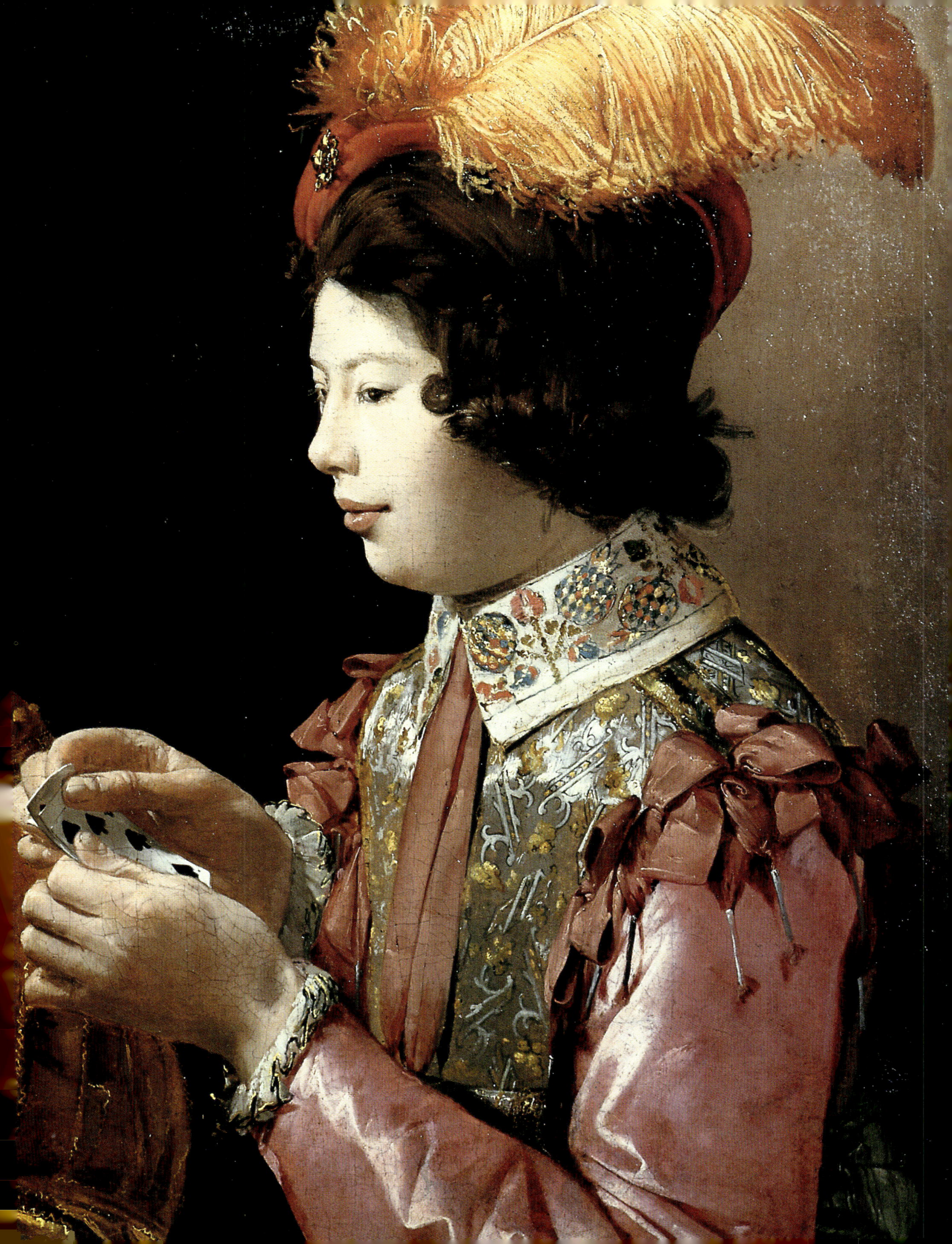

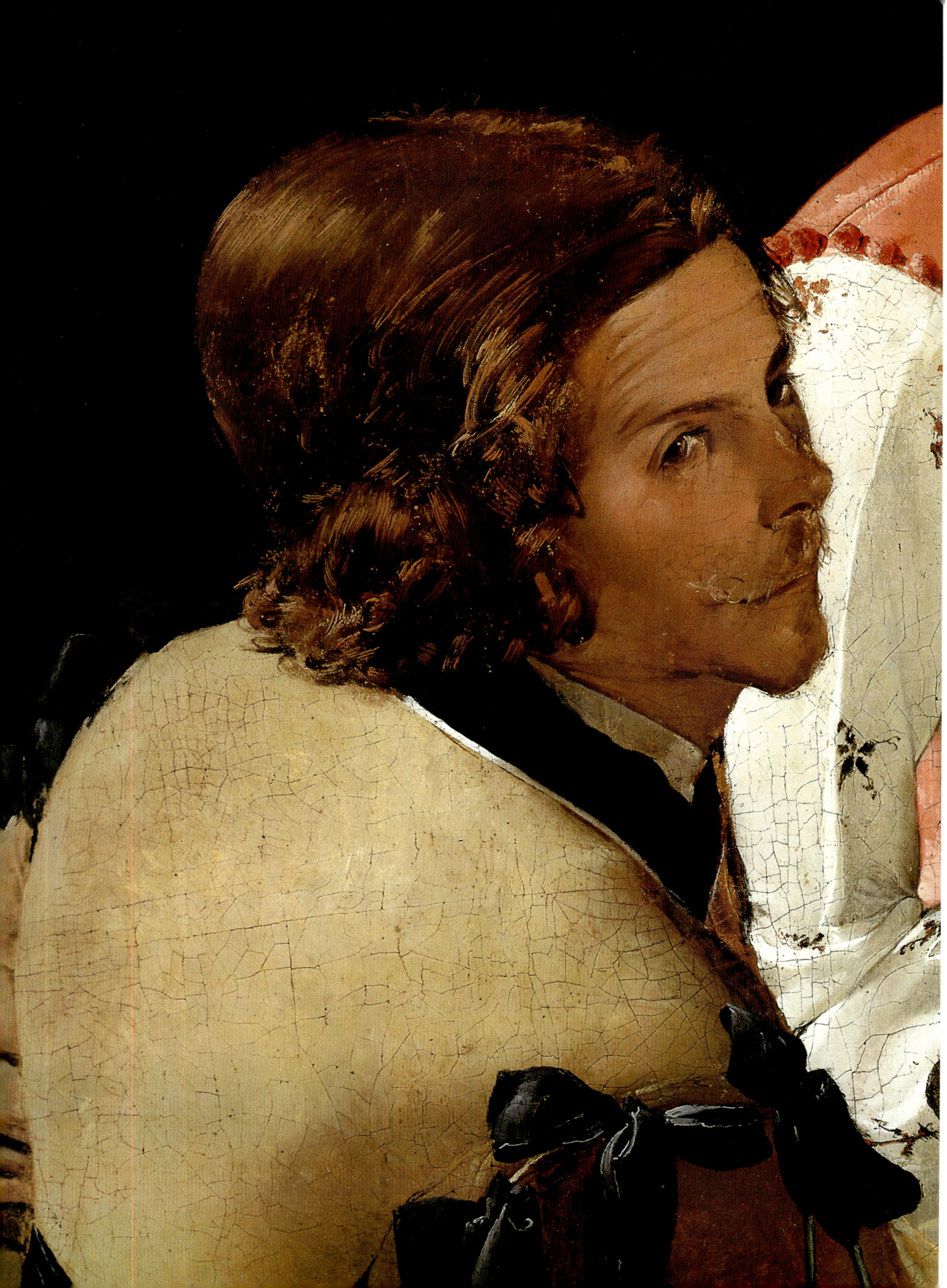

14

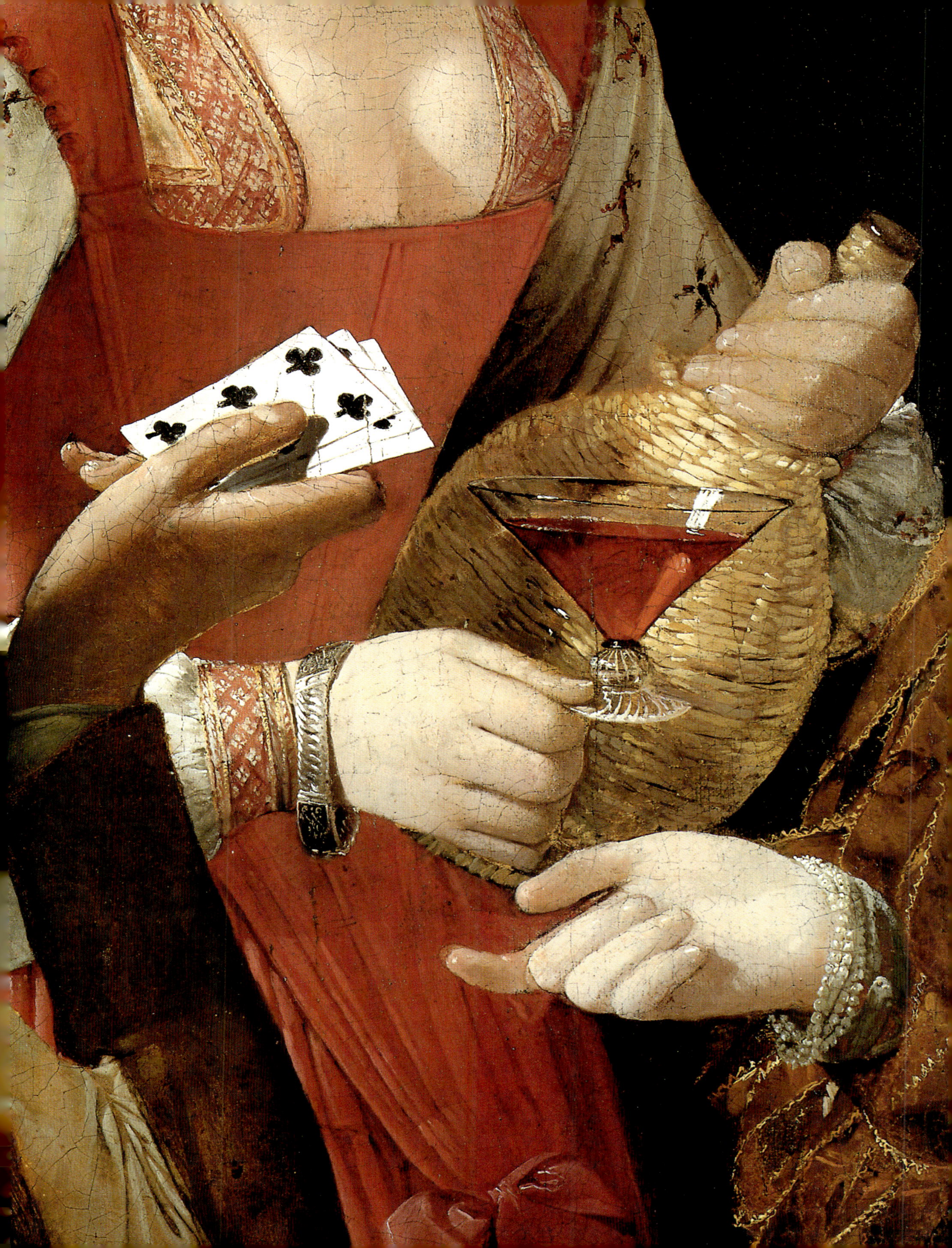

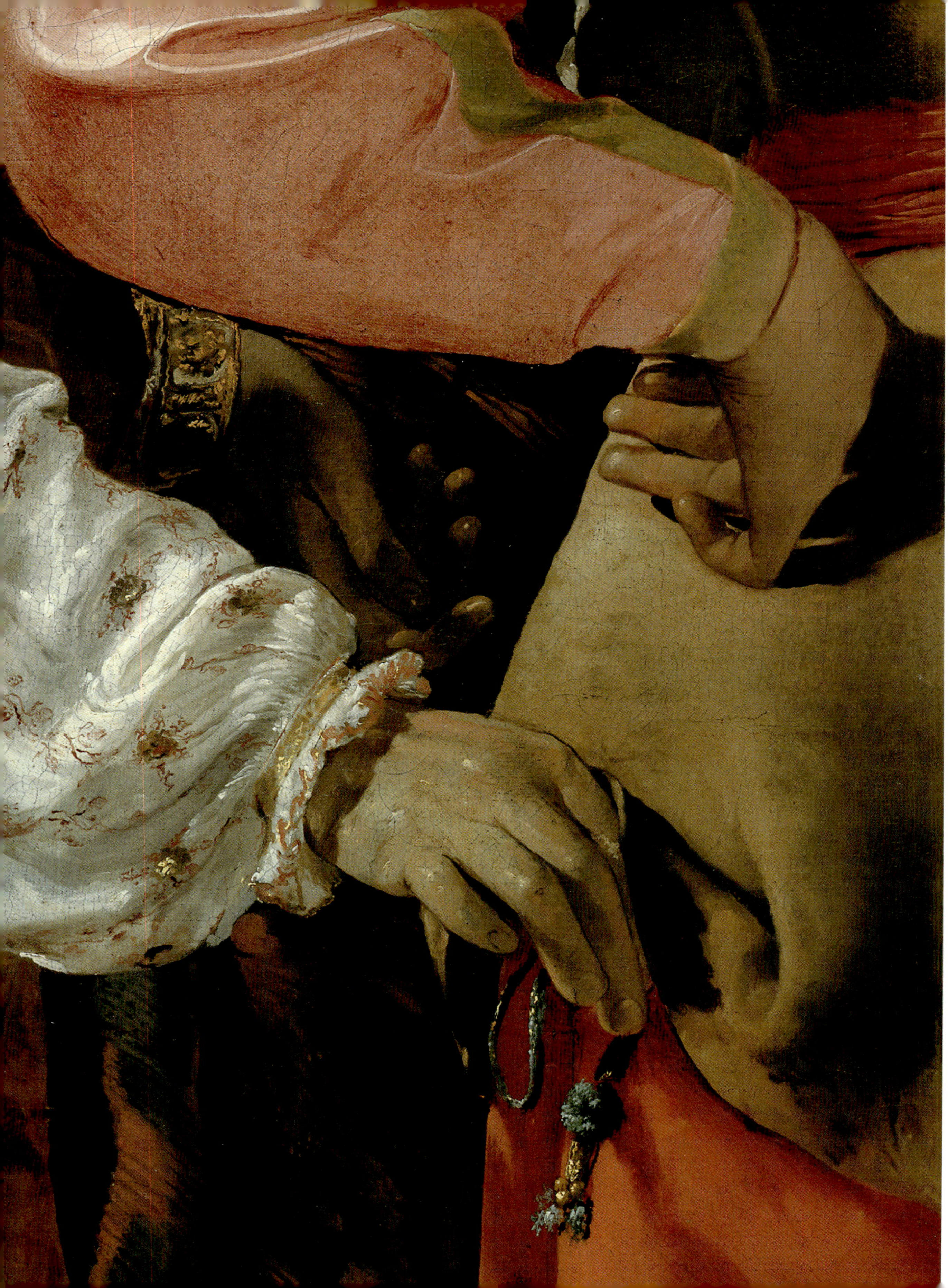

14

14

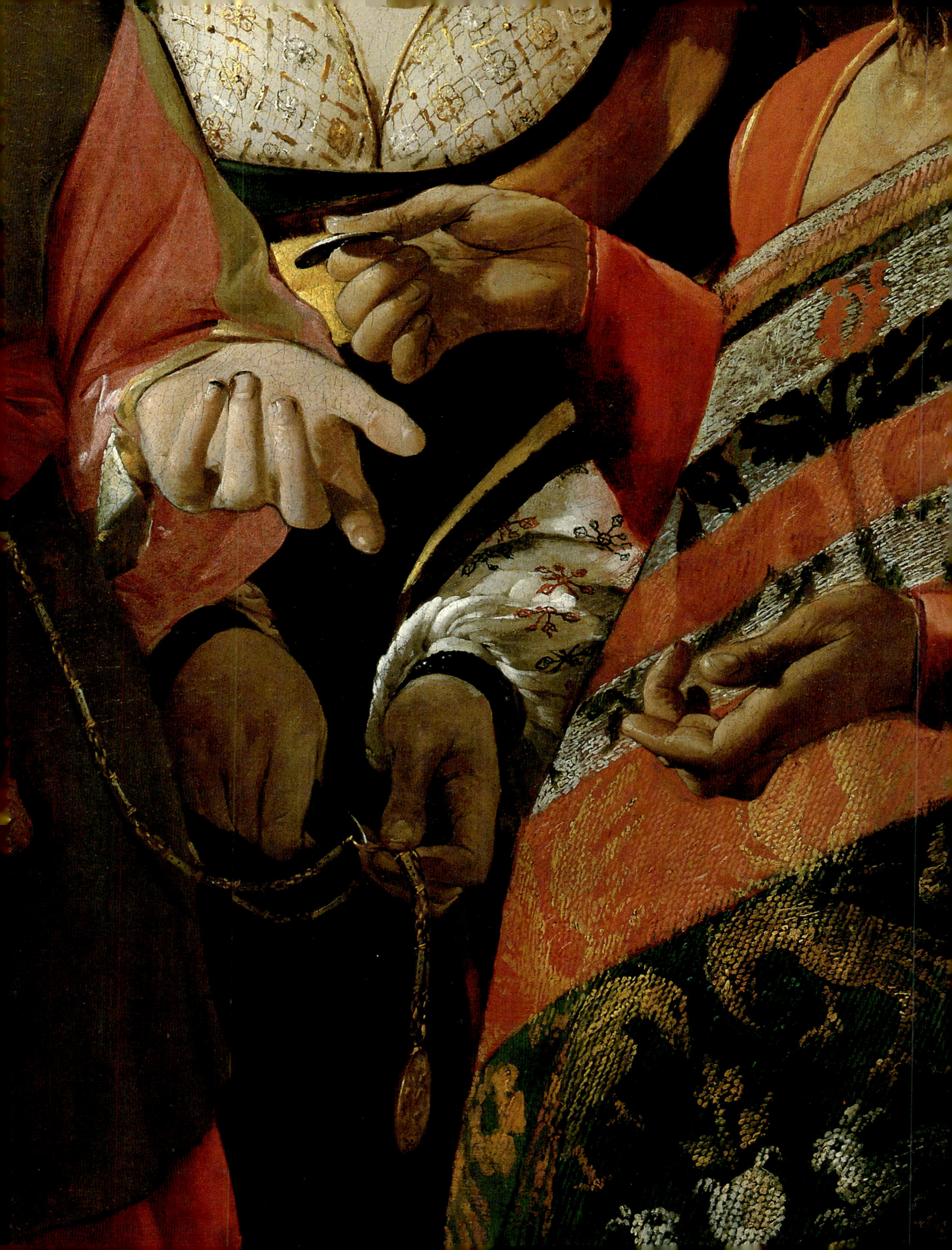

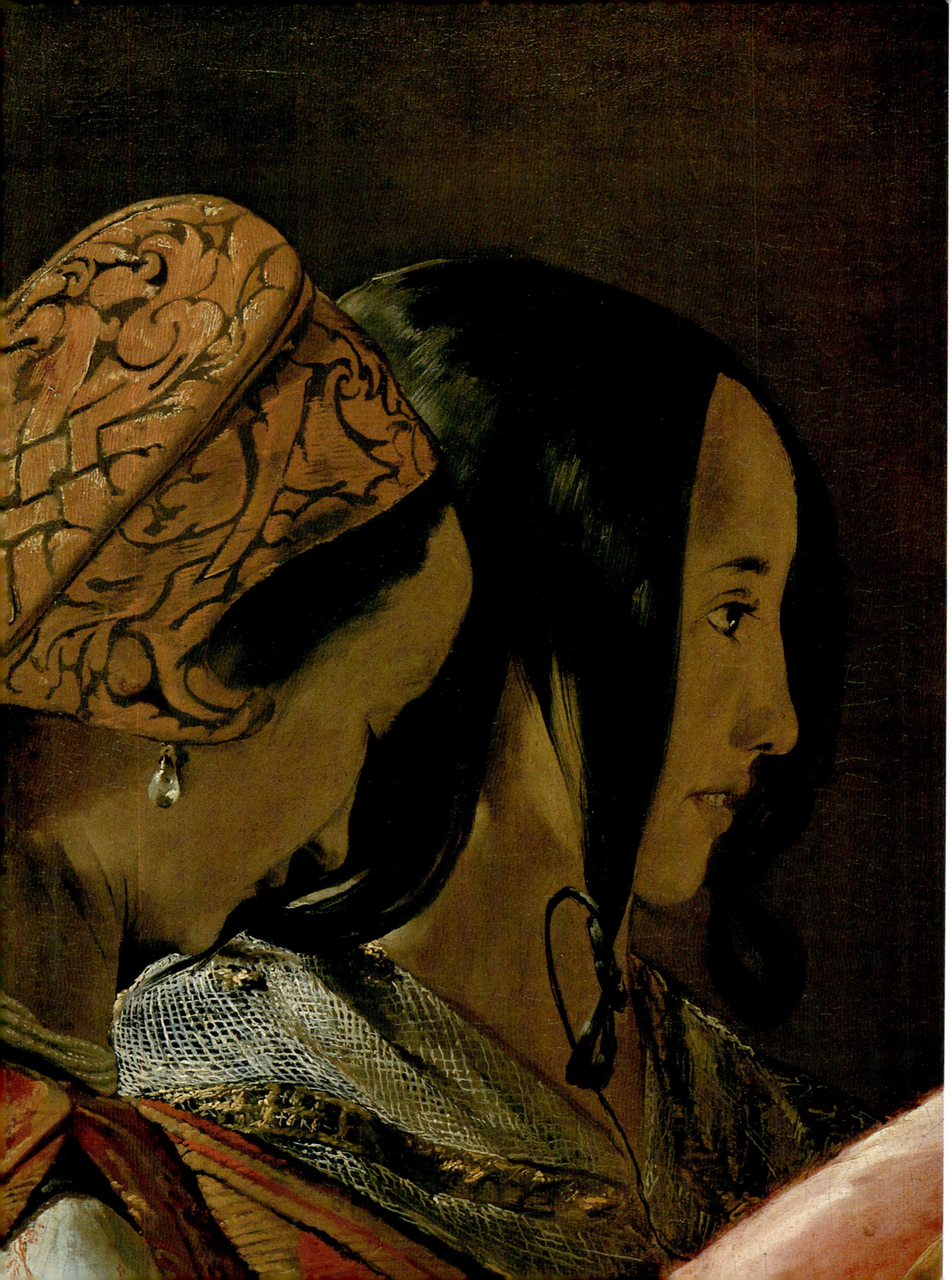

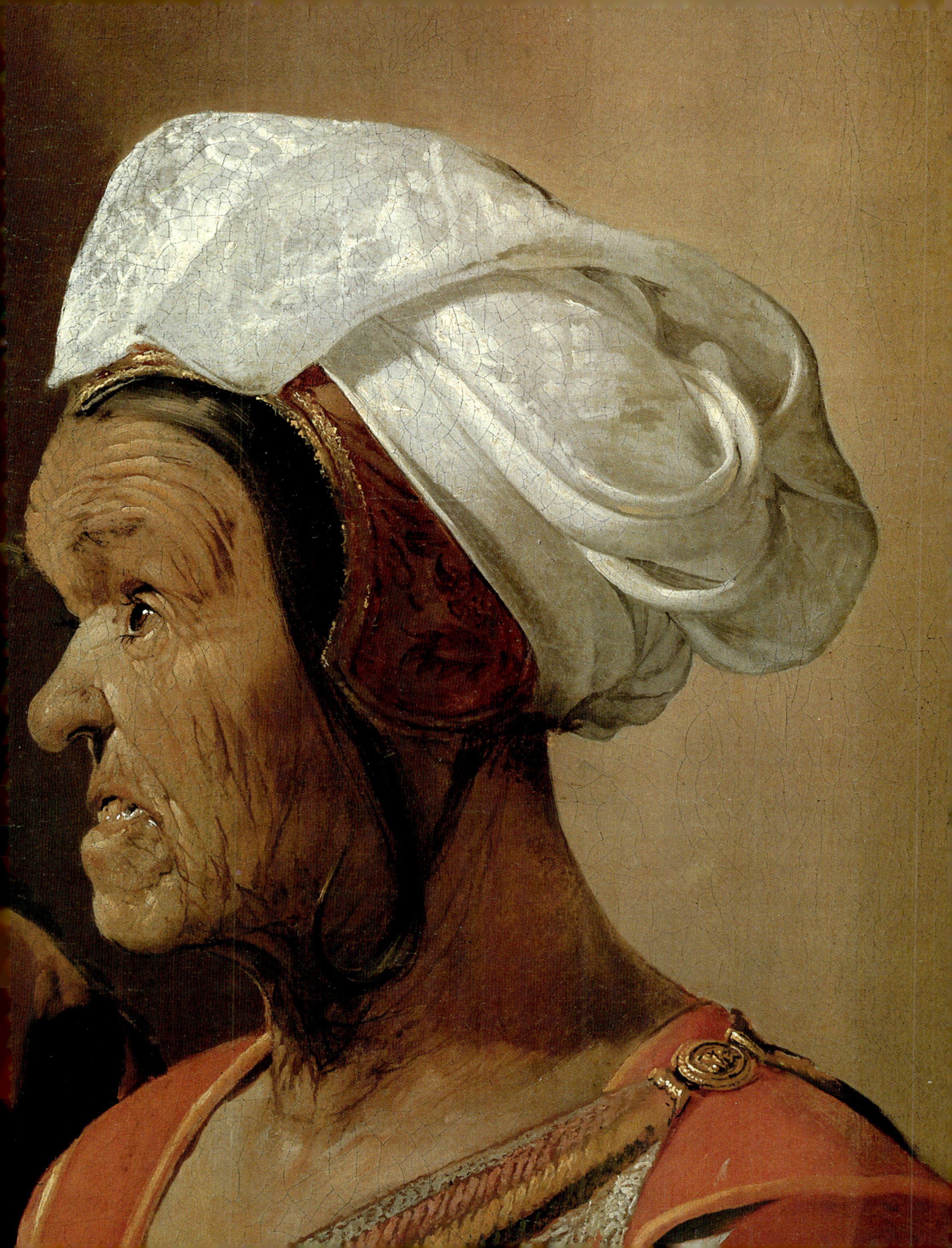

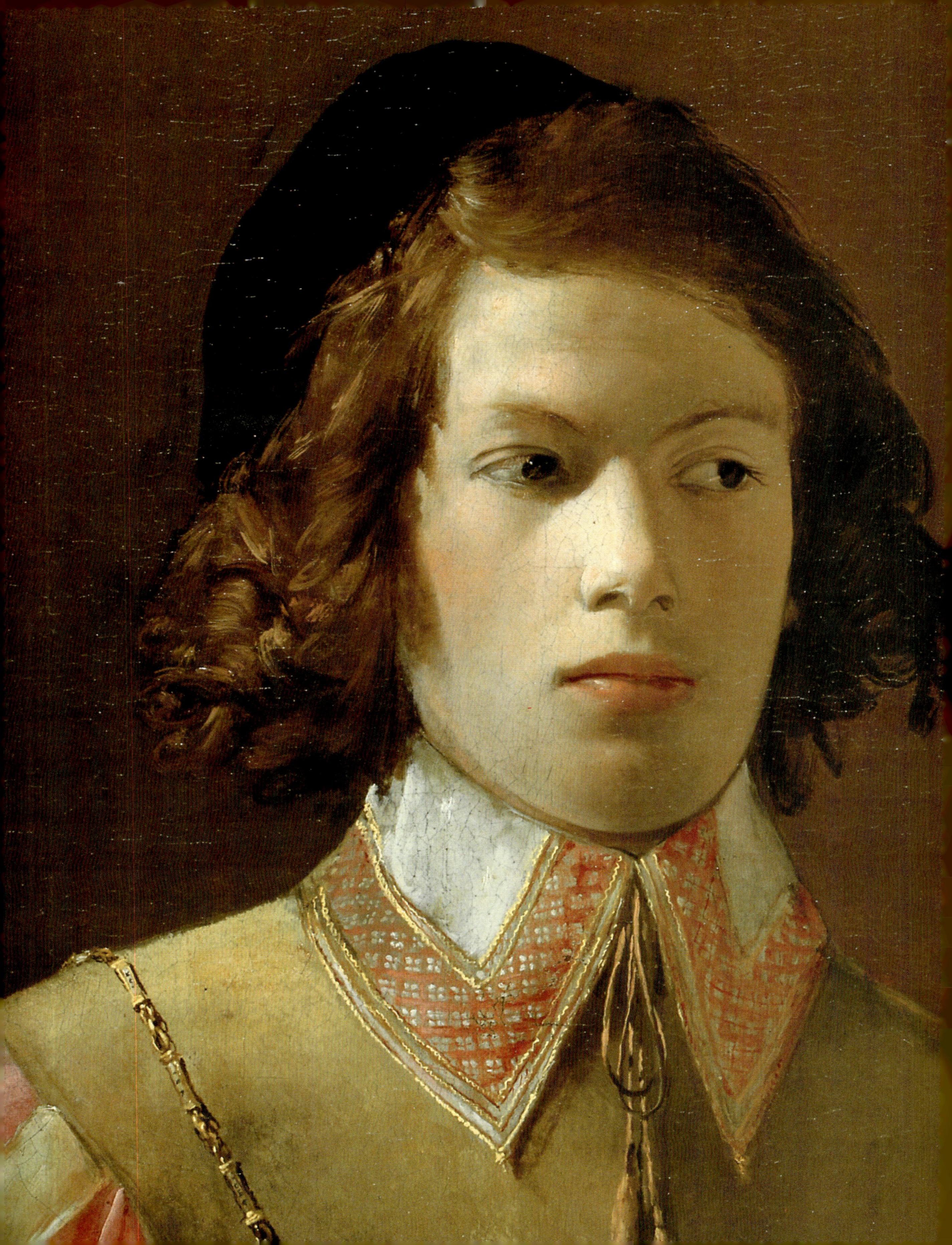

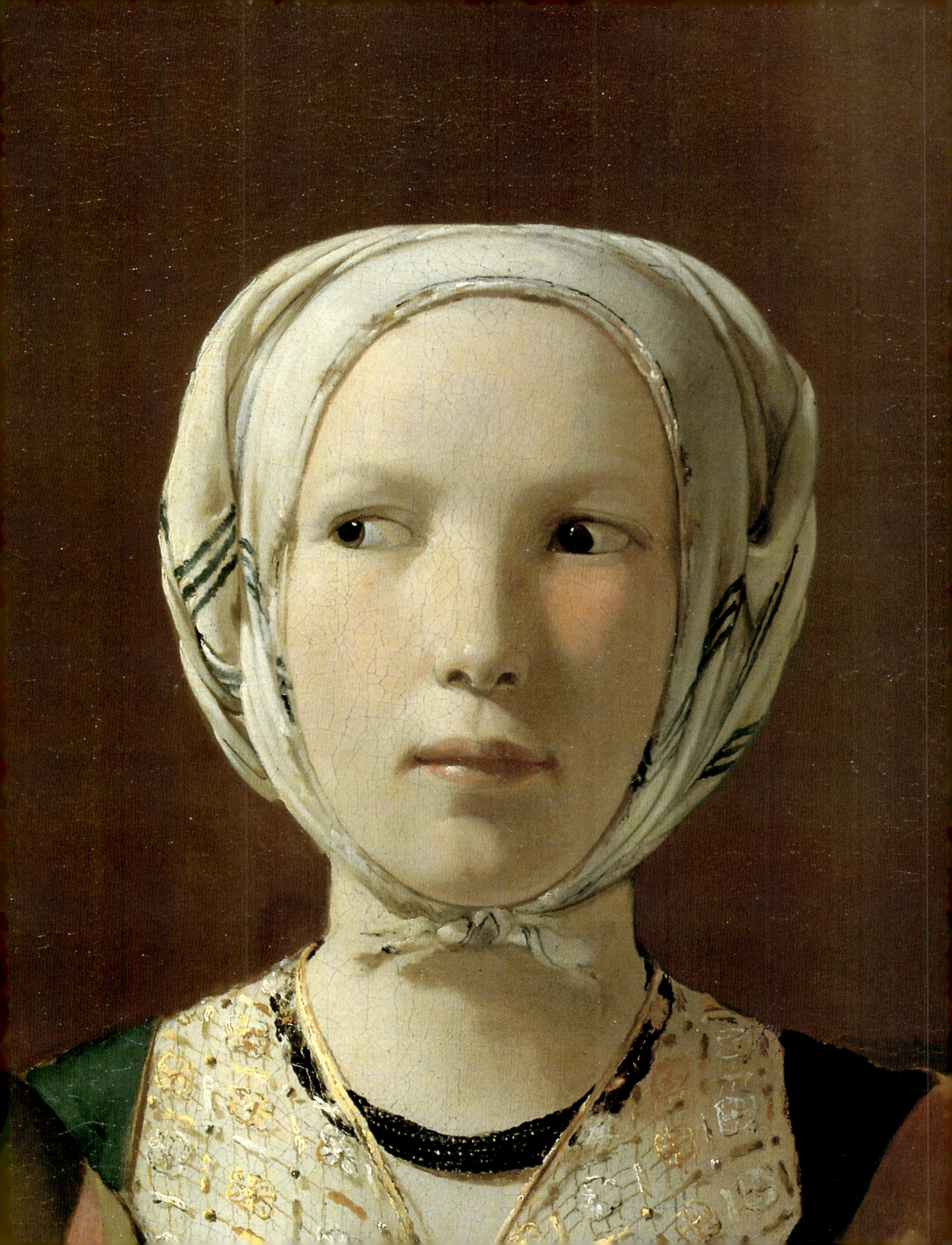

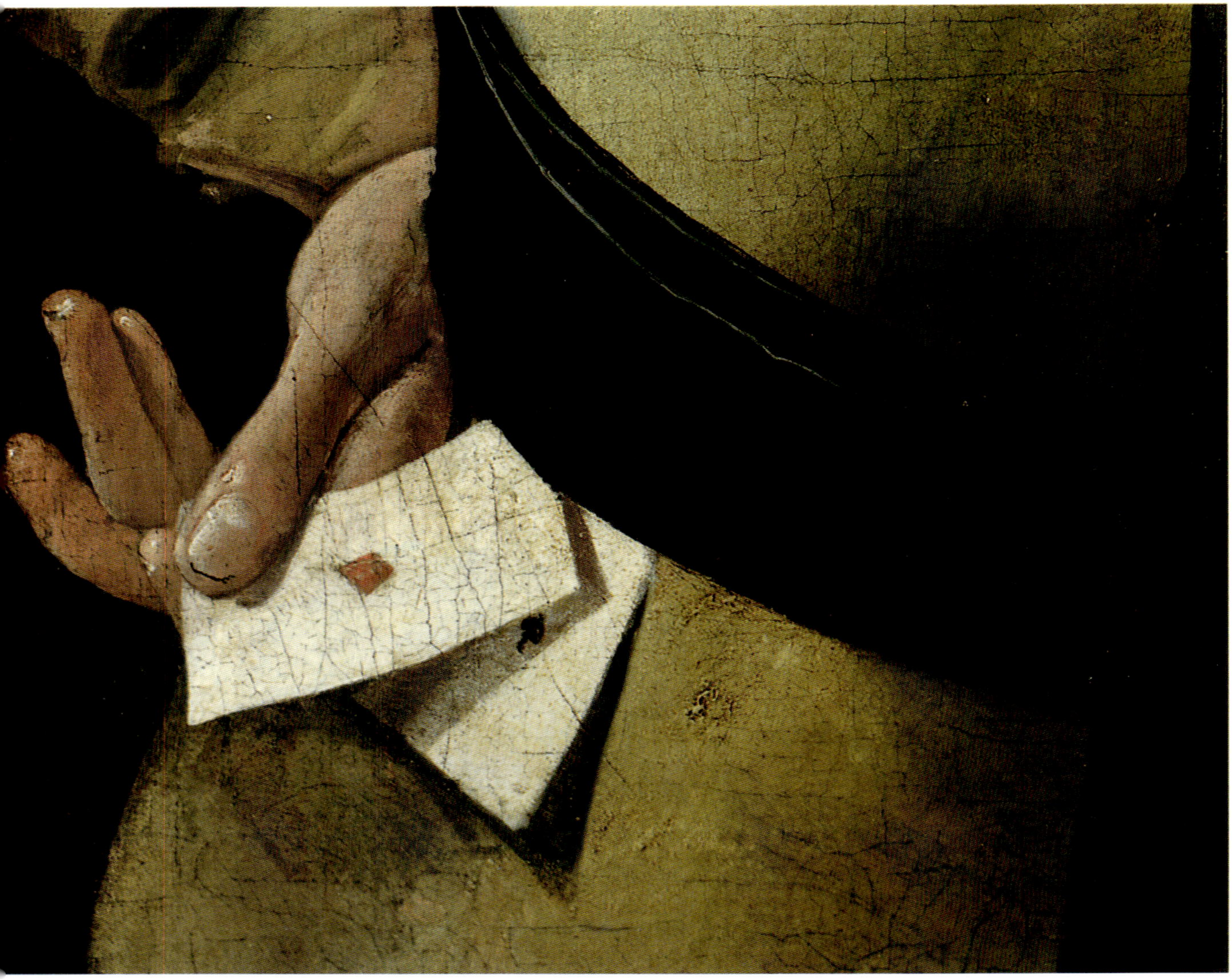

pp. 148-151:
The Cheat with the Ace of Diamonds, details.

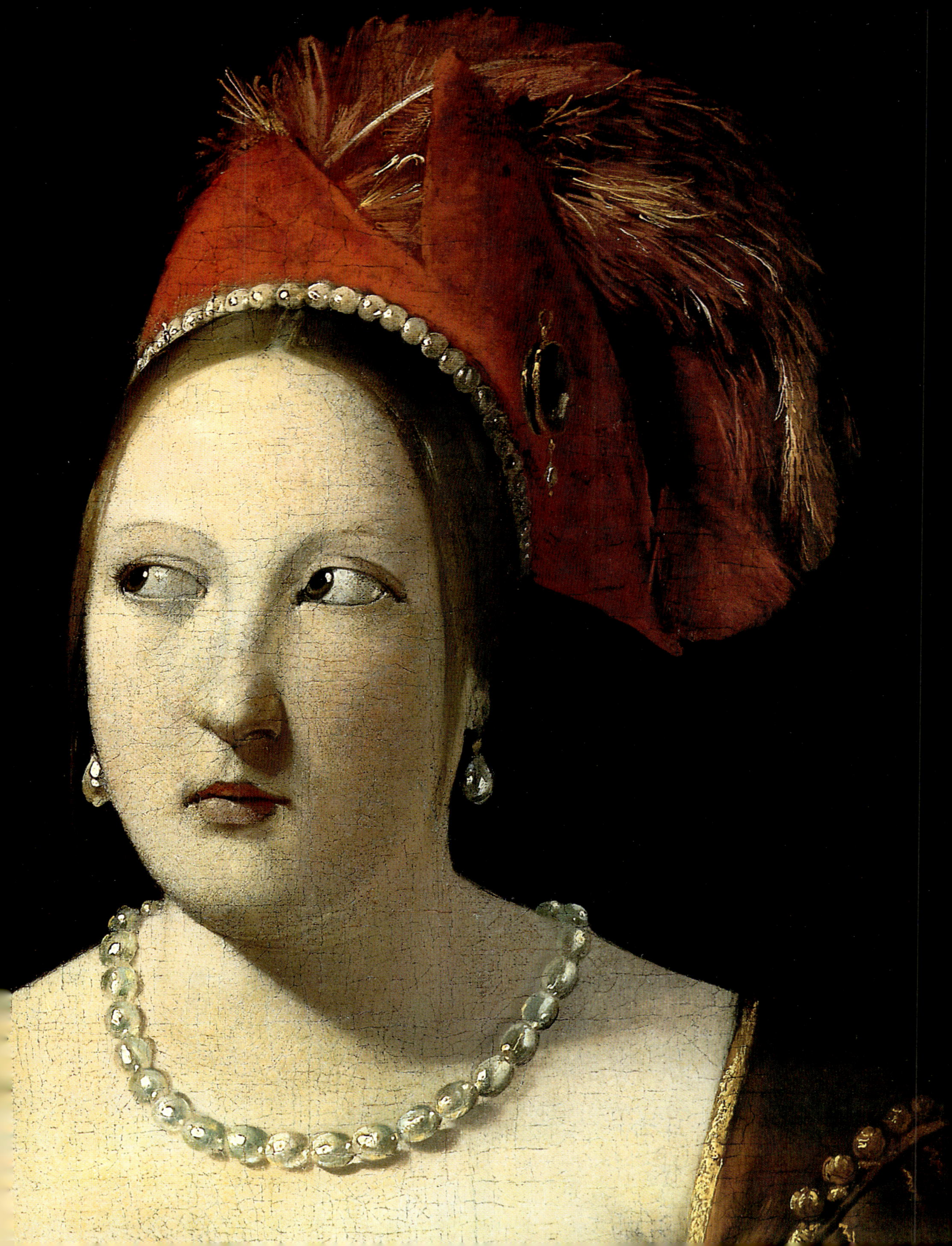

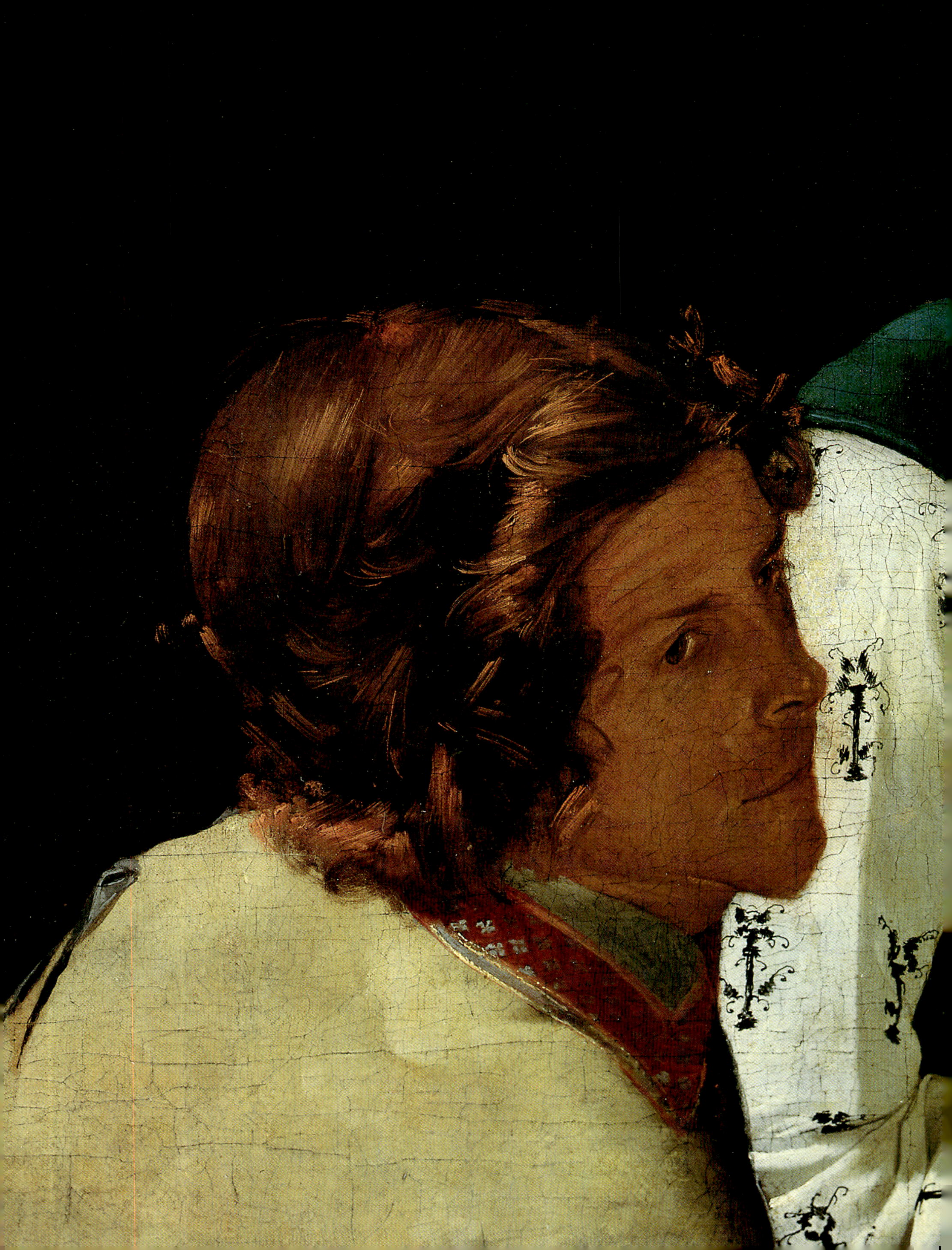

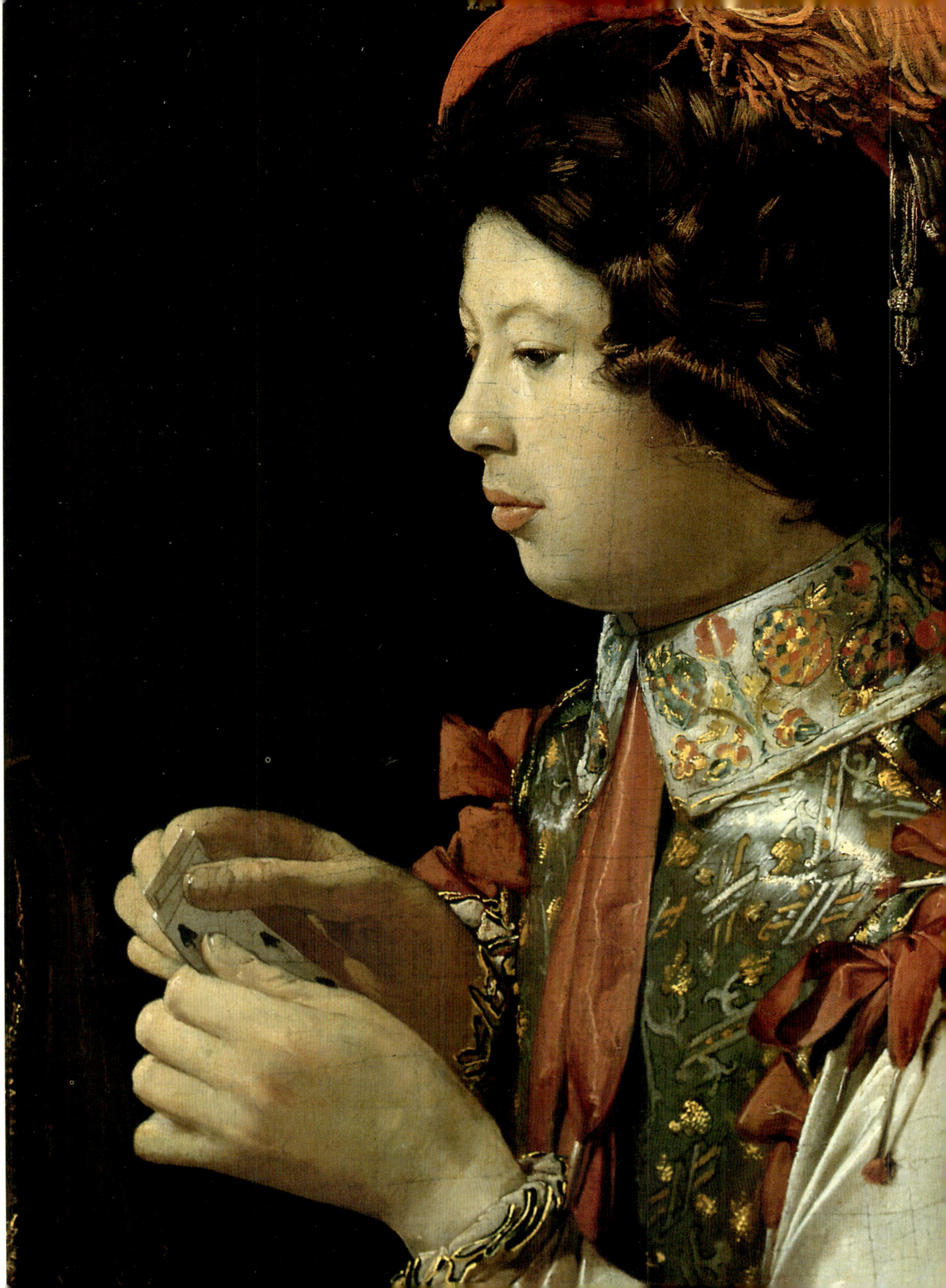

60
61

THE DEVELOPMENT OF THE NOCTURNES

There is little doubt that this slow transformation, of both style and thought, coincided with the increasing numbers of "night" paintings. It has sometimes been suggested that it was prompted by them. Distinguishing between cause and effect, however, is almost impossible when it comes to an artist's creation. Very often the artist only becomes aware of his own thought as he begins to paint, but nevertheless it is an inner feeling that has guided his hand. La Tour devoted himself increasingly to painting "night" scenes, doubtless in response to external demand, but also out of a fundamental instinct of his own, the same one that prompted him to make such decisive modifications in the daylight paintings. His subjects also began to change at the same time. Paradoxical though it may seem, as poverty became widespread in Lorraine, beggars disappeared from his paintings. We have no "night" pictures of beggars or blind musicians, and there is nothing in the archives to suggest that La Tour ever painted any. The "nocturnes" deal with totally different themes: they are meditations on human frailty and the mutability of fate, on suffering, death, and the steadfastness fitting to the just.

Guy François (attributed to).
The Repentant Magdalen.
Musée du Louvre, Paris

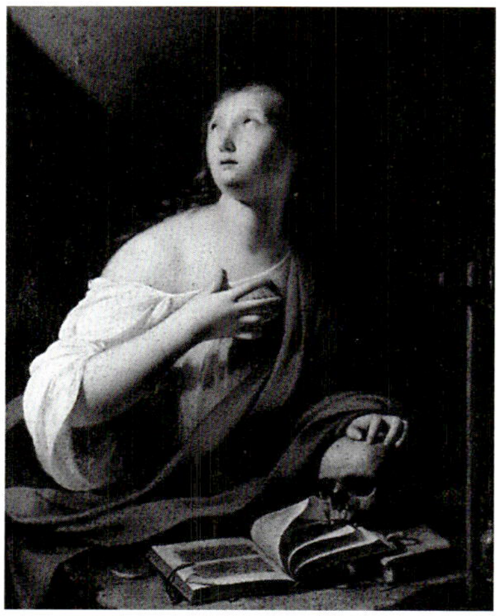

Three engravings of lost works provide a kind of proof of this assertion. These are the only engravings thus far known with certainty to have been produced in the seventeenth century after paintings by La Tour. All three, manifestly by the same hand and close in date, represent "nocturnes," and all three offer subjects that are entirely new.

There are very few surviving copies of the engravings. Those of *The Newborn Child* (also called *Madonna and Child with St. Anne*) bear the name of a publisher, François van den Wyngaerden, and credit Jacques Callot with the composition. This is patently fraudulent: no one but La Tour could have produced it. It is also a later fraud: Wyngaerden was not born until 1614 and died in 1679, so it seems that this Dutch dealer put his name on plates he did not commission. As to when and where he acquired them, nothing is known for certain. The style of the engravings seems to indicate a date somewhere between 1640-1650, and there is nothing to suggest that the engravings are by La Tour, as has been rashly propounded, or by Le Clerc, as Pariset believed, or necessarily even by an engraver in Nancy at all. Although Bellange and Callot increased engraving's importance in Lorraine, it should be remembered that these two masters intended to engrave their own work, and they hardly gave rise to a great printed reproduction industry there. The source of our engravings is far more likely to have been some operation in Paris. Perhaps La Tour himself decided to have his work reproduced as a way of getting it publicized. Alternatively, it may have been a project initiated by one of his admirers and halted on his return to Lorraine. For two of the three engraved subjects, there are corresponding paintings listed in Jean-Baptiste de Bretagne's collection. Is this a mere coincidence? In any case, they seem to represent three of the first "night" pictures that found their way to Paris and that date from around 1638-1642.

Artemisia Gentilechi.
The Repentant Magdalen.
Palazzo Pitti, Florence

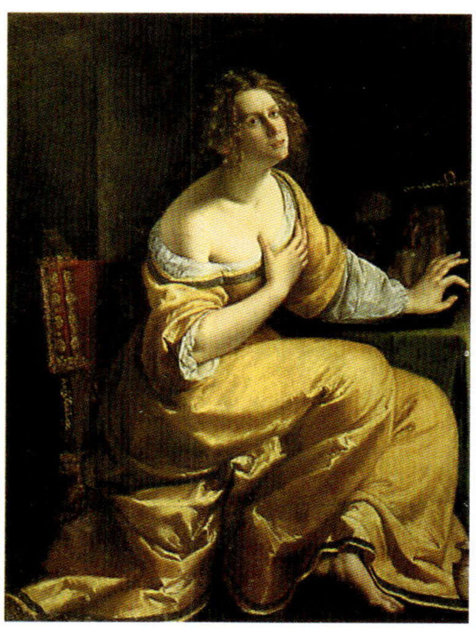

One of the three engravings shows the Magdalen in meditation. It was in fact at the time of the "nocturnes" that the *The Repentant Magdalen* series first appeared. It is the most famous of all La Tour's series, and also one of the best represented.

The series could have started fairly early and developed rapidly in the late 1630s, and it met with no less success in Paris than in Lorraine. It came at a particularly propitious time. The cult of the Magdalen, worshiped since ancient times at the famous grotto of St. Baume in Provence, was then enjoying a revival and had been given a new theological justification. In the great tradition of mystical thought in the early part of the century the Magdalen represented pure love. Historically and symbolically, she was the human being who, sinful in both nature and deed, is elevated through love, without any need for doctrine or argument, to God, and cleaves to Truth. The Magdalen thus emerged as the highest in the spiritual hierarchy, coming immediately after the Virgin, who was born without any sin, and before John, the favorite of the Apostles, before St. Joseph, St. Peter, and St. Paul. This at least was the belief of Cardinal de Bérulle, who, around July 1625, composed his *Elevations* on the holy Magdalen, one of the most beautiful mystical poems in the French language. In

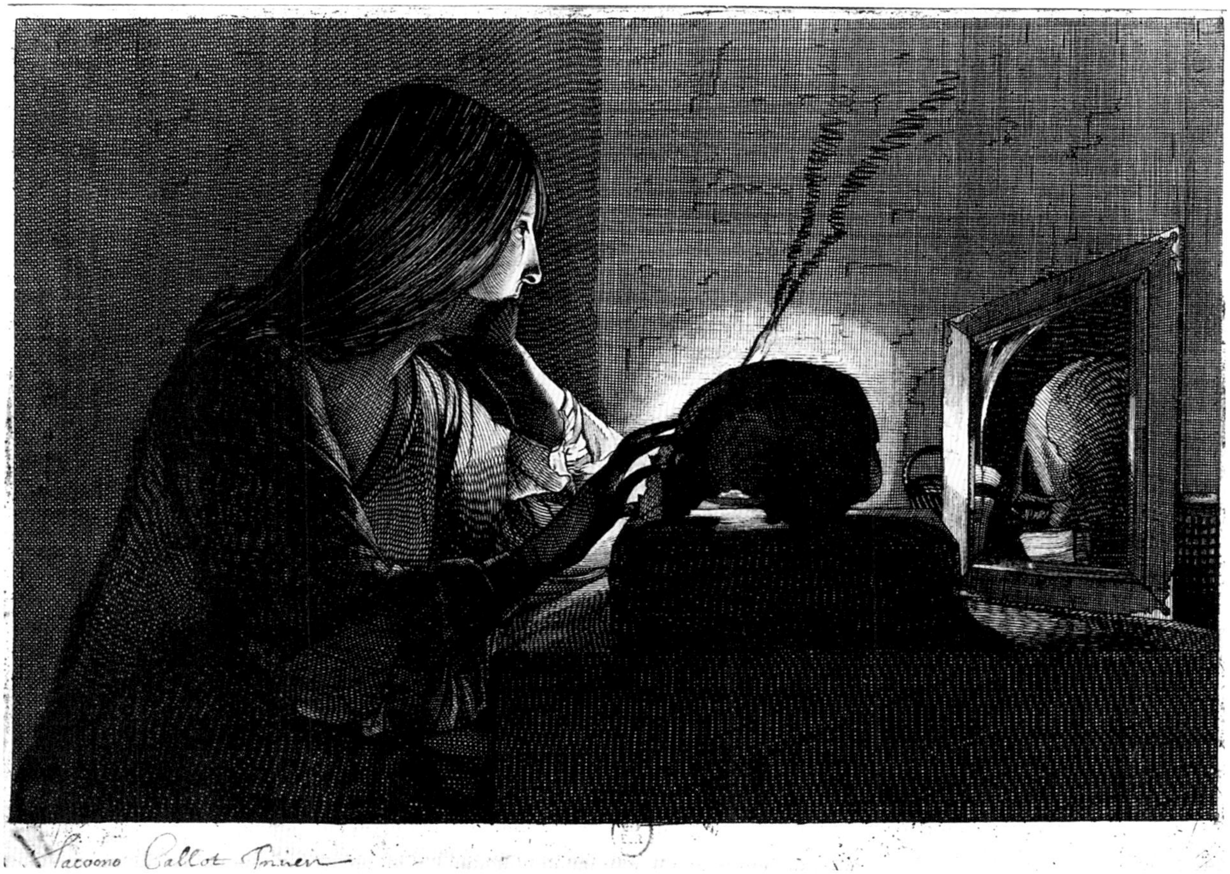

After Georges de La Tour.
The Repentant Magdalen (with a Mirror).
Anonymous engraving.
Cabinet des Estampes, Bibliothèque Nationale, Paris

it he celebrates "the spiritual union of Jesus and Mary Magdalen" and describes how the Magdalen is first impelled by love in "humble and saintly ignorance," and how she pursues Christ to supper with Simon:

> She enters the house of the Pharisee; but she thinks only of you, she sees only you, in this hall, at this table, and she dissolves at your feet . . .

then to Calvary, where:

> She is riveted and fixed to Jesus on the cross, and this streaming blood of Jesus is the cement which binds the hearts of Jesus and Magadalen together,

and after the Resurrection:

> The disciples and Apostles followed you faithfully, but when they were called . . . This woman came in search of you, followed you, ran to you, without being called by you with any direct word luring her and directed to her. And now, you want her to be the first to hear your voice.

Finally comes the separation that was to determine the rest of the Magdalen's life, the austerity of which was less meditation and penance than a perpetual union of love:

> You go back into the secrecy of your inaccessible light. . . . She can no longer see you, find you, hold you, it seems. . . . At the very moment she finds you, she finds in you a stone harder than the stone of your sepulchre that your angels had lifted for her. You are a stone to her . . . of separation, . . . [but] for a greater love. . . .
>
> In your love, by depriving this soul of the fruit of her love, you give her a

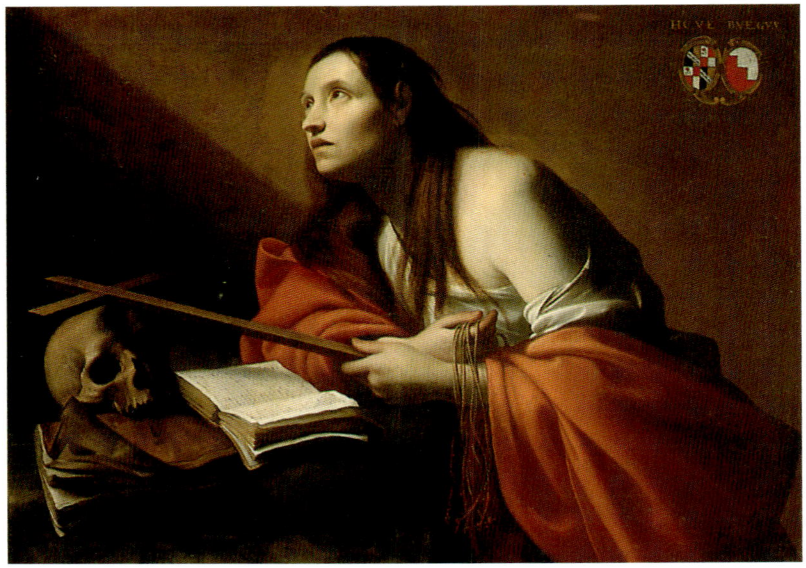

Johan Ulrich Loth.
The Repentant Magdalen, 1630.
Alte Pinakothek, Munich

> new strength, and the strength of love to bear this deprivation, this hardship and this separation: a separation which secretly and imperceptibly joins her soul to you in a new way. O pure, celestial, divine Love, which needs no maintence and no feeling; love which subsists by its very being, and not by maintenance, exercise, and operation; love which, like the fires of heaven, endures in her soul like in his very element, without movement or nourishment, whereas the terrestrial fires are in perpetual motion, and need food to maintain them and to keep them going here below, as they are in a place which is alien to them. . . .

These passages are worth quoting, with their remarkable combination of the very highest spiritual thoughts and the most direct, sensual images possible, and with the constrast between the calm of pure love that burns and glows "by its very being," impervious to all things terrestrial, and terrestrial flames that go out if they are not kindled—for all of this is found in painting too, with a wide variety of interpretations and emphases. Leaving aside Italian and Flemish art, suffice it to recall the moving *Magdalen* of Johann-Ulrich Loth in Munich, signed and dated 1630, and which is enough to gain him notoriety. In Paris, Vouet painted his *Repentant Magdalen* about 1633 and his surprising *Magdalen in Ecstasy* in 1638, followed by Le Nain's *Magdalen in the Grotto* around 1641-1643. La Tour's series must date from about the same time. A 1641 document refers in fact to a *Magdalen*, doubtless painted around 1637-1638, which had not been paid for at the time of the purchaser's death, and which La Tour wanted personally to get back from the dead man's family. It would not be surprising if numerous versions continued to be turned out over a good ten-year period. La Tour was alone, however, in always treating the subject as a "night" scene, as though for him the Magdalen's meditation required the darkness, which obliterates all vanity, and the flame, real and lively, yet immaterial like the spirit, and like love.

In one rather strange version, known to us only through a copy in a private collection, the Magdalen is shown holding a crucifix in an attitude very like that of the two versions of *St. Jerome*. A reproduction published by Rosenberg gives us only a rough idea of the original. It appears, however, to be the most rhetorical of all the versions, and to belong to the beginning of the series.

After Georges de La Tour.
The Repentant Magdalen (with the Crucifix).
Private collection, France

The engraved version, where the Magdalen is half-length, is the first to incorporate the poetic device of the mirror in which the saint contemplates the empty-eyed skull on which she rests her hand. This rendering must have met with great

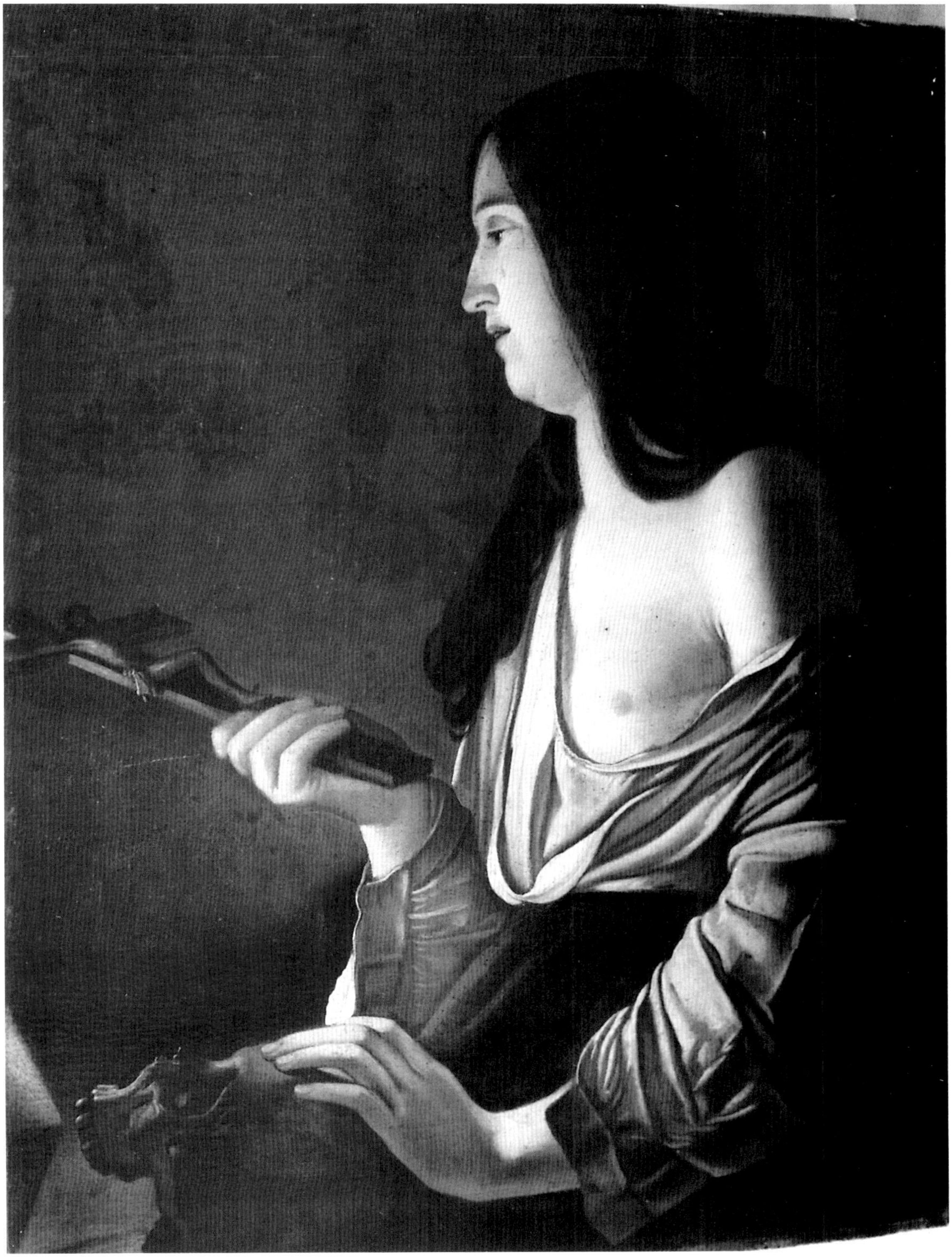

Right:
The Repentant Magdalen
(also called the *Fabius Magdalen*).
The National Gallery of Art, Washington, D.C.

success. We have at least two fairly faithful old copies, and it seems to have given rise to a whole series of replicas differing only in minor detail. Thus, along with the lost original known from the engraving, there must have been a second original with a half-length figure: there is yet another copy in the museum in Besançon with too many minor but subtle differences—in the fall of the hair, the folds of the clothing, and the play of shadows—for a simple case of negligent copying. A third variation showing the Magdalen full-length was in the Fabius Collection in Paris from 1936 to 1974, when it was acquired by the museum in Washington. This time the painting is an original, owned by the marquise de Caulaincourt in the nineteenth century; the composition basically corresponds to the engraved version, but once again there are some modifications.

Another, starker version was first known through a rather mediocre copy on wood. The original has recently been discovered. Painted on canvas, it is signed in the upper part but is in very poor condition. The background has had to be entirely restored. Only a few light areas, painted with a full brush, have remained intact. It is by these lighted portions that we must judge the painting, and also by its moving effect. In the solitude of night, the Magdalen is shown virtually naked, her face invisible behind her hair except for an unattractive, expressionless profile, as she meditates before the skull and book, this time posed on a heavy rustic table. The austerity of the composition and the stylization of the forms would tend to suggest a late date, but this is contradicted by the somber tonality that remains devoid of any color accents.

The Repentant Magdalen.
Private collection

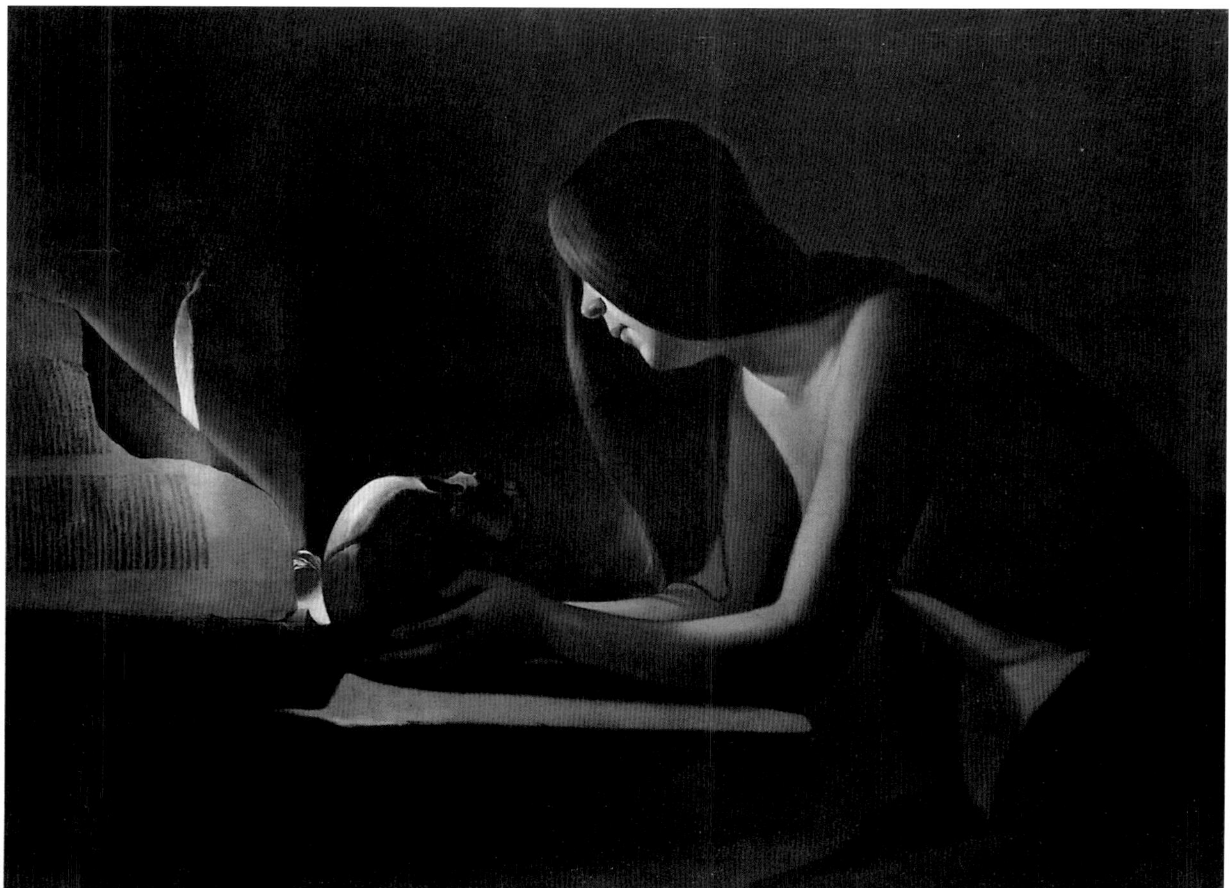

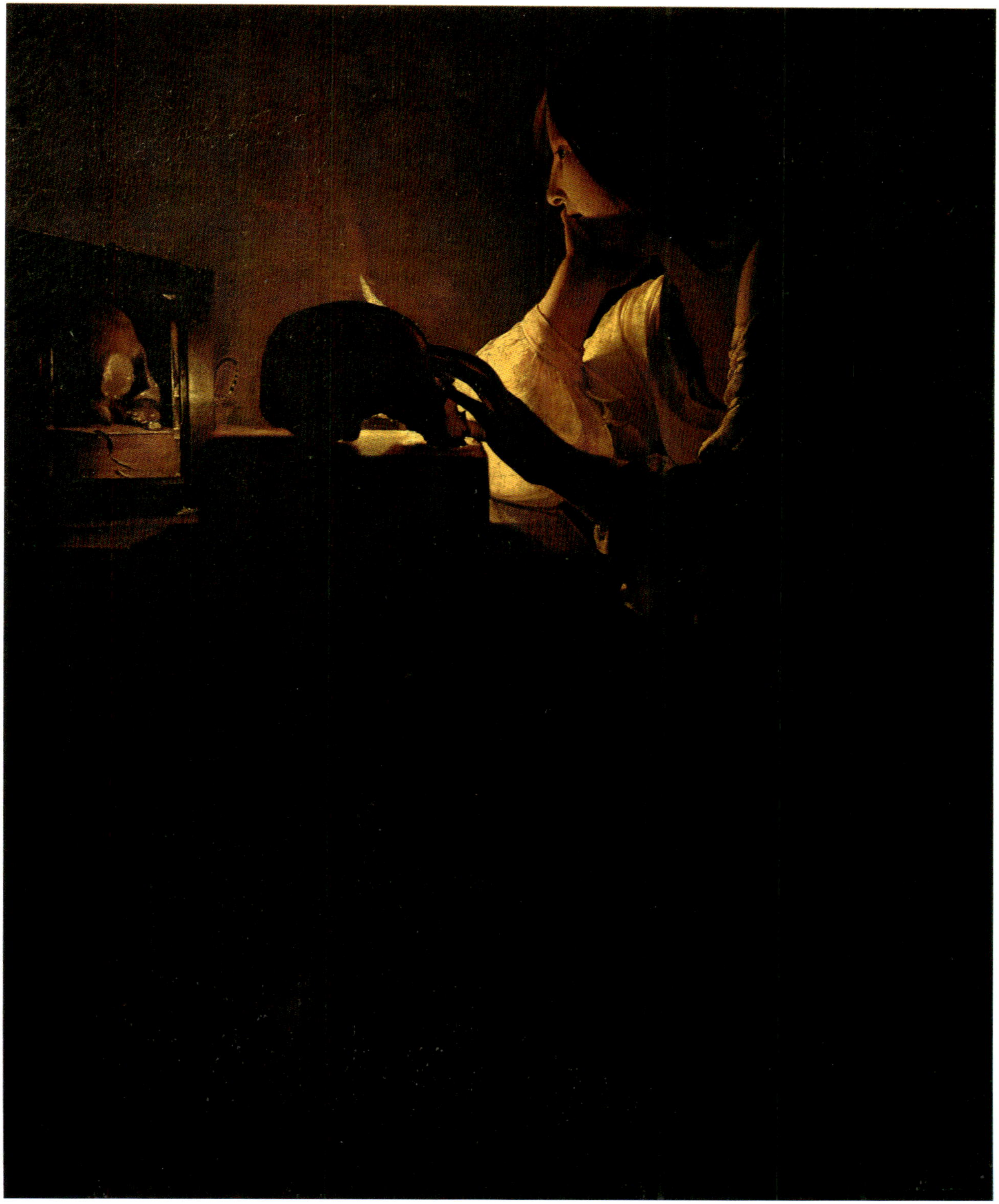

After Jacques Blanchard. *The Repentant Magdalen with Jewels*. Etching by Charles David.

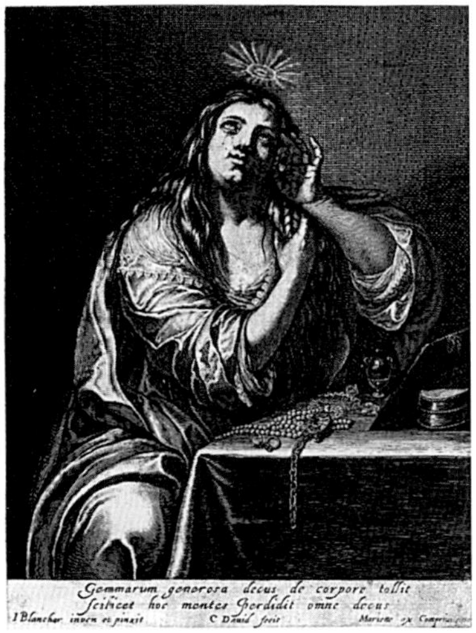

A fourth version also preserved through a small old copy in good condition, belonging to a private collection in the south of France, is now known through two slightly different originals, both of which are signed. One of these, discovered at the time of the 1972 exhibition, has been acquired by the Los Angeles County Museum. In this composition the Magdalen is shown communing with Christ in the glow of a night light, before a cross, a pile of books, and a rope. The other painting is very similar, but various changes in the details and the lighting give it a more subtle lyrical quality. The sobriety of the still life, for instance, reduced here to a set of lines and angles, suggests a later date, undoubtedly the early 1640s. This is the famous *Terff Magdalen* in the Louvre.

The fifth known version probably belongs somewhere between these two very similar originals. The mirror has reappeared, but it is the candle's flame that the spectator sees reflected in it. This is the Magdalen at the beginning of her penance, before the Passion and the Resurrection. She has not yet divested herself of her skirt with its embroidered hem, her mirror in its carved and gilded frame, and a metal candlestick, and tossed aside though not flung far away are her jeweled laces, her pearls and various jewels. This is the most elegant of all La Tour's versions of the *Magdalen*, with something of the look of the courtesans in his daylight paintings. Everything else, however, points to it being later in the series: the extreme simplification of the volumes, the strict geometry of the composition, with its rectangles and trapezoids just barely softened by the sweeping curve of the hair and sleeve, the harsh contrast of light and dark. Was La Tour trying to revive a subject that had been too often repeated, or was he rather bringing a new spirit to bear on a version he had devised sometime earlier? The very idea of the series makes any hypothesis seem possible; only new (and in this case unlikely) documents could determine which is the right one.

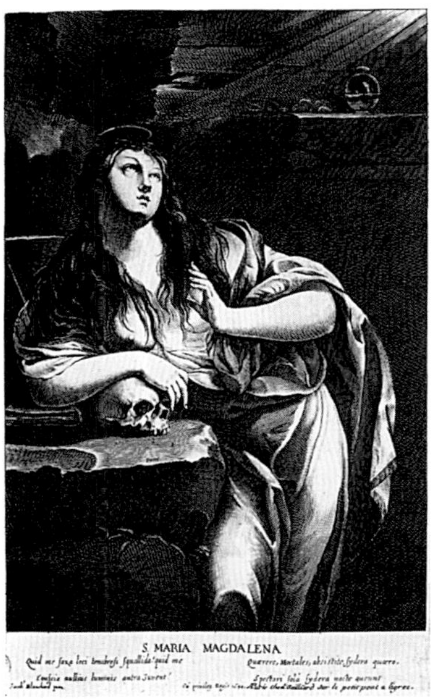

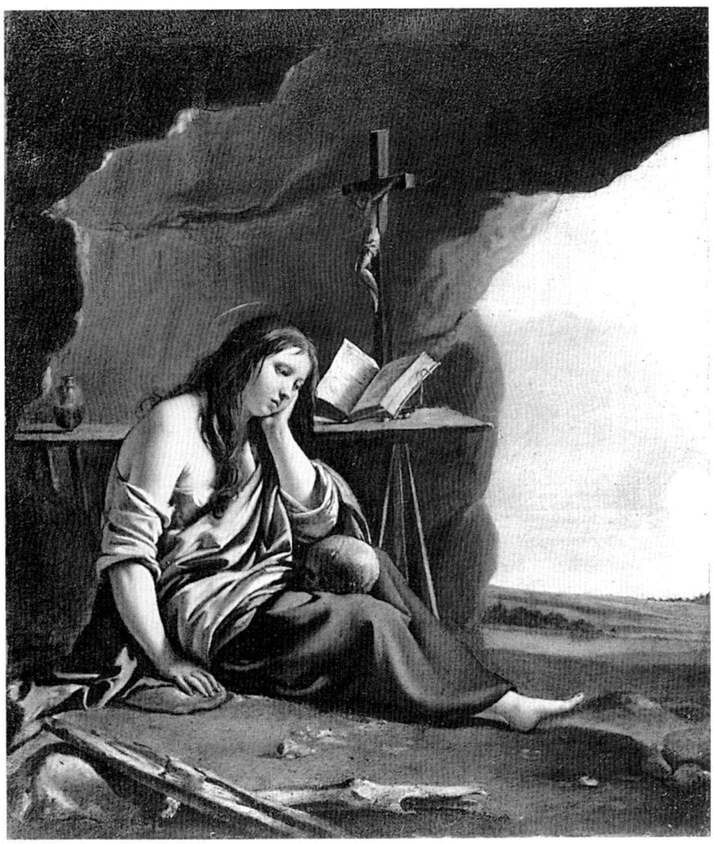

Above: After Jacques Blanchard. *The Repentant Magdalen (With a Skull)*. Engraving by Pierre Daret.

Opposite: Le Nain. *The Repentant Magdalen*. Private collection

pp. 159-161: *The Repentant Magdalen* (also called the *Wrightsman Magdalen*). The Metropolitan Museum of Art, New York

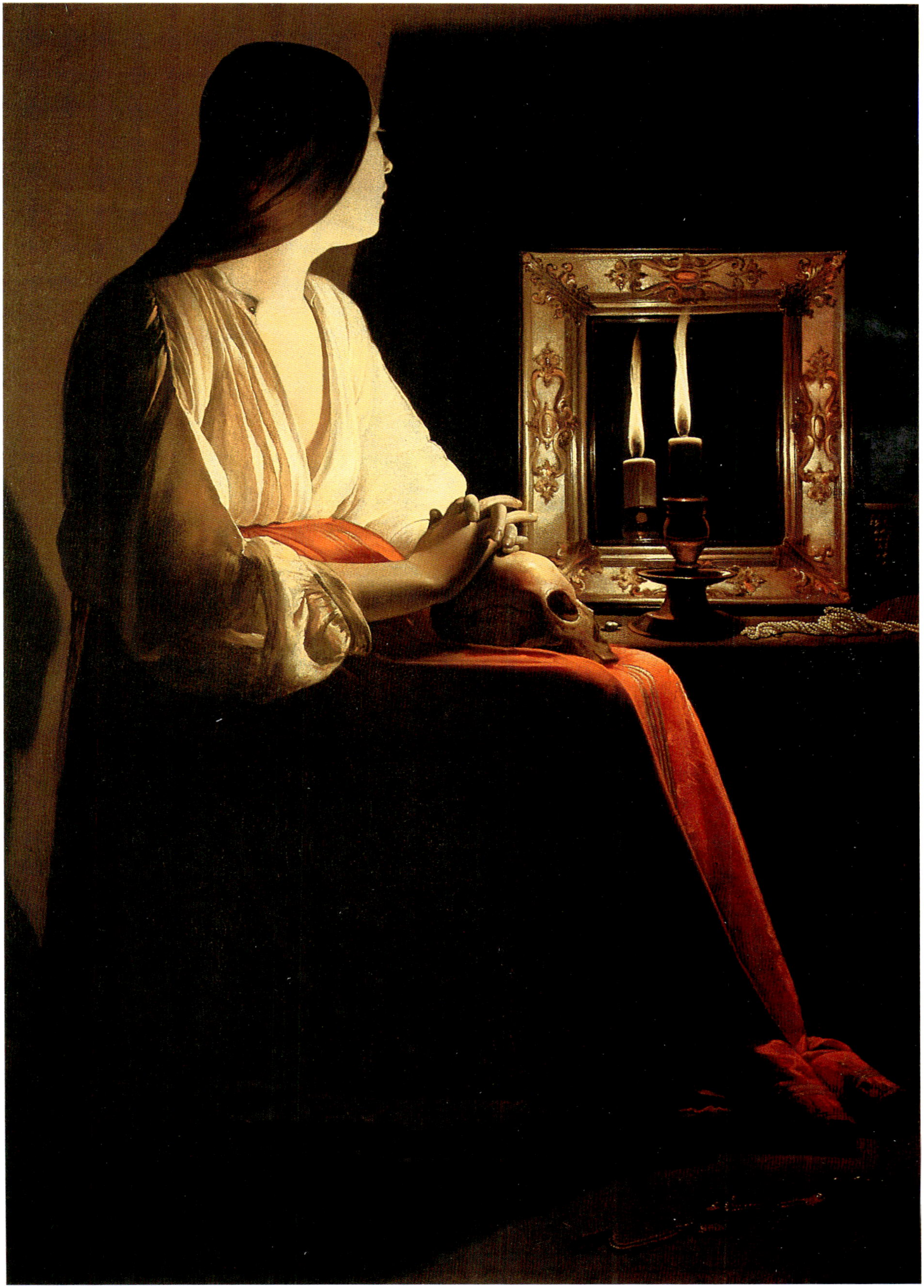

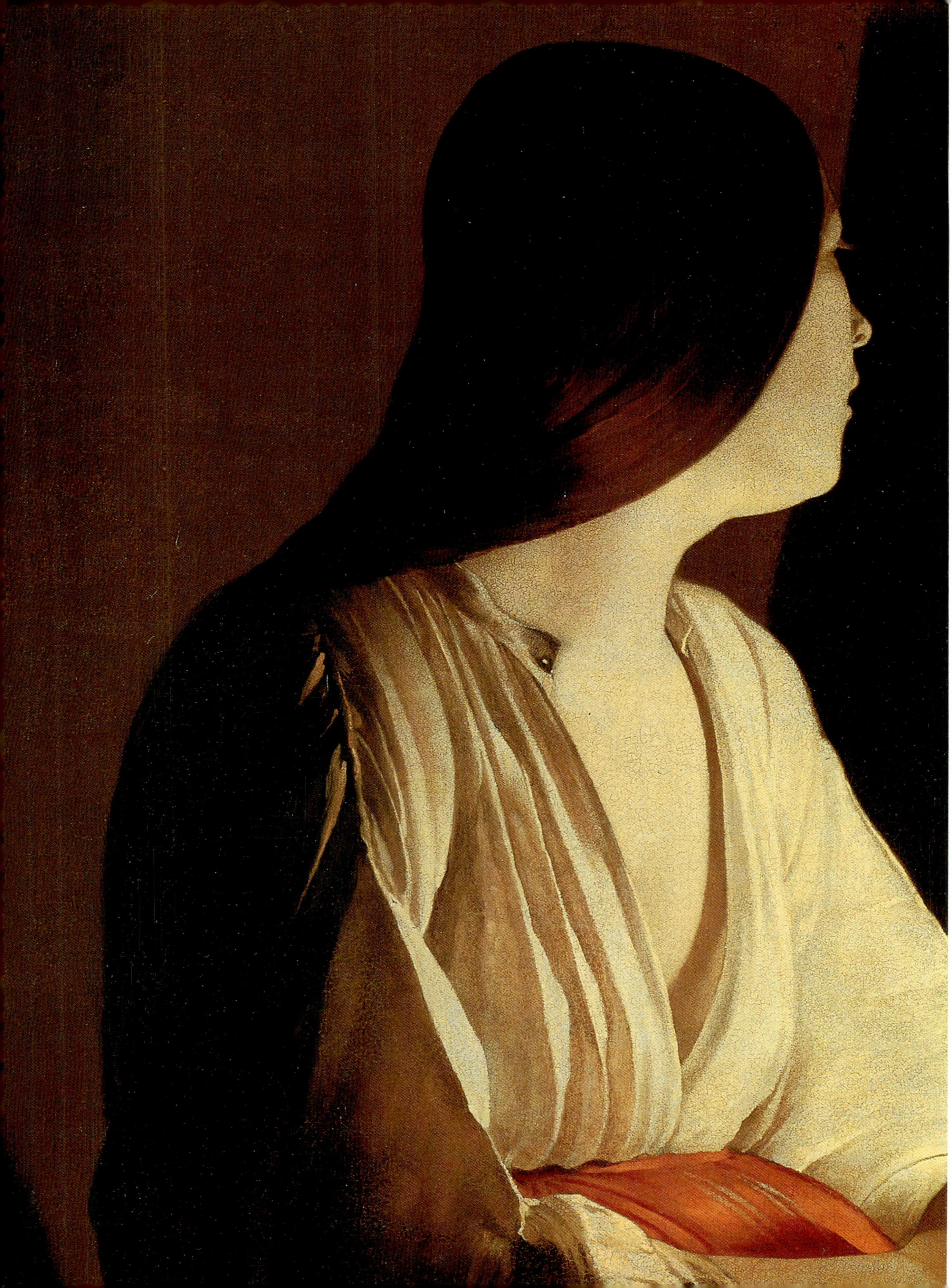

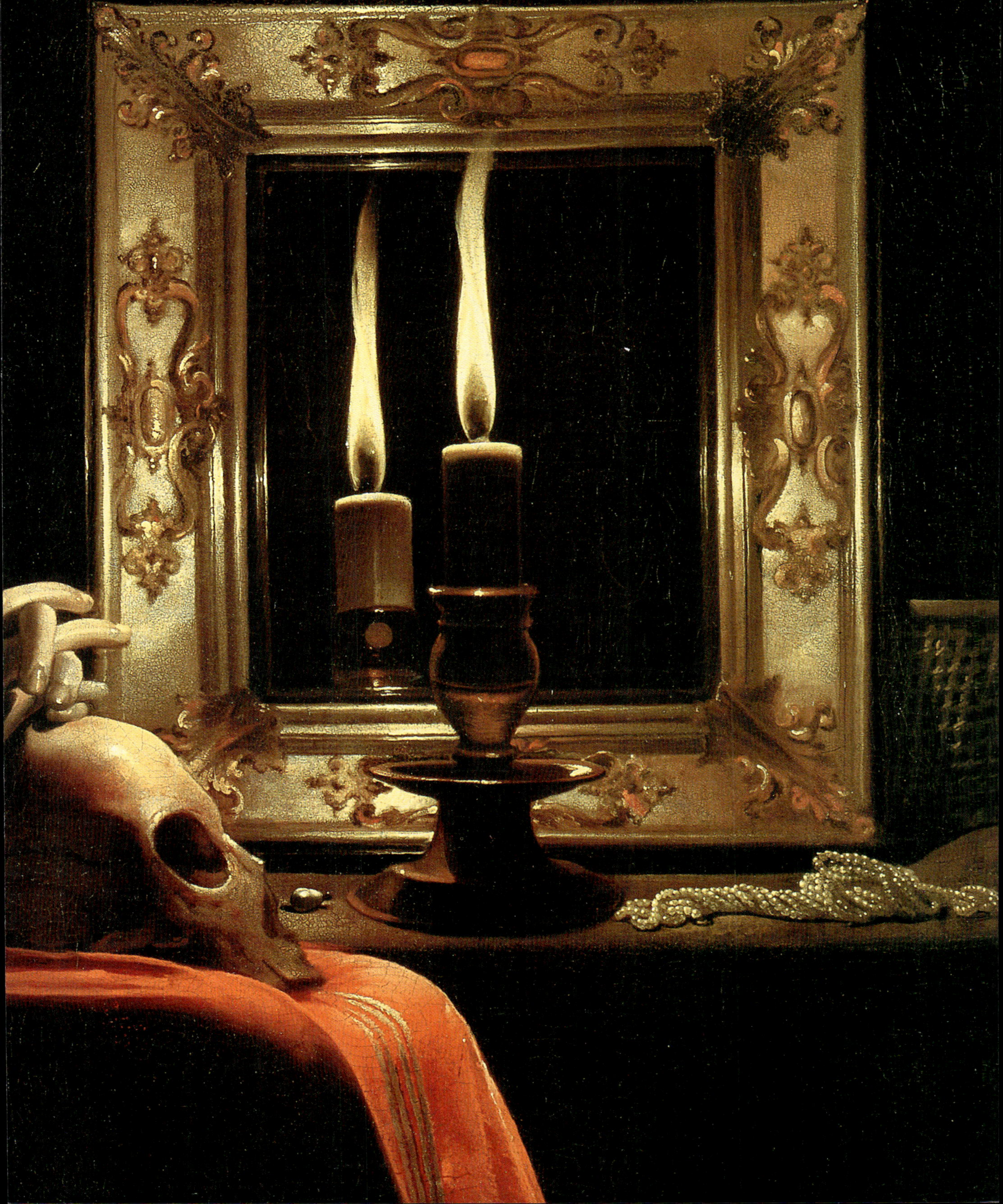

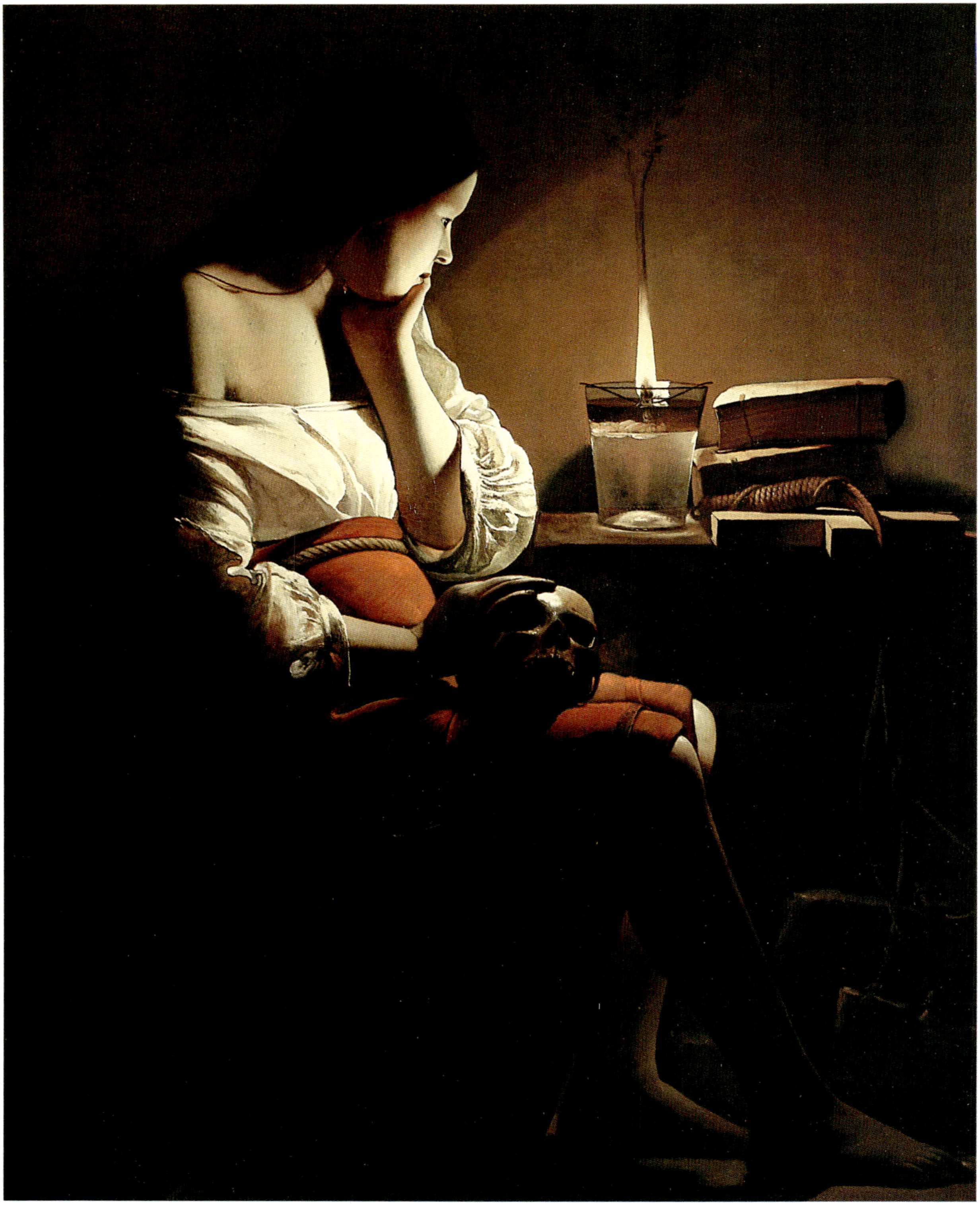

pp. 162, 164, and 165:
The Repentant Magdalen with the Night Light, complete work and details.
County Museum of Art, Los Angeles

pp. 163, 166, and 167:
The Repentant Magdalen with the Night Light, complete work and details.
Musée du Louvre, Paris

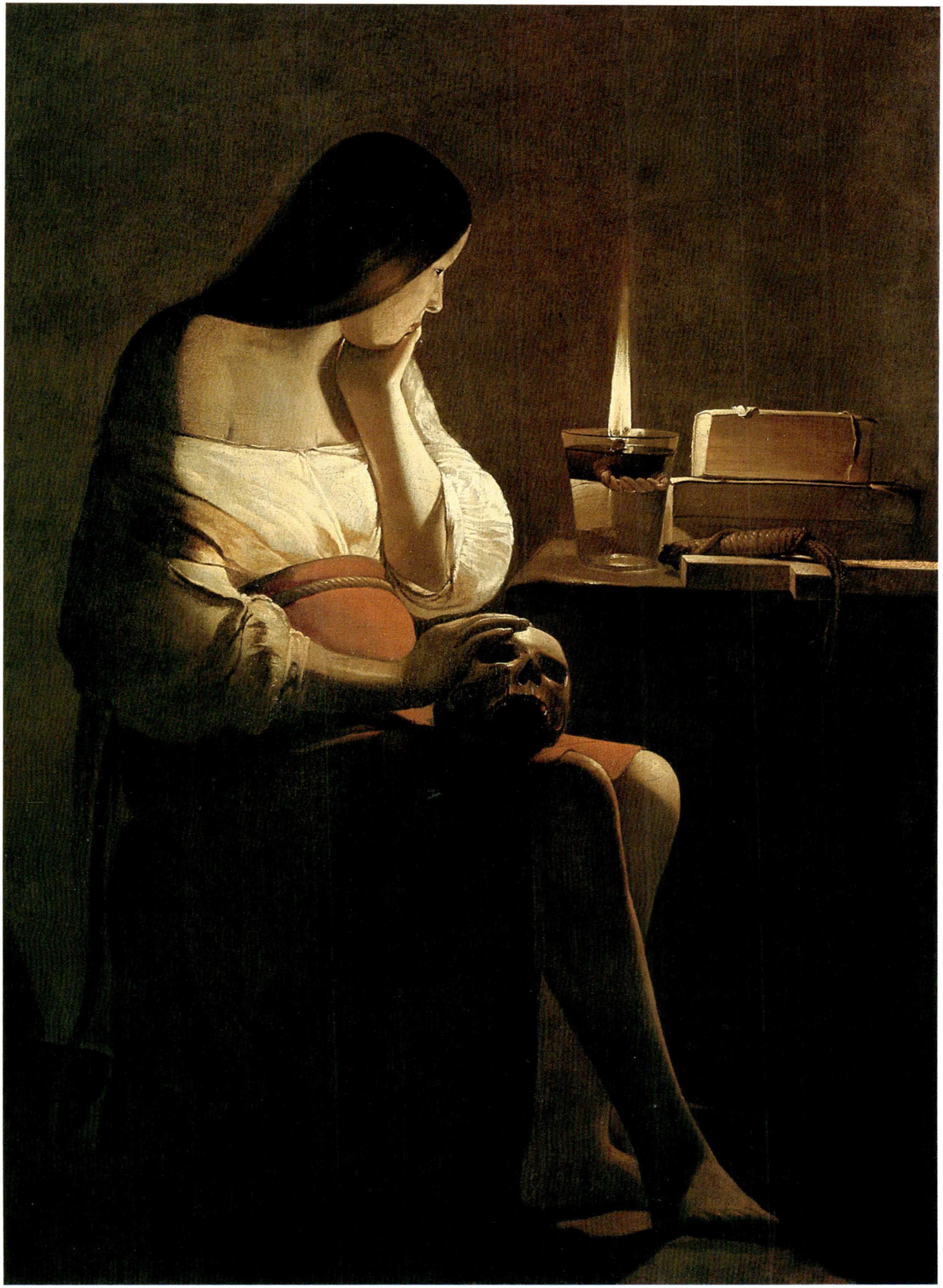

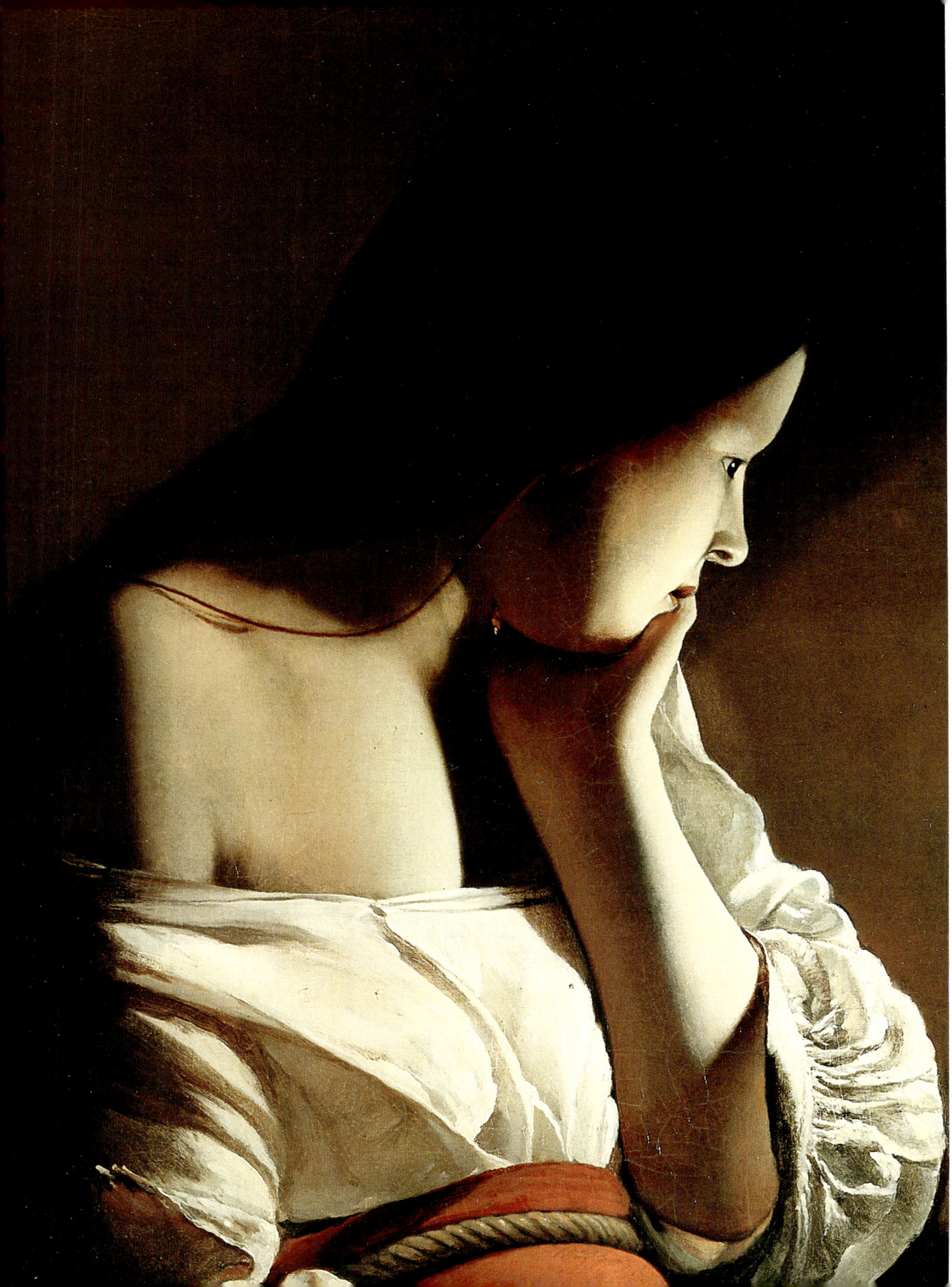

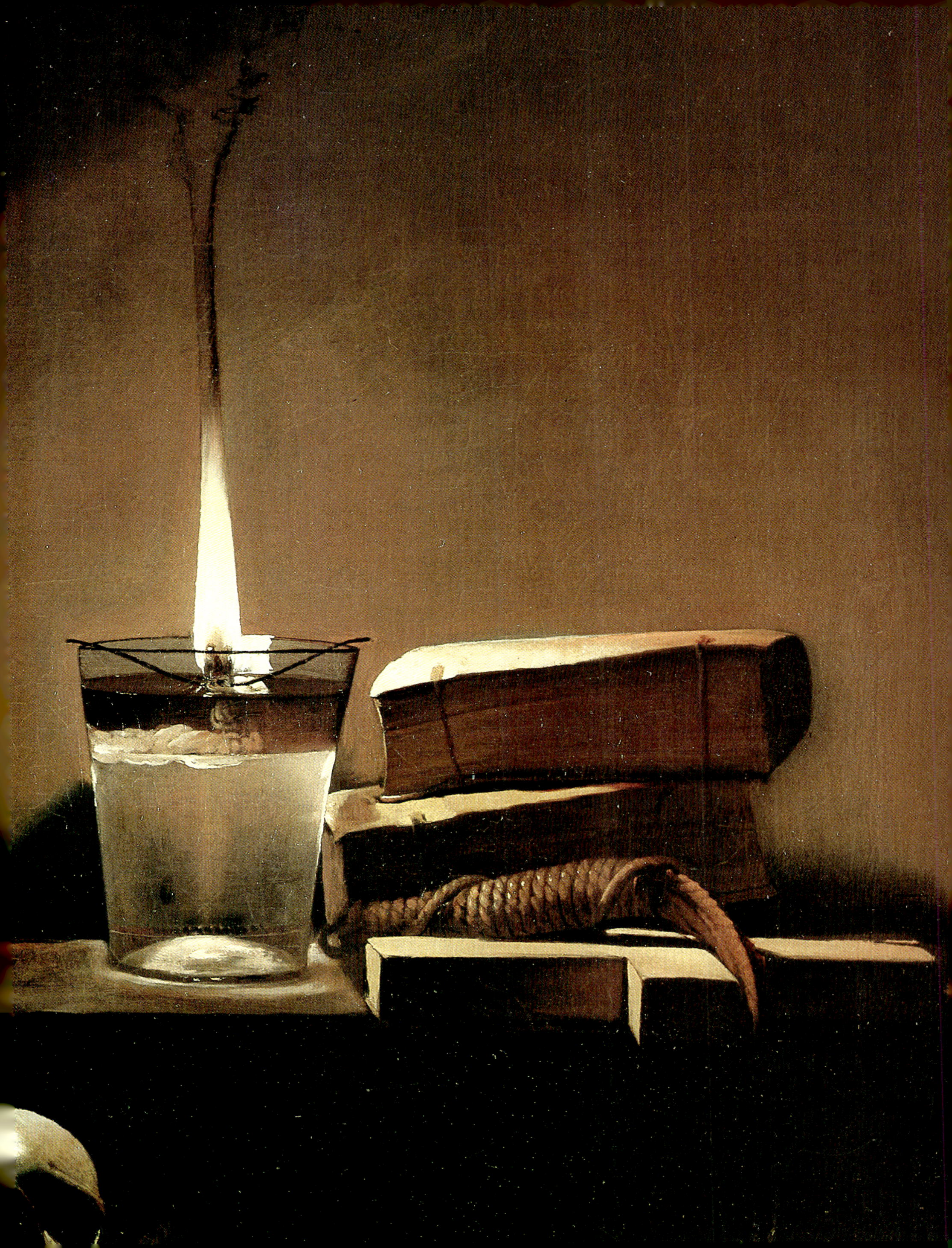

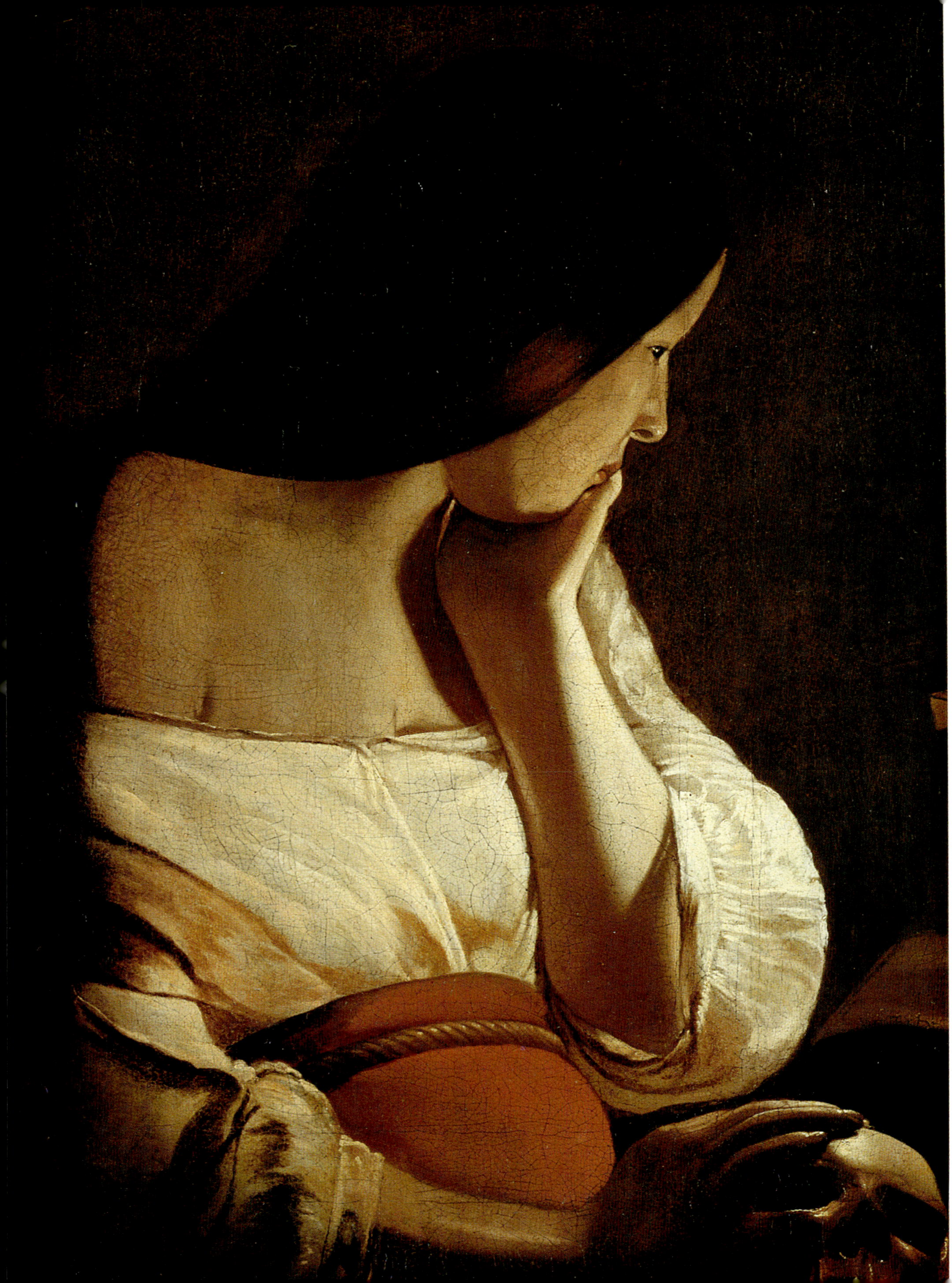

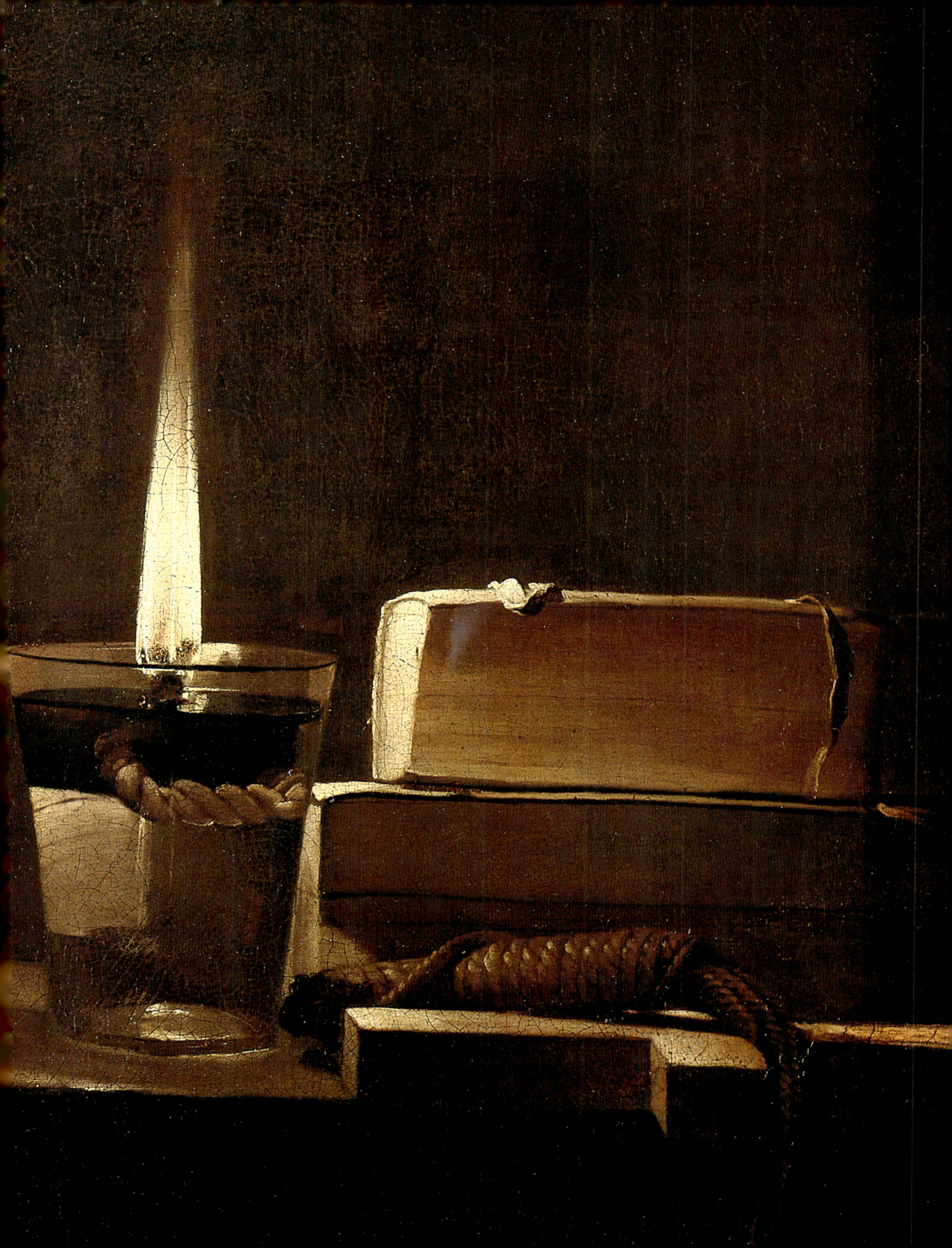

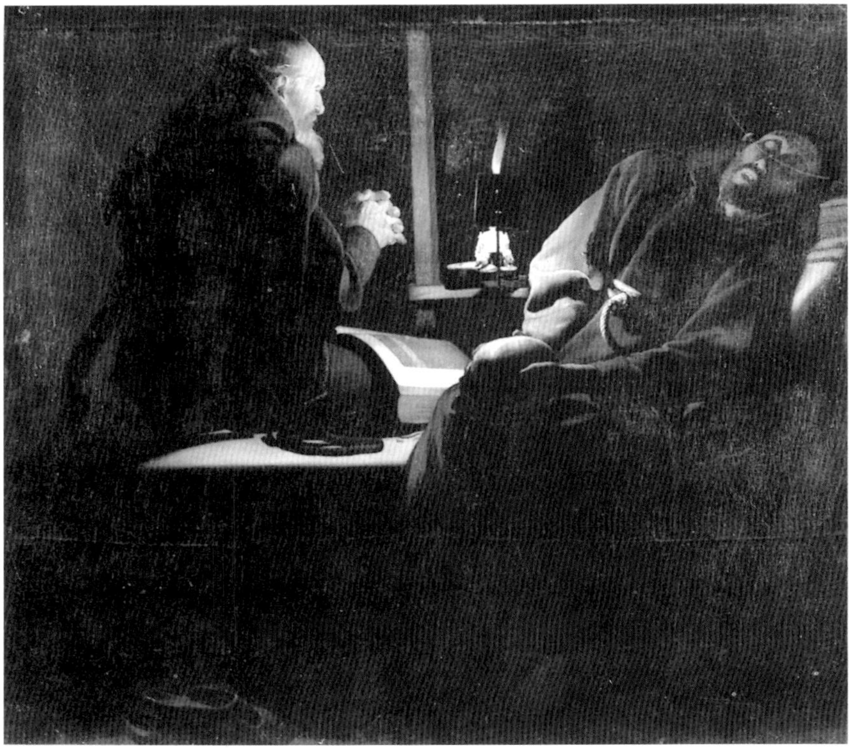

After Georges de La Tour.
St. Francis in Ecstasy.
Musée Tessé, Le Mans

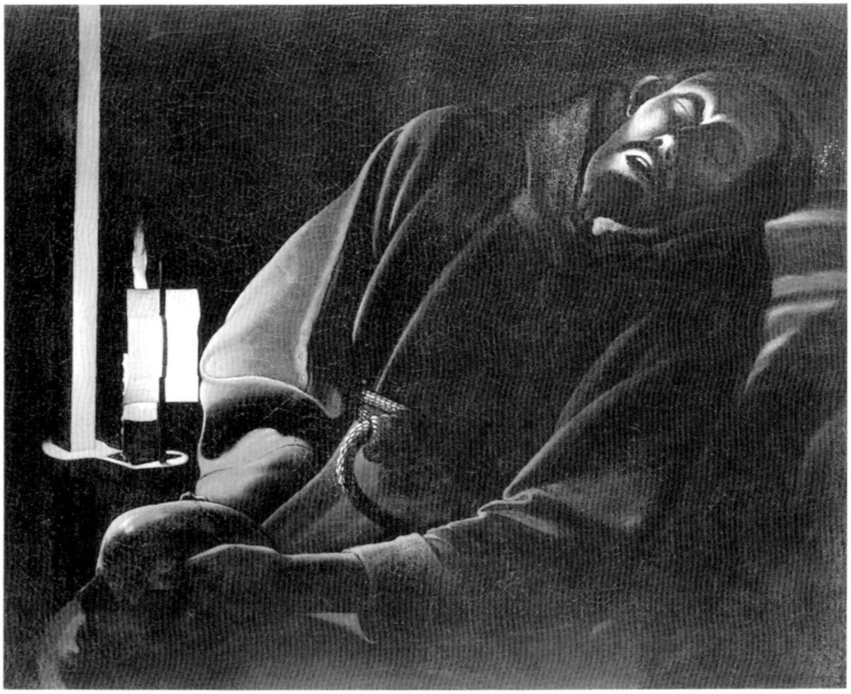

After Georges de La Tour.
St. Francis in Ecstasy.
Wadsworth Atheneum, Hartford, Connecticut

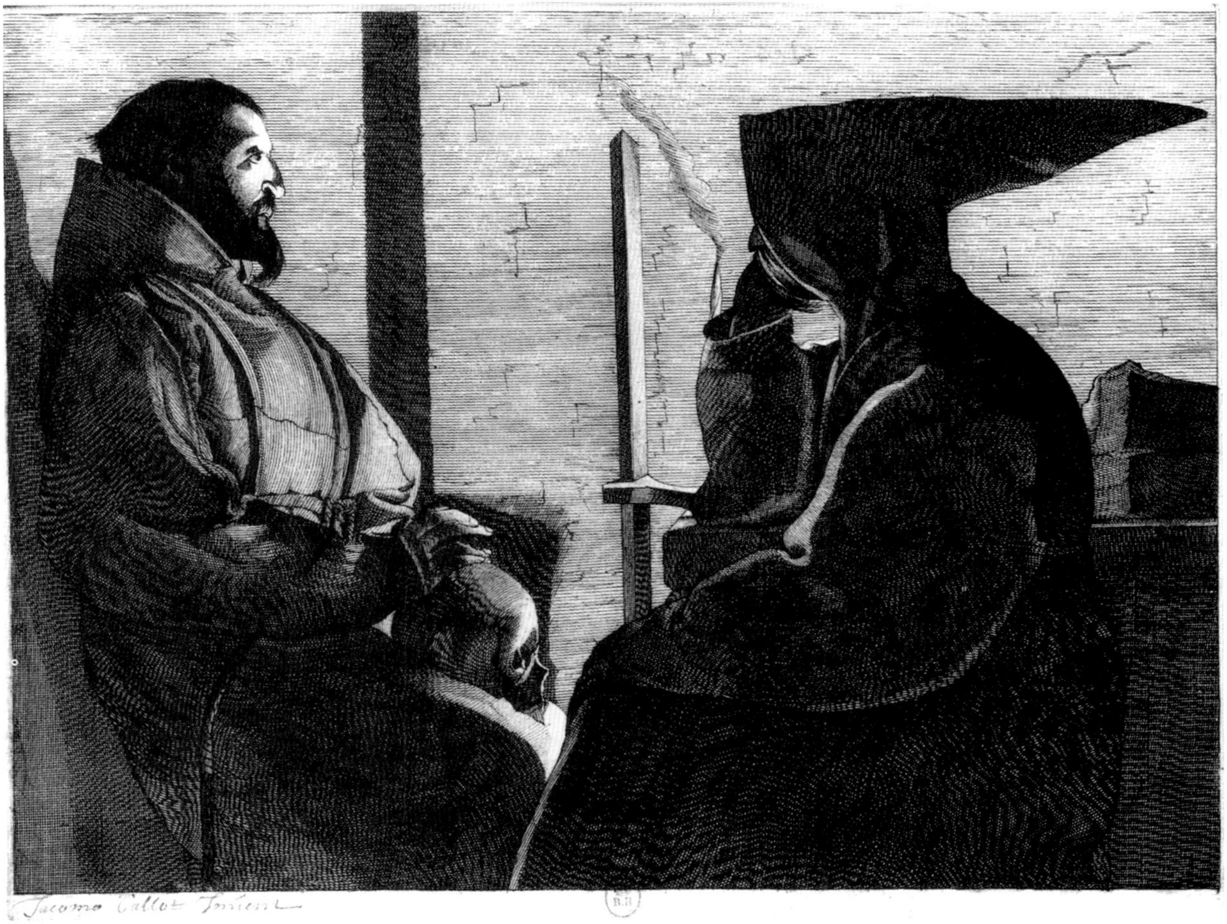

After Georges de La Tour. *St. Francis Meditating.* Anonymous engraving.
Cabinet des Estampes, Bibliothèque Nationale, Paris

The second print relates to the *St. Francis* series, which was not so rich. No originals survive, but there were at least three different versions. All three depict the meditation that transports the saint into an ecstasy of love bordering on death. This ecstasy is often represented by a single angel playing music or a choir of angels, as seen in a painting by Le Clerc that has come down to us. But it is also common to show Francis deep in meditation, with Brother Leo praying or reading at his side: this is how El Greco repeatedly chose to portray him. La Tour seems never to have painted sky or clouds, at least not after his return to France, and he seems to have been even less taken with apparitions. Uncompromising in his realism, like Courbet some two hundred years later, he was reluctant to paint winged angels and parting skies. The lost painting that we know through the engraving shows the saint meditating, a death's head on his knees. He is a powerful figure, more like a lord than a monk, his stiffness accentuated by the harsh light of the candle, while Brother Leo with his long pointed hood is silhouetted dramatically against the wall of the cell. The lighting is enough to give the scene a supernatural quality. It was doubtless one of the finest among the myriad representations of the saint.

A second, very different version is known to us only through two copies. The larger of these, now in the Le Mans museum, was published by Charles Sterling in 1938. It has often been accepted as an original, wrongly in my opinion: the painting is too heavy-handed and the light too opaque. The mistake is understandable, though, for this large painting with its full-length figures preserves something of what must have been a very striking work. This time it is the figure of Brother Leo that is singled out by the light, while on the other side St. Francis, sunken into his chair, slips away toward the night in an ecstasy that closes his eyes and draws his lips. The glimmers of light that filter onto his face turn it into a death's head. There is nothing here but darkness and the somber earth color of his habit. Hidden by a screen, the flame casts a dull light; time seems to have stopped.

Despite its austerity, or perhaps because of it, the painting must have aroused great admiration. Another copy, showing only the figure of St. Francis, is housed in the Wadsworth Atheneum in Hartford. There are enough differences here to suggest the existence of a third version that was very close to the second, but with a slightly modified lighting scheme and a more prominent position for the candlestick. It could be a fragment from a larger composition, but not necessarily. The cult of St. Francis called for smaller paintings as well as large, and La Tour readily reverted to his single, half-length figures. It is also worth remembering that Jean-Baptiste de Bretagne's collection included both a painting described as *Two Capuchins Meditating by Candlelight*, which would seem to fit with the engraved version, and another of *A Sleeping Monk*, seemingly a picture of St. Francis alone, which could very well be this third version, or one very like it.

The last of the three engravings has a different but no less solemn poetry about it. It is generally called *The Newborn Child* or the *Madonna and Child with St. Anne*. It shows a cradle watched over by a young woman with a book on her lap and an old woman who, candle in hand, lights up the face of the child lying tightly bound in swaddling clothes. Great shadows are cast on the bare wall and floor. This could be seen as a simple maternity scene, with a mother and grandmother watching over a newborn child still plunged in the darkness of pre-life. It is tempting to go further, however. Notwithstanding the engraver's somewhat awkward transposition, the woman with the slightly rounded nose and full little mouth bears a marked resemblance to the Fabius *Magdalen*, and the old woman with the hooked nose also seems familiar. La Tour appears to have drawn his models from his entourage, if not from his immediate family. His youngest daughter, Marie, was baptized in March 1636, and she may well have had a special place in his affections, which would then give the painting a very simple and personal meaning. It is clear, however, that La Tour also freely exploits the ambiguity of the scene's religious connotations, in that he refuses to describe or translate them by means of supernatural effects. The open book is enough to suggest the Virgin meditating on the infant Christ's destiny, while the grandmother's admiring gaze at the newborn child readily evokes St. Anne contemplating the Savior. Such is the virtue of realism. All this aside, beyond the ambiguities, the painting is clearly a meditation on birth, on the fragility of this being scarcely emerged from the limbo of matter, on the uncertainty of the fate that will soon take him beyond the protection of the cupped hand and the quivering circle of light.

Indeed, light plays an essential role in these paintings. Whether still, or slightly curved by a breath, or hidden behind a screen but no less present, the flame has become the very focus of the scene—which was not at all the case in *The Payment of Dues*, where all the light was concentrated on the double page of the register. La Tour undoubtedly found light fascinating in its own right, apart from any precise meaning it might have. His *Boy Blowing on a Charcoal Stick* in the Granville Collection, in the museum in Dijon, takes up an old luminist theme, treated by the Bassanos and El Greco and repeated by the northern Caravaggists from Terbrugghen to Stomer. A signed original that is still on its old canvas (which is unusual for La Tour), the Granville painting is an uncompromising representation of a child's face, distorted by effort, yet at the same time lit up by the glowing firebrand toward which he raises his oil lamp. There is something here of La Tour's earlier relish for materials, now brought to bear on the boy's leather apron or the half-charred lump of wood that glimmers into life. Nowhere, however, does La Tour take his study of light further than in the first version of *St. Sebastian Tended by Irene*, where light becomes the very means of an entirely new treatment of the scene.

This is the first version that we know of at least; there may well have been others. St. Sebastian was widely worshiped in Lorraine, as in the rest of France, moreover. Nursed back to health by the widow Irene after being shot with arrows, the

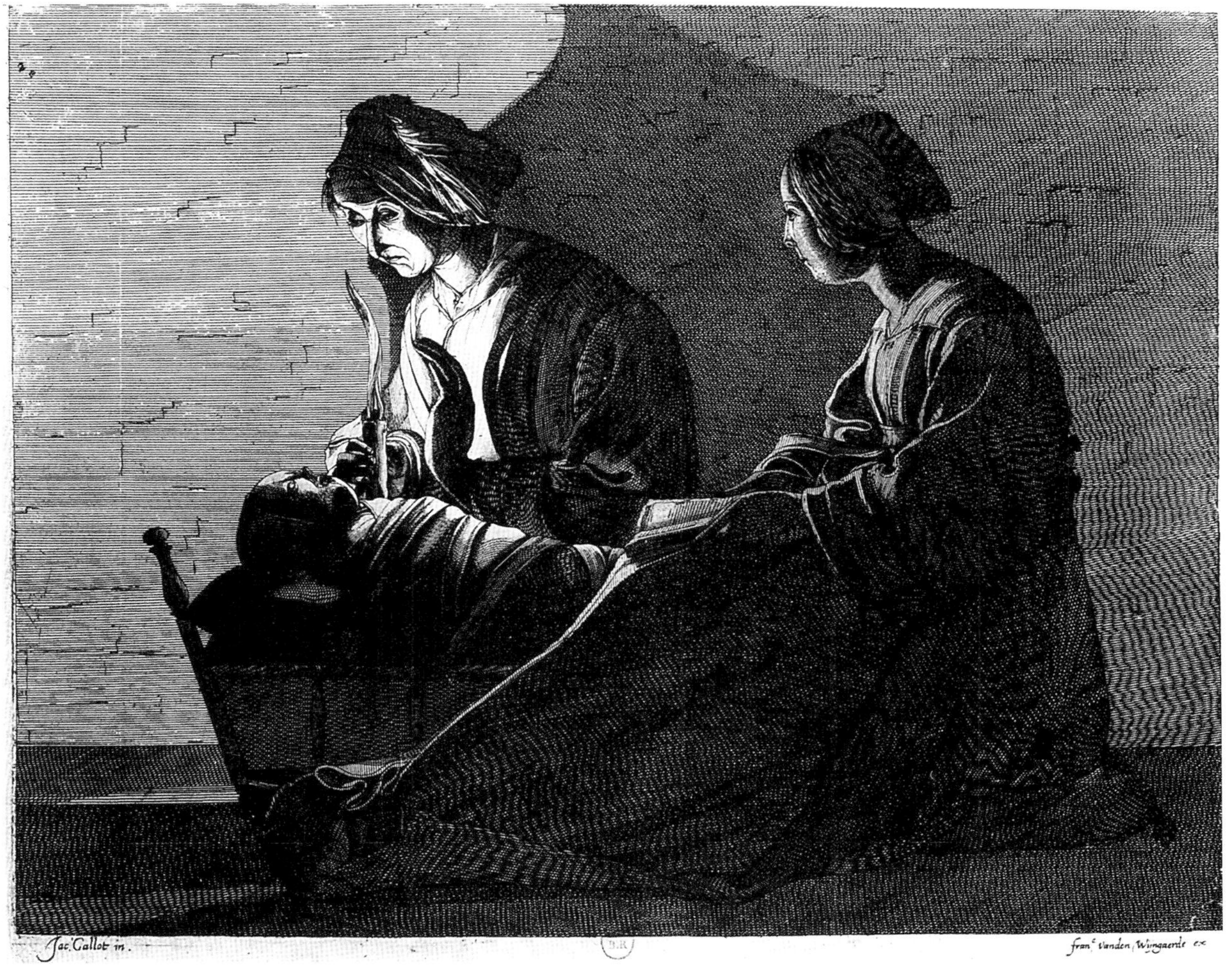

After Georges de La Tour,
The Newborn Child (also called *Madonna and Child with St. Anne*).
Anonymous engraving.
Cabinet des Estampes, Bibliothèque Nationale, Paris

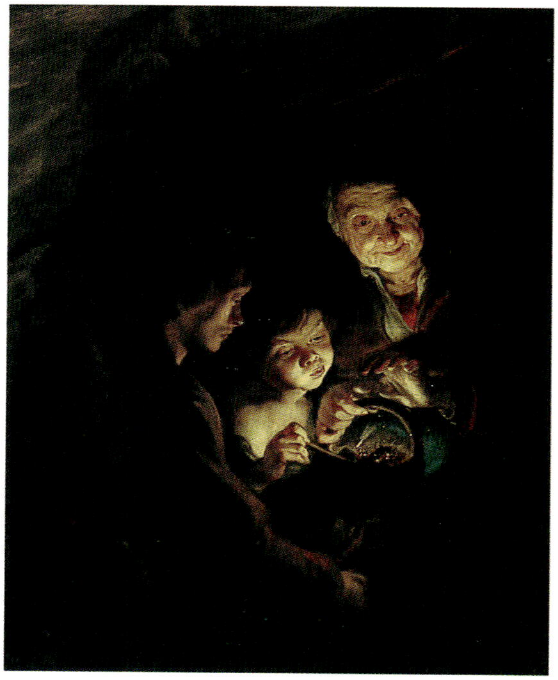

PAINTINGS OF *SOUFFLEURS*

Left:
Peter Paul Rubens. *Woman with a Brazier.* *c.* 1618-1620.
Gemäldegalerie, Dresden

Below left:
Jan Lievens. *Man Blowing on a Flame.*
National Museum, Warsaw

Below right:
El Greco. *Boy Blowing on an Ember.*
Museo di Capodimonte, Naples

p. 173:
Boy Blowing on a Charcoal Stick.
Musée des Beaux-Arts, Dijon,
Pierre and Kathleen Granville bequest

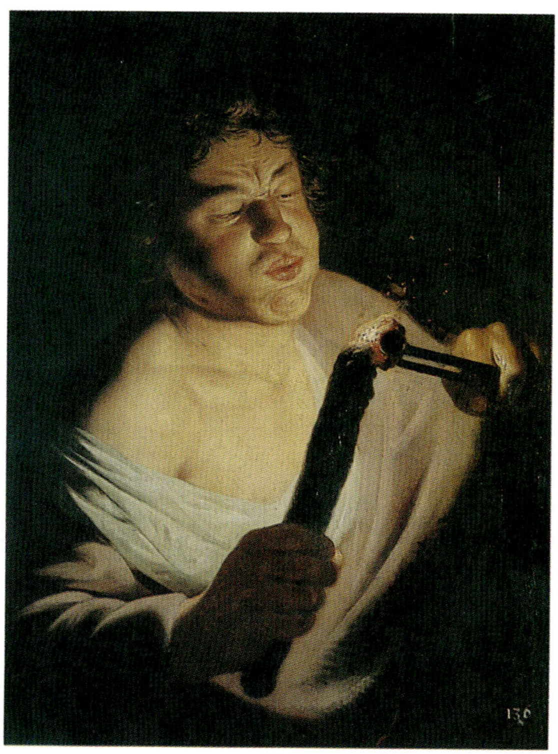

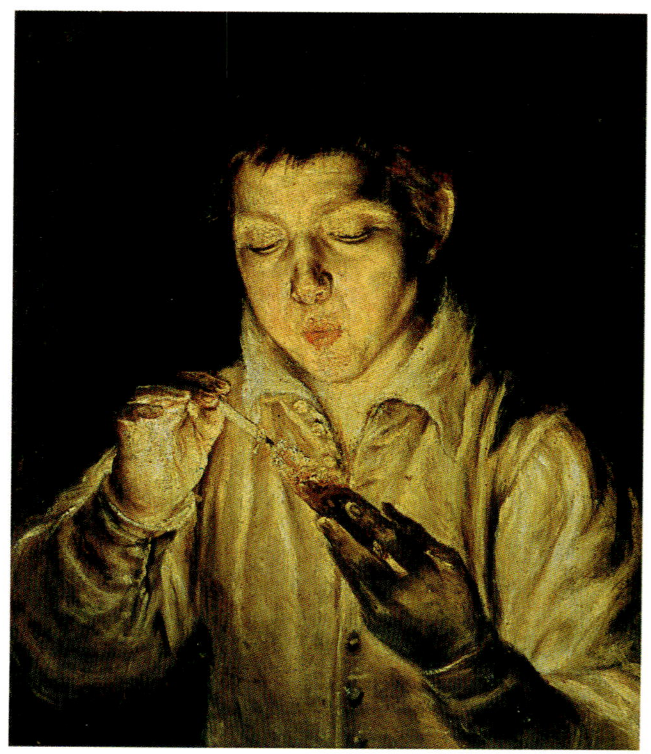

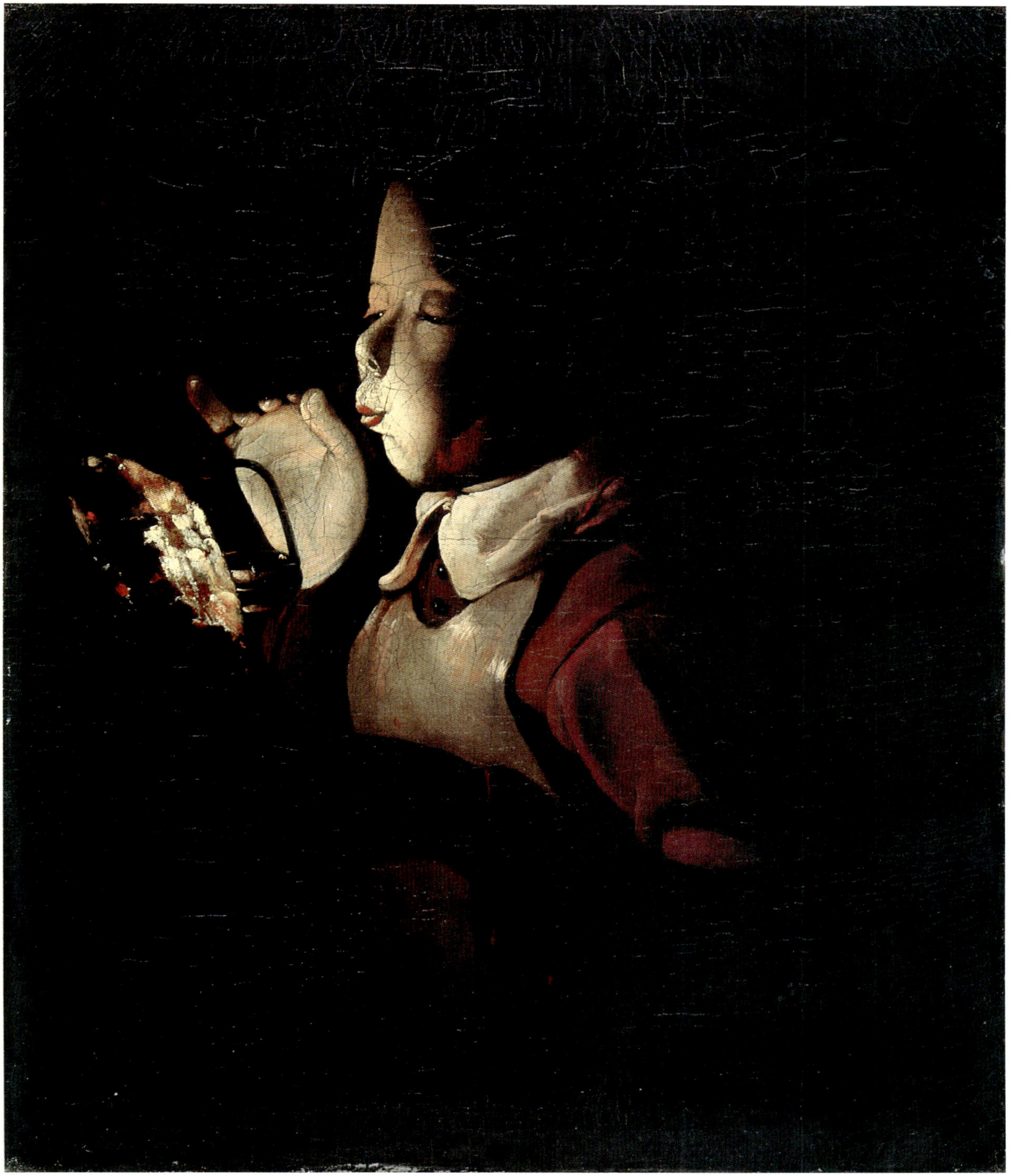

ST. SEBASTIAN TENDED BY ST. IRENE

Above: Giuseppe de Ribera.
The Hermitage Museum, St. Petersburg

Far right: Trophime Bigot.
The Vatican Museum, Rome

Right: Hendrick Terbrugghen.
Allen Art Museum, Oberlin, Ohio

Below, from top to bottom:
Pierre Brébiette. Etching.

After Jacques Blanchard. Engraving by Antoine Garnier.

After Rutilio Manetti. Engraving.

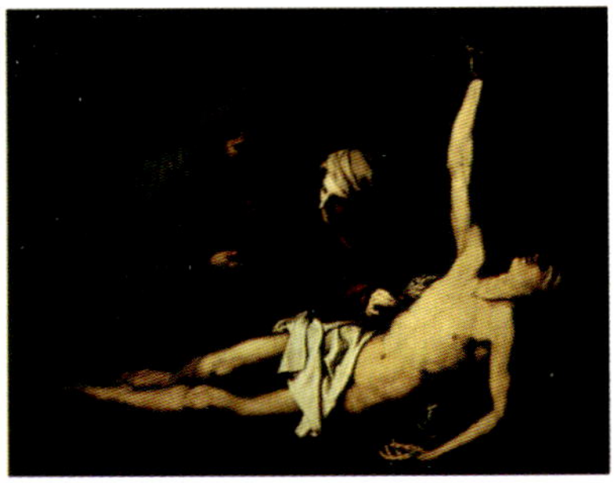

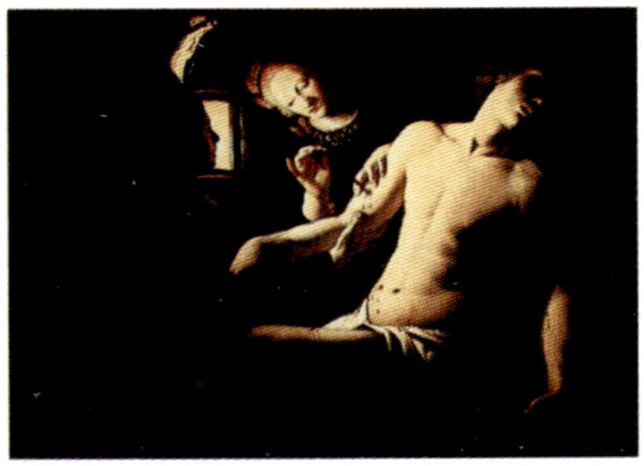

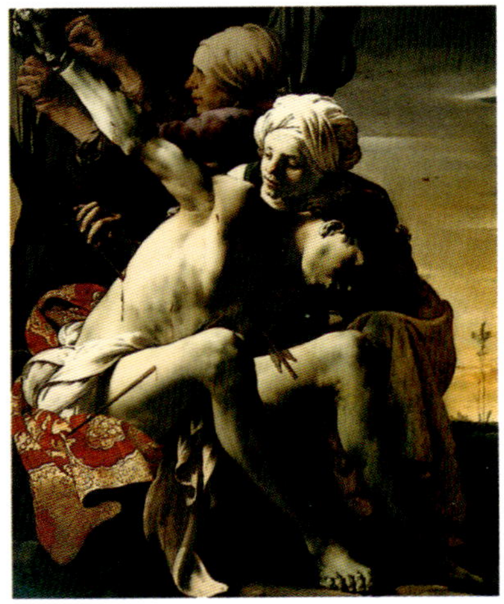

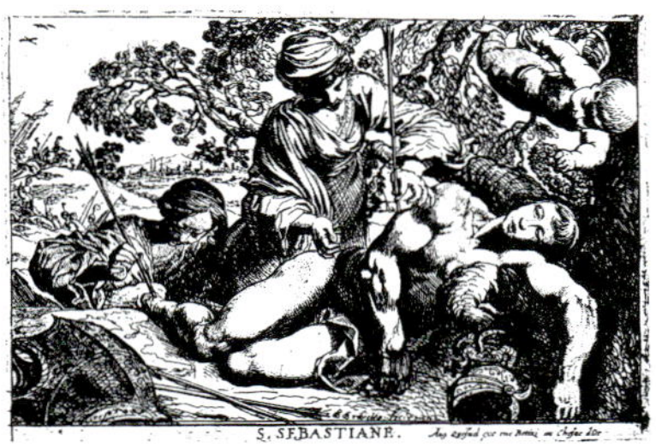

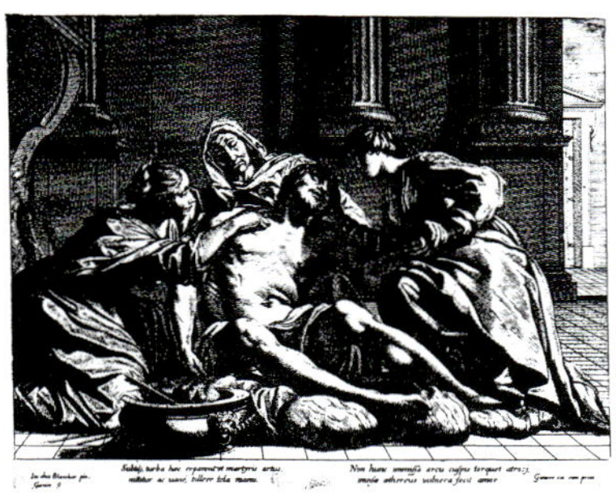

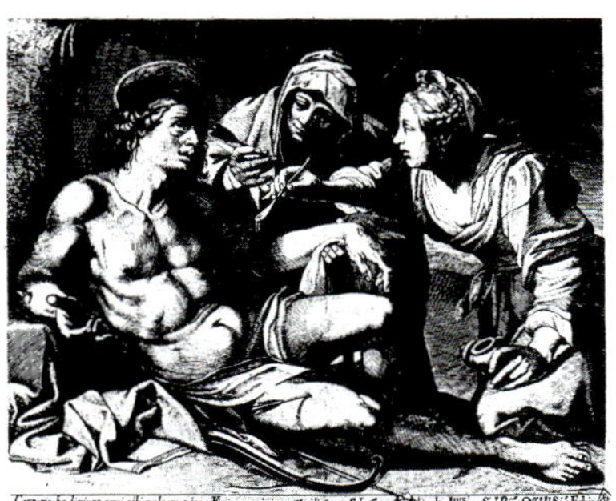

Roman soldier was invoked against the plague. The epidemic of 1631 and the repeated outbreaks that followed seem to have brought about a revival of the saint's cult, and to have prompted La Tour to tackle this theme. It is not impossible that he produced some daylight treatments of it in the early 1630s, and that these were followed soon after by the first night versions. According to Dom Calmet, La Tour presented Duke Charles II with a picture of St. Sebastian, which would have to have been painted before 1634. The horizontal version that we know was copied so often (the original is lost, but there are reports of at least a dozen copies), and appears to have been so highly regarded in France (there are examples in Orléans, Rouen, Evreux, Honfleur, etc.) that it could well be the painting that La Tour presented to Louis XIII and which, according to Dom Calmet, was "of such perfect taste that the king removed all the other pictures from his chamber, so that this one might hang on its own." In such a case, this version, if not the composition itself, would have to date from about 1638-1639.

At the center of the composition is a lantern shielding a candle. The glow of the hidden flame filters over the young man's bared body and lights up Irene's hand, her attentive face framed by veils, and the arrow that she draws from the wound. It is reflected on the servant's dress and the wounded soldier's helmet. The haphazard rays escaping through the dark bars of the lantern's frame binds the silent trio together in the darkness as it focuses on the point of pain indicated by the feathered arrow. Relying on the shadows to banish any impropriety, La Tour makes his St. Sebastian a nude, as convention allowed, but however young and handsome the figure is, it owes nothing to the antique tradition; the inspiration remains realist. There is even a certain ambiguity at work: with no halo, angel, or martyr's crown, there is nothing to signal that this is a religious scene. The widow Irene is also very young and very beautiful, and perhaps one of the most moving figures La Tour ever painted. Indeed, it is difficult to rid one's mind of similar scenes where compassion is inspired less by piety than by love, such as the episode of Erminia nursing Tancred in *Jerusalem Delivered* that was so often treated by painters,

> *Mira e tratta le piaghe e, di ferute*
> *Giudice esperata, spera indi salute. . . .*

Here, however, a strict geometrical structure suspends all movement, imposes a silence on the scene, and gives it a restraint that a great many paintings of *St. Sebastian* lack. This is almost certainly La Tour's finest and most moving composition of the entire period, and the one that displays his poetic talent to the full.

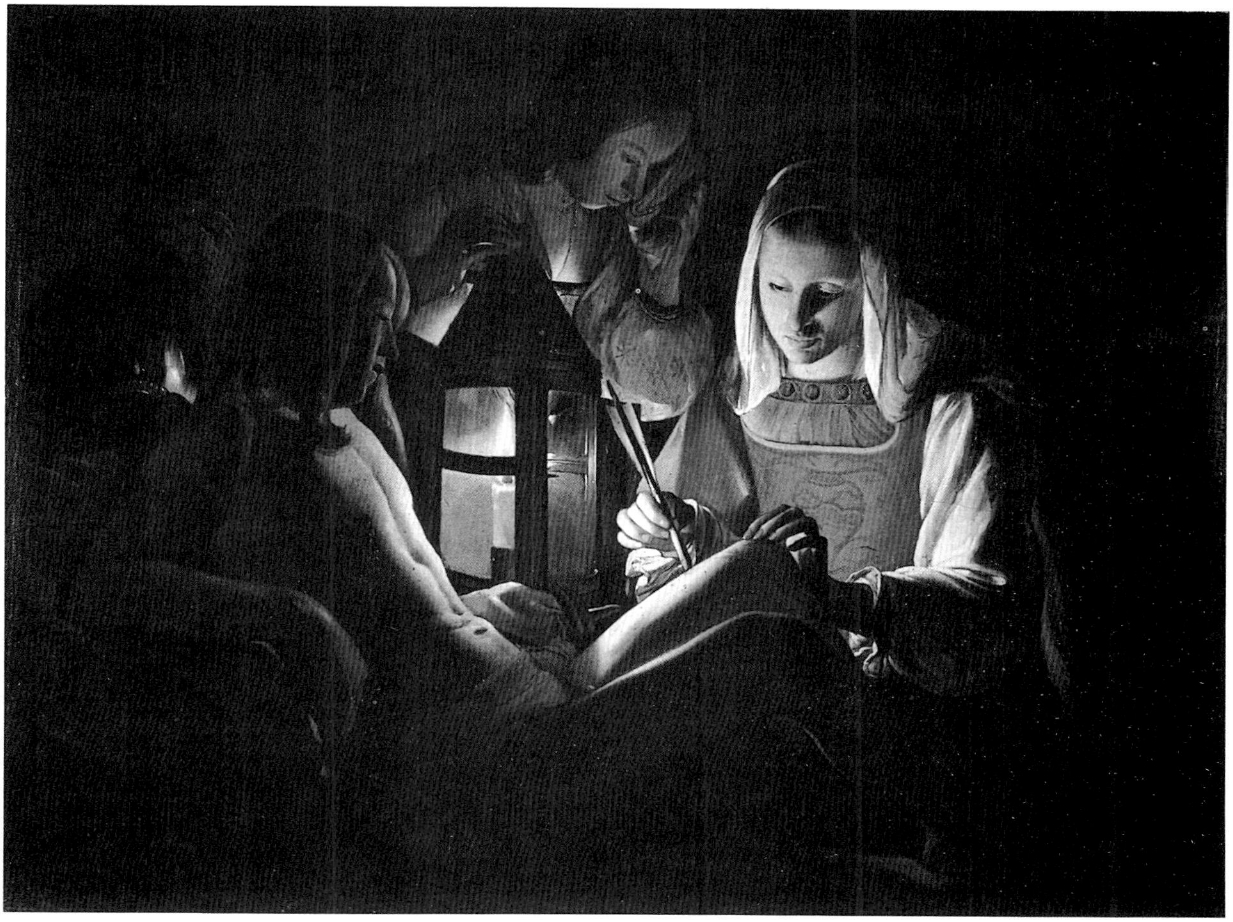

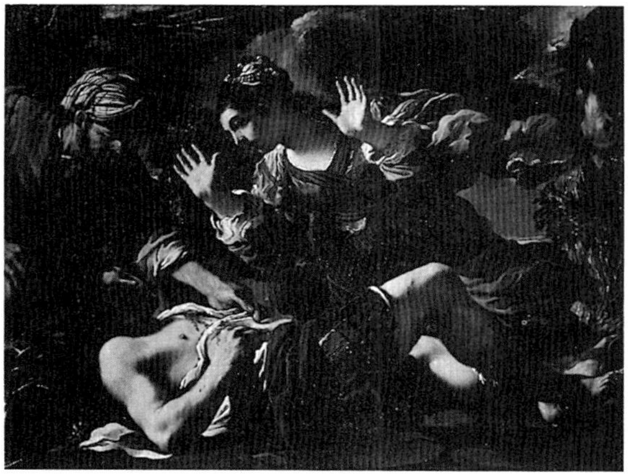

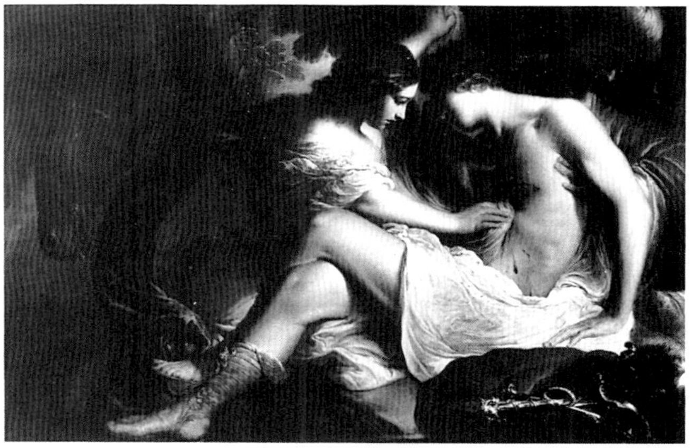

It also gives us the key to that talent. La Tour, the La Tour of *The Cheat* and *St. Sebastian*, has not yet turned his back on the real world, on its outward charms or even its sensual appeal. He still revels in the sheen of satin, the intricacies of embroidery, and the glimmer of light. He still observes faces minutely and seeks out the human presence—but he does so differently.

Everything he once took such delight in capturing with his brush—the unpredictable diversity, the vitality, crude and unattractive though it may have been, the tactile quality of matter, stray wisps of hair on a neck, the coarseness of a rough-hewn staff—seems to interest him less and less. Or rather, he introduces it into a tight geometric design in which reality, human impulse, and passion, good and bad alike,

Top: After Georges de La Tour. *St. Sebastian Tended by Irene (with the Lantern).*
Musée des Beaux-Arts, Rouen

A THEME BOTH SACRED AND PROFANE

Left: Il Guercino. *Tancred and Erminia.*
Galleria Doria Pamphili, Rome

Above: Pietro Ricchi. *Tancred and Erminia.*
Residenzgalerie, Salzburg

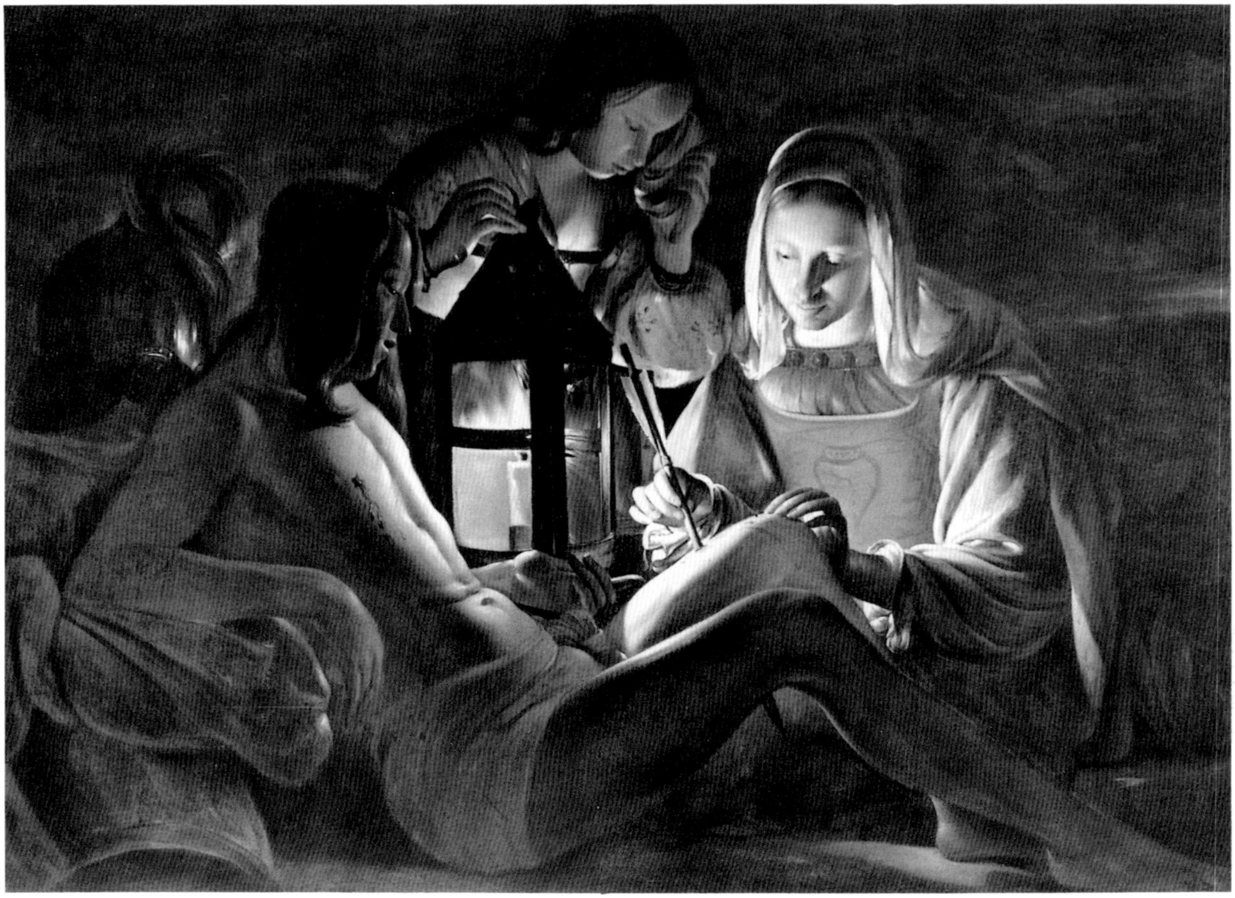

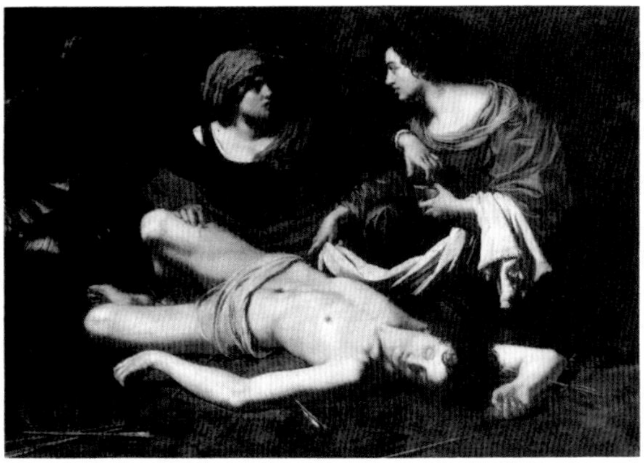

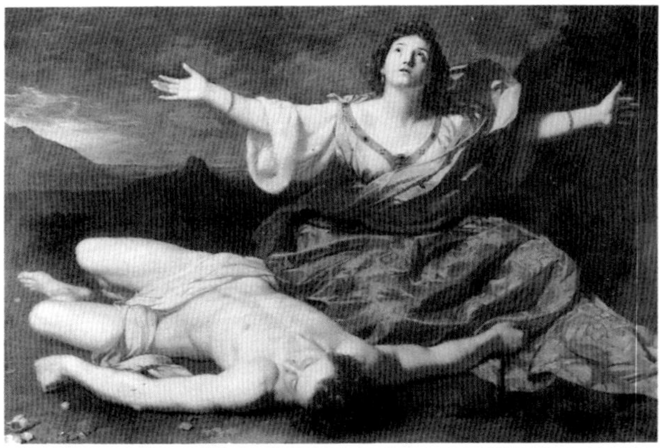

Above: After Georges de La Tour. *St. Sebastian Tended by Irene (with the Lantern).*
William Rockhill Nelson Gallery of Art, Kansas City

A THEME BOTH SACRED AND PROFANE

Left: Nicolas Régnier.
St. Sebastian Tended by Irene.
Musée des Beaux-Arts, Rouen
Right: Nicolas Régnier. *Hero and Leander.*
National Museum of Victoria, Melbourne

assume the inevitability of destiny. Even the misshapen body of St. Jerome flagellating himself is held between two sharp parallel lines and surrounded—indeed propped up—by the two great splashes of cardinal scarlet. This is still a very glittering world, in a way even more so than before: it is not so much the rugged face of everyday reality that now preoccupies La Tour as its artificial aspect—jewels, fantastic embroidery, showy dress. Because of its artifice, however, it is a world that La Tour can all the more readily bend to suit his purposes.

The nocturnes do away with this deceptive glitter and impose further limits on a universe where nature and greenery had never found a place. They dispense with color and return to essential form. The Magdalen's hair, for instance, is reduced to a heavy, dark, glossy mass, while wrinkles and whiskers are barely visible. The world recovers a primordial simplicity: that of the idea.

It is difficult not to see these increasingly pronounced stylistic choices of the 1630s as the expression of a deep psychological change. La Tour was becoming richer, more famous, and more sure of himself and of his art. Yet at the same time the world around him was constantly threatened by sickness, war, and death; it revealed itself to be instable and disappointing. For the masses of common people lamentation and suffering was natural; for the young, life was made of revolt and adventure. Wisdom rather than action behooves a man of maturity; wisdom consisted of recognizing the vanity of everything here below, and of enduring the ills of life that were not within his power to avoid.

Even the new subjects La Tour chooses are revealing. The prodigal son has gone off to discover the world and its pleasures: riches, love, sensual gratification. The game is rigged, however: he is hoodwinked by the partner who takes his gold; he is hoodwinked by the Gypsy woman who promises him a life of happiness and reduces him to tending pigs, and he is hoodwinked by the feminine beauty that ensnares him, causing him to forget that such attractions will be reduced to the toothless mouth and bloodshot eyes of an old hussy. The only refuge is internal: Francis steals away from the world to be with God, while Mary Magdalen, forgetting wealth, beauty, pleasure, forgetting her body to the point where she is no longer conscious of decency, burns with a purely spiritual fire that will not go out when the flame of the night light begins to flicker. Nothing is durable or certain but the three Virtues: Faith, which enables man to transcend appearances and attain the ideal; Hope, which allows one to believe that the future is always open, and that the frail newborn child still suspended in the void will grow up and know happiness and pain in his turn; and Charity, which, like Irene, looks to the wounds of others and tries to assuage their pain.

Did La Tour give these virtues their religious meanings? The exhortations of the psalms—which he could well have known in Malherbe's unforgettable translation—might have served as his credo:

Trust no more, soul, in the promises of the world;
Its light is a glass and its favor a wave
Ever tossed by the wind, never still:
Let us leave these vanities, cease pursuing them,
    It is God who makes us live
    It is God we must love.

It is indeed possible that La Tour retreated into Christian thought of this kind, but not certain. Stoicism, with its motto *sustine et abstine*, similarly denounced the vanity of a deceptive world and called for steadfastness. The Libertines of La Tour's generation espoused a stoic philosophy and looked down on the common people for taking refuge in religion at the first sign of trouble. But at the same time, stoicism permeated religious thought, and the ancient dictums even found their way into sermons. The two philosophies shared a common disdain for the vicissitudes of the world, called for the same meditative withdrawal into oneself, and generated the same gravity, often coupled with a kind of familiar simplicity found only in beings detached from futile pretensions and anxieties. In the absence of personal testimony, it is difficult to distinguish between the influence of classical philosophy and Montaigne and what depends on the certainty of faith. In La Tour's case, we have no letters, no testimony from friends or enemies.

It is true that where this might be critical in the case of a writer or philosopher, it matters less in the case of an artist, who expresses himself through the image. Images are both precise and ambiguous. Their virtue is that they are not limited by narrow concepts, that they can convey values in a way that is general enough to transcend systems. An image does not have to state whether it is religious or philosophical in substance. It has only to propose ideas and to direct our thinking toward them by means other than reasoned argument. Painting defies the headstrong commentator who would pretend to extract an ideological interpretation. A great painter does not preach moral doctrine—working with forms, not words, he designates attitudes. In Georges de La Tour's case, there can be little doubt: the whole of his work during this period, from the paintings of *The Cheat* to those of *The Magdalen*, is a rejection of the world and a return to the self and to spiritual certainties. Through them, the painter, offers us an ascetic vision as the only refuge worthy of man.

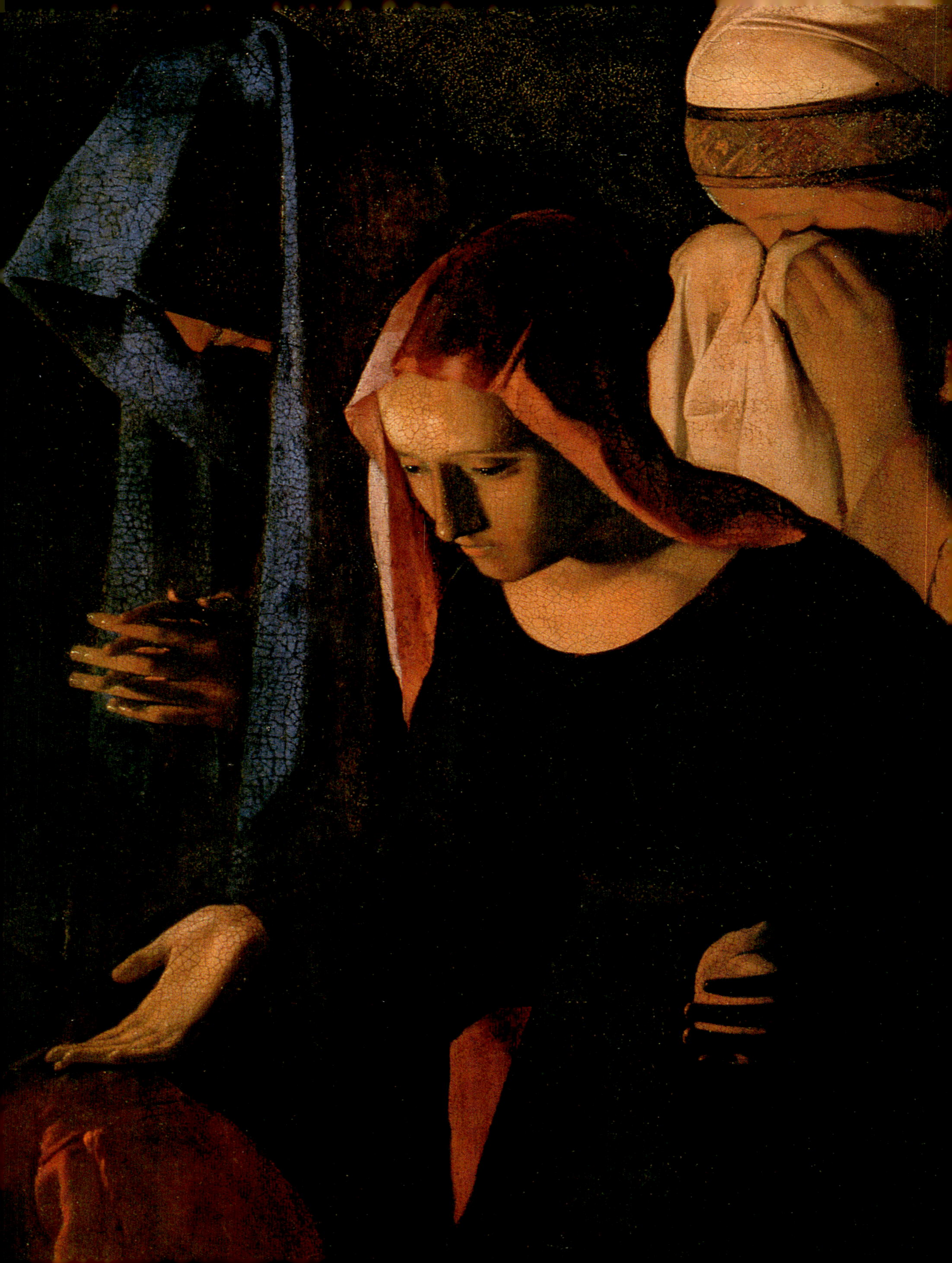

MEDITATION SHATTERED

HARD TIMES IN LORRAINE

The year 1643 found La Tour already turned fifty, settled once more in Lunéville; his house was apparently put to rights, all his privileges resolutely won back. With Richelieu and Louis XIII dead, Paris was moving slowly toward civil war. Nor had the situation in Lorraine improved.

In 1641 the king concluded a new agreement with his brother-in-law Charles IV restoring some of the latter's powers and a number of fortified towns that he promptly set about repairing, only to take flight again before long and resume hostilities. Less concerned with securing peace for his duchy than with pursuing his own ambitions, Charles was banking this time on a regency that would effectively place the power in the hands of Gaston of Orléans. Indeed, Richelieu died in December 1642 and Louis XIII in May 1643. No one had foreseen that Anne of Austria, apparently weak and inexperienced, would display the prudence and firmness of a great queen, discerning in Mazarin the only political genius around her and securing his complete devotion. The Spanish queen was quite French when it came to politics. There was no more question now than in Richelieu's day of tolerating an alliance between Lorraine and the Holy Roman Empire when Lorraine was all that barred the latter's way to Paris. The French were too aware of Lorraine's sense of identity to think of annexing it and too preoccupied with upheavals in Paris to take a firm stand against the claims the duke was making from his retreat in Luxembourg. The war was at its height. The most they could do until negotiations began was to hold on firmly to their strategic positions, control the country as best they could, and try to improve a state of affairs that they knew to be devastating. The situation was impossible. Lorraine was caught between two opposing powers. The governor, installed in Nancy in the name of the king of France, was forced to levy tax after tax during this period of continuous warfare, and to maintain considerable troops who were quartered with the locals. The French presence was not simple military conquest: there was a parliament with its headquarters in Metz, and an administration endeavoring to check the tide of economic disaster and famine. On the other hand, however, the duke also sought to govern Lorraine from Luxembourg, and was giving orders, levying taxes, maintaining a council that administered justice, and systematically opposing all measures undertaken by the governor. His troops harassed the French troops from a handful of strongholds where they were firmly entrenched. Poorly paid, they treated the population as cruelly as the foreign armies did.

The result was a strange confusion. A single example says it all. On 22 September 1643 Charles ordered a general levy in Lorraine and the duchy of Bar. All noblemen and soldiers who had borne arms in the last twenty years were commanded to join the duke "on penalty of having their homes set on fire, and the mayors and communities of these said places, together with all their relatives, branded guilty of treason." The riposte was not slow in coming: on 29 October the governor issued a counter-order in which he "expressly forbids all noblemen and soldiers to obey the duke's orders, on pain of being branded guilty of treason, and orders the bailiffs to punish all those who contravene his ruling and, where they cannot take them in person, to drive out their wives and children, seize their possessions, and raze their houses to the ground." In fact, neither the duke, who had taken refuge abroad, nor the governor, who was incapable of imposing his rule outside the towns, was in a position to enforce such decrees. Nevertheless, this exchange of order and counter-order has its dangers. From time to time, an example had to be made. The most striking of all was perhaps the siege of La Mothe in 1645. This was a fortified town that had remained in the duke's possession, and, together with Longwy, it was one of the most important in his control. He kept a heavy garrison there, and the French did not dare venture too close. The duke profited from the situation to maintain his administration there and to levy taxes that fed his budget. The stronghold was a base for deadly raids and unexpected forays that devastated the countryside and even threatened the towns. The town's governor, Laurent Cliquot, was a colonel in Charles IV's service who was also a friend of Louis de Rambervillers and certainly well known to La Tour; his bravery and daring finally made the situation intolerable. La Mothe was besieged and held out for seven months but finally had to yield. The fortress and the town were burned to the ground. Lorraine never recovered from the loss of this ancient stronghold.

Preceding page:
St. Sebastian Tended by Irene, detail.
Musée du Louvre, Paris

What could the population do? Caught between two powers that were not entirely enemies—the duke was the brother-in-law not only of the late king, but also of both the queen regent and Gaston of Orléans, and was forever negotiating—nor for the time reconcilable, they had no choice but to put up with the situation. Even in Lunéville, they paid the monies demanded by the governor and the taxes levied by the duke. They put up with it and hedged. The times demanded it. Forced to cope with two governments the Lorrainers endeavored to loosen the noose around their necks by playing one against the other. They simultaneously petitioned both the council in Luxembourg and the parliament in Metz; they had French decisions quashed by the ducal authorities and vice versa. Very few formal documents from this period have a ring of sincerity, because almost all of them are written in function of the intended reader. There was hardly anyone who, as the saying goes, did not run with the hare and hunt with the hounds.

These sorry, shifting times were not limited to Lorraine—the whole of Europe was sliding into unrest, war, and bloodshed. Between 1647 and 1649 the world was to see the young king of France driven from the capital by the fishwives, Naples proclaimed a people's republic, Poland rocked by a formidable revolt of the cossacks of Dnieper on the sudden death of Ladislaus IV, and the king of England lose his head. Noblemen rebelled, parliaments plotted, the people rose up, crowns teetered, even the pope waged war. From his retreat in Rome, Poussin, only partly reassured, writes in January 1649: "It is a great pleasure to live in such an eventful century, provided you have a nice little secluded spot somewhere to sit back in comfortably and watch the drama." Even if they were no longer at the center of the storm, the people of Lorraine continued to feel its effects cruelly. It would be a long time before the sky began to clear, before any sort of future looked possible. For the moment, it was not a question of hoping, but simply of avoiding the worst, of dressing wounds, which were deep, of holding fast for the sake of future generations.

GEORGES DE LA TOUR, "LORD" OF LUNÉVILLE

It was in this time of anxiety over the present and uncertainty over the future, in this land where simply to survive and secure the survival of one's line required selfishness and tenacity, that La Tour lived out his last years.

Gone was the prosperity of the past. That is to say, the poor and the low-ranking "burgers" had become poorer still. They were overcome by the different taxes and special levies, notably for the quartering and upkeep of the troops, which included not only those of the garrison, troops who were more or less accepted, but also those who were going back and forth to the theater of war in Germany, and who were a terror to the population. The privileged classes and the various people who were exempt, by contrast, got away without paying ordinary and extraordinary taxes alike, and were trying to salvage what they could of their fortunes. La Tour, having escaped death with his wife and four of his children, was among these. The petition of 1646 to which we will return later declares that the various religious foundations in Lunéville, mistresses Des Fours and de Chargey, and "Master George La Tour painter" owned "between them a third of the livestock to be found in the aforementioned Lunéville" and "plow and sow more than all the other inhabitants in the place." This helps to explain why the Paris episode did not convince La Tour to exile himself there.

The experience was not a waste of time, however. As well as opening up a new clientele, it brought him the title of "*peintre ordinaire du roi,*" one that he was the only artist to hold (and indeed ever to have held) in Lorraine. Despite an odd notarial reference to the contrary in 1647, it does not seem that the title gave him a royal pension of any sort. Nonetheless, the prestige it brought was obvious. The title even appears in baptism registers, which were normally quite succinct, and one of them, in December 1644, goes as far as to describe La Tour as a "famous painter." The title must have helped La Tour considerably in his dealings with the Parliament of Metz, and it must have carried great weight with potential collectors, both near and far. This French title is not likely to have been greatly appreciated by the common people of Lorraine, however, who saw Georges de La Tour not only maintaining his position but actually growing perceptively richer at a time of widespread hardship.

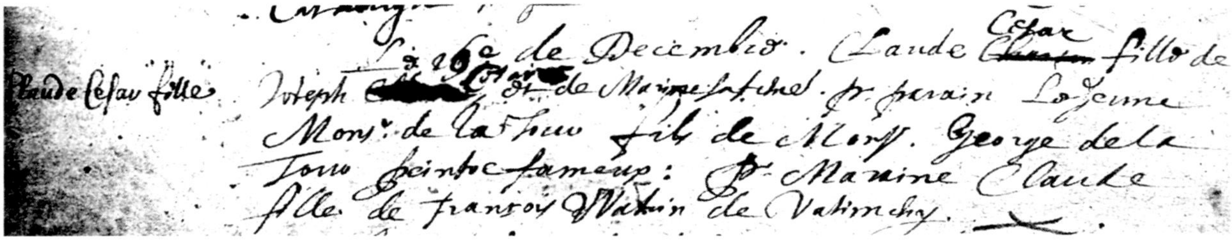
Claude César fille. Le 19e de Decembre. Claude César fille de Joseph [redacted] de Mainefatche. pr parain Le jeune Monsr de la Tour fils de Monsr George de la Tour peintre fameux: Mr Marine Claude fille de François Watin de Vatimchy.

LA TOUR'S REPUTATION
Mention of La Tour's name as a "famous painter" in the record of Claude César's baptism in Lunéville on 19 December 1644.
Archives Municipales, Lunéville

The last ten years of La Tour's life, from the end of 1642 to January 1652, must have been the most strained in social terms. Driven by poverty and want, the poor easily turned to theft and pillage, and a constant watch had to be kept on property. There were more and more clashes, more and more lawsuits. La Tour defended his interests and those of his family. In 1643, he embarked on a case (not to be settled until 8 August 1645) to recover six hundred francs that his brother-in-law had lent some time before to the community of Tonnois. The same year he instituted proceedings to recover two hundred francs that Chrétien Georges's guardians still had not paid him. In January 1651, he obtained a down payment of ten francs on a debt of forty. La Tour seems to have become tougher with age and did not shy away from trouble. At the beginning of 1646, and although he was well over fifty, he apparently gave a sergeant such a beating that the man had to be treated by a doctor and subsequently sought compensation from the town. There was a more serious incident in July 1650, when La Tour caught a plowman from Lunéville by the name of Fleurant Louys messing about in one of his fields and beat him thoroughly—a quicker and much more effective way of teaching him a lesson than going through a judge. Unfortunately for La Tour, Fleurant took to his bed, summoned a surgeon, Jacques de La Chambre, and appealed to the judge. Things could have turned out very badly, because La Tour's neighbors cannot have been particularly well disposed toward him, and perhaps the magistrates as well, and it is not impossible that the victim secretly had their backing. Georges's son Etienne had to step in and pacify Fleurant and his wife, Fleuratte, who would only settle for the sizeable sum of 140 francs—almost certainly more than the plowman earned in a year.

Nevertheless, La Tour gave in. It is easy to see why from the petition of 1646 mentioned earlier. This is an extraordinary document that can only be understood in the context of Lorraine. We have to remember that Charles IV was continuing to wage an administrative war with the French authorities from his retreat in Luxembourg and that the people of Lorraine were capitalizing on this. They would petition the parliament set up by the French in Metz (which was then sitting at Toul), and address the same petitions, couched in different terms, to the sovereign court in Luxembourg: two decisions were clearly better than one when the future was so uncertain, and if they were contradictory, the better of the two could always be used to challenge the other. Thus, the present petition was addressed by the inhabitants of Lunéville to the duke, although Lunéville was under royal rule. Its object was to get the exemptions abolished and to make all inhabitants pay their share of ordinary and extraordinary taxes alike. The petitioners emphasize the damages caused by the French troops, while overlooking the fact that the troops of the duke and the Holy Roman Empire were no less violent and evoking Charles IV's "longed for" return. Obviously, people known to be in sympathy with the French and favored by the governor were blamed more than people who professed their allegiance to Charles IV. All the same, the main facts must be true, even if the presentation is somewhat biased. It is worth reading the text in full:

To His Highness
The people of the Council and the Police of Lunéville very humbly remonstrate, Saying That, given that since the beginning of these wars the costs to the Town have been very high, the armies of France having camped there during various times and years, and

[that] the inhabitants have since been crushed by a garrison swollen some years by five companies, and in others by more, and in 1639 by a whole regiment, always at the expense of the townspeople, who had already been subjected to three days of pillaging, and vexed year after year by troops passing through on their way to Germany, and finally so ill-treated by different troops billeted in various quarters over the winter, especially the winter just past, that they are now reduced to unprecedented extremes of poverty, and are in the hapless position of seeing those who collect the fruits and benefits of the land thereabouts by the amount of livestock they own in horses, oxen, cows, and pigs refuse to bear some of the costs of the said town; of this number are the monks and nuns, who have whole fields and teams, the noblewomen Des Fours and de Chargey, and Master George de La Tour, painter, who own between them a third of the livestock to be found in the aforementioned Lunéville, and who plow and sow more than all the other inhabitants of the place, which gives the town the air of having some means of subsistence and has consequently led to an increase in both ordinary and extraordinary taxes in winter. The said mistress de Chargey and the said La Tour (who renders himself "odious to the people by the number of dogs he keeps, both greyhounds and spaniels, as if he were the local lord, hunting hares through the cultivated fields, trampling and spoiling them) have obtained exemption from quartering soldiers, she from Monsieur the governor of Nancy, and he too, and from all taxes. Following their example, the prosecutor Jean Cousson has obtained similar exemption from the King, as bursar of the Abbey of Saint-Rémy in the aforementioned Lunéville, as has another prosecutor, Jean Bressade, as bursar of the Abbey of Beaupré. Nicolas La Cour, as farmer of Mehon, has by favor of the local lord had his last winter's quarter's contribution reduced by half; Claude Voirin, tenant of the mills in the aforementioned Lunéville, has also obtained a similar reduction. Sire Thiriet, magistrate, has also been granted a reduction of a third in his share and since, having petitioned sire Intendant to be granted exemption from all taxes as resident in a free house where he went to live with the connivance of the tenant, has instigated proceedings against the town that have yet to be decided. The widow of the late sire de Boucquenomme, having tried the same course and failed, has petitioned your Highness's sovereign Court for exemption from all quartering and taxes, and has summoned the town before sire provost de Blamont for him to hear the parties' contentions and settle the case when he has examined these. All this at the expense of the said town.

And so the lower ranks and the poorest of the poor, who are not granted any favors, bear the costs of the said town, which mount as the war lasts and continues, and all the more so for them, [with the result] that, seeing themselves crippled by poverty, they will in the end be compelled to abandon their home, and have to take refuge with those inhabitants who have the means to bear the joint costs, the strong coming to the aid of the weak, without exception. This disunion is the source of great stirrings and will bring disorder among the people of poor Lunéville, which is threatened with ruin if provision is not made against this on this occasion by the goodness and prudence of Your Highness, out of the care you may have for its preservation.

This is why the said remonstrants beg in all humility and with hands clasped that it may please Your Highness [to] revoke all exemptions and rebates that have or may yet be obtained by whomsoever, and [to] ordain that all the residents of the said Lunéville, whatever their rank, shall bear their share of the town's expenses, past and future, during the war, it not being reasonable that [the war] should be the ruin of some to the profit of others, since all are subjects of Your Highness, so that by observing this equality the said town may survive in some way, until your said Highness's longed for return to his States. And they will pray to God unceasingly to preserve him in health and prosperity.

Even if it cannot all be taken for gospel, such a document gives us a far better idea of the situation in Lorraine at this time than all the texts. The "crippling poverty," the "threat of ruin," the "great stirrings," and the desire for "equality" in misfortune were all very real, so too were the privileged classes' strenuous efforts to preserve their status and fortune, coveted on all sides and already cruelly depleted as a result of the fire and looting.

The duke, moreover, settled matters once and for all on 18 July 1646, in his own typically shifty way. He ruled that all the inhabitants of Lunéville would pay their share, with the exception of members of religious orders and persons duly exempted by himself—thus contriving to affirm his authority against the royal administration while changing nothing. For his part, La Tour had his letters of exemption from the duke, which he had validated all the same by the French authorities as a safety precaution. Although Charles IV could rely on the support of the Capuchins and the common people, he was not keen on alienating any of the leading citizens. Some had proved to be his most loyal servants: the mistresses Des Fours, mentioned in the petition (but not coming in for specific accusation), for instance, represented the rest of the family in Lunéville of Jean Des Fours, who was one of several noblemen to attach themselves to the duke and follow him into exile. The others were still very influential, and the French would have been only too pleased to seize this opportunity in order to win them over once and for all.

It was by no means certain that it would be wise to withdraw their privileges, even though this might be in the general interest of the population. Too many had already abandoned the duchy, taking with them what was left of their fortunes and therefore a large part of the meager funds still available. Too many towns and villages, bereft of influential people, had quite simply died, and the fields left to fallow. The document proves this: it was the privileged who were the first to recover, who made Lunéville habitable again, who were able to get farming going, and who thus permitted a gradual reconstruction effort and the struggle against the ever-present threat of famine. Without them, there would have been no one to employ servants, who would otherwise have been reduced to vagabondage, no one to bring back a bit of commerce and industry, no one, moreover, to maintain a minimum of lucidity in the face of the wild impulses and sometimes even collective madness overtaking the region, as well as the religious life and political relations indispensable for survival. In an era of such profound poverty, exemptions seemed more unjust, scandalous even, than ever. At the same time, however, they recovered their original raison d'être, which was to favor the living structure of a country, that solid and active part that is its very backbone and stands firm even in the midst of disaster. Lorraine's weakness, as every observer pointed out, was precisely that it did not have enough of a hierarchy or enough of an elite, as recent events had shown. The plague, the wars, and voluntary exile had decimated this meager elite still further, with potentially dire consequences for the future. Neither the duke nor the French underestimated its importance.

One has the impression, moreover, of an increasingly close society, aware of its smallness and its isolation, sticking together and presenting a united front. In February 1644, for example, La Tour contracted with the Order of the Commandery of Jerusalem in Nancy to rent the commandery of Saint-Georges in Lunéville for a period of six years—apparently not so much to live there himself (the family was now down to six, and there do not seem to have been many servants) as to work the land abandoned by the monks. By August 1645, however, while reserving all rights, exceptions, and exemptions, he had transferred the rental of the house to Théodore Thiriet—none other than the magistrate whom the 1646 petition accuses of seeking to obtain exemption from taxes on the grounds that he lived in a tax-free house "with the agreement of the tenant. . . ." It seems likely that La Tour was the tenant in question, and that the rental of the commandery was designed to be of double benefit, allowing one notable to expand his estate and retain the option of using the exemption should his own be withdrawn, while giving the other the grounds for seeking an exemption he did not already have, but which the French might confer on him as a magistrate in a town where the duke still wielded too great an influence.

Étienne's marriage seems equally typical of the period. Born in 1621, Étienne had recently come of age. In its ruinous state, Lunéville certainly did not offer anything like the range of suitable marriage opportunities it once had. The family looked once more to Vic, with which it had never wholly lost touch, even though La Tour's brother, François, who had contented himself with the rather lowly job of beadle at the ecclesiastical court, had died there in 1636. Étienne married the damsel Anne-Catherine, daughter of the honorable Jean Friot, merchant of Vic. He was one of the richest people in the area, one of the rare few to have managed to keep a little trade at a time when there was no money to be seen and the roads were no longer safe. The contract was signed on 23 February 1647. The future bride received a dowry of two thousand francs, together with four hundred francs for furniture, not to mention a trousseau for the occasion and her deceased mother's estate. Above all, she had great expectations on her father's side. However hard the times, the couple could count on being well off. For his part, Georges de La Tour promised among other things to give the bride "a hundred écus' worth of jewels." The marriage contract was signed in the presence of a distinguished collection of people. On the bride's side, the mayor of Vic and the painter Jean Dogoz, who was her cousin, were joined by a number of rich merchants, while Étienne's side included the chancellor and the attorney general at the bishopric of Metz, as well as various lords such as Chrétien d'Anglure and Nicolas de Saint-Livier, captain of Sampigny. There was not the slightest hint that they were still in one of the worst times in Lorraine's history.

Étienne's marriage did not break up the unity of the family—quite the contrary. The contract stipulated that La Tour should support the young couple for two years, as was the custom. Nor did Étienne leave Lunéville when these two years were up. In 1649 he rented a house near the Church of Saint-Jacques for six years, and managed to secure from the town, rather than the status of "burgher," the privileged status of "refugee," which he had renewed in February 1651. As early as April 1646 he is described in a document as "painter," and in another of 1648 he and his father are jointly described as "*peintres ordinaires du roi.*" This title reappears a number of times, and it looks very much as if Georges de La Tour managed, through his connections, and perhaps at the very time the Academy was being founded in Paris, to get the title he had been given bestowed on his son as well.

In fact Étienne seems to have become increasingly involved in his father's doings, and undoubtedly had a direct hand in executing his paintings. We do not know if La Tour kept Chrétien Georges on for a time after he came to the end of the three-year apprenticeship undertaken in September 1641, or if he took on another apprentice who has managed to escape us. We do know, however, that in September 1648 he engaged the young Jean-Nicolas Didelot, nephew of the parish priest in Vic, and that there was a new clause in the contract, quite unlike any other I have ever come across: "Because the nature of the profession demands that it be pursued according to the same principles and precepts, sire Étienne de La Tour, son of the said sire Georges de La Tour, being also present, has agreed and undertakes, in the case of his father's death, to take on and keep the said Nicolas for the remainder of his time, on the above conditions." It is clear that La Tour—and probably the public at large—saw his son Étienne not only as a competent assistant, but also as the natural heir to his art. It is also possible—but this is perhaps stretching the point somewhat—that, now that he had turned fifty-five, he was beginning to feel the weight of age or illness. In any case, the man who had so often painted a death's head was certainly not afraid to consider his own death.

The epidemics continued, moreover, felling people all around. A month earlier, little Marie, who was baptized on 28 March 1636, died of "the small pox" before she reached the age of thirteen. She was La Tour's youngest daughter, and her death must have been a cruel blow. It left him in 1648 with only Étienne and two unmarried daughters, Claude who was then twenty-five, and Chrétienne, also called Christine, who was twenty-two. This was to be compensated for to some extent, it is true, by the birth of a grandson (and apparently Étienne's first child, though he had by then been married for almost three years), Jean-Hyacinthe, in September 1650. La Tour need no longer worry: the family line was secure. *Nunc dimittis*. . . .

We have no way of knowing whether this is how he thought. He continued to look after his affairs, which do not seem to have been in danger. He continued to paint, and must have been conscious of attaining a greater sureness and perfection in his art than ever before. There is no reason to suppose, in spite of the prophetic clause in the contract, that he did not want and expect to live to a ripe old age. Fate, however, decreed otherwise. Diane died on 15 January 1652 "of a fever accompanied by a palpitation of the heart." She was followed on the twenty-second by a servant, Jean, known as de Montauban, stricken with "pleurisy." On the thirtieth, La Tour succumbed to "pleurisy" as well. The epidemic, also dubbed "pulmonia" and "false pleurisy," was doubtless fairly close to the "Spanish influenza" of the nineteenth century. It spared Étienne and his wife, who lived on their own, the two sisters Claude and Chrétienne, the apprentice Jean-Nicolas Didelot, an important figure in the household, and Anne Rocque, a servant and companion who had been practically one of the family for seventeen or eighteen years.

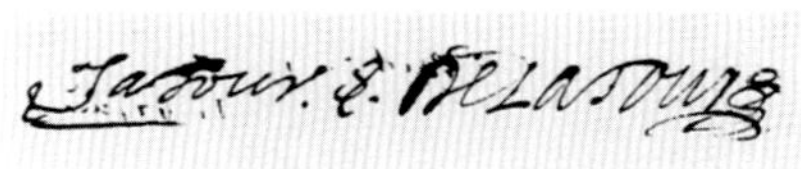

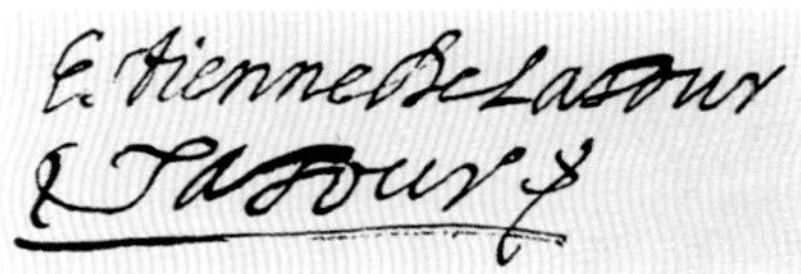

ÉTIENNE DE LA TOUR'S GROWING ROLE:

The appearance of joint signatures on legal documents.
From top to bottom:
Acts from 1647 and 1648.

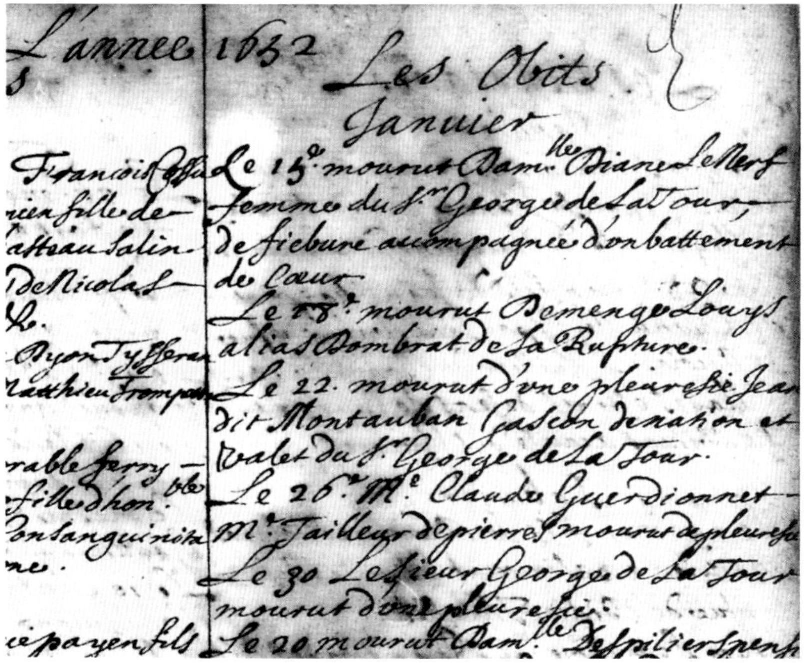
L'annee 1652 Les Obits
Janvier
Le 15e mourut Dam.lle Diane le Nerf
femme du Sr George de La Tour
de fiebure accompagnée d'un battement
de Coeur
Le 18e mourut Demenge Louys
alias Dombrat de La Rupture
Le 22 mourut d'une pleuresie Jean
dit Montauban Gascon de nation et
valet du Sr George de La Tour
Le 26e Me Claude Guerdionnet
Me Tailleur de pierre mourut de pleuresie
Le 30 Le sieur George de La Tour
mourut d'une pleuresie

DEATHS IN GEORGES DE LA TOUR'S HOUSEHOLD
On the same page, mention of the deaths of Diane (15 January), of the servant Jean (22 January), and of Georges (30 January).

There was no will, and no inventory of the contents of the house has been found. The three heirs, who seem to have been very close, declared that their father had, by "verbal bequest," left to the Capuchin fathers of the town "a *meix* and a garden" at the spot known as "the old sheep-folds." They ensured that Anne Rocque was properly settled and provided her with a dowry of five hundred francs, together with one hundred francs' worth of furniture (the amount Diane had when she married Georges), as a gift from their father in recogniton of her loyal service.

Étienne, who had been given an advance of 6,200 francs on his inheritance by his father-in-law in 1651, left Lunéville to settle in Vic. In 1654 he is again described as "*peintre ordinaire du roi,*" but there is no reason to suppose that he continued to paint much. In 1660 he bought the tax-free estate of Ménil or Mesnil, near Lunéville. After another about-face that allowed Charles IV to take advantage of the general peace cleverly negotiated by Mazarin, the duke came back to reclaim his states and appointed Étienne lieutenant of the bailiwick at Lunéville. Étienne returned to Lunéville, but this time with the very highest rank. In 1669 Charles IV elevated the Mesnil estate into the fief of Mesnil-La Tour, and on 19 March 1670 he granted Étienne his patent of nobility, which was registered on 26 June.

Death had robbed Georges de La Tour of the noble status he had so ardently desired and which his life and art had consistently confirmed. He undoubtedly desired it less for himself, however, than for his descendants, who did achieve it and kept their title for generations. La Tour had also wanted recognition of the talent he knew he had, and, failing Nancy, it was Paris that gave him his first glowing acclaim. He could not have realized that it would take three centuries for his name to reappear in the annals of art, but this time among the greatest painters of his day.

GLORY AND ISOLATION

It is not easy to imagine how La Tour continued to produce his art on his return to Lunéville, in a Lorraine overrun with the military and strewn with ruins. Granted that he is described as a "famous painter," even in the registers of births, marriages and deaths. But where was his clientele?

There can be no doubt that his fame was real enough in Paris and that he had collectors there. Paris itself was entering a difficult period, however. The Regency had gotten off to a difficult start, and the Fronde was soon to follow with all its uncertainties. These were to be precarious times for Parisian artists. Le Brun, for instance, had to produce drawings for popular prints, and Bourdon finally gave in to the invitation of the Swedish court. Poussin, meanwhile, took care not to return to France, and no one thought of asking him back. The situation went from bad to worse, and the crisis was not really over until the end of the Fronde and Mazarin's return in 1653—in other words, after La Tour's death. If La Tour continued sending work to Paris, this would undoubtedly have been around 1642-1648, and not in the very last years of his life.

What sort of clients could he have had in Lorraine? The few Lorrainese who had managed to remain rich were unlikely to have cared about buying paintings in such uncertain times. The churches, pillaged and impoverished as they were, would have had more pressing needs. La Tour would more likely have found collectors among the French officials brought into Lorraine by the war. Some of them may have followed the example of the governor of Lorraine, who wanted not just one but at least six canvases by La Tour, and probably more. He is an exception among La Tour's collectors: we know not only his name, but what he was like, the subjects of the works he acquired, what they cost, and the date they were painted. This is a very special case, but one worth pausing over.

The governor appointed by the queen regent in 1643 to lead Lorraine was the son of Henri de Senneterre or Senectère (or Saint-Nectaire), a rather eminent figure who had made his fortune in the shadow of the count of Soissons. As knight of the king's orders, lieutenant general to the government of Champagne, ambassador to England and Rome, and minister of state, this first Henri de Senneterre was an important figure at court. "During Cardinal Richelieu's life," Tallemant Des Réaux tells us, "Senneterre, Chavigny, and Mazarin lived in each other's pockets." After Louis XIII's death, old Senneterre faithfully continued paying court to the queen regent. His elder son, Henri II, had distinguished himself at La Rochelle as the head of Soissons's regiment, and had led the left wing of the French army at Rocroi. The Marquis de Lenoncourt's death during the siege of Thionville on 25 July 1643 left the governorship of Lorraine vacant, Mazarin, who was suspicious of the other contestants, appointed him to the post. The example of the father sufficed to instill confidence in the son's loyalty, and in January 1651 Mazarin was to elevate him to the rank of maréchal of France. From then on he was known as Maréchal de La Ferté, or La Ferté-Senneterre, from the marquisate of La Ferté-Nabert that had belonged to his family since the sixteenth century. He died on 27 September 1681 at the age of eighty-one.

La Ferté-Senneterre was a flamboyant figure. His affair with the beautiful Marion de Lorme was the talk of Paris. It was said that he wanted to take her with him to Lorraine, but that she refused, lest he should keep her "in a seraglio." His quarrels with his wife were famous, and he ended up having her locked up as a lunatic. He displayed courage in war and steadfastness in times of crisis. His greed was often reckoned excessive, even for the period. He used his position in Lorraine, as most governors did, to consolidate his family's relatively recent, but nevertheless substantial fortune and in the process had few qualms about heaping additional taxes on a population already bled dry. This was the norm at the time, and his fiercest critics seem to have been those who would have been only too happy to obtain his position in order to do the same. It remains true that in return for the most prudent of measures and most slender of favors, he generally expected a tidy New Year's tribute from the towns, and Nancy above all. In Lunéville's case, however, and apparently at his suggestion, the annual tribute was waived in favor of a painting by Georges de La Tour—an extraordinary arrangement without parallel during that century. The first of these paintings was commissioned and delivered toward the end of 1644. The custom was fixed from then on until La Tour's death, with the painting delivered at the end of 1651. Interestingly, however, there is no record of a gift to the governor at the end of 1646, the year of the petition discussed above, when the town seems to have been exempted, while at the end of 1647 a gift of six hundred livres was paid in cash, perhaps because La Tour was away or indisposed. The governor took great care of these paintings, and, with the exception of one religious subject, they all appear in the inventory of his effects drawn up at the time when his first wife was declared insane in 1653.

At the end of 1644, then, we know that La Tour painted a *Nativity* for the governor that was worth seven hundred francs. At the end of 1645, he painted another work, the title of which is not recorded, but which could have been the *St. Anne and the Virgin*, and which was worth six hundred francs. In 1648 there was a *St. Alexis*

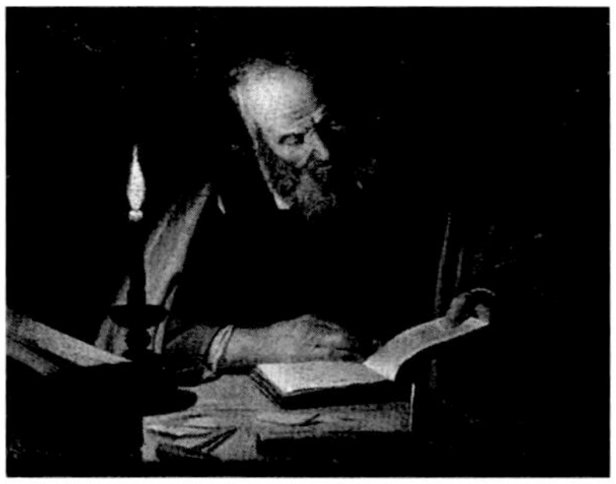

Anonymous. *St. Joseph Studying.*
Galleria Dona Pamphili, Rome

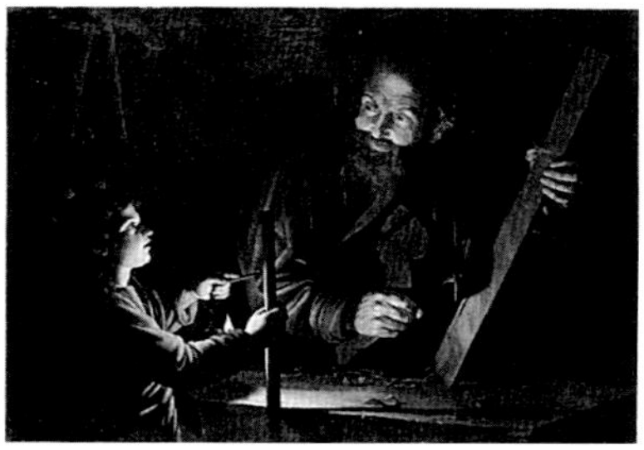

Matthias Stomer. *St. Joseph in his Workshop.*

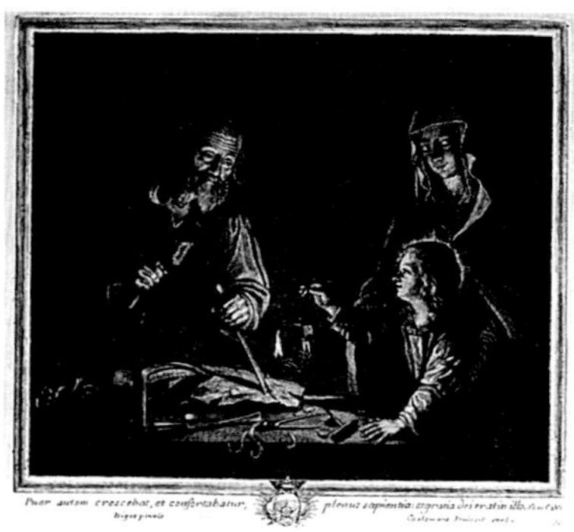

After Trophime Bigot. *St. Joseph in his Workshop.* Engraving by Jacques Coelmans.
Private collection

Right:
Christ with St. Joseph in the Carpenter's Shop
Musée du Louvre, Paris

noted at five hundred francs, and in 1649 a *St. Sebastian* estimated at seven hundred francs and which could reasonably have been the version with the torch, even the canvas that found its way to Bois-Anzeray and from there to the Louvre. In 1650 there is a *Denial of St. Peter*, priced at 650 francs, which could correspond to the composition in the Nantes museum, fittingly signed and dated 1650. Finally, in 1651, La Tour painted a canvas estimated at five hundred francs, the subject of which is not given, but which seems to have been one of the two others by La Tour listed in the governor's inventory—*Christ Blindfolded Being Struck by a Jew* or *Two Card Players with (? a Smoker)*, a composition now known only through two bad copies, but the original of which must have been painted around this date. Along with Jean-Baptiste de Bretagne, La Ferté was clearly the foremost collector of La Tour's work. Moreover, all this cost the inhabitants of Lunéville a great deal: 8,650 francs at the very least. There is no indication that La Tour gave the town a discount on the agreed price, even secretly as was sometimes the case. It is hardly surprising that his fellow citizens might have felt some resentment towards him, even if they knew from experience that it would have cost them the same, possibly even more, had the tribute been paid in cash.

On the other hand, over a seven- or eight-year period, this was a fairly meager income for a man like La Tour, and we can assume that he had clients other than the governor. He must have continued to paint a great deal, because he took on apprentices and seems to have had Étienne working with him by 1646 at the latest. The preserved paintings that can be placed in this period represent a sizeable proportion of what we know of La Tour's oeuvre as a whole. And they are masterpieces in which his genius finds its very finest expression.

Although he was by then over fifty, La Tour seems to have kept his physical strength: we are told in 1646 that he pursued the pleasures of hunting with gusto, and it is clear from the apprenticeship contract of 1648 that he was ready to leap into the saddle at any moment to attend to his affairs. Should we think of him as a man of wisdom, painting mainly for his own pleasure and perfecting a few long-pondered works in isolation for honorary commissions or works drawn from his own inspiration, with the results being fought over by a handful of loyal collectors? The image seems slightly anachronistic. This was certainly the case for Poussin, however, who was back in his house by the Pincio in Rome at the end of 1642, like La Tour in Lunéville, and who was also drawn to a stoic philosophy, manifest in his *Extreme Unction* of 1644, *Moses Saved from the Water* of 1647, and the *Landscape with Diogenes* of 1648. It is worth remembering, moreover, that Poussin and La Tour were only a year apart in age.

Obviously Rome was not Lunéville, and Poussin lived in a wealthy capital. Established in the heart of the artistic center that would continue, for a short time at least, to be the most brilliant in Europe, he was cherished by groups of highly cultured individuals who swore by him alone and surrounded by a trade that was beginning to speculate in his paintings—all of which would encourage an artist's creation. La Tour in Lorraine, on the other hand, certainly had to work harder to find a market for his work, and small compositions like the *Smoker* and the *Girl Blowing on a Brazier* (there are signed versions of both dating from this period) seem to have been specifically conceived for a less sophisticated public. It is not impossible, however, that La Tour, seeing Lorraine deprived of its duke and Paris rocked by the Fronde, gave up some of his ambitions, much as Poussin—though not without regret—gave up his position as first painter to the king of France. Acquiescing to circumstance, he would thus have devoted himself to refining a few paintings to perfection.

These are all "night" scenes. The success that they met with in Paris encouraged La Tour to develop this form. His daylight paintings were also well received there, however. Not only did Richelieu probably own a *Night Scene with Musicians* listed in the 1643 inventory of his château at Reuil, but, as we have seen, the *St. Jerome*, recorded as hanging in his personal dressing room in the Palais Cardinal, must have been a daylight painting. Jean-Baptiste de Bretagne is also known to have acquired some *Fortune Tellers* that were unlikely to have been the subject of a "night" scene, along with a number of "candlelight" paintings. If Georges de La Tour stopped painting daylight pictures, to our knowledge at least, after about 1642, it was certainly not because he was pandering to a particular fashion or tailoring his art to public taste. The "nights" answered some inner need and suited his meditations at the time. More than ever before, in fact, these paintings seem to be meditations on man and his fate.

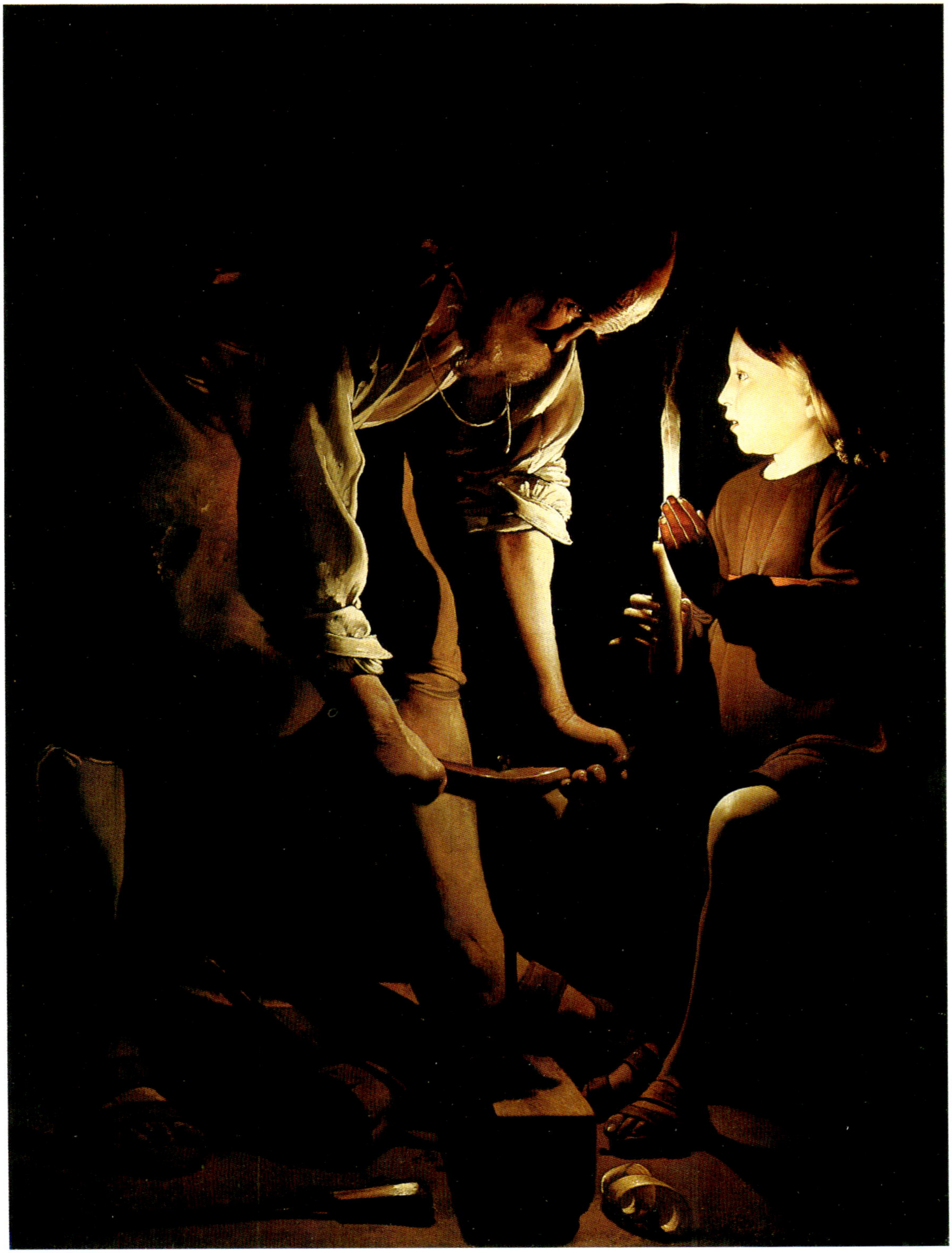

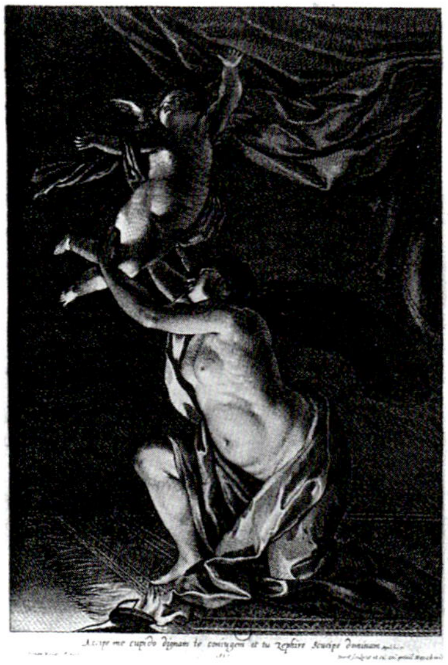

After Simon Vouet. *Cupid and Psyche.* 1637. Engraving by Pierre Daret.

Jean Valentin (also called Jean de Boulogne or Moïse Valentin). *The Dream of St. Joseph.* Formerly Matthiesen Gallery, London

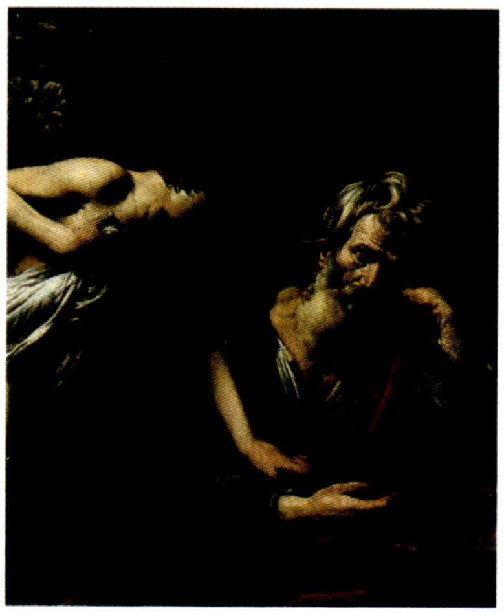

THE GREAT NOCTURNES

One of the finest of all these "night" scenes is the painting of *Christ with St. Joseph in the Carpenter's Shop* given to the Louvre by Percy Moore Turner in 1948 (a good early copy is located in the museum in Besançon). There is no doubt about the subject. La Tour has not introduced any halos or any other identifying features—at most, the two beams the carpenter is working on suggest the idea of the Cross in their perpendicular arrangement. The theme is far too common, however, and the tenor too serious, for any confusion with a genre scene. Honthorst painted a famous version of this subject as did Trophime Bigot, and it is worth remembering that the Serrone canvas had already treated it rather more explicitly. The worship of St. Joseph was becoming increasingly widespread at this time. Jesus' foster father was seen as the unpolished man who earned his living by the sweat of his brow and through his contact with the Virgin and Child rose up to a truth that was beyond his understanding, which sometimes shocked him, but whose mysteries he finally fathomed. With all his doubt, struggling and groping, Joseph came closer than anyone else and served the cause of the Holy Spirit more effectively with a love more complete than any other being. Thus he provided a model for the priest who devotes himself to the service of the Church, without having to know perfect union with the divine essence, since it is enough for God to bring whatever enlightenment and grace he needs day by day.

La Tour's genius lies precisely in capturing the very earthly nature of the old man, a bald-headed giant bent over his task and incapable of perceiving the mystery of the Cross he is prefiguring, to which he contrasts the spiritual simplicity of the Child with his face bathed in light and his translucent hands. In the process, a pious image becomes the most profound evocation of the human condition.

The work is solidly constructed in a narrow space animated by flickering shadows cast by the candlelight; volumes are powerfully modeled as in the carpenter's massive arms, and the palette is kept to a dark monochrome of reddish brown, with color all but banished by the light. It could be dated around 1642-1644. It does not have the poetic sensitivity of the *Magdalen* series, but it is richer and more powerful and as such one of the most impressive masterworks in this series of "night" paintings.

The idea behind *The Dream of St. Joseph* is very similar and is treated in the same tone and spirit, although this signed painting now in Nantes is probably slightly later in date. Its exceptional quality, both poetic and plastic, easily allows it to compete with the great masters of La Tour's day and, thereafter, Rembrandt and Vermeer.

This time the subject is not so immediately identifiable, which adds to the poetry of the painting. It has been variously interpreted, but all are agreed that the young girl on the left is an angel, even though La Tour, faithful to his realist principles even in the midst of the very highest spirituality, refuses to give her wings. The light illuminating her profile (which in itself is not at all idealized), her attitude, at once delicate, familiar, and ethereal, and the cascade of pearls and jade that the candlelight brings out on the embroidered end of her sash are enough to convince us of the celestial character of the young messenger. What of the old man to whom she speaks? He has been variously identified as Elijah, St. Matthew, and St. Peter, but once again, he seems far more likely to be St. Joseph, who is so often depicted book in hand, hoping to discover the key to the mysteries that elude him. Weary, and overcome by his earthly nature, the old man has fallen asleep. His eyes are closed as the angel appears before him. Is this the first vision, informing him that his suspicions are unfounded and that Mary has conceived without sin? It seems more likely to be the second, telling him to leave for Egypt with Mary and the Infant Jesus and thus making this humble fugitive carpenter the Savior's savior. La Tour has introduced nothing in the way of identifying details, or rather he has rejected all the traditional signs used to indicate the episode and the circumstances in which it takes place. For him, the essential lies elsewhere. It is to be found in the angel's appearance before Joseph at the very moment when, exhausted by his struggle to understand the spiritual truths of the Spirit, he relapses into his torpor. It is the unforeseeable gift that so preoccupied the entire seventeenth century: the mystery of grace.

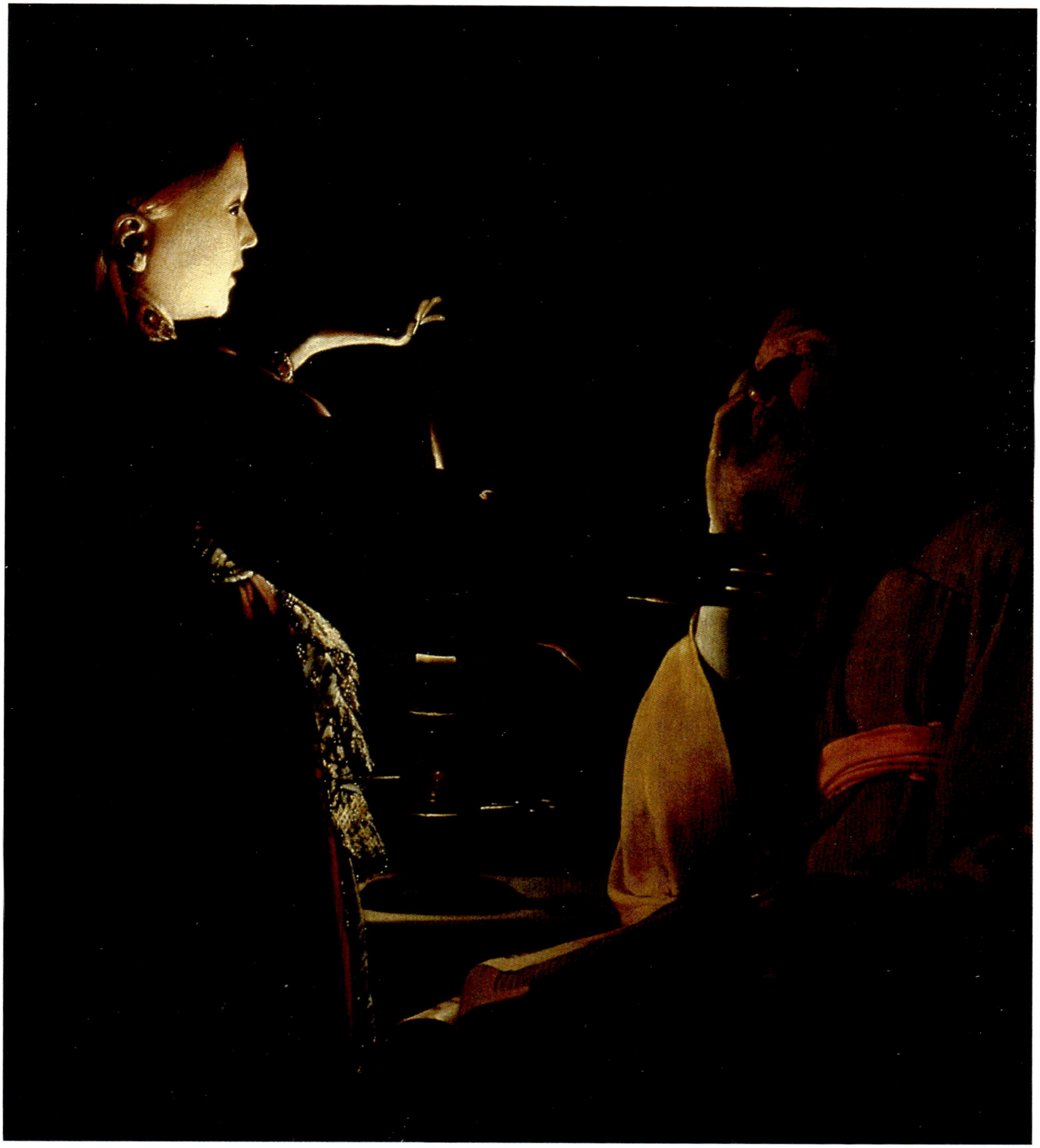

Above:
The Dream of St. Joseph.
Musée des Beaux-Arts, Nantes

pp. 192-195: *Christ with St. Joseph in the Carpenter's Shop* and *The Dream of St. Joseph*, details.

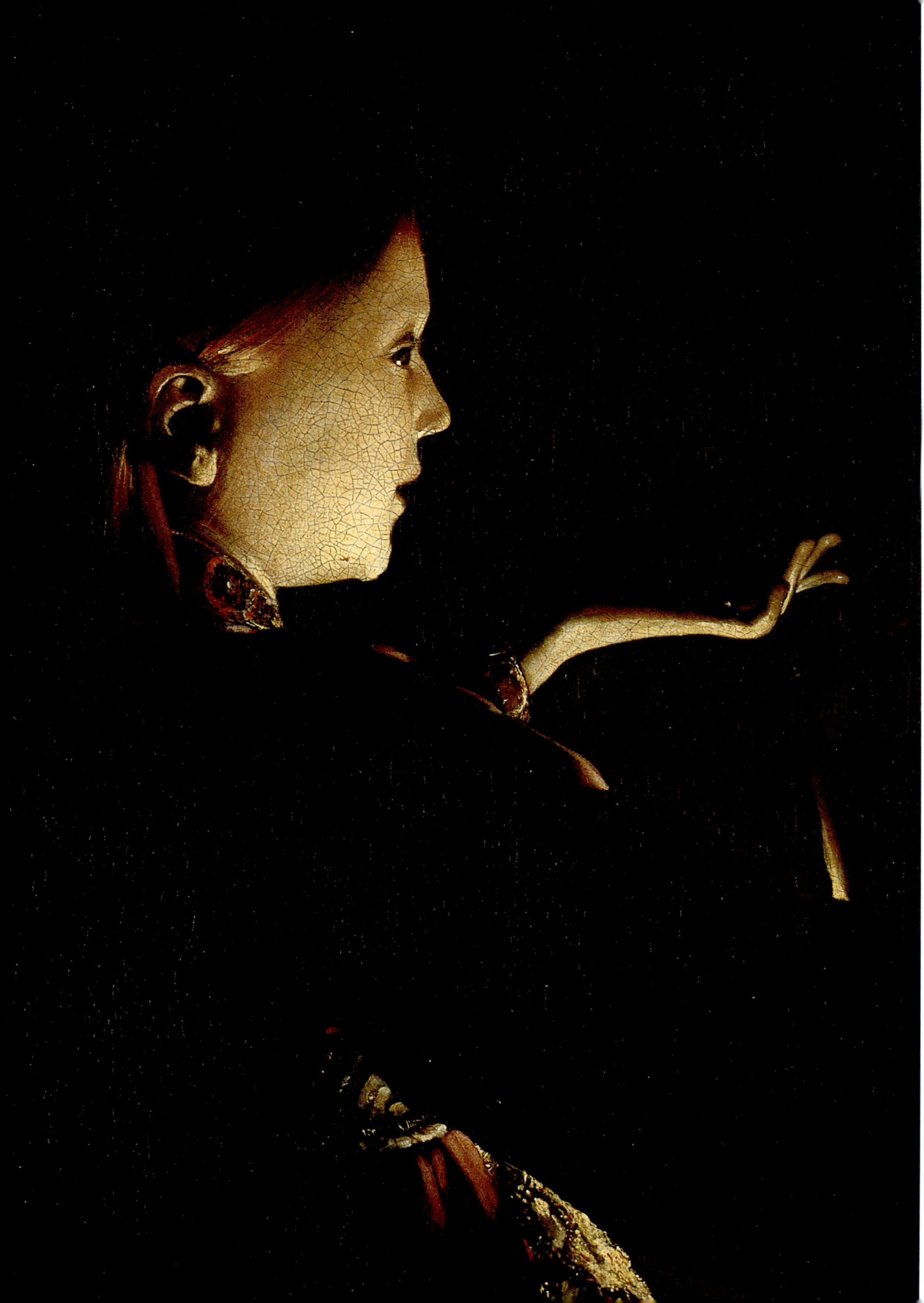

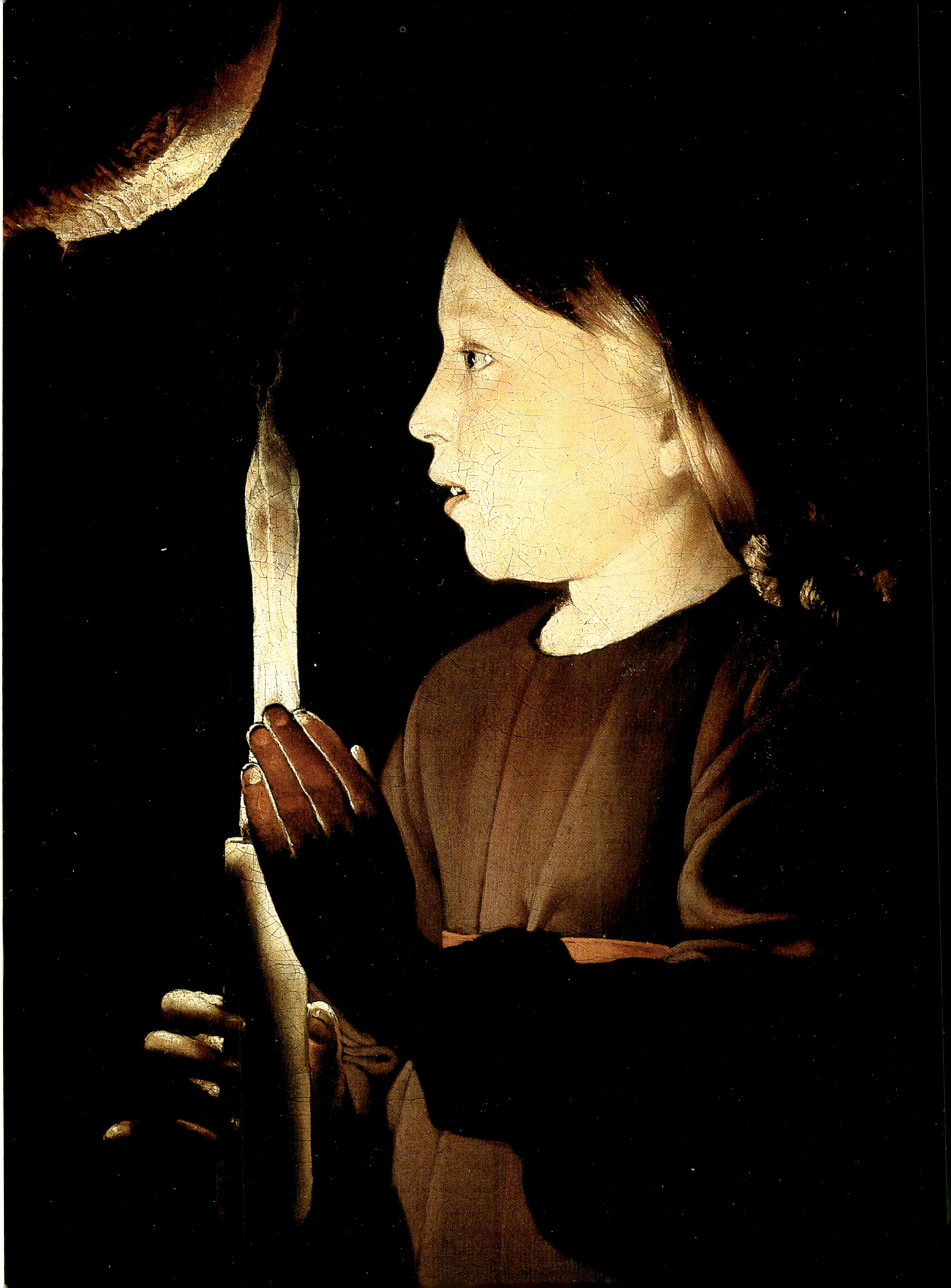

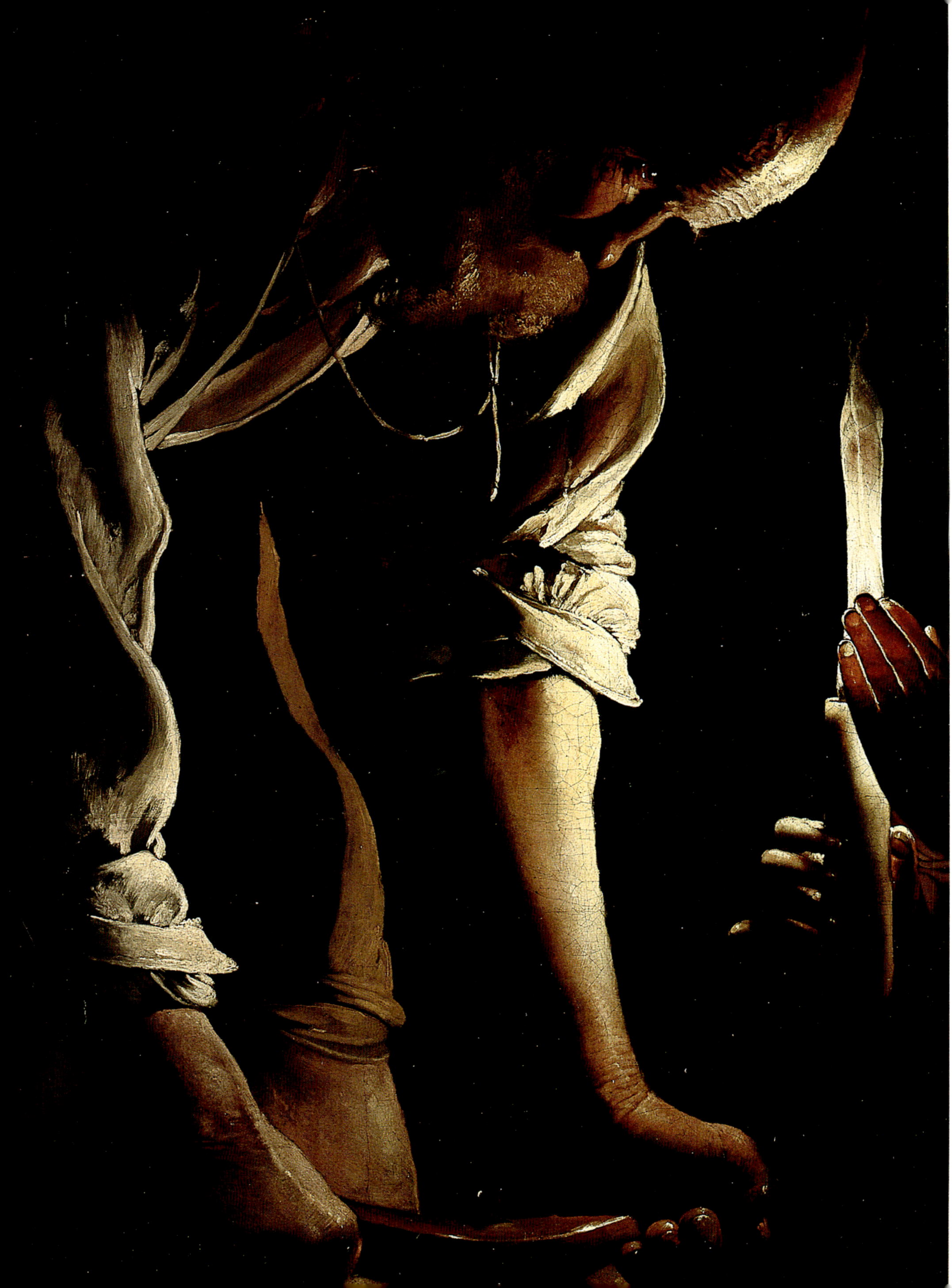

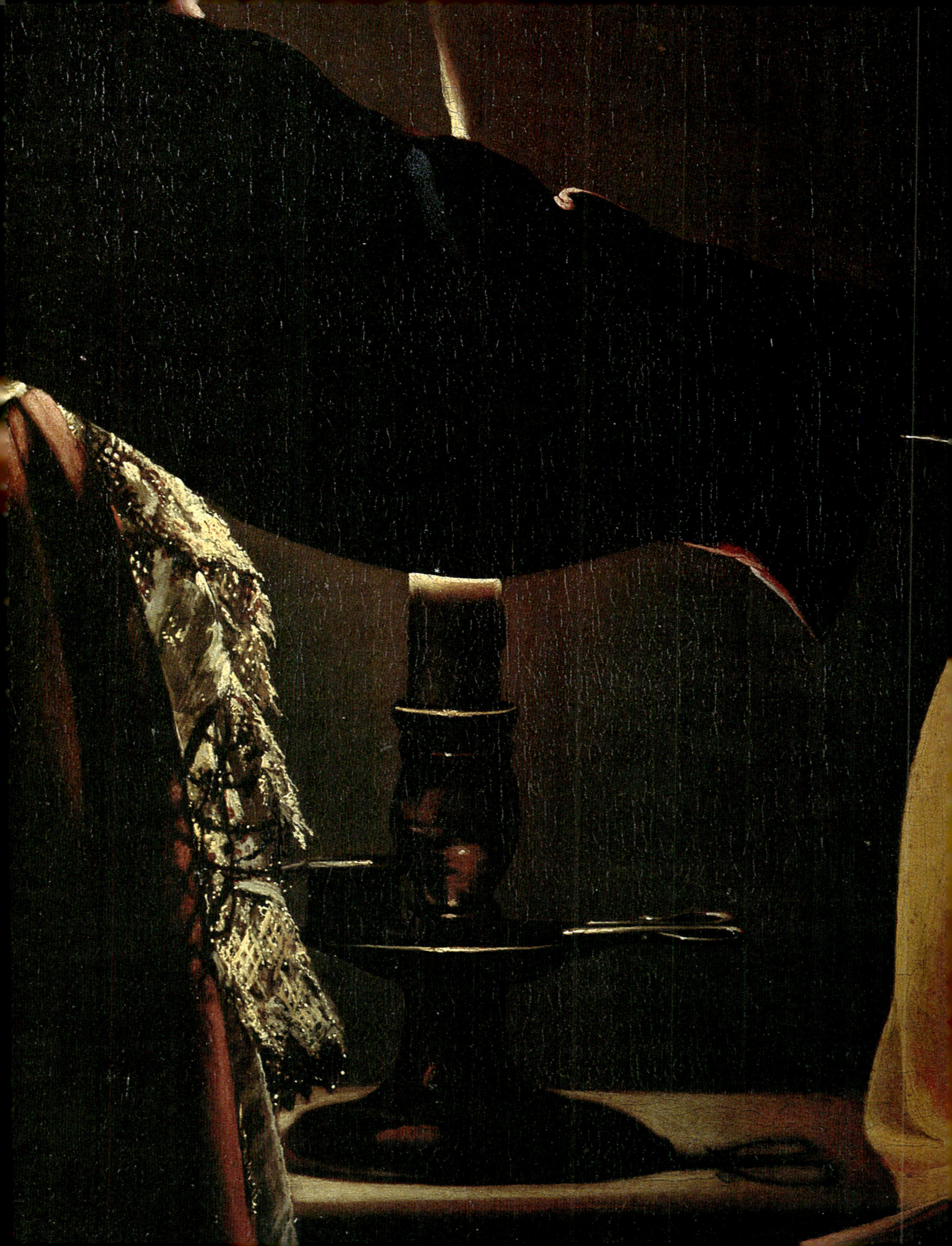

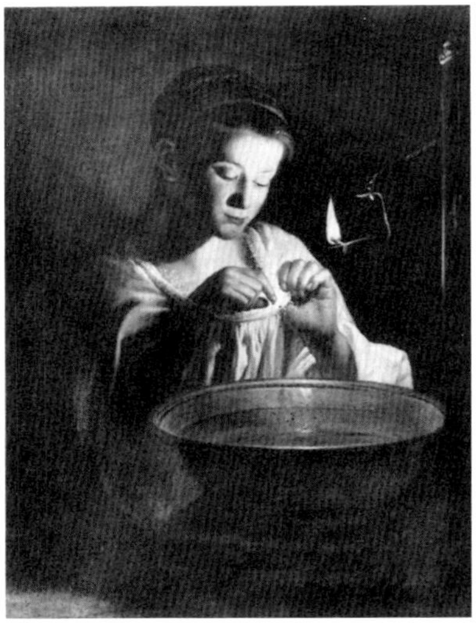

Trophime Bigot. *A Flea Catcher.*
Galleria Doria-Pamphili, Rome

In his genius, La Tour thus succeeds in creating works that appear to be simpler than ever but which are so removed from conventional iconography that they clearly spring from a deep personal meditation and, at the same time, defy specific interpretation. This, however, is the hallmark of certain artists of genius, such as the elderly Rembrandt, the late Hugo, and the great Mallarmé. By deflecting the commonplace they give new meaning to the iconography of their tribe. La Tour does just this in another masterpiece in which the subject, this time, is simple, even crude, and the iconography easy to identify. It is represented literally, but in such a new spirit that it is quite transformed, and even today very few people are prepared to recognize it for what it is. It is the famous *Flea Catcher* in the Musée Lorrain in Nancy.

Discovered in 1955 in Rennes rather than in Lorraine, this painting was so disconcerting that the museum was able to step in and buy it before the rest of the art world had reacted. I can still remember its presentation to the public of the Société de l'histoire de l'Art français by François-Georges Pariset, and the uncomfortable shock it produced among all those who knew and loved *The Newborn Child* in Rennes and *The Adoration of the Shepherds* in the Louvre. The reason is that it quite clearly shows a woman ridding herself of fleas before going to bed. There is no mistaking the flea she is squashing between her nails, nor that La Tour really painted that flea. In an age when vermin were ubiquitous, this was a daily ritual, at every level of society. It was a popular subject with painters in the seventeenth through the nineteenth centuries. It was also popular with poets, who composed little verses around it, such as those in the collection entitled *The Flea of Madame Desroches* published by Etienne Pasquier in 1583. Artists were usually quick to exploit the sexual innuendo and ribaldry implicit in the undress the scene entailed, the contrast between the woman's white skin and the insect's dark body, and the intimacy of the places where it tries to hide. Honthorst was no exception. Perhaps Trophime Bigot alone sought to conjure up no more than the melancholy of a lonely night in his strange painting, now in the Galleria Doria in Rome, showing a chaste, earnest-looking girl drowning her fleas in a basin of water. La Tour does far more. He brings to the scene a stillness, a strength, and a solemn severity that are not readily associated with the subject. Critics have balked at the facts and tried desperately to come up with other explanations such as the saying of the rosary (which unfortunately does not appear on the canvas), the pregnant servant girl's regret, or the sorrow of Hagar.

The contrast between style and subject matter is certainly enough to disconcert. The composition is severe, stripped of all accessories apart from a jade bracelet around the woman's wrist, with large, flat areas of red dissipating the darkness. Set against this is the realism of the subject, and the realism, too, of the woman's face and body that rejects all conventions. The thick simplified forms of the nude seem less like a painting, even an unfinished one, than like a rough wooden sculpture. This could not be further from Bellange, or indeed from *The Fortune Teller.* Why should La Tour choose this subject? It is surely that in his pursuit of human truth, he has to use this silence and this light, so alive and so pure as the candle nears its end, to capture the everyday reality of an ordinary human being reduced to the most humble and common of activities, but a human being nonetheless, a soul. This represents an important evolution from the *Hurdy-Gurdy Player* of Bergues or Nantes which, though similar in import, seem quite superficial in their perfection by comparison. It will be a source of perpetual astonishment that there were then any takers for such a work, which is one of the most difficult in all of western painting.

There are worse things than solitude and dereliction: error, fear, cowardice, human beings in a state of sinfulness and recognizing their sinfulness, their sinful nature. La Tour seems to have been drawn once again to the theme of St. Peter, the apostle who denied Christ three times before the cock crowed. He dealt with it before but had always focused primarily on the distraught face of an aged man. Now the hands will be the same as in the earlier works, clasped in an attitude that combines surprise, suffering, and supplication, but La Tour takes the theme much further, going beyond a simple study of psychology to conjure up the utter baseness of the daring man who had told Jesus, "I am ready to follow you to prison, and to death," who cut off the right ear of the high priest's servant, and who ultimately betrayed three times over without even realizing it, to his own disgrace. There are at least three known ver-

pp. 197-199:
A Flea Catcher, complete work and details.
Musée Historique Lorrain, Nancy

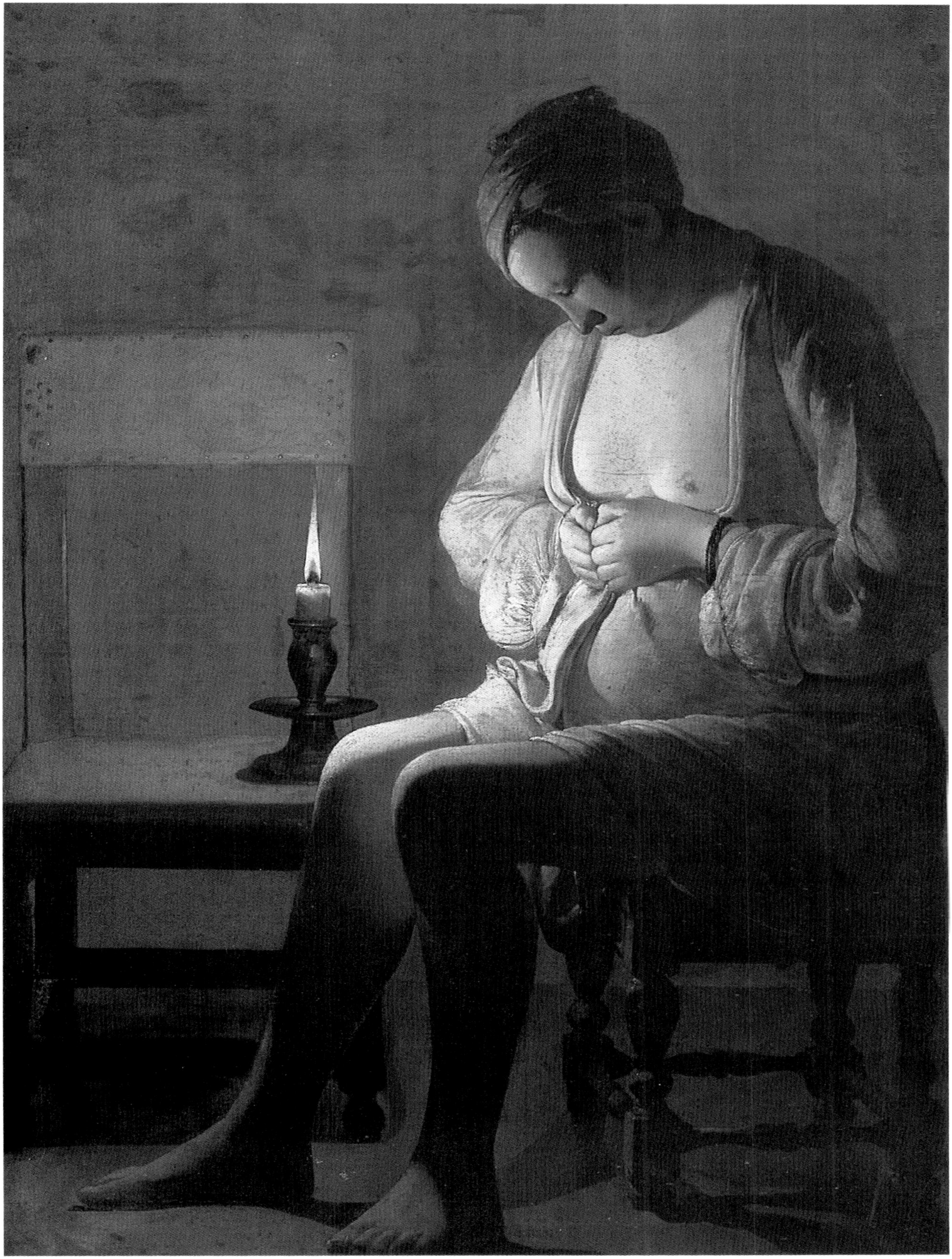

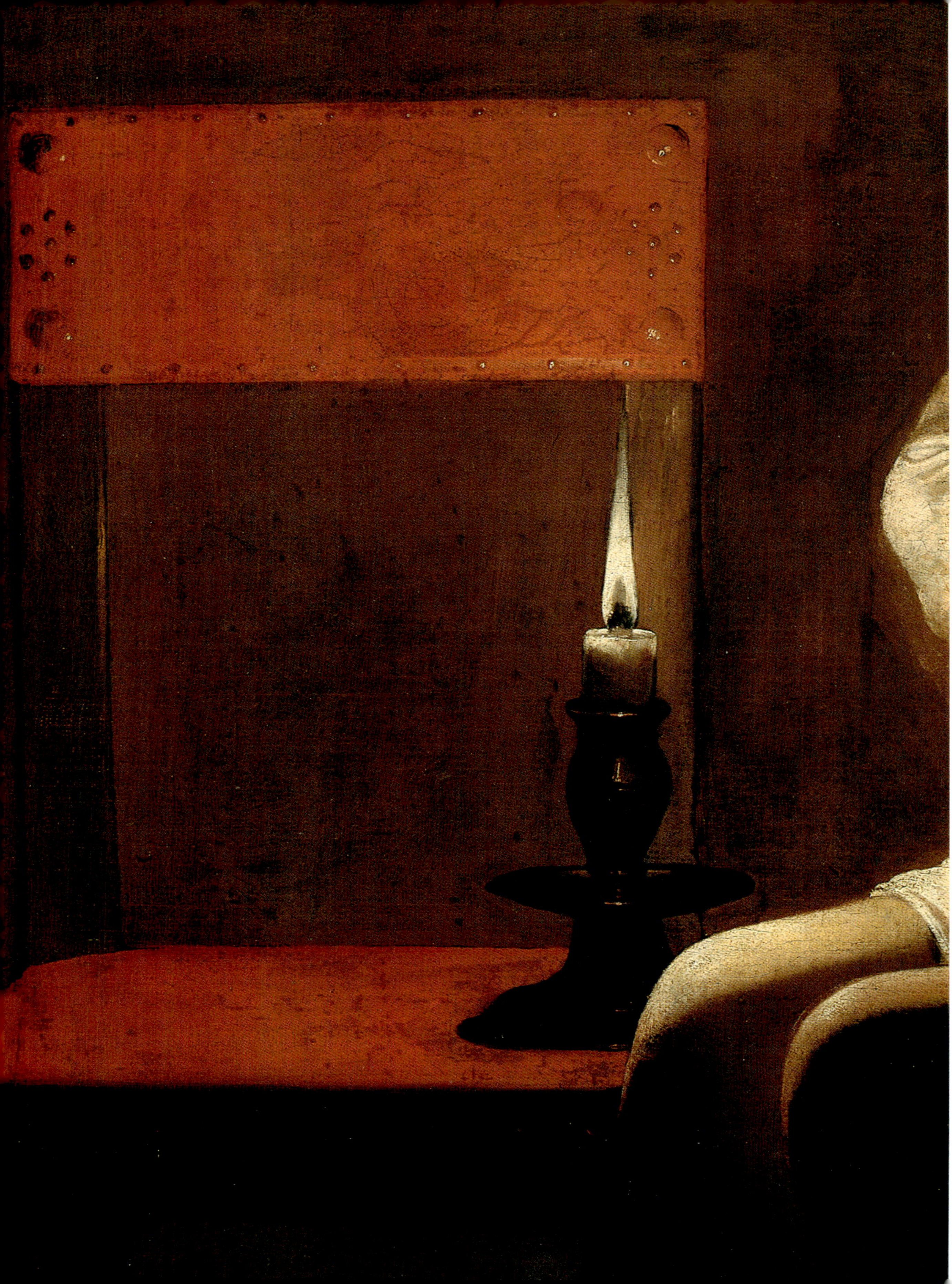

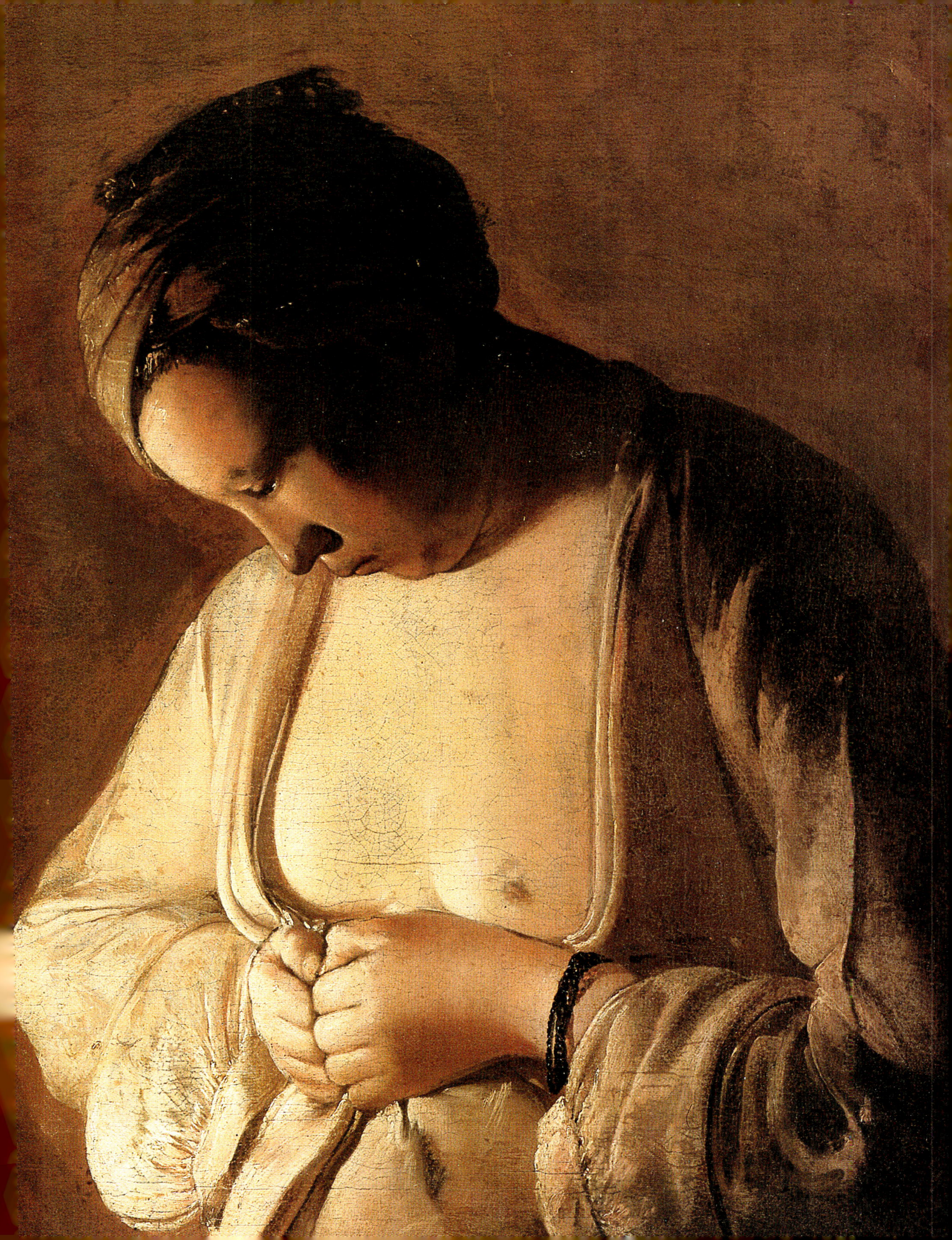

sions of the subject from this period. The earliest and most complete is undoubtedly *The Penitent St. Peter,* signed and dated 1645, and more accurately called *The Weeping of St. Peter.* The picture reappeared on the London art market around 1950 and was acquired by the Cleveland Museum in 1951. The seated profile pose of the saint is reminiscent of the various versions of *The Repentant Magdalen* with the night light, but the composition is tighter, the figure more monumental, and the darkness around him less dense. The old man's legs and habit are lit by a lantern on the ground, the same as in *St. Sebastian Tended by Irene.* Above it sits the cock, whose crowing has just filled the old man's eyes with sudden tears. It sits there placidly, staring with its beady little eye, the stupid instrument of God. This is a striking animal figure, comparable to the dog in the Bergues *Hurdy-Gurdy Player.* La Tour refuses to play with iridescent plumes and sweeping tail feathers; with magistral restraint, he captures the profile of a common farmyard fowl from some corner of Lorraine, cockscomb bristling, ready to scuttle off, as far removed from standard convention as the docile hens of the Le Nain brothers. Above the cock hangs a broken, withered branch of ivy, one of the rare plants that La Tour painted—a symbol, apparently, of broken faith, and, as such, a poetic exception as well for La Tour, who avoids symbols as a rule.

This nocturnal world might become unbearable were it not for the increasing number of children who appear in it as a sign of innocence and hope. Of La Tour's ten sons and daughters, he had already lost six by this time. It is possible that a very personal element underlies these paintings. The earliest preserved child's image is probably *A Boy Blowing on a Charcoal Stick,* and we have already seen how, in *Christ with St. Joseph in the Carpenter's Shop* and *The Dream of St. Joseph* the child embodies the very intervention of grace in human life. In *The Nativity (The Madonna and Child with St. Anne),* La Tour had also shown the child, in the form of a newborn baby, as the image of a destiny to be fulfilled amid the joys and sorrows of an uncertain future. This theme of birth inspired one of La Tour's great series. In one instance, a solitary figure watching over the newborn child—perhaps *St. Anne with the Virgin in Swaddling Clothes* this time—appears to be a fragment of an old copy or of an original stiffened by overpainting (I have never been able to study this painting, which is in a private collection in America), and undoubtedly goes back to a fairly late variation. Another fragment showing a tender, serious-looking woman bending toward the light was identified in the Schloss Fasanerie in Adolphseck, near Fulda, and appears to come from another *Nativity.* A third fragment, of a woman's head with the lit areas of the profile well preserved, but the volume regrettably overrestored, may have been part of a large *Adoration of the Shepherds.* The records themselves tell us that the town of Lunéville gave the governor a *Nativity* by La Tour at the end of 1644. There is no proof that this was *The Adoration of the Shepherds* now in the Louvre, but the hypothesis is at least plausible.

Discovered in Amsterdam around 1926, this painting has suffered somewhat in the lower part and has been trimmed along the bottom and on two sides. A very mediocre copy in Albi shows that the figures were originally set in a much larger space, which gave them far more room to breathe, and that they were shown full-length rather than three-quarters. Although the picture may now have lost some of its balance, its charm remains intact. What La Tour has sought here is not the rugged truth of the Albi *Apostles,* but a simplicity that is not unreminiscent of the lingering medieval sweetness of a painter such as Bourdichon. The entire scene—the contemplative faces of the shepherds, the Virgin with her red dress bathed in light from the candle, the bowl of milk, the lamb's head nudging toward the child with a wisp of straw in its mouth, the child himself, tightly bound in white swaddling clothes, his eyes shut—is permeated by a serenity, a quiet certainty that we do not expect in La Tour's works. The simple, Virgil-like gesture of the shepherdess with the bowl and the smiling face of the shepherd with the pipe who tips his hat seemingly hark back to that happy Lorraine that La Tour had never celebrated at the time. This is in fact the only unequivocal smile in all of La Tour's work, for he preferred to depict the seriousness of people deep in their own thoughts and had never gotten beyond the simper on the face of the *Prodigal Son* in the Kimbell Art Museum in Fort Worth or the amused snickering of the beggars as they watch the brawl in the Malibu painting.

The Penitent St. Peter.
Cleveland Museum of Art

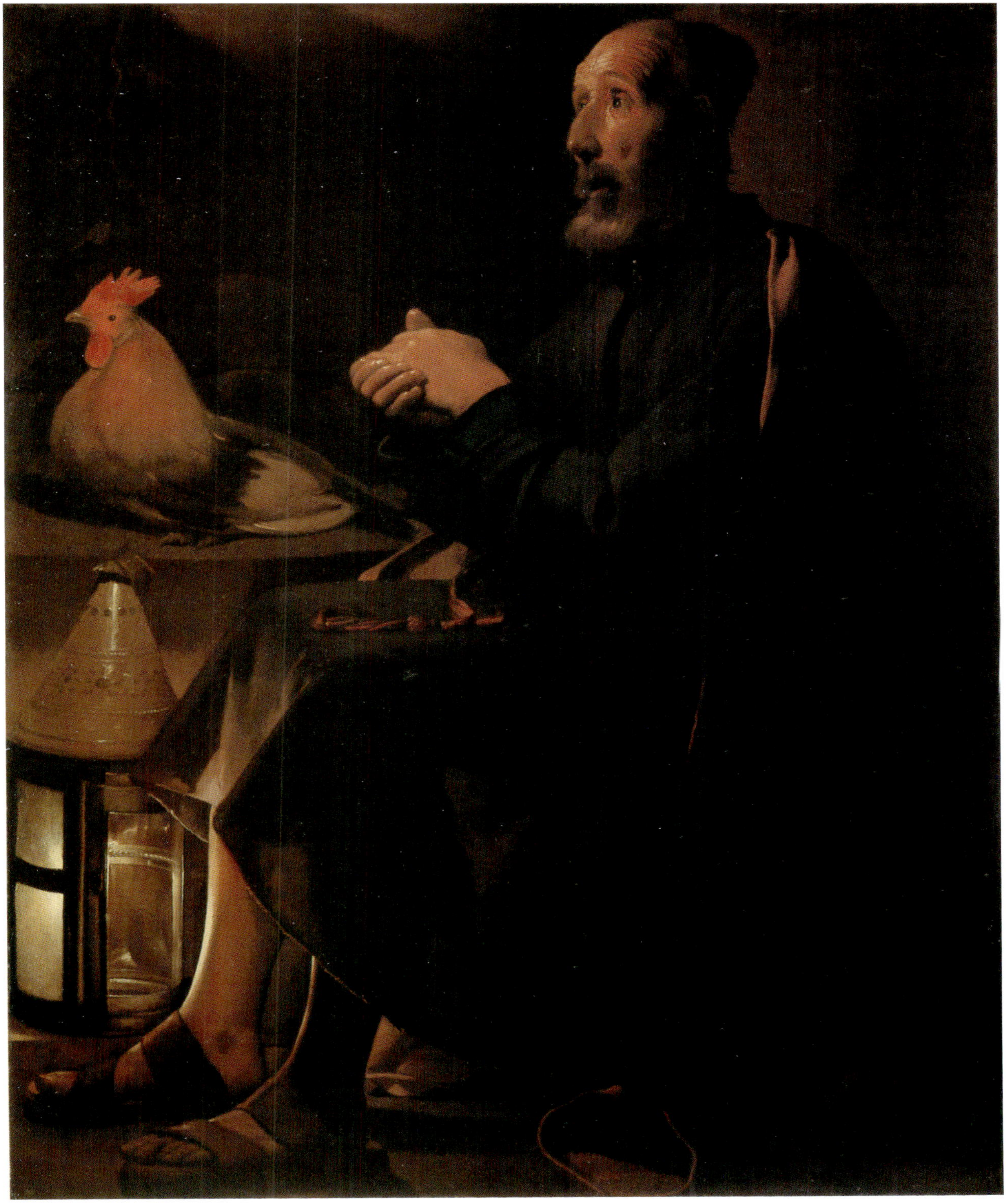

Head of a Woman, fragment (?).
Schloss Fasanerie, Adolphseck (near Fulda)

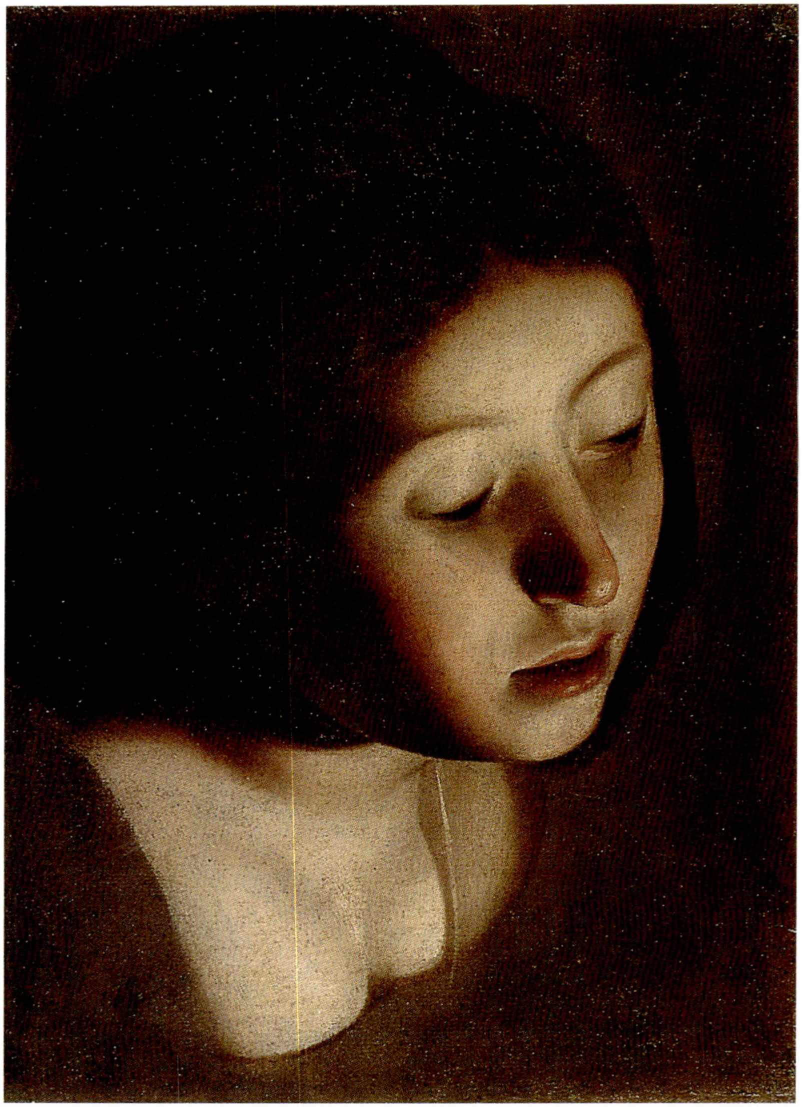

The Newborn Child, copy (?).
Private collection

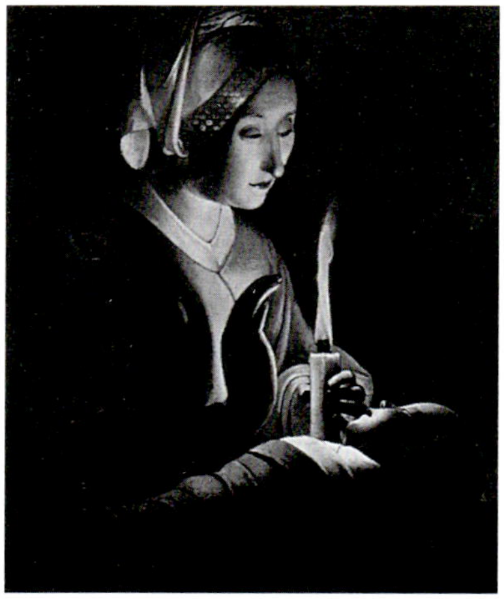

THE PROBLEM OF CUT-UP PAINTINGS

The Adoration of the Shepherds in the Louvre, *The Newborn Child* in Rennes, and the engraving of the *Madonna and Child with St. Anne* suggest that La Tour painted a succession of works on the theme of birth and motherhood. Only two have survived, but it is possible that the works on these two pages come from similar compositions. Even when La Tour painted a canvas with several figures, he liked to set each face in a space of its own. This habit encouraged the cutting up of paintings so commonly practiced by art dealers in the past.

Once La Tour was forgotten, most of his canvases often went unrecognized. In the "night" pictures the backgrounds are touched in with a quick glaze, while the light areas are thickly painted with highlights emphasizing the brightest parts. In certain cases, these dark backgrounds have crumbled away, leaving only most closely worked areas. It is thus easy to see how a number of pictures came to be trimmed (*The Adoration of the Shepherds* in the Louvre and *St. Alexis* in Nancy, for instance, both trimmed at the bottom), and how others survive as mere fragments: the two versions of the *Hurdy-Gurdy Player* in Brussels

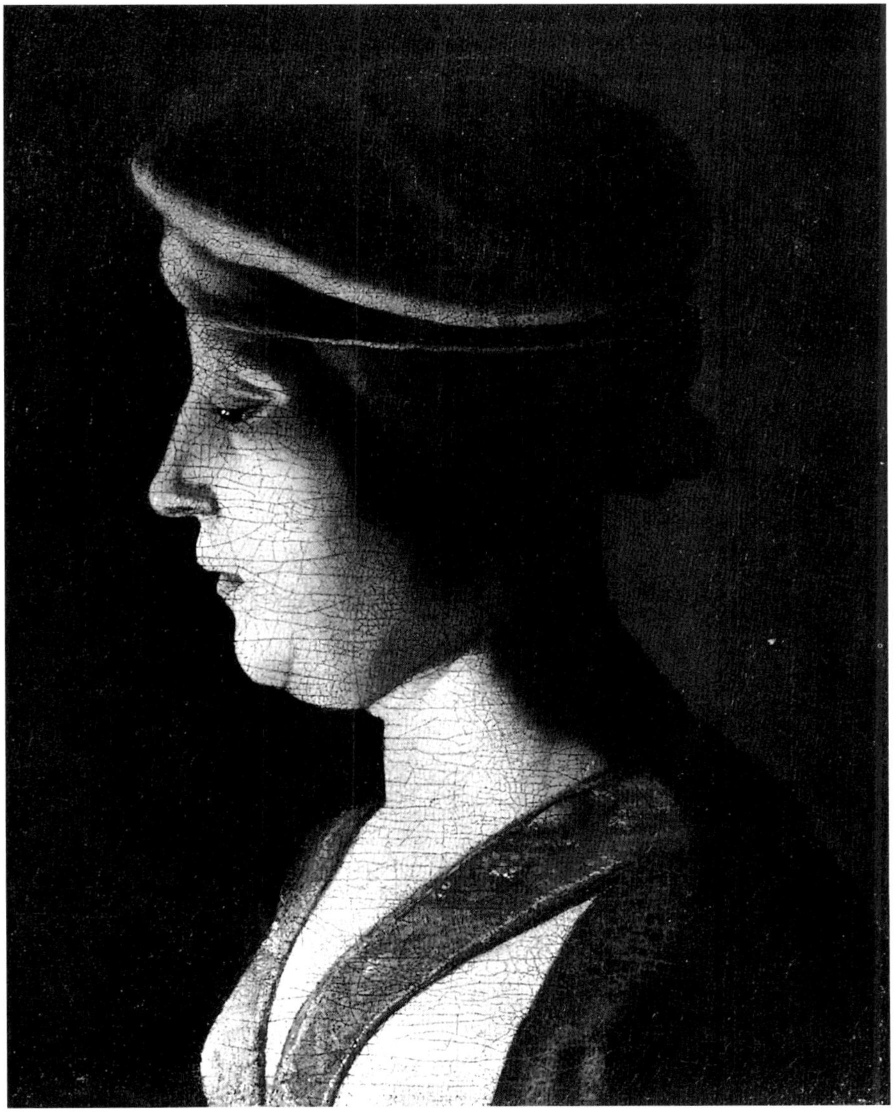

Head of a Woman, fragment.
Formerly Pierre Landry collection

and Madrid are both cut from larger works, and as we will see later on, *The Girl with a Taper* now in Detroit is all that remains of an *Education of the Virgin*.

La Tour's Nativity scenes were even more vulnerable to such savage treatment. With only fragments to go on, it is often difficult to know whether we are looking at parts of an original or of a copy. This is particularly true of the work often called *St. Anne with the Virgin in Swaddling Clothes* acquired earlier this century by Pierre Landry. Only the profile is original; the back of the head has doubtless been wrongly restored and has lost all seventeenth-century character as a result. Benedict Nicolson has attributed the head in the Schloss Fasanerie to La Tour, although he does not seem to have studied it firsthand. Like him I know it through a photograph. Only a scientific analysis of the picture could tell us whether it is a fragment of an original (perhaps even from an unfinished canvas, some of which must have remained in La Tour's studio at the time of his death) or probably a later study made from a lost work, like the pastel study of a figure in *The Beggars' Brawl* that came to the Musée Lécuyer in Saint-Quentin as part of the Quentin La Tour collection.

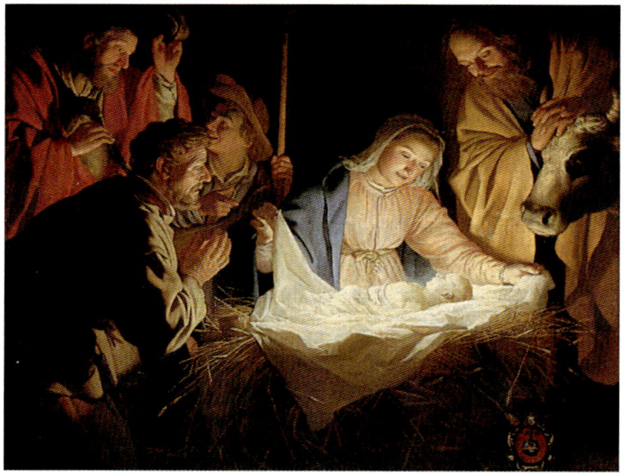

Gerrit van Honthorst.
The Adoration of the Shepherds. 1622.
Wallraf-Richartz Museum, Cologne

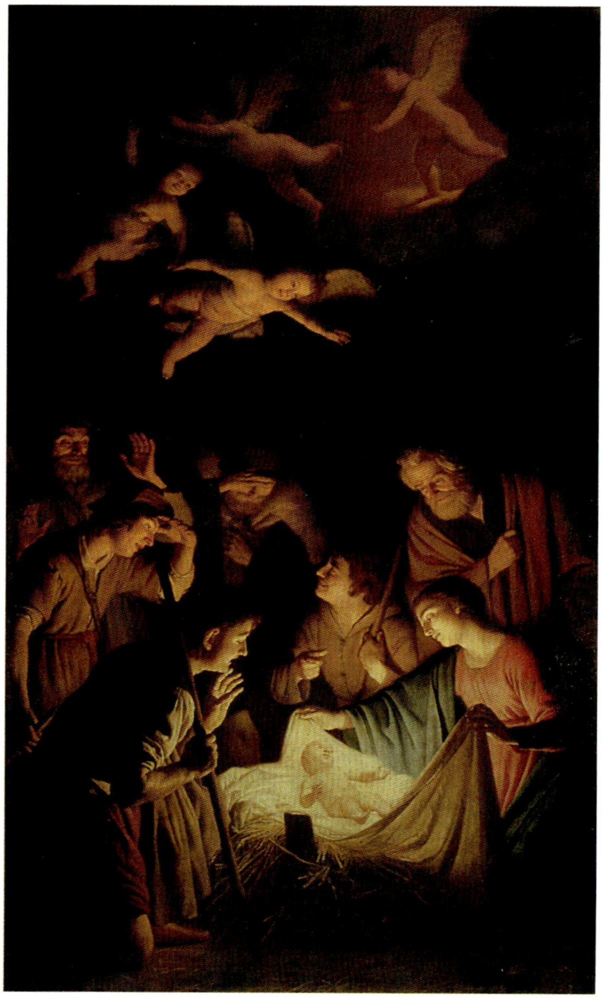

Gerrit van Honthorst.
The Adoration of the Shepherds. 1620.
The Uffizi Gallery, Florence

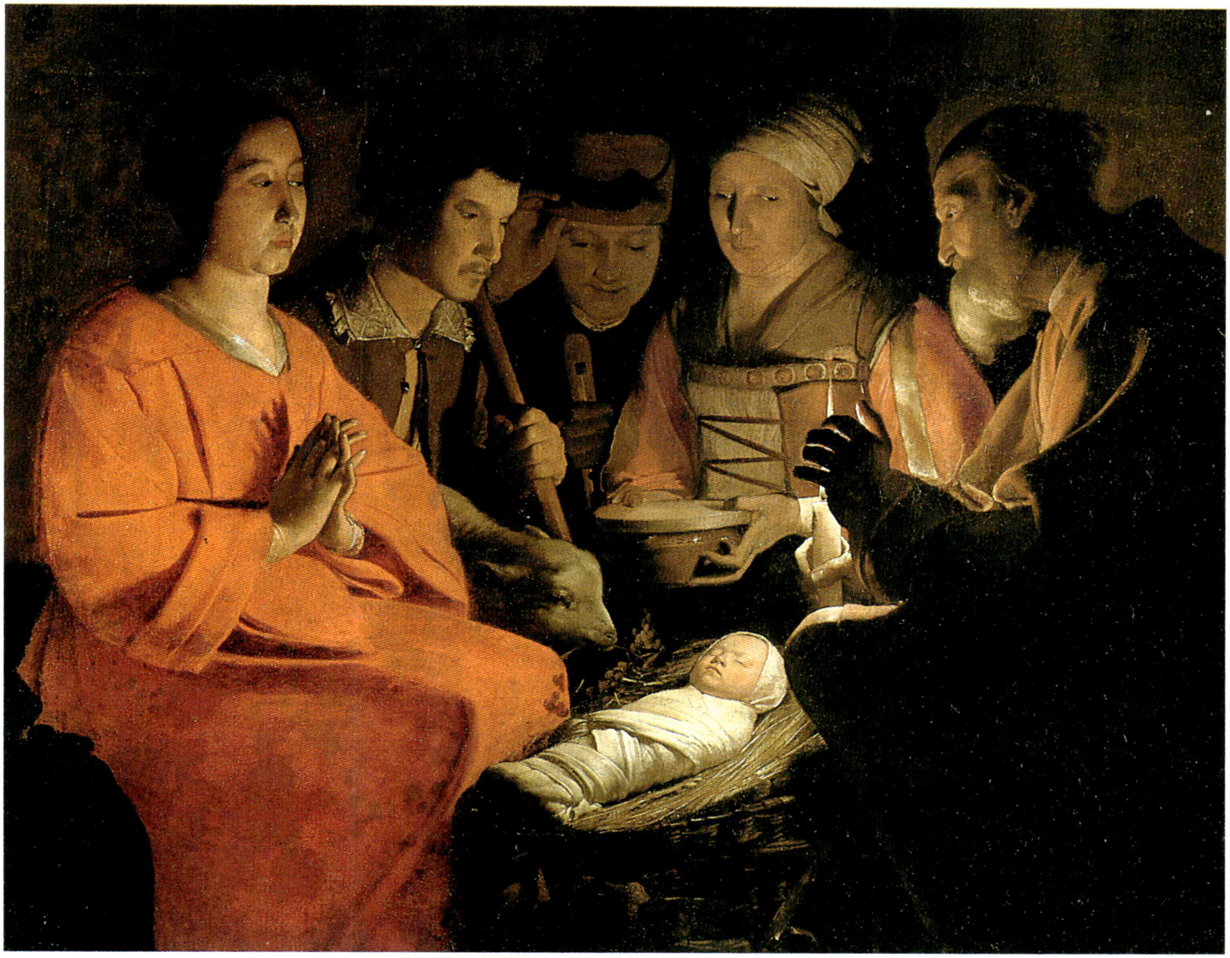

Above and pp. 206-209:
The Adoration of the Shepherds,
complete work and details.
Musée du Louvre, Paris

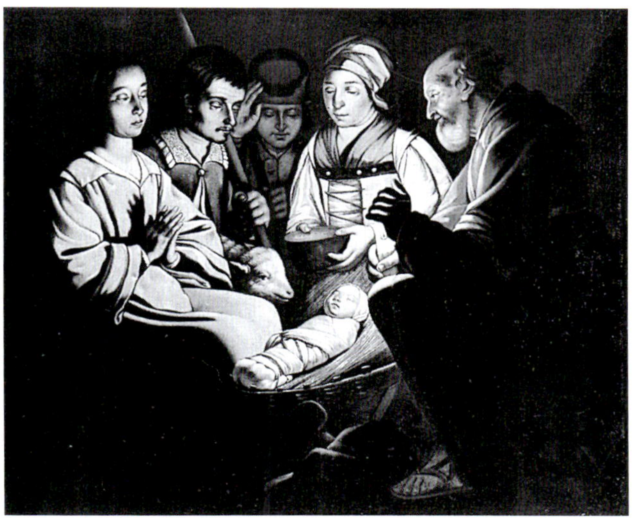

The Adoration of the Shepherds, a copy
showing the complete original composition.
Musée Toulouse-Lautrec, Albi

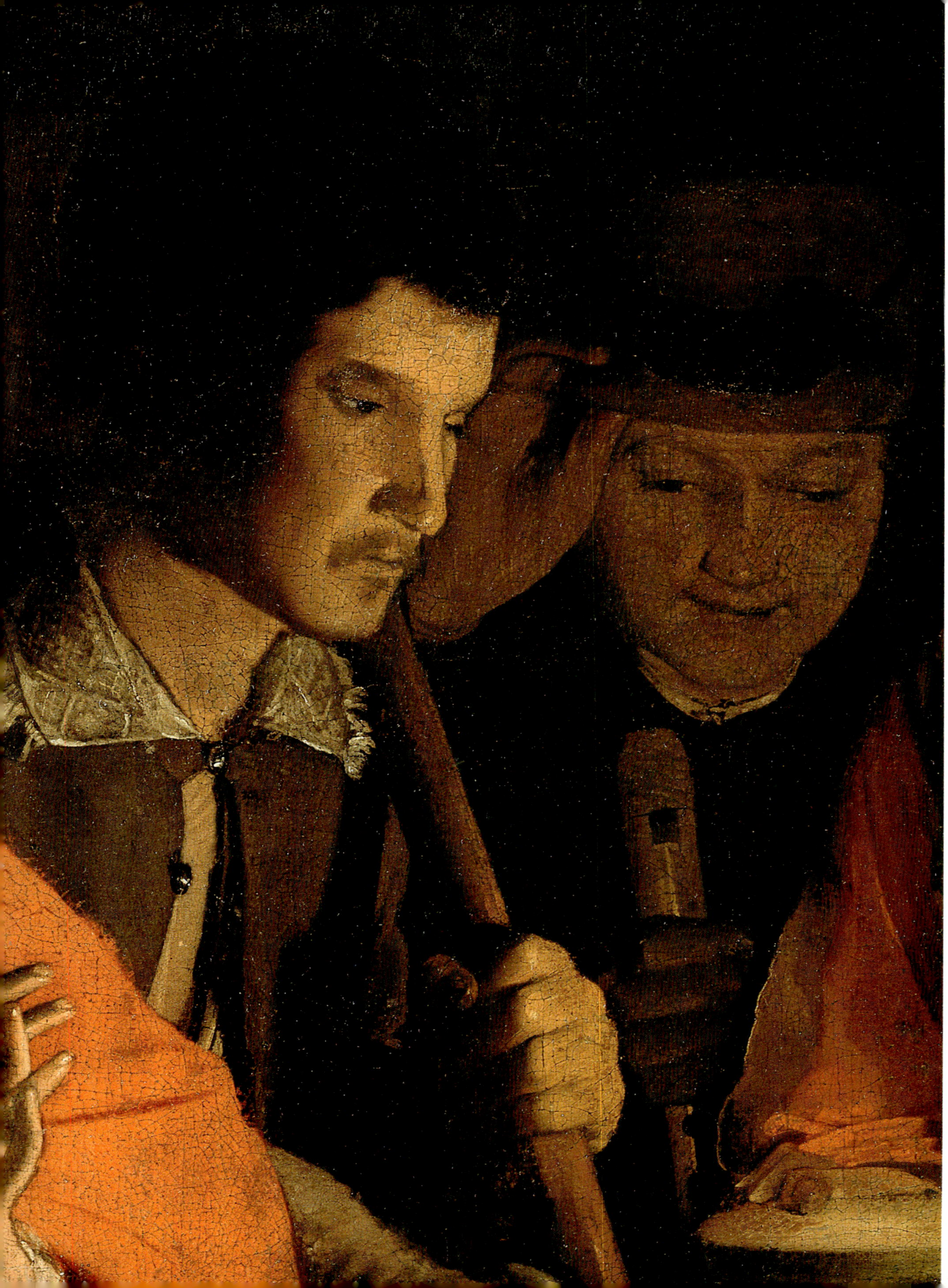

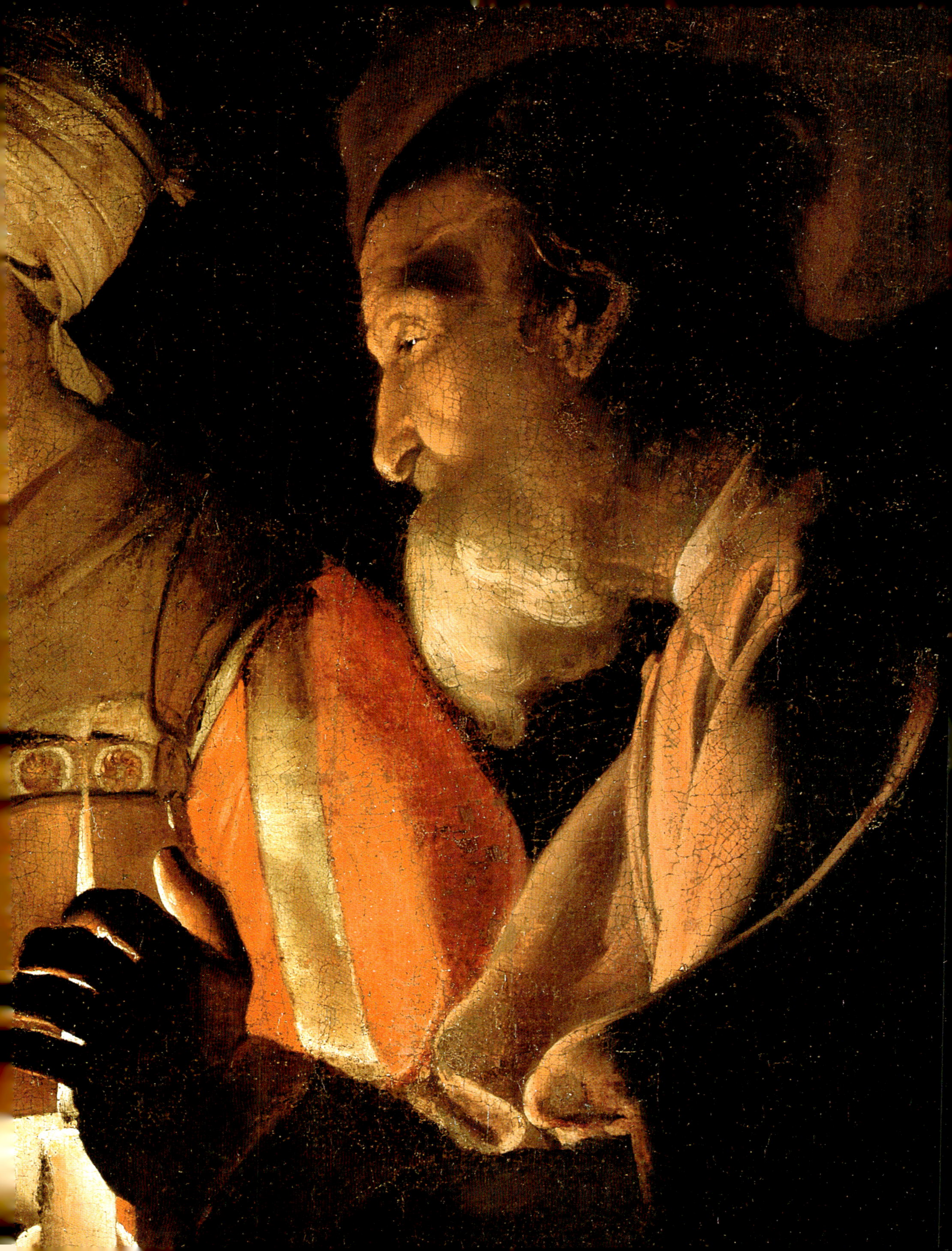

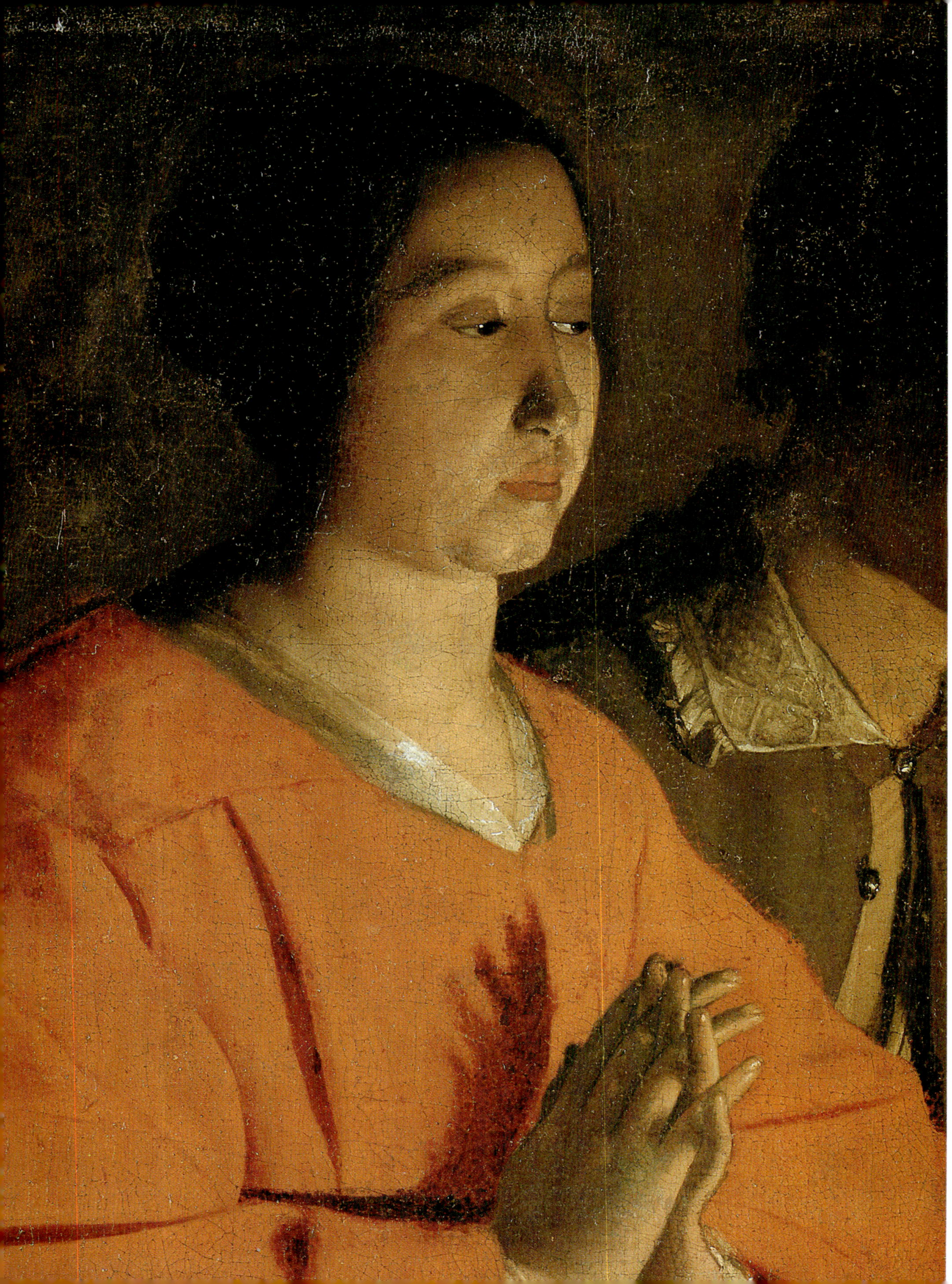

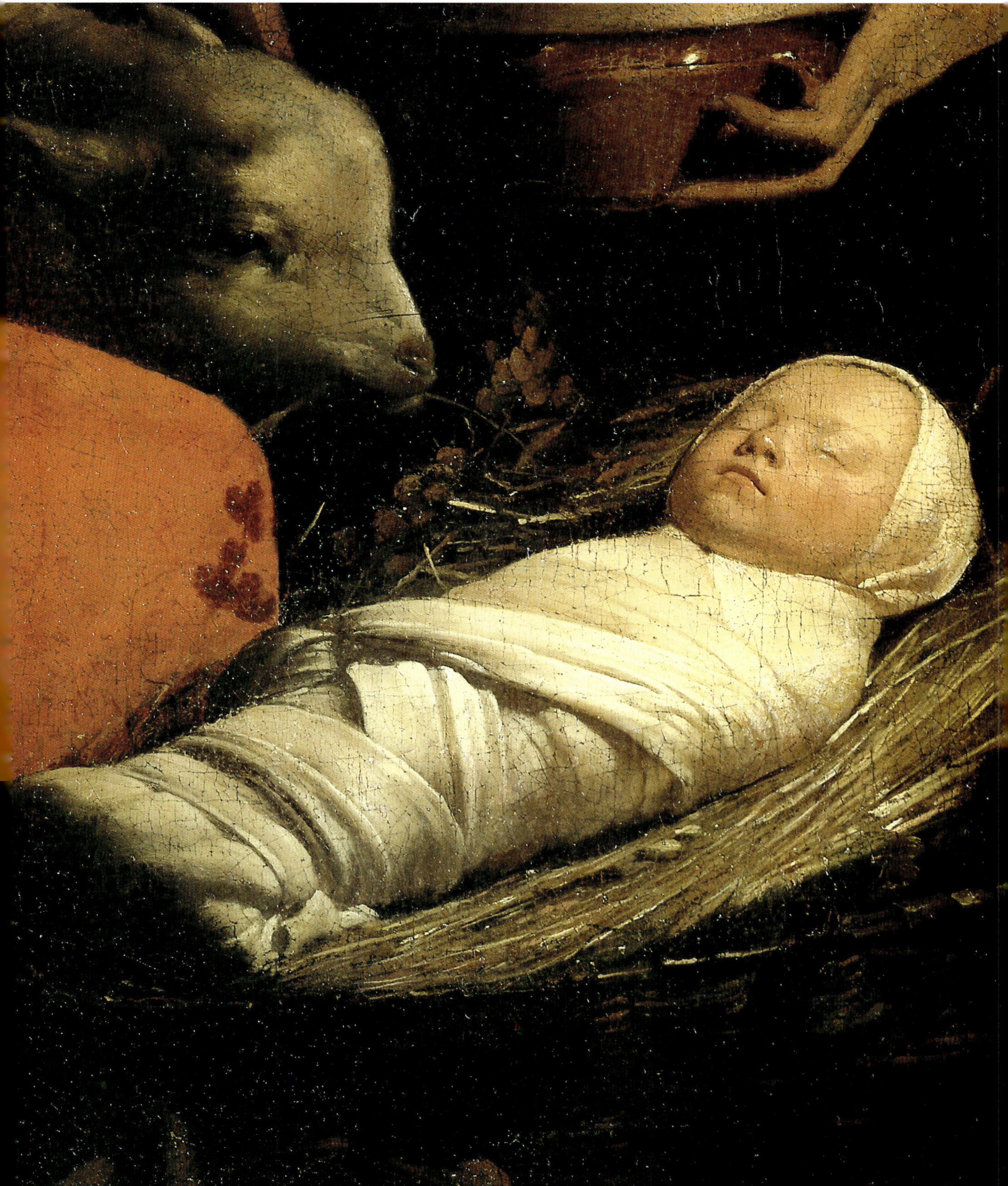

There is a greater tension in that masterpiece among masterpieces, *The Newborn Child* in Rennes. The composition is tighter and simpler, and all the more striking as a result. Here again a strict geometry dictates the arrangement of figures and forms refined almost to the point of rigidity. The candle placed in the foreground lights up the mother's dress in a blaze of red that sets the whole picture aglow and blocks out all other color except for the faintest hint of yellow in the baby's swaddling clothes and the slightest touch of purple on the grandmother's dress. Never has La Tour achieved a light as simple and palpable as this; never has the flame hidden behind a protective hand conveyed more powerfully the presence, amid the silence and shadows, of life itself, hidden in the little sleeping form. The mother's face is expressionless: she is locked in communion with what was just a short time ago a part of herself. The grandmother's face is calm and meditative, and her gesture is enough to conjure up all the care and dedication that this destiny barely underway will need in the face of the dangers already lying ahead. The resulting image is so profound, so deeply rooted in the real world that however natural it is to see it as a *Nativity with the Madonna and St. Anne*, this reading adds little to the painting. What is presented here is the mystery of all birth, whether that of God incarnate or that of any ordinary child, in its patent mystery beyond time, beyond all explanation: light and night.

Another composition featuring a child, this time six or seven years old, also gave rise to a series. There is one version in the Frick Collection in New York. It is signed, but decimated by a restoration so extreme that most critics cannot accept it as anything more than a copy—probably erroneously, since the few small areas that survive unscathed have the authentic stamp of an original. It is clear from a surviving old copy that there must be another version, with the figures shown full-length and great areas of shadow filling the whole lower portion of the painting. Another copy, in the museum in Dijon, reveals several differences in the embroidery on the headdress and the style of the collar that could only have come from La Tour himself, and seems therefore to correspond to a third original that is now lost. Yet another version radically altered the composition: the arrangement is the same, but the book is replaced by a needlepoint cushion and the candle by a taper. A fragment in the Detroit Art Institute showing the girl's head and hand almost certainly comes from the original, which can be reconstituted from a copy. This sewing lesson is more informal, taken more directly from ordinary life, but it lacks the great sweep of light that descends from the woman's face to the open book and gives the other version its poetic force.

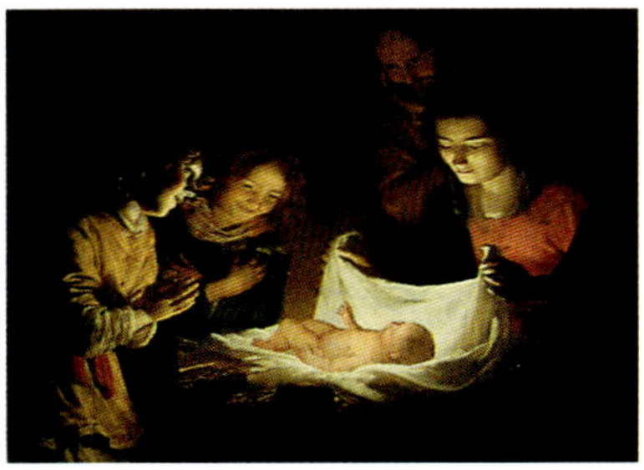

Gerrit van Honthorst. *The Nativity.*
The Uffizi Gallery, Florence

Here too we are faced with an ambiguity: this is a woman teaching her young daughter, but also the *Education of the Virgin*. Indeed, the *St. Anne* listed in Maréchal de La Ferté's collection must have corresponded to one of these versions. The subject was a common one, and it was regularly treated by painters and sculptors from the sixteenth century onward. It turns up among Bourdichon's miniatures, Rubens's oils, and Brébiette's engravings, and in almost every case the artist highlights the bond between mother and daughter, the strong protective figure of Anne on one hand, and the frail young girl already *gratiae plena* (full of grace) on the other. By transposing the scene into a nocturne, La Tour has not simply added the poetry of darkness to the scene—he has changed the interpretation. The narrow circle of light does lock mother and daughter together, but around the holy book. Instead of merging the two figures together into a single mass, like Rubens, La Tour deliberately separates them, and almost opposes them: on one side, the innocence and the purity of the child; on the other, sitting upright and seeming saddened, the mother. The adult sits upright and foresees the misery and sorrow that her love would like to ward off, but that are the only and inescapable ways to glory.

Despite St. Anne's melancholy and that extraordinary expression of hers combining knowledge of life, a sense of destiny, and womanly gentleness, these paintings could seem to herald a kind of release for La Tour. We might be tempted to think that the appearance of children and human affection, so utterly foreign to the world of the penitent *St. Jerome* and the *Magdalen*, finally came to temper the harshness of his stoic asceticism. In fact, however, these first appeared in the early 1640s, and it is perhaps no more than chance that has permitted only relatively late versions of such subjects to come down to us. Indeed, the last great surviving masterpieces seem to show that La Tour's vision became increasingly tragic and increasingly bitter.

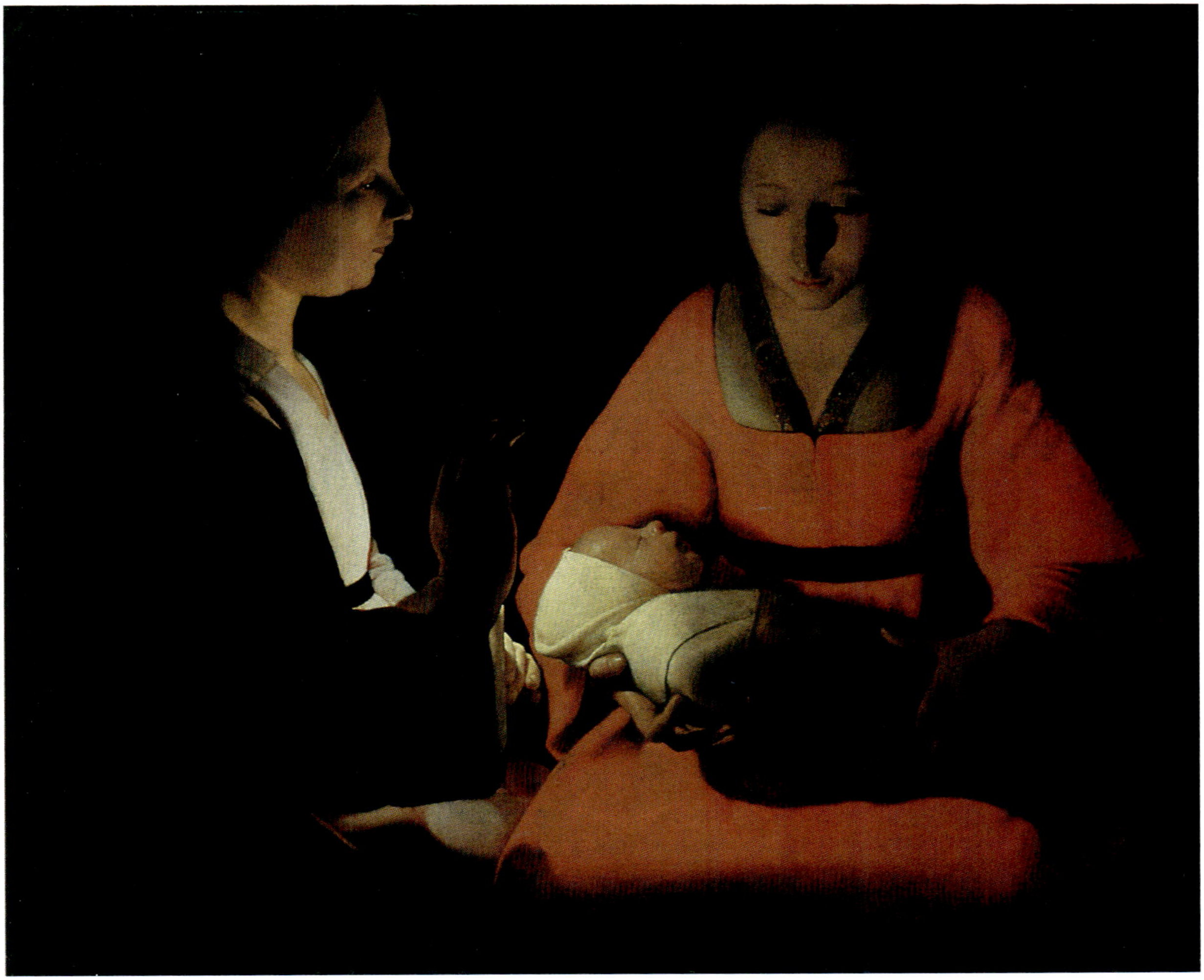

Above and pp. 212-213:
The Newborn Child,
complete work and details.
Musée des Beaux-Arts, Rennes

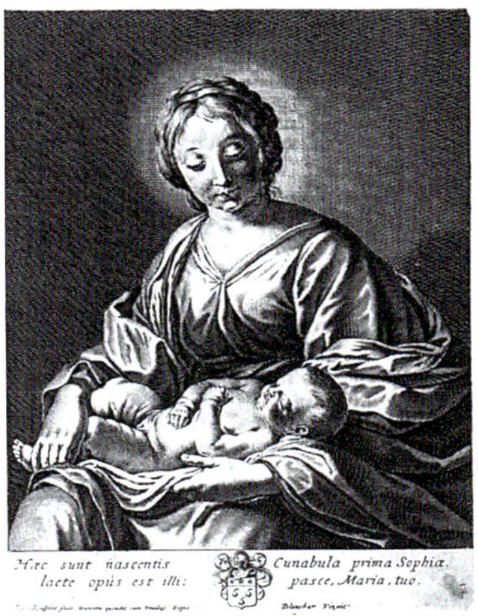

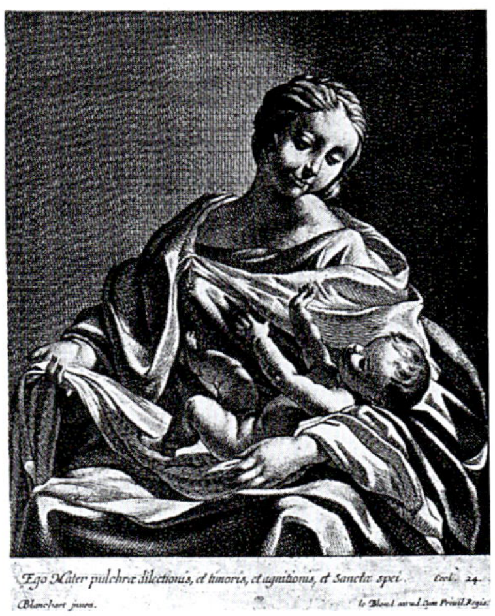

Opposite:
After Jacques Blanchard. *Virgin and Child*.
Engraving by Gilles Rousselet.

Right:
After Jacques Blanchard. *Virgin and Child*.
Engraving by Antoine Garnier.

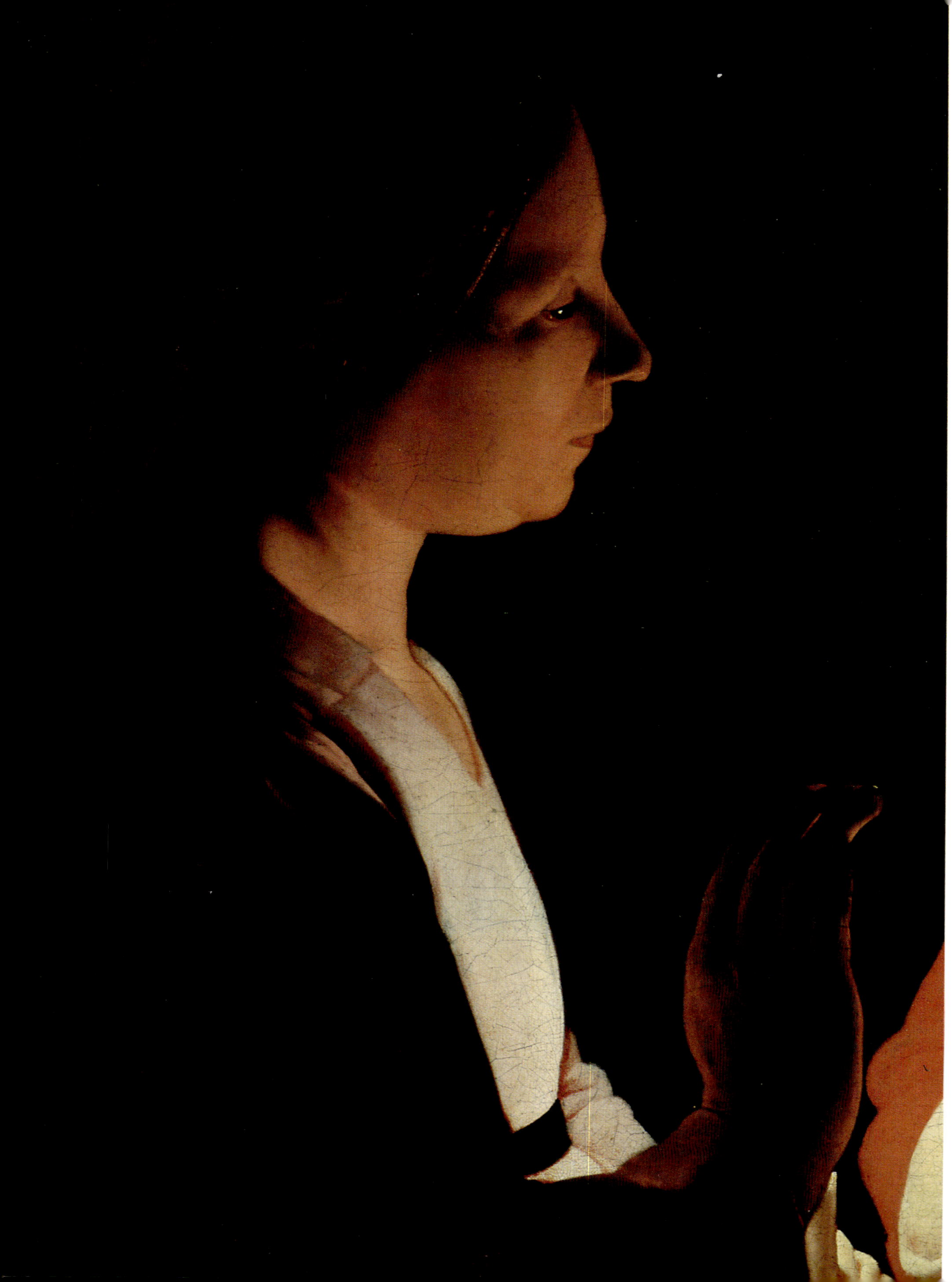

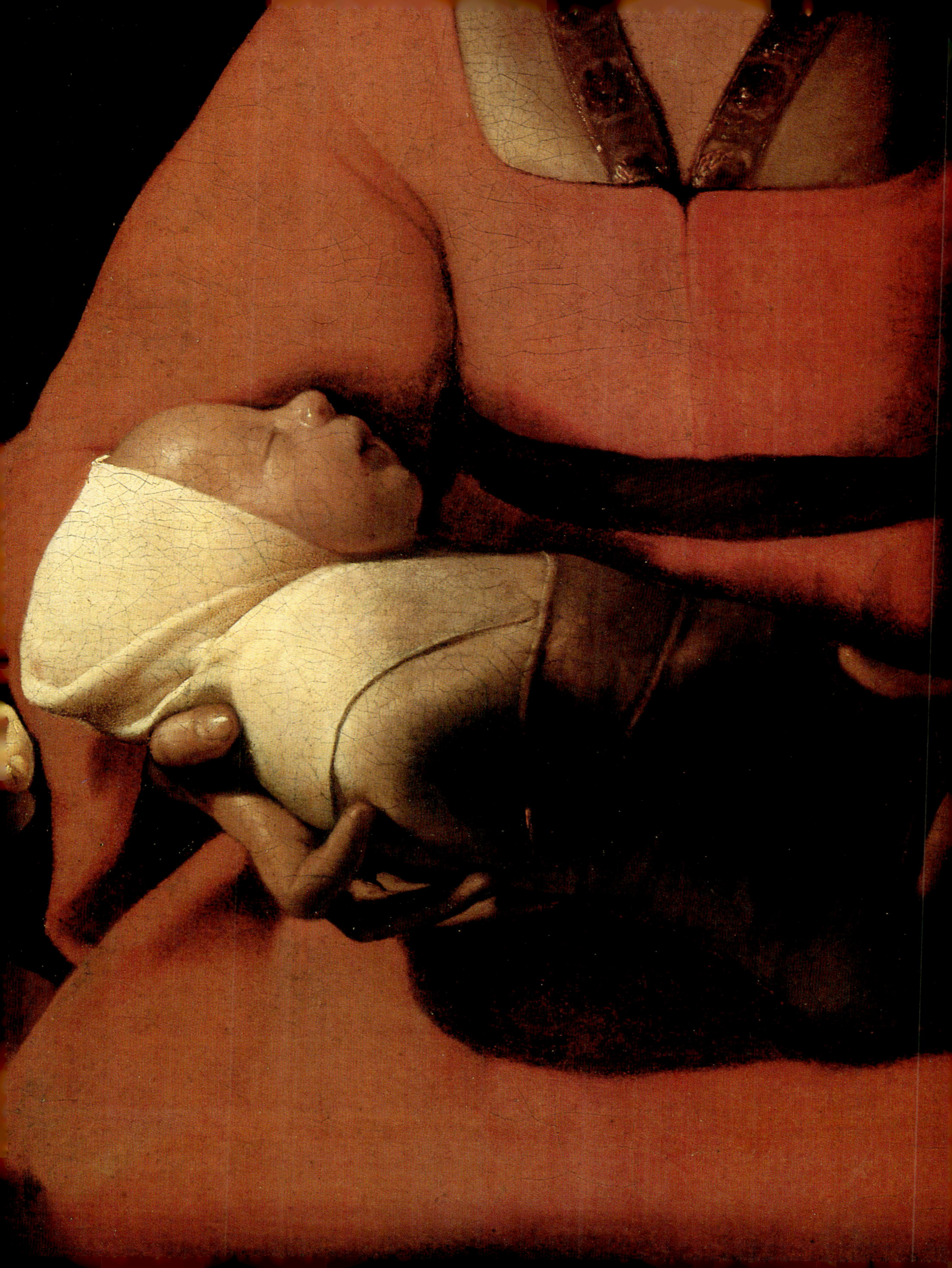

After Georges de La Tour.
The Education of the Virgin.
Heinz Kister Collection, Kreuzlingen

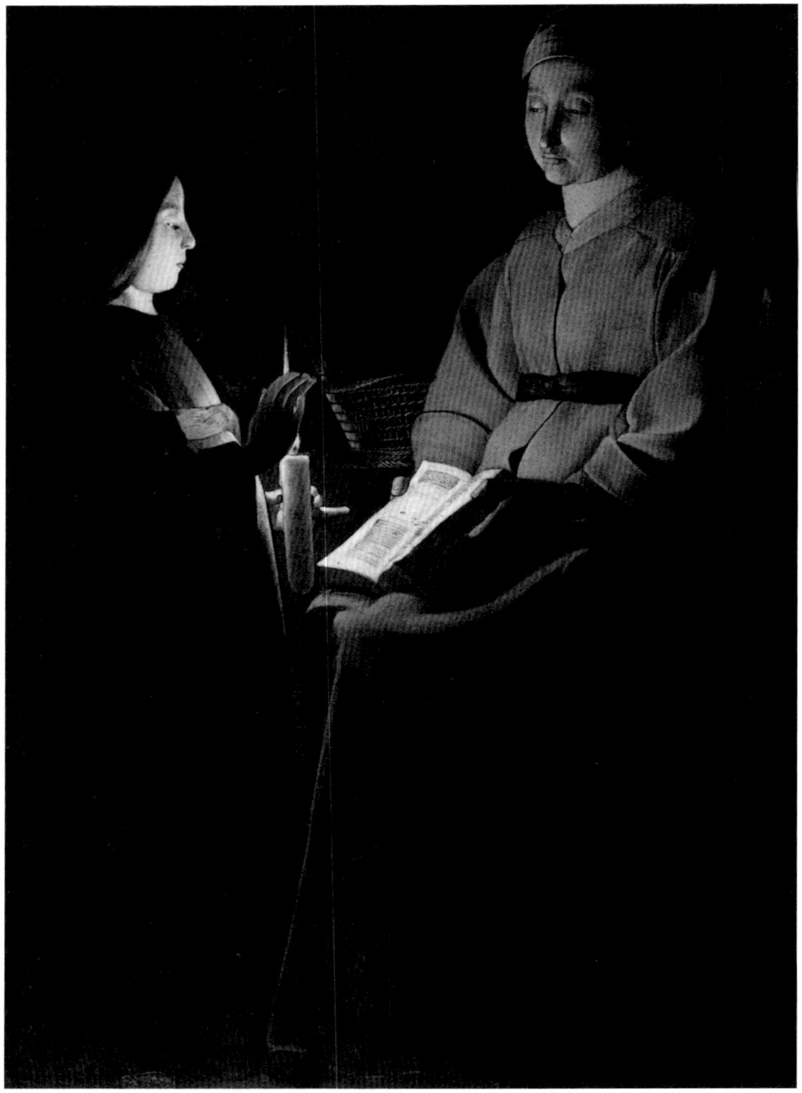

Peter Paul Rubens.
The Education of the Virgin.
Musée des Beaux-Arts, Antwerp

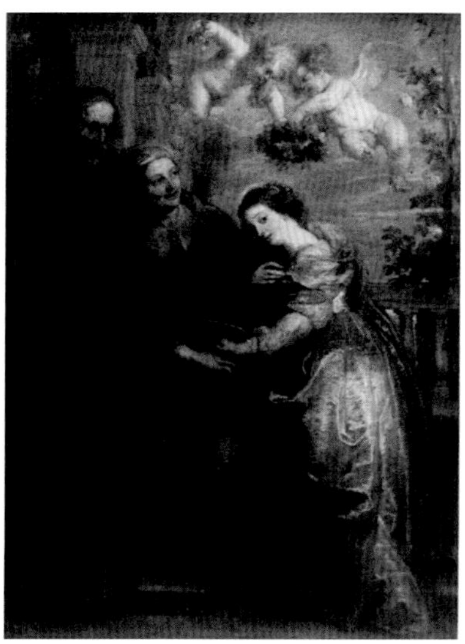

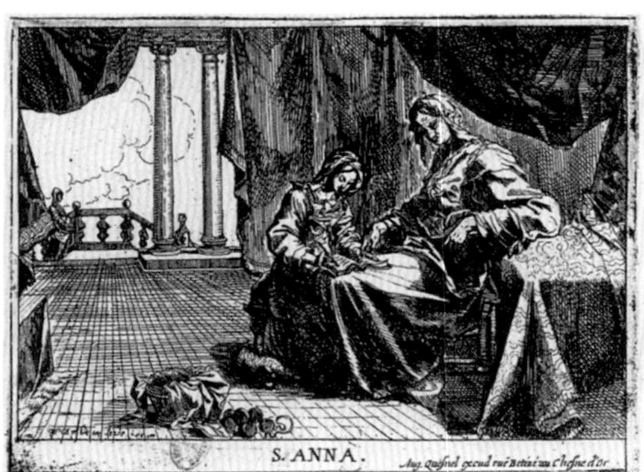

Pierre Brébiette. *The Education of the Virgin.* Etching.
Cabinet des Estampes, Bibliothèque Nationale, Paris

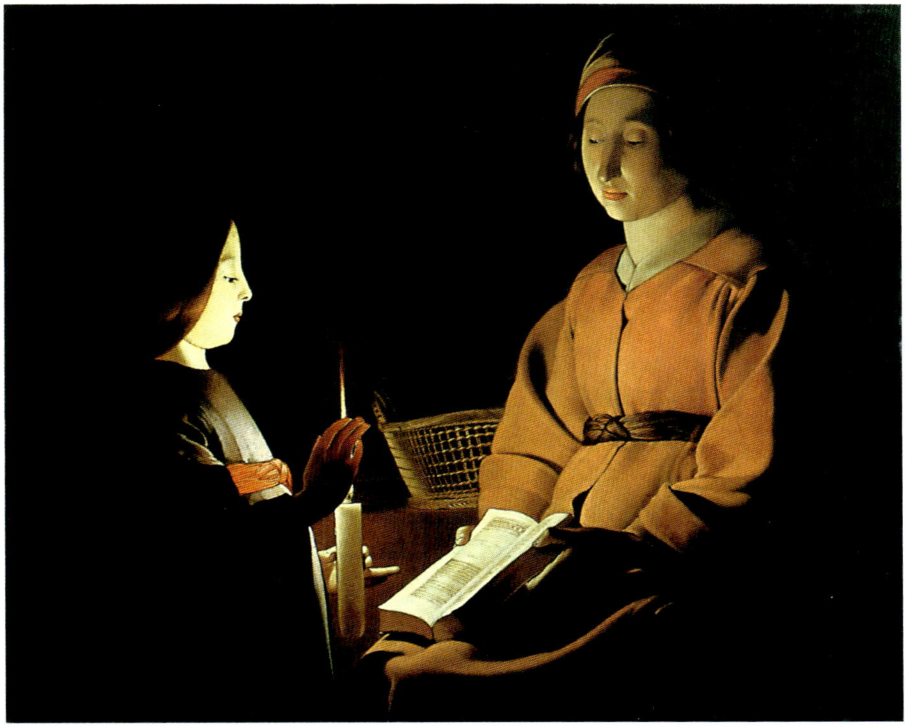

The Education of the Virgin.
The Frick Collection, New York

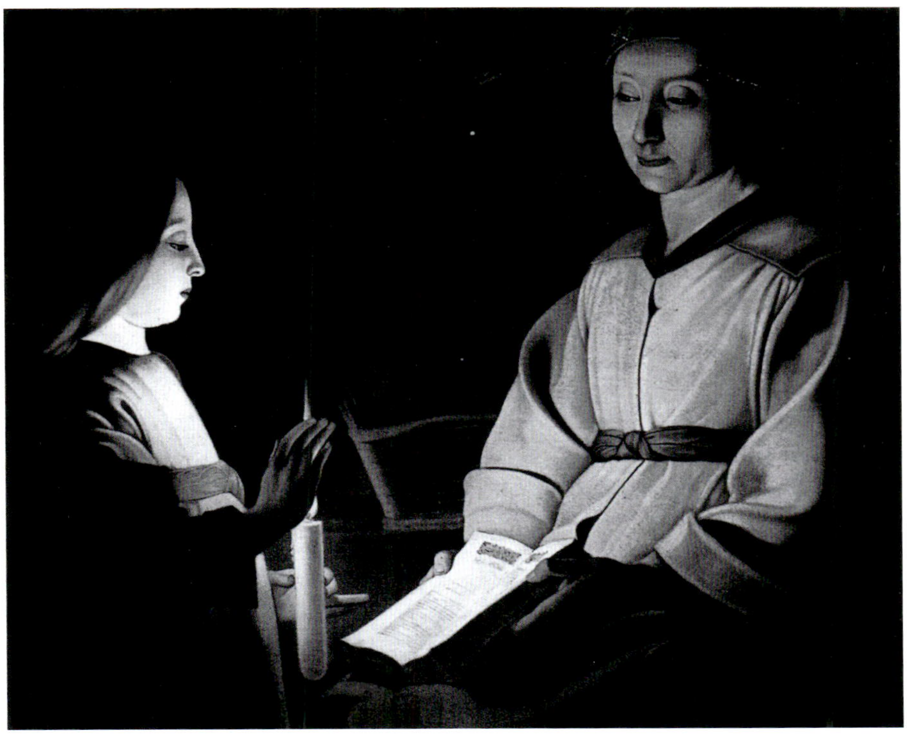

After Georges de La Tour.
The Education of the Virgin.
Musée des Beaux-Arts, Dijon

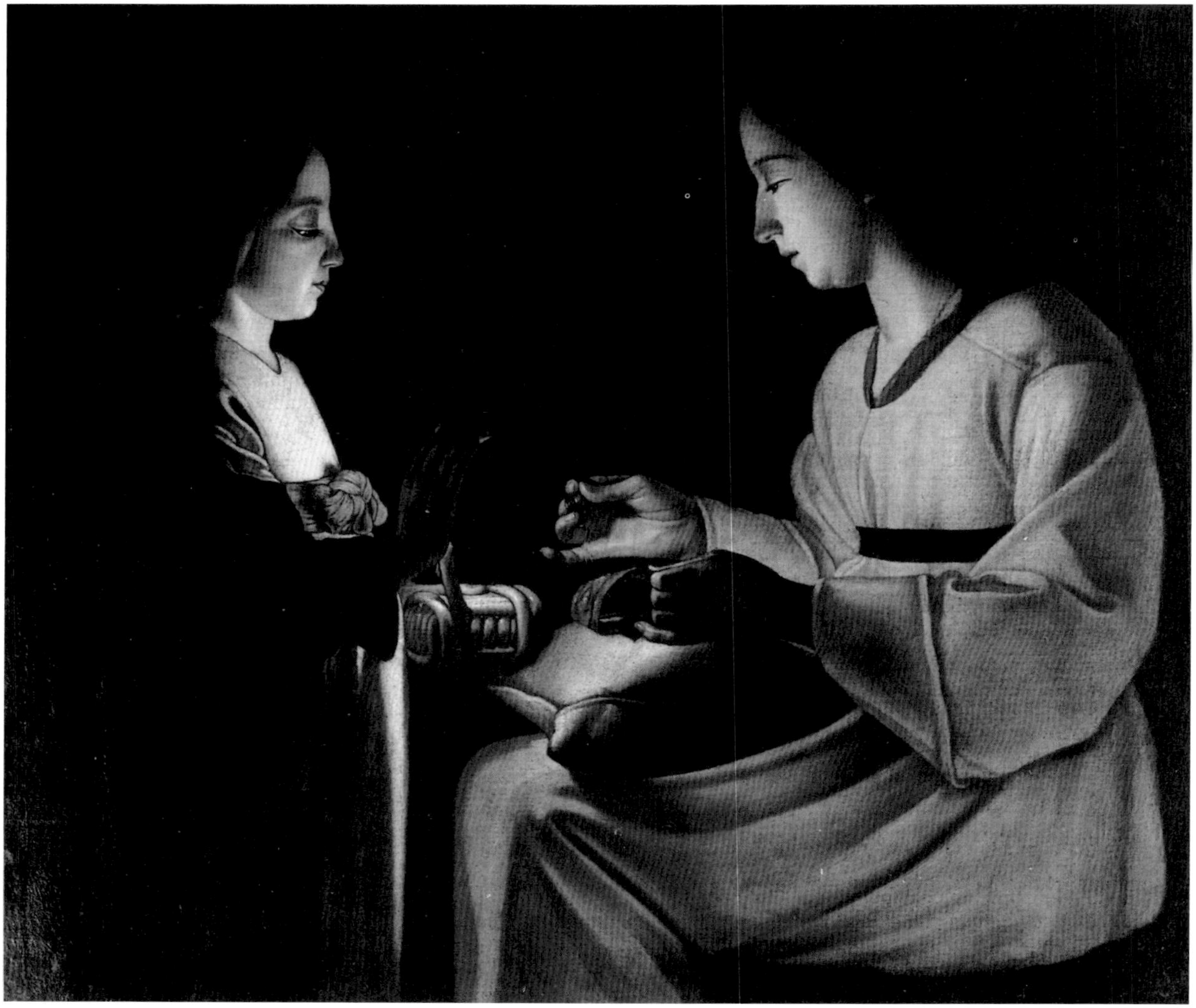

After Georges de La Tour.
The Sewing Lesson.
Collection Marquess R. del Carretto,
Cisano sul Neva (Savona)

The Sewing Lesson, fragment,
also called *The Girl with the Taper.*
Detroit Institute of Arts

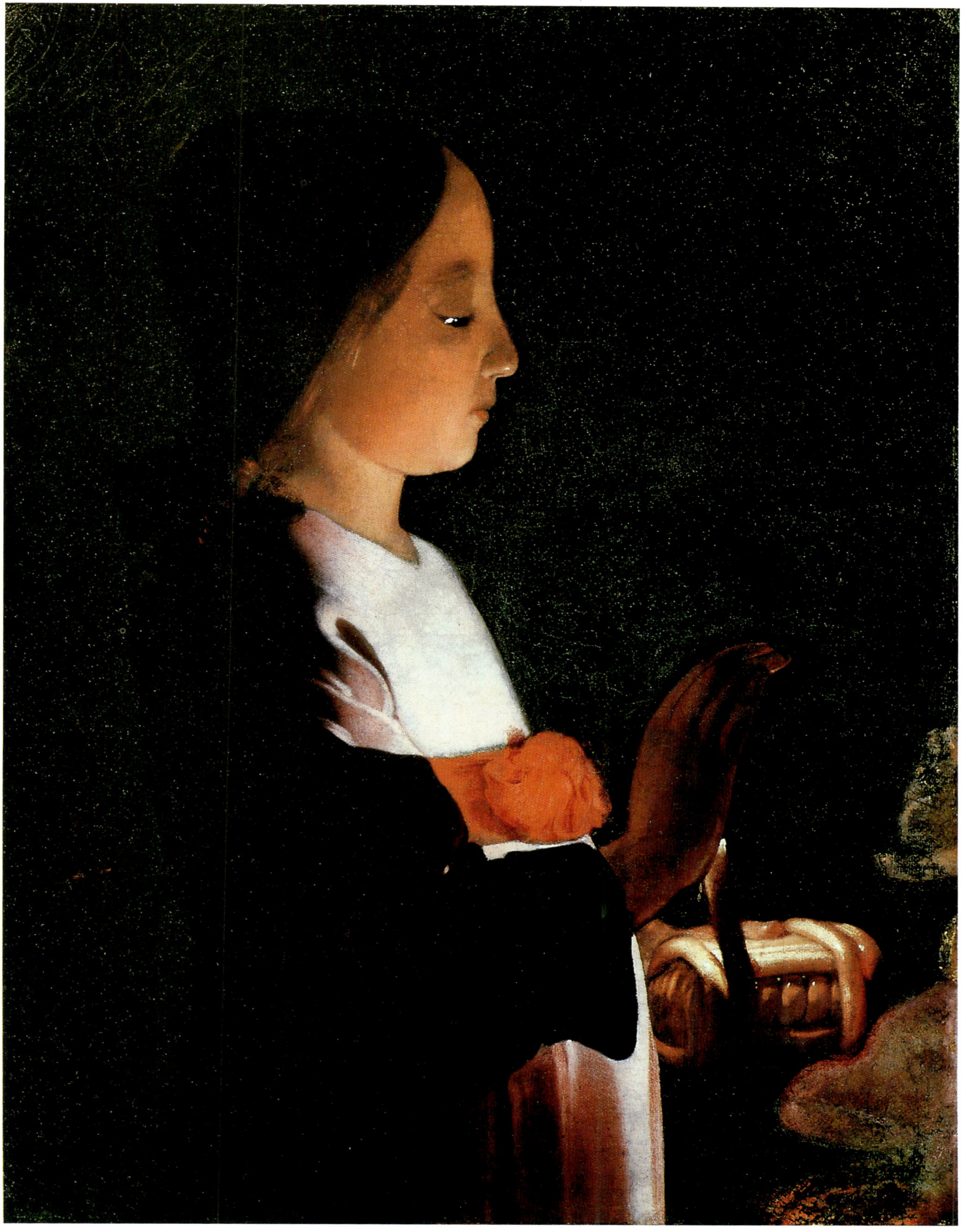

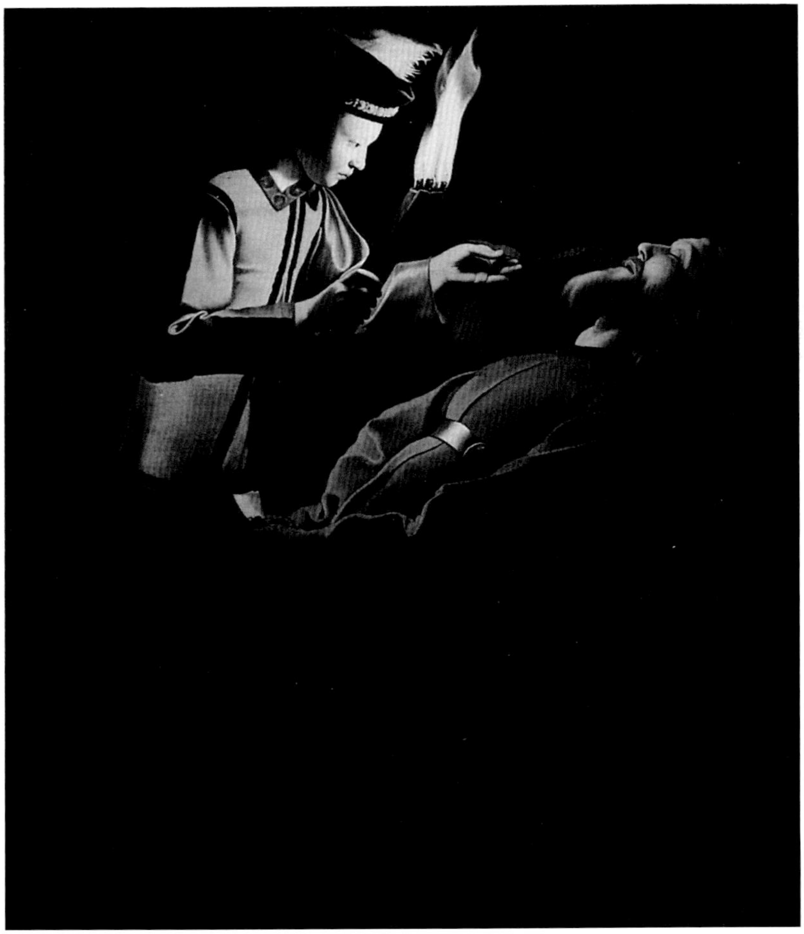

St. Alexis, a copy showing the original format of the composition.
National Gallery of Ireland, Dublin

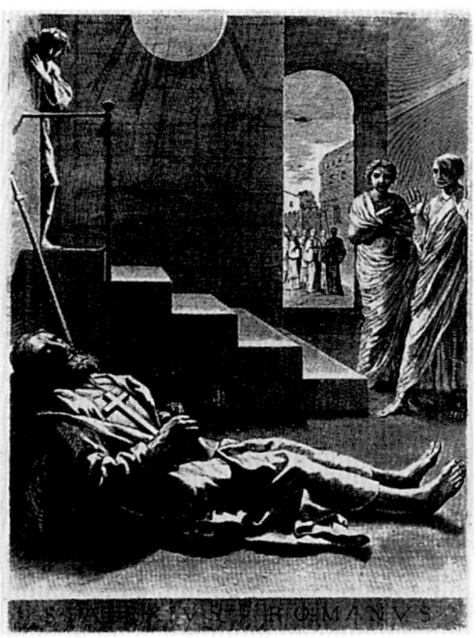

Claude Mellan. *St. Alexis*. 1649. Engraving.
Private collection

St. Alexis probably dates from the end of 1648. The complete composition is known only through a rather leaden copy acquired several decades ago by the Dublin museum. The version in the Musée Lorrain, with a section unfortunately cut away from the bottom and another added to the top, may well be the original, but only a scientific study, which has yet to be performed, could make the determination. It was an "image St. Alexis" that the governor of Nancy received as his New Year's present for 1649, and everything suggests that this was the composition in question. The subject is relatively rare, although it was treated by both Pietro da Cortona in Rome and Claude Mellan in Paris, as well as by numerous provincial painters. The story of St. Alexis, related in *The Golden Legend,* was very well known at the time. It was the very example of asceticism taken to the point of paradox and absurdity. Alexis, a young Roman nobleman, the cherished only son of devout and charitable parents, married a beautiful young girl who loved him, and left on his wedding night to live far away in poverty, penitence, and charity. Seventeen years later, he came back to Rome and to his parents' house, where his wife was still hoping for his return, but, without making himself known, he slipped in among the lowest of the servants, who scorned and mistreated him. After another seventeen years, he died in the hole under the stairs where he had his bed, and it was only then, through a paper found in his hands and telling his life story, that both his identity and saintliness were discovered. Quite interestingly, the legend is very close in parts to that of Bernard de Bade, who was particularly venerated at Vic (where there is a statue of him to this day). La Tour would almost certainly have heard his

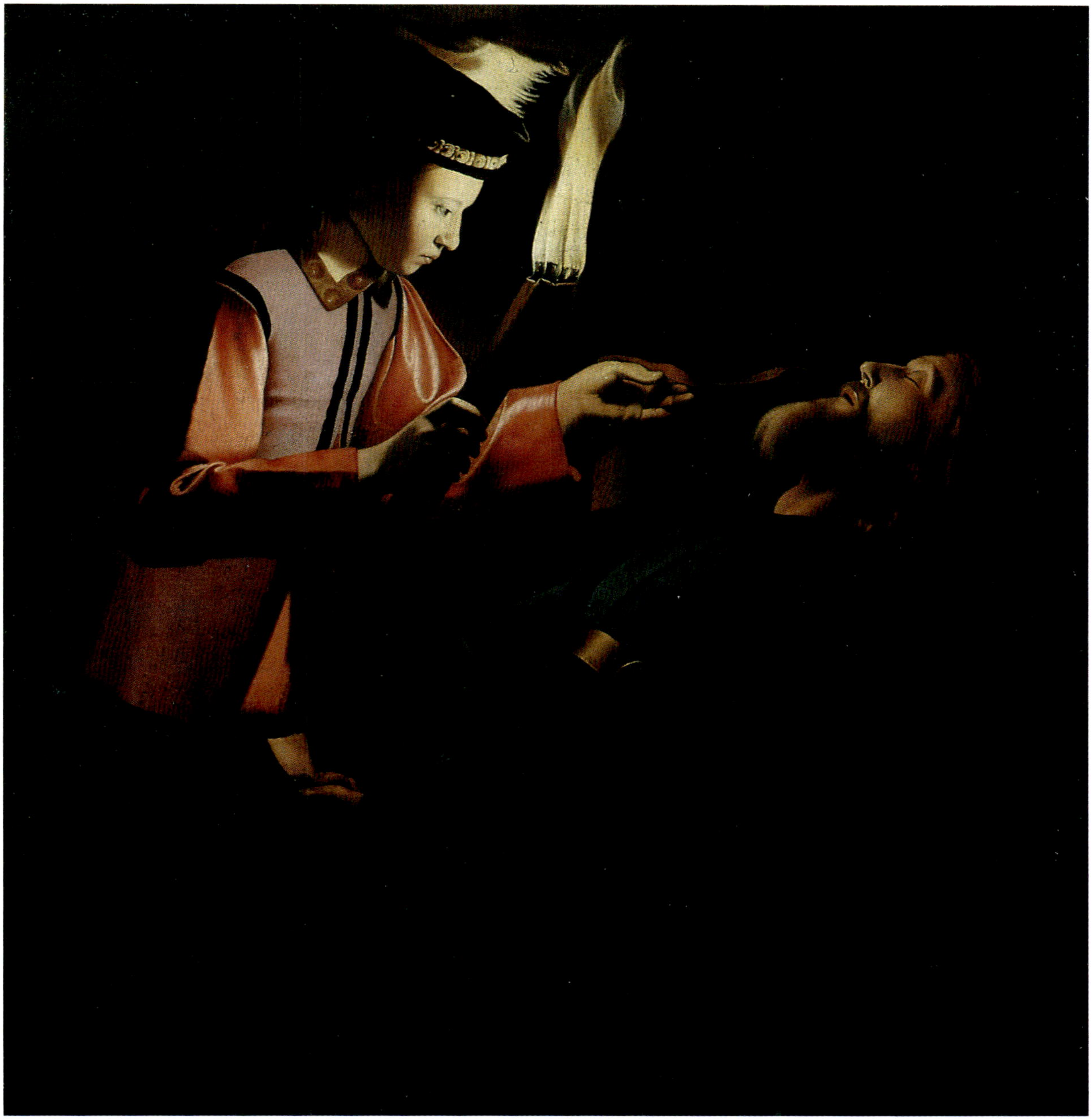

St. Alexis.
Musée Historique Lorrain, Nancy

story, which was quite likely to strike the mind of a child: this young fifteenth-century lord, son of the margrave of Baden and the duke of Lorraine's daughter, was due to marry Princess Madeleine, daughter of the king of France, but he gave everything up to devote himself to God. Miracles took place at his grave after his death in 1458, and he was beatified by the Pope in 1481. The cult of St. Alexis was so large in Vic that at the end of the sixteenth century the cardinal of Lorraine ordered his statue to be removed from the altar where it stood in the collegiate church and relegated to the sacristy, and forbade his worship. This peremptory act did not have much effect, and as late as 1699 the bishop of Metz was obliged to take new steps to contain this popular local cult.

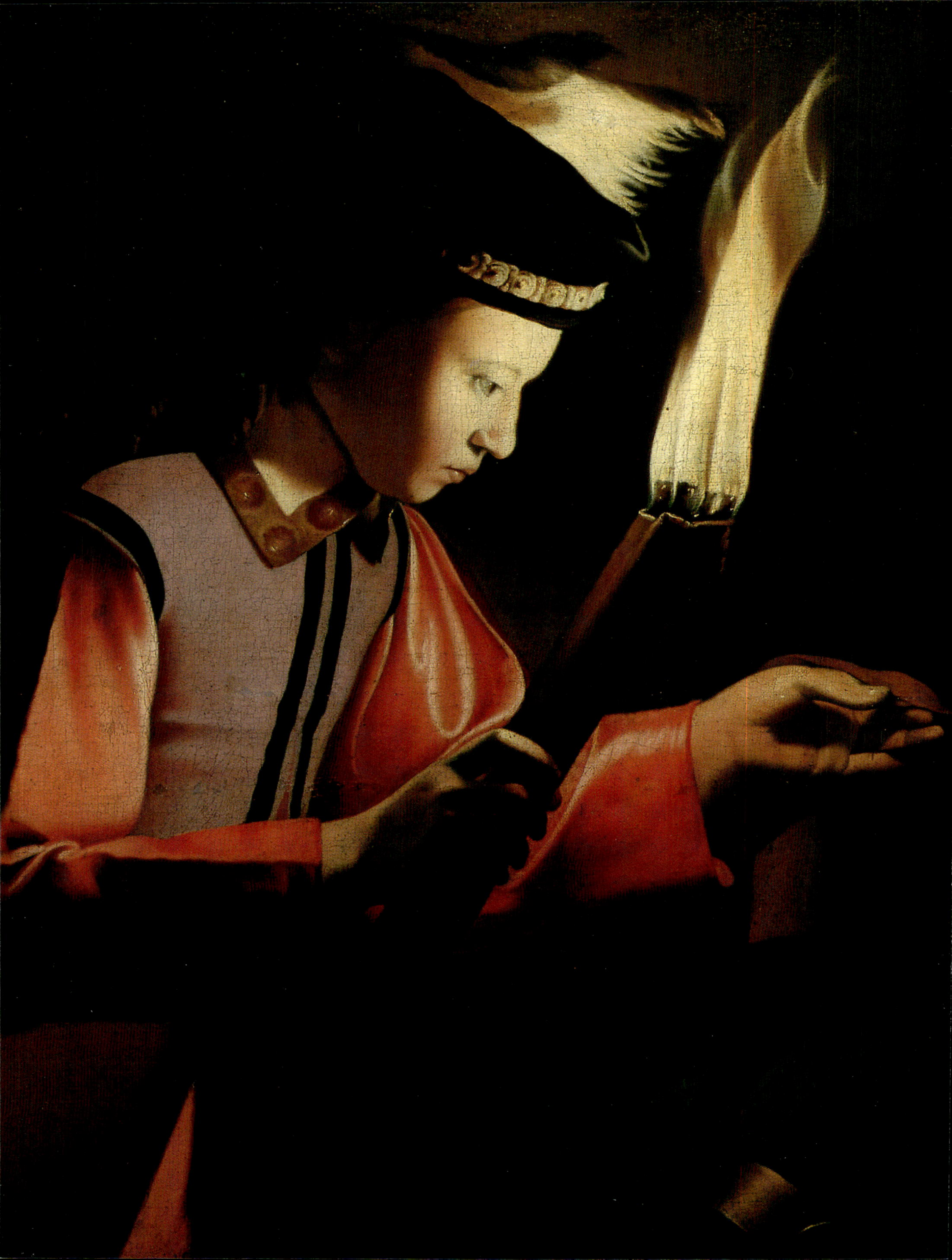

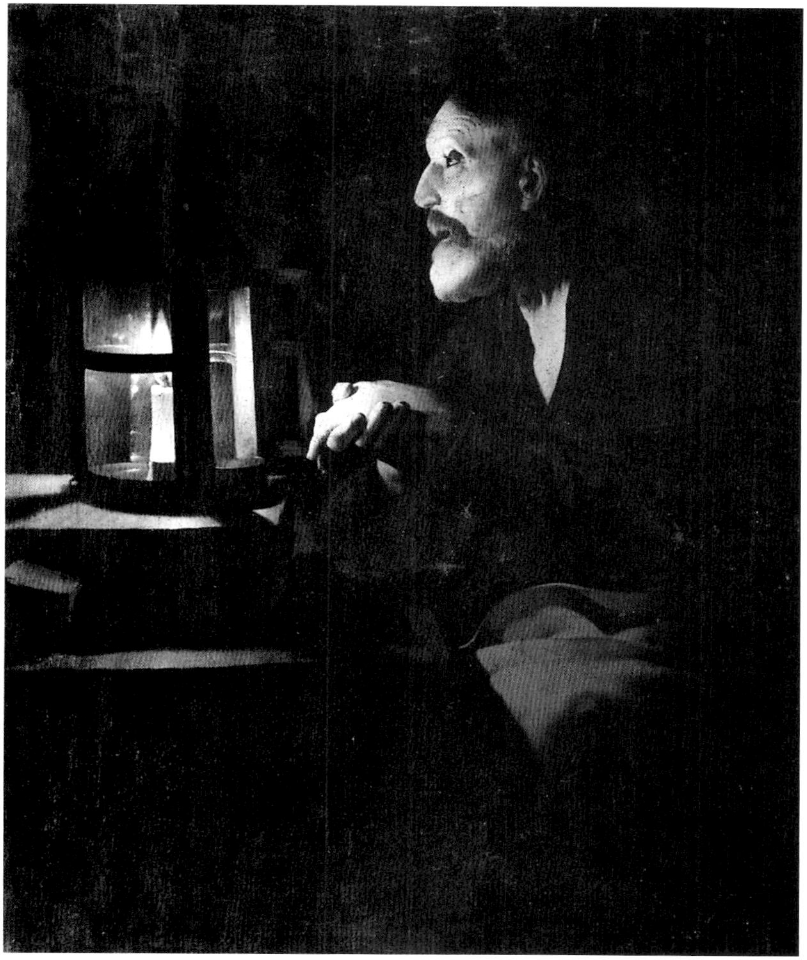

After Georges de La Tour.
The Penitent St. Peter.
Private collection, France

It is not strange therefore to see La Tour tackling the subject of St. Alexis. His approach is unique, however, in that he departs completely from *The Golden Legend,* in order to make the discovery of the body take place at night. He does not show the despair of the parents or the wife, the astonishment of the pope and the two emperors warned by a miraculous voice, or the excitement of the crowd. Instead, the body is found by a young page, scarcely more than a boy, who comes upon it by chance and discovers both his true master's death and the noble ascetic lesson he bequeathes by his example. Once again there is a silent exchange between a man who has lived a long life and a child with a face full of light. This time, however, ignorance and anxiety accompany the one embarking on life, while truth, cruel but assuaged, lies on the side of the one taking his leave.

Undoubtedly close in date is yet another version of *The Penitent St. Peter,* known only through what would seem to be an excellent copy. As in the Cleveland paintings, the subject is treated as a night scene, but stripped of all pathos and reduced to the three essential elements: face, hands and light. This is certainly a handsome image, but, after so many other versions, it lacks that unexpected extra something, the stroke of genius that surprises and captivates in La Tour's other paintings. By contrast, in the two paintings that appear to have come immediately after *St. Alexis,* the approach has never been more of a surprise, nor La Tour's genius more manifest.

St. Alexis, detail.
Musée Historique Lorrain, Nancy

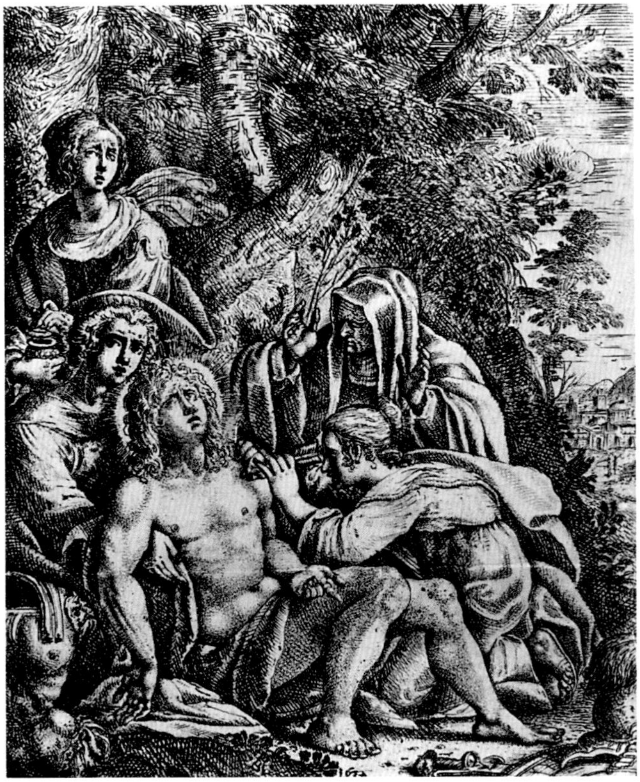

Anonymous (wrongly attributed to Pierre Brébiette).
St. Sebastian Tended by Irene. 1634. Etching. Private collection

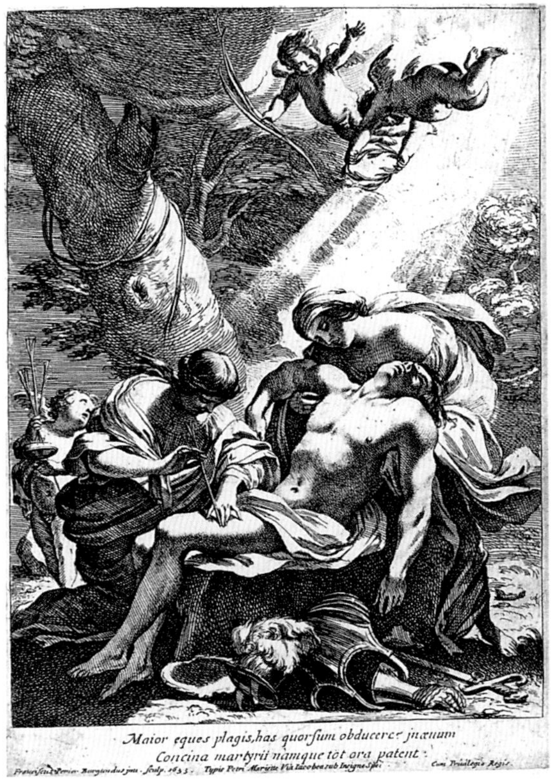

François Perrier. *St. Sebastian Tended by Irene.* 1633.
Etching. Private collection

The second version of *St. Sebastian Tended by Irene* should correspond, as we have said, to the painting presented to the governor of Lorraine at the end of 1649. The subject treated ten years earlier is taken up this time with a more complex composition with five figures in a vertical format. The painting that was discovered in the chapel at Bois-Anzeray in Normandy, and went from there to the Louvre is unquestionably the original. The subtlety of the light, the quality of the brushwork, and the significant changes revealed by the X-rays prove this beyond all doubt. I do not believe, however, that we should therefore relegate the Berlin painting, long admired by some of the very best authorities as an original, to the ranks of mere copies. It is quite different from all the other copies that we know, and, as I shall argue below, I believe it was painted at the very least under La Tour's supervision, and probably with his help. The unexpected beauty of the composition suffices to explain why a replica should have been immediately desired.

Ever faithful to Caravaggist principles, La Tour has no qualms about setting the classical Roman scene in contemporary dress. In fact, St. Irene's tight bodice and braid-edged sleeves are barely noticeable, if at all, for the scene has a grandeur that transcends time. Despite countless lamentations over the dead Christ and entombments, La Tour manages to bring something new to this encounter between womanly

Right:
St. Sebastian Tended by Irene.
Musée du Louvre, Paris

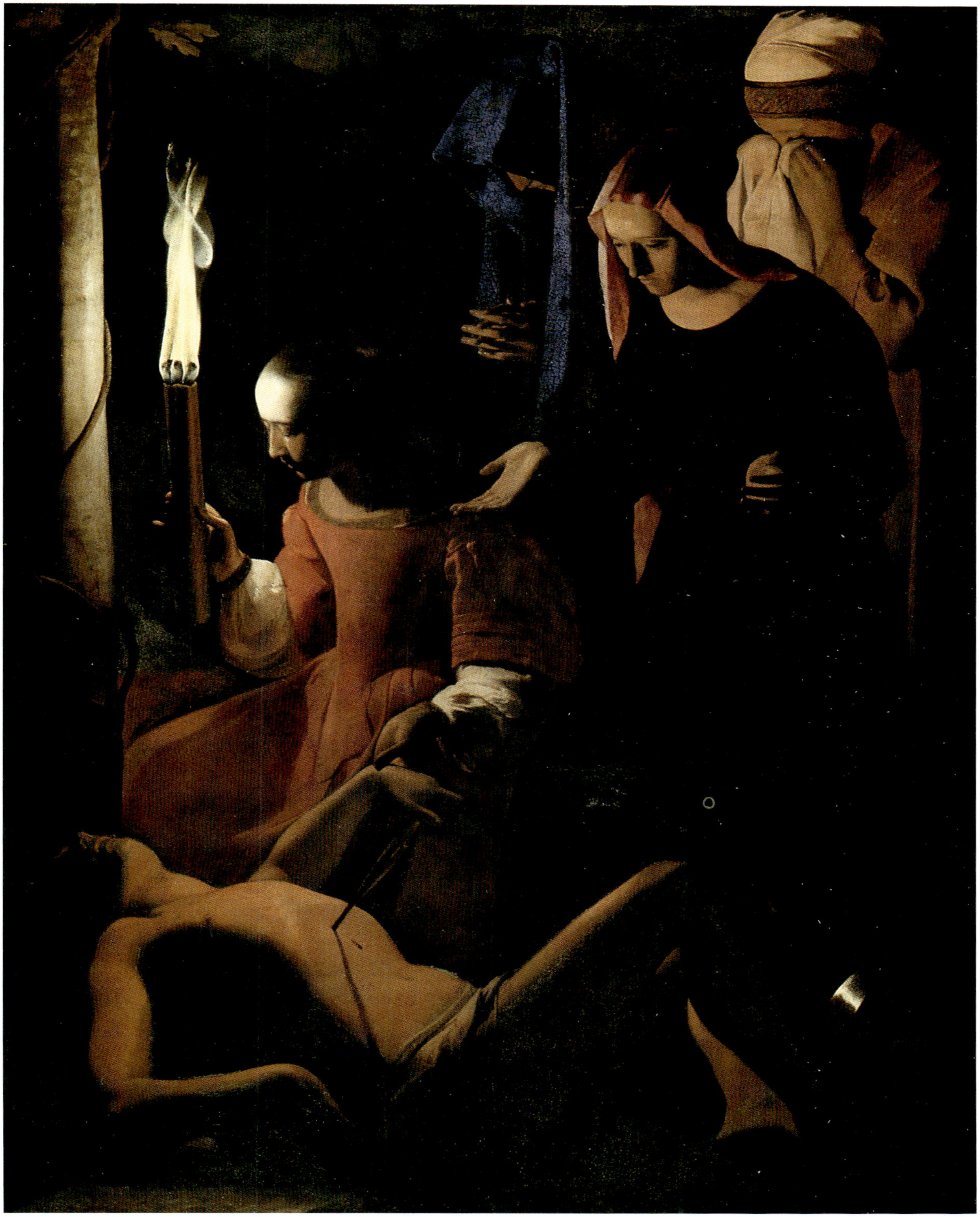

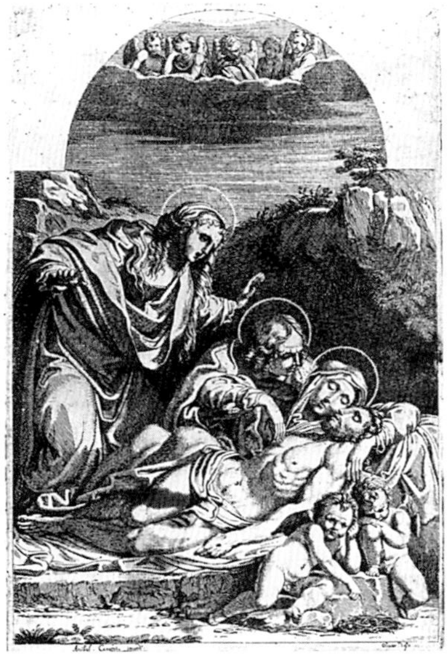

After Annibale Carracci.
The Lamentation. Etching
by Olivier Dauphin.
Private collection

compassion and the tortured victim, and to produce an image as harmonious as it is tragic. In a stroke of singular boldness, the scene is constructed along one great diagonal, so that the silent lament seems to descend from the standing woman who weeps to the kneeling St. Irene, and from her to the victim spread out on the ground. There is no longer any trace of the tender dialogue previously springing up between compassionate young nurse and wounded man. Sebastian has fainted from pain; he is no longer really there, no longer involved in the world of will and faith, which is the world of the men. Irene does no more than take up an inert wrist. The tear she lets fall from her lowered gaze is a tear of pity for the Christian hero who has followed his faith through to the end, the sort of hero we find in Corneille's *Polyeucte* three years later. Once again, there are no martyr's crowns and no angels. La Tour does not show us the heavens parting to reveal the celestial triumph awaiting Sebastian. He gives us only the suffering and the compassion, which are all the more profound for the limited recourse to gestures and cries. The triple-wicked torch fails to penetrate the gloom of this vast stark scene. It leaves the naked body of the wounded soldier in shadow, and struggles to pick out a hand here, a forehead there, and a few hidden profiles. These weeping women know that nothing they can do, even if they save Sebastian this time, can help him escape the sole destiny that his duty dictates, which is death.

Not long after *St. Sebastian* almost certainly came the boldest and most cruel of all La Tour's works, the *Job Mocked by his Wife* now in the Épinal museum. The signature only came to light in 1972, but there was never any doubt concerning the attribution—no one but La Tour could have conceived such a singular work.

It is unlike anything else we encounter in painting that century, and is surprising even in the context of La Tour's own work. This time La Tour does not simply impose a rigid geometry: the great realist arrives at the very boldest of stylization. With an expansive freedom reminiscent in its own way of Bellange, La Tour transforms the wife into an enormous mass taking up two-thirds of the canvas and has forced the figure to bend at the waist and neck to stay within the frame. Her head, covered with a coif half-shrouded in darkness, is reduced to a profile and a pearl. Job, emerging painfully from the darkness, recalls the thin, creased body of St. Jerome, but one that is now flaccid and emptied of all its strength. Yet for all this, Job opposes his wife's indignation with acceptance and steadfastness. La Tour follows the words of the Bible: "Then said his wife unto him, Dost thou still retain thine integrity? curse God, and die. But he said unto her, Thou speakest as one of the foolish women speaketh. What? shall we receive good at the hand of God, and shall we not receive evil?" Thus speaks the Stoic philosopher in the face of misfortune, thus too the saint before the sorrows of the world.

The work is so strange, and so little calculated to appeal to collectors, that it must be seen as a reflection of La Tour's deepest beliefs. The fact, however, that the sage's steadfastness has been evoked through such extreme means—his repulsive naked frame, the enormous red dress—hardly suggests that wisdom brings serenity. We are far from St. Jerome and his impassive countenance. This face pitted more by shadows than by sores, this toothless mouth voicing lament rather than certainty, is hardly the Job who dismissed his wife and "did not sin with his lips," but the Job of the next chapter of the Bible, who complained before his three friends:

> Let the day perish wherein I was born, and the night
> In which it was said: there is a man child conceived. . . .
> Wearisome nights are appointed to me.
> When I lie down, I say: When shall I arise, and the
> Night be gone? and I am full of tossings to and fro
> Unto the dawning of the day. . . .

It is the Job who submits to the afflictions sent by God, yet questions their purpose:

> I would despise my life.
> This is one thing, therefore I said it, He destroyeth
> The perfect and the wicked.
> If the scourge slay suddenly, he will laugh at the
> Trial of the innocent.
> The earth is given into the hand of the wicked: he
> Covereth the faces of the judges thereof; if not,
> Where, and who is he?

Right:
St. Sebastian Tended by Irene.
Staatliche Museen, Berlin

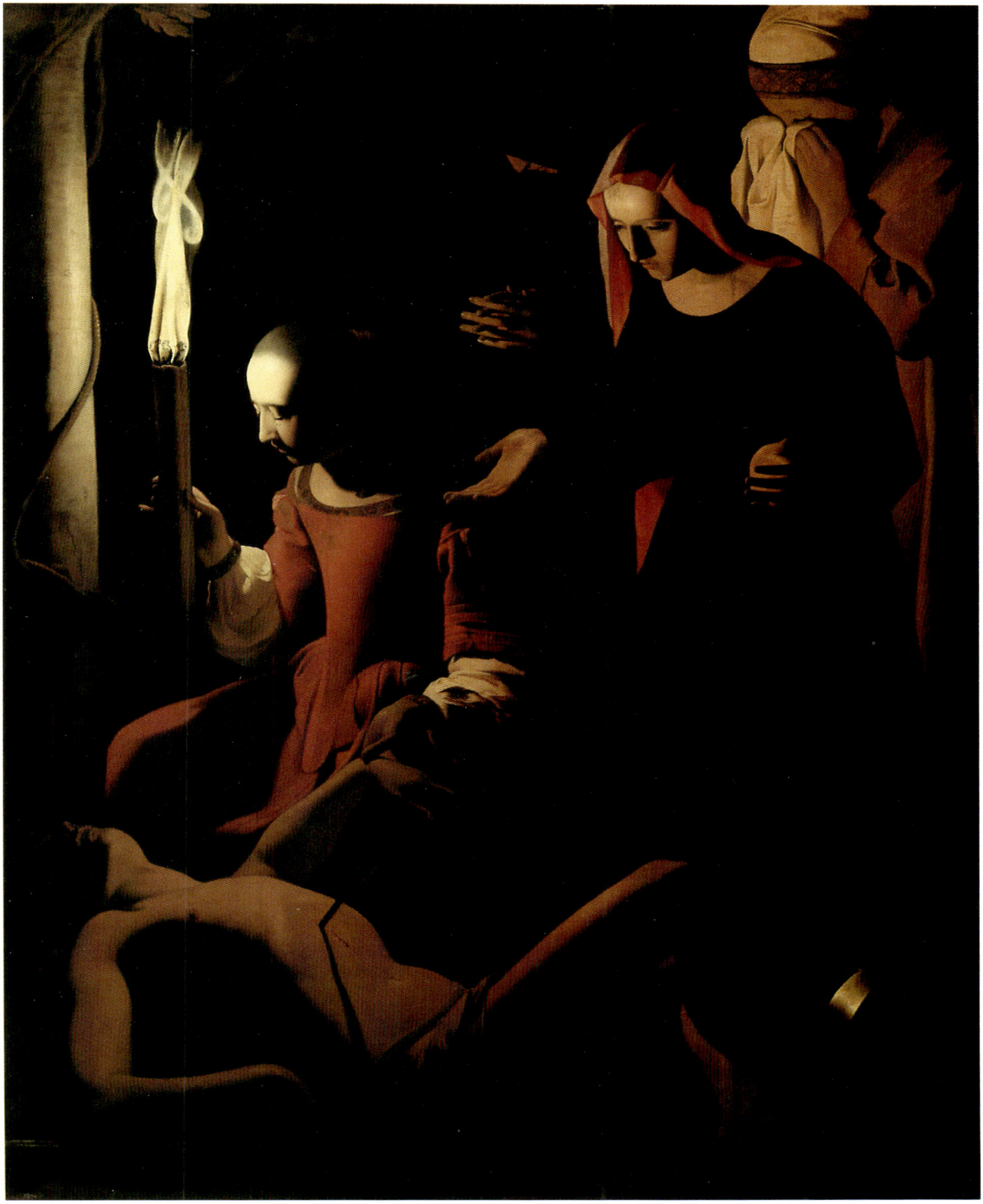

The Book of Job was read regularly in the seventeenth century, and Pierre Fourier cited its passages to the nuns of Lunéville to sustain them through the upheavals. Some of the verses must have had an uncanny resonance in Lorraine, which was once so flourishing and was now stricken on all sides:

> Behold, I cry out of wrong, but I am not heard: I cry
> Aloud, but there is no judgment.
> He hath fenced up my way that I cannot pass, and he
> Hath set darkness in my paths.
> He hath stripped me of my glory, . . .
> He hath destroyed me on every side, and I am gone:
> And mine hope hath He removed like a tree.
> He hath also kindled His wrath against me, and he
> Counteth me unto Him as one of His enemies.
> His troops come together, and raise up their way
> Against me, and encamp round about my tabernacle. . . .

It is true that Job finally submits and accepts that God's purpose is unknowable:

> Therefore have I uttered that I understood not;
> Things too wonderful for me, which I knew not.

Yet he is the man who, without cursing or swerving from the path of righteousness, poses the question in the face of misfortune. It is tempting to think that La Tour reacted to the dire events of those cruel years like the stricken Job, who remains steadfast yet questions fate. But why would La Tour have made Job's wife this sharp-profiled figure indignantly questioning in her crimson skirts, why would he have pleated her apron into such powerful verticals or cupped her hand in such a gentle gesture if he were not also on her side, if she were not also the scolding wife who wants the cowering old man to rise up and set out to recover his health and his fortune. The call of this great Lorraine that rebels against misery and poverty is louder than all of Callot's engravings, and all of Heraudel's verses. In times of extreme hardship, the debate between the indignant soul and the patient soul never ends.

Gaspare Traversi. *Job Mocked by His Wife.*
National Museum, Warsaw

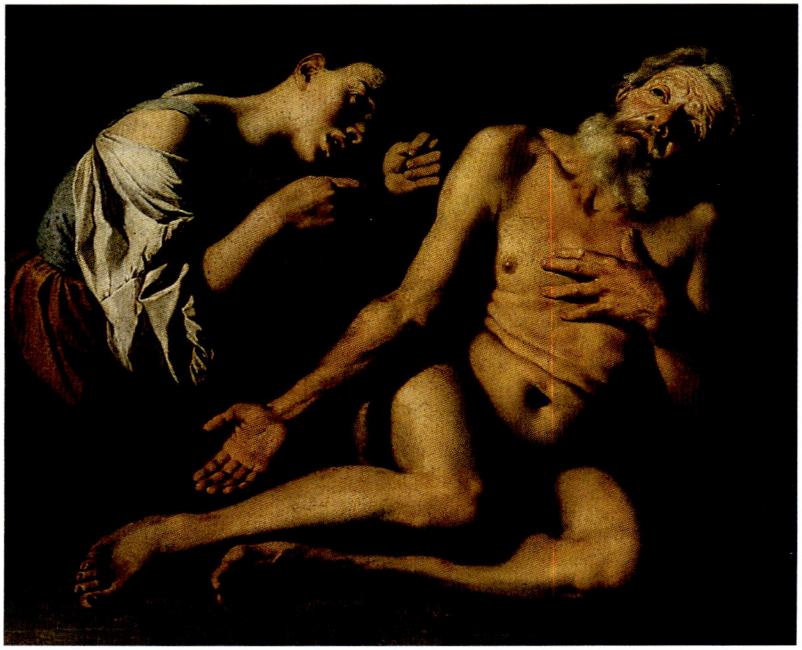

Right:
Job Mocked by his Wife.
Musée Départemental des Vosges, Épinal

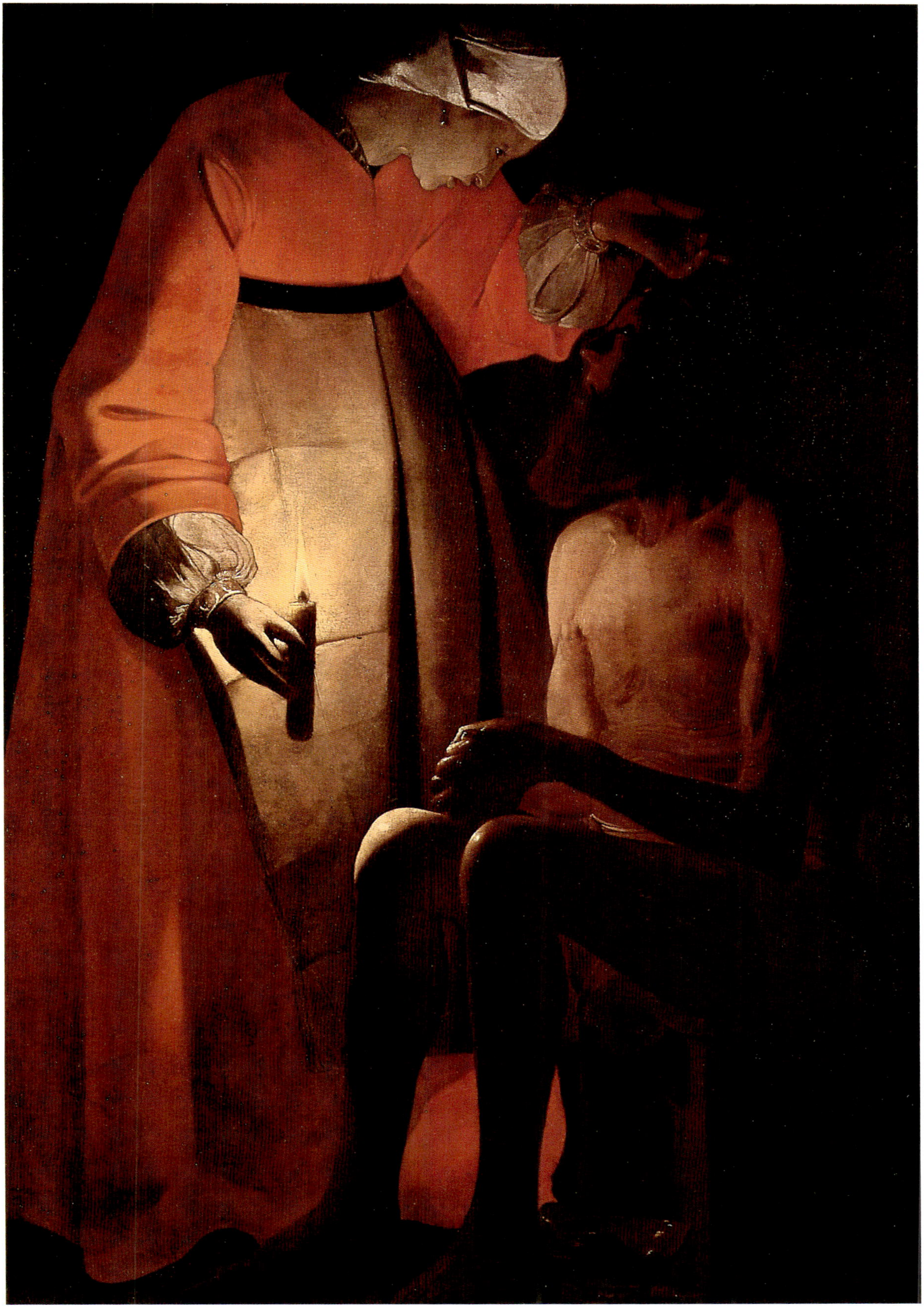

FROM GEORGES TO ÉTIENNE DE LA TOUR

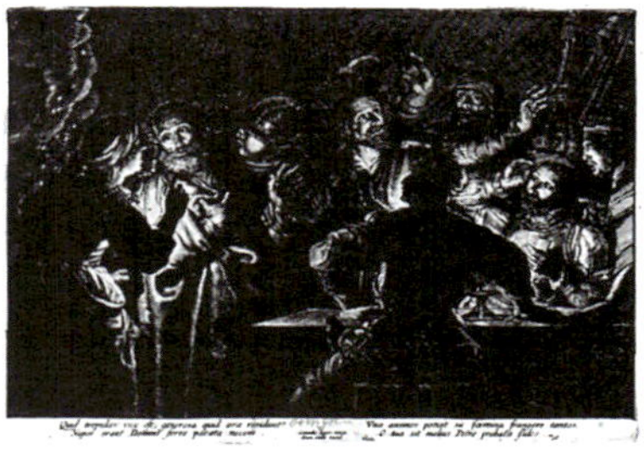

After Gerard Seghers. *The Denial of St. Peter.* Engraving by Joan Galle.
Private collection

If we are not mistaken about the dating of this singular canvas, it has to be La Tour's final masterpiece. There are several paintings that appear to be later, but they have neither the quality nor the originality of the *Job*. Interestingly enough, these are paintings that must be dated late because of their execution, but in terms of subject and composition, they could well have been painted twenty or thirty years earlier.

The most important of these is the famous *Denial of St. Peter*, now in the museum in Nantes, signed and dated 1650. The theme is the one we have seen so many times before, but here St. Peter is relegated to the sidelines and the guards given pride of place—a classic Caravaggesque arrangement widely diffused by the likes of Manfredi, Valentin, and Honthorst. There is no reason to doubt the authenticity of the work, particularly since it was a *Denial of St. Peter* that was commissioned from La Tour at the end of 1650 and given to the governor in March 1651. The Nantes painting could have been a forerunner or model of the one given to La Ferté, signed because it was sent away to Paris. All the same, the brushwork is not as subtle as usual, and the image yielded by X-rays is different from the one we get, for instance, from the *St. Sebastian* in the Louvre. Moreover, it is surprising that, after such personal paintings, La Tour should revert to a type of composition so commonplace in Europe for several decades. Certain stylistic details, such as the simplifying of the hands and faces, fit perfectly with this late date, but others are not at all what we would expect, notably the complex structuring of the space and the broad pattern of light emanating from a double light source. Despite the obvious power and quality of this work, we may wonder whether we are not witnessing a new phenomenon: the studio painting.

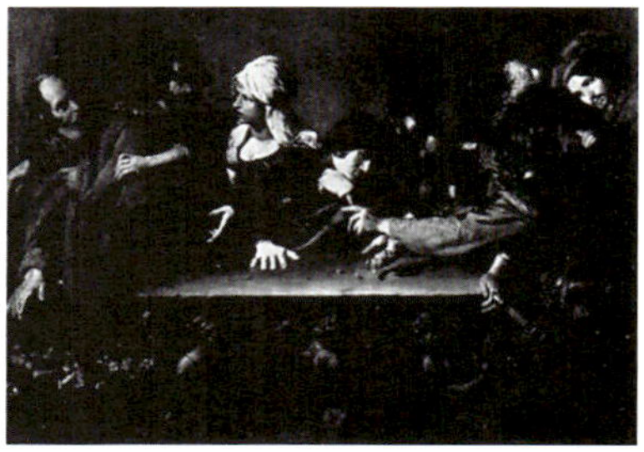

Jean Valentin (also called Jean de Boulogne or Moïse Valentin). *The Denial of St. Peter.*
The Longhi Foundation, Florence

I have said that for a very long period the term "studio" is meaningless as far as La Tour is concerned. He worked alone, with no one but a young and inexperienced apprentice. In September 1648, however, he took on Jean-Nicolas Didelot, the nephew of the parish priest in Vic, and judging by the position the young man seems to have occupied in the house, he appears to have made rapid progress. More important, Étienne, then twenty-seven and newly married, seems to have started to play a greater part in his father's studio at this time. He was trained by La Tour, and must have painted in exactly his manner, as the contract for the young Didelot's apprenticeship would seem to testify. Paintings like the *Smoker*, signed simply "La Tour," and the *Girl Blowing on a Brazier*, which were probably reworkings of earlier compositions, have a kind of dryness that could well signal the son's involvement. Similarly, the Berlin version of *St. Sebastian Tended by Irene*, which is quite beautiful though less subtle than that of the Louvre, yields an X-ray image that is strikingly different and free of pentimenti. I do not think this is a copy, but rather, as I have said, a replica executed in great part by Étienne under his father's supervision, and quite possibly finished off by Georges himself.

Something of the same sort must have happened with *The Denial of St. Peter*. I could easily imagine an earlier composition recast by Georges himself in the style of his later years, and executed partly in concert with Étienne. This would certainly make sense if it were indeed a replica of the painting presented to the governor. Moreover, we cannot rule out the possibility that La Tour had help from his son on the original as well.

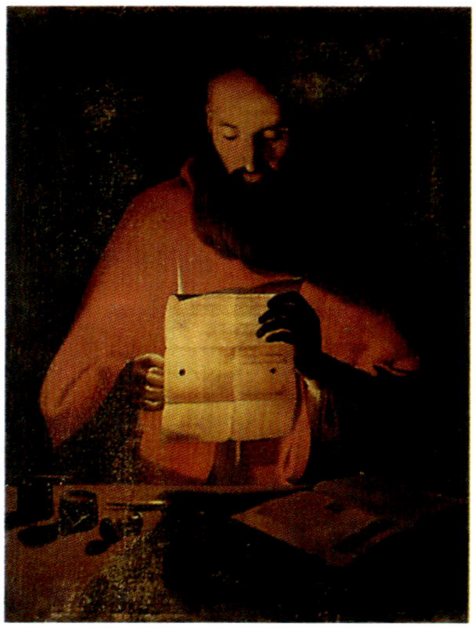

St. Jerome Reading.
The painting's condition upon its discovery, photographed by the Laboratory of the Louvre and the Museums of France (RMN).
Musée Historique Lorrain, Nancy

The *Dice Players*, discovered in England in 1972 has features very close to those of the Nantes *Denial of St. Peter*. The subject—a naive young man being cheated at dice while another villain steals his purse—seems to be a "night" version of *The Fortune Teller* with an all-male cast. It is certainly very similar in spirit, but stylistically, on the other hand, The *Dice Players* displays a number of features we associate with the later years, and the brushwork, for all of its supreme refinement, manifests certain awkward passages as well. It looks very much as if this painting too were a late version of an earlier composition produced in collaboration with Étienne. In spite of the beauty of certain faces, we are missing the profound conviction that underlies all of Georges de La Tour's true creations.

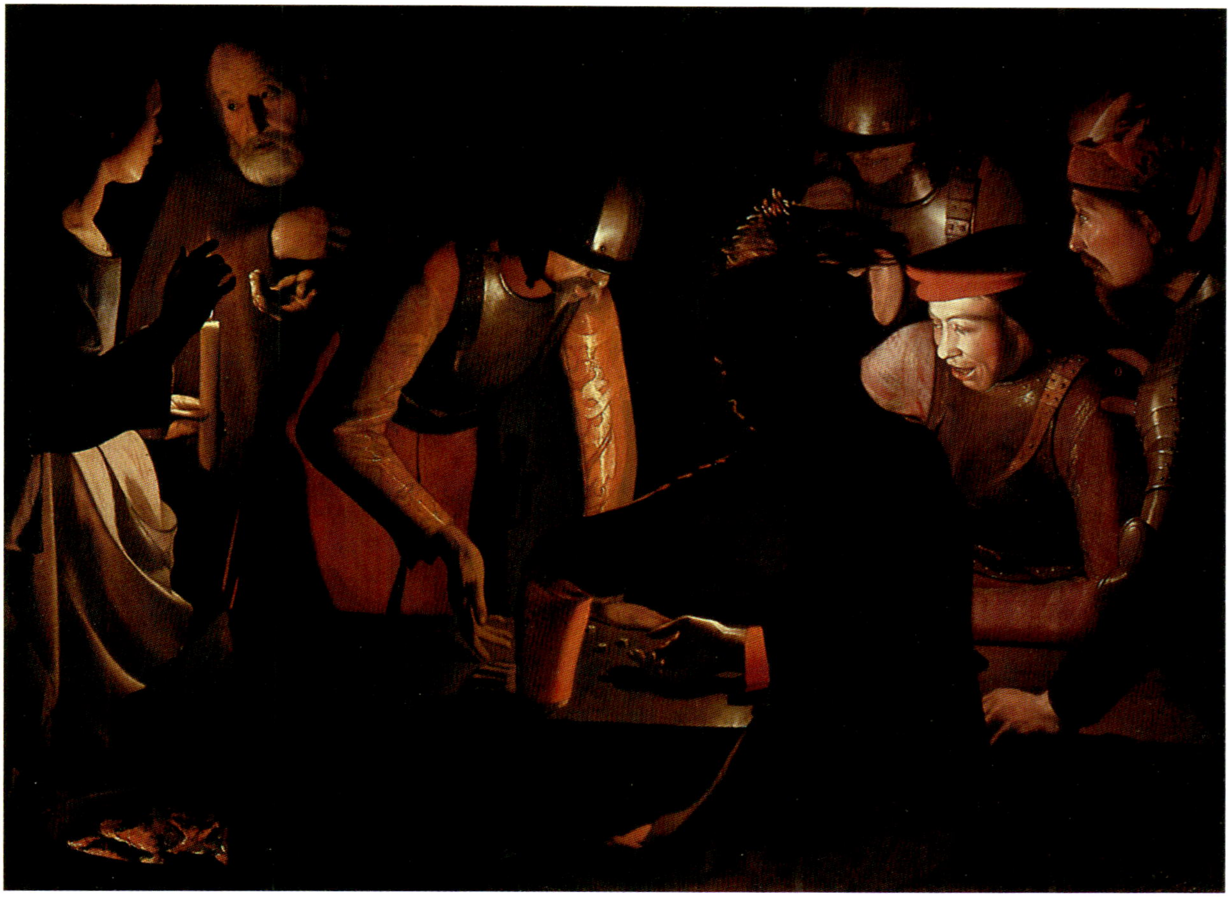

Above and pp. 230-233:
The Denial of St. Peter,
complete work and details.
Musée des Beaux-Arts, Nantes

The same is true of an even more recent discovery, the *Young Singer* now in the Leicester Art Gallery, which was published by Christopher Wright in 1984. La Tour's "musicians" made it seem likely that he had also painted singers, as Bigot and Honthorst did, for instance, but there was no known example. This one has many of the features of an original, and yet there is a kind of dryness about the treatment, a certain weakness and stiffness about the design. The face has nothing of the realism so characteristic of La Tour's figures. Étienne probably had a hand in it, or indeed, this time it could even have been his own creation, since he must have aspired to do more than paint copies and might well have produced a pendant to one of his father's singers or musicians. If this is the case, Étienne de La Tour was certainly well equipped with what his father called his "principles and precepts"—but not with his inspiration, which rarely passes from one generation to another. Inspiration does not come from the hand or the head; it springs from an inner necessity, feeds on struggles and failures, on the experiences of a lifetime, that can no more be handed on than relived. Georges de La Tour had no school and left no heir.

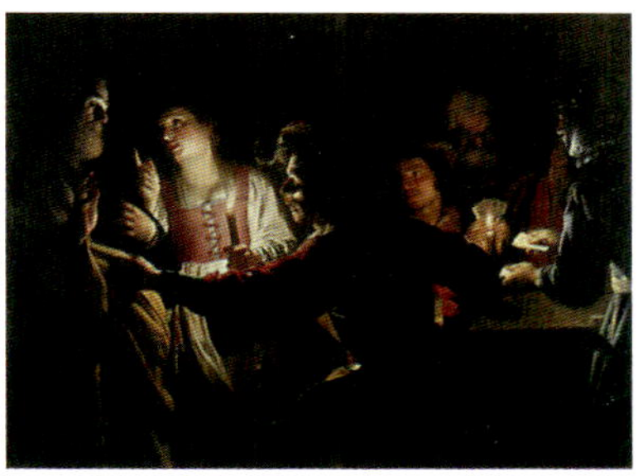

Gerrit van Honthorst.
The Denial of St. Peter.
Musée des Beaux-Arts, Rennes

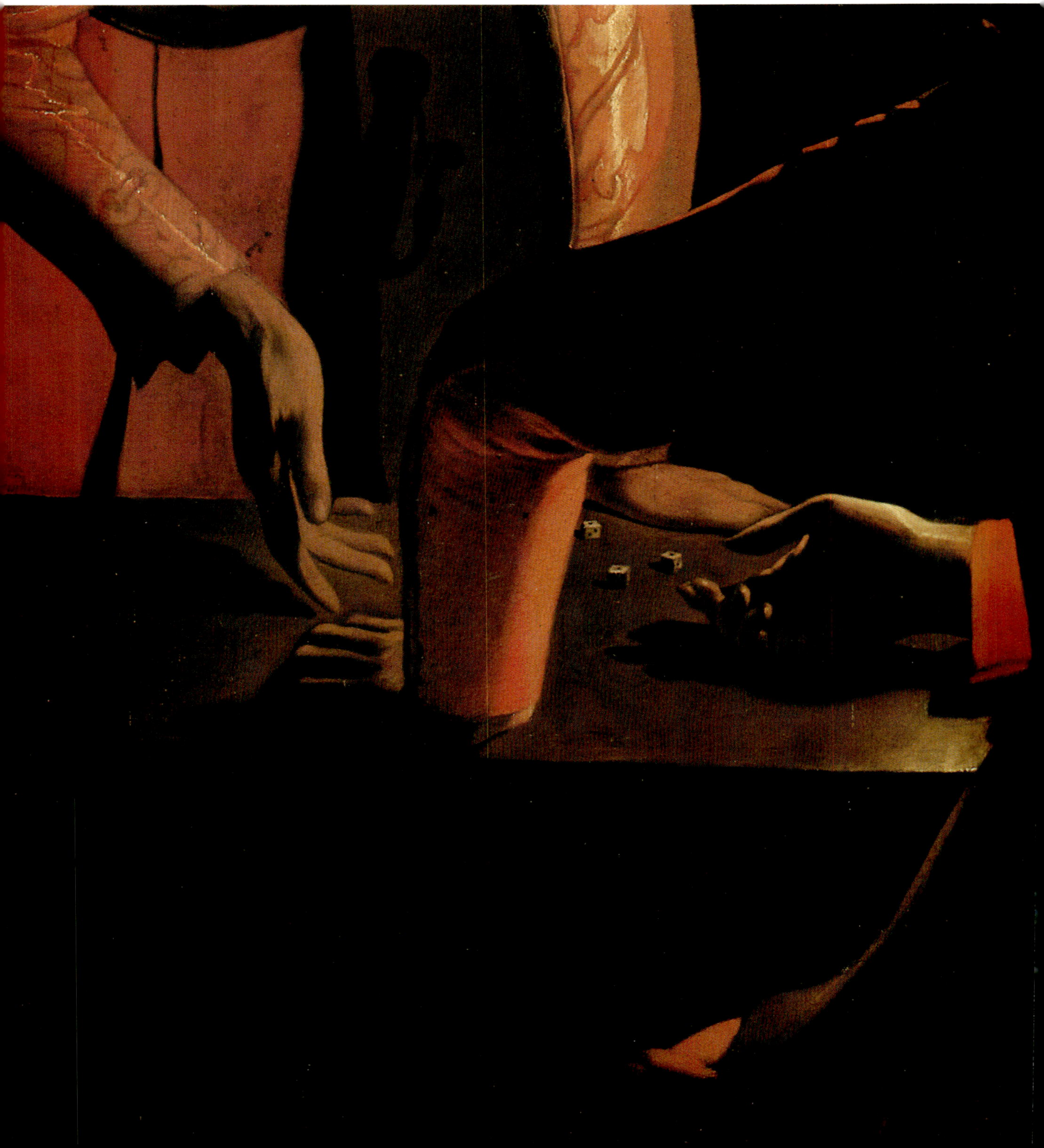

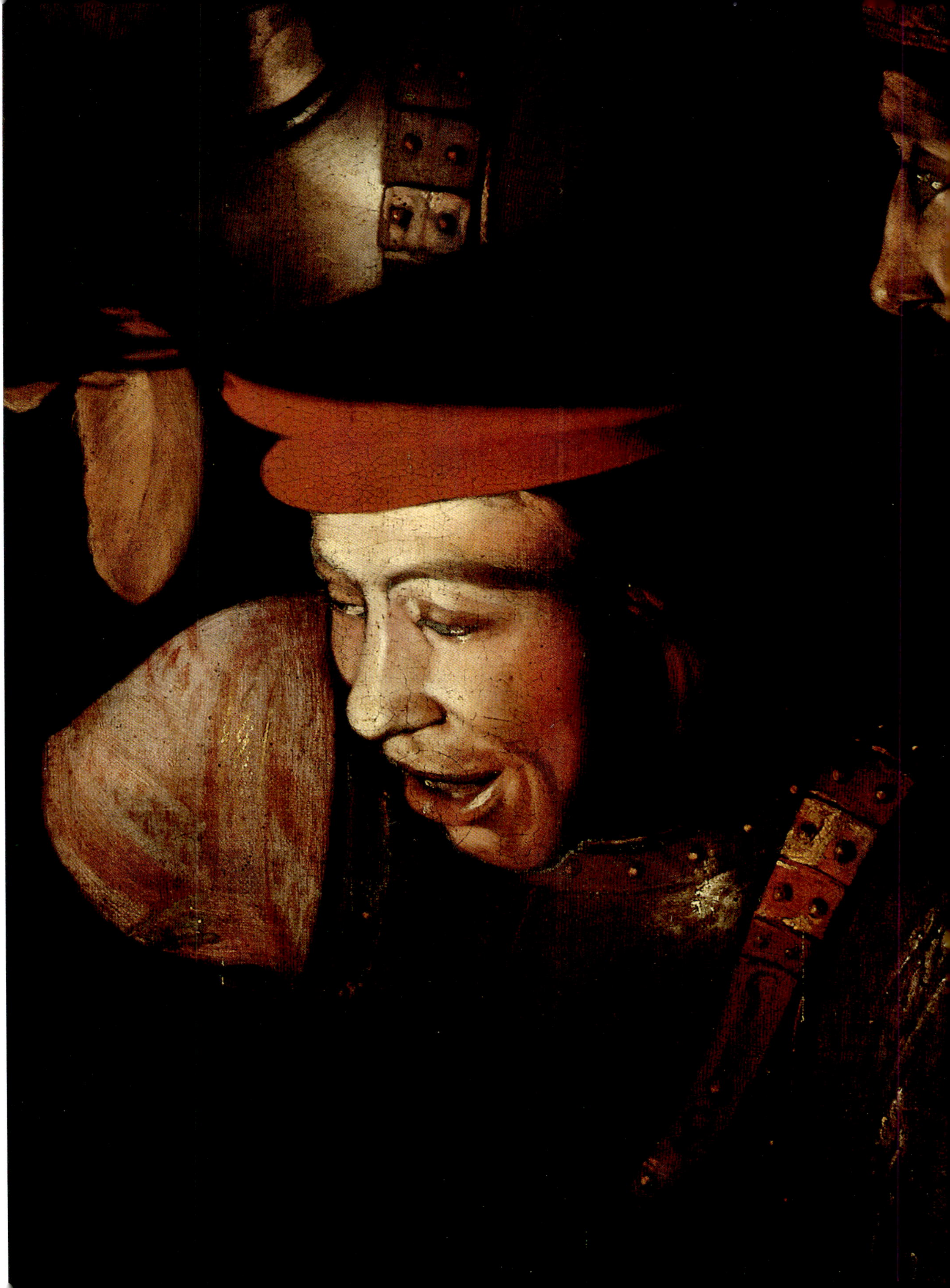

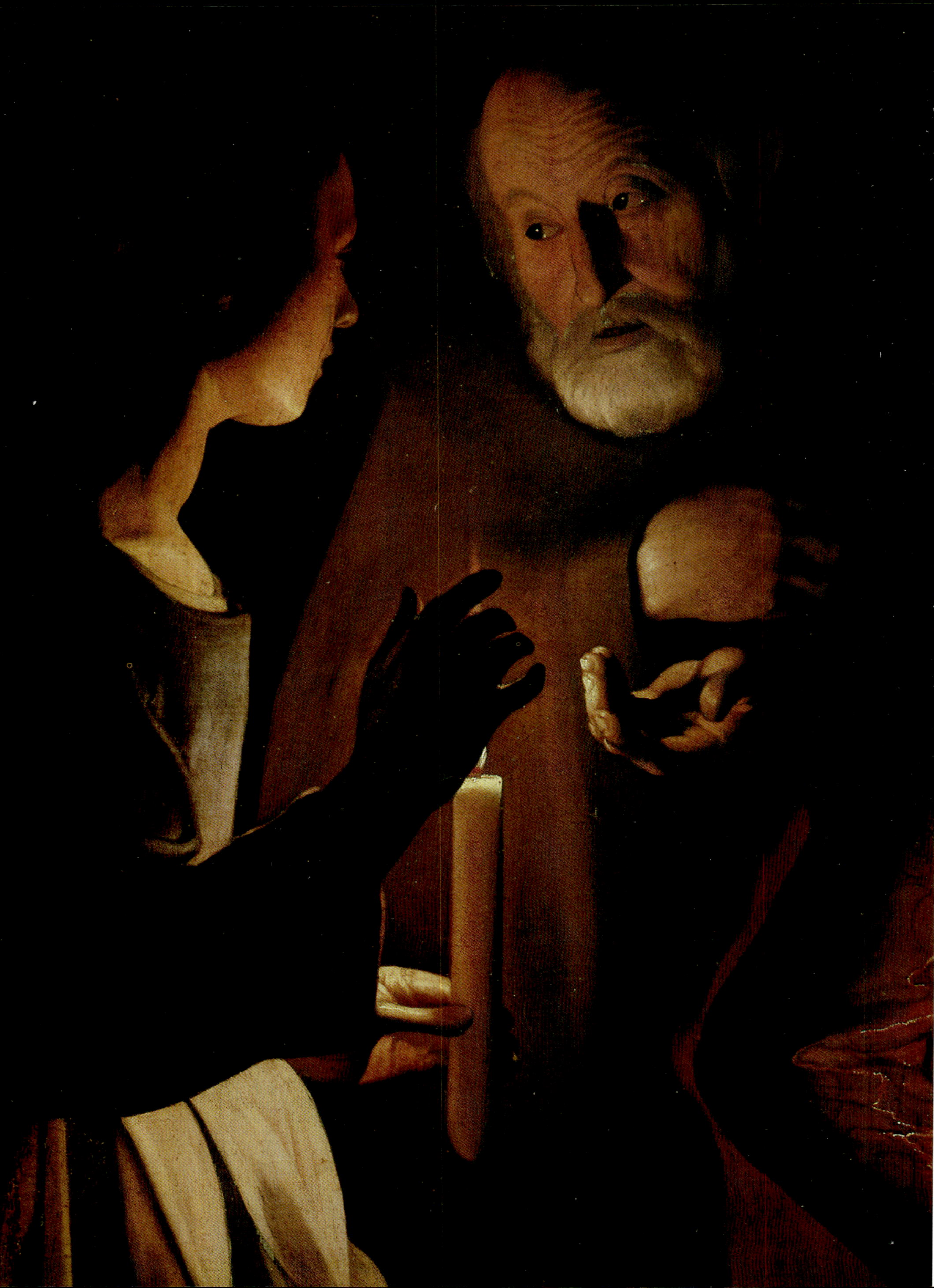

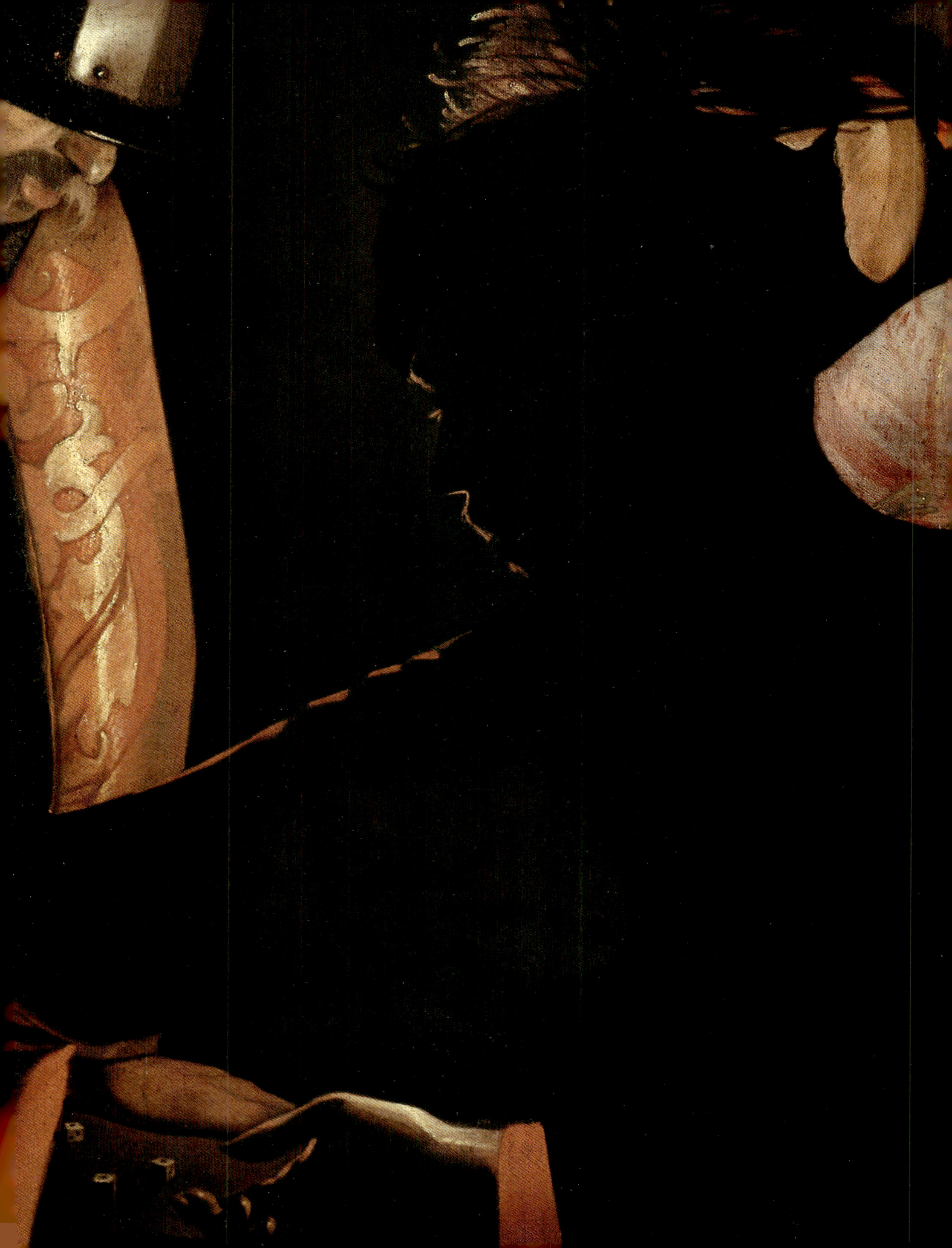

A Girl Blowing on a Brazier.
Private collection, U.S.A.

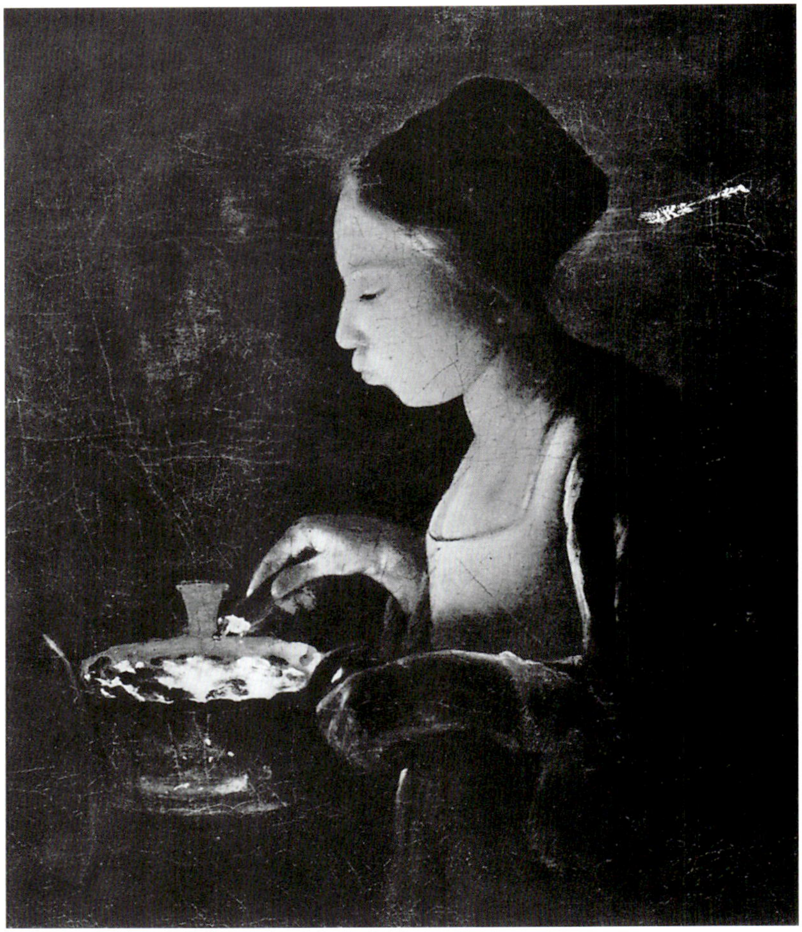

Matthias Stomer.
Soldier Lighting a Candle.
National Museum, Warsaw

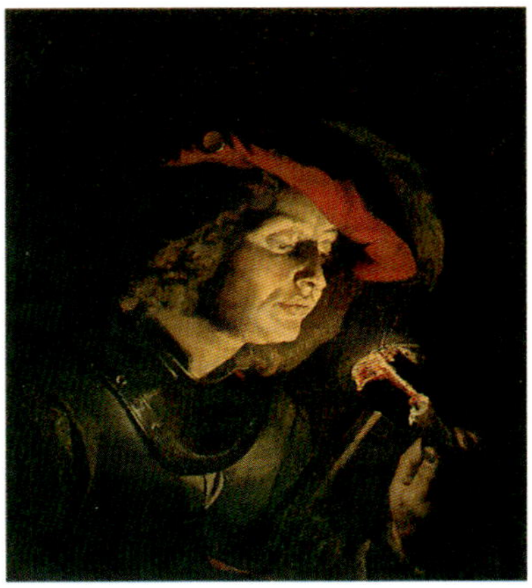

THE "SOUFFLEUR" TRADITION IN LORRAINE

As we have seen, the theme of "souffleurs" was by no means peculiar to Lorraine. Painters and collectors alike appear long to have been fascinated by the effects of blowing on a flame—the sudden glow of light and the striking facial distortion it produces. The subject makes its first appearance with "Mannerist" painters such as El Greco (see p. 172) and Varin in France (*The Circumcision*, in Beauvais). Its popularity seems due to the works of the Bassano family, who liked to slip young "souffleurs" into corners of their paintings. Caravaggio was not attracted to it, but Rubens showed some interest, and the Caravaggesque painters took it up frequently, isolating the image as El Greco had done, and turning it into a genre subject. This oft-repeated theme became a simplified "night" scene with a broad popular appeal.

It enjoyed a significant success in Northern Europe, where there was a constant demand for little paintings for a relatively unsophisticated market (Terbrugghen, Honthorst, Lievens). It was no less popular in Lorraine, as Michel Sylvestre's study of seventeenth-century estate inventories in Nancy proves. La Tour, however, approaches the subject in quite a different spirit. He dispenses with all that is most superficial in the genre scene, as we can see clearly if we compare his treatment and Stomer's. La Tour dwells less on the purely visual aspect, the momentary lighting up of a face in the darkness produced by the glow of a flame, and focuses instead on the opposition of profile and flame in a time suddenly stopped. As several copies of *A Girl Blowing on a Brazier* and *A Smoker* have survived, it is possible to think that these two La Tour inventions were replicated not only by the painter himself and by his son, but also by many second-rate copyists.

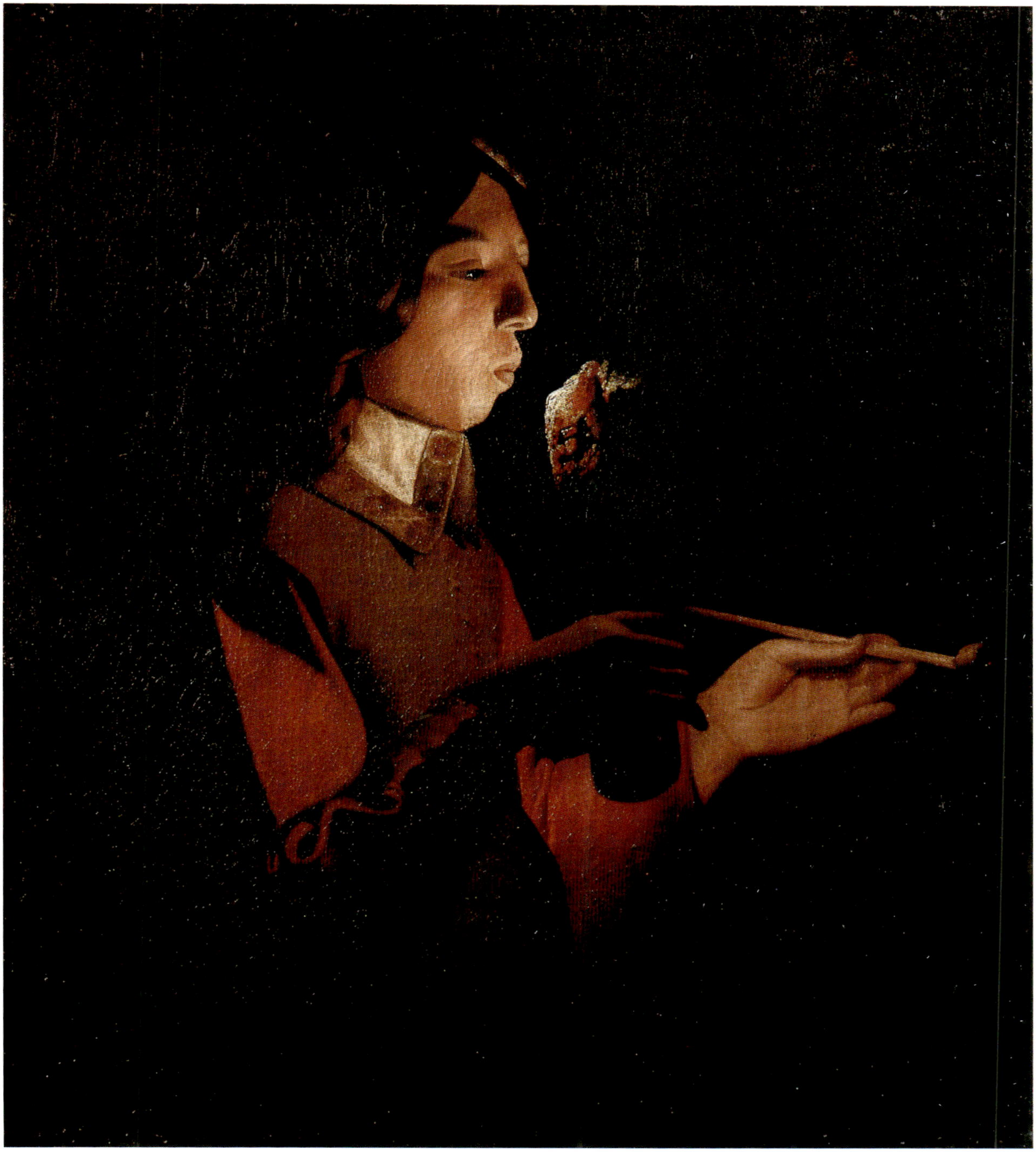

A Smoker.
Private collection, France

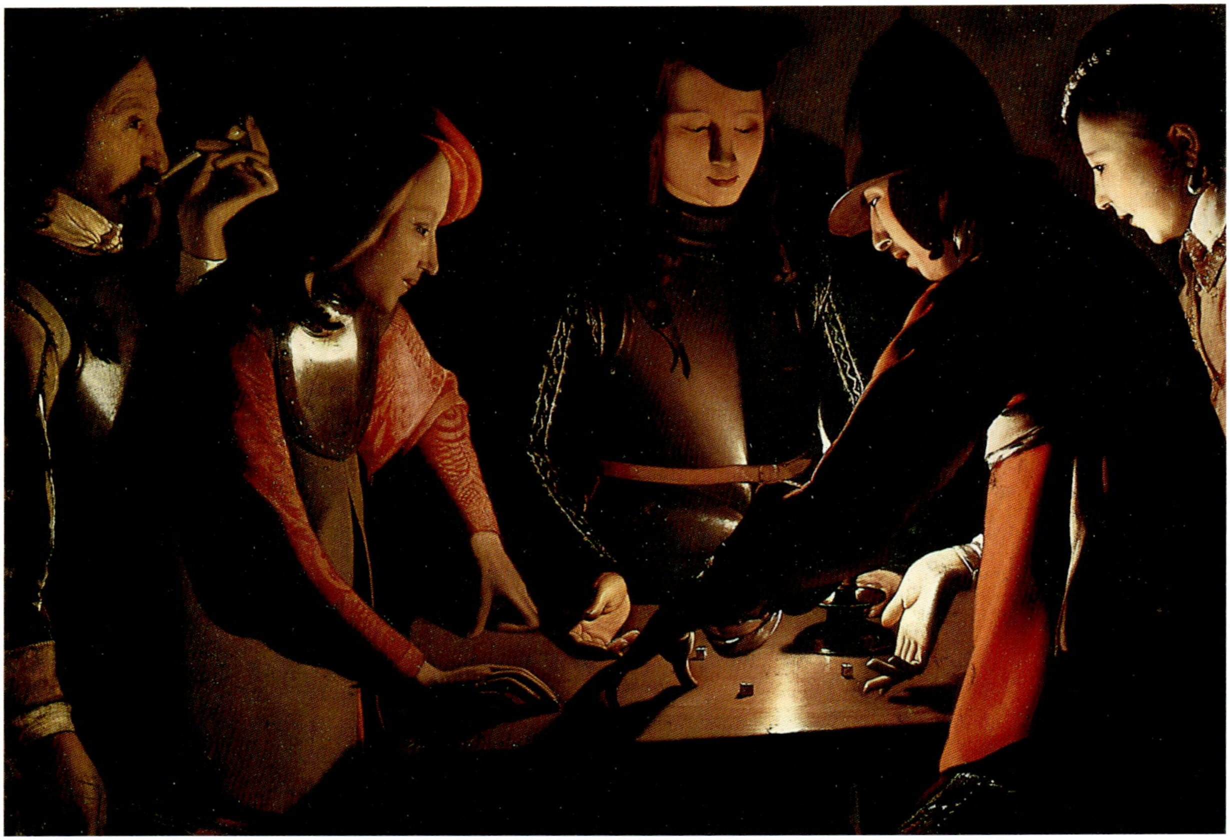

Georges de La Tour (and Étienne de La Tour?). *Dice Players (Five Figures).*
Teeside Museum, Middlesbrough (England)

Étienne de La Tour (?). *A Young Singer.*
The Leicester Museum and Art Gallery, England

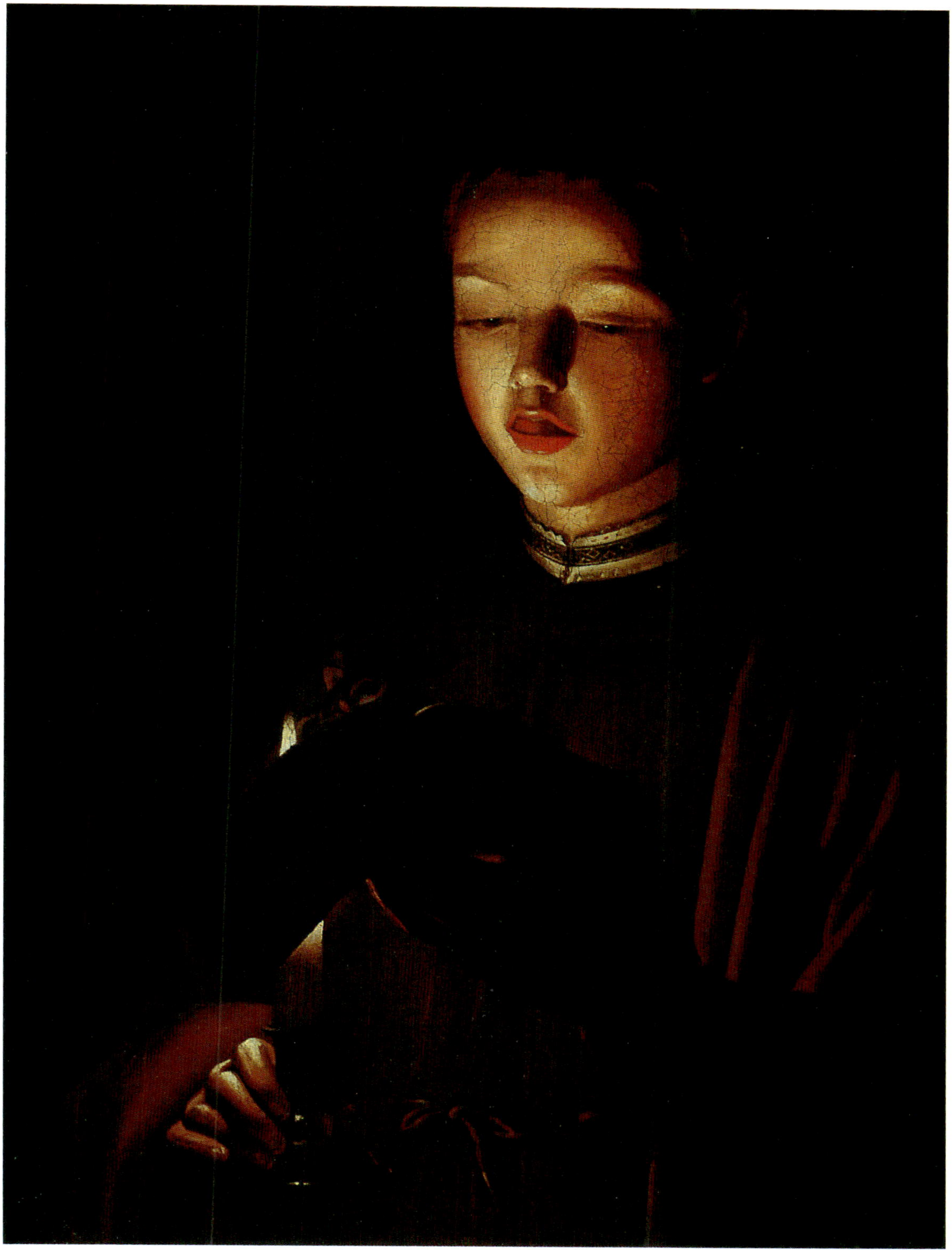

LA TOUR TODAY

Jean Le Clerc died before his time in 1633, and Jacques Callot by 1635—late enough to have recorded the beginnings of Lorraine's ordeals, too early to have lived through its torment. Only Claude Deruet lived on to 1660 to see the first glimmer of light after the storm. Lorraine's artistic activity, however, was over. The brilliant flame that Charles III and Henri II had taken such care to kindle with their patronage had disappeared without a trace. From the 1630s on Lorrainese painters and sculptors fled the ruins of their country. Those who managed to get to Rome abandoned virtually all thought of ever returning to their homeland. They preferred to stay on the other side of the mountains where the torch of Lorrainese painting had just passed from Charles *Lorrain*—that is to say, Charles Mellin, who died in 1649—to Claude *Lorrain*—otherwise known as Claude Gellée, already long considered to be one of the greatest living landscape painters, if not the greatest of all. Others went to Paris, where Claude Henriet and his line, in the person first of Israël and then of Sylvestre, made comfortable niches for themselves. It was not until the eighteeenth century, under the good king Stanislas, that Lorraine began to burgeon once more with palaces, festivals, and new churches, and that it once again gave the lead to the rest of Europe with the matchless décor of the town of Nancy, the château of Lunéville, and that great master of wrought iron, Jean Lamour. It was not until the end of the nineteenth century that another painter from Lorraine managed, without in any way renouncing his roots, to make a name for himself in Paris and to reach an international public, this time from Portugal to Russia; notably Jules Bastien-Lepage. One hundred years after his death, he has found an assiduous biographer, and it will undoubtedly not be much longer before he too, on a more modest level, certainly, recovers the public acclaim no less unjustly denied him.

La Tour's death did not simply mark the moment when the art of Lorraine vanished from the European stage for many a long year. It coincided with the obliteration, throughout Europe, of a great generation of artists with its own ideals and incomparable prestige. Among La Tour's contemporaries, the painters he may have come across, who was left? Valentin and Tournier had died by the 1630s, while Régnier, in Venice, was to die in 1657. Ribera died a few months after La Tour, and Honthorst four years later. It was the same in Paris: Blanchard was the first to go, in 1638, followed by two of the Le Nain brothers in 1648, and by Vouet and Perrier in 1649. In Rome in August 1655, Poussin, who still had ten years to live, made no bones about declaring to Fouquet "that there was nobody left in painting who was tolerable, and that he did not even see anybody coming along, and that this art would suddenly disappear altogether." This could be taken as no more than a splenetic outburst from a sick old man plagued with a trembling hand that rendered all work painful. The fact is, however, that Domenichino had died in 1641, Guido Reni in 1642, and Charles Mellin in 1649, and there too all that was left of that magnificent generation was a handful of tottering old men not long for this world: Albani was to die in 1660, Sacchi in 1661, Guercino in 1666, and Pietro da Cortona in 1669. Neither the reputation Mignard had already gained in Rome, especially as a portrait painter, nor the growing fame of *Il Carluccio* (Carlo Maratta), was enough to generate the feeling that the inevitable void these masters would leave behind could easily be filled. This was all the more true because with their passing a concept of art was being lost, and people rightly sensed that the rising generation, with its very different preoccupations, would scarcely seek to take it up.

La Tour's generation was born at the end of the Wars of Religion, wars that had started as doctrinal disputes before turning into appalling massacres. In terms of art, it came on the heels of a "Mannerist" tradition which sought to capture the "idea" but which had, through intellectual speculation, gradually degenerated into the emptiest of conventions. In reaction, the new generation was deliberately realist and harbored a tremendous mistrust of abstraction of all kinds. With the astonishing example of Caravaggio firmly in mind, these artists were not afraid to tackle the problem of art on its simplest and most direct level: how to combine a representation of "reality"

St. Sebastian Tended by Irene, detail.
Musée du Louvre, Paris

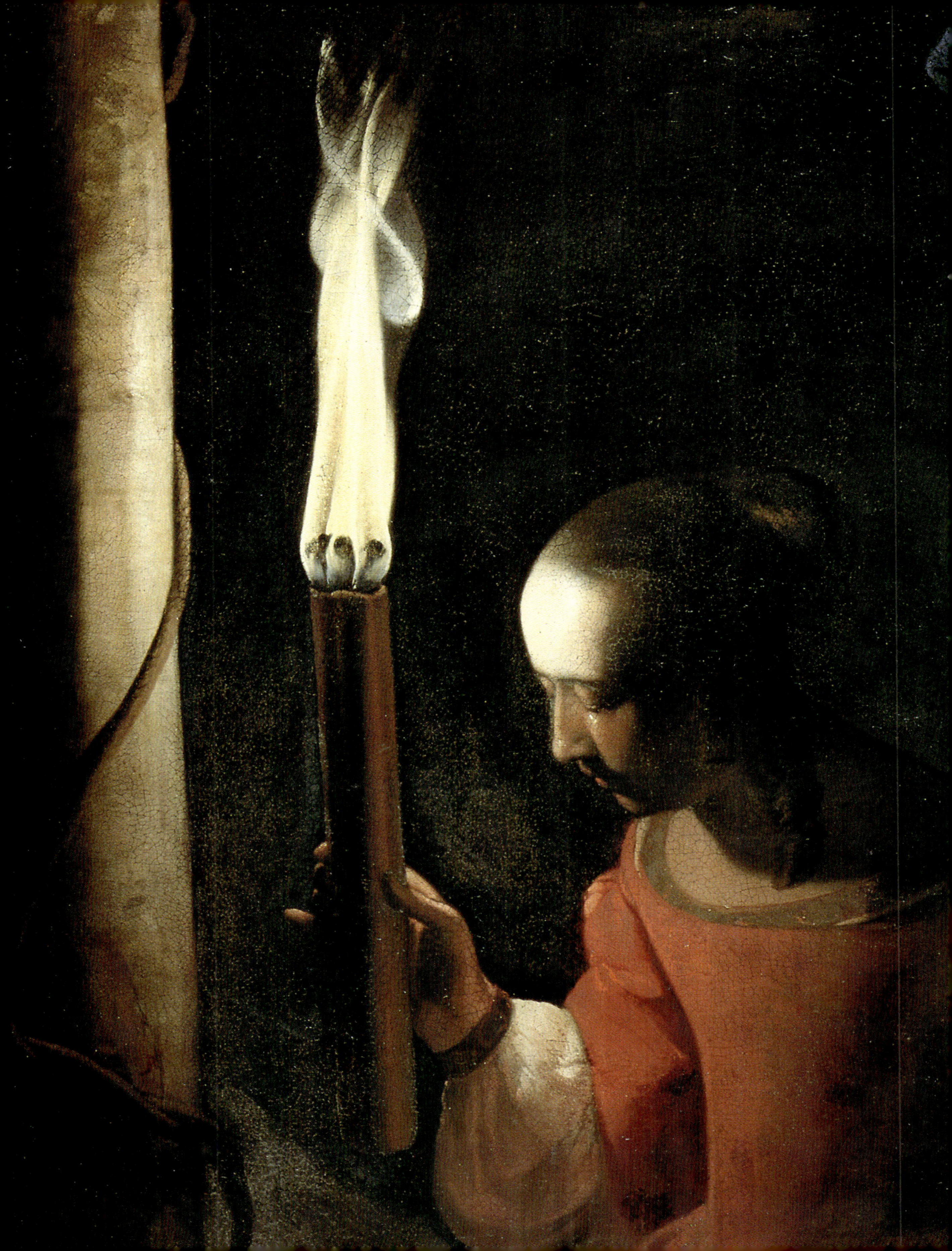

with the creator's "idea" in a single indissoluble whole. Rarely has the very nature of painting been so comprehensively called into question, not by theoreticians but by painters themselves. The result was an extraordinary range of works, for this reexamination, by its very nature, precluded the creation of "schools." But all these works sought to render nature with a new exactness and precision, and to imbue it with a personal vision. It was an astonishing period, when painters preoccupied with the effect of light on form also dealt with human passions, predestination, and divine grace. It is just this fusion that accounts for Poussin's greatness, and, in an utterly different way, that of La Tour.

As we have seen, each of La Tour's pictures, in this sense, was a new proposition to be tested. He sought to capture the tactile reality of form, but in order to conjure up the image of humanity confronted with destiny. This double purpose gave rise not to a style, but to a constant changing of methods and results, an ever-increasing depth of response. From minutely sharp descriptions of individuals, La Tour went on to reach a point where a motionless face touches us more than any cry, the mere flame of a torch says more and moves us more than a long, detailed narrative. Nowhere is this clearer than in the "night" scenes, where the more pared down the image becomes, the greater the sense of presence it creates, not only of people and things, but of a spiritual truth. And this is undoubtedly why they have so persistently fascinated our contemporaries.

They must also sense that this intimate union of reality and idea, which artists today dismiss so easily, had strange powers, and perhaps still has them. What good is a painter's message if there is no medium through which to communicate it? What good is a sensible form without a message? The pointless babble of so many modern works, justified by endless theorizing, is surely not unlike that of late "Mannerism." Is the time not coming to reexamine the very nature of painting? The great lesson of La Tour's generation, nowhere more vividly or clearly exemplified than in his paintings, may once again become the most timely as well.

DOCUMENTARY SOURCES

Our knowledge of Georges de La Tour is based entirely on archival material. There are no contemporary biographies, accounts, or appraisals of him, nor any literary references to him. Until 1863 all we had were eleven very short lines by Dom Calmet in column 947 of his *Bibliothèque Lorraine* (1751). Alexandre Joly was the first to search through the Lunéville records, and in that sense he was the true "discoverer" of La Tour. Little by little the shadowy figure of the painter began to take shape. After 1915, paintings began to emerge and add to the evidence, but to put them in any order or to understand them, we always have to go back to the records.

These precious documents are for the most part divided among four collections: the municipal archives of Vic and Lunéville, the departmental archives of Metz, where the notarial records for Vic and the judicial documents relating to the former episcopal bailiwick are preserved, and the departmental archives of Nancy, where the equivalent notarial records and judicial papers for Lunéville are kept. In point of fact, because of the king of France's creation of a parliament in Lorraine and the subsequent removal of the ducal records to Vienna (and their later return), the records are not always located where they might be expected. In addition there are the Paris archives, with their notarial records in particular, and although these have yielded only a handful of deeds to date, records we must hope that they may still have important documents to add.

The archival material is not easily accessible, less because of its dispersion than because of its particular character. In almost every case we are faced with documents written in an execrable hand, which take hours of patient effort to decipher. Very few people, even specialists, are familiar with them, not least because they have been for the most part reported or summarized without being published. Great theories have often been elaborated on the strength of a few sentences taken from a longer document that in fact gives them quite a different meaning. François-Georges Pariset studied almost all of these records when he was putting together his thesis and drew his own conclusions from them, but was prevented by his publisher from supplying us with anything more substantive than a cursory reference and the occasional brief quotation. The key documents were published in full in the catalogue of the 1972 exhibition (in the Chronology, pp. 59-84), and new documents have since been discovered and published by Henri Tribout de Morembert, Marie-Thérèse Aubry and Canon Jacques Choux, Michel Antoine, Hubert Collin, Michel Sylvestre, Anne Reinbold, and Paulette Choné. The rest of the archival material, of which there is a great deal, remains practically unpublished, and some of it, indeed, has never even been fully deciphered. This is how the myth that Georges de La Tour's estate was called "La Licorne," owing to a rushed and incomplete reading of the original document, has been perpetuated to the present day.

My purpose here has been simply to bring together all the main documents in order to provide a solid base for future research and scholarship. I have not sought to produce a complete "corpus." In such a field this does not exist. On the one hand, more and more records will certainly reappear in coming years, notably when the judicial archives are gone over with care. On the other hand, even with the documents that have already been uncovered, it is necessary to impose limits. Already some of the documents in the following pages no longer relate directly to the painter, but simply indicate his presence, illustrate how his property was administered, or shed some light on the milieu in which he lived. These are all precious pieces of information, but to go any further is to enter into a study of a family and its fortune, which very quickly moves beyond the realm of art history.

At the same time, I have made every effort to provide reliable documents. Wherever it could be done without making this section of the book unduly long, I have given documents in their entirety, and in their original spelling (except for the use of capital letters when this seems too inconsistent). I have added a minimum of punctuation, but without altering the often tortuous and confusing sentence structure at all. Any difference between a text as I give it here and as it appears in earlier publications is the product of a conscious decision: unless otherwise stated, where a transcript exists, this has been checked against the original document. Although I have read and reread them, I am sure some mistakes remain, but in practical terms, such errors should not affect the essence of these invaluable texts—their meaning and their contribution to our knowledge of Georges de La Tour.

I

GEORGES DE LA TOUR A PAINTER FROM VIC 1593–1620

1583, 9 January: The first marriage contract of Georges's mother, Sibylle (Vic).

We still know fairly little about Georges de La Tour's ancestors. Reproduced here is the contract relating to his mother's first marriage, as transcribed by Tribout de Morembert and published by him in 1972 (p. 224). It gives us an insight into the lower-middle-class society of Vic, in which ownership of a vineyard or two was often the most important part of someone's fortune.

Le IXe jour de janvier 1583. En traictant et accordant le mariage futur et espéré à faire par et entre Nicolas Bizet, jeune filz, filz de Jean Bizet, demeurant à Vic, assisté dudict son père, de noble homme messire François Lescamoussier, greffier au bailliage de l'evesché de Metz et de Thoussainct Pracat, demeurans audit Vic d'une part, et Sebille, fille de feu Milian courier luy vivant demeurant audit Vic, assistée de Marguerite Trompette sa mère, de Jean Trompette son oncle, de Jacquemin de Cropsal et de Jean Lhuillier demeurans audit Vic, proche parens à ladite Sebille d'aultre part, lesquelz sont recongnuz avoir traictez et accordez les poinctz et articles que s'ensuyvent. Et premier que lesdits Nicolas et Sebille se prendront et espouseront en face de notre mère saincte Eglise le plustost que faire se pourra. Et après ledit mariage consommé, ilz mettront tous leurs biens par ensembles pour en user comme gens de bien doibvent faire. Item a esté passé et accordé que ladite Margueritte sa mère habillera et meublera sadite fille selon son estat et encor luy donnera la somme de cinquante frans, la moitié à la Sainct-Remy prochain, et à l'aultre Sainct-Remy suyvant après l'aultre moitié. Et cas advenant fortune sur les vignes de sadite mère, lesdits futurs conjoinctz auront esgard ad cela et ne la presseront pour le terme escheu, neantmoins que ledit terme escheu sera dheu pour l'année séquente. Item ladite mère leur laisse jusques à partage une vigne contenant demy jornal ou environ à prendre sur sesdites vignes à la disposition de leurdite mère, à condition que lesdits futurs conjoinctz seront tenuz de bien entretenir ladite vigne, et aultrement seroit loisible à ladite Margueritte leur mère de leur oster ladite vigne sans aultres formes de procès. Item ont accordez que de tous acquestz qui se feront constant leurdit futur mariage, ladite Sebille sera acquesteresse pour la moitié soit dénommée ès lettres ou non. Promettans lesdites parties de tenir soubz l'obligation, etc. In forma. Presens vénérable et discrette personne messire François Boucher, chanoine de l'église Saint-Etienne, Mathieu Mirbel couvreur et Symon Relinguer menuisier, demeurans audit Vic, tesmoings.

(Metz, Archives de la Moselle, 3 E 8146, fol. 2)

1590, 31 December: Marriage contract between Georges's parents, Jean de La Tour and Sibylle (Vic).

This document, similarly published by Tribout de Morembert in 1972 (pp. 223-224), gives little information about the painter's father. Jean de La Tour is not attended either by his parents, both of whom were presumably dead, or by any brothers or sisters, nor is there any mention of goods in his possession or due to come to him. The contract is essentially concerned with safeguarding the rights of Sibylle's two children by her first marriage (who are not even referred to by name).

Le mesme jour [dernier décembre 1590] ont comparus en personnes Jean de Latour, jeusne filz, assisté de Claudon de Latour masson, son oncle, de Claudin Philippe boulangier, demeurans à Vic d'une part, et Sibille de Cropsaulx, vefve de feu Nicolas Bizet, sienne dame, assistée de Margueritte, vefve de feu Melian, corrier, sa mère, de Jean Bizet, Jean Trompette et Christophe Bizet, tous ses parans bien veuillans d'autre paft. Ont recongnus que, en traictant et accordant du mariage futur et espéré à faire par et entre le dit Jean et la dite Sibille, ont esté passés et accordés les pointz que s'en suyvent. Scavoir que ledit Jean prandra la dite Sibille pour sa loyalle femme au plus tost, et leur mariage confirmez il en a esté accordé entre lesdites parties, que touchant les enfans délaissés par ledit feu N. Bizet et ladite Sibille, lesdits futur conjoinctz seront tenus nourir et entretenir lesdits enfans jusques à l'estat de mariage, et lors dudit mariage iceulz conjointz seront attenus de donner à chacun desdits deux enfans la somme de quatre vingtz frans, pour la part et advenant de leur part des meubles à eulx obvenus et délaissiés par le décès dudit feu Bizet leur père, iceulx meubles appréciés par gens an congnoissantz à pareils biens susdits, comme il a esté dict et desclaré par honorable homme Claude Thiebauld, commis clerc juré et depputé à cest estat, en présence de moy et des tesmoings cy après, lesquelz meubles seront et demeureront à ce moyen et ès conditions cy dessus ausdits futurs pour en disposer comme de leurs propres. Ils en ont accordés que pour le fait de la maison cy devant acquestée par ledit feu Nicolas Bizet, dont il y a desia la somme de quatre centz cinquante frans de payé, et qu'il reste encore à payer la somme de cinq centz frans pour ladite maison, ledit Jean de Latour et ladite Sibille paracheveront ce qu'il reste à payer d'icelle maison, pour, ayant hoirs procréés en leurs mariage, pouvoir joyr de ladite maison selon l'advenant de ladite somme desdits cinq centz francs, après le décez d'iceulx conjointz. Néantmoing ont accordés que les enfans dudit feu Bizet et de ladite Sibille auront chois et option de prendre ladite maison après le décès de ladite Sibille leur mère, en satisfaisant ausdits cinq centz frans que se restitueront es enfans dudit second mariage, si aulcun en y a, sans aultre empeschement et conditions de les recepvoir chacun an cent frans, comme ilz les auront payés, et tiendra ladite maison jusques à ce que il sera satisfait de ladite somme de cinq centz frans, en payant par chascun an la moitié du louage de ladite maison depuis le commencement de ladite restitution. Et ny ayant enfans procreés en leur dit mariage, et advenant que ladite somme de cinq centz frans fut payée, et que l'ung desdits futur conjointz vint à décéder sans hoirs, les héritiers du premier décédé auront la somme de cent frans, à prandre sur les plus clairs et apparans biens desdites parties lors dudit trespas. Et au cas que ladite maison ne seroit parachevée de payer, ladite donation de cent frans sera nul, tant envers l'une des parties que de l'autre. Item que en tous acquestz et conquestz ladite Sibille sera acquisteresse pour la moitié, soit dénommée ès lettres ou non. Et advenant le décès de ladite Sibille avant que ladite maison ne fut parachevée de payer, ledit Jean ne sera tenu de parachever ladite paye se faire ne le veult, ny nourir davantage lesdits deux enfans du premier mariage de ladite Sibille, en luy rendant ce que par luy sera esté payé de ladite maison depuis ledit traicté de mariage. Item advenant le décès dudit Jean sans hoirs avant ladite Sibille, elle pourra disposer de deux pièces de ses meilleurs habillementz ou bagues. Si ont promis lesdites parties, soubz l'obligation, etc.

Presens vénérable personne Messire François Boucher, prestre, et Noel Touillat, recouvreur, demeurans à Vic, tesmoings à ce requis et appellés.
[Signed] Breton

(Metz, Archives de la Moselle, 3 E 8141, fols. 118-119)

1591, 26 October: Baptism of Diane Le Nerf, Georges's future wife (Lunéville).

This is no more than a mention, but it establishes quite unambiguously the identity of the woman who was to become the painter's wife.

Octobre 1591
Dianne fille de M. le Nerf et de dame Catherine sa femme. P(arrain) Francois Morcel, M(arraine) Mougeotte femme de Pierre de Moirry. Le 26me.

(Lunéville, Archives Municipales)

1593, 14 March: Baptism of Georges (Vic).

After a fruitless search in Lunéville by Alexandre Joly, Georges's baptismal certificate was eventually tracked down in Vic, thus giving us the possibility to reconstruct, at least partially, La Tour's early years.

It is important to realize that in spite of their peasant-sounding names, Jean Desboeufs [i.e. John of the Oxen] and Nicolas Le Meusnier [Nicholas the Miller] were people of some standing in Vic; the latter, indeed, was a municipal magistrate.

George, filz de Jean De la tour boullengier et Sybille sa femme fut baptizé le 14 de mars. Parrin Jean desboeufs mercier. Marinne Pentecoste femme a Nicolas Le meusnier, tous de Vic.

(Vic-sur-Seille, Archives Municipales)

1594–1600: Baptisms of Georges's younger brothers and sisters (Vic).

Apart from her children by her first husband, Nicolas Bizet (we know of two, Catherine and François), Sybille had a total of seven sons and daughters by Jean de La Tour. The oldest child was Jacob, who was baptized on 15 January 1592, with a haberdasher by the name of Jean Balthazar as godfather and the wife of Master Jacob, surgeon of Château-Salins, as godmother. Georges followed in 1593, and after him came the five whose baptismal records are given below. Georges must have grown up surrounded by children, but also by death. François, born in 1598, seems to be the only one of his siblings to have survived childhood.

All the godparents came from the family's circle, which was relatively modest, but nevertheless of sufficiently high standing to include the parish priest and the mayor's wife.

1594. Jean, filz de Jean de la tour boullengier et de Isabeau sa femme fut baptizé le mesme ior (14e d'aoust). Parain Vian (?) Forcelle courier marrine Barbe femme a Thiebault taillet.
1596. Françoise, fille de Jean de la tour Boullengier et de Sybille sa femme fut baptizée le 19 d'april. Parrin Jean Hannet clerc iuré de ce lieu de Vic marrinne Françoise Guillet femme au sieur Boutaucour de moyenvic.
1598. François, fils de Jean de la tour boullengier et d'Ysabillon sa femme fut baptizé le douzieme du mesme mois (de febvrier). Parrin le soubsigné curé de ceste église. Marine dame Madgeleine pierson femme au Sr David bourguignon maire de Vic.
1599. Margueritte, fille de Jean de la tour boullengier et de Sybille Melian sa femme fut baptizée le quartorzieme septembre. Parrin Didier Cugnin bouchier. Marine Margueritte femme à Aubertin anthoine bouchier.
1600. Maurice, filz de Jean de La Tour boullengier et de sybille sa femme fut baptizé le 29 novembre. Parrin Bastian Leloup marchant, marinne Margueritte femme a Demenge michel meulnier aux moulins de ce lieu.

(Vic-sur-Seille, Archives Municipales)

1596, 12 June: Division of the estate of Marguerite Trompette, Georges's maternal grandmother (Vic).

This deed of settlement for the estate of Marguerite Trompette, mother of Sibylle, gives us a clear picture of Georges de La Tour's relations on his mother's side. The text given here represents the beginning of the deed and follows the transcription made by Tribout de Morembert (1972, p. 224).

Le XIIe juing 96 ont comparus en leurs personnes honnorables hommes Jean Trompette boulangier et Claudon de La Tour, masson, demeurans à Vic, au nom et comme tuteurs de Marguerite, fille de feu Demange Henry luy vivant salpétrier demeurant audit Vic, Jean de Latour, boulangier, au nom de Sibille sa femme, et François Melian, fils de feu Melian courier, et tous enfans de feu Marguerite Trompette, femme quand vivoit en première nopce audit feu Melian et en secondes audit Demange Henry ; lesquelz ont recongneu et confessé de leur pure et franche volonté, sans forces ny contraintes, tant lesdits tuteurs, Jean de La Tour que François, avoir faict entre eulx les partages et accordz et divisions de tous et chacun les héritaiges à eulx escheus et obvenant tant de par lesdits feu Melian et Demange Henry, comme de ladite Margueritte leur mère, comme cy à présent déclarés. . . .

(Metz, Archives de la Moselle, 3 E 8142, fol. 171)

1613, 1 June: Jean de La Tour, father of Georges, as guardian to the children of Claudon de La Tour the younger (Vic).

This hitherto unpublished document throws some light in turn on the paternal side of La Tour's family. It becomes clear that Jean de La Tour, Georges's father, rather than being the son of Claudon de La Tour the Elder, was in fact only his nephew. We still do not know who Georges's grandfather was, but the document does show that the family was relatively wealthy.

Copie de la req[ues]te et decret cy devant mentionné.
A Monsieur, Monsieur le procureur général de l'evesché de Metz, Demonstrent très humblement Claudon de La Tour le vieil demeurant à Marsal et Jean de La Tour bourgeois de ce lieu de Vic, comme tuteurs de quattre enfans délaissés par feu Claudon de La Tour le jeune, fils audit de la Tour le vieux, dont deux d'iceulx seroient mariés, désirant faire leur plus grand proffictz, tant de leur part que de celle des deux qui demeurent en tutelle, de quelques pièces d'héritage qu'ils ont eues impartageables, ce qu'ils ne peuvent sinon par la vente totalle d'icelles, pour à quoy parvenir vous supplient treshumblement vouloir permettre par votre noble volonté qu'elles soient vendues au lieu accoustumé, à l'esteincte de la chandelle, pour mettre l'argent premièrement de la part desdits mineurs en rente a leurs proufficts, et les deux autres susdits mariés recepvoir leur part pour en faire leur prouffict comme ils pourront mieulx. A quoy inclinant seront tenus prier Dieu pour votre santé, prospérité et très noble estat.

Veu la présente req[ues]te le soubscript procureur général de l'Evesché de Metz, consent pour le regard de Claude et Nicolas, enfans mineurs de feu Claudon de La Tour, à ce que les pièces d'héritage a eulx délaissé qui ne leur apportent grand prouffict et qui commodément ne peuvent estre partagées en sorte que les deniers en provenant leur deussent tourner en plus grande utilité, soient publiées et vendeues à l'estaincte de la chandelle, a charge de rapporter par les tuteurs d'iceulx leur advenant en compte avec la rente au taxe dudit evesché. Faict à Vic le premier jour de juin 1613. Ainsy signé. F. Dabocourt.

(Nancy, Archives de Meurthe-et-Moselle, Bj 1547 (2))

1616, 20 October: Georges as godfather (Vic).

This is the first known document since the certificate of baptism that refers directly to Georges. By this time, however, he was already twenty-three. Everything points to his having lived far from Vic at least since adolescence.

Margueritte fille de Claude fontaine et de margueritte barrier sa femme fut baptizée le 20ᵉ dudit octobre. Parrin George de Latour, marrine Margueritte fille de feu Demenge Cugnin.

(Vic-sur-Seille, Archives Municipales)

1617, 21 February: Georges de La Tour as witness for Claude de Lisseras (Nancy).

Michel Sylvestre discovered this document in 1983 (1985, pp. 47-49). Insignificant in itself, it reveals a connection between La Tour and Claude de Lisseras, lord of Anderny, and gentleman of the duke of Lorraine's bedchamber. It is an acknowledgment of two debts, for 9,170 francs and 1,000 francs, respectively, made out by the young lord to a merchant in Nancy by the name of Pierre Dautré. La Tour acted as witness, clearly demonstrating that, in this early stage in his career as a painter, he had some some very fine connections.

Ce jourduy vingtunième fevrier mil six cents dix sept, en présence du tabellion soubsigné, et des tesmoins en bas nommés, est comparu honoré seigneur Claude de Licerasse, seigneur Danderni, Capitaine Baillif de Chastel sur mozelle et gentilhomme de la Chambre de Son Altesse, lequel a recognu et vollontairement confessé debvoir et estre attenu paier de bonne et juste debte à honorable homme Piere Dautreÿ, marchant, demeurant à Nancy, créditeur pour luÿ, ses hoirs et ayans cause, la somme de neufs mil cents soixante dix francs monnoye du pais, pour cause de marchandise a luÿ sieur debteur vendue et délivrée et de prix faict et arresté avec ledit Dautreÿ à ladite somme de neuf mil cents soixante et dix francs, dont ledit Seigneur de Licerasse a déclaré se tenir pour contant de ladite marchandise ; laquelle somme pour cause que desus il a promis paier audit créditeur, sesdits hoirs et ayant cause, sçavoir la moitié à la Sᵗ. Jean Baptiste prochaine, l'autre moitié faisant ladite somme dans Noel dict Nativité notre Seigneur immédiatement suivant, à peine de tous despends, domages et intérets. Et advenant que ledit sʳ Danderni fut en demeure de paier lesdites sommes dans la fin de la présente année, il promet de là en avant en paier la rente au fueur des ordonnances et à mesure du temps, sans préjudice néantmoins à la contraincte au principal lesdits tems expirés, et d'une autre obligation d'autre somme de mils francs que ledit Dautreÿ a ce jourd'huÿ presté audit sʳ Danderni, receue par ledit soubsigné ; pour laquelle somme pour ce que dessus fournir et satisfaire ledit Seigneur debteur en a par ces présentes obligé et oblige tous ses biens, terres et seigneuries présents et advenir par tout, qu'il a submis et submect a toute justice pour ÿ pouvoir faire exploiter comme pour chose y jugée, tant pour ladite somme que frais de poursuite. Renonceant par exprès quand ad ce et sur ce ledit seigneur Danderny à garend, arrière garends, et à toutes autres singulières et généralles exceptions contraires à ces présentes. Que furent faictes et passées audit Nancy en présence d'Isaac Nicot, tailleur d'habits, demeurant à Nancy, et le Sʳ George de la Thoure, de la suitte dudit Sʳ Danderni tesmoingts.
[*A line has been drawn through this text by the notary, who has written in the margin* "effacée du consentement dudit créditeur pour estre acquictée, tant en principal qu'interets. . . ." *The second record follows immediately after:*]

Fut présent en sa personne par devant le tabellion soubsigné demeurant à Nancy et des tesmoins en bas nommés honoré Seigneur Claude de Licerasse, Seigneur Danderni, Capitaine Baillifs de Chastel sur Mozelle et gentilhomme de la Chambre de Son Altesse, estant de présent audict Nancy et y demeurant, lequel a recognu debvoir de bonne et juste debte à honorable homme Piere Dautreÿ, marchant demeurant à Nancy, créditeur pour luÿ, ses hoirs et ayans cause, la somme de mil francs monnoÿe du pais, pour pareille et semblable somme à luÿ seigneur debteur prestée et délivréee par ledit Dautreÿ, ainsÿ qu'il a recognu, dont il s'en tient pour contant. Laquelle somme de mille francs telle et pour cause que dessus il a promis rendre et restituer audit créditeur dans la Sᵗ Jean Baptiste prochaine, avec la rentte en deniers au fueur des ordonnances et à mesure du temps, à peine de tous despends, domages et interests, sans préjudice d'une autre obligation portant somme de neufs mils cents soixante et dix francs que ledit seigneur Danderni a ce jourdhuÿ passé au proffict dudict Dantreÿ par devant ledit soubsigné. Pour laquelle somme telle et pour cause que dessus fournir et satisffaire ledit Seigneur Danderni en a par exprès obligé et oblige tous et chacun ses biens, terres et seigneuries présens et advenir par tout, qu'i a submis à toutes justices pour ÿ faire exploiter comme pour chose ÿ cognue tant pour ladite somme que frais de poursuitte. Renonceant ledit seigneur debteur à garend, arrière garends et a toutes autres exceptions contraires. Que furent faictes et passées audit Nancy l'an de grâce nostre Seigneur mil six cents dix sept le vingtunième febvrier en présence d'Isaac nicot tailleur d'habitz demeurant audit Nancy, et le sʳ George de la Thoure de la suitte dudit sʳ Danderni, tesmoins.

(Nancy, Archives de Meurthe-et-Moselle, 3 E 1286, fol. 39-40)

1617, 2 July: Georges's marriage contract (Vic).

This important certificate was discovered by Tribout de Morembert in 1955. The marriage obviously marked a crucial turning point for La Tour, whose future was thereafter firmly anchored in Lorraine. It is clear from the details of the contract that this marriage was the first step in a steady progression up the very complicated social ladder in Lorraine. There are a number of puzzling elements, however, such as the absence of Diane's parents.

Du IIᵉ Juillet 1617
En traictant, pourparlant et accordant etc. par et entre honnorable maître George de la tour paintre Jeune filz d'honnorable Jean de la tour boulangier demeurant a Vic assisté dudit son pere, de Messire Jean Gallavaux, prebstre chanoinne de l'église collégiale St Estienne dudit Vic, de Noble Jean Martinÿ maire audit Vic et conseillier etc., de Jean Gomin portier de la porte (de la porte, *répété*) d'Annal dudit Vic, de Vaultrin Larcher paveur, et de Claudin Remÿ bouchier demeurant audit Vic, tous ses parentz et bons amys d'une part, Et Dÿanne le nerf fille de Noble Jean Le nerf et damme Catherinne Lamance demeurants a Luneville, assistée de Damoiselle Dyanne Beaufort vefve et relicte de feu le Sʳ Nicolas de Saulcerotte, vivant Sʳ dudit lieu, Lesse, Fremerÿ en partye, et du Sʳ Alphonce de rambervillier Sʳ de Dairlem, de Vaucourt en partie, conseillier aux conseils d'estat et privé et lieutenant général en l'evesché de metz ; du Sʳ Jean du halt escuyer Sʳ de Henamesnil et Cryon en partie conseillier aux conseils d'estat et privé et tresorier général audit evesché, et du Sʳ Didier Marsal, advocat au bailliage dudit Esvesché, tous ses cousins parentz aliez et amys d'autre part, ont estés passes les articles que cÿ après :
Premier que lesdits deux futurs coniointz se prendront fianceront et espouseront en face de notre mere sainte Eglise sÿ Dieu et Icelle sÿ accordent au plustost que commodement faire se pourra ;
Que ledit mariage consommé ils seront uns et communs en tous biens meubles et immeubles acquestz et conquestz, soit que ladite Dÿanne soit dénommée aux contractz d'iceux ou nom *[sic]* ;
Qu'en contemplation d'iceluy mariage ladite damoiselle de Beaufort donra a ladite Dÿanne la somme de quatre centz francs monnoye en outre les centz francs qu'elle luy a ja cy devant donné, lesquels elle a

mis en mains dudit Sr Jean Le nerf son pere, qui font en tout cinq centz francs, la moitié desquelz s'employera en acquestz qui tiendra nature d'ancien et de propre a ladite future espouse et a ses enfans apres le deces d'icelle ses hoirs et ayants cause ; en outre luÿ donra encor par dessus les habitz qu'elle a présentement une robe et une couste pour le jour de son festin, outre deux vaches et une genixe dont elle l'auroit ja cÿ devant gratifiée, et finallement luÿ donra quelques meubles à sa discrétion et volonté, le tout sans déroger en rien que se soit a tel mariage que ses sœurs ont heu de sondit père, qu'elle pourra repeter après le decès d'iceluÿ, et sans prejudicier au droict de succession qui luÿ pourra obvenir de ses parentz.

Au reciprocque et en récompense de quoy ledit Jean de La tour père a promis de donner auxdits futurs conjoincts la quantité de six paires de grains moitié bled et aveinne mesure dudit Vic de rente annuel attendant l'ouverture de sa succession, et de continuer encor la mesme rente en cas que ledit son filz vienne à predeceder ladite Dÿanne, tant et sy longtemps qu'elle vivra au cas qu'il ÿ ait enfants procréés dudit futur mariage, et pendant la viduité de ladite Dyanne (en) cas que sondit filz passe de vie à trespas sans laisser hoirs de son corps, luy reservant toutesfois le douaire coustumier sÿ le cas y eschet ; de plus d'habiller sondit fils decemment selon sa qualité et condition, de le meubler competanment a la volonté toutesfois et discretion de sa femme, s'obligeant aussy à faire le festin de nopces.

Promettants lesdites partyes respectivement etc, sçavoir lesdits futurs conioincts comme aussy ladite damoiselle de Beaufort et ledit Jean de la Tour et sadite femme chacun a son egard, d'avoir et tenir, faire avoir et tenir pour aggreable ferme stable et inviolable le contenu au présent traicté sans y contrevenir ny souffrir estre contrevenu directement ou indirectement, au contraire en facon maniere et condition etc., soubz l'obligation etc., présens venerable et dicrette personne Messire Didier Soinlet prebstre chanoinne de ladite eglise et George Guanat coordonnier, demeurants audit Vic, tesmoings a ce requis priez et appelez.

(Metz, Archives de la Moselle, 3 E 8176, fol. 238-239)

1618, 16 May: Georges as guardian to the children of Colin Chérier and Babillon de La Tour.

Henri Tribout de Morembert (1974, pp. 221-222) refers to several deeds drawn up by a notary in March, April, and May 1618 and which show Georges de La Tour acting as guardian to the orphaned children of Colin Chérier and his wife, Babillon de La Tour, who appear to have been his cousins living in Moyenvic. The deed reproduced here, in the text published by Tribout de Morembert, concerns the division of the house. The two others (3 E 5803, fols. 28-30, 40-41) relate to the division of the vines and a meix.

Du XVIe maye 1618. Comparurent en leurs personnes honnorable homme Georges de la Tour, peintre, demeurant à Vic..., comme tuteur de Babillon, Marguerite, Claude et Jean, enfans de feu Colin Cherier et de Babillon de La Tour, quand ils vivoient demeurant à Moyenvic, leurs père et mère, et Nicolas Cogubu à cause de Claudatte sa femme, demeurant à Einville, estant muni du consentement de sadicte femme..., d'une part, et Toussaint Grandidier, demeurant audict Moyenvic, dernier mary à la deffuncte Babillon, d'aultre part ; lesquels ont recogneu avoir faict entre eulx partage et division d'une maison située au lieu dudict Moyenvic en la rue de l'Estang, monsieur Humbert de Nancy d'une part, et Demange Mansuy d'aultre part, scavoir que ledit Toussainct a et emporte pour luy, ses hoirs et ayant cause le corps du logis avec les usaires du devant et la moitié du meix de derriere (...) et pour le reste de ladite maison, consistant en estable, grainge, allée d'icelle, usuaire du devant et l'autre moitié du meix de derrière, le susdit de La Tour et ledit Nicolas, pour et aux noms comme dit est, demeure pour contre-partage pour eux, leurs hoirs etc. et à charge que ledit Toussain retournera... esdits pupils deux cent quatre vingt francs monnoye de Lorraine, si comme ledit George de La Tour a confessé avoir heu et receu dudit Toussainct... Présens honnorable homme Peltrement Demange, maire audit Moyenvic, et Thiriet Thiriet masson, demeurant à Vic, tesmoings.

(Metz, Archives de la Moselle, 3 E 5803, fol. 50-53)

1618: Death of Jean de La Tour, Georges's father, at an unknown date before 25 May, and death of Jean Le Nerf, Diane's father, 30 July.

Anne Reinbold (1991, p. 35) refers to various deeds dated 25 May, 20 August, and 5 and 6 September relating to litigation following the death of Jean de La Tour, from which we can safely infer that this took place before 25 May 1618 (Nancy, Meurthe-et-Moselle Archives, Bj 1589). We know rather more precisely from other deeds that Jean Le Nerf died on 30 July of the same year (cf. Denis, 1899, p. 21).

1618, 8 November: Georges as witness to his brother François's apprenticeship contract (Vic).

François was apprenticed to Nicolas Saulnier, merchant tanner of Saint-Nicolas-du-Port. Georges appended his signature to the contract, which was subsequently annulled on 7 February 1619 (cf. Reinbold, 1991, pp. 36, 186).

1619, 5 August: Baptism of Philippe, Georges's son (Vic).

Although there was no specific clause to this effect in their marriage contract, local custom would have dictated that Georges's parents house and feed the young couple for two years. Because Georges's father died before the first year was up and before the hundred francs promised them on the occasion of the marriage were paid (Tribout de Morembert, 1955), Georges and his wife may well have stayed on in the family home while preparing to move to Lunéville.

A marked change is evident between the baptism certificates of La Tour's brothers and sisters and this one. Jean Philippe de Myon, lord of Gombervaux, who married Anne Du Halt on 14 January, was an influential figure. Diane de Beaufort, lady of Saulcerotte, was the aunt who had given Diane Le Nerf her dowry and who apparently continued to keep a watchful eye over the couple.

Augustus 1619 – Philippe filz de George de la tour et de Diane Le nerf sa femme fut baptizé le 5me d'aoust. Parain noble Jean Philippe demion, Seigneur de Gombervaux et Maraine dam[ois]elle Diane de Baufort.

(Vic-sur-Seille, Archives Municipales)

1620, 18 April: Georges as godfather to Royenne Ferry (Vic).

La Tour's acting as godfather to Royenne, daughter of Jean Ferry, in Vic, would seem to indicate that the painter was still living in his native town.

1620, 10 July: Decree of exemption granted to Georges (Nancy).

This is another key document. In the absence of the originals, which La Tour must have kept jealously in his possession, we have this excellent copy executed no doubt at his request by his neighbor and relative, the notary Étienne Gérard. The petition is undated, and may even go back to the previous year. The decree was made on 10 July, although it is not clear whether La Tour and his wife had already moved to Lunéville by then. These documents were not only of great importance to La Tour, who from then on enjoyed a privileged social status (and one that he subsequently found hard to defend). Like the favors granted by Henri II to Deruet, Le Clerc, and Callot, they reflect a fundamental change in attitude: long before other countries, Lorraine recognized the "nobility" of art and the rank artists deserved to hold in society.

A Son Altesse.
Remonstre en toute humilité, George de la Tour, Peintre natif de Vic, ou il demeure, qu'ayant espousé une fille de qualité noble à Lunéville, il desireroit s'y retirer pour y rendre ses très humbles services à V.A., ny ayant la ny aux environs personne de l'art et profession du Remonstrant. Et bien que cet art soit noble de soy, si n'oseroit-il esperer de demeurer en vostre souveraineté exempt des tailles ordinaires et autres sujettions, s'il n'a l[ett]res d'exemption de V.A., laquelle il suplie très humblement luy vouloir accorder de grace speciale, a fin qu'il ne soit inquiété ny molesté pour cet égard, et qu'il iouïsse de toutes les franchises, dont usent les autres frans de vostre souveraineté. Et il supliera N[ost]re Seigneur pour la grandeur et prosperité de V.A.

Veue la presente requeste, Nous, en faveur de la profession de notre cher et bien aymé George de la Tour supliant, et de la résidence qu'il expose avoir choisie en nostre ville de Lunéville, Avons de grace speciale et authorité souveraine affranchy et affranchisons par cestes ledit supliant de tous traitz, tailles, redevances et prestacions personnelles, revenantes a nous et a nostre dommaine, ensemble de tous aydes et subsides generaulx, personnels, ord[inai]res et extraord[inai]res imposés et a imposer. Mandons a nos tres chers et feaux les Srs commis et deputez a la direction de nos Aydes generaulx, Presidens et Gens des Comptes de Lorraine, Procureur general de nostredit duché ou ses Substituz Receveur et Controlleur dudict Lunéville, et a tous autres nos officiers et justiciers qu'il appartiendra de faire et souffrir jouyr ledit supliant de l'effet de nostre present decret d'affranchissement sa vie naturelle durant, sans luy mettre ou donner ny souffrir luy estre mis ou donné aucun trouble ou empeschement, au contraire, et en rapportant et representant par nosdit Receveur et Controleur copie deuement collationnée de cestuy nostre decret ou il appartiendra elle leur servira de descharge des cottes dudit supliant, Car ainsy nous plaist, Expédié à Nancy, le dixieme jour de juillet mil six cent vingt, Les Srs comte de Tornielle grand maitre en l'hostel et surintendant des finances, et Rennel président de Lorraine presents. Ainsi signé Hanry et plus bas pour secrétaire Janin.

Copié et traicté et dheuement collationné a l'original des presentes par le tabellion soubscript, – en se concordent. [*Signed*] Gérard

(Nancy, Archives de Meurthe-et-Moselle, Série 3 F 320, fol. 36r)

II

GEORGES DE LA TOUR IN LUNÉVILLE: GOOD TIMES IN LORRAINE 1620–1633

1620, 19 August: Apprenticeship contract of Claude Baccarat (Lunéville).

Once settled in Lunéville, the painter obviously needed someone to help him. He took as an apprentice the son of a tailor in the town who did not need to lodge with him, and to whom he therefore offered only board and instruction. This is why the terms were relatively low.

Le XIX[e] jour d'aoust 1620 au lieu de Luneville comparurent honn[ora]ble homme George de La Tour peintre demeurant audit lieu d'une part, et maitre Jean Baccarat tailleur d'habits demeurant au dit lieu d'autre part, lesquelz ont recongneu volontairement avoir faitz et font entre eux les conventions cy après. C'est assçavoir que ledit La Tour a promis et promect par ces presentes de monstrer et apprendre fidellement et diligemment a Claude filz dudit maître Jean l'art de peinture, le nourrir et entretenir seulement de sa bouche, luy fournir les couleurs nécessaires à faire son apprentissage dudit art pendant le temps de quatres années que ledit La Tour le tiendra enseignera et nourrira (à prendre au jour et datte des présentes). Et en consideration de ce que dessus ledit maître Jean Baccarat est obligé luy payer et delivrer la somme de deux cents frans monnoye Lorraine aux termes cy apres, a sçavoir la somme de cent frans dicte monnoie dans le jour de feste Nat[ivit]é nostre Seigneur du Noël prochainement venant, et les autres cent frans sçavoir cinquante frans audit jour de Noël suyvant que l'on dira 1621 et les derniers cinquante frans parfaisant ladite somme entiere de deux cent frans audit jour de Noël 1622.
Est convenu et accordé entre lesdites parties que cas arrivant le décès dudit La Tour ou dudit Claude pendant lesdits quatre ans ledit maître Jean sera tenu payer de ladite somme de deux cent frans au rata du tems qu'il l'aura tenu. Et sy tant estoit que ledit Claude apprentif abondonnât ledit La Tour sans subiet legitime, ledit maître Jean est et sera tenu payer et satisfaire a ladite somme entiere, et reciproquement aussi s'il avoit subiect legitime de l'habandonner et quicter pour quelque mauvais traictement ou négligence de l'enseigner diligemment dans ledit art, il ne sera tenu payer qu'au rata du temps de sa résidence en son logis. Promettant lesdites parties respectivement de tenir, etc. satisfaire aux conditions susdites, etc., soubs l'obligation des parties, etc.

(Nancy, Archives de Meurthe-et-Moselle 3 E 795)

1620, 31 August: Repurchase by Georges de La Tour of a *meix* from the Sisters of St. Francis.

We know from other documents (see for example the deed of gift of 16 February 1652) that the subject of this deed of repurchase, not specified in the text, is a modest dwelling known as a meix. *Acquired in 1604 by Jean Le Nerf and sold on 3 September 1619, that is to say, shortly after his death, by his wife and son (Catherine Lamance and the parish priest François Le Nerf), to the Sisters of St. Francis, it was now being taken back from them by La Tour. He and his wife could hardly have considered this* meix *with its enclosed garden, situated between the town ramparts and the convent to which the nuns belonged, as a fit place to live. Georges La Tour's motive must have been to either mark his establishment in Lunéville straight away with the purchase of some land, or, more likely, to find somewhere suitable to set up a studio.*

Le dernier jour d'Aoust 1620 Sœur Catherine Gagny, Sœur Philippe de Belieu, et Sœur Elisabeth Simon, religieuses au couvent Saint François à Lunéville, en l'absence de Dame Anne T..., mère d'iceluy couvent, ont recognu que Maistre George de La Tour peintre demeurant à Lunéville, a retiré dudit couvent pour luy, damoiselle Diane Le Nerf, etc, les actes au vendage passé au profit d'iceluy couvent par Dame Catherine Lamance, vefve de feu Noble Jean le Nerf vivant demeurant audit Lunéville, et Noble François Le Nerf son fils, au troisième de septembre année dernière 1619, portant de deux cents vingt quatre francs, cy avant soub le seing du tabellion soubscript ; cette retraite faite moyennant pareille somme... ... [*this is followed by standard guarantees; the deed is ratified by the mother superior of the convent, Anne, whose signature appears in the margin, dated 3 and 8 October*].

(Nancy, Archives de Meurthe-et-Moselle, 3 E 801, fol. 66r)

1620: Payment of "burghers" dues (Lunéville).

With the payment of this tax La Tour became one of the "burghers" of Lunéville, with all the duties and obligations that title entailed.

Entrées de ville,
Le Sr de La Tour painctre ayant de mesme esté reçu bourgeois a payé au comptable 33 fr. 4 gros.

(Lunéville, Archives Municipales, Série CC 5, fol. 6 (8)r)

1621, 24 May: La Tour as witness for the notary Étienne Gérard and his wife, Marie Le Nerf (Lunéville).

This is the first evidence of the close links that developed between Georges de La Tour and his cousin by marriage, the notary Étienne Gérard.

Le 24 may 1621. Nicolas Paris tisserand demeurant à Huthelut, se faisant fort de Sibille sa femme, a reconnu debvoir à honorable Estienne Gerard tabellion demeurant à Lunéville, créditeur pour luy, damoiselle Marie le nerf sa femme etc., la somme de trente trois francs monnoye de lorraine, pour cause de trois reseaulx de bled a lui vendu et delivré, dont est a payer au jour de S[t] Martin prochain. En obligeant pour ce faire tous ses biens etc. Les submettant etc. Renonceant a tous garands etc. Presents George de La Tour painctre, demeurant audit Lunéville, et honorable Martin Schreck archer des gardes de S[on] A[ltesse], demeurant à Barth, te[moing]s.

(Nancy, Archives de Meurthe-et-Moselle, 3 E 726; see also a similar act dated 26 June)

1621, 2 August: Baptism of Étienne, Georges's son (Lunéville).

Étienne was La Tour's second son and the only one to carry on the line.

Aoust (1621)
Estienne, filz de Maistre George de La Tour et Diane sa femme. P. le sire Estienne gerard. M. Dame Catherine Le nerfz. 2e [du mois].

(Lunéville, Archives Municipales)

1622, 16 May: Marriage of François de La Tour, Georges's brother (Vic).

François married Jeanne Huelle, daughter of the Honorable Claudon Huelle of Jevaincourt-lès-Mirecourt and sister of a canon of the collegiate church of Vic. He is described as mace-bearer at the spiritual court (record cited by Tribout de Morembert, 1955; Metz, Archives de la Moselle, 3 E 8177, fols. 23-24.).

The couple had a son, Claude, baptized on 18 May 1623 (record cited by Reinbold, 1991, p. 51; Vic-sur-Seille, Archives Municipales).

1623, 21 February: La Tour as witness to the loan of a black cow and its heifer calf (Lunéville).

From this point on, La Tour appears very often in the notarial records of Lunéville, as a witness for family or friends. Only some of these are given here, mostly hitherto unpublished; they are of little importance in themselves, but they help to give us a better sense of everyday life in a small town in Lorraine, where the soil was still all-important. This one relates to Marie Le Nerf, Diane's first cousin and wife of the notary Étienne Gérard.

Le mesme jour damoiselle Marie Le Nerf espouse d'honorable Estienne Gérard, demeurant à Lunéville, se disant avoir charge d'iceluy, a congneu avoir laissé à tiltre de bail à maître Demenge Lucart demeurant a Crion et Elisabeth sa femme, une vache noire avec une genisse d'un an pour les nourrir traicter et [...] avec les fruicts qu'elles produiront pendant la présente laisse ; laquelle est faict pour le terme de trois ans, commenceant au jour de S[t]. George prochain, moyennant la somme de vingt francs pour prix desdites bestes, que ledit preneur sera tenu et a promis de donner a ladite dame renonçant etc. au bout desdits trois ans, et avant faire partage desdites bestes en deux moitiés esgalles, dont ledit laisseur aura le choix de prendre l'une d'elles ; et cas que ladite vache ne soit propre pendant lesdits trois ans, ledit S[r] laisseur en remestra une autre en place. Promettant etc. Garandir etc. obligeant respectivement leurs biens etc. Présents Claude Henry cousturier et honorable George de La Tour peintre demeurant audit Luneville tesmoings.

(Nancy, Archives de Meurthe-et-Moselle, 3 E 727, fol. 31 recto and verso)

1623, 12 July: Purchase of a painting by the duke (Nancy).

This record is proof that Henri II was a patron but unfortunately does not specify the subject of the painting he bought.

Parties de peintres et graveurs (...)
A... [*the space for the first name is left blank*] . . . [*the word replaces something that has been crossed out, possibly "ce lieu"*] pour le prix d'ung Tableau que Sadite altesse a achepté de luy de prix faict par elle mesme à ladite somme, comme appert par mandement absolut du XIIe juillet 1623. cy rendu icy... CXXIII fr.

(Nancy, Archives de Meurthe-et-Moselle, B. 1429, fol. 287r)

1623, 13 October: Baptism of Claude, Georges's daughter (Lunéville).

Claude was one of two daughters to survive infancy. Her godfather was François Le Nerf, Diane's brother and parish priest of Tonnoy, and her godmother, the daughter of Anne Raoul, Diane's first cousin, who was first married to Nicolas Berman, and then to Alphonse de Rambervillers.

Octobre -
Claude fille de Mre George de Latour peinctre et Diane sa femme. P. M[re] françois Le nerfz Curé de Tonnoy. M. damoiselle Claude Berman fille de feu noble Nicolas Berman. 13

(Lunéville, Archives Municipales)

1623, 7 December: Purchase of a house and meadow by Georges de La Tour (Lunéville).

Georges and Diane bought a house with outbuildings and a meadow from Diane's mother; this seems to have been the Le Nerf family home, for the widow Le Nerf declares that she has left Lunéville and gone to live in Tonnoy, apparently with her son François who was parish priest there. The boundaries of the property are defined by the adjoining properties, and it is not given any name. Pariset believed the house was called "La Licorne," and everyone followed him, but he was in fact mistaken (see below, under 14 February 1628).

Du septième décembre 1623
Par devant le tabellion soubscrit au duché de Lorraine et dem[euran]t à Thonnoy comparut en personne noble Catherine Lamance, vefve et relictz de feu noble Jean Le nerf, vivant dem[euran]t à Lunéville et elle dem[eurant] pr[ésen]tement à Thonnoy, sienne dame et matresse [*sic*] usant librement de ses droicts de viduité co[mme] elle a dict, et assistée de noble messire François Nerf [*sic*], prestre et curé dudict Thonnoy, honorable homme Estienne Rony demeurant a la Gaillard ad cause de damoiselle Claude Le Nerf et promectant la faire consentir et ratifier le contenu es présentes sy mestier faict tous et quantefois que requis en sera, et de noble George Le Nerf dem[euran]t à Dieuze, iceulx faisant partie des enfans dudict feu le Sieur Jean le Nerf et de ladite Catherine Lamance, qui ont consenty et agreé a ce qui s'enssuitte [*sic*] :
A recogneu et confessé avoir vendu pour toujours en propriété et treffond à hon[ora]ble homme George La Tour bourgeois demeurant à Luneville [...] acquesteur pour luy, Dianne sa femme, leurs hoirs et ayant cause, une maison avec ses usuaires devant et derriere, puis la grange au derrière d'icelle avec le meix au derriere de ladicte maison, le tout scis audict Lunéville, lieudict en la rue S[t]. Jacque, les hoirs de feu Claudin Ferriet d'une part et les héritiers de la vieille recepvesse d'Einville d'autre part ; item encore un preys comme il se contient scis au ban dudict Lunéville, lieudict es preys David, le sieur prevost Maillard d'une part et Claudon bouxart bouchier d'autre part, chargé ledict preys de trois gros de cens chacun an, au reste le tout franc et quicte de toute rente, servitude et obligation quelconque. Le présent vandaige faict pour la somme de deux mil cinq cents francs monnoie lorraine en principal et cent frans au vin avec le coustant des présentes, dont ladicte venderesse s'en a tenu pour contant ; promectant icelle venderesse tenir et avoir pour agréable le présent vandaige et le bonnement garandir audict acquesteur, ses hoirs, etc. Soubs l'obligation de tous ses biens meubles et immeubles présents et advenir par tout etc. In forma... Présents Jean Couta, alias Bourguignon, et Laurent Audieu, demeurant audict Thonnoy, tesmoings..
Pour copie prinsse a son original.

(Nancy, Archives de Meurthe-et-Moselle, 3 E 795)

1624, 23 January: Loan of one hundred francs to Georges de La Tour (Lunéville).

We do not know why exactly La Tour borrowed this money. Could it really have been directly related to the 2,600 francs that La Tour promised to pay his mother-in-law for the property she sold them? What we do know is that La Tour did not bother to free himself from this bond, which remained unredeemed until 1667 when his heirs finally paid the heirs of the parish priest of Roselieure.

Le 23 janvier 1624 honnorable George de la Tour paintre dem[euran]t à Lunéville et damoiselle dianne le nerf sa femme a r[econnu] avoir

vendu et constitué pour toujours jusques au rachapt, au proffict du Sr Natalis curé à Rozelleure absent, stipulant et arrestant pour luy etc. venerable Nicolas Girard, prevost de l'esglise colégialle de Haussonville, curateur estably par monseigneur de Toul, se faisant fort du Sr Gaulthier curé de Frameville son cocurateur, la somme de sept franc de rente annuelle, payable par chacun an au jour de Noël, dont le premier terme de payement sera audit jour prochain venant et ainsi continuant jusques audict réachapt faisant ; en obligeant le dict S^r de La tour pour asseurance de ce par principal abbout ung meix comme il se constitue au ban dudict Lunéville dans l'enclos des rampartz, les dames religieuses d'une part et Jean Cousson chirugien d'autre part, chargé de trois gros de cens à l'abbaye S^t. Remy [...], guallement tous ses autres biens, en les submettant, etc. pour y faire, etc. [...] Est faict ce present vendage et constitution de rente pour la somme de cent francs que ledict S^r. de La Tour a confessé avoir cy-devant receu dudict S^r venerable, dont etc. Promettant iceluy de tenir et avoir etc., de bien payer icelle par chacun an audict jour ou un mois après pour tout delay à peine d'estre contrainct à la restitution du principal, et garandir etc. Est assavoir que iceluy S. de La Tour, etc. en pourront à toujours à leur bonne volonté reachepter lesdicts sept francs de rente en rendant ladicte somme de cent francs auxdict S^r venerable, etc. par mesme jour de Noel [...] Pour meilleure asseurance du tout honorable Estienne Gérard, tabellion demeurant audict Lunéville, se faisant fort de damoiselle Marie Le Nerf, sa femme, s'en est rendu caution principal, et pour ce en oblige ses biens, etc. [...]
Presents Jacques M... le vieil et Jacques M... son fils, dem[euran]t audict Lunéville, tesmoings.

[*in the margin*]
Ce jourd'hui neufième aprvil mil six cent soixante sept la constitution cy de costé a esté rayée par le soubscript gardenotte à Lunéville sur la quittance endossée à la grosse d'icelle, passée par devant N. La Court Tabellion, par Anne Huguet, vefve de Ferry Sibille, dudict Lunéville, comme heritier du feu Sr Natalis, curé de Rozelieure, en datte du premier septembre 1661, tesmoing le seing dudict Gardenotte.
[*signed*] J. Cousson gardenotte.

(Nancy, Archives de Meurthe-et-Moselle, 3 E 727)

1624, 6 February: Georges as godfather on behalf of Jean Berman (Lunéville).

Like the various notarial records, certificates of baptism give us an insight into La Tour's world. Chrétien George appears several times in the records. Claude Berman was the cousin by marriage who had acted as godmother to Claude the year before and for whom La Tour was to act as witness on 16 April; Jean Berman was her brother.

févbrier 1624 – Jean filz de Chrestien George et Nicole sa femme. P. honorable George de Latour au nom de Noble Jean Berman. M. damoiselle Claude Berman. 6

(Lunéville, Archives Municipales)

1624, 16 April: La Tour as witness for one of Jean Berman's sisters (Lunéville).

Jean Berman sold a large estate at Xermamesnil valued at 12,000 francs, and here his sister Claude ratifies the deed drawn up before Étienne Gérard, with La Tour as her witness.

(This follows the agreement signed by Jean Berman)

... Conséquemment le XVIe apvril 1624 Damoiselle Claude Berman cy dessus mentionnée, suffisamment aagée, hors de toutes tutelles et curatelles, néantmoins assistée dudict sieur Berman son frère et du sieur Paul Fabry, substitut de Monsieur le proqureur général de Lorraine à Luneville, de leur advis et consentement icelle damoiselle ayant heu lecture du vendage cy-dessus, elle a recongnu et confessé volontairement sans aucune contraite ou séduction, par lesdits consentement et advis, avoir ratiffié, advoué et corroboré, et par ces présentes ratiffie, advoue et corrobore le contenu audit vendage et veult et desclaire iceluy sortir son plain et entier effet par tout [...] comme si elle même l'avoist passé avec ledit sieur son frère, et a cest effet a promis et promect par cestes la garandie dudit vendage, se tenante pour contante de la somme y portée et contenue, soubs l'obligation expresse de tous ses biens meubles et immeubles présents et futurs. Et de mesme ledit sieur Berman pour asseurance plus grande aux acquesteurs susmentionnés avec ladite garandye a obligé tous ses biens meubles et immeubles, presens et advenir avec iceulx de ladite damoiselle sa sœur.
Le tout fait et passé au lieu de Lunéville en présence d'honorable George de La Tour peintre et maitre Claude Henry, tailleur d'habits, demeurant à Lunéville, tesmoings ad ce requis.
[*signed*] Gérard

(Nancy, Archives de Meurthe-et-Moselle, 3 E 795)

1624, before 31 July: Purchase of an "Image of Saint Peter" by the duke (Nancy).

This is a record of another purchase by the duke, which must have been made before his death in July. This time the subject of the work is specified.

Aultre despence extraordinaire faict par ce Comptable tant pour le faict de sa charge par mandement, comme aultrement durant l'an de ce compte.
(...)
Il est encore en despense la some de cent cinquante frans qu'il a payé a George de la Tour paintre demeurant a Luneville pour un Tableau de l'Image St Pierre que feu S.A. a faict prendre de luy et ordonné a ce Comptable luy payer ladite somme ainsy qu'il appert par son noble mandement... CL fr.

(Nancy, Archives de Meurthe-et-Moselle, B 5374, fol. 145)

1624, 22 July: La Tour as witness for the collector of the Abbey of Beaupré (Lunéville).

This record, of slight interest in itself, was cited but not published by Pariset. It was signed "honorable Demenge Matrin, recepveur général de l'abbaie de Belprey, demeurant à Lunéville" *in the presence of* "Maîtres François" *[sic]* de La Tour peintre demeurant audict Lunéville et Demenge Prevost demeurant à Blainville temoings". *Everything implies that it is Georges who is meant, and that he is simply given his brother's first name by mistake.*

(Nancy, Archives de Meurthe-et-Moselle, 3 E 870)

1624, 1 October: La Tour as witness for the governor of La Neufville-aux-bois (Lunéville).

La Tour was twice present as a witness relating to a loan; the deeds are cited but not published by Pariset.

1625, 11 January: Baptism of Marie, Georges's daughter (Lunéville).

René Gaspar had been governor of the hospital at Lunéville, and the munipal magistrate Didier Clément was one of Pierre Fourier's most loyal friends and supporters.

Janvier 1625.
Marie, fille de Maistre George [*these two words were inserted later into a gap left for the purpose*] de La Tour peintre et Diane sa femme. P[arrain] Monsr Didier Clement m[aît]re eschevin. M[arraine] Dame Halenne femme de René gaspar. 11^e

(Lunéville, Archives Municipales)

1625, 16 March: Georges de La Tour as witness to a sale.

It is not possible to present all the deeds for which La Tour served as witness, generally before the notary Étienne Gérard. They are very often similar to this one.

Le XVIe jour de Mars 1625 Mengin Philletier tanneur demeurant à Lunéville, se faisant fort d'Annet sa femme, a recongnu et confessé etc., avoir vendu à Gille Purion, serurier demeurant à Anville acceptant pour lui, Claudon sa femme, leurs hoirs, etc. une pièce de vigne comme elle se contient lieudit à Rambour, ban dudict Luneville, Philletier boulengier d'une part et Didier Claba d'autre part, encore une autre pièce de vigne audit ban comme elle se contient, lieudit audit Rambour autre part appellé aux sept Journaulx, entre Claudon Forgery le vieil dudit Anville d'une part et Denis Gardon de Ronviller d'autre part, franche et quitte etc. Et est faict ce present vendage pour la somme de deux cent cinquante trois francs huict gros m[onnoie] l[orraine] de principal, et trente francs de vin, dont ledit vendeur s'en est tenu contant etc. Promettant garandir etc. Obligeant etc. In forma. Presents honn^ble homme George de La Tour peintre demeurant à Luneville et honn^ble Nicolas Doyen, soldat, demeurant audit lieu, tesmoings.

[*signed*] Gérard

(Nancy, Archives de Meurthe-et-Moselle, 3 E 795)

1625, 22 August: Diane as godmother (Lunéville).

Georges was not the only one invited to be a godparent: Diane was too, and later their son Étienne and their daughters as well.

Le 22e – Jean fils de Jean poiresson et Parise sa femme. Parain Jean Comman de Mesnil, maraine Diane femme de George de La Tour peintre.

(Lunéville, Archives Municipales)

1625, 27 October: Georges de La Tour as witness for Jean Chamant and Jean Berman (Lunéville).

Here Jean Chamant of Vic, husband of Marie Berman, then deceased, sells Jean Berman, probably his brother-in-law, half of a meix *in Lunéville, part of the property left by Marie to her son, who was then still under guardianship.*

Le XXVIIe octobre 1625 noble Jean Chamant demeurant à Vic, au nom de Jean Chamant son fils, procréé au corps de feu damoiselle Marie Berman vivant sa femme, promectant faire advouer le vendage cy après par le sieur substitut du sieur procureur général de Lorraine à Lunéville et faire ratiffier ledit son filz quand il sera parvenu en aage et qu'il en sera requis, a recongnu et confessé volontairement en ladicte qualité avoir vendu pour tousiours à Noble sieur Jean Berman chappellain episcopalle de Metz et Viguier de Toul et y demeurant, acquesteur pour luy ses ayans cause, la moictié par indivis d'un meix situé en la ville fermée de Lunéville appelé le meix du mollin, entre Jean Thibesme et Lazar Lhuillier d'une part et les heritiers feu Jean Gerard d'autre part, frappant des deux poinctes sur les chemins et usuaires de ville, (franche *barré*) parmy les charges anciennes et accoustumées, au reste franc et quite de toutes autres charges, hipothèques et obligations. Et est faict ce present vendage pour la somme de deux cent francs monoye lorraine pour principal, dont ledict vendeur audict nom s'en a tenu contant, promettant de tenir etc. garandir etc. obligeant tous ses biens etc. In forma meliory. Presents hon[ora]ble George de La Tour peintre demeurant à Lunéville et le sieur Jean Nicolas de Ramberviller, demeurant audict Vic, tesmoings.

[*signed*] Gérard

(Nancy, Archives de Meurthe-et-Moselle, 3 E 795)

1626: The episode of the grain for the poor (Lunéville).

A great deal has been written about these few lines. Pariset misread "la serrure du sieur La Tour" for "du grenier La Tour," and "les grains estant audit sieur" instead of "audit grenier." As a result, people were led to believe that La Tour was an unscrupulous hoarder, buying up grain when it was cheap to sell at a profit when it was scarce (the record is not dated, but seems to relate to the beginning of June), and that the town had to use force to make him yield.

The actual text is considerably less specific. To make any sense of it we need to read it in conjunction with another record cited by Pariset (1948, p. 46) for the same year: . . . This time the wood clearly belongs to the commune. Is it not likely that La Tour rented one of his two meix *to the town? If this were not the case, La Tour would have been compensated for giving up his grain, even if he had been forced to do so, and there would be some reference to this in the accounts. In the absence of any such reference, it is difficult to come to any final interpretation of this too ambiguous passage.*

Encore despence en deniers
Payé a ung serurier de Luneville ung gros huict deniers pour avoir arraché la serrure du grenier La Tour, peintre pour faire livrer les grains estant audit grenier aux pauvres, et pour avoir fourny ung cadenet. Icy... I gr. VIII d.

(Lunéville, Archives Municipales, CC 5, fol. 229 [12])

1626, 7 March: Georges as godfather (Lunéville).

Claude Ely was a master mason who worked on many of the buildings in Lunéville, notably the ducal château and the church. He appears also to have been related to René Gaspar (see baptism of Marie, 2 January 1625).

Mars. le 7e. George fils de Claude Ely tailleur de pierre et Heillouix sa femme. Parain George de La tour peintre. Maraine Anne femme de Dominic Harman serrurier.

(Lunéville, Archives Municipales)

1626, 6 May: Georges as witness to the marriage contract between Étienne Gérard's daughter, Catherine, and Nicolas Bouillon, master of the duke's harbingers (Lunéville).

La Tour's cousin by marriage made a brilliant match. The friends and relatives listed at the head of the contract represent pretty much the élite—markedly different from the "old nobility"—of which La Tour now seems to have been a part.

Du sixième may 1626
Pour parvenir au mariage futur et espéré à faire si Dieu et notre mère sainte Eglise s'y accordent par et entre le sieur Nicolas Bouillon, maitre des fourriers de monseigneur le duc, jeune fils, présent iceluy assisté de Noble Francois du Tr..., controlleur en l'estat de mondit seigneur, du S^r. Daniel Coppyet tabellion et substitut général en la prevosté de Prugny ses oncles, iceulx munis de procuration sur eux passée par

damoiselle Elisabeth Noel mère audit sieur Bouillon apparues en datte du jourd'hui signée J. Cardinal, insérée à la fin des presentes, de nobles Francois Coltier admodiateur a Haussonville son beau frère et maître Claude (...), licencié en droict et advocat a Nancy, son bon ami, d'une part ; et damoiselle Catherine Gerard, jeune fille, assistée du Sieur Estienne Gérard tabellion et (...) de Luneville, son père, de vénérable et discrette personne messire Nicolas Gerard bachelier en teologie et prévost de l'église colégialle, Monsieur Saint Claude dudit Haussonville son frère, de Noble Daniel le Nerf son oncle, du sieur Louys de Ramberviller gruyer, sieur de Pulgny, Sainctrey et Voinemont en partie, et du sieur George de la Tour ses coussins, demeurant audit Luneville d'une part, sont esté passés, promis et accordez les points et articles cy après (*this is followed by the usual clauses covering joint estate and the rules on the division of the estate in the event of the death of either spouse and the settlement of debts; the record was not signed by either party*).

(Nancy, Archives de Meurthe-et-Moselle, 3 E 728)

1626, 12 June: Apprenticeship contract of Charles Roynet (Lunéville).

This contract is unusually brief. It does not specify whether La Tour is to house the apprentice, although the sum agreed upon for the three years is relatively high.

Le XIIe Jour de Juing 1626 au lieu de Lunéville sont comparus personnes honnorables George de La Tour peintre demeurant a Luneville d'une part, et honnorable Philippe Roynet bourgeois de Remyremont d'autre part, entre lesquels ont esté faicts les marchés et conventions qui ensuyvent. C'est assçavoir que ledit Sr de La Tour a promis et promect par cestes de monstrer et instruire fidellement et diligemment l'art de peinture a Charles fils dudit Sr par l'espace de trois annees qui ont ja commencé au Jour de Noel dernier et finissant au pareil Jour, pendant lesquels ledit Sr de La Tour est obligé de le nourrir et entretenir de la bouche seulement, et luy fournir des couleurs requises a cest art. Et en consideration de ce ledit Sr a promis et promet luy payer, rendre et delivrer la somme de cinq cents frans aux termes suyvants, sçavoir deux cent francs dite monnoye a l'entrée et les autres trois cent francs par chacun jour de Noel mesme somme de cent francs. Et ainsi l'ont ils promis et promettent, soubz l'obligation respective de tous leurs biens etc. Les submettans etc. Reconnoissant etc. In forma. Présents Noël Chéz (...) demeurant à Lunéville et Honorable René Gaspard demeurant audit lieu tesmoings.

[*Added at the bottom*] Item est aussi accordé entre lesdites parties qu'arrivant que ledit Charles s'absente sans subiect ledit Sr Roynet est obligé de payer ladite somme en entier.

(Nancy, Archives de Meurthe-et-Moselle, 3 E 795)

1626, 21 June: Baptism of Christine, Georges's daughter (Lunéville).

The Anne Le Nerf here must be Diane's sister, born in 1581 and married first to Claude Nardoyen.

Chrétien de Nogent married Louise de Xaubourel, granddaughter of Diane de Beaufort. We know from a record of 1641 (see below) that he liked Georges de La Tour's painting.

Juin – Cristine, fille de Jean [*sic*] de La Tour et Diane sa femme, le 21e. Parain le Sr Crestien de Nogent gentilhomme de S[on] A[ltesse]. Maraine Anne Le Nerf.

(Lunéville, Archives Municipales)

1627, 2 July: Georges as godfather (Lunéville).

Gaspard Billery or Bellery was a master mason who worked on many of the buildings in Lunéville. It is not known whether Joseph Tiriet was related in any way to the Thiriet family, and more particularly to the municipal magistrate Théodore Thiriet, with whom La Tour was closely involved.

Juillet – Marie, fille de Gaspard Billery et Claudon sa femme, de Luneville, ce 2[e] Juillet. Le Parain le S[r] George de Latour paintre dem[euran]t a Luneville. La Maraine Marie femme a Josef Tiriet.

(Lunéville, Archives Municipales)

1627, 22 September: Diane as godmother to Nicolas Bouillon in the parish of Saint-Epvre in Nancy (Nancy).

This record is cited by Reinbold (1991, p. 204). Nicolas Bouillon was the son of Nicolas Bouillon and Catherine Gérard (see 6 May 1626).

(Nancy, Archives Municipales, GG 84, Parish of Saint-Epvre, fol. 383v)

1628, 11 January: Georges as godfather (Lunéville).

This is further evidence of La Tour's good relations with the leading citizens of Lunéville.

Claude fille du sieur Demenge Mougenot procureur et de Claude sa femme. Le 11e. Le parain le Sr Henri [*sic*] de La Tour peintre et la maraine dame Phelippe vefve de feu Bastien Cognard.

(Lunéville, Archives Municipales)

1628, 14 February: Settlement of an annuity by Georges de La Tour.

Georges and Diane settled an annuity of 17-1/2 francs, against a capital sum of 250 francs, on the Abbey Saint-Rémy at Lunéville, with their house as guarantee.

The money the monks invested in this way came from the redemption of an earlier annuity, against a capital sum of 240 francs, settled on Saint-Rémy by "sieur Chauvenel de Saint-Nicolas," and the capital sum was rounded off to 250 francs by the prior. It is difficult to say whether La Tour saw this as a good way of obtaining some cash to invest, or whether he was simply helping the abbey, which was anxious to invest its capital wisely and could be sure of his ability to meet his payments.

The interest of this document lies elsewhere, however. It was brought to public attention by Pariset, who does not appear to have deciphered it from beginning to end or to have understood what it was about. An over-hasty reading of a note in the margin led him to endow La Tour's house with the name "La Licorne." In fact it was Chauvenel's house that was so named. It seemed like a poetic twist of fate that Georges and Diane should live in a house called "The Unicorn," and nobody bothered to check the text. Sadly, this is a fiction we have to abandon.

Le XIIIIe jour de febvrier 1628 honnorable George de La Tour peintre demeurant à Luneville et Dianne Le Nerf sa femme, a ce présente licenciée quand a ce faire, laquelle licence elle a receue aggréée et eue, ont recongneu etc. avoir vendu constitué et assigné jusques au rachapt aux sieurs Reverands pères religieux et profes de l'abbaye Monseigneur Saint Remy audit Lunéville, acceptant par Reverand père Jean Petitjean, prieur en ladite abbaye, pour eulx, leurs successeurs religieux et ayant causes, la somme de dix sept francs et demy de rente annuelle jusques audit rachapt, assise et assignée pour les avoir prendre et tenir par chacun an [*in the margin*: au terme purification

notre dame dicte la Chandelleur] sur une maison grange estable et herbier au derriere d'icelle la totalité, entre Demenge Mengenot procureur audit Luneville d'une part, et George Bocquenomme d'autre part, frappant sur la rue devant l'eglise St Jacques du devant, et du derrière sur la rue dicte derrière ledit St Jacques. Dont le premier terme de payement de ladite rente sera et commencera audit jour de feste purification prochaine que l'on dira 1629, et ainsi continant d'an en an et de terme en autre sans aulcun deffault. Et est faict ce présent vendage et constitution de rente pour la somme de deux cent cinquante francs monnoye lorraine [*en marge*: que lesdits vendeurs ont receue dont ils se tiennent contens], laquelle provient du réachapt d'une autre constitution faict par le sieur Chauvenel de St Nicolas et montant en son principalle a deux cent quarante francs*, a laquelle ledit sieur prieur a adjousté dix francs pour faire ladite somme de deux cent cinquante francs, promettans lesdits vendeurs de bien payer ladite rente par chacun an audit terme sans aulcun deffault [...] soubs l'obligation expresse de tous leurs aultres biens meubles et immeubles presens et advenir partout [...]
[*In the margin*]
* assignée sur sa maison appellée vulgairement de la Licorne ou ledit sieur est domicilié, icelle rente dependant de la chappelle Notre-Dame de pitié erigée en ladite eglise S^t. Remy.

(Nancy, Archives de Meurthe-et-Moselle, 3 E 795)

1628, 24 February: Reference to La Tour's studio.

This extract from a letter from Pierre Fourier at Pont-à-Mousson to Fathers Guinet and Lemulier then on a mission to Rome can only be about one of La Tour's apprentices. Is the boy in question Claude Baccarat, who made his profession with the monks of Saint-Sauveur on 7 October 1630?

... un jeune garçon qui se mêle de peindre et apprenoit jadis à Lunéville, d'où il est natif et d'honnêtes parens, chez le peintre de là avec le fils de M. le Maître Echevin (...) Il n'est pas ouvrier parfait, ny tel que l'on puisse se servir de ses tableaux, et nonobstant qu'il soit âgé de vingt ans, il a le corps petit et fort grêle et sans beaucoup de force, ce semble, pour faire autres ouvrages. Ledit Père ajoute qu'il pourroit enseigner l'arithmétique aux enfans ; aussy en a-t-il vu quelques règles.

(Saint Pierre Fourier, *Correspondance, vol. II, p. 551 ; letter of 24 February*)

1628, 2 May: La Tour as witness for Jacques Triplot (Lunéville).

This is a document cited but not published by Pariset (1948, p. 48). According to Reinbold (1991, p. 204), the nobleman Jacques Triplot was one of the Thirteen at the court of Metz, and his mother, Barbe Dodot, widow of the nobleman Jean Triplot, council member in the bailiwick of Vic, lived in Lunéville.

(Nancy, Archives de Meurthe-et-Moselle, 3 E 795)

1628, 6 July: Georges as godfather (Lunéville).

Noël Chés has yet to be identified.

Elizabeth, fille de Noël Chés et Alizon sa femme. Le 6e. Le parain le Sr George la tour peintre et la maraine Elizabeth fille du Sr Gerard jadis receveur de Turquestain.

(Lunéville, Archives Municipales)

1628, 7 October: Baptism of Louis, Georges's son (Lunéville).

The godfather, Louis de Rambervillers, son of Alphonse, was still based in Vic; the godmother, "Demoiselle Lucie," was Diane's older sister.

Octobre – Louïs, fils du Sr George La Tour peintre et dame Diane sa femme nacquit le 5e et fut baptizé le 7e. Le parain noble Louis de Ramberviller dem[euran]t a Vic et la maraine Damoiselle Lucie fille de Noble Jean Le nerf, de ce lieu.

(Lunéville, Archives Municipales)

1629, 7 November: Georges de La Tour as witness for Louis de Rambervillers (Lunéville).

Louis de Rambervillers sold a house and meadow; La Tour and Chrétien George acted as witnesses to the deed of sale, cited by Pariset (1948, p. 50).

(Nancy, Archives de Meurthe-et-Moselle, 3 E 871)

1629, 25 December: La Tour as witness for Nicolas Gérard (Lunéville).

This is a document cited but not published by Pariset (1948, p. 50). Together with Father Petitjean, by then parish priest of Lunéville, La Tour witnessed the will that Nicolas Gérard, one of Étienne Gérard's sons, made on his sickbed. Nicolas Gérard died shortly afterward. La Tour's signature, surname only, but in a firm and steady hand is the main interest of the document.

(Nancy, Archives de Meurthe-et-Moselle, 3 E 722)

1629: Fine imposed on Georges de La Tour for not removing rubbish.

This document gives us an insight into daily life, but we should beware of reading too much into it.

Amandes d'immundices
Chacun bourgeois qui faict et laisse des immundices devant sa maison, et son usuaire, est obligé de les faire aussytost oster à peine de dix sols d'amande pour chacune fois estant rapporté et y ayant plaincte, et ceulx et celles qui en portent sur les usuaires d'aultruy de cinq francs à partager entre le sieur prévost pour un tier, un autre à la Ville, et l'autre tier au rapporteur, pouvantes touttes personnes en faire rapport. Dont pour l'an de ce compte s'ensuivent ceulx qui ont esté rapportez d'en avoir tenu sur leurs usuaires seulement

Demenge Dron	VII gr. VIII d.
Le fournier de la rue Gargault	VII gr. VIII d.
Le sieur George de La Tour	VII gr. VIII d.
Le fournier de la porte St Jacques	VII gr. VIII d.
Le vefve du sieur Mougenot	VII gr. VIII d.

(Lunéville, Archives Municipales, CC 5, 1629, fol. 5)

1630, 21 January: Diane as godmother to Jeanne Cousson (Lunéville).

Jeanne was the daughter of the public prosecutor Jean Cousson, one of the leading citizens denounced with La Tour in the petition of 1646; the godfather was Jean de Villaucourt, who held the important position of forest warden in Lunéville, and was related by marriage to the Callot and Rambervillers families.

(Lunéville, Archives Municipales)

1630, 4 August: Baptism of Nicolas Georges, son of Georges de La Tour (Lunéville).

Here again we come across Nicolas Bouillon and the family of Étienne Gérard, all very much part of the Le Nerf family circle. La Tour must have been quite set on having the duke's harbinger there to have delayed the baptism for several days.

Aoust. Nicolas George fils du Sr George La Tour peintre et de dame Diane sa femme, nacquit le 30e de juillet et fut baptizé le 4e d'aoust. Le parain le Sr Nicolas Bouillon fourier de monseigneur le duc François, et la maraine Elizabeth fille du Sr Estienne Gerard, de ce lieu.

(Lunéville, Archives Municipales)

1630, 19 November: Fine imposed on Georges de La Tour for failing to do guard duty (Lunéville).

La Tour incurred this fine for refusing to take his turn at guarding the gates and walls: he must have been among those who claimed "exemption from guard duty." This record was cited by Pariset (1948, p. 51).

(Lunéville, Archives Municipales, CC 5, fol. 12v)

1631, 11 February: Georges de La Tour as witness (Lunéville).

This deed was drawn up before the notary Gérard. Although he signed it, the document is not in his writing. The magnificent hand is not that of Jean Du Parc either, but looks remarkably like that of the third signatory, La Tour. Pariset believed the document to be written by La Tour.

L'onzième jour de febvrier 1631 au lieu de Lunéville environ les dix heures du matin, Jean des bois demeurant à Mesnil, se faisant fort de Marguerite sa femme, a recognu debvoir à jean Haumant demeurant à Lunéville, créditeur pour luy, Claudon sa femme, leurs hoirs, etc. la somme de vingt quatre francs pour cause de grain et de bon compte fait par ensemble sans préjudice d'autres obligations cy devant passée qui demeure en leur force, laquelle somme de vingt quatre francs il a promis payer dans le jour de feste S[t]. Martin prochainement venant avec la rente au taxé de S. Altesse, et si crédit luy est fait davantage il payerera ladite rente au prorata du temps sans préjudice neanmoins de luy faire payer ladite somme audit terme ; obligant etc. submettant etc. renonçant à garand etc. In forma. Present honorable George de La Tour peintre et Messire Jean du Parc tous deux demeurant à Luneville.
[*Signed*] Jean du Parque La Tour Gérard

(Nancy, Archives de Meurthe-et-Moselle, 3 E 795)

1631, 18 February: Georges de La Tour as witness (Lunéville).

The nobleman Claude Aubertin was an influential figure: Pariset tells us that at the time of his death in 1635 he held the office of governor and representative of the town.

Le 18 fébvrier 1631 Claude Claudinet courdonnier demeurant à Lunéville, se f[aisant fort] de francoyse sa femme, a congneu debvoir à noble Claude Aulbertin demeurant auditlieu, acceptant pour luy, dame Zabillon sa femme etc., la somme de quarante deux francs pour grains à lui vendu et délivré, dont etc. a payer au jour de S[t]. Remy prochain, en obligeant ses biens, etc. les submettant, etc. Renonçant, etc. Présent le Sr George de La tour peinctre demeurant à Lunéville et Colin Maire demeurant à Baptselemont tesmoings ; à huict du matin.
[*Signed*] La Tour

(Lunéville, Archives de Meurthe-et-Moselle, 3 E 730, fol. 44)

1631, 5 March: Georges de La Tour as witness (Lunéville).

Here again we have an illustration of the intricate family relations typical of a small town.

Le ve Mars 1631 a Lunéville sur trois heures de relevée Nicolas Perin le vieil (...), pour aider et subvenir à la necessité des enffants naiz aux mariages de Jean Perin son fils, dudit Luneville, avec Catherine Montfort et Catherine Jacquet ses deux premières femmes, iceulx au nombre de six et de chacun des licts trois, et a ceulx de Jacques Sellier et Marie fille dudict recognoissant, en nombre de trois, et à ceux de Nicolas Montfort de Viller et de feue Marie aussi fille dudit recognoissant, aussy au nombre de sept, il leur a donné par bonne et irrévocable donnation faite entre vifs pour eulx chacun par thiers de ces trois mariages [...] la somme de dix huict cents francs monnoie de Lorraine, qui est pour chacun des trois [...] la somme de six cents francs partageables [...]
Présents le s[r] Estienne Gerard tabellion et le s[r] George de La Tour peintre, demeurants audit Luneville, tesmoings.
[*Signed*] E. Gerard Latour J. Cousson
[at end of doc.]
La Tour also signed the following deed by which this same Nicolas Perrin made a special gift of two hundred francs to his granddaughter Marguerite, his son's daughter by his first marriage.

(Nancy, Archives de Meurthe-et-Moselle, 3 E 781, fol. 14v)

1632, 21 January: Confirmation of an annuity by Georges and his wife (Lunéville).

This deed was discovered by Canon Choux in a bundle of old papers relating to the district of Lunéville. It concerns a loan of one hundred francs made to Jean Le Nerf in 1614 in return for an annuity. By a succession of legacies and transfers, liability for the loan came down to La Tour and his wife, and the title to the money to a notary in Lunéville. The latter demanded that the annuity be redeemed, which La Tour promised to do within three years. However, this was followed only by a legal detour to prove title. The debt was not discharged until October 1654, when the money was eventually paid by Étienne La Tour to the notary's widow. A copy of the deed was drawn up at that time, with a receipt on the back for the one hundred francs paid by Étienne. This copy has come down to us, and through it we have been able to trace the original in the departmental archives, which was crossed out in April 1667 and bears one of the finest of La Tour's signatures.

Du XXI janvier 1632. Environ deux heures apres midy.
Comme ainsy soit que Noble Jean le Nerf, vivant demeurant à Lunéville, ait le seizieme d'Aoust mil six cent et quatorze, par devant J. Guerin, passé obligation de cent francs au profict des enfants du feu sieur Joseph Serrier, vivant demeurant audit lieu, et que le sieur George de la Tour peintre demeurant audit Lunéville, beau filz audit fut sieur le Nerf, auroit tousiours paié l'interest depuis la mort d'iceluÿ comme il a dict, laquelle obligation estante venue a la part de Noble Francois Feriet, Trilleur aux Sallines de Moyenvic, comme marit de l'une des filles dudit fut sieur Serrier, en auroit faict transport à Thirion Parterre tabellion demeurant audit Lunéville, ainsy qu'il en a faict apparoir audict sieur de la Tour qui a l'instant s'est tenu pour signiffié dudict transport, surquoy, luy Parterre l'ayant interpellé au payement dedicts cens francs, luy a dict de l'attendre encore quelque temps en paiant tousjours l'interest comme du passé, a quoy il a condescendu et sans innover a ladicte obligation ; est-il que comparans par devant le tabellion soubscript et tesmoings cy aubas dénommez ledit sieur de la Tour et damoiselle Dianne Le Nerf sa femme de luy licenciée, laquelle licence elle a receue et eue aggreablement, lesquels ont declairé qu'ils se sont chargez et chargent, tant pour eux que leurs frères et sœurs héritiers dudict feu S[r]Le Nerf, de paÿer ladicte debte audict Parterre dans trois ans à prendre dès le seizieme d'Aoust dernier, toute rente satisfaite et acquictées du paravant jusques audict jour. Et si tant est que credist leur soit faict plus longtemps, ils en paieront la rente au prorata du temps, le tout sans préjudice de ladicte novation. Soubs l'obligation de tous leurs biens... (*this is followed by the usual legal phrases*).

[*On the copy*:]
Que furent faictes et passées pardevant E. Gérard vivant Tabellion le Vingt Unième janvier mil six cent trente deux, environ deux heures après midy, présent maistre Jean du parque menuisier et Mengin Babel courdonnier demeurant à Lunéville qui n'a l'usage d'ecrire, tesmoins.
Jean du parque E. Gérard George de La Tour

(Nancy, Archives de Meurthe-et-Moselle, 3 E, liasse)

1632, last day of February: Baptism of André Georges, son of Georges (Lunéville).

André Doyen was steward to Mgr de Gorze in Lunéville, and his father was an officer of the cardinal of Lorraine in Blainville-sur-l'Eau. Jacques de Mory, described here as an apothecary, seems to be the Lunéville nobleman exempted from guard duty in 1630 and related to the La Tour family through the marriage of Daniel Le Nerf to Marthe de Mory.

André George, filz du Sr George de La Tour et Diane sa femme, le dernier febvrier. Pour parrain Noble André Doyen et pour marraine, Claude femme du Sr Jacques Mory Apothecaire.

(Lunéville, Archives Municipales)

1632, 17 April: La Tour as proxy for his brother-in-law François Le Nerf (Lunéville).

This document relates to the restoration of the Sainte-Barbe chapel in Einville, the chaplain of which was François le Nerf, La Tour's brother-in-law and parish priest of Tonnoy. The restoration work prompted a string of documents bearing La Tour's signature: 17 April 1632, 28 July 1632, 16 February 1633.

(Nancy, Archives de Meurthe-et-Moselle, 3 E 730 and 3 E 876)

1632, 22 August: La Tour as witness to Elisabeth Gérard's marriage contract.

Elisabeth Gérard married François Vaultrin, the son of a master gold- and silversmith of Nancy. As we have seen, she became godmother to one of George and Diane de La Tour's children, Nicolas-Georges, on 4 August 1630. She had a dowry of 1,400 francs, and in addition to La Tour the contract was witnessed, among others, by Nicolas Bouillon and Chrétien de Nogent.

(Nancy, Archives de Meurthe-et-Moselle, 3 E 722)

III

THE TROUBLED YEARS
1634–1640

1634, 5 February: Baptism of Madeleine, Georges's daughter (Lunéville).

Forest warden Jean de Villaucourt was a prominent figure in Lunéville (see under 21 January 1630). We have no further information concerning the identity of Nicolas Chevalier.

Magdeleine, fille du Sr George La Tour et Dianne sa femme. le 5e. Par. Noble et p[uissan]t Jean de Villaucourt gruyer. Mar. Damoiselle Magdeleine fille du Sr Nicolas Chevalier.

(Lunéville, Archives Municipales)

1634: Georges as guardian to the Nardoyen children (Lunéville).

After the death of her first husband, Claude Nardoyen, Anne Le Nerf, Diane's sister, married Jean Maire, the tenant farmer of Nouveaulieu. La Tour was appointed guardian of her two sons, Antoine and François Nardoyen, by the courts on 23 April 1631. The question of their inheritance was complicated by the deaths of their grandmother, Catherine Lamance, and of their uncle the parish priest, and generated quantities of documents, of limited interest in themselves, but useful in helping us to chart La Tour's movements. We have only reproduced a few in this book, and those for 1634 are assembled here.

1634, 10 May: Lawsuit over the estate of Catherine Lamance.

Du dixième May 1634 a Thonnoy sur les sept heures du matin.
(...) presents Mathias Weistroff Ch[ate]llain de fauquemont, se portant fort des enfans de feu damoiselle Marie le Nerfz vivante vefve du feu s[ieu]r Bernard Maillard vivant receveur a dalem, Claude Peltre clerc juré dem[eurant] a Bures, au nom et comme tuteur establj a Paul et Jeanne le Nerfz enfans mineurs de feu Noble George Le Nerfz vivant admodiateur a Biedestroff, se portant fort de dam[oiselle] Catherine le Nerfz sa belle mere vefve de feu Henry Stoique vivant dem[eurant] a Avricourt, George de la Tour peintre dem[eurant] a Luneville et dam[oiselle] deanne le Nerfz sa femme, estant led[it] s[ieu]r De la Tour tuteur d'Anthoine et francois les Nardouins, enfans mineurs du premier mariage de feu dam[ois]elle Anne le Nerfz avec feu Noble Claude Nardouin, Pierre Maire greffier des terres et seigneur de hombourg et St Avold a cause de dam[oiselle] Anne Nardouin sa femme et se portant fort de Nicolas Maire son fils mineur d'ans, tous heritiers de feu Noble et venerable personne Messire francois Le Nerfz vivant licencé en Theologie et Curé de ferrieres et Thonnoy (...) Ilz ont faict, créé, nommé, constitué et establi pour leurs procureurs g[é]n[ér]aux et speciaulx C'est ascavoir lesd[its] sieurs George de la Tour, Mathias Weistroff, & Pierre Maire (...) [pour] assumer poursuivre et soliciter la vuidange d'un proces intenté tant par le[dit] feu s[ieu]r Curé leur beau fils et oncle, que par lesd[its] constituans et coheritiers en la succession de feu damoiselle Catherine Lamance vivante femme a feu Noble Jean Le Nerfz dem[eurant] a Luneville contre les sieurs heritiers du feu sieur Gaillard vivant Ch[ate]llain a Albestroff et damoiselle dianne de Beaufort son espouse, auparavant vefve du feu s[ieu]r de Saulcerotte, au sujet de la réintégrande par lesd[it]s pretendants en la moictié d'une maison et gagnage de jambrot et de trois anciens gagnages provenans du propre & ancien de ladite dam[oiselle] Catherine Lamance, l'un soit au ban de Vic, un autre au ban de Juvrecourt et la troisieme au ban de Burthecourt (...) passé aud[it] Thonnoy le jour dixieme May mil six centz trente quatre. En p[rese]nce de francois Thirion et Nicolas Bourlet dem[eurant] aud[it] Thonnoy tesm[oings].
Les sieurs Constituans ont recognu av[oir] passé procura[ti]on avec pouvoir de substitution sur la personne de Claudin Genot Mayeur a Thonnoy (...)
[*signed*] Estienne de Rony
Claude le nerfz
George de La Tour
diane le nerf M. Weystroff
C. Peltre P. Maire

(Nancy, Archives de Meurthe-et-Moselle, 3 E 3108, fol. 36)

1634, 10 May: Joint gift to Claude de Ronny.

Du dixième May 1634 a Thonnoy sur les dix heures du matin.
Comparurent personnellement seign[eu]r Mathias Weistroff Chastelain a faulquemon, tant en son nom que se portant fort de ses coheritiers enfans de feu damoiselle Marie le Nerfz, Claude Peltre Clerc juré a Bures tant du chef de damoiselle Catherine Le Nerfz de laquelle il s'est porté fort, que comme tuteur de Paul et Jeanne enfans mineurs de feu Noble George le Nerfz, George de la Tour et dam[ois]elle dianne Le Nerfz sa femme dem[euran]tz a Luneville tant du chef de lad[ite] dam[ois]elle que comme estant led[it] sieur de la Tour tuteur establj a Anthoine et francois les Nardouins enfans du premier mariage de damoiselle Anne le Nerfz, Pierre Maire greffier de St Avold tant du chef de dam[ois]elle Catherine Nardoien sa femme que se portant fort de Nicolas Maire son beau frere, tous heritiers de feu Noble et vennerable personne Messire francois le Nerfz vivant curé de Thonnoy, ont recognu volontairement quilz ont ceddé renoncé et transporté pour tousiours a Claude de Ronny jeune fille demeurant aud[it] Thonnoy a ce p[rese]nte et acceptant pour elle ses hoirs et ajant cause leur part de contengente en une somme de deux cents frans que le sieur Estienne de Ronny son pere doibt a la succession dud[it] feu s[ieu]r Curé par obliga[ti]on passée par devant J. Curty [*en marge*: le sixi[em]e May 1626 au proffict du sieur Jean Maire et à luj paié par led[it] feu s[ieu]r Curé ainsy quilz ont dit, et laquelle obliga[ti]on] quilz ont consenty estre deboursés a lad[ite] acceptante pour luj valloir et servir co[mm]e de ra[is]on, et est faict ce present transport cession et renoncia[ti]on en recompense des bons et aggreables services que lad[ite] Claude a heu rendu aud[it] feu s[ieu]r Curé son oncle pendant le temps quelle a residé avec luj. Promettant de tenir et garandir de leurs faictz et promesses et non plus avant, Soubz l'obliga[ti]on de tous leurs biens etc. In forma. passé en p[rese]nce de Claudin Genot Mayeur Messire Germain Cunin vicaire de ferrieres tesmoings.
[*signatures*] George de la tour
M. Weystroff
P. Maire Germain Cunin tesmoing
C. Genot C. Peltre

(Nancy, Archives de Meurthe-et-Moselle, 3 E 3108, fol. 31)

1634, 10 May: Lawsuit over the estate of the parish priest François Le Nerf.

Ce jourd'huy dixieme May Mil six cents trente quatre au lieu de Thonnoy sur les dix heures du matin, Claude Peltre N[otai]re juré a Bures au nom et comme Tuteur establj par le s[ieu]r Procureur general de Lorraine a Paul et Jeanne Le Nerfz enfans mineurs de feu Noble George Le Nerfz vivant demeurant a Biederstroff, addressant ses parolles aux sieurs Estienne de Ronny, George de La Tour, Mathias Weistroff, Pierre Maire, et aux damoiselles femmes desd[its] sieurs de Ronny et de La Tour comme aussy a Claude le Nerfz jeune fille, heritiers de feu Noble et venerable personne Messire francois le Nerfz lors qu'il vivoit curé de Ferrieres et Thonnoy, leur a declaré quil est obligé a l'acquit de sa charge de les interpeller comme il faict, de prester serment avec tous ceulx qui ont hanté et frequenté en la maison mortuaire dud[it] feu s[ieu]r curé tant auparavant qu'appres son deces, et declarer s'ilz ont distraict ou faict distraire quelque chose provenante de la succession dud[it] feu s[ieu]r Curé, en tant quilz en auroient distraict ou faict distraire directement ou indirectement, le repre[se]nter et remettre pour estre partagé entre sesd[its] heritiers a la conserva[ti]on du droit desd[its] mineurs, lesquelz sieurs de Ronny, de La Tour, les damoiselles leurs femmes et lad[its] Claude, ont declaré ne defferer de prester led[it] serment, mais qu'ilz ny veulent saisf[air]e quant a present et jusque a ce que tous leurs au[tr]es coheritiers qui ont hanté et frequenté en lad[ite] maison viennent et se representent pour conjoinctement avec eulx prester led[it] serment ainsy quilz y sont obligés, s'offrant allors de le prester avec eulx. Et a l'esgard desd[its] sieurs Weistroff et Maire, Ilz ont offert led[it] serment et le presté a linstant entre les mains de Claudin Genot Mayeur aud[it] Thonnoy, et soustenu par iceluj n'avoir distraict ni faict distraire par au[tr]es, et a l'instant comparant Demenge Bouchier, Idatte Pierron et Anne du Chastel domestiques et servantes dud[it] feu s[ieu]r Curé ont presté mesme serment et soustenu n'avoir prins ni distraict aulcune chose de lad[ite] succession, Comme aussy ont faict en mesme temps lesd[its] sieurs de Ronny, lad[ite] damoiselle se femme, le s[ieu]r Jean de Ronny filz et la femme dud[i]t s[ieu]r de la Tour, avec led[it] Peltre pour son chef par protesta[ti]on que led[it] Peltre a faict de contraindre a prester pareil serment tous ceulx qu'il appartiendra. Et de quoy led[it] tuteur ayant demandé acte au tabellion soubscript luj en a esté octrojé le present, saulf tous droictz (...)

(Nancy, Archives de Meurthe-et-Moselle, 3 E 3108, fol. 35)

1634, 31 May: Investment of the sum of two hundred francs.

In this two-part document Georges de La Tour appears first as witness for Pierre de Leschassier and his wife, then as guardian of the Nardoyen children, anxious therefore to invest their their inheritance as profitably as possible.

Le dernier jour de May 1634, environ dix heures du matin, le sieur Pierre de Leschassier, escuyer, sieur de Vertpres et de Fes en partie, demeurant à Enville, et damoiselle Chrestienne d'Enville sa femme, ont r[recognu] avoir faict, nommé, constitué, créé et estably et par ces présentes etc. pour leurs procureurs generaulx et spéciaux, asscavoir le sieur Paris procureur à Bruyeres [*a line is left blank*] ausquels procureurs par chacun d'iceuls r[recognus] lesdicts sieur et damoiselle constituans ont donné et donnent plain pouvoir et mandement de comparaistre etc. partout etc. [*this is followed by the standard legal short forms*] soubs l'obligation etc. Presens le sieur George de La Tour et Claudon Harmant demeurant audit Luneville, tesmoings
[*Signed*] Deverpred Christinne denville
Colin George de La tour

Le mesme jour et heure à Luneville, le sieur Pierre de Leschassier, escuyer, sieur de Vertpres et de Fes en partie, demeurant a Enville [*in the margin:*] et damoiselle Chrétienne d'Enville sa femme] ont r[ecognu] debvoir aux enfans pupils de feu noble Claude Nardouin vivant dem[euran]t au Nouveaulieu, absens et stjpulant pour eulx etc. par le sieur George de La Tour dem[euran]t a Lunéville leur tuteur, la somme de deux centz francs pour cause de pareille somme a luy prestée et délivrée, dont etc., à paier d'huy en un an ladite dette etc. et à continuer etc. sans etc. obligeant etc. qu'ils ont submis etc. renonçant a garands etc. Presens Claudon Harmant et Claudon Pienat demeurant audit Luneville tesmoings, qui ont dict ne sçavoir escrire
[*Signed*] Colin Devertpred Christinn denville

(Nancy, Archives de Meurthe-et-Moselle, 3 E 775, fols. 197rv)

1634, 18 November: Extension granted by La Tour for the repayment of a loan.

This is typical of the countless transactions that arose from the business of settling annuities. It is even possible that La Tour's purpose in going through this procedure was not actually to obtain repayment of the capital, but simply to secure formal recognition of his possession of title to this bond that he had inherited, together with a guarantor.

Du dix huictieme Novembre 1634 a Thonnoy sur les huict heures du matin. Comme il soit que francois Laurent Rouyer demeurant a Thonnoy se soit trouvé redebvable a la succession de feu Noble et venerable personne Messire francois le Nerfz, vivant Curé dud[it] Thonnoy, de la somme de Cinquante francs par obligation du septieme Mars 1633 par devant d. Aubrj, et que ceste somme soit obvenue en partage a honn[ora]ble George de la Tour peintre demeurant a Luneville a cau[s]e de dam[ois]elle deanne le Narfz sa femme (...) a la priere dud[it] Laurent debteur et de Jean Pierson son beaufrere dud[it] Thonnoy a ce p[rese]ntz Led[it] s[ieu]r de la Tour a prorogé terme aud[it] debteur pour f[air]e le payement de la somme p[rincip]alle jusques a la sainct Jean Baptiste p[ro]chainement venant, a condition que led[it] debteur acquitera la rente pour une année au septie[m]e Mars p[ro]chain, et continuera la rente a courir au prorata du temps, s'estant led[it] Jean Pierson pour plus grande asseurance de tous tourné caution et p[ri]n[cip]al payeur de lad[ite] somme p[ri]n[cip]alle et rente, pour y estre le premier contrainct et poursuivy au choix dud[it] s[ieu]r de la Tour (...)
[*signed*] George de la tour

(Archives de Meurthe-et-Moselle, 3 E 3108, fol. 90)

1634, 8 November: La Tour swears allegiance to Louis XIII, king of France.

Reinbold has shown (1984) that La Tour, like all the other citizens of Lunéville (with the exception of the Capuchins), agreed to take the oath of allegiance demanded by Louis XIII. He presented himself and signed in good company along with the leading citizens of the town, and on that occasion we find him described as "nobleman Georges de La Tour."

(Paris, Bibliothèque Nationale, Cabinet des Manuscrits, Collection de Lorraine, MSS 795, fol. 156r)

1635: Payment made to Georges de La Tour for a delivery of oats (Lunéville).

This is one of the rare pieces of evidence we have of the La Tour's other business: like all the noblemen and prominent figures of Lunéville, he had an estate that he worked, which saved him from potential penury and provided him with a sizeable income. Given the dearth of information on this subject, it is impossible to say just how big his estate was (and of what it consisted). It would seem to have brought him security in those troubled times, but also, because of an ever-increasing incidence of crop-pilfering and cattle-stealing, a constant source of worry.

Despense pour aveine acheptée par la ville des cy-après desnommés : (...)
Au sieur George de La tour de ce lieu, pour six reseals d'aveine qu'il a eu deslivré pour Monsieur le Gouverneur de ce lieu, à quatorze francs l'un, icy par quictance... IIII^{xx} IIII frs

(Lunéville, Archives Municipales, CC 6, fol. 200)

1636, 23 January: Submission of accounts for guardianship of the Nardoyen brothers by La Tour (Lunéville).

La Tour acted as guardian to his nephews, brothers Antoine and François Nardoyen, from 23 April 1631 (see above, 1634). He seems to have treated them as his own children and perhaps even to have had them living with him (cf. the will made by Antoine before a trip "in the direction of France," 31 April 1632, 3 E 781, before the notary Cousson). In 1636 the older of the two, Antoine, reached his majority, and the guardianship accounts therefore had to be rendered. This hitherto unpublished document (cited by Pariset, 1948, pp. 27, 344) gives us a detailed picture of the constant juggling with loans and accumulated interest that people engaged in to preserve the value of their fortunes. La Tour comes across as something of a past master at all this.

Antoine received his share, but François could not receive his until he came of age. He died, however, a few months later while an apprentice with La Tour (see under 28 February and 26 May 1636), and his death brought further financial complications.

Comme dès le 23e apvril 1631, par devant le sieur Vincent substitut de Monsieur le procureur général de Lorraine à Nancy, le sieur George de La Tour, maître peintre, demeurant à Lunéville ait esté créé et institué tuteur à Anthoine et Francois les Nardoyens, fils mineurs de feu noble Claude Nardoyen, et de damoiselle Anne Le Nerf, et depuis ledit temps à jusques à luy, [ait] touché et receu les biens desdits enffans, lesquels désirants en avoir l'estat, et esclaircissement, ont depuis quelques jours ença demandé audit sieur de La Tour compte et satisfaction desdits biens, luy au réciproque désirant se descharger de ladite tutelle et s'acquicter de ce qu'il s'en trouvera relicquataire, comparants ce jourd'huy par devant le Tabellion Royal soubscript et tesmoings bas nommés, ont convenu et confessé, scavoir lesdits Anthoine et Francois Nardoyen d'une part en reddition de compte tutélaire, ledit Anthoine suffisamment aagé ocmme il a dict, et à ce mois émancipé, et ledit sieur de La Tour le tuteur et présentant ledit compte, que dès le 17 du courant janvier 1636, s'estant trouvé par devant les sieurs Théodore Thieriet eschevin, Claude Henriet greffier, Jean Bresade tabellion et procureur, ensemble lesdits soubscrips, tous agréés et convenus pour entendre ledit compte, et reigler de commun consentement les difficultés qui s'y eussent pu rencontrer, il en ont sorty dès ledit jour à leur gré et consentement reciproque, comme s'ensuit.
En premier lieu ledit sieur de La Tour aiant présenté et mis en évidence l'estat dressé des biens communaux d'entre le sieur Jean Maire, admodiateur du Nouveaulieu et ladite damoiselle Le Nerf sa seconde femme, contenant tout leur advenant esdits biens, accepté par Noble et Vénérable personne Messire Francois Le Nerf, oncle maternel desdits Anthoine et Francois [...] mars 1631, avec un autre estat abrégé des choses contenues en iceluy susdit non encore vendues, et du depuis converties en denniers, avec le contract de transaction advenu entre ledit sieur de La Tour en ladite qualité de tuteur et ledit sieur Maire le xe janvier 1632 par devant le tabellion greffier de Rosières, leur acquérant droict pour quelques prétentions contre ledit s^{r} Maire, qu'est tout ce de quoy il avoit à faire recepte en sondit compte, et rien plus, il s'est trouvé redebvable de la somme de six mils cinquante neuf francs sept gros, à laquelle joinct une de sept cents arrestée pour toutes rentes des capitaux qui faisoient ladite recepte, faict qu'il doit six mils sept cents cinquante neuf francs sept gros pour toute recepte, de laquelle lesdits Anthoine et François les Nardoyens se sont contantez, et faict acceptation.
Et en après aiant faict veoir la despense [...] supportée chacun en particulier desdits Anthoine et Francois, tant d'argent desboursé que pour pensions, entretiens et autrement, et tout par le menu, il s'est trouvé qu'à l'esgard dudit Anthoine sa despense monte à mils quatre cent soixante et quinze francs deux gros douze deniers, et celle dudit Francois à mils sept cens soixante et quinze francs neuf gros quatre deniers, comprinse la somme de trois cents francs pour le payement d'une année de sa pension escheante seullement à la St Remy prochaine, de sorte que par ladite recepte leur estant echeu à chacun trois mils trois cents soixante dix neuf francs neuf gros huit deniers, et déduction [...] faite de ladicte despense, il ne leur vient plus qu'audit Anthoine mils neuf cents quatre francs six gros douze deniers, et audit François mils six cents quatre francs quatre deniers, qu'est tout ce que ledit sieur de La Tour s'est trouvé debvoir de ladite tutelle, a cause des biens receus, gérés et maniés appartenans auxdits Anthoine et Francois. Moiennant la satisfaction de quoy, de leur consentement franc et absolu, il sera deschargé de toutes recherches et prétentions que de ceste cause et esgard lesdits Anthoine et Francois les Nardoyens pourroient avoir contre luy, ses hoirs ou aiant cause, et ainsy l'ont ils accordé des le jour susdit 17e du courant en présence desdits sieurs leurs amis et bien veuillants de part et d'autre convenus. Sur et après la recognoissance et justification faicte de point en point tant des choses a mectre en recepte que despense audit compte et tous à présent le veullent et accordent tous de mesme et de rechef en présence dudit soubscript et desdits tesmoings, et veullent au surplus le présent depart leur en estre et à chacun d'eulx donné, comme fut résoult ledit jour, pour asseurance à l'advenir de toutes les choses susdites ; et par ainsy lesdits Anthoine et Francois les Nardoyens quictèrent et quictent par ces présentes ledit sieur de La Tour de la reddition de compte de ladite tutelle, à la charge de leur satisfaire des reliquaux susdits chacun pour leur cotte et advenant ainsi qui est desclairé cy dessus.
Et pour y satisfaire par ledit sieur de La Tour en ce qui tousche ledit Anthoine, il lui a laissé, assigné et cédé les debtes cy après provenues de ses biens communaux d'entre ledit sieur Maire et ladite damoiselle Le Nerf sa mere et qui ont enflé et grossi ladite recepte, estant ledit Sr Maire obligé par ladite transaction du x janvier 1632 de les garandir, premier quatre cents francs de principal sur plus grande (somme) dheue par Pierson Gomay de Charleville, et cinquante un francs deux gros de rente escheus, soixante cinq francs de principal dheus par Dar... de Lassas et sept francs sept gros de rente, cent francs de principal dheus par Nicolas de Charmois Mr de Ferrières, et dix huict francs huict gros de rente, cinq cents francs de principal dheubs par ledit s^{r} Maire de plus grande somme et vingt trois francs quatre gros de rente, cinquante francs de principal, touchés par ledit s^{r} Maire de Messire Louys de Thonnoy, et quatre francs de rente, soixante francs de principal dheus par Claudin Marenser bouchier demeurant à Rosieres, et dix neuf francs neuf gros de rente, vingt sept francs six gros de principal dheus par la vefve Jean Mariette dudit Rosières, et six francs trois gros de rente, treize francs sur Demenge Burtenot dudit Rosières de principal, et trois francs de rente, plus encore deux autres debtes d'argent qu'il a presté provenu des denniers de ladite recepte, l'une de deux cents francs de principal dheus par Mr de Verdprey d'Einville et vingt trois francs quatre gros de rente, l'autre de cent vingt francs de principal dheus par la demoiselle Crochot dudit Einvile, et deux francs huit gros de rente, le tout desdites rentes escheant au dernier apvril prochain, lesdites sommes revenantes à une de mil six cents quatre vingt quinze francs trois gros, ledit Anthoine aiant pris et accepté sur la parolle et promesse dudit sieur de La Tour de l'en garandir en cas qu'il y soit empesché pour chose de son faict et non autrement.
Et pour l'esgard dudict Francois ledit sieur de La Tour luy demeure tenu de sa somme de relicqua pour laquelle il lui fournira assignat

d'autres debtes ou luy paiera autrement. En en tesmoing de tout quoy les présentes sont scellées.
Faites et passées au lieu de Lunéville ce vingtroisième janvier 1636 sur les dix heures du matin, presents Nicolas Jacquinon tailleur d'habits et Didier Ferry aussy tailleur d'habits demeurant audit Luneville tesmoings, bien cognus et soubscripts avec lesdites parties.

George de La Tour A Nardoyens [*sic*]
F Nardoyn [*sic*] Nicolas Jacquinon Didier Ferry
J. Cousson

(Nancy, Archives de Meurthe-et-Moselle, 3 E 782)

1636, 28 February: Apprenticeship contract of François Nardoyen (Lunéville).

The boy we find La Tour taking on as his apprentice was his own nephew, who was still under his guardianship. Even considering the reduction of one hundred francs, the rate he charged was very high, but François was the son of a nobleman and a familiar visitor to his uncle's house, and as such had to be treated in a manner "befitting his rank and station."

Le vingt huictiesme jour de febvrier 1636, au lieu de Luneville, sur les huict heures du matin, entre le sieur George de La Tour maître peintre demeurant audit lieu d'une part, et François Nardoyen, jeune fils de feu le sieur Claude Nardoyen vivant admodiateur au Nouveaulieu, assisté du sieur Anthoine Nardoyen docteur en droitz, son frère, et du sieur François Vaultrin, marchant, demeurant audit Luneville, son cousin d'autre part, a esté convenu et accordé que ledit sieur de La Tour prendra et retiendra en son losgis ledit François Nardoyen pendant le temps et espace de trois ans sept mois, comenceantz au premier de Mars prochain finissanz apres lesdits trois ans sept mois revolus et expirés, le nourrira honnestement selon sa qualité et condition, et pendant ledit temps luy enseignera bonnement et diligemment ledit art de peintre, ainsy et comme doit et est obligé de faire en concience un bon Maître ; et au reciprocque qu'à cause de ce, ledit François Nardoyen sera obligé et tenu de payer audit sieur de La Tour la somme de sept cents frans monnoie de Lorraine, outre une couppe d'argent qu'il a donné à la damoiselle sa tante femme dudit sieur de La Tour, et outre aussy cent frans que pour l'encourager a bien faire et servir ledit sieur de La Tour a quicté des huict qu'il debvoit avoir au lieu des sept cents sudits, lesquels sept cents francs se paieront scavoir quatre cents francs contant, deux cents francs d'huy en un an, et les autres cent restant un an apres, le tout sans deffault de part ny d'autre. Sy ont promis lesdites parties respectivement de tenir la présente convention et accord agréable ferme et stable et d'y satisfaire chacun à son esgard, soubs l'obligation etc. Et advenant que l'une ou l'autre des parties vienne à déceder avant l'accomplissement de ladite convention et accord, ce qui aura esté receu ne pourra estre reversé ; et advenant aussy que ledit François Nardoyen vienne a s'absenter dudit losgis dudit sieur de La Tour, et quicter les services et debvoirs qu'il debvoit sans cause suffisante ny légitime, en ce cas ledit François Nardoyen seroit obligé et tenu de payer audit sieur de La Tour, pour dommaiges et interestz, la somme d'huict cent francs dicte monnoie. Présents Jean Morel et Dieudonné Colas, eulx deux charpentiers, demeurant audit Luneville, tous bien cognus au soubscript, ledit Colas n'aiant l'usage d'escrire.
Nota qu'en ladíte convention n'est comprinse la pension dudit François d'icy à la St Remy prochaine, jaceoit que l'a paiée jusques à là audit Sieur de La Tour.

[*signed:*] Georges de La Tour. F Nardoyen. A Nardoyen. Vaultrin.
J. Cousson. J.M.

(Archives de Meurthe-et-Moselle, 3 E 782, fol. 76v).

1636, 28 March: Baptism of Marie, Georges's daughter (Lunéville).

Diane was forty-five when this her last child was born. The girl was christened Marie: the first Marie, born in 1625, must already have been dead. The second was spared by the plague which struck several weeks after her birth but died in 1648.

This record is of particular interest because of the choice of godfather: the governor of Lunéville, representative of the king of France. La Tour was clearly not afraid of demonstrating his sympathy with the royal administration, at a time when his neighbor, the nobleman Jean Des Fours, had left the country to devote himself to the service of the duke.

Marie fille du Sr George de la Tour, et damoiselle Diane sa femme. Le 28. Par. Sanbat de Pesdamond Capitaine au regiment de Picardie et Gouverneur de Lunéville pour le service du Roy, et damoiselle Marie fille du Sr Estienne Gérard, de ce lieu."

(Lunéville, Archives Municipales)

1636, 13 April: Georges as godfather (Lunéville).

Jean Calquehousse, father of La Tour's fellow godparent Lucie, was the owner of the "Black Eagle" inn and a local notable. We have not been able to identify Jacques Amaldo. The baptism took place two weeks before the outbreak of the great plague.

(Lunéville, Archives Municipales)

1636, 26 May: Death of François Nardoyen (Lunéville).

The plague broke out in Lunéville around 30 April. Étienne Gérard's house was struck, and one of his daughters died, perhaps Marie, who was godmother at the baptism on 28 March. La Tour's house was also struck.

This blunt administrative record had already been discovered by Joly. It has sometimes been unfavorably interpreted, with the La Tour family accused of taking off to the country and leaving the orphaned nephew to look after the house alone, and thus exposed to the infection. There is no justification for such an extrapolation. The epidemic seems to have been even harsher in the villages than in the town. We do not know where La Tour and his family were at the time, or whether or not any of his children died during this outbreak, since we do not have a list of the victims of the epidemics. It is not impossible, however—we know that five of his ten children were no longer alive by about 1640 and we have yet to find any record of their deaths.

[In the section on visits made "Pendant la contagion" *by the surgeon Master François Thomassin, under 26 May:]*

Fut visité le valet de la Tour estant mort au logis et fut trouvé tout chargé de pourpre.

[In the statement of the amounts owed to the town by the families of the victims:]

Le Sr de la Tour peintre a cause d'un sien nepveu mort de peste visité par maître François mené hors sur la charette et enteré par les happechars.
Ledit Sr doibt audit nom les 4ᵉ, 5ᵉ et 7ᵉ desdicts articles revenans à quatorze frans cinq gros quinze deniers. Icy... XIIII fr. V gr. XVd.
Oultre ce doibt encor une journée à raison de quinze gros que le petit (?) Claude a employé a aérer sa maison, Icy... 1 fr. 3 gros.
Les deux sommes revenantes à une de quinze francs huict gros quinze deniers, partant Icy... XV fr. VIII gr. XV d.

(Lunéville, Archives Municipales, G.G. 30)

1636, August–September: Death of Georges de La Tour's brother and settlement of his estate by Georges (Vic).

Pariset (1948, pp. 62-63, 345) cites various documents indicating that François lived in Vic, was married in 1622, and had a child in 1623; he was to lose both wife and child, before dying himself, probably around the end of August 1636. He left the bulk of his estate to his brother. Georges began the execution of the will immediately, but at the same time challenged its validity before the courts. His challenge was ultimately rejected, but in fact, the move was probably designed to get legal endorsement for the will.

(Nancy, Archives de Meurthe-et-Moselle, 3 E 731, 3 September 1636 ; Metz, Archives de la Moselle, BJ 8198, 13 September 1636)

1637, 27 August: Georges's daughter Claude as godmother (Lunéville).

This is the only document we have for 1637, and it indicates only that young Claude, then almost fourteen, was at Lunéville at the time. Where was La Tour? Had he left, or at least been away for a good part of the year? Was he already trying his luck in Paris, where so many Lorrainese had found refuge?

Aoust 1637 – Henry fils d'honnorable Vincent Traver et Catherine sa f^{e}. le 27. Par. Henry de Vergy, seigneur de Henamesnil. Mar. Claude fille du Sr George de La Tour.

(Lunéville, Archives Municipales)

1638, 14 January: Georges's son Étienne and daughter Claude as godparents (Lunéville).

Here again it is La Tour's children, Étienne, aged seventeen, and Claude, aged fourteen, who are asked to act as godparents.

Janvier 1638 – Dominique fils a Demenge Croupsal et Chrestienne sa f^{e}. le 14. Par. Estienne fils au Sr George de La Tour, et Claude sa fille.

(Lunéville, Archives Municipales)

1638, 19 May: Agreement between Georges de La Tour and Jeanne Aubry (Lunéville).

This is one of the documents that best illustrates the tragic situation in Lorraine. A wealthy widow decides to flee the country for the duration of the war and take refuge in France. She sells La Tour all her furniture and rents her house to him for two years for what seems like a song. La Tour, moreover, is careful to stipulate that he will not be responsible for any damage that may occur—a precaution he must have been quite glad to have taken a few months later. The agreement seems to have been drawn up somewhat on the spur of the moment, for the document shows signs of changes and additions.

Was La Tour simply helping a neighbor on her own with good cause to fear in those disastrous times? Or was he trading on her anxiety to get his hands on some of her property? It is not easy to deside. In addition, people all over Lorraine were shutting up their houses and fleeing the country, only too pleased to know someone who could keep even the tiniest eye on their property; "agreements" like this one must have abounded.

Subsequently, this incident would provoke a lawsuit, for which a number of relevant papers have been discovered by Marie-Thérèse Aubry and Jacques Choux (see under 20 January 1642).

Le XIXe jour de may 1638 damoiselle Jehennon Albry, veufve de feu le Sieur Saffroy Vaultrin, vivant Recepveur et admodiateur a Henamesnil, sienne maîtresse, a r[ecognu] avoir laissé a tiltre de loue au Sr George de La tour peintre, dem[euran]t à Lunéville, présent acceptant pour luy, damoiselle Dianne Le nerf sa femme, etc. une maison comme etc., au lieu de Lunéville, sans en rien réserver, en la rue de la boucherie, entre Jean Romet d'une part et Marion Vernet d'autre part, encore ung jardin fermé de muraille, l'héritage de l'abbaye d'une part, et joindant la muraille de ville d'autre part, pour en jouyr et disposer pendant le tems de deux ans a commencer dès le jour de la panthecoste prochaine [*in the margin:*] sans estre attenu à nul refections, ains la reprendre au bout desdits deux ans en l'estat qu'elle se trouvera] comme aussy luy a vendu pour une fois sans fraude ny cautionnement tout les mobiliers indifférament qu'elle delaissera du jour d'huy tant audit Luneville qu'à Nancy et partout ailleurs, dequel espèce et qualité ils soient, qu'on les puisse nommer et desclarer partout ; et est faicte la présente loue et vendage pour et moyennant la somme de [deux, *deleted*] trois cent [cinquante, *deleted*] vingt francs de principal, dont ladicte dame s'est tenue contante et à ce moyen demeure quicte envers ledict S^{r} de La tour des deniers qu'elle luy pouvoit debvoir et le surplus à elle délivré pour subvenir à faire son voyage en France, comme a esté dit, promettant icelle de tenir ladite loue et vendage pour agréable etc. Et font bonnement garandie, en obligeant ses biens etc. submettant etc. Renonceant a tous garands. In forma etc. Presents Chrestien du bas et Nicolas du bas a la St Martin, tesmoings, qui ont signé

Chrestien du bas Nicolas du bas
George de la Tour
Jeanne aubry
N. Bidault.

(Nancy, Archives de Meurthe-et-Moselle, 3 E 731)

1638, 5 July: Georges's daughter Claude as godmother (Lunéville).

Was Georges de La Tour once again away? Here yet again we find his daughter called upon to act as godparent. There is nothing to say for certain that he was in Lunéville on 30 September, the fateful day the town went up in flames.

Juillet – Pierre fils de Francois Michel et Anne sa femme. le 5. Par. Pierre Du bois. Mar. Claude fille au Sr George de La Tour.

(Lunéville, Archives Municipales)

1639, 23 March: Diane de La Tour as godmother in Nancy.

Diane Le Nerf and her children undoubtedly took refuge in Nancy and quite probably managed to save and store there at least some of the property that had been cleared out before the fire. Jean Capchon was a painter who seems to have had quite a respectable career, although none of his work has been identified. He subsequently became La Tour's representative in Nancy and perhaps already filled this role. Basile Mus was the director of the Mont-de-piété and an important figure who turns up in connection with Callot and Deruet (see also under 18 July 1646).

Charle, fils de Jean Capchon peintre et d'Anne Breton sa fe[mme]. le p[arrain] Basile Musse, la m[arraine] Diane Le Nerf.

(Nancy, Archives Municipales, Parish of Saint-Epvre, Baptisms, GG 85)

1639, 17 May: Order by the Conseil d'État for payment to Georges de La Tour (Paris).

We owe the propitious but unexpected discovery of this document to Michel Antoine (1979, pp. 17-26). It provides clear confirmation that La Tour was in direct contact with Paris at this time. Though this "Georges

de La Tour" is not identified as an artist, and the reason for his visit not specified, it is difficult to imagine that it relates to anyone or anything but the painter and his decisive meeting with Louis XIII and Richelieu.

Roolle de plusieurs parties et sommes de deniers que le Roy a commandé à Mre Gaspard de Fieubet, conseiller du Roy en son Conseil d'Estat et trésorier de son espargne païer, bailler et dellivrer comptant ou assigner par ses mandemens portans quictances durant les quartiers de janvier, febvrier et mars de la présente année mil six cent trente neuf aux personnes, pour les causes, selon et ainsy qu'il s'ensuict.
(...)
17 mai 1639
Voyages
A Georges de La Tour, la somme de mil livres à luy ordonnée pour le voïage qu'il est venu faire de Nancy à Paris pour affaires concernans le service de Sa Maiesté, y compris son séiour de six sepmaines et son retour.
. . . *[roll passed by the Conseil d'Estat du Roy for Finance in Paris, 17 March 1639; signed by Séguier, Claude de Bullion, Claude Bouthiller, and Jacques Tubeuf]*

(Paris, Bibliothèque Nationale, Cabinet des Manuscrits, N. Acq. Fr., 165)

1639, 14 September: Settlement of the Nardoyen case by Georges de La Tour (Lunéville).

François Nardoyen's death in 1636 during his apprenticeship with La Tour created a series of financial problems. On the one hand, François was a boarder with La Tour and under contract to him. On the other, in his capacity as guardian to the Nardoyen boys, La Tour had been waiting for François to come of age to turn over his share of his father's estate, which the painter subsequently had to give to the boy's brother. The troubled times seem to have led to a delay in the settlement, which further complicated matters through cumulative interest and the difficulty of enforcing some debts. An agreement was signed on 14 September 1639, but Catherine Nardoyen was not present, having almost certainly taken refuge somewhere outside Lorraine (Nancy, Archives de Meurthe-et-Moselle, 3 E 782). It was only ratified on 28 January 1642.

La Tour has so often been suspected of exploiting his nephew's minority in every way he could and of trying to make off with his inheritance that it seems useful to publish the complete text of this last document. It shows that these were complicated financial arrangements and that while this was a sphere in which La Tour was clearly well-versed, he seems to have been motivated by devotion rather than greed. Moreover he was dealing with professionals who were more than capable of knowing and defending their rights. In addition, it can be seen that La Tour was probably back in Lunéville, or at least in Lorraine, by September 1639.

Par contrat du quatorzième septembre mil six cents trente neuf, signé J. Huet, d'entre le sieur George de La Tour Mre peintre demeurant à Lunéville d'une part, et le sieur Pierre Maire greffier de St Avolt d'autre part, icelui agissant tant de son chef au nom de damoiselle Catherine Nardowin sa femme, que du sieur Anthoine Nardowin son frère absent, portant de faire ratiffier la damoiselle Catherine et de s'estre faict fort dudict son frère pour les choses y contenues representées à la passation des présentes par lecture audict instrument faite à cet effect ; Il est ainsy qu'aujourdhuy, datte de ceste, par devant Jean Cousson tabellion demeurant à Lunéville et tesmoings bas nommés, ledict sieur Maire et ladite damoiselle sa femme comparant personnellement, ladite damoiselle dhuement licenciée dudit sieur Maire son mari, et laquelle licance elle a accepté pour agréable, a dict advouer, confirmer, approuver et corroborer pour tousjours ledict contract en toute sa teneur, tout comme si alors de la passation d'iceluy elle avoit esté présente, et le conforter sans pouvoir à l'advenir d'y contrevenir à quel prétexte ce soit ou puisse estre, promectant de le tenir à tousjours stable et inviolable, comme chose sainement advenue, fete et passée, ce que ledit sieur de La Tour aussy comparant a accepté pour luy ses hoirs et aiant cause, et en conséquence dudict contract faict et advenu, non seullement pour l'égard desdits sieurs Maire et ladite damoiselle sa femme, et encor dudict Anthoinne Nardowin, mais aussi pour tout le droict que Francois Nardowin le frère avoit à prétendre contre ledict sieur de La Tour pour raison de compte à rendre de sa tutelle qu'il avoit gérée conjoinctement avec celle dudict Anthoine son frère, et lequel mort avant l'événement dudit contract leur faisoit escheutte de sa part de prétention, pourquoy s'est entendu la transaction spécifiée. Jaceois que nommément ny plus particulierement il n'y soit déclairé, en telle sorte que générallement ledit sieur de La Tour en demeure, luy ses hoirs et ayant cause, quicte et sans plus de recerches, il a délivré audit Sieur Maire et à ladite damoiselle sa femme acceptans pour eulx tant en leurs noms que dudit Anthoine et tant de ces chefs que comme héritiers dudit Francois Nardowin, la scedulle portant cinq cents francs passée le 8e mai 1634 signée J. le Maire au proffict dudict sieur de La Tour mentionnée audit contract, consenty que l'obligation de cinq cents francs passé aussi à son profict par les héritiers de feu le Sr Estienne Gérard dudit Lunéville le 29 d'aoust 1634 par devant le tabellion Lhoste de Nancy, leur soit délivré pour estre annexé aux presentes ou bien à ladicte transaction, et s'en servir comme de chose passée et a quoi il n'a plus rien par tradition des présentes et d'icelle transaction, tant en principal que rentes, encor leur a délivré l'obligation de quatre cents francs passé par Claudin Jeunet de Tonnoy qu'est à tiltre de constitution signée à Rouxel du 2e mars 1632 passé au profict de son frère Curé de Tonnoy, et de plus consenti qu'un autre obligation portant deux cent vingt cinq francs passé à même proffict par George Mourlat dudict Tonnoy le 18e novembre 1633 signé D. Maire Didier Tabellion demeurant à Nommeny, leur soit delivré comme dessus,et d'abondant ledit sieur de La Tour at aussy consenti que les autres sommes assignées par autre transaction que la susdite du 23e janvier 1636, passée par devant le Tabellion des présentes, soient receu par lesdits sieur Maire et damoiselle Catherine sa femme, et (...) celle dheue par le sieur de Verdprey d'Einville portant deux cent frans principal est par obligation signée D. Collin du dernier may 1634, l'autre par la damoiselle Bergot dudict Einville de cent vingt francs par obligation du [*deletion and blank space*] signée dudict Collin, est ainsy ladite transaction du 4 septembre 1639 entièrement et plainement subsistante, ayant ledit sieur de La Tour promis que si pour son faict propre et particulier il s'y trouvoit troubles ou empeschements de son costé, d'en porter garandie auxdits sieur Maire et damoiselle sa femme etc. soubs l'obligation etc.
Présents Nicolas Perin margulier et Jean Marchal (...) demeurants audict Lunéville tesmoings, tous de la cognoissance du soubscript et ont les parties signé. Passé à Lunéville ce vingt huitieme janvier mil six cents quarante deux sur les trois heures après midy.
[*signed*] La Tour. Maire. Nicolas Perin. Catherine Nardouin.
J. Cousson

(Nancy, Archives de Meurthe-et-Moselle, 3 E 782, fol. 74)

1639, 25 September: Diane de La Tour as godmother in Nancy.

This record was published by Sylvestre (1983 [1985], p. 55). Everything seems to suggest that in spite of being a "refugee," Diane retained both her social standing and her friends in Nancy.

Baptesmes. Septembre 1639. – Francois fils de Barthelemy Laurent et de Claude Didon sa femme a esté baptizé le 25e. Le Parin noble François du Bois cy devant audit[eu]r des Comptes de Loraine Seig[neu]r d'Oheville Heyncourt et Semy Bezange et la marine Damoiselle Diane Le Nerf.

(Nancy, Archives Municipales, Parish of Saint-Sébastien, Baptisms, GG 4)

1639, 22 December: Georges as godfather (Nancy).

One small detail makes this record all-important: it is the first occasion La Tour is credited with the title of "peintre ordinaire du roi," *which could only have been justified by a warrant from Louis XIII.*

Baptesmes. Décembre 1639. – Georges fils de Jean Husson et de Marguerite sa femme a esté baptizé le 22. le Parin George de La Tour Peintre ordinaire du Roy et la Marine Mengeon Despieres.

(Nancy, Archives Municipales, Parish of Saint-Sébastien; Baptisms, GG 4)

1640, 25 August: Reference in Paris to an "agent" of Georges de la Tour.

This is the simple apprenticeship contract relating to an orphan by the name of Guillaume Ré, who wanted to learn the cooper's trade. The document, discovered by Michel Antoine, is almost illegible. The person responsible for the contract, Baptiste Quarin, does not just give a brief indication of his occupation after his name in the normal way, but a lengthy title that seems to read "agent of Monsieur de La Tour peintre ordinaire du roi.*" In theory, "resident in the the galleries of the Louvre" could apply as well to Quarin as to La Tour, but the term* résident *seems deliberately to have been used instead of the more customary* demeurant *[inhabitant]. Similarly, the term* commensal *[table companion] of the king, which La Tour himself sometimes used (16 January 1643, for instance), can only be accounted for by his having been granted lodgings in the Louvre. Then again, was Quarin acting here in his own name or as La Tour's agent? In the latter case, what possible reason could La Tour have had for supporting the son of a currier from Angers? We can only hope that the appearance of additional Parisian records throw some light on this text. As it stands, this document raises as many questions as it answers, and we must beware of interpreting it too simplistically.*

xxv[e] aoust 1640
Fut présent en sa personne Baptiste Quarin, facteur de Monsieur de La Tour peintre ord[inai]re du Roy résident aux galleries du Louvre, par[roiss]e S[t]. Germain auxerrois, lequel pour le proffict faire à Guillaume Rué, fils de feu Marin Rué, vivant maître coroyeur à angers, et de Marye jadis sa femme à présent sa ve[uf]ve [...] a baillé et mis en service et apprentissage d'aujourdhui jusque a cinq ans prochains venant [...] a Jacques Charton, maître tonnelier, dechargeur de vins à Paris y demeurant rue de Beauvais, present et acceptant, qui l'a pris et retenu pour son service et apprenti, et auquel pendant ledict temps il promet montrer et enseigner a son pouvoir sondict mestier de tonnelier et tout ce qui se mesle et entremet en icelui, et fournir à lui ses vivres et aliments corporels, et ledit apprenty s'entretiendra d'habits, linge, chaussures et autres ses nécessités. [En faveur : *barré*] Sans que pour rien du present apprentissage soit baillé et payé [...]
A ce présent ledit apprenty agé de dix-neuf ans [...] promect servir sondict maitre audict mestier en toutes autres choses licites et honnestes qui lui seront commandées, faire son proffict et éviter son dommage et l'advertir du necessaire s'il vient a sa cognoissance [...] Et en cas de fuite [devra] estre pris et apréhendé au corps et estre ramené à sondict maître pour parachever le temps et restes dudict présent apprentissage [...] Le présent acte faict et passé en la présence de Pierre Pinson maître tonnelier [...] le vingt cinquieme jour d'aoust avant midi mil six cent quarante. Et ont signé fors ledit apprenti qui a dit ne scavoir ecrire ni signer

Baptiste Quarin Jacques Charton
Pierre pinson
Briquet Bauldry

(Paris, Archives Nationales, Minutier central, XIX, 420)

IV

RETIREMENT AND FAME 1640–1652

1641, 4 February: Legal action taken by Georges de La Tour over one of his paintings (Lunéville).

This quite exceptional document was discovered and published by Aubry and Choux (1976, p. 155), and it is given here in their transcription. La Tour had sold his friend Chrétien de Nogent (see under 21 June 1926) a painting of Mary Magdalen—whether or not it was a "night" picture is not specified—for approximately three hundred francs. This must have been around 1637-1638. Shortly after the sale, disaster struck Lunéville, and later that same year, 1638, Nogent died, before he could finish paying for the work. When life began to return to normal, La Tour set about recovering his money. De Nogent's widow, though unwilling to pay the outstanding sum, refused to return the painting, which had been left with the Minims for safe keeping, or to allow La Tour to sell the painting for her and give her the profits. Did she hope to make more by selling it herself? It is likely that the value of La Tour's works had greatly increased, thus allowing speculation.
The affair comes up more than once in the rediscovered register (4 February, 4 and 26 March), but the outcome remains unknown. This does not matter: what is interesting is the importance La Tour clearly attached to his "original" works (from which we can infer that there were already copies in existence), the considerable price he could get even before 1638 for a canvas with a single figure, and the reputation his representations of the Magdalen must have had even then.

Remonstre le sieur George de La Tour, maître peintre demeurant en ce lieu, disant qu'il auroit vendu et délivré à feu honoré seigneur Chrestien de Nogent, seigneur de Chanteheu etc., un tableau représentant la sainte Magdelaine, de son propre travail, pour la somme de quatorze pistolles, desquelles il paya en deux fois quatre quadruples à la femme du remonstrant, rien plus, de sorte qu'il demeura redebvable de six restantes, et après son décès, ayant interpellé la dame sa veuve de luy payer, et elle en [ayant] faict quelque refus, ledit remonstrant pour n'estre frustré de son travail, ou du prix en convenu, luy auroit faict faire offre par sadite femme de reprendre ledit tableau, duquel il faisoit cas et estime (pourveu que ce soit en son original) et de le mettre en estat pour le vendre. Ce qu'estant, et luy paié desdites six pistolles restantes, il luy donneroit le surplus pour se rembourser du surplus desdits quadruples. A quoy ladite dame ayant déféré et accordé, elle envoia des aussy tost en la maison des RR. PP. Minimes dudit Lunéville, où ledit tableau estoit en refuge, pour l'avoir et luy mettre en mains. Mais le Père correcteur ne s'y estant lors trouvé, et bien qu'elle ait aussy donné parolle de le renvoier audit remonstrant à son retour, si est-ce que du depuis, ny encores présentement, il ne l'a peu avoir. C'est pourquoy il faict instance envers ladite dame d'avoir son payement desdites six pistolles, de quoy elle faict refus. Supplie, partant, qu'elle soit adjournée à l'extraordinaire, pour aux fins de despens et intérests se voir, en suite de l'accord susdit, condemner à luy remettre ledit tableau en mains, pour le vendre et se païer desdites six pistolles, et après, luy rendre le surplus...

(Nancy, Archives de Meurthe-et-Moselle, Bj 427)

1641, 14 May: Georges's son Étienne as witness at Rosières.

Étienne acted as a witness for Nicole Chauvenel, widow of Simon Rennel, who was probably a lesser-known member of the same family as Bonaventure Rennel, the secretary of state to Duke Charles III who signed La Tour's letters of exemption in 1624. The document is interesting because it shows that the painter and his family continued to be very much in evidence after the troubles (see records below).

(Nancy, Archives de Meurthe-et-Moselle, 3 E 3109)

1641, 25 May: Georges's daughter Claude as godmother at Lunéville.

Dominique, daughter of sire Dominique Bourget, surgeon, had as godparents sire François Nicolas Morcel and "Claude, daughter of sire Georges de la Tour, all of Lunéville." The record is cited by Pariset (1948, p. 68).

(Lunéville, Archives Municipales)

1641, 23 July: Georges's children, Étienne and Claude as godparents in Lunéville.

This record is similarly cited by Pariset (1948, p. 68). Jacques Étienne Charien is registered as godchild of Étienne and Claude "son and daughter of sire Georges La Tour, painter, all of Lunéville."

(Lunéville, Archives Municipales)

1641, 15 August: Georges de La Tour as witness to Claude de Ronny's marriage.

In spite of all the recent disasters and the uncertain future ahead, life resumed its normal course in Lorraine. Claude de Ronny was the daughter of Claude Le Nerf, Diane's sister. Her father, Captain Étienne de Ronny, was dead. So too was the groom's father. The bride's mother, Claude, displays remarkable caution over the dowry, promising to give "as much as the present times and her means reasonably allow" and stressing the difficulty of recovering any sums owed in those times. The document was published in 1987 by Paulette Choné, and it is given here in her transcription.

Du quinzieme Aoust 1641 a Rosieres sur les deux heures apres midy. En pourparlant et discourant du mariage futur et esperé a faire sy dieu et n[otr]e mere s[ain]te Eglise sy accordent, Par et entre honnorable Claude Nicolas jeune filz de feu honnorable Francois Nicolas vivant admodiateur a Mont, assisté d'honnorable francois Regnault tabellion demeurant a Rosieres son oncle d'une part, Et Claude de Ronny jeune fille du feu sieur Estienne de Ronny et de Noble Claude le Nerfz sa femme ses pere et mere, de present residente a Rosieres, assistée de lad[ite] damoiselle sa mere et du sieur George de La Tour son oncle peintre ord[inai]re de sa Majesté demeurant a Luneville d'au[tr]e part (...) Que des l'instant de la solempnisa[ti]on dud[it] mariage ilz seront ungs et communs en tous acquetz et conquetz immeubles quilz pouront faire (...) Qu'au surplus douaire venant a escheoir et quil n'y ayt enfans issus dud[it] mariage pour lors vivans lad[ite] future espouse aura pour douaire prefixe et limité la quantité de huict paires de grains par moictié bled froment et aveine mesure de Nancy a delivrer par un jour de sainct Martin au lieu de Mont ou a deux lieues de distance (...) Et pource qui touche lad[ite] dam[ois]elle Claude Le Nerfz mere de lad[ite] future espouse, elle a promis de meubler convenablem[ent] sad[ite] fille d'autant raisonnablement que la condition du temps et ses facultés luy pouront permettre et non plus, et de luy assigner sur les debtes les plus claires et apparentes que luy peuvent estre dheues une somme de cinq centz francs pour s'acquicter envers elle, scavoir de trois centz frans a elle donnés par la feu dam[ois]elle de Saulserotte tante de lad[ite] dam[ois]elle Claude Le Nerfz et les au[tr]es deux centz francs par le feu s[ieu]r Curé de Thonnoy son oncle, et en cas que de son vivant elle ne toucheroit lesd[ites] debtes actifves a elle dheues elle aura droict de les prendre sur les plus clairs et apparents biens de sa succession, avant aulcun partage, le surplus remis aux us et coutumes du pays (...)"

[*signatures*] C. Nicolas Claude de Rosny
claude le nerfz
La Tour
Thovenin
F. Regnault
Michel
Husson

(Nancy, Archives de Meurthe-et-Moselle, 3 E 3109)

1641, 22 September: Georges's son Étienne as godfather in Lunéville.

In this the third baptismal record cited by Pariset for that year (1948, p. 68), Étienne Hilaire has as godfather Étienne, "son of M. Georges de La Tour, Painter of this place."

(Lunéville, Archives Municipales)

1641, 12 November: Georges's daughter Claude as godmother in Lunéville.

On this occasion Claude was godmother to Claude Lhuilier, of Moncel (record cited by Reinbold, 1991, p. 117).

(Lunéville, Archives Municipales)

1642, 20 January: complaints lodged against Georges de La Tour (Lunéville).

This affair is cited by Aubry and Choux (1976, p. 157). It arose as an unexpected consequence of the agreement that La Tour signed in 1638 with Jeanne Aubry (see under 19 May). We do not really know what became of the lease, whether in fact the widow reclaimed possession of her estate at the end of the two years stipulated in the contract, or what state it may have been in by then. There was a clause in the contract allowing La Tour to dispose of the widow's furnishings and other belongings; her servant, Anne, daughter of the late Claude Henry, of Lunéville, claimed, however, that La Tour had made off with some goods that were rightfully hers. There were various hearings between 20 January and 9 May, but both beginning and end of the register are missing, and we do not know how the case, minor in itself, eventually turned out. One detail that makes this document more interesting is the reference to "Anne Roc" as servant in the La Tour household at this date (for more on this young woman, probably first employed in the family from as early as the 1630s, see below, 1652-1660).

(Nancy, Archives de Meurthe-et-Moselle, Bj 7054)

1642, April–1643, January: Challenge to Georges de La Tour's letters of exemption.

The calamity in Lunéville, the state of war in Lorraine, the economic ruin and the constant and crippling burden of taxes imposed by force, not to mention the dual government of the country, had utterly destroyed the social equilibrium. People were wary of challenging the privileges of the Church, but they openly attacked those of the nobles, and more readily still of anyone who did not have the excuse of a long tradition of privilege. La Tour was particularly singled out. He clearly knew this, as well as the fact that giving way on the slightest point would mean the end of the special status granted to him in happier times by an art-loving duke. If he stresses his title of "peintre ordinaire du roi," *it is because it was one that could have some weight at a time when Lorraine was occupied by French troops. But it could also irritate his fellow citizens.*

No sooner was he back in Lunéville, it seems, than an attempt was made to make him pay a tax levied on the inhabitants of Lunéville according to the number of heads of cattle they owned. He refused. On 9 April, a sergeant was dispatched to him with a writ. La Tour slammed the door in his face, after dealing him "a sharp kick" and a torrent of abuse (document 1). On 3 May the lieutenant of the bailiwick went before the deputy public prosecutor. La Tour was summoned "that he might be heard in his own tongue, without the intermediary of a lawyer." He promised to come but did not appear. He was judged in absentia, but this delaying tactic had not been in vain. When the sergeant brought him a second summons on 28 May he declared "that he was engaged in an appeal before Parliament." He made the same reply on 4 June and "declared the nullity of everything done or which might be done prejudicial to this appeal." He managed to get the town of Lunéville summoned before the Parliament of Metz, then based at Toul, and the town was forced to dispatch both the deputy public prosecutor Georges Alba and sergeant Pierre Manvisse there (document 2). The matter was indeed raised in Parliament (document 3). In point of fact La Tour had some effective support behind him and an excellent knowledge of legal procedures; ultimately the town was unable to strip him of his privilege.

The affair was a complex one, involving a number of different suits, further complicated by La Tour's tendency to make use of every possible circumstance, favorable and unfavorable alike. We do not yet have the full story, but Pariset (1948, pp. 68-69, pp. 348, note 2), Tribout de Morembert (1974, p. 222), and more particularly Aubry and Choux (1976, p. 157) have in turn uncovered various episodes. We have taken the most significant texts from them.

1642, 9 April: Report by Pierre Manvisse, sergeant of the bailiwick, to Didier Clément, the bailiff's lieutenant and chief magistrate in Lunéville, about the delivery of a writ to Georges de La Tour.

Je soubsigné sergent bailliager à Lunéville, certifie et faict ce très humble rapport à vous, Monsieur Clément, commis lieutenant de Monsieur le bailly de Nancy audit Lunéville et à tous autres qu'il appartiendra, que par vertu du noble décret de Monseigneur de Vignier cy joinct, en datte du iiij janvier dernier, et requis par vous Jean Roville,

au nom et comme sindic de ville dudit Lunéville, de contraindre plusieurs particuliers délayant de satisfaire à ce qu'ils sont cottisés pour leur bestail, au contenu du rol aussy cy joinct, pourquoy faire je me suis ce neufième apvril 1642, assisté de Jean Corpey, sergent de ladite ville, transporté au domicil du sieur George de La Tour, peintre audit lieu. Où estant dans l'allée de sa maison et parlant à luy, je l'ay à l'amiable et par plusieurs fois interpellé au payement de la somme de seize frans six gros à quoy il est cottisé pour sondit bestail ; lequel a faict response qu'il n'en vouloit rien paier. Et après l'avoir prié de ce faire, ou que je serois contrainct de le gager, a faict response que je le gage. Et m'estant mis en debvoir pour ce faire d'entrer plus avant dans sa maison, m'a donné un grand coup de pied et fermé sa porte, disant avec colère que le premier qui entreroit plus avant, il luy donneroit un coup de pistolet, cause que je n'ay peu faire autre exploict. Et en faict ceste relation, que j'atteste contenir vérité, pour y estre ordonné par qui il appartient.
[text published by Marie-Thérèse Aubry and Jacques Choux]

(Nancy, Archives de Meurthe-et-Moselle, Bj 7054)

1643, 10 January: Municipal accounts relating to the summons to the Parliament of Toul served on Lunéville at La Tour's request.

Dix huict francs paiez a Pieron Manvisse sergent et à lui accordez pour et au subiect d'un voiage par lui faict a Toul a l'assignation y donnée contre la ville par le s[r] George de La Tour au subiect de ses contributions, appert d'ordre datté du dixième janvier 1643 et quittance, cy... XVIII fr.

[...]

Fait despence de vingtcinq francs paiez a George Alba et a lui accordez pour un voiage par lui faict a Toul a une assignation impétrée a requête du S[r] de La Tour, cy... XXV fr.

(Lunéville, Archives Municipales, CC 7, fol. 23r)

1643, 16 January: Judgment delivered by the court concerning the appeal put forward by Georges de La Tour.

Audience de Lorraine.
Entre George de La Tour, peintre ordinaire de la Majesté du Roy, appelant des taxes et cottizations de sa personne adjournement personnel et de tout ce qui s'en est ensuivy, faict et ordonné par les Gens de justice de Lunéville d'une part et les habitans et communaulté dudit Lunéville inthimés d'autre part.
Après que Viry, pour l'appelant, a dict qu'au préjudice des privilèges et immunités particulières qui luy ont esté octroyés par le deffunct duc Henry de Lorraine et mesme confirmé par sa Majesté qui a voulu, en considération de l'expérience qu'il s'est acquise au faict de peinture, le tenir du nombre de ses commansaulx, les inthimés l'auroient compris en leurs contributions et voulu forcer d'exécuter le payement de sa quotte, ce qui à l'instant donna lieu à l'adjournement personnel pour avoir jetté dehors le sergent exécuteur et fermé la porte sur luy ; ouy Lefebvre pour les inthimés qui a soustenu ledit appelant non recepvable, après avoir procédé volontairement par devant le sieur intendant de justice, lequel sur les pièces produites de part et d'autre auroit, conformément au mandement de Sa Majesté, ordonné que ledit appelant payeroit, et que ce prétendu privilège n'avoit lieu pendant la ruyne des guerres ; ouy Forcal pour le procureur général du Roy, la Cour, en tant que touche l'appel de adjournement personnel, a mis et met l'appellation... au néant et les parties hors de Cour et de procès.

(text published by Henri Tribout de Morembert)

In the end, then, La Tour both lost and won his case: lost because the Parliament declared his privilege invalid in time of war, and won because by the same token his privileged status was officially recognized. This may well have the object of the entire exercise. In fact the Parliament of Toul's ruling was almost certainly based on the royal edict of November 1640 that decreed the "suspension of privileges and exemptions for all Officers, Domestics and Commensals of the King." This suspension was lifted and abolished by royal proclamation on 26 November 1644. We find La Tour securing another exemption for himself in February 1644 by renting the Commandery of Saint-Georges, but by the end of the year his privilege was legally restored to him.

(Metz, Archives de la Moselle, B 521, fol. 3)

1642, 10 September: Georges de La Tour is summoned for receiving and concealing a sow (Lunéville).

Life in a small town like Lunéville was still largely dominated by peasant concerns and attendant disputes involving crops, cattle, and damage caused by neighbors. Aubry and Choux (1976, p. 158) have discovered a fragment in an incomplete register that relates to one such dispute: a summons dated 10 September to appear at a hearing two days later regarding a lost sow. Unfortunately we have only the complaint; it seems likely, however, that if La Tour was indeed responsible for abducting the sow, he had a good reason for impounding the unfortunate animal.

Didier Clément [...] à vous, le sieur George de La Tour, peintre demeurant audit Lunéville, salut. Jean Gaillard de Haudonviller nous a dit et remonstré que Mougeon Gaillard de Haudonviller, son frère, luy ayant laissé en son logis une truye d'environ demi an pour la nourrire, il est ainsy que vous ou vostre commandement l'aurié prin ou faict prendre, comme elle estoit parmy la ville, lundy dernier, et différés indheuement de luy rendre, occasion qu'il nous a resquis vous faire adjourner pour y voire condamner et aux despens et intérests de poursuitte...

(Nancy, Archives de Meurthe-et-Moselle, Bj 7054)

1643, 17 October: Georges's son Étienne as godfather (Lunéville).

Once again it is Étienne who is called on to be a godparent. These records shed no light on the young man's character, but they do convey the impression that he was popular in all quarters, with the ordinary people and the nobility alike, in Lunéville itself and the district around it, as well as in Vic.

It is interesting to note that here, at the age of twenty-two, he is still not described as "painter," but simply as "son of the honorable Georges de La Tour painter."

Octobre. – Anne, fille de Maistre Augustin Simonet Cordonnier et Anne sa femme. Parrain M. [barré] Estienne fils d'honorable George de La Tour peintre. Maraine Elisabeth fille d'honorable Ferry Sibile, tous de Lunéville. Le 17 oct."

(Lunéville, Archives Municipales)

1643, 10 November: Apprenticeship contract of Chrétien George (Lunéville).

Although the contract is dated 10 November, it appears that the apprenticeship had begun on 16 September. La Tour was evidently settled in Lunéville once again and intent on resuming his activity of painting there by the autumn—although of course this did not preclude his making visits to Paris. He was more insistent than ever on his title of "peintre ordinaire du roi," *and here we see the notary start to write "master" [painter], immediately cross it out, and replace it with the requisite form, which was clearly an unusual one in Lorraine.*

Chrétien George belonged to the solid middle class of Lunéville. His father, who was also called Chrétien George and was the tenant farmer of the Blamont estate, was recently deceased. Because of complications over the will, La Tour did not receive the sum he was promised and only succeeded in getting the money a good many years later. Chrétien George, who subsequently married and entered the service of the marquis de Ville, apparently gave up painting.

This very detailed record gives us invaluable information about the kind of life La Tour led in his last years, as both landed gentleman and painter.

Le dixieme jour de Novembre 1643 au lieu de Luneville avant Midy, entre le sieur George de La Tour [maître, *deleted*] peintre ordinaire du Roy demeurant audit lieu, d'une part, et Claude Coullon demeurant a Varangeville au nom de Chrestien George son beau-frere, jeune fils de feu Chrestien George vivant admodiateur du domaine de Blanmont, d'autre part, a l'adveu et assistance de honorable personne messire Gorgonne Coullon prebstre, du sieur Philippe George advocat a Nancy, et d'honorable Claude Connadelat bourgeois dudit Luneville, parents et bien veillantz dudit Chrestien, a esté traicté, convenu et accordé que ledit sieur de la Tour prendra, losgera et nourrira ledit Chrestien en son losgis pendant le temps, terme et espace de trois ans ja commencez des le seizième septembre dernier, pour et pendant luy enseigner et apprendre bonnement et diligemment l'art et science de peintre sans luy rien cacher, aux charges, conditions et modifications cy apres ; premier que pour raison de ladite nourriture et losgement il sera paié audit sieur de la Tour, par chacun desdits trois ans, la somme de cent francs, dont le premier payement se debvoit a l'entrée, lequel non faict neantmoins jusques icy que pour quarante francs, s'acquerera pour les soixante restans a Noel prochain, qu'il sera fourny pour les autres deux payements au terme du seizième septembre à chacun cent francs des annees prochaines 1644 et 1645, que les habits honnestes et decents convenables audit Chrestien pour servir ledit sieur son maître luy seront fournis sans retard ny manquement, comme encor ses linges, et autres hardes a luy necessaires, qu'il sera tenu de le suivre en ville, et hors de ville, ou ses affaires l'appelleront, et d'aller aux champs pour son service quand ses negoces le requerront, de le servir a table, et penser diligemment et a bon point son cheval de monture soir et matin, le tout avec la fidelité et diligence que doit un bon et affectionné serviteur. Que si ledit Chrestien par sa faulte, et sans subject légitime vient à sortir dudit service avant l'expiration desdits trois ans, il sera tenu et obligé de payer outre ce qui l'auroit peu estre desdits trois cents francs pour interests dudit sieur de la Tour, la somme de quatre cents francs incontinent [*this is followed by guarantees from the apprentice's family*] Lui present ayant promis aultant que son aage peut permettre a l'assistance desdites personnes ses parents de bien satisfaire a son debvoir quant aux choses susdites (...)
[*Signed*] La Tour   Claude Conadelat   Claude Colon
Marguerite George   Touloy   Georges   J. Cousson

(Nancy, Archives de Meurthe-et-Moselle, 3 E 782, p. 106v-107r)

1644, 6 February–1645, 30 September: Rental by Georges de La Tour of the Commandery of Saint-Georges in Lunéville.

As a result of the events of the day, large estates were abandoned in Lunéville as they were throughout Lorraine, and buildings and land alike left to ruin. La Tour for his part felt that his right of exemption would always fall under attack, and as the petition of 1646 proved, his fears were well grounded. So it was that he came to rent a commandery of the Order of St. John of Jerusalem consisting of a large house in the town itself, exempt from tax, together with a meix *and plowed land that were similarly exempt, but this time by virtue of an ancient religious privilege. If the need arose, La Tour could avail himself of the "rights, exemptions and franchises" that went with the commandery. The contract was signed in Nancy on 6 February 1644 with Louis de Thonnoy, canon of the cathedral church of Verdun on behalf of "Messire Ferri-Antoine Saladin d'Anglure, knight of the Order of St. John of Jerusalem, commander of the Commandery of Saint-Jean [John] of the Old Star in Nancy." (Nancy, Meuthe-et-Moselle Archives, 3 E 2234)*

It seems, however, that this property was too much for La Tour to farm, on top of his other holdings. Heartened, for the time being at least, by the royal proclamation of 26 November 1644 that reinstated the privileges of "commensals," he reassigned the land to Théodore Thiriet, a magistrate and one of the notables remaining in Lunéville. Thiriet, who was not a nobleman, then tried to use the transaction to secure an exemption that he did not hold. La Tour, meanwhile, was free to take back the exemption if he happened to need it. This was a cunning ploy, understandable enough in those troubled times, but not one that fooled the inhabitants of Lunéville. The petition of 1646 was to denounce it openly.

Given here is the second of the two contracts, the agreement signed in September 1645 between Théodore Thiriet and La Tour and his wife, which discloses the operation.

Le dernier de septembre 1645 au lieu de Lunéville trois heures après midy, le s[ieur] Georges de La Tour peintre ordinaire du Roy demeurant à Lunéville, ce faisant fort de Dam[oiselle] Diane le Nerf sa femme, a recognu avoir cédé et transporté au S[ieur] Theodore Thiriet, Eschevin en la justice ordinaire dudit Lunéville, acceptant pour luy et Dam[oiselle] Nicolle sa femme tant seulement le contenu en un tiltre de bail passé à son profict le 6 febvrier 1644 par devant Vodot tabellion pour l'admodiation du gaignage franc quappartient [*sic*] a M^r le Commandeur de St Jean au ban et finage de Lunéville, dict et appelé le gaignage de St George, dépendant de ladicte Commanderie avec les droicts, examptions et franchises y appartenants, le tout conformément au bail duquel reste a faire cinq années et duquel aussy ledit s[ieur] acceptant a dict n'ignorer les charges et conditions.
La présente cession et renonciation faicts moyenant qu'iceluy a promis et sera tenu de décharger et porter quicte ledit s[ieur] recognoissant de toutes et chacune les charges portees audit bail, sauf des points exceptés lesquels derechef ledit s[ieur] acceptant a dict bien scavoir. Si a promis ledit s[ieur] recognoissant de tenir la présente renonciation pour agréable et de la garandir pour ses faicts et promesses tant seulement soubs l'obligation, etc. et ledit s[ieur] acceptant de satisfaire auxdites charges soubs l'obligation, etc., qu'il a submis, etc. et renoncé à garand. Presents Claude Cousson jeune fils et Nicolas Doyen aussy jeune fils dudit Lunéville tesmoings, tous de cognoissance et soubscripts
[*Signed*] La Tour.   Thiriet
J. Cousson
C. Cousson.   Nicolas Doyen

Audit jour et lieu ledit s[ieur] Thiriet, se faisant fort de sadite femme, a recognu que, non obstant la cession et transport cy dessus, il a néantmoins promis, comme par les présentes il promect, audit s[ieur] de La Tour acceptant pour luy, ladite Damoiselle sa femme, leurs hoirs et ayans cause, qu'au cas qu'ils ayent nécessité pendant les cinq années à venir de ladite admodiation de jouyr de la franchise et exemption appartenante audict gaignage, de leurs [*sic*] laisser icelle librement, jaçois ledit transport, et de ce contenter pour les terres dudit gaignage d'une pièce de neuf jours dict en la rue hargault entre le s^r Géneval d'une part et les meix d'autre part, encore de quatre jours [...] tout en un tenant, et quatre jours joindant le cimetiere hors de la ville, le surplus de la consistance dudit gaignage estant par ledit s[ieur] Thiriet [...] laissé audict s[ieur] de La Tour.
Aussi ledit S[ieur] Thiriet ne payera il du canon de ladite admodiation que la moictié du canon y porté, l'autre moictié demeurant audit S[ieur] de La Tour avec les autres charges exprimées audit bail. Si ont promis

iceux respectivement de ce tenir, garandir et faire valoir reciproquement l'effect de leurs presentes promesses, à peine de tous despens dommages et interests contre le contrevenant, soub l'obligation etc. Et est entendu que si ledit S[r] de La Tour venoit à reprendre la jouissance de ladite franchise pour besoing qu'il en ait, qu'en ce cas ledit s[ieur] Thiriet sera deschargé dudit canon et non tenu plus avant que du moyage des terres qu'il auroit ensemencé ou amandé. Presents lesdits tesmoings
[*signed*] La Tour. Thiriet.
J. Cousson.
C. Cousson. Nicolas Doyen.

(Nancy, Archives de Meurthe-et-Moselle, 3 E 782, fol. 12v)

1644, 26 April: Death certificate of Georges's servant, Nicolas Daniel (Lunéville).

We know very little about La Tour's innermost circle, particularly the servants who lived with him. Other records, as we shall see, indicate that Anne Rocque, in her double role of servant and companion, was almost certainly part of the family from about 1634-1635 and remained so until her masters' death. This death certificate shows that the household also included Nicolas Daniel, who seems to have been a native of Chanteheux, a small town not far from Lunéville, though whether he was an old retainer or a young valet is not clear. We know too from an entry in the register in January 1652 that La Tour had another servant at that time, one Jean, known as Montauban. Was he already in La Tour's service in the 1640s, or even before? Pariset identified him, with good reason, with the "Jean Bergier, known as Montauban, supposedly native of L'Imbessac in Languedoc, presently soldier in the company of sire de Fressinet, captain of the garrison at the said Lunéville in the service of His Majesty," who in October 1636 (the marriage contract is dated the fourteenth), attended by a number of comrades known variously as du Laurier, l'Esperance, La Fortune, and so on, married in Lunéville "Catherine Gaspard, widow of Jean Painblanc, her own mistress, attended by Jacques Godard and Hugo Connadelat, her cousins." For one reason or another, he must have decided to leave the army and settle in his wife's native region.

L'année 1644
Les obits
Apvril
Le 15me mourut Claudon, vefve de Jean Barthelemy de Chanteheu, et fust enterré au petit cimetier de S[t]. Jacques.
Le 26me mourut Nicolas Daniel de Chanteheu serviteur du Sieur De La Tour peintre et fust enterré au grand cimetier hors la ville.

(Lunéville, Archives Municipales)

1644, 20 October: Georges's son Étienne as godfather to one of Claude Didelot's sons (Lunéville).

Once again we find Étienne called upon to be a godparent, which could mean that La Tour was still often away.

Octobre 1644
François fils de Claude Didelot et Nicole sa femme. Parrain Mr Estienne fils d'honorable Georges de La tour peintre, marraine Damoiselle Marie fille d'honorable Chrestien Hanet, de Rosier, les autres de Lunéville. Le 20 octobre.

(Lunéville, Archives Municipales)

1644, December: Georges de La Tour supplies provisions and fuel to the Oysonville regiment garrisoned in Lunéville (Lunéville).

Pariset (1948, pp. 71, 350) discovered records in the Lunéville accounts of payments made to Georges de La Tour for his contribution to the maintenance of the garrison (because of his exempted status, La Tour could claim reimbursement from the town). The supplies recorded did not amount to much: around 6 December: "1 franc 9 gros paiez au Sr de la tour pour pain fourny. . . . ; *on about 14 December,* 2 francs 6 gros au sr de La Tour pour une charriée *[of firewood]*.

(Lunéville, Archives Municipales, CC 7, fol. 138 et 140)

1644, 16 December [?]: Étienne de La Tour as godfather (Lunéville).

This is yet another instance where Étienne, rather than Georges, was called upon to be a godparent. What makes this record particularly interesting is the surprising reference (quite exceptional in a certificate of baptism where even the highest-ranking individuals are referred to only by title) to "Georges de La Tour the famous painter," a reference all the more remarkable given that he is not even the godfather but only the godfather's father. "Knights" though they were, neither Bellange, nor Le Clerc, nor even Deruet is known to have been favored in this way.

Le 19e [ou Le 16e : surcharge] de décembre. – Claude Cesar fille de Joseph Cesar et de Marine sa femme. Pour parain le Jeune Monsr de la Tour fils de Monsr George de la Tour peintre fameux ; p. Marine Claude fille de François Watrin de Vatimchy.

(Lunéville, Archives Municipales)

1644, end–beginning of 1645: Municipal accounts relating to the *Nativity* presented to the governor (Lunéville).

Mazarin appointed Henri de La Ferté Senneterrre governor of Nancy and of Lorraine towards the end of 1643, following the death of the marquis of Lenoncourt in Thionville on 25 July. Through his father, La Ferté was in close touch with the court of Louis XIII, where painters were encouraged in all manner of ways, and which rivalled the great Roman families in its taste for collecting paintings. A soldier by profession, La Ferté was also a lover of art. In distinguishing La Tour, he was undoubtedly following the example set by the late king and cardinal, winning over to the French cause a particularly influential figure in a town that was far from secure. We should not let this make us think, however, that he had no taste—after all, here was a man with a reputation for greed who actively preferred paintings as his New Year's gift to the sackfuls of écus normally required by provincial governors. From January 1645 until the artist's death (with the exception, perhaps of 1647, and of 1648, when his present took the shape of six hundred francs in cash), the town of Lunéville was under orders to make its annual New Year's gift to him a painting by La Tour. The accounts clearly describe the system that was set up from the start.

The first of these gifts was a picture of the Nativity—by all accounts the painting now in the Louvre, or at least the same composition. A banquet was held in honor of the commission, paid for out of public funds, and apparently with no expense spared.

Faict despence au comptable de quarante francs paiez au sieur receveur Joli, pour despense faicte en son logis lorsqu'il fut traicté avec le Sieur de la Tour, peintre en ce lieu, pour le tableau représentant La Nativité Nostre Seigneur, donné par don et présent a Monsieur le gouverneur de Nancy, appert d'ordre du vingttieme janvier et quittance du 13 mars suivant, cy... XL fr.

(Lunéville, Archives Municipales, CC 7, fol. 27)

. . . The painting was acquired for the considerable sum of seven hundred francs. Pariset (1948, p. 350) discovered the following document,

dated 12 January 1645, in which the town acknowledges that it still owes La Tour six hundred of the agreed-upon seven hundred francs. The second entry shows that the balance was duly paid.

Du XIIe Janvier 1645 avant midi à Lunéville
Les sieurs Claude Bagat commis de ville de Luneville, Dominicq Longet, Joseph Geneval Gouverneur de l'hospital, Claude Guerin son Controlleur, Louys Malbourant, Loys Sibille, Nicolas de la Court, Claudon Hierosme, Jean Hierosme, Nicolas le clerc, Demange Mourits, Nicolas Thiry et Claude Voirin conseillers de ville dudit Lunéville, et le sieur Teodore Thiriet eschevin en la justice ordinaire dudit lieu, ont recogneu et confessé debvoir au nom de la Communaulté dudit Lunéville au sieur George de la Tour peintre demeurant audit lieu, présent créditeur de la somme de six cents francs restant de sept cents francs d'accord du prix faict avec lui pour un tableau que ladite Communaulté veult faire présent à Monsieur le marquis de la ferté, Gouverneur de Lorraine, laquelle somme de six cents francs telle et pour entier (au cas que mondit sieur le Gouverneur aggrée et accepte ledit tableau) lesdits recognoissans au nom de ladite Communaulté ont promis de la paier audit S^r de La Tour, sçavoir la moitié d'huy en trois sepmaines, l'autre moitié d'huy en sept sepmaines.
Pour assurance de quoy lesdits debteurs en ont obliges les biens Communaulx dudit Lunéville et les leurs propres qu'ils ont submis solidairement [...] Et arrivant que Monsieur le Gouverneur n'accepte ledit tableau ledit sieur de La Tour sera tenu de rendre à ladite Communaulté les cent francs par luy receu. Soub pareille obligation submission et renonciation etc. In forma.
Présens Gerard Burté sergent de ville et Pierre Jofroix menuisier demeurant audit Luneville tesmoings.

[*signed*]	C Bagat.		
	Longa	J. Geneval	
	C Guérin	Beurte	Sibille
	pieriofroy	T Thiriet	
	N. Thiery	C. Hierosme	N. La Court
	La Tour		
	J. Hierosmet	N. Le Clerc	
	Bressade	Domange Mourise	
	Loys Malbourant	C. Woirin	

(Nancy, Archives de Meurthe-et-Moselle, 3 E 749)

De la somme de sept cent francs paiés audit sieur de La Tour pour le prix dudict tableau, suivant la convention en faicte avec luy et pour asseurance de laquelle y avoit obligation passé par les sieurs du conseil par devant le sieur Bresade, tabellion, qui par le moien dudit paiement demeure cassé, rapportant icy plusieurs quittances dudit sieur de la Tour pour lesdits sept cent francs par lui touchez tant du comptable que de Claude Merinet et son compagnon et de Gérard Burté, des deniers du roolle levé pour paiement de ladite somme, duquel roolle ledit comptable a faict estat en la recepte cy devant au chapitre des roolles et contributions, feuille 12 verso. Cy donc lesdits... VIIc fr."

(Lunéville, Archives Municipales, CC 7, fol. 27)

As the following record shows, the governor's New Year's gift—in this case, the painting by La Tour—was paid for by public subscription, mainly levied, it seems, on those who had recently managed to avoid paying a share toward the billeting of the troops.

Pour taxe d'argent remi par Burté du roole de ceulx qui n'avoient eu logement du régiment d'Oysonville, délivré audit la Tour... II fr. V gr.

(*Ibid.*)

. . . The work had been painted at Lunéville and was sent to Nancy around the beginning of January, as these other records prove:

Pour une planche à faire un casson pour ledit tableau et façon... I fr. X gr.
Le comptable a paié audit sieur Bressade trois francs tant pour la casation dudit obligation que pour estre en grosse à queue pendante a requeste dudit sieur de La Tour, cy... III fr.
Encore audit sieur fiscal, autre somme de dix huit francs de même, pour trois jours de voïage faict audit Nancy pour porter le tableau présenté et donné a Monsieur le Gouverneur, appert d'ordre du XX dudit janvier et quittance, icy... XVIII fr.
Payé un fran six gros audit V... au voiage faict portant un tableau donné à Monsieur le Gouverneur... 1 fr. VI gr.

(*Ibid.* and fols. 39 and 41)

1645, 12 January: Georges's daughter Claude as godmother to one of Didier Gérard's sons (Lunéville).

Yet again we find one of La Tour's children called upon to be a godparent. Didier Gérard appears to have been part of the extended Gérard family.

Janvier 1645.
Jacques, fils de Didier Gérard et de Anne sa femme. Jacques fils de Claude Hubertin (?) parain. Claude fille du sieur La Tour Maraine. 12 janvier.

(Lunéville, Archives Municipales)

1645, 8 August: La Tour's settlement of his lawsuit against the people of Tonnoy.

La Tour's recourse to the court at the Parliament of Toul over the matter of a debt of six hundred francs incurred in 1632 by the people of Tonnoy and his subsequent victory on 5 September 1643 have prompted talk of La Tour's "callousness" toward a community already reduced to dire straits by the war, his "brutality," his "harshness," his litigious and "implacable" character. We must not be misled by the legal language, however: the fact is that having secured a court ruling against the people of Tonnoy in September 1643, La Tour did not demand payment from them until August 1645, and even then only in installments. More importantly, we have to remember that the money was not La Tour's, but had been lent to the town by his brother-in-law, the parish priest of Tonnoy. La Tour was executor of his brother-in-law's estate, from which he could hope only for a small inheritance. However, he not only advanced the money for the legal costs, as recorded in these documents, but also almost certainly for the unofficial but no less onerous costs that were customary at the time.

We cannot reproduce all the documents here, so we have limited ourselves to the end of the 1645 record, the one that has prompted the most criticism. Set in their proper context, there is clearly nothing incriminating about these terms—they are typical of the language commonly used in "treaties" of this kind.

Ce jourd'huy huitiesme aoust mil six cents quarante cinq, au lieu de Lunéville, sur les six heures de relevée, après ledit compte faict et arresté entre ledit sieur de La Tour d'une part, et lesdits habitans de Tonnoy par Jean Doyt et Claudin Voiriot leurs [...] munis de procuration spécialle dattée du jourd'hier apparue et à eulx rendue signée C.M. Claude d'autre part, par devant le tabellion soubscript, et tesmoings bas nommés, les parties se sont accordées, scavoir que lesdits habitans paieront audit Sieur de La Tour cens francs dans d'huy en trois septmaines, deux cents francs à la Saint Luc proche, a Pasques suivante cent cinquante deux francs huit gros, et de la S^t. Remy venant en un an, deux cents francs, le tout rendu à chasque terme audit Lunéville en mains dudit sieur de La Tour avec les intérests à la ratte d'un chacun payement, lesquels termes il a accordé auxdits habitants pour

leur faciliter l'acquis desdits six cents francs du principal de cinquante deux francs huit gros restans des rentes à payer, sans nonaction de son obligation, arrests et exploicts ensuivis, et a charge auxdits habitans de payer provision lesdits jours auxdits termes sur peine d'estre contraincts pour le tout et a rigueur, sans attendre l'expiration des autres termes non escheus et sans espoir d'autres respit obtenu ou a obtenir pour quelle cause ce puisse estre. A quoi les habitans par les susidts en vertu de leur procuration ont renoncé expressément, tant du chef de leurs constituans que du leur.
Presens Henri Hilaire manouvrier dudit Lunéville et Claude Margot aussi manoeuvrier de Henniet proche Sarbourg, lesquels ne scavent signer ni aussy ledit Voiriot.
[*signed*] La Tour. Jean Doibts J. Cousson

(Nancy, Archives de Meurthe-et-Moselle, 3 E 782)

1645–1646: Municipal accounts relating to the painting presented to the governor (Lunéville).

The governor was presented with another painting for his New Year's gift in 1646, though the subject is not recorded. The intermediary on this occasion was M. du Monnerot, who was governor of Lunéville in 1639.

Un fran six gros à Didier Eilrick pour avoir esté envoyé à Nancy le 20e janvier dernier porter le procès que le sieur Thiriet avoit contre la ville, comme aussy pour porter les répartitions faictes sur les villages de la recepte de Lunéville et la faire authoriser par Monsieur l'Intendant, et pour porter au sieur de Monnero l'indemnité de cautionnement qu'il avoit presté pour la ville envers le sieur La Tour, auquel voyage il auroit employé trois jours
Icy... 1 fr. VI gros
Un fran trois gros a Nicolas Couroux pour porter lettres à Nancy le 4e janvier au sieur Henriot afin de veoir Monsieur de Monnero pour le Tableau que Monsieur le Gouverneur demandoit a la ville, icy...
1 fr III gr.
Quatre francs au fils de Toussainct Pano envoyé icy expres par mondit Sieur de Monnero au subject dudit tableau
Trois centz francs au Sr de la Tour sur ce que la ville lui est attenue du prix d'un Tableau, en appert par ses quittances. Icy... IIIc fr.
A Claude Hilaire un fran six gros pour porter led. Tableau a Nancy et un franc six gros a Pierre Geoffroy pour faire une boeste a mestre ledit Tableau, cy : III fr.

This appears to be the same painting referred to in the accounts for 1646:

A Claude Gagat, trois francs, au nom de Nicolas Thomas, pour lequel il a tenu compte d'aultant, qu'il devoit pour sa cotte part d'une contribution qu'on a levé pour un tableau donné à Monsieur le Gouverneur, ladite contribution de trois francs ayant esté comprise au traicté faict par ledit Thomas avec la ville pour l'an de sa sortie...
Au Sr Georges de La Tour la somme de trois cent francs pour payement entier de la somme de six cent du prix d'un tableau donné a M[r] le Gouverneur, appert de la cedule du Sr de Monnereau et quictance au bas d'icelle desdits IIIc fr.
Audit la Tour vingt francs pour son remboursement de pareille somme qu'il a esté obligé suporter au suiect de la ville, appert d'ordre et quictance desdits... XX fr.

(Lunéville, Archives Municipales, CC 7 (1645), fol. 23, 34, 44-45 (1646), fol. 25, 44-45)

1646, 7 April: Georges and his son Étienne as witnesses for Catherine Gérard, widow of Nicolas Bouillon.

What makes this document particularly interesting is that we see Georges and his son appearing together, and described as "painters living in Lunéville." From this time one, Georges and Étienne very often would appear and sign together.

Le septième apvril 1646 à Lunéville sur les dix heures du matain, George Gassel, Mayeur à Vitumont, se faisant fort de Margueritte sa femme, a reconnu debvoir à damoiselle Catherine Gérard, relicte de feu le sieur Bouillon vivant Maitre des fouriers de l'Altesse Monseigneur le duc François acceptant, etc, la somme de cent huict francs pour cause de l'accord fait entre eulx tant pour principal que despens et interests résultant du procès intenté par ledit sieur deffunct contre ledit débiteur, en la justice du bailliage dudit Lunéville, pour graines et vin qu'il lui avoit vendu, lequel demeure estainct et assoupi par le moien des présentes, de quoy ledit debteur s'est tenu content ; laquelle somme ledit debteur a promis paier, scavoir, la moictié a la S[t]. Martin prochaine, et l'autre à la St Remy suivante qu'on dira 1647. Obligeant etc. Submectant etc. Renonceant à garand, benefice de respit, et toutes autres deffences contraires. Présents les sieurs de La Tour père et fils, peintres demeurant audit Lunéville, tesmoings, qui ont signé, et sont tous de cognoissance.
[*signed*] Gazel. C. Gérard. La Tour. Estienne de La Tour.

(Nancy, Archives de Meurthe-et-Moselle, 3 E 782, fol. 19v)

1646, 20 April: Étienne de La Tour as godfather on behalf of his father (Nancy).

This record was published by Sylvestre (1983 [1985], p. 55). This time, Étienne acts as a godparent in Nancy simply as a stand-in for his absent father. The Silly and La Tour families had known each other a long time (cf. record of 22 September 1627). Antoine Grandpère was a Nancy merchant. Interestingly, both Georges and his son are referred to with the title of "noble."

Le 20 [avril] a esté baptisée Françoise fille de Anthoine Grandpère et de Jeanne Charles ; le parain noble Estienne de la Tour au nom de noble George de La Tour peintre ordinaire du Roy ; la marraine demoiselle Francoise de Silly femme de monsieur de Collignon.

(Nancy, Archives Municipales, Parish of Saint-Epvre, GG 84)

1646: Petition by the inhabitants of Lunéville to the Duke (Luxembourg).

This famous document has been discussed above. It is important to remember the context in which it was written. There were two powers to contend with: on the one hand, the French administration, and on the other, the ducal authorities, temporarily transfered to Luxembourg but still powerful, and to whom the petition is addressed. Then there was the dire poverty to which the people had been reduced, which provoked violent tensions and left people vulnerable to manipulation. The petition provides us with an invaluable list of important figures in Lunéville, but there is no guarantee that it is complete. We do not know who drew it up, or what rivalries afflicted the town. It would be a mistake to see it as a reflection of either the social divisions or the major political conflicts of the day.

Petition on behalf of the inhabitants and community of Lunéville
A Son Altesse
Remonstrent treshumblement les gens du Conseil, et Police de Luneville, Disans, Que comme dés le commencement des guerres les charges de la Ville ont esté très grandes, les Armées de france y ayans campé a divers temps, et années, et depuis les habitans ont esté foulés de garnison enflée de cinq compagnies en quelques années, en d'autres de plus grand nombre, et en 1639 d'un Regiment entier, tousiours aus fraix de la Bourgeoisie, laquelle avoit ia esté donnée au pillage pendant trois iours, et d'année a autre vexée du passage des Troupes pour l'Allemagne, enfin si mal traittée par logements divers en

quartiers d'hyver, notamment au dernier, quelle est sans pareille reduite a l'extremité, et si infortunée que ceux qui y perçoivent les fruicts, et emoluments du ban, et finage, par la quantité du bestial quils ont, en chevaulx, boeufs, vaches, et cochons, ne veullent supporter peu, ny point des charges de ladite Ville, de ce nombre sont les Religieux, et Religieuses qui ont charues entieres, les Dames des fours, et de Chargey, et Me George la Tour peintre, ayans ensemblement un tier du bestail qu'on voit audit Luneville, lesquels y labourent, et sement plus que tout le reste des habitans du lieu. Ce qui faict paroistre la Ville en quelque estat de subsistance, et par consequent a accreu les contributions tant ordinaires, qu'extraordinaires en hyver ; ladite dame de Chargey, et ledict la Tour, (qui se rend odieus au peuple par la quantité de chiens quil nourit tant levriers, qu'espagneus, comme s'il estoit Seigneur du lieu, pousse les lievres dans les grains, les gaste, et foule) ont obtenu exemptions de logements de gens de guerre, elle de Monsr. le Gouverneur de Nancy, et lui aussy, et de toutes contributions. Et a leur imitation Jean Cousson procureur, comme Receveur de L'Abbaye St Remy dudit Luneville a obtenu pareille exemption du Roy, Jean Bresade aussy procureur, comme Receveur de l'Abbaye de Beauprey, en a obtenu une mesme, Nicolas la Cour comme fermier de Mehon a par la faveur du Seigneur du lieu, obtenu moderation de la moitié de sa cotte du quartier dhyver dernier, Claude Voirin fermier des moulins dudit Luneville aussy obtenu pareil, Le Sr Thiriet Eschevin a obtenu aussy par faveur moderation du tier de sa cotte et depuis ayant presenté Requeste au Sieur Intendant a ce d'estre exempt de toutes contributions comme resident en une maison franche, ou il sest logé par intelligence avec le fermier dicelle a suscité un proces a la Ville encores indecis. La veuve du feu Sr Boucquenomme ayant tenté la mesme voye et rebutée, a presenté Requeste a la Cour Souveraine de V. A. tendante a exemption entiere de losgements, et contributions et a obtenu assignation contre la Ville pardevant le S[r] prevost de Blamont pour recevoir les contestations des parties et envoier le proces instruict pour y estre ordonné. Ce sont aultant de fraix pour ladite Ville. Si bien que les mediocres, et les tout pauvres supporteront (privés de faveur) les charges de ladite Ville, qui croissent a mesure que la guerre dure, et continue, et d'autant plus pour eulx, que se voyant accablés de miseres ils seront en fin contraints d'abandonner leur résidence, et se retirer chés ceux qui par egalité de biens, le fort aydant le foible, sans exception d'aucuns portent les charges communes. Ceste desunion cause un murmure grand, et apportera un desordre parmy les habitans de la pauvre Luneville qui est menassée de ruine, s'il ny est prouveu a ceste fois par la bonté et prudence de V. A. pour l'interest quelle peut avoir a la conservation dicelle.
C'est pourquoy lesdits Rem[ontr]ans supplient en toute humilité, et a mains iointes quil plaise a V. Altesse revocquer toutes exemptions et descharges obtenues et a obtenir par qui ce soit, et ordonner que tous les residens audit Luneville de quelle qualité ils soient porteront leurs cotteparts des charges d'icelle, passées, et futures, pendant la guerre, n'estant raisonnable quelle soit la ruyne entiere des uns, a l'advantage des autres puisque tous sont subiects de V. A., affin que par ceste egalité observée, ladite Ville puisse subsister aucunement attendant le retour de Vostredite A. dans ses estats, si fort souhaité. Et ils prieront Dieu incessamment qu'il la conserve en santé, et prospérité.

La Cour conformement aux ordonnances de Son Altesse ordonne que tous les habitans et residants a Luneville payeront leurs courses des contributions, a la reserve de ceux qui sont fondés en exemption de Sad[te] Altesse, Enthérinés par la Cour, ou en exemption octroyée par Lad[te] Cour, et des Religieux et Religieuses Labourants sur les biens de leurs maisons et ne faisants autre traffic. Faict à Luxembourg le dix huictieme de Juillet 1646.

[*Signed*] Gondrecourt
J. Ruliard

(Lunéville, Archives Municipales, CC 1b, no. 6, art. 4).

1646, 18 July: Georges de La Tour as godfather (Nancy).

One of the effects of the disaster of 1638 seems to have been to tighten rather than loosen La Tour's links with Nancy. Basile Mus was a prominent figure. A native of Liège, he married Marie Bergeron, niece of Claude Bergeron, the widow of Jacques de Bellange, and was known to be on friendly terms with Callot and Deruet. He acted as godparent along with Diane at the baptism of Jean Capchon's son on 13 March 1639. It is possible that he was eager to have La Tour as his son's godfather and that he deferred the baptism for nine days until the painter could be there in person.

George Joseph, fils du sieur Basile Mus, administrateur du Mont de pieté, et damoiselle Margueritte Masson sa femme. A été baptisé le 18 juillet, estant venu au monde le 9e dudit mois. Le sieur George La Tour peintre p. Damoiselle Helenne Graffis marreine.

(Nancy, Archives Municipales, Parish of Saint-Sébastien)

1646, 21 July–1647, 20 May: Records concerning Jean Barthelemin.

A series of records affords us a glimpse of another servant in the La Tour household, by the name of Barthelemin. Probably the son of a peasant from Henarmesnil, and illiterate, Barthelemin is clearly described as the painter's "servant" in the record of 15 July 1647. He seems to have had little to complain of in his master. La Tour was present at his marriage with a young girl from Barthélemont, who was attended for her part by the municipal magistrate Thiriet, which makes one wonder if the match was carefully arranged with Barthelin's best interests in mind. When a daughter was born to the couple on 20 May 1647, Étienne and Christine acted as her godparents. It is not impossible that La Tour housed the young couple under his own roof: it is only on 15 July of that year that we find Barthelemin moving to a house of his own, on the strength of his refugee status. It is clear from his tax level that, though by no means rich, he could not be called poor either, and in those dire times he can hardly have regretted his stay in the La Tour household. All three records are given here, each one illuminating the others.

1646, 21 July: Georges de La Tour and his son Étienne present at Jean Barthelemin's marriage contract.

Le XXI juillet 1646 au lieu de Luneville après midy, en parlant du mariage espéré, si dieu et Sainte Eglise l'accordent, d'entre Barthelemin Jean Barthelemin [*sic*] jeune fils de Henamesnil, fils de feu Louys Barthelemin dudit Henamesnil, assisté du Sieur La Tour peintre ordinaire du Roy demeurant audit Luneville, et Margueritte jeune fille de feu Jean Huillier vivant demeurant à Barthelémont, aussi assistée du Sieur Théodore Thiriet, eschevin audit Lunéville d'autre part, a esté accordé et promis qu'ils se prendront, fianceront et espouseront en face de notre mère Sainte Eglise aussitost que faire se pourra. Qu'en après ils entreront en communaulté de meubles, acquet et conquets soit faicts au pays ou dehors, quand mesme ladite Margueritte n'y seroit dénommée. Qu'ils payeront chacun leurs debtes contractées avant ledit mariage de leur fond et propre sans interests de ladite communaulté. Qu'arrivant la dissolution dudit mariage les meubles et acquests se partageront entre le survivant et les enfants dudit mariage s'il y en a et où il n'y en auroit appartiendront pour le tout au survivant si le premier mourant n'en a disposé par testament. Que ledit Barthelemin ne pourra disposer par testament et ordonnance de volonté dernière que de sa part de moitié desdits meubles et que ladite Margueritte en pourra faire de mesme pour la moitié, à quoy faire elle est authorisée dès a présent. Que si ledit Barthelemin vient à déceder le premier et qu'il n'y eut enfans de leur mariage, il donne a ladite Mar-

gueritte comme par forme de douaire la somme de trois cents francs pour les bons services qu'il prétend recepvoir d'elle, et ou il y auroit enfans ladite somme sera restraincte à une de cent cinquante, ce qu'il luy a assigné sur le meilleur et plus clair de son fond dudit Henamesnil et ailleurs où il en pourra avoir au choix de ladite Margueritte, le surplus de ce qui n'est contenu au présent traicté estant remis aux us et coustumes du pays. Si ont promis etc. se le garandir et faire valloir etc. soubs l'obligation respective etc. Presents le Sr Estienne de La Tour fils dudit Sieur de La Tour et Nicolas Cagnard manouvrier demeurant audit Lunéville tesmoings, tous de cognoissance, lesdits futurs ne scachant escrire ny aussi ledit Cagnard.
La Tour Thiriet Delatour J. Cousson

(Nancy, Archives de Meurthe-et-Moselle, 3 E 782, fol. 23v)

1647, 15 July: Barthelemin Jean Barthelemin seeks refugee status (Lunéville).

Barthelemin Barthelemin, cy devant serviteur du S[r] La Tour peintre de ce lieu, a traitté avec les s[rs] de Police dudit lieu pour une année de refuge en ceste Ville à commencer au quinze du courant et à finir à pareil jour, pour laquelle il a promis payer vingt quatre francs en mains desdits Commis de Ville en charge, a quatre termes que seront six francs par chacun quartier, et fera advance d'un chacun afin de ne fournir caution pour l'asseurance du payement... [*this is followed by the standard conditions and phrases*]
Faict à Lunéville ce quinzième de juillet mil six cent quarante sept, soubs la signature du soubscript greffier
+ marque dudit Barthelemin Henriot

(Lunéville, Archives Municipales, BB 2)

1647, 20 May: Étienne and Christine as godparents to Barthelemin's daughter (Lunéville).

Mense Maio.
20. Christine, fille de Barthelemy Jean Barthelemy, et de Marguerite sa femme, fut baptisée le 28 May : et eut pour parrain le Sr Estienne de la Tour : et pour Marraine Damoiselle Christine fille au Sr George de La Tour.

(Lunéville, Archives Municipales)

1646, 10 November: Georges as godfather to one of Théodore Thiriet's daughters (Lunéville).

In these desperate times, when the very survival of individuals and families alike was uncertain, it was essential for the leading citizens to stick together. There were very few now in Lunéville: the only representatives of the nobility seem to have been women, their men having gone off to war, while countless members of the wealthy merchant class had retreated to the safety of Nancy and even Paris. The Thiriet and La Tour families became increasingly involved with each other over the years (see also 23 February, 20 April 1647, 9 March 1649).

Novembre 1646
Catherine, fille de Mons[r] Thiriet et de Damoiselle Nicole sa femme. Pour p. Monsieur George de la tour Peintre Ordinaire du Roy et pour m. Made[moi]selle Alizon femme de Mons[r] Joly Receveur du domaine. ce 10 nov. 1646.

(Lunéville, Archives Municipales)

1647, 23 February: Marriage contract of Georges's son Étienne (Vic).

This marriage was without doubt one of the key events in Georges de La Tour's life. Étienne was his only son, and the entire future of the line rested on him: it was through Étienne and his future children that the determined pursuit of social elevation that had governed so much of the painter's own life would bear fruit.

This was not a noble match but it was a rich one, and in such difficult times, that was apparently the best bet. With the exception of his father and his cousin François Gomien, all the witnesses on Étienne's side were nobles; for her part Anne-Catherine had mainly merchants (and a painter, Jean Dogoz). The contract makes no mention of the future husband's property or even of his profession: his father simply undertakes to clothe him and to provide the wedding feast, and promises, as custom dictated, to support the young couple for two years. La Tour would have been known as a man of sound fortune, however, and Étienne no longer had any brothers, but only three sisters. Moreover, La Tour gave the bride "a hundred écus' worth of jewels"—a fairly handsome gift in itself, which testified to liquid assests that were distinctly rare in those years.

Du XXIII febvrier MCI[c] quarante sept

En traictant et pourparlant du futur et espéré mariage à faire si dieu et notre Mère Sainte Eglise s'y accorde entre le Sieur Estienne de La Tour, fils du sieur George de La Tour Peintre et pensionnaire du Roy, demeurant à Lunéville, son père, assisté d'iceluy sieur son père, d'honor[able] François Gomien bourgeois de Vic [*ajouté en marge*], de noble Daniel Le Nerf cy devant Maire à Maiziere, d'honorable Seigneur Crestien d'Anglure seigneur de Chambrey, Nicolas de Saulbourel, s[eigneur] de Saint Lipvier, Bailly d'Apremont et Cap[itai]ne de Sampigny, de Louys de Ramberviller seigneur de Darlem et Waucour, Con[seill]er au Conseil d'Estat et privé de l'Evesché de Metz et Chancellier en iceluy, du sieur Claude Thiriet escuyer, Con[seill]er au Conseil dudict baillage dudict evesché et Maire de la ville dudict Vic [*ratures*] et du Sieur Theodoricq Dietreman escuyer aussy Con[seill]er audict Conseil d'Estat et privé et procureur général audict Evesché, ses parents, alliés et bons amis d'une part, Et Dam[oise]lle Anne Catherine fille d'hon[ora]ble Jean Friot marchant dem[eurant] audict Vic son pere, assisté d'iceluy, d'hon[ora]ble Barthelemy Claus jeune fils, son frère, d'hon[ora]bles Jean Sauveget, Charles Godefroid, marchants dem[euran]ts audict Vic ses oncles, de Jean Dogoz peintre dem[emeuran]t audict lieu son cousin, Francois Anthoine cy devant Ch[ate]llain de Habondange, d'Adolphe Cardel maître vicier, ses cousins, parants et alliés, de noble Jean Huyn licentié en doict et advocat audit baill[age], d'hon[ora]ble Claude Thiriet Eschevin en la justice localle dudict Vic et con[seill]er es gruyeries dudict Vic, Lagarde, Fribourg et Albestroff, Claude Hannet Maitre apothicaire, Martin Kremer marchant, et Claude Schaumert bourgeois dudict Vic, ses bons amis, d'autre part. Sont esté traictés, convenus et accordés les poinctz et articles cy après :
Scavoir, que lesdicts futurs conjoinctz se prendront fianceront et espouseront en face de nostre Mere Ste Eglise, au plustost et comodément que faire se pourra.
Qu'incontinent et après la solemnisation dudict futur mariage, ils seront uns et communs en tous biens meubles, acquests et conquets qu'ils auront et feront pendant et constant ledict futur mariage, pour après la dissolution d'iceluy estre partagés par moitié entre le survivant et les heritiers du prémourant, à la charge des debtes de la Co[mmun]aulté, des frais funéraires de mesme par moitié. Saulf que si ledict futur espoux survit il emportera par preciput ses habitz, armes et cheval de service, et si c'est ladicte future espouse, ses habitz, bagues et joyaulx avec sa chambre garnie selon sa condition.
Sera ladicte future espouse acquesteresse pour la moitié, desnommée es lettres d'acquest ou non, et nonobstant toutes coustumes faisantes au contraire.
En faveur et contemplation dudict futur mariage, ledict sieur de La Tour père acquitera ledit futur espoux de toutes debtes, l'habillera décemment et selon sa qualité, fera le festin de nopces à sa discretion,

et entretiendra lesdicts futurs conjoints pendant l'espace de deux ans sans obligation d'aucun raport ; en cas qu'il vivroit pendant lesdictes deux années et aussy sans que sa vefve soit chargée dudict entretien.
Au réciproque ledict sieur Friot père, donnera a ladicte futur espouse la somme de cent pistolles vallantes deux mille frans barrois et quatre cents frans pour meubles, ou bien meubles en espèces, jusques à la valeur d'iceulx, l'habillera décemment et selon sa condition, et lui rendra bon et fidel compte de la succession meubiliaire et immeubiliaire de feue sa Mère, à la réserve, quant à présent, à l'égard de l'immeubiliaire, des acquests faictz avec elle, dont par son traicté de mariage il doit avoir la jouissance par usufruict.
Et comme la part de ladicte future espouse est marchandise à elle obvenue du chef de sadite Mère, ne competents audict futur espoux ny a elle, ains sont plus propres audict Sr Friot son père, iceluy s'est submis de les retenir, suivant l'estimation qui en a esté tiré es inventaires pour ce cy devant dressés, et dont il fera le payement auxdicts futurs conjoinctz, scavoir le tier en argent dans un an, et les autres deux tiers contant, en bonnes debtes exigibles et portant rentes, qu'il garandira, fournira et fera valloir, mesme sera obligé aux poursuittes à ses frais, après interpellation juidiciaire et refus des debiteurs de payer.
Donnera ledict sieur de La Tour père, a ladicte future espouse, pour cent escus de joyaulx, desquels et de ses habits, et autres joyaulx qu'elle aura, ensemble de sa chambre garnie, elle pourra disposer, par testament, en faveur de qui bon lui semblera, pourquoy et comme d'icy pour lors elle est auctorysée.
Ne pourra ledict futur espoux disposer par testament que de la moitié des meubles de la Co[mmun]aulté, l'autre moitié devant en tous cas demeurer saulve a ladicte future espouse, avec sondict preciput.
Douaire escheant, ladict future espouse aura pour douair préfix la somme de deux cents francs, soit qu'il y ayt enfants ou non, pourquoy ledict Sieur de La Tour père en a obligé ses biens, entendu que la contingenté héréditaire dudict futur espoux en demeurera chargée, en cas d'ouverture de succession, et la généralité tous les biens dudict S[r] de La Tour père en deschargée, et ce au cas que la contingenté susdicte y suffise ; sera néanmoings loisible a ladicte futur espouse de prendre et opter le coustumier, si faire le veult.
Ne pourra ledict futur espoux vendre le bien ancien de ladicte future espouse, escheu et a escheoir, qu'à charge de remploy, qui se prendra sur les biens de la co[mmun]aulté, et subsidiairement sur les propres dudit futur espoux pour la moitié seulement
Le surplus non icy réglé, estant remis aux us et coustumes desdits lieux où ils feront leur résidances, sy ont promis lesdictes parties, chacune en droict soy, d'avoir pour aggréable, ferme et stable les présents articles et conditions, aux charges y portées, sous l'obligation de tous leurs biens, qu'ils ont pour ce submis a l'exécution de toutes cours et juridictions, pour l'entier accomplissement de tous ce que y est porté, ren[onçant] a tout ce qui pourroit faire au contraire.
Qui fut faict et passé audict Vic le vingt troisième febvrier mil six cents quarante sept, en présence d'honorable Christophe Fontenoy Maître orphebvre et Martin Virion Maitre tailleur dem[euran]ts audict Vic tesm[oings] a ce requis et appelés, qui se sont icy soubsignés avec lesdicts futurs conjoincts, parents, assistants et tabellions.

Etienne de La Tour   Anne Catherine Friot
La Tour   J. Friot   F. Gomien
D'anglure Chambrey
N. de Sabourel de Sainct Livier   De Ramberviller.   B. Clause
C. Thiriet   T. Dietremans
Jean Sauveget   C. Godefroy
J. Dogoz   Antoine   Jean : huyn   Adolphe Cardel
C. thiriet   C Hannet
C. Fontenoy tesmoing   Marien Virion tesmoing   Martin Kremmer
Claude Schomert   Collot tabellion

(Metz, Archives de la Moselle, 3 E 8227, fol. 107-109)

1647, 20 April: Anne-Catherine as godmother (Lunéville).

Anne-Catherine's fellow godparent at this baptism was one of the Thiriet sons. La Tour's daughter-in-law seems to have settled quickly into her place in Lunéville society.

Mense Aprili
15. Nicolas, fils de Claude Gau, et d'Anne sa femme, fut baptizé le 20me d'Apvril : et eut pour parrain Nicolas Thiriet ieune fils de Lunéville : et pour Marraine Damoiselle Anne Catherine femme au sieur Estienne de La Tour.

(Lunéville, Archives Municipales)

1648, 21 June: Georges and his son Étienne as witnesses to the marriage contract between Claude Vaultrin and Nicolas de Chamagne (Lunéville).

This record was first cited by Pariset (1948, p. 77). Claude Vaultrin was the widow of an archer in the duke's guards, Jean Ga, and Nicolas de Chamagne, a widower and neighbor of the La Tour family, was also an archer in His Highness's personal guards.

(Nancy, Archives de Meurthe-et-Moselle, 3 E 782)

1648, 10 July: Remittance by Georges de La Tour of his niece Marie Le Nerf's inheritance (Lunéville).

Marie was the daughter of Georges Le Nerf, La Tour's brother-in-law, who was born in 1588 and became tenant farmer of Badestroff. Both her parents and her brother Paul were dead. We gather from the text that La Tour took her in, almost certainly in the capacity of a "companion," since we hear that he gave her a dress for services rendered. This is La Tour once again in his role as executor of the estate of the parish priest of Tonnoy, the young girl's uncle, here remitting her share of the estate on her coming of age.

(Nancy, Archives de Meurthe-et-Moselle, 3 E 782)

1648, 24 August: Death of Georges's daughter Marie (Lunéville).

This is the only death certificate we have for any of the seven La Tour children who died before their parents. The cause of death was smallpox, the scourge of the seventeenth century, which wiped out rich and poor alike. Born in 1636, godchild of Sambat de Pesdamont, Marie was the youngest of the family and had just turned twelve.

L'année 1648
Les obits
Aoust. Le 24me Aoust mourut Marie fille du Sieur George de La Tour peintre, de la petite verolle.

(Lunéville, Archives Municipales)

1648, 10 September: Apprenticeship contract of Jean-Nicolas Didelot (Vic).

Jean-Nicolas Didelot was La Tour's last known apprentice. His apprenticeship was unlike any other: La Tour's price for four years was a mere hundred francs, together with a ring for Diane. Nephew of the parish priest of Vic and apparently an orphan, but described in a later record as noble, Didelot seems almost to have been adopted rather taken on as an apprentice, and we see him later taking part in family decisions.

The contract, however, is very precise and describes his duties in detail, which were as much those of a page as of an apprentice painter. Two points are particularly noteworthy: the stipulation that Jean-Nicolas should "serve in his person as a model for drawing or painting as the occasion arises," and more important, La Tour's anticipation of his own death and the continuation of the apprenticeship under Étienne "according to the same principles and precepts." We can conclude from this that Étienne must have thoroughly mastered his father's manner by this time.

Du xme septembre 1648
Par devant le Tabellion Général en la Cour et Chatelainie de Habondanges soubsignez et en presence des tesmoings embas nommez sont comparus venerable sieur Messire Christoffle Didelot Curé de Vic et Conseiller au Bailliage de l'Evesché de Metz d'une part, et le sieur George de La Tour peintre ordinaire du Roy residant a Luneville d'autre part, lesquels ont faict le traicté, marché et convention que cy apres pour et au subject de Jean Nicolas Didelot nepveu dudit Sr Curé, sçavoir que ledit sieur de La Tour prendra et recevra ledit Jean Nicolas en apprentissage de l'art de peintre pour le terme et espace de quattre années à commencer des ce jourd'huy et l'instuira bonnement et fidelement en ce qui est de ladite proffession, moyennant la somme de vingt cinq escus barrois que ledit Sr curé baillera pour une fois et pour une bague à la damoiselle femme audit sieur de La Tour, lequel au surplus pour la consideration particulière dudit Sr Curé a voulu gratiffier ledit Jean Nicolas de ce qu'il auroit peu legitimement demander pour la recognoissance de son aprentissage ainsy qu'il se praticque, à charge pourtant qu'iceluy sera obligé de bien penser un cheval soir et matin, d'avoir soing de sa nourriture et enharnachement, de suyvre son Maitre la part où il poura avoir affaire, tant pour avoir soing de sa personne que de son cheval et luy rendre autres services, qu'il ira en campagne porter quelques lettres ou autres affaires sy l'occasion s'en presente, servir a table par le mesnage et autres choses qu'un aprentif est obligé, qu'il sera aussy attenu de broyer les coulleurs, imprimer les toilles, faire et d'avoir soing de tout ce qui depend de la peinture, de servir de Model a peindre ou designer sur sa personne aux occurences qui se presenteront, et que ledit Sieur Curé (hors le vivre) l'entretiendra de tout ce qui luy sera necessaire. Lequel Sr Curé s'est aussy obligé outre les cent francs avant dicts de payer audict Sr de la Tour la somme de quattre cents francs barrois au cas que ledit Jean Nicolas viendroit à sortir au paravant lesdictes quattre années plainement courues, quand mesme il n'en manqueroit que trois mois ou moins, pour asseurance de quoy il en a affecté et obligé tous ses biens presents et futurs et specialement le revenu de son gagnage de Vic et les deux cents francs qu'il perçoit annuellement sur les dixmes dudit Vic, lesquels d'icy comme pour lors pour les années 1651 et 1652 il consent estre mises en sequestre ez mains du Sr Huyn advocat audit Bailliage, ami commun et entremetteur du present traicté, Et a l'esgard desdits cent francs pour la bague sus mentionnée ledit Sieur Curé les payera a la Saint Jean Baptiste prochaine soubz la mesme obligation et affectation, Et pource que la nature de la profession demande d'estre continuée soubz les mesmes principes et preceptes, le Sieur Estienne de la Tour filz dudit Sieur George de la Tour aussy present a aggréé et s'oblige, cas arrivant la mort dudit Sr son pere, de prendre et retenir ledit Jean Nicolas pour le restant de ses années, aux conditions avant dictes ; et s'est ledit Jean Nicolas pareillement present volontairement soubmis et obligé a touts le contenu des presentes et de faire son possible pour donner audit sieur de la Tour touttes sortes de satisfaction. Promettantes les partyes chacune endroict soy d'avoir pour aggréable le present traicté et iceluy suyvre en tout son contenu soubz l'obligation de leurs biens respectifs. Faict et passé en presence des sieurs Claude Hanet Maître Appothicaire et Jean Friot Marchand audit Vic, tesmoings etc. qui ont signé avec lesdictes parties.
[*Signed*] Didelot. La Tour. De La Tour.
J.N. Didelot. C. Hannet Appothicaire tesmoing. J. Friot.

(Metz, Archives de la Moselle, 3 E 8216)

1648, 22 November: Georges and Étienne present at Barbe Dogoz's marriage contract (Vic).

Barbe Dogoz was the daughter of Claude Dogoz, the painter from Vic who had married one of Jean Friot's sisters. Dogoz was dead and seems to have left his wife and children rather badly off. His widow mustered a dowry of 150 francs all told and undertook to keep the couple for only a few months. Barbe's rich uncle, a merchant brother-in-law, and Étienne de La Tour joined together to provide another 150 francs "as pure gift," and so furnish their young relative with a more respectable dowry. Georges de La Tour's presence added considerably to the occasion, and although he was not strictly speaking a relative of the bride, his name was added—as an afterthought—to the list of witnesses, which threw off the wording of the record somewhat. At the end of the contract the magnificent signatures of La Tour father and son stand out from all the others.

Du vingt deuxieme de Novembre MVI^c quarante huict
En traictant et pourparlant du mariage futur et esperé a faire si Dieu et notre Mère Sainte Eglise s'y accorde, par et entre honorable Jean Honin, Maître chirugien, jeune fils [...] et Barbe fille de feu honorable Claude Dogoz vivant Maître peintre [...], assistée de Dame Elisabeth Friot, sa mere, d'honorable Jean Dogoz aussy M^re peintre son frere, des Sr Jean Maillard Marchand demeurant a Dieuze son beau frere, Jean Friot Marchand demeurant audit Vic son oncle, et des sieurs George et Estienne de La Tour, Peintres ordinaires du Roy son cousin [*sic*], d'Adolphe Cardel, maître greffier, et Nicolas Vaultrin, aussi ses cousins, de noble Fiacre Foust, maître eschevin, Jean Calay et Charles Denas, ses bons amis, résidant audict Vic, d'aultre part.
Sont esté arrestés les poincts et articles cy après : [...]
Qu'en faveur dudit futur mariage ladite Dame Elisabeth mère a promis de donner audit Sieur Honin, incontinent la consumation [*sic*] dudit futur mariage, la somme de cent cinquante francs barrois et la meublera decemment selon sa condition et avec ce sera obligée de les nourrir jusques a pasques prochain, comme aussi de les loger en la maison où elle réside pendant et durant une année.
Comme aussi au réciproque ledit sieur Jean Friot oncle à ladite future espouse a promis de luy donner incontinent ledit mariage consumé [*sic*] cent francs, qu'il lui a donné en pur don.
De mesme aussy lesdits sieurs Estienne de La Tour et Maillard sont aussi obligez de delivrer audit temps chacun vingt cinq francs aussy en pur don.
[...]

(Metz, Archives de la Moselle, 3 E 8227)

1648: Compensation paid by the town to Drouin Bastien, beaten by Georges (Lunéville).

This is the second occasion recorded in the archives (which give only a partial account) on which La Tour's somewhat summary fashion of settling disputes got him into trouble. There were almost certainly many others. It seems likely that La Tour suffered a great deal from pilfering on his land and from people challenging his rights on his estates as they did his privileges of exemption. Disputes of this kind were the order of the day in the country, as they still are today. La Tour seems to have been determined to secure the respect not just of the yokels but of the sergeants too, with whom he was on far from friendly terms, as we have seen (cf. under April 1642). There are no known portraits of La Tour, but the story of this beating conjures up an image of a great burly fellow worthy of Corot or Courbet.

This document was first noted by Joly in 1863. It is given here, not in the transcription published by Pariset (1948, p. 354, note 24), but in Reinbold's fuller, more comprehensible text (1991, p. 142).

A Drouin Bastien dix francs pour l'indemniser de sa cure des blessures par luy receues des coups de baston a luy donnés par Mr George de la Tour estant au droict et devoir de banvard [*de la surveillance*] des contrées des sables l'an present et pourquoy y a proces comencé a requeste dudit Drouin joinct a luy ledit substitud, non vuidé sur l'apel dudit La Tour, et saulf à recouvrer ledit appel vuidé, suivant l'ordre du VIIe janvier 1649, cy rendu icy... X fr.

(Lunéville, Archives Municipales, accounts of 1648, fol. 43v)

---

late 1648–1649: municipal accounts relating to the painting of *St. Alexis* presented to the governor (Lunéville).

La Ferté was given an "image St. Alexis" in January 1649. The painting was bought from La Tour for the price of five hundred francs, even though it appears to have contained only two figures. The Nancy painter Capchon, who as we know (cf. record of 23 March 1639) had links with La Tour, was responsible for the canvas once it arrived from Lunéville. A great deal of importance was clearly attached to the frame, produced by a gilder in Nancy, which alone cost twenty francs.

Aultre despence faicte en l'an de ce compte.
Le comptable faict despence de la somme de cinq cent francs delivrés au Sr George La Tour peintre pour le prix convenu d'un tableau représentant l'image St Alexis, acheptė de luy pour faire present a Monsieur le Marquis de la Ferté Gouverneur de Nancy, pour en recevoir protection au bien et soulagement de la Communauté de ce lieu, au contenu de l'ordre du VII[e] janvier 1649, cy-rendu servant tant pour ceste article que les suivants et quictance desdits V[c] fr.
De trente francs pour le cadre a poser ledit tableau faict a Nancy par le nommé Me Jean le doreur XXX fr.
Quatre francs un gros donnés au Sr Capchon peintre audit Nancy pour ses peines d'avoir tendu ledit tableau, l'avoir verny avant le presenter et faict faire ledit cadre, cy IIII fr. I gr.
Quinze francs pour trois jours de voiage audit Nancy par le sieur Mayart allant présenter ledit tableau XV fr.
Cinq francs pour trois journées de louage d'un cheval et despence d'iceluy audit voiage, cy V fr.
Trois francs a Jean Houillon qui a porté led. tableau audit Nancy, III fr.
Pour la caise a mettre ledit tableau I fr. IIII gr.
Trois francs pour le faulx-chassis sur lequel ledit cadre a esté faict affin d'avoir la juste mesure III fr.
Pour le port d'iceluy en octobre III fr.
Pour le disner du Sr Capchon le jour que l'on fist marché dudit cadre II fr.
Payé : V[c] LXVI fr. V gr.

(Lunéville, Archives Municipales, CC 7, fol. 44r)

1649, 9 March: Anne-Catherine as godmother to one of Thiriet's sons (Lunéville).

This time Théodore Thiriet chose Anne-Catherine and her father as his son's godparents. A close friendship developed between the Thiriet family of Lunéville and the La Tour in-laws. But it is also possible that the Thiriet family of Vic had favored the marriage.

Mense Marsio
17. Jean George fils du s[r] Théodore Thiriet échevin et de Damoiselle Nicolle Remy sa femme fut baptizé le 9 mars : et eut pour parrain le s[r] Jean Friot, Marchand demeurant à Vic : et pour Marraine Mademoiselle Anne Catherine femme au Sieur Estienne de La Tour.

(Lunéville, Archives Municipales)

1649–1650: Étienne sets up house in Lunéville.

The conditions laid down in the marriage contract were duly observed: Étienne and his wife were housed and supported for two years by Georges and Diane. Étienne had continued to work with his father and was now recognized as a painter in his own right. The time had come for him to find a home of his own.

On 14 April Étienne took out a six-year lease on a house belonging to the Gérard family near the Church of Saint-Jacques (record 2). His purchase of some planks (record 3) may have been connected with the refurbishment of this house, which had apparently suffered in the Lunéville fire.

He did not seek to be granted "burgher" status. In view of the prevailing conditions and the need to repopulate the city, Lunéville, like a great many other provincial towns, had instituted an additional and temporary "refugee" status. In return for a sort of variable fee, this enabled people to take up residence in the town without being subject to the crippling taxes and duties that burdened the rest of population. Étienne secured this status for two years on 11 April (record 1). Records of payments made in this connection follow the other documents (records 4 and 5).

1649, 11 April: Étienne leaves his father's house and seeks temporary exemption from taxes (Lunéville).

Du onzième apvril 1649. En la Chambre du Conseil, Ville de Luneville.
Le sieur Estienne de La Tour peintre résidant en ce lieu, ayant faict déclaration de sortir du logis du sieur George de La Tour peintre en cedit lieu, son père, auquel en sont deux ans et plus escoulés il a jusques icy esté entretenu avec son mesnage, desirant s'habituer en maison particulière avec sondit mesnage, et avant ce faire désir de scavoir ce qu'à l'occasion de la continuation de sa résidence en cedit lieu avec sondit mesnage il pourra estre abutté par année des deux qu'il a devant icelle pour toutes les charges tant ordinaires qu'extraordinaires de guerre et autres qui lui pourroient estre imposées ou demandées pendant icelles sans estre pour ce comprins aux roolles et charges ;
Le Conseil de ville, au respect dudit sieur de La Tour, l'ont modéré et quitté pour une somme de soixante francs par année des deux qu'ils lui ont laissé ladicte résidence a commencer dès le jour de St Georges prochaine, a paier ladite somme par quartier et par advance, moiennant quoy il demeurera quitte de toutes lesdittes charges ordinaires et extraordinaires et logemens de gens de guerre qui se feront par billet et ordre de la Ville, et toutes autres, à la réserve de la garde des portes à son tour. Et pour quoy a esté dressé le présent acte pour servir audit sieur de la Tour et a signé
de la Tour
J. Coquard.

(Lunéville, Archives Municipales, BB 70v)

1649, 14 April: Étienne rents a house in Lunéville.

Du quatorzième Apvril 1649
A Lunéville avant midy
Le Sr Francois Vaultrin marchand, demeurant à Dompbasle, et demoiselle Catherine Gerard vefve de feu sieur Nicolas Bouillon demeurant à Nancy, tant en leurs noms que se portans fort d'Estienne Chaulson pupil, ont recognus et confessez avoir laissé pour six années, l'année commenceante à la sainct George prochaine et finissante à pareil jour lesdictes six années expirées, au sieur Estienne de La Tour demeurant à Lunéville, preneur pour luy et ses ayans cause, une maison avec toutes ses commodités et appartements, scise audict Luneville, proche la paroisse sainct Jacques, les héritiers Nicolas Bienolat d'une part, et

ceux de Demenge Haron d'autre. En payant pour lesdictes six années cent huict francs, qu'est pour chacune d'icelles dix huict francs, ayant esté accordé entre ces parties que ledit sieur preneur pourra faire faire toutes les réparations nécessaires en ladite maison suivant et conformément à la déclaration qui s'en fera par lesdictes parties et qui sera signée d'eulx, et que ce qu'il y emploira se desduira sur lesdicts cent huict francs, mesme que s'il y a mis plus qu'iceulx il lui sera rendu par lesdits s[rs] et damoiselle laisseurs, à la fin du présent baux.

[*The customary guarantees follow, but this time they are written out in full*]

Présent le Sr Jean Friot marchand à Vic et Dominique Levesque dudict Lunéville tesmoings

[*signed*] Friot Vaultrin Gerard
Delatour

(Nancy, Archives de Meurthe-et-Moselle, E 833)

1649: Étienne's purchase of some planks from the town (Lunéville).

Cinq francs du sieur Estienne de La Tour pour le prix de quelques planches provenantes de la Tour de la porte St Jacques... V fr.

(Lunéville, Archives Municipales, CC 8, fol. 22v)

1649: Étienne's settlement of part of his "treaty" with the town for his first year of residence (Lunéville).

De quarante cinq francs du s[r] Estienne de La Tour, peintre en cedit lieu, des soixante qu'il a deu paier pour sa cotte aux charges dudit lieu pour la première des deux années qu'il a traicté avec lesdits sieurs de police, Ladite première année commencoit au jour de St George 1649 suivant ledit traité qui est du unzieme apvril précédant, le surplus se debvant recevoir et rapporter par ledit successeur cy... XLV fr.

(Lunéville, Archives Municipales, CC 8 (1649), fol. 20r)

1650: Étienne's settlement of the second part of his "treaty" with the town for his first year of residence and the whole of his second (Lunéville).

Quinze francs du s[r] Estienne de La Tour pour le dernier quartier de la première année de son refuge expirée à la St George 1650, cy... XV fr.

Soixante francs dudit S[r] La Tour pour la seconde et derniere année de son traicté expiré à la St George 1651, cy LX fr.

(Lunéville, Archives Municipales, CC 8 (year 1650), fol. 18r)

1649, 26 October: Anne-Catherine as godmother to Jean Mauvis (Lunéville).

Anne Marie was the granddaughter of one of Diane's sisters, so to some extent this was still a family affair, but there were also connections with Paris.

Mense octobri

47. Jean, fils du Sr Nicolas Mauvis, fils du conseillier de la Cour de parlement de Paris, et d'Anne Maire sa femme, fut baptizé le 26 d'octobre : et eut pour parrain le s[r] Jean feraint de Vic : et pour Marraine eut Anne Catherine, femme au Sr Estienne de la Tour.

(Lunéville, Archives Municipales)

1649–1650: Municipal accounts relating to the painting of *St. Sebastian* presented to the governor (Lunéville).

The painting presented to La Ferté as his New Year's gift for 1650 was the famous St. Sebastian. *It was an ambitious composition with five figures and cost the town seven hundred francs, paid to La Tour the following June. The frame alone, commissioned from the sculptor Jean Grégoire, cost forty-five francs. Once again, we have a detailed account of the transaction. The deal included a bonus for one of La Tour's daughters (did she obtain her father's assent for the commission or agree to pose for the figure of St. Irene?) and was toasted at his house with three pots of wine, which does not at all conjure up the image of a moribund or misanthropic old man.*

Quatre francs paiez au sieur Joly pour trois potz de vin qu'il fournist pour boire chez le sieur de la Tour peintre lorsque l'on fist marché avec lui pour ledit tableau de saint Sébastien pour un present a Monsieur le Gouverneur de Nancy IIII fr

Trente six francs trois gros, scavoir vingt cinq audit sieur Mayart pour cinq jours en deux voiages audit Nancy, le premier d'un jour pour veoir Monsieur le Gouverneur a son retour de la campagne, et le second de quatre jours pour lui presenter le tableau de Saint Sébastien duquel la ville lui a faict don, en decembre de l'année du present compte, et onze francs trois gros pour la journée et despence du cheval que ledit sieur Mayart emploia en ces voiages, faisant lesdits trente six francs trois gros dont appert d'ordre du douzième dudit decembre et de quittance, cy XXXVI fr. III gr.

Trente deux francs quatre gros allouez au comptable pour plusieurs voiages par lui faicts, l'un à Nancy le XXIIe Juin, un à Saint-Nicolas et Rozieres le 3 Juillet, un autre à Nancy le XIIIe aoust, pour porter argent à Saint-Arnoult sur les contributions, et un autre audit Nancy le 24 Novembre pour y marchander le cadre a poser le tableau de Saint-Sébastien donné à Monsieur le Gouverneur, le tout suivant l'ordre dudit XXI decembre cy rendu XXXII fr. IIII gr.

Aultre despence pour l'achapt du tableau de St Sébastien donné en present à Monsieur le Gouverneur de Nancy

Le comptable faict despence de la somme de sept cent francs pour le prix dudit tableau, convenu avec le sieur George de la Tour, peintre residant en ce lieu, qui l'a ouvragé, appert de sa quittance dudit prix, lequel a esté accordé avec les sieurs du conseil et police de cedit lieu, ladite quittance en datte du IX[e] juin 1650, cy... VII[c] fr.

Pour un cadre à mettre ledit tableau marchandé a quarante cinq francs au nommé Jean Gregoire sculteur à Nancy sont cy rapportez sur la quittance dudit Gregoire XLV fr.

Six francs donnez a la fille dudit sieur de la Tour pour recognoissance a elle promise au subiect dudit tableau, cy VI fr.

Pour le faulx chassis sur lequel ledit cadre a esté faict affin d'en prendre la juste mesure. III fr.

[Le 7, trois francs six gros pour avoir porté le tableau de Saint Sébastien à Nancy : III fr. VI gr.]

Pour la caisse ou ledit tableau fust mis pour le porter à Nancy. I fr. VI gr.

Quatre francs donnez au sieur Capchon, peintre audit Nancy, pour ses honnoraires d'avoir tendu ledit tableau sur ledit cadre et le porter audit seigneur gouverneur. IIII fr.

Plus le comptable rapporte en despence trente quatre francs cinq gros pour despence de bouche faicte et supportee au logis de luy comptable tant desdits sieurs du conseil de ville que des sieurs la Tour pere et filz au subject du prix dudit tableau, et ainsy qu'il en fust convenu lors du traictié, y a de ladite despence parties reglees le douziesme decembre 1649 cy rapportees XXXIIII fr. V gr.

(Lunéville, Archives Muncipales, CC 8, fols. 45 to 56)

1650, 23 July: Settlement between Étienne de La Tour and Fleuratte Louys (Lunéville).

This curious document is the only record we have of another dispute that La Tour had gotten himself into, and one that he preferred to bring to close with an expensive settlement: payment of all the medical and legal costs and 140 francs in cash.

The sequence of events can more or less be reconstructed from the deed of settlement. A Lunéville laborer by the name of Fleurant Louys caused some damage in one of the fields of the commandery of St. Georges, which La Tour was still renting. Whether he caught Louys in the act or simply believed him to be responsible, La Tour gave him such a thrashing that he had to be seen by a surgeon. Clearly, at over fifty-seven La Tour was still fighting fit. The laborer unfortunately lodged an official complaint, and though he may well have been illiterate, there can have been no shortage of people ready to tell him how best to do battle with the painter, who must have amassed quite as many enemies as friends among his fellow citizens. Neither side could lose face: Étienne arranged a compromise with the plaintiff's wife, who probably had never laid her hands on so much money before.

Le XXIII juillet 1650 avant midy a Luneville le sieur Estienne de La Tour peintre demeurant audit Luneville, se portant fort du sieur George de La Tour son pere y demeurant, a recogneu avoir promis comme par ceste il promect de paier a la descharge de Fleurant Flouys laboureur demeurant audit Luneville les peines et medicaments de Me Jacquin de la Chambre chirurgien demeurant audit lieu qui a traicté et médicamenté ledit Louys et traictera jusque a entier guerison des coups a luy donnéz par ledit sieur Georges de la Tour, en outre de faire deporter des plainctes qu'il a faict contre luy et de paier la ou les amendes s'il y en a sorte que ledit Louys soit deschargé et exempt de toutes choses, mesme des pretentions que ledit sieur George de la Tour peut avoir contre luy au subiect du ou des dommages pretendus faict en un champ dudit Sr de la Tour deppendant de la commanderie ; et a ledit sieur recognoissant delivré et paié contant a Fleuratte femme dudit Louys la somme de sept vingts francs pour les domages et interestes des fraix de poursuitte que ledit Louys avait intenté contre ledit Sr de la Tour père au subiect desdits coups.
Moiennant laquelle somme et descharge avant dicte ladite Fleuratte se disant avoir charge et pourvoir dudit Louys son mari s'est ainsi deporté et deporte desdits Interests et fraix par luy exposé a ladite poursuitte de laquelle elle s'est deporté et renonce a icelle et promet de le faire advouer par ledit Louys son mari.
Ainsi les parties sont demeures d'accord et hors de difficultes soub les conditions et charges avandictes. Pour assurance de tout quoy les parties en ont obligés respectivement leurs biens, etc. (...).
Présents le sieur Théodore Thiriet eschevin en la Justice ordinaire dudit Luneville et honorable Demenge Pierre marchand y demeurant tesmoings qui ont signé avec ledit sieur de La Tour et non ladite Fleuratte pour n'en avoir l'usage et bien cognue au tabellion soubscript.
[*signed*] : De la Tour. Thiriet. D Pierre. Bressade.
A l'instant apres que ledit Louys a recu lecture de l'accord cy-dessus il la advoué ratiffié et confirmé sous les conditions et modifications y portées et promet de l'avoir a tousiours pour agreable soub l'obligation de tous ses biens. Presents lesdits tesmoings, ne scachant ledit Louys signer.
[Signed]: Thiriet. D Pierre. Bressade

(Nancy, Archives de Meurthe-et-Moselle, 3 E 749)

1650, 28 September: Baptism of Jean Hyacinthe de La Tour, grandson of Georges de La Tour (Lunéville).

With the birth of his first grandson, Georges de La Tour could consider his family line assured. In fact Anne-Catherine gave Étienne at least seven children. Étienne's choice of godmother for his son is interesting: the daughter of Jean Des Fours, one of Duke Charles IV's most loyal supporters, who died in his service.

Mense Septembri
35. Jean Hyacinthe, fils du Sieur Estienne de la Tour et de Dam[ois]elle Anne Catherine sa femme, fut baptizé le 28 septembre. Et eut pour parrain le sieur Jean Feriet de Vic ; et pour marraine Mademoiselle Jeanne, fille de feu honnoré seigneur Jean des fours, seigneur de Mont."

(Lunéville, Archives Municipales)

1650, 29 September: Jean Friot's gift of a bond for four hundred francs to his daughter Anne-Catherine, La Tour's daughter-in-law (Lunéville).

This first gift from Jean Friot came just two days after the birth of his grandson, which must have been the fulfillment of his dearest wishes.

Le pénultième jour de septembre 1650 à Lunéville après midy, le sieur Jean Friot marchant, demeurant à Vic, se faisant fort de barbe sa femme, a reconnu avoir donné, cédé, quicté et transporté à Anne Catherine sa fille, espouse au sieur Estienne de La Tour Maitre peintre demeurant audit Lunéville, acceptante par ledit sieur son mari pour elle, ses hoirs et ayant cause, la somme de quatre cents francs de principal à lui dheue par obligation passé à son proffict le 24 fébrier 1640 par devant P. Maire tabellion par Noble Claude Rattel d'Einville soubs le consentement presté par le sieur Chamant son beau-frère et damoiselle Marie Rattel sa sœur, le dernier dudit mois et an par devant C. Brichoux aussy Tabellion, ensemble les intérests des dheus dès le temps cotté audit obligation, la subrogeant pour le tout en ses droits desdits contracts, qu'il a promis de fournir à ladite sa fille, voire audit sieur La Tour, son mari pour s'en prevalloir et servir quant au payement desdits interests tant escheus qu'à escheoir cy apres.
Et est faite ladite donation, cession, quictance et transport pour bonne cause à ce mouvante ledit recognoissant, et particulièrement qu'ainsy il le veut et luy plaist et à sa charge que si ladite Anne Catherine sa fille venoit à décéder sans hoirs de son corps, ladite somme principalle de quatre cents francs demeurera et appartiendra à Jen Francois, Jean Jacques et Jean Nicolas ses frères procréés du dernier mariage dudit recognoissant avec ladite Barbe sa femme ; et sy aulcun d'iceulx estoit décédé, il en seroit esheutte aux autres ; mesmes si tous venoient à mourir, en ce cas ladite somme principalle de quatre cents francs retournera aux parents plus proches dudit recognoissant, sans préjudice des intérests qui appartiendront audit sieur La Tour, tant escheus comme dict est que ceux à escheoir du vivant de ladite Anne Catherine sa femme. Sy a promis ledit recognoissant de tenir, garandir et faire valloir ladite donnation, cession, quictance et renonciation, soubs l'obligation etc.
Present le sieur George de La Tour peintre ordinaire du Roy demeurant à Lunéville, et Nicolas Collat cuisenier demeurant audit Luneville tesmoings, tous de cognoissance, et soubsignes a la minutte, Et depuis ledit obligation en la quarte a esté delivré par ledit sieur Friot audit sieur La Tour son beaufils au nom de ladite Anne Catherine sa femme
[*signed*] J. Cousson. F. Friot. La Tour
De La Tour. N. Colas

(Nancy, Archives de Meurthe-et-Moselle, 3 E 782, fol. 127v)

1651, 22 February: Jean Friot's gift of 6,200 francs to his daughter.

This was an advance on Anne-Catherine's inheritance of her deceased mother's estate (cf. the marriage contract of February 1647). Jean Friot did not die until 1660, and he too left a will in his daughter's favor (Metz, Archives de la Moselle, 3 E 8197, fol. 19), as well as a sizeable fortune to be divided between Anne-Catherine and her half-brothers (Ibid. 3 E 98197, fol. 49).

1651, 23 June: Georges's daughter Claude de La Tour as godmother (Lunéville).

Interestingly, the godfather on this occasion is La Tour's apprentice Jean-Nicolas Didelot.

Mense Junio
23. Jean Anthoine, fils d'Anthoine fery et d'Anthoinette sa femme, fut baptizé le dernier de juin : et eut pour parrain Jean Nicolas Didelot ieune fils de Vic : et pour Maraine Claude fille du sieur Georges de la Tour de Lunéville.

(Lunéville, Archives Municipales)

1651: Municipal accounts relating to the *Denial of St. Peter* presented to the governor (Lunéville).

La Ferté's New Year's gift for 1651 was a painting of the Denial of St. Peter, for which La Tour was paid 650 francs. The picture consisted of seven figures, but in half-length only. The arrangements were the same as for the previous paintings.

"Six cent cinquante francs paiez a plusieurs fois a defunct le sieur George de La Tour pour le prix accordé avec luy d'un tableau par luy ouvragé representant le reniement de saint Pierre et qui fust presenté et donné à monsieur le mareschal de la Ferté, au nom de ceste ville, en l'année du comptable, ledit prix accordé ayant esté du gré et consentement des sieurs de la police, appert de quittance dudit sieur de La Tour cy rendue VI^c L fr.
Neuf gros pour un faulx chassis envoié a Nancy pour faire le cadre a mettre ledit tableau IX gr.
Pour ledit cadre a esté paié quarante cinq francs a maître Jean Gregoire menuisier et doreur a Nancy suivant sa quittance du 25e mars rendu. XLV fr.
Un fran six gros a Nicolas Badelat pour une cassette par luy façonnée et a mettre ledit tableau pour l'envoier a Nancy. I fr. VI gr.
Neuf francs donnéz au sieur Capchon peintre audit Nancy pour recognoissance de ses peines d'avoir servy la ville en plusieurs rencontres au subiect dudit tableau, appert d'ordre pour ce chef couché avec iceluy pour le voiage de Coquard allant presenter ledit tableau cy-après escript au chapitre des voiages IX fr.

(Lunéville, Archives Municipales, CC 8, fol. 181b [1651, fols. 49 and 49b])

Trente francs au procureur Coquard pour un voiage de cinq jours a Nancy au mois de mars pour presenter un tableau a Monsieur le Mareschal de La Ferté de la part de ladite communauté, et pour autres affaires de d'icelle, appert d'ordre du 12 apvril avec quittance XXX fr.

(*ibid.*, CC 8, fols. 49 to 56)

1651, 30 December: Georges and Étienne as witnesses to Catherine Gremel's marriage (Vic).

Catherine Gremel was the daughter of Daniel Gremel, a laborer of Vic, then deceased, and Catherine Gérardin, who was a relative of Georges de La Tour. She married Didier Heulay, son of Didier Heulay, a laborer in Gremecy, also deceased, and Didière Friche, who had married Simon Dupuis, known as La Treille, "sergeant in command at the château of Vic." La Tour and Étienne were among the witnesses. This record was first cited by Tribout de Morembert (1974, p. 223). Its chief interest lies in the fact that it bears La Tour's last known signature.

(Metz, Archives de la Moselle, 3 E 8222, fol. 15)

1651-1652: Municipal accounts relating to the last painting presented to the governor (Lunéville).

We do not know the subject of the painting La Tour was commissioned to produce for the 1652 New Year's gift, but it was priced at about five hundred francs. La Tour seems to have had time to complete it and received an advance of one hundred francs.

As often happened, the painting was not delivered to the governor until March. Étienne would only release it on payment of another 155 francs, and he managed to secure the balance of 245 francs in April, but only by instigating legal proceedings. The painting may have been the Card Players listed in the inventory of La Ferté's collection two years later.

[Faict depense] de deux cent cinquante cinq francs paiez tant a defunct le sieur de La Tour son pere qu'au sieur Estienne de La Tour son filz, en tant moins des cinq cents francs du prix du dernier tableau que la ville a eu de luy, et presenté a monseigneur le mareschal de la Ferté, le surplus ayant este satisfaict par le sieur Roville successeur au comptable, appert de deux quittances et de billetz cy joinctz pour la justification de paiement desditz 255 fr. cy... IIc LV fr.
De... [*left blank*] pour les fraics faictz à la poursuitte du paiement des quattre cent francs qui restoient à paier de prix dudit tableau, ainsi qu'appert par extraict et exploitz rendus, cy [*the paragraph is crossed out, and the following written in the margin*].
Trois fr. six gr. à Nicolas du Bois pour avoir en mars porté le tableau que l'on donna à monsieur de La Ferté... III fr. VI gr.

(Comptes Municipaux, vol. VIII, fol. 186 (1651), fol. 54)

Deux cent quarante cinq francs paiez au sieur de La Tour peintre a present residant a Vic pour le parachef des cinq cent francs convenus avec defunct le sieur son pere pour le dernier tableau qu'il a fourni a la ville en 1651 pour presenter a Monsieur le Mareschal de La Ferté, le restant ayant esté paié par le comptable Prendat, appert de quittance du 9 apvril avec l'adveu de conseil de ce paiement cy II^c XLV fr.
Pour les frais de la poursuitte faicte par ledit la Tour pour paiement de son deu, lui a esté paié six francs cinq gros huict derniers appert de quittance. VI fr. V gr. VIII d.
Et au sergent Colin pour plusieurs exploits faicts a ce subiect et non comptez par ledit la Tour V fr. [*rayé*]
[*in the margin:*] réglé à trois francs, cy... III fr.

(Lunéville, Archives Municipales, CC 8, (1652), fol. 23)

1652, January: Deaths of Diane, Georges, and their servant.

The closeness of these three deaths, each a week apart, surely points to an epidemic, known as "pleurisy." These are by no means the only deaths attributed to this cause: the registers for this period are full of others.

1652, 15 January: Death certificate of Georges's wife, Diane (Lunéville).

L'année 1652
Les Obits
Janvier
Le 15e mourut Dam[ois]elle Diane Le Nerf, femme de Sr Georges de La Tour, de fiebvre accompagné d'un battement de cœur.

(Lunéville, Archives Communales)

22 January: Death certificate of Georges's valet, Montauban (Lunéville).

L'année 1652.
Les Obits.
Janvier.

Le 22 mourut d'une pleurésie Jean, dit Montauban, Gascon de nation et valet de S^r. George de La Tour.

30 January: Death certificate of Georges de La Tour (Lunéville).

L'année 1652
Les Obits
Janvier.
Le 30 Le sieur Georges de La Tour mourut d'une pleurésie.
[Le 26 Me Claude Guerdionnet M^e tailleur de pierres mourut de pleurésie.
Le 20 mourut Damoiselle Despiliers pensionnaire perpétuelle des sœurs de S^t. Francois et le 27e la mère desdites sœurs mourut d'une fausse pleurésie.
Febvrier.
Le 22 mourut Genefviève femme de Claude Marin d'une pleurésie.
Mars
Le 4 Henriette fille de S^r. Nic[olas] Francois Morcel prevost de ce lieu mourut de fiebvre continue...]

1652, 26 February: Gift made by Georges's children to the Capuchins of Lunéville (Lunéville).

La Tour seems to have died suddenly and without leaving a will. Étienne and his sisters averred that he had declared his intention of giving the Capuchins of Lunéville one of his meix, *situated in a part of Luneville territory known as "the old sheepfolds." This was the* meix *that Georges de La Tour and his wife had bought back for 224 francs in 1620 (see that date). It was not a paltry gift, but nor was it particularly large. The dowry given to Anne Rocque amounted to more than twice as much.*

Le vingt-sixième jour de febvrier 1652 à Luneville cinq heures de relevée, le sieur Estienne de la Tour demeurant présentement à Lunéville et damoiselles Claude et Chrestienne ses sœurs, enffantz de deffuncts le sieur George de la Tour et damoiselle Diane le Nerf, vivants demeurant audit Lunéville, leur père et mère, lesquels ont rattifié, confirmé et approuvé la donnation testamentaire faict verballement par ledit feu sieur leur père au couvent des Rds Pères Capucins érigé en la ville noeufve dudit Lunéville d'ung meix et jardin fermé de murailles et palissades comme il se contient en lad. noeufve Lunéville ou qu'on dit es vieilles bergeries, entre les rampartz dud. lieu d'une part et les religieuses du tiers ordre St. François d'autre, parmy trois gros de cens dheus chacun an au revenu de l'abbaye dudit Luneville, au reste franc et quicte, et ce pour par lesdits sieur et damoiselle deffunctz ensemble lesdits recognoissans participer aux bonnes prieres, messes, oraisons et autres œuvres pieuses desdits Rds Pères et de leur successeurs audit Couvent.
Laquelle donnation ensemble ceste présente rattification lesdits recognoissans veullent et entendent sortir leur plain et entier effect par tout en jugement et dehors comme sy ladite donnation avoit estée receue et stipulée par tabellion ou autre personne publique, et ont promis d'avoir et tenir le tout pour aggreable, ferme et stable sans y contredire, et le garandir a toujours ausdits Reverends pères et à leurs successeurs audit lieu contre et envers tout jusques au droict. Sous l'obligation de tous leurs biens etc. Auquels Reverends pères sont esté delivrées et mises en mains les lettres d'asseurence dudict meix faites et passées par Révérend père en Dieu Messire Jacques Magnier vivant abbé dudict Luneville au proffict de feu noble Jean Le Nerf et damoiselle Catherine Lamance sa femme en date du 27 janvier 1604 signée Virietz. Comme aussy les lettres d'acquest que les dames Religieuses du tiers ordre St François dudit Luneville avoient faict dudit meix des mains de ladite damoiselle Lamance et du sieur Francois le Nerf son fils datées du troisième septembre 1619 signées J. Guerin, et celles de la retraicte en faicte par lesdits feus sieurs et damoiselle deffunctz datée du dernier aoust 1620 signée desdicts et toutes trois garantiguée du scel de S[on] A[ltesse] etc. pour servir ausdits Reverends peres comme elles pouvoiet faire auxdits sieur et damoiselle recognoissants avant la passation des présentes.
Faict et passé en présence de Noble Jean Nicolas Didelot jeune fils de Vic et Mengin Colot Bourgeois dudict Lunéville, qui a dict ne scavoir escrire et sont tous de cognoissance
[*signed*] Delatour. C. de La Tour
Chrestienne de La Tour J.N. Didelot

(Nancy, Archives de Meurthe-et-Moselle, 3 E 776)

1652-1660: Gift to Anne Rocque by Georges's children (Vic).

Along with the gift to the Capuchins, chief among the concerns of La Tour's children was to make provisions for Anne Rocque, and here too they were almost certainly acting on their parents' wishes. Anne Rocque had probably lived with the La Tour family since 1634-1635; we know for certain that she was with them in 1642 (see document under 20 January). She was probably little older than La Tour's own daughters, and in her combined role as servant and companion she must have become almost like one of the family by the time it was broken apart by the deaths of Diane and Georges. La Tour's children provided her with a capital of six hundred francs—roughly the total amount Diane received for her dowry, and considerably more than did Barbe Dogoz—thus enabling her to marry into the bourgeoisie. Both records, recently published by Reinbold (1985, pp. 239-241), are given here.

1652, 2 December: Gift of six hundred francs.

Par devant le soussigné tabellion, conseiller en la cour et châtellenie de Vic, sont comparus le sieur Estienne de La Tour, et damoiselle Claude et Christienne La Tour ses sœurs, lesquelles ont volontairement recogneu debvoir a Anne Rocq présentement demeurante chés ledit sieur La Tour, la somme de cinq cents francs [*added above*: et cent francs de meubles] en suitte de la donnation a elle faicte par le feu sieur George de La Tour leur père, pour les bons services qu'elle luy avoit rendu depuis dix sept a dix huict années ; laquelle dite somme de [cinq *crossed out*] six cents francs ils doibvent chacun par tiers, [*the reader is directed to a note in the margin, which reads*:] au moyen de quoy elle a quitté et renoncé à touttes les pretentions qu'elle pouvoit avoir contre eux. approbo *signed*: Anne Rocque] et laquelle dite somme ladite Anne Rocq veult et entend que si elle venoit a mourir pendant la demeurance et résidance qu'elle faict ches ledit sieur La Tour [et – *crossed out*] ou lesdites damoiselles, ladite somme de [cinq – *crossed out*] six cents francs leur demeurera avec tout ce qui luy restera, en faisant faire ses services et prier dieu pour elle ; promettants etc. renonçants etc. présents le sieur Charles Vostelet marchand et Vaultrin Phulpin residants audit Vic tesmoins a ce requis. [*this is followed by the signatures and Phulpin's mark*].
In the margin: Rayé du consentement de ladite Anne Rocq au moyen de pareille somme a elle promise par traicté de mariage passé le 6e janvier présente année auquel jour elle auroit consenty a ladite rature.
[*signed*] Claudon.

(Metz, Archives de la Moselle, 3 E 8228, fol. 106r)

1654, 6 January: Marriage of Anne Rocque, Georges's legatee (Vic).

"Registrata Du VIe janvier 1654.
En traictant etc. par et entre Simon Tabourin jeune fils de Jean

Tabourin bourgeois de ce lieu de Vic, assisté dudit son père, de Claudin Martin, Pierre Marchal ses oncles, et maître Georges Nicaise armurier son maître d'une part,
Et Anne fille de Jean Roch vivant bourgeois de Lunéville, icelle demeurante présentement au logis de noble Estienne Joseph La Tour, peintre ordinaire du roy, présentement résidant audit Vic, assistée d'iceluy sieur son maître, du sieur Charles Vautellet marchand [*the reader is directed to the margin:* "approbo. damoiselle Chrestienne de La Tour jeune fille suffisamment agée"], Jean Friot aussy marchand, Claude Nicolas greffier au marquisat de Blainville ses bons amys d'aultre part, sont esté passés etc. les poincts et articles etc. scavoir,
Que lesdits futurs se prendront et espouseront en face d'église, que le mariage consommé ils seront uns et communs en tous meubles acquests et conquests qu'il feront constant leur mariage, ladite Anne sera acquéteur pour la moitié, dénommée es lettres ou non.
Pour arrivant la dissolution dudit mariage estre lesdits meubles acquests et conquests partagés partagés [*sic*] entre le survivant et les enfants procréés audit mariage s'il y en a, mais n'y ayant enfants lesdits meubles et acquests demeureront pour le tout audit survivant, et saulf encor au premier cas que ledit survivant emportera le preciput ordinaire, scavoir,
Sy c'est ledit Simon qui survit, il emportera ses habits armes ordinaires et outils de sa profession, et sy c'est ladite Anne ses habits bagues et joyaux et (?) que lesdits sieurs Estienne Joseph et Charles Vaultellet ensemble ladite Chrestienne ont promis et se sont obligés chacun pour un tiers de donner à ladite Anne, scavoir ledit sieur Estienne Joseph la somme de cent soixante six francs et huict gros dans Pasques prochain or argent, et pour trente trois francs quatre gros en meubles, et lesdits sieurs Vaultellet et Chrestienne chacun aultant dans la pantecoste aussy prochain, le tout faisant la somme de six cents francs, desquels six cents frans deux cents francs prendront nature de propre a [ladite ?] Anne et aux enfants procréés dudit mariage s'il y en a, et au cas qu'il n'y en auroit, lesdits deux cents francs retourneront auxdits sieurs Estienne Joseph, Vautellet et à ladite Chrestienne ou à leurs héritiers et ayant cause, qu'iceluy Simon sera obligé de leur rendre et payer huict ans apres le deces de ladite Anne future espouse, charge neantmoins d'en payer la rente par chacun an, autrement pourra estre contraint au payement desdits deux cents francs,
Le surplus remis aux us et coutumes du pays,
Promettant lesdites parties d'avoir etc. tenir etc. sans en contrevenir etc. et iceluy faire réussir chacun endoict, soubs l'obligation etc., tesmoins et présents Mariem Virion bourgeois audit Vic et Clément Jacob domesticque audit sieur Friot tesmoins à ce priés.
[*this is followed by the signatures and Jacob's mark*].

(Metz, Archives de la Moselle, 3 E 8228)

1660, 19 March:

Ce jourdhuy dix neufvième mars mil six cent soixante est comparu maître Simon Tabourin dénommé au traicté cy dessus, lequel a confessé avoir esté satisfaict des sieurs Estienne de La Tour, Charles Vautellet et Damoiselle Xrienne de la Tour des six centz frans a luy promis par ledits sieurs et damoiselle, dont il s'en tient pour bien payé et satisfaict, pourquoy en ayant desja donné quelques quictances elle ne pourroit servir avec la presente que pour un mesme effect. Faict audit jourdhuy dix neufviesme mars mil six cents soixante et trois en presence de Caesar Vautrin jeune filz et Nicolas Thiebault demeurants audit Vic tesmoings."
[*this is followed by the signatures and Tabourin's mark*]. (*Ibid.*)

CATALOGUE OF WORKS

Chronological list of paintings by or attributable to Georges de La Tour

The process of piecing together La Tour's oeuvre began hardly more than seventy-five years ago. In 1850 the Société de l'Union des Arts in Nancy begged in vain for someone to come up with a work by the "Dumesnil de La Tour" whose name Dom Calmet had mentioned in his illustrations of Lorraine. Writing in 1863 in the *Journal de la Société d'Archéologie Lorraine*, Alexandre Joly rounded off his reconstruction of La Tour's life with the hope that "one day or another . . . hanging on the walls of some country church" someone would discover "a dilapidated canvas by this artist." In 1883 the curator of the Musée de Nantes, Olivier Merson, carefully recorded the signature "G. de La Tour" on *The Dream of St. Joseph* and *The Denial of St. Peter* in his catalogue of the museum's collections: "We draw the attention of researchers and scholars to the author of these two pictures. It would be worthwhile and interesting to discover something about such an artist of considerable merit, yet so totally overlooked that there is no mention of him anywhere, in the catalogue of another museum or in any biographical work. . . ." Olivier Merson had not heard of Joly's research, nor had he consulted either Nagler or Fiorillo, both of whom duly include La Tour's name (as does Siret, whose *Dictionnaire* was published in the same year). An excellent article on Dumesnil de La Tour had come out in Pierre Larousse's *Grand Dictionnaire universel du XIXe siècle* as early as 1870, but it did not occur to anyone to put paintings and text together.

It was a young German scholar named Hermann Voss who first made the connection. In a famous one-page article published in 1915 he linked the facts provided by Dom Calmet and Joly to the signed paintings in Nantes, and, with a wonderful stroke of intuition, *The Newborn Child* in Rennes and the engraving known as *Madonna and Child with St. Anne*. In 1922 Louis Demonts added the Épinal *Job* (which Gonse had suggested in 1900), the Rouen *St. Sebastian* (at Longhi's suggestion), and, less happily, *The Denial of St. Peter* in the Louvre. In 1926, Pierre Landry discovered *The Cheat with the Ace of Diamonds* (no. 39), and *The Adoration of the Shepherds* (no. 55) was identified by Voss.

From then on, the process gathered steam. Writing in *Formes* in 1930, Vitale Bloch lists seven "night" pictures. In 1931 Voss added a number of "daylight" canvases that had gone unmentioned in the documentary sources but which were authenticated by the signature on *The Cheat*. Charles Sterling's catalogue to the "Peintres de la Réalité" exhibition of 1934 cites thirteen paintings, and Thérèse Bertin-Mourot's 1942 book, collating all of Jamot's research, illustrates twenty-two compositions. Finally, in his major Ph.D. thesis of 1948, François-Georges Pariset cited, discussed, and reproduced several dozen works, including both originals and copies. In the exhibition devoted to La Tour in 1972—the first such—there were thirty-one originals and thirty-one related works. The present catalogue embraces eighty compositions altogether, of which about half are known to us only through copies or references in documents. Future discoveries may yet increase this number by bringing to light lost originals or even quite unknown works. Such is one of the hopes and aims of this book.

This slow piecing together has been far from straightforward, and problems of attribution and classification are rife. Only a dozen works are signed; only two are dated. La Tour has sometimes been credited with paintings that have nothing to do with him. There is still disagreement over the chronology of the works.

My intention here is to marshal all the material amassed to date into critical and chronological order. Pierre Rosenberg and I embarked on the task together with our joint catalogue to the Orangerie exhibition (May 1972). Since then I have had the opportunity to study paintings firsthand and see X-rays, and have thus been able to revise and correct a great many details. Nothing, however, has led me to alter our basic framework.

The guiding principle I have adopted in this catalogue is essentially twofold, assessing the work in terms of both its plastic and spiritual quality. I have laid great emphasis on the development of color, paint quality, and brushwork. At the same time, however, I have believed it imperative, in the case of an artist like La Tour, to take into account the development of his inspiration. It is only on the basis of these two aspects that we can safely determine whether and where a given painting belongs in La Tour's oeuvre.

My approach is thus to start from within the works. To go from the outside in and attempt to establish a chronology from supposed encounters with different artists (whether Le Clerc, Terbrugghen and the other northern painters, Bigot, or anyone else) seems to me a dangerous way to proceed. Lorraine was a bustling thoroughfare to which new ideas quickly found their way. To assume the visit of a certain artist on the basis of the paintings and to date the paintings based on that visit is circular reasoning. Certainly we have to take account of external circumstances, not least the misfortunes that engulfed Lorraine from 1631-1634 on, bringing with them a radical change of perspective and forcing artists to seek out a new clientele. It would be unsound, however, to base a chronology on a sequence of outside influences alone.

The chronology I present here remains both approximate and general. In most cases, it seems to me distinctly dangerous to give precise and definitive dates. There are three reasons for this, all of them particular to La Tour:

1. *The dearth of fixed points of reference.* There are only two dates which are absolutely certain (*The Penitent St. Peter*, 1645, and *The Denial of St. Peter*, 1650), and two others that can be counted as very likely (*St. Alexis*, 1648, and *St. Sebastian*, 1649). All four, moreover, fall within a mere six-year period in a career that spanned at least thirty-five.
2. *The paucity of surviving originals.* Only half the known compositions are represented by originals, and it is always very risky to attempt to establish a chronology on the basis of engravings or copies that are generally a good deal less than perfect.
3. *The remarkable existence of "series."* La Tour returned to compositions again and again, recreating them more or less faithfully after long intervals and in a distinctly different style. Elements of the initial version clearly persist in the later ones, but color, technique, and spirit are all profoundly altered. As a result, these paintings pose a serious and tricky problem in terms of dating. Not even X-rays can provide us with a conclusive answer here. Given that La Tour probably adopted a Caravaggesque way of working—straight onto the canvas, without any preliminary drawing—we can expect the image X-rays yield of these "repeats" to be rather different—lighter, not so worked, and with fewer pentimenti—from that of new "creations" of the same date. However, so many paintings have been destroyed that when faced with a given work, we have no way of deciding if it is a second or even a third version.

In these circumstances, the notion of being able to produce a minute chronology seems to me not only to be pure whimsy but to stem from an utterly misguided approach. To my mind attempting to establish the main tendencies in La Tour's creation is already quite an undertaking in itself.

In order to give the clearest and most complete idea possible, I have included in the catalogue every composition that I believe to be by La Tour, one after the other. Wherever the original exists, it is reproduced; otherwise I have opted for the engraving or the copies that seem truest to a lost original.

The authentic works will, I hope, be obvious both from the entries and from the color plates that reproduce most of them. Appended to the catalogue is a list of lost works cited in documents but about which we have so little information that they are impossible to sort into any order (List A).

The entries have been kept as brief and factual as possible. Almost all the paintings have been the subject of a host of different theories. Many of these have now been shown—particularly since the 1972 and 1993 exhibitions—and on their authors' own admission—to be quite obsolete. I therefore make only occasional reference to them but always indicate the year of publication. The reader can then locate the relevant book or article under that date in the bibliography at the end of this volume.

The Albi Apostles

This was a series of thirteen canvases (Christ and the twelve Apostles) identical in conception to the series of *apostolados* that have come down to us by artists such as El Greco and Zurbarán, and close to the engraved series by Bellange, Callot, and others. It is mentioned at the cathedral of Albi as early as 1698, when it hung in the chapel of St. John and was believed to have been the gift of Canon Nualard. A laboratory study (1972) allows us to reconstruct the subsequent history with some degree of certainty. An inventory after the French Revolution confirms that the series was virtually complete until at least 1795. Some time before then, however, toward the end of the eighteenth century, or more likely, at the beginning of the nineteenth, it suffered a rather common fate at the time: all but a few of the originals (nos. 7 and 10) were removed, almost certainly because they were in very poor condition, and replaced with copies presumably commissioned from a local painter. That artist seems to have held on to at least some of the discarded originals, which he then repaired and sold, as was common practice among restorers at the time. When the series was rediscovered at the museum in Albi and published by René Huyghe in 1946, there were only eleven canvases including nine copies and two originals. Three other originals have since reappeared for sale (in 194[illegible] and 1991). Nevertheless, the series as it stands provides us with an invaluable index of the type of figures La Tour created in the first part of his career and enables us to evaluate his early realism.

1. LE CHRIST BÉNISSANT. Salvator Mundi.

Original lost.
Copy: oil on canvas, 67 x 53 cm.
Musée Toulouse-Lautrec, Albi
[Or. 34]

This figure is undoubtedly the least expected from La Tour, in that he has adopted a very traditional schema. X-rays of the Albi canvas have confirmed that it is indeed a copy and reveal that it was painted on top of a reused piece of canvas (formerly showing a nobleman in seventeenth-century dress and a kneeling monk).

2. SAINT PIERRE. St. Peter.

Original lost.
Copy: oil on canvas, 67 x 53 cm.
Musée Toulouse-Lautrec, Albi
[Or. 35]

This has a certain amount in common with no. 28, notably the very particular gesture of the hands clasped one over the other, which La Tour uses in all the versions of the *Penitent St. Peter* (cf. nos. 28, 58, 68).

3. SAINT PAUL. St. Paul Reading.

Original lost.
Copy: oil on canvas, 67 x 53 cm.
Musée Toulouse-Lautrec, Albi
[Or. 36]

Although St. Paul was not one of the Apostles, he is generally included in the *apostolados* as a counterpart to St. Peter, and he is designated here by the sword and the letter. This painting is close to both the Hampton Court and Louvre versions of *St. Jerome Reading* (nos. 15 and 36, respectively).

4. SAINT JEAN.
St. John.

Original lost.

There are no known copies of this canvas, but St. John would undoubtedly have been included in the *Apostles* series.

5. SAINT JACQUES LE MAJEUR.
St. James the Great.

Original lost.
Copy: oil on canvas, 63 x 51 cm.
Musée Toulouse-Lautrec, Albi [Or. 37]

This figure, more than any other in the series, exemplifies the Caravaggesque tradition in its deliberate use of contemporary dress (the pilgrim's habit, staff, and gourd).

6. SAINT ANDRÉ.
St. Andrew (also wrongly called St. Bartholomew).
Private collection.

Copy: oil on canvas, 67 x 53 cm.
Musée Toulouse-Lautrec, Albi [Or. 42]

The original, which was long unknown, appeared for sale at Sotheby's Monaco on 21 June 1991; it was said to have come from an old family living in the region of Albi for a many years. The cleaning clearly revealed a St. Andrew's cross in the background which had not been understood by the copyist, and as a result this Apostle was wrongly identified as St. Bartholomew.

7. SAINT JACQUES LE MINEUR.
St. James the Less (also wrongly identified as **St. Jude**).
Musée Toulouse-Lautrec, Albi.

Oil on canvas, 66 x 54 cm. [Or. 4]

This is one of the two originals still in Albi. The 1972 X-ray confirmed its quality and revealed that La Tour made a fairly major change in the composition (the head was originally leaning to the left). La Tour's brushwork is at its most complex here and his palette at its most subtle, avoiding all local color.

8. SAINT THOMAS.
St. Thomas (also wrongly identified as **St. Matthew** or **St. Bartholomew**).
Ishizuka Tokyo Collection.

Copy: oil on canvas, 65 x 53 cm.
Musée Toulouse-Lautrec, Albi [Or. 40]

The original, which was long unknown, went up for sale at Christie's Monaco on 22 June 1991. This is the most Caravaggesque compostion in the series: only the saint's bald, wrinkled head is illuminated, while the rest of his face is in shadow. The Albi copy is among the best and is painted, as X-rays reveal, on part of a canvas originally used for a larger composition.

9. SAINT PHILIPPE.
St. Philip (also wrongly identified as **St. Andrew**)
Chrysler Museum, Norfolk.

Oil on canvas, 63 x 52 cm. [Or. 6]
Copy: oil on canvas, 67 x 53 cm.
Musée Toulouse-Lautrec, Albi [Or. 38]

Both the original and a copy of this work survive. The original, which reappeared in 1941, has been slightly trimmed at the top, where a strip of canvas about 2 cm wide has been added. It is very worn but still has some fine passages. The copy which remains in Albi to this day, was painted over part of an earlier work that is visible on the cross-section of the canvas.

10. SAINT JUDE THADÉE.
St. Judas Thaddeus (or **St. Matthew**).
Musée Toulouse-Lautrec, Albi.

Oil on canvas, 62 x 51 cm. [Or. 5]

This is the second of the two originals still in Albi. The powerful realism of the painting suggests the northern tradition more than Caravaggesque models and even harks back, in the palette and the delicate highlights applied with the tip of a brush, to Dürer's figures of old men.

11. SAINT MATTHIAS.
St. Matthias.

Original lost.
Copy: oil on canvas, 67 x 53 cm.
Musée Toulouse-Lautrec, Albi [Or. 41]

This is very close to the *St. Thomas* in its obvious kinship with specifically Caravaggesque figures of bald, wrinkled old men, as well as in its lighting effects.

12. SAINT SIMON.
St. Simon.

Original lost.
Copy: oil on canvas, 65 x 53 cm.
Musée Toulouse-Lautrec, Albi [Or. 39].

This figure is the most brutally realist in the series.

13. SAINT BARTHÉLEMY or SAINT MATTHIEU.
St. Bartholomew or
St. Matthew.

Original lost.

There are no known copies for the twelfth Apostle, but the series would normally be completed by one of these two saints.

14. RIXE DE MUSICIENS.
The Beggars' Brawl.
J. Paul Getty Museum, Malibu.

Oil on canvas, 94.4 x 141.2 cm. [Or. 8]

The painting was discovered in an English collection where it was listed in 1928 as a Caravaggio; although its existence was made known in 1958, it was only published by Benedict Nicolson in 1971. It was put on sale at Christie's in London on 8 December 1972 and acquired for 380,000 guineas by Paul Getty. This was the first major La Tour to come up for public auction.
The composition was already known through a handsome old copy (Chambéry, Musée des Beaux-Arts, oil on canvas, 83 x 136 cm. [Or. 46]), formerly regarded as the work of the Le Nain brothers, but justly attributed to La Tour by Charles Sterling and exhibited at the Orangerie in 1934 (no. 55). The violence of the theme and the way the figures are presented in half-length and without any depth led some critics (Philippe, 1935; Landry, 1937; Blunt, 1950) to question whether this was La Tour's composition, but all doubts were finally quelled when the original was revealed at the Orangerie in 1972, and the canvas has been unanimously accepted ever since.
The quality of the execution is impressive despite certain worn areas in the clothing (notably that of the musician in the center, where only the bottom remains) and we have to rely on the Chambéry copy for a closer idea of the original colors.
The subject had been treated with a very different sort of violence in an engraving by Bellange. One copy bears the caption *Mendicus mendico invidet* (literally, "the beggar envies the beggar," in other words, "however badly off you are, there will always be someone worse off

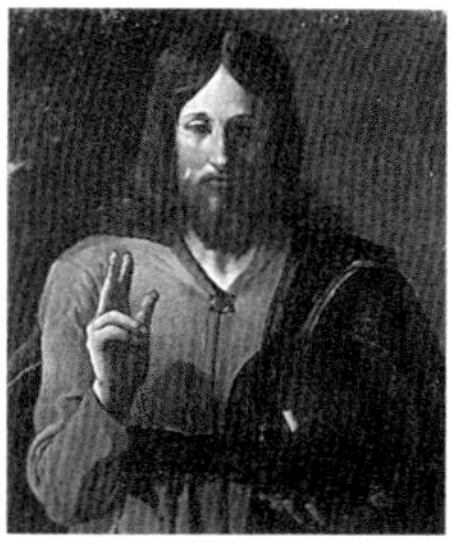

1 copy

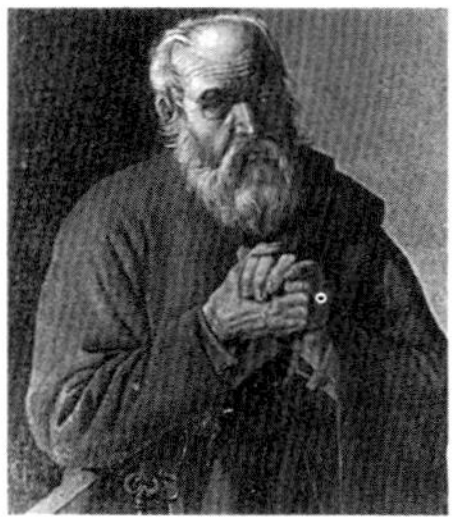

2 copy

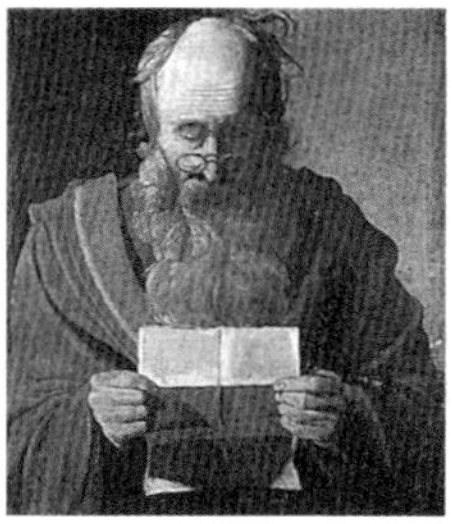

3 copy

4 lost

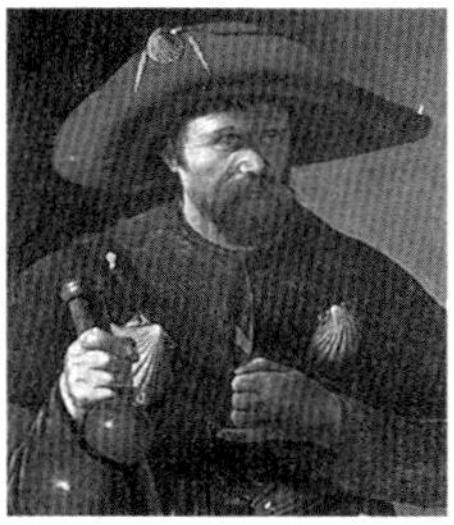

5 copy

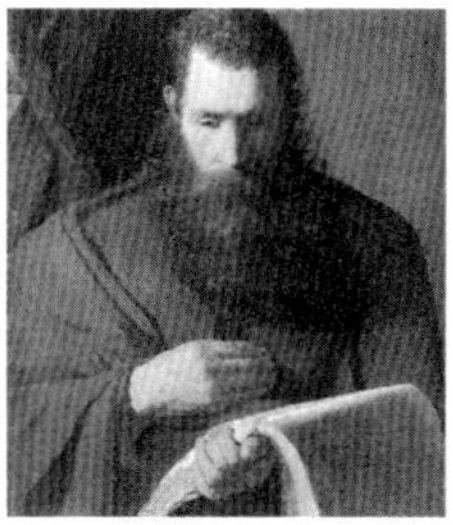

6

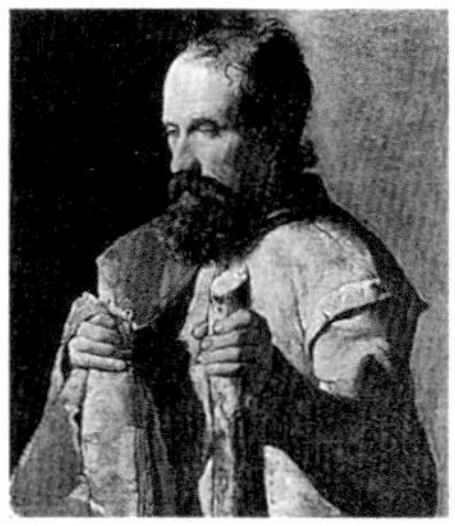

7

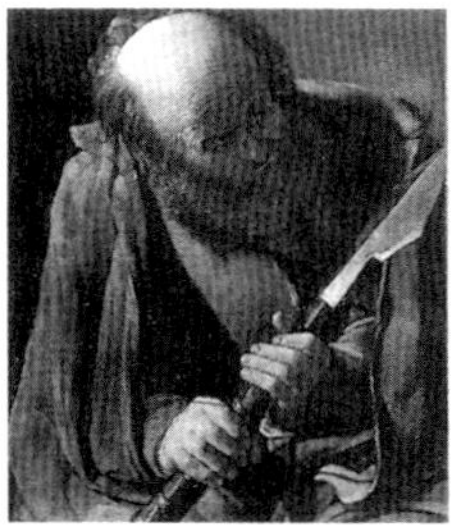

8

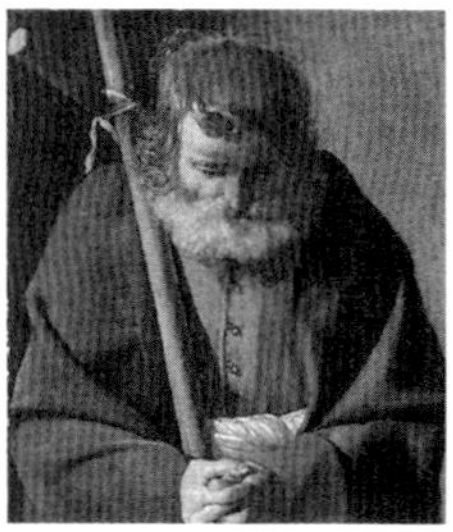

9

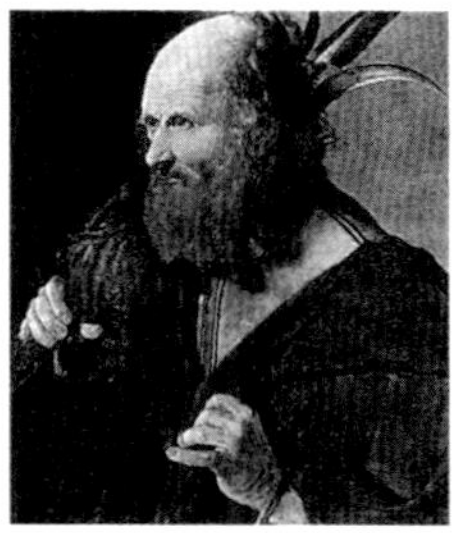

10

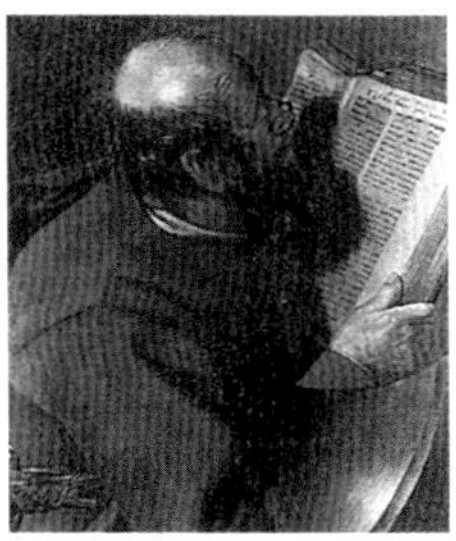

11 copy

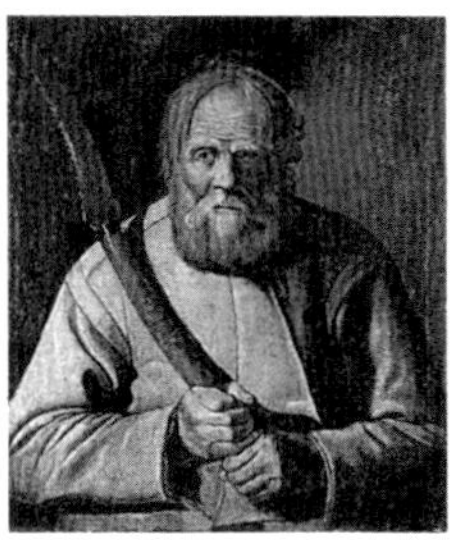

12 copy

13 lost

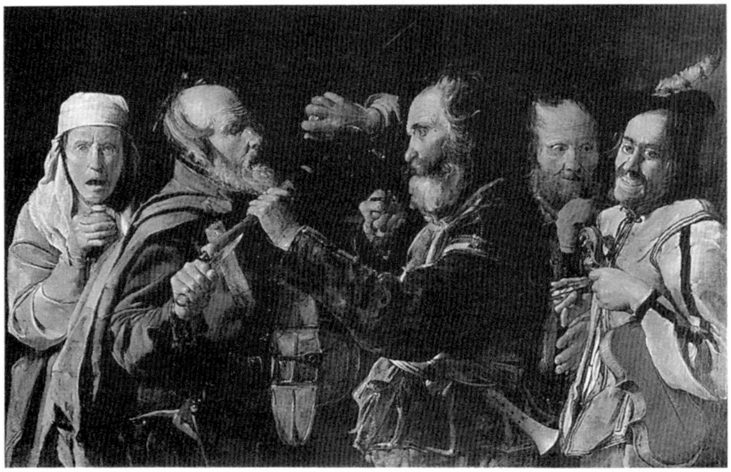

14 with later additions

to envy you"), and this moralizing proverb perhaps provided a pretext for such a representation.

15. SAINT JEROME LISANT.
St. Jerome Reading.
Royal Collection, Hampton Court Palace, England.

Oil on canvas, 62 x 55 cm. [Or. 7]

This painting, presented as "manner of Durer," was bought for 150 florins by Charles II, who acquired it with William Frizell's collection no later than 1662. It has remained in the royal collections ever since under various attributions (Catalani, etc.). It was identified as a copy of La Tour by Gerson as early as 1942. Recent restoration work (1972) suggests that it is in fact a very worn original, probably on account of over-vigorous cleanings in the past. These have resulted in the ground showing through and the highlights all but disappearing (from the hair, beard, and so on), which has given the picture an uncharacteristically blurred appearance. In fact the technique used here seems very close to the one we see in the *Apostles* series (notably in nos. 9 and 10). The motif of the old man with spectacles, already used by Caravaggio in *The Calling of St. Matthew* and widely treated by both his followers and the northern Mannerists, was one that La Tour took up on several occasions (cf. nos. 3 and 36).

16. LE VIELLEUR AU CHIEN.
A Hurdy-Gurdy Player with His Dog.
Musée Municipal, Bergues.

Oil on canvas, 186 x 120 cm. [Or. 3]

The painting was recorded among the Revolutionary seizures in 1791 as originating from the Abbey of Saint-Winoc in Bergues and was allocated to the museum in 1838. It was discovered in 1934 by Pierre Landry, and most critics agreed with him in seeing it as a studio copy. The restoration of the work (1972) has made it clear that the painting is in ruined condition, no doubt as a result of brutal cleaning in the nineteenth

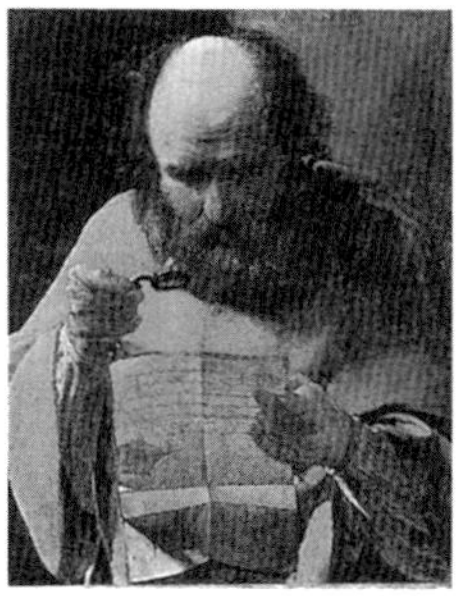

15

century. At the same time, however, the quality of the best-preserved areas (the face and dog) and the significant pentimenti (the right leg) that it has revealed point to this being an original, and the work now seems to be accepted as such. This must be La Tour's earliest surviving representation of a beggar musician, an extremely popular subject among artists in Lorraine at the beginning of the seventeenth century (Bellange, Callot, and others) and one that La Tour was to tackle several times (cf. nos. 14, 17-20). The sober palette, strong tonal contrasts, and the care given to textures that are apparent in the preserved areas link this work directly to the *Apostles* series.

17. GROUPE DE MUSICIENS.
Group of Musicians.

Original destroyed.
A fragment survives:

"Le Vielleur" (The Hurdy-Gurdy Player).

Oil on canvas, 85 x 58 cm. signed?
Musées Royaux des Beaux Arts, Brussels [Or. 45]

Discovered around 1948 in a private collection in Brussels, this painting was immediately published by Greindl, and acquired by the Brussels museum in 1949. X-rays (17a) reveal that this is the right-hand part of a composition depicting several figures, with a violinist discernible next to the hurdy-gurdy player (we can clearly make out a hand, instrument, and bow). The work as we see it has been totally overpainted and presents a thoroughly deceptive appearance. Even the signature, oddly placed as it is, seems suspect. The X-rays, however, show the quality of the work underneath to be good enough for it to be a fragment cut from an original La Tour similar in composition to the frieze of *The Beggars' Brawl* (no. 14) and close in date to *A Hurdy-Gurdy Player in Profile* (no. 18).

18. LE VIELLEUR A LA SACOCHE.
A Hurdy-Gurdy Player in Profile (the Waidmann Hurdy-Gurdy Player) Musée Charles Friry, Remiremont.

Oil on canvas, 157 x 94 cm. [Or. 44]

This composition seems to have preceded and paved the way for the Nantes painting (no. 20). The

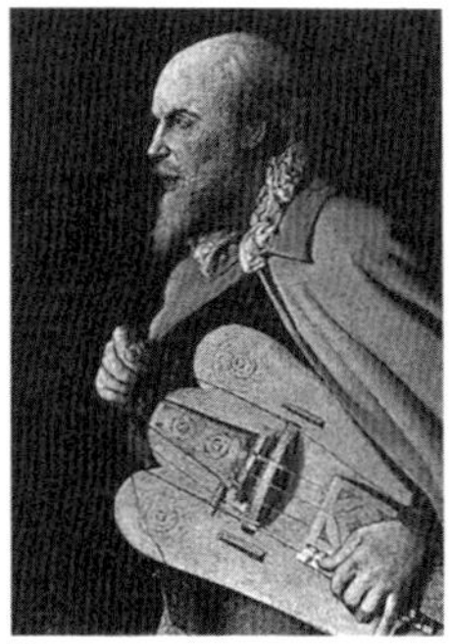

17

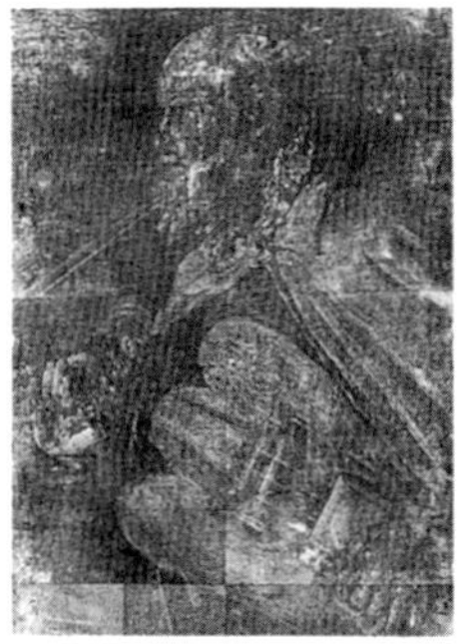

17a X-ray photograph

Remiremont version was in Lorraine at the beginning of the nineteenth century; it was bought in 1848 by Charles Friry (as Spanish School) and etched by him and subsequently passed through the Friry family to the museum that they founded. It has always been thought to be either a studio work (for example at the Orangerie exhibition of 1934) or a copy (Arts Décoratifs exhibition of 1948). It is of high quality, however, and since the cleaning of the canvas and the exhibition in Nancy in 1993 can be considered

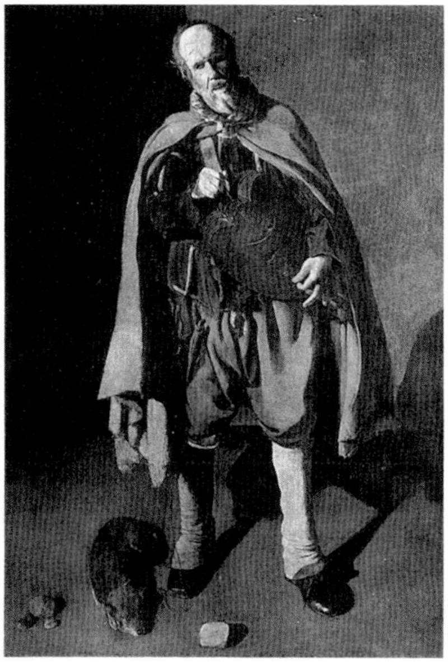

16

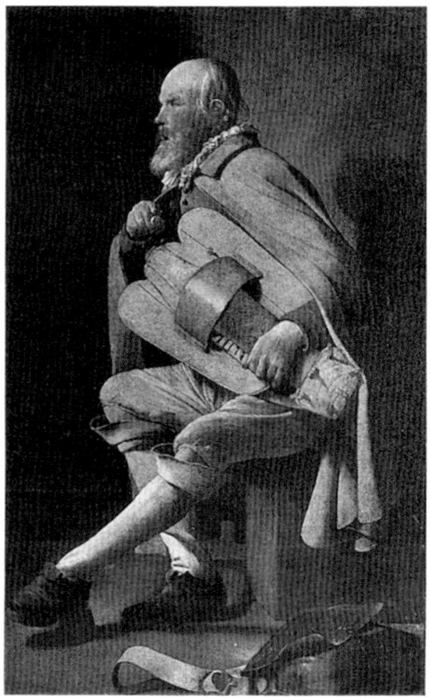

18

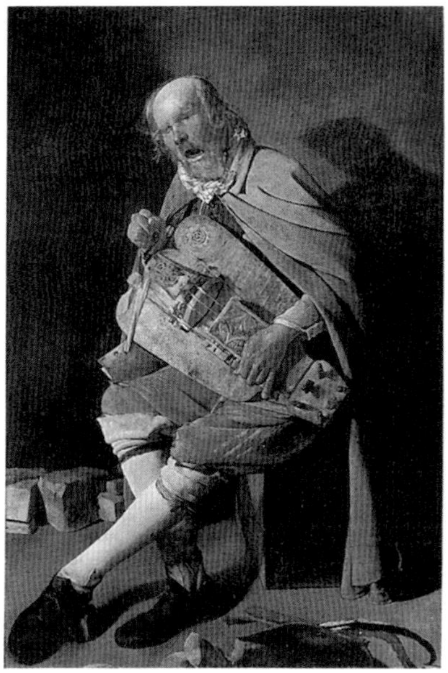

20

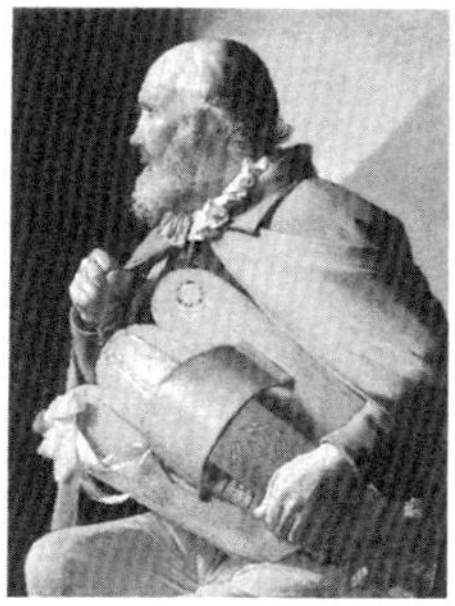

19

an original whose execution is less refined and tonality different from those of the Nantes painting.
Another painting (oil on canvas, 159 x 97 cm) was found in a house in Troyes bought by the Jesuits around 1880; known since 1934, it was bought by the Musée Historique Lorrain de Nancy in 1960. It is more cursory in execution and must be considered an old copy.

19. LE VIELLEUR AU RUBAN.
A Hurdy-Gurdy Player with a Ribbon.
The Prado, Madrid.

Oil on canvas, 84 x 61 cm.

This painting recently came to light in England and was restored in London before being bought by a private Japanese collector. It was published by Pierre Rosenberg in 1990. Subsequently it came back to London, where it was sold at Christie's on 16 December 1991 and acquired by the Prado Museum. Everything points to its being part of a full-length figure, similar to the Remiremont *Hurdy-Gurdy Player in Profile* (the model seems to have been the same blind musician), but differing from it in a number of details, notably the head shown in *profil perdu*, and the broad band attached to the hurdy-gurdy.

20. LE VIELLEUR (au chapeau).
A Hurdy-Gurdy Player.
Musée des Beaux-Arts, Nantes.

Oil on canvas, 162 x 105 cm. [Or. 9]

This is one of the most important and well known of La Tour's works. It was part of the Cacault Collection toward the end of the eighteenth century or the beginning of the nineteenth. Acquired with the whole of the collection in 1810 by the town of Nantes—as a Murillo—it was much admired by Mérimée (1835), Stendhal (1837), Clément de Ris (1861), and Gonse (1900). It was successively attributed to Ribera, the young Velásquez, Herrara the Elder, Zurbarán, Mayno, and Rissi, to name but a few, before being formally given to La Tour by Voss in 1931. Voss's attribution slowly became accepted (though not without a good deal of heated debate) and is now no longer disputed. In its restrained use of color, this work represents one of the masterpieces of the realist tradition in Lorraine and of that entire, often burlesque current that takes wretched beggars and small artisans as its subject, from Carracci's *Cries of Bologna* to Brébiette's *Cries of Paris*. It is tempting to see it as the *Hurdy-Gurdy Player* recorded as hanging in the king's bedroom in the château of Commercy in Lorraine in 1764 (General Inventory of Furnishings in the royal château of Commercy, Archives Nationales KK1131), but even assuming that this picture was indeed a La Tour, as seems quite likely, there is no way of knowing if it was this one rather than another *Hurdy-Gurdy Player*. No copy has been found, other than a smaller version (32 x 23 cm), rather mediocre in quality, that is now in a private collection in Paris. A possible date would be about 1631-1636.

21-22. VIEILLARD. VIEILLE FEMME.
Peasant. Peasant's Wife.
The Fine Arts Museums of San Francisco, Roscoe and Margaret Oakes Collection.

Oil on canvas, each 90.5 x 59.5 cm. [Or. 1 - 2]

Identified in a Swiss collection around 1949 and published in 1954 by Vitale Bloch, the two paintings were acquired in 1956 by the De Young Memorial Museum. They were viewed initially with some scepticism because of their polished technique and small size and subsequently accepted by Sterling (Rome exhibition, 1956), categorically rejected by Isarlo, who declared that they were fragments cut out of a "fairground theater curtain" (1957, 1972), and regarded as dubious by Spear (Cleveland exhibition, 1971). In fact, these two paintings seem to offer precious evidence of an output intended to grace modest interiors, and at the 1972 exhibition, their authenticity no longer seemed to be called into question by serious critics. They have been likened to the kind of studies of contemporary characters so popular with Callot, whose engravings of such subjects were equally unaffected. The two figures are not so much peasants, as has been said, as carefully dressed people from a small town. The woman's headdress has prompted some people to see these works as studies of Roman peasants (Fiocco, 1954) going back to the presumed stay in Italy, but in fact everything suggests that these costumes are typical of Lorraine. The complex technique in some parts of the paintings and the tortured folds, in the woman's sleeves, for instance, in the manner of Le Clerc, suggest a date that is perhaps somewhat earlier than has always been admitted.

23. L'ARGENT VERSÉ.
The Payment of Dues.
Lvov (Lemberg) Museum.

Oil on canvas, 99 x 152 cm. Signed [Or. 32]

Acquired for the Dombsky Collection in the first quarter of the nineteenth century as a Honthorst, attributed to La Tour by Cherbatova in 1970, and exhibited for the first time at the Orangerie in 1972, this remarkable painting was accepted as being by La Tour by many scholars (Bloch, Blunt, Rosenberg, Nicolson, etc.), in spite of various reservations (Pariset, etc.). The discovery of the signature has confirmed the work's authenticity, but it has not solved all the problems.
To date no satisfactory explanation has been provided for the subject. There are obvious similarities with *The Calling of St Matthew*, but the figure of Christ is missing. Other biblical possibilities might include: Matthew at his usurer's table, although this is extremely rare, or the parable of the laborers in the vineyard, but there is only one laborer and a pile of coins rather than a single one (cf. a very different treatment in the painting attributed to Ryckaert in the Stockholm museum). Alternatively, it could be a simple genre subject: the usurer, for instance, as Cherbatova suggests, or, more likely, the payment of taxes.
The dating of the painting remains problematic as well. It was first thought to belong to the very beginning of La Tour's career, around 1616-1618 according to some art historians, or around 1621-1624, which would show that La Tour was painting nocturnes by this time. Unfortunately, the date that follows the recently discovered signature is damaged: it has been interpreted variously as 1634 (Vsevolzhskaya and Linnik, 1975) and 1641 (Zolotov, 1976), but a laboratory analysis has proven that no reading is possible. All we can really do is to consider this painting the earliest of La Tour's known surviving nocturnes, with its precise date remaining uncertain, but we believe it to be relatively early.

24. LES MANGEURS DE POIS.
Old Peasant Couple Eating.
Gemäldegalerie, Staatliche Museen, Berlin-Dahlem.

Oil on canvas, 74 x 87 cm.

Identified in a collection in Lugano and published by Bologna in 1975,

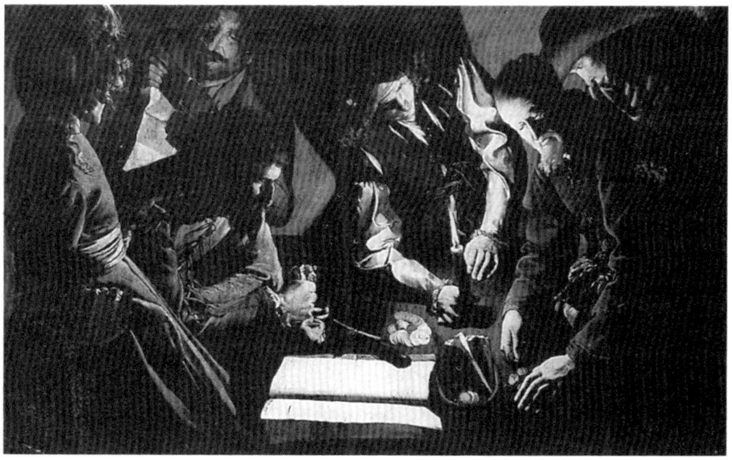

23

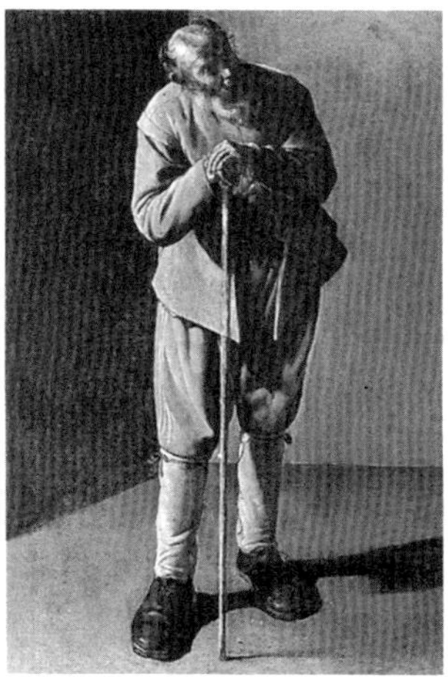

21

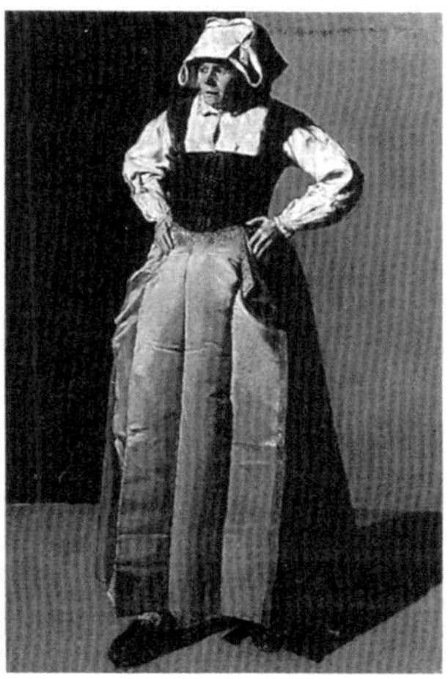

22

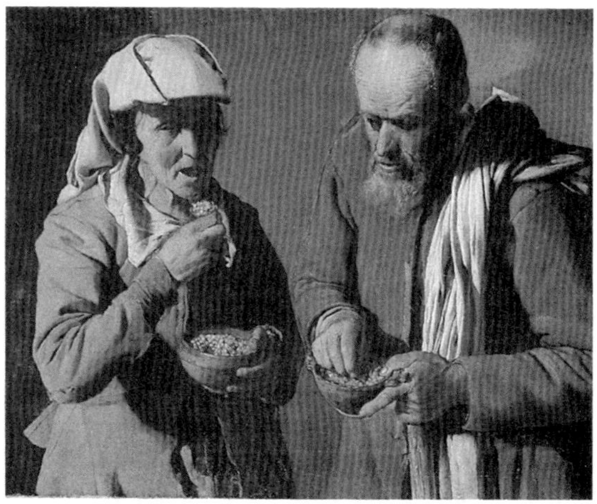

24

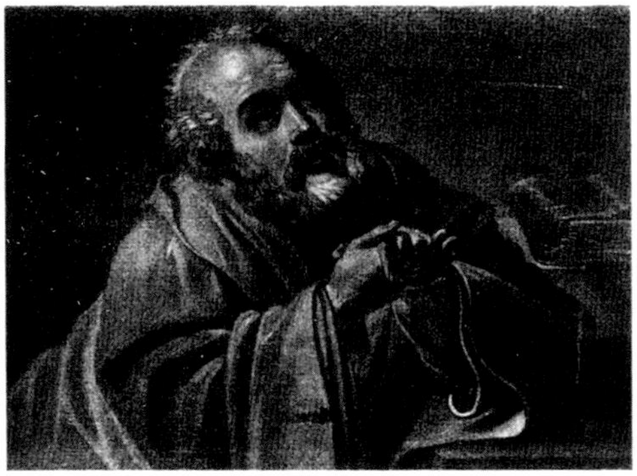

28 engraving

the painting was acquired shortly after by the Berlin museum. When it was discovered, the two figures were separated as counterparts. They were reunited when restoration work was carried out; a small and mediocre copy (Nancy, Musée Lorrain) ensured the accuracy of the reconstitution. This is unanimously believed (by Bologna, Schleier, Rosenberg, etc.) to be one of La Tour's earliest surviving works. Strongly realist genre subjects of this type were common in France in the early seventeenth century (see Lallemant's *George and the Bowl of Broth* in the National Museum of Warsaw) as evidenced in a great many engravings. According to Sylvestre, a Nancy inventory from 1635 precisely indicates a painting depicting *"pea eaters"* but does not identify the artist.

25. SAINT PHILIPPE.
St. Philip.

Original lost.
Copy: oil on canvas, 102 x 85 cm.
Switzerland, private collection.

This canvas was sold as a La Tour in Lucerne in 1951 and authenticated by Voss in 1962, but justly regarded by Nicolson in 1974 as a very mediocre copy of a lost work by La Tour. This latter hypothesis seems reasonable. The half-length presentation, the elongation of the head, and the vertical folds suggest that the original was not very far removed from the *Old Peasant Couple Eating*.

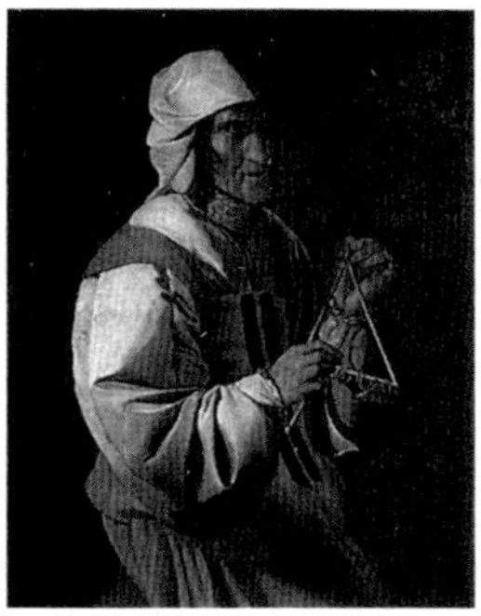

26 copy

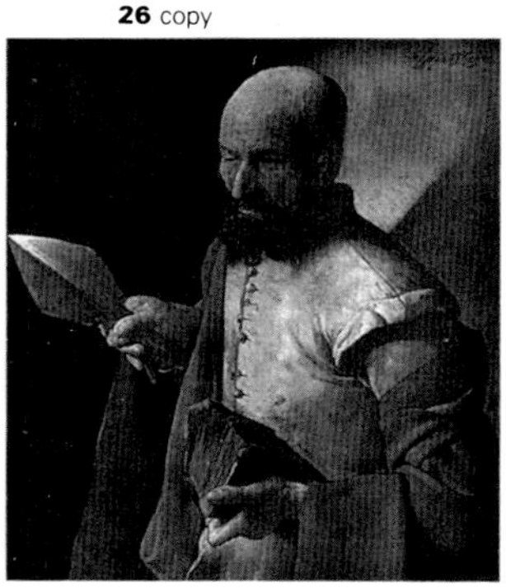

29

26. LA JOUEUSE DE TRIANGLE.
Woman Playing a Triangle.

Original lost.
Copy: oil on canvas, 88.5 x 66 cm.
Private collection, Antwerp.

This copy of a lost work was published in 1991 by Pierre Rosenberg (pp. 703-705). It goes back to one of the genre paintings of musicians that La Tour seems to have produced in great numbers in the early period and which, as seventeenth-century inventories show, often decorated Lorraine homes.

27. SAINT PIERRE.
St. Peter.

c. 1623-1624.

Referred to as "Image [of] Saint Peter" in the accounting records, this painting was bought from the artist by Duke Henri II of Lorraine for 150 francs before July 1624. Grossmann (1958) tentatively suggested that this could be the *Penitent St. Peter* in the collection of the archduke Leopold Wilhelm (see no. 28). Lepage (1875), however, appears to have known a document (yet to be rediscovered) indicating that the painting was presented by the duke to the Minim order of Lunéville as a gift for their church. If this is the case, the composition in question is unknown to us and was probably destroyed in the Lunéville fire of 1638.

28. LES LARMES DE SAINT PIERRE.
The Penitent St Peter.

Lost original: oil on canvas, approx. 135 x 160 cm.

In the collection of the archduke Leopold Wilhelm in the seventeenth century and described in its 1659 inventory as a La Tour, the painting then passed into the imperial collections in Vienna. It featured in two sets of engravings of the latter (see the mezzotint by Anton Joseph Prenner [G5] from *Theatrum artis pictoriae*, vol. III, 1730). There is no record of the painting after the end of the eighteenth century, but it may still exist. Grossmann (1958) suggested that it might be the "Image [of] Saint Peter" bought by the duke of Lorraine in 1624, but this remains open to question (see no. 27). In any case, it should be dated in the 1620s: the composition is similar to the horizontal canvases with half-length figures of saints produced, for example, by Terbrugghen around 1621.

29. SAINT THOMAS.
St. Thomas (also known as **Saint with a Spear**).
Musée du Louvre, Paris.

Oil on canvas, 71 x 56 cm. Signed.

The existence of this painting, which is signed *Georgius de La Tour fecit*, was made known in 1950 by Madeleine Pré, and it was subsequently mentioned and reproduced by Pariset (1955, 1963), Huyghe (1960), Tanaka (1969, 1972), and others. Access to the work in the château de Gallerande in the Sarthe region of France was persistently denied to art historians by its owner, who refused to lend it to the exhibition at the Orangerie and left it to the Order of Malta. It was offered for sale by the latter, and eventually bought by the Louvre in 1988 after a national subscription campaign. A composition that is more expansive and fluid than those of the Albi *Apostles* suggests that it is appreciably later in date and already prefigures the style of *The Fortune Teller* (no. 31).

30. LE TRICHEUR (à l'as de trèfle).
The Cheat with the Ace of Clubs.
Kimbell Art Museum, Fort Worth.

Oil on canvas, 96 x 155 cm. [Or. 13]

This painting was in a private collection in Geneva from at least the end of the nineteenth century and known since 1932, but it was either disregarded completely or considered a copy by most art historians, with the exception of Pariset (1948, 1963). Publically displayed for the first time at the Orangerie in 1972, it has been accepted as an original ever since, and was acquired by the museum in Fort Worth in 1981. Although parts of the canvas are unfortunately damaged, it still contains many passages of the highest quality.

La Tour takes up the subject of the cheat pioneered by Caravaggio and frequently treated by artists after him (Valentin, etc.), but, as in *The Fortune Teller*, seems to add that of the prodigal son, and at the same time brings together three major temptations of the seventeenth century—wine, women, and gambling. The work has been variously dated, and sometimes

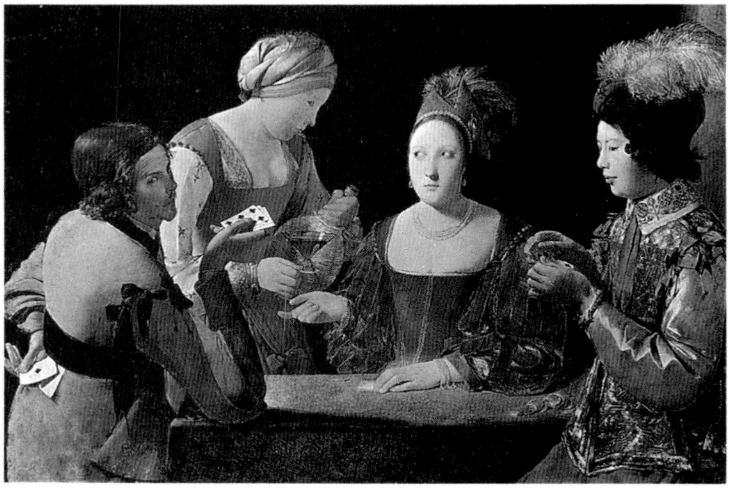

30

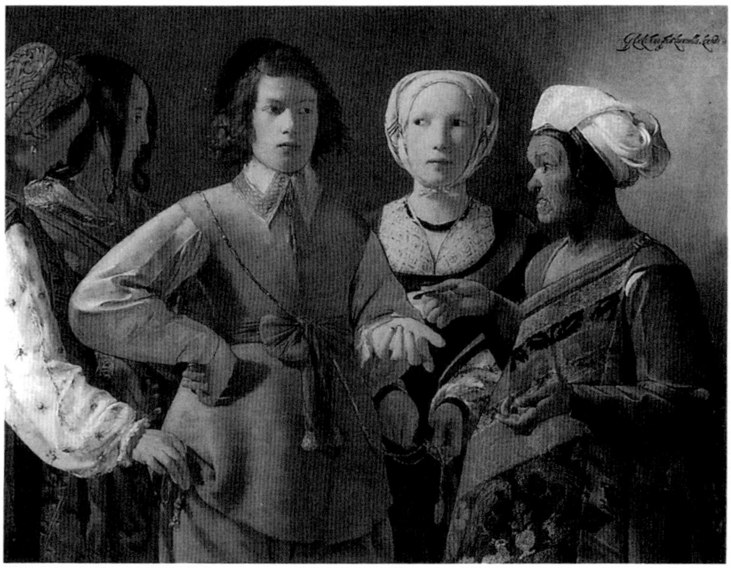

31

even thought to be later than the Louvre version (no. 39). It seems far more likely, however, from the lighter palette, and the delicate handling of the paint, as well as the number of pentimenti, to be earlier than the signed version and even earlier than the *The Fortune Teller*.

31. LA DISEUSE DE BONNE AVENTURE.
The Fortune Teller.
The Metropolitan Museum of Art, New York.

Oil on canvas, 102 x 123 cm. Signed. [Or. 12]

The painting is signed *G. de La Tour Fecit Lunevillae Lothar.* It was discovered during the Second World War in the château of La Vagotière (in the Sarthe region of France), which was owned by the family of General de Gastines. Purchased by the Galerie Wildenstein in 1949, it was exported ten years later to the United States, where it was acquired by the Metropolitan Museum in March 1960. The news of its export evoked keen emotions in France, and gave rise to a media campaign that provided a measure of La Tour's rise to fame. The work's authenticity was subsequently questioned (Diana de Marly, 1970) but was confirmed by the 1972 exhibition, where it received particular admiration, only to be challenged again in the United States in 1980 (when Christopher Wright and Diana de Marly contended that it was a modern forgery executed shortly before the Second World War). The media in turn tried to transform the affair into a scandal, but Rosenberg put an end to this campaign in 1981 when he produced precise documentary evidence that the painting was already in existence in 1879, at a time when La Tour was still thoroughly neglected.

The Caravaggesque theme of fortune-telling was quite widespread in the first half of the seventeenth century (Caravaggio, Gentileschi, etc.) and often embroidered, as here, with touches of sexual innuendo and sly pickpocketing by the Gypsy women (Vouet, Valentin, Brébiette, etc.). To this, La Tour seems to add, as he does in no. 30, the theme of the prodigal son being relieved of his possessions by women, which was equally popular at the time. It has been suggested that this painting dates from the period immediately after La Tour settled in Lunéville (Pariset, 1961; Nicolson). In my view, however, it represents the very best of the daylight scenes and could therefore be pushed back as late even as 1636-1638. The reference to *Lunevillae*, in keeping with contemporary convention, appears to have indicated that the picture was for a collector from outside Lorraine. We are also reminded of Jean-Baptiste de Bretagne's collection where" a large canvas painting . . . portraying fortune tellers" was described as "an original by La Tour" in 1650 (cf. no. A13).

32. SAINT JÉRÔME PÉNITENT (à l'auréole).
St. Jerome.
Musée des Beaux-Arts, Grenoble.

Oil on canvas, 157 x 100 cm. [Or. 10]

Confiscated during the Revolution, this work probably came from the Abbey of Saint-Antoine-de-Viennois in the Dauphiné region. La Tour is mentioned in two local manuscripts dating from the early eighteenth century as one of a number of artists whose work the church owned. The painting was long claimed for one artist of the Spanish School or another (Ribera, Mayno), before finally being attributed to La Tour by Voss (1931) along with the Stockholm version (no. 38). After a great deal of opposition (La Tourette and others), and doubts as to its authenticity—which seems incomprehensible given the stunning quality of the execution—the painting is now universally accepted as one of La Tour's masterpieces. This is perhaps the work that best demonstrates La Tour's skill as a draftsman: here more than anywhere else we see the sharpness of his line and the steady swiftness of his brush, both of which can be fully appreciated due to the paintings's excellent condition and which are emphasized by the X-ray as well.

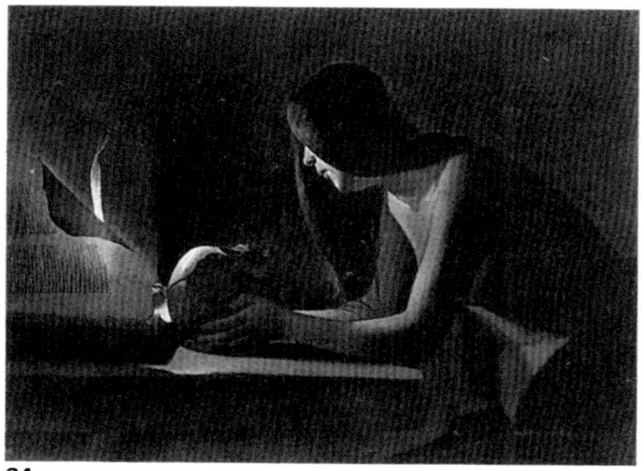
34

33. LA MADELEINE PÉNITENTE AU CRUCIFIX.
The Repentant Magdalen with the Crucifix.

Original lost.
Copy: oil on canvas.
Private collection, France.

This hitherto unknown composition was published by Rosenberg in 1976 (p. 453, fig. 1) as a copy of a lost original by La Tour. The Magdalen is depicted in darkness, one breast bared, one hand resting on a death's head, the other grasping a crucifix in a gesture reminiscent of *St. Jerome*. The original, which was undoubtedly by La Tour, must have been one of the earliest of the *Repentant Magdalen* series.

34. LA MADELEINE PÉNITENTE.
The Repentant Magdalen.
Private collection.

Oil on canvas.

When this painting was discovered recently, the dark areas were found to be completely altered, but the light areas were better preserved, and part of a signature survives. The composition was already known through a rather mediocre copy on wood in Nancy. It seems probable that this work falls rather early in his long series of nocturnes.

35. LA MADELEINE.
The Magdalen.

In February 1641 La Tour himself referred to this painting as "representing the holy Magdalen, by his own hand" and indicated that it had been sold for 14 pistoles (approximately 290 Barrish francs) to Chrétien de Nogent, lord of Chanteheux and chamberlain of the duke of Lorraine, who resided in Lunéville and was a friend of the painter (cf. Aubry and Choux, 1976, p. 155). Since Chrétien de Nogent died in 1638 without having finished paying for the painting, it could reasonably be dated to 1636-1638. It could likewise be assumed that payment was initially suspended because of the harsh events of those years, which would also explain why the painting, which escaped the burning and pillaging of Lunéville, was found "in refuge" in 1641 with the Minim Fathers. The *Magdalen* series painted by La Tour is too large for us to connect this text with one of the surviving examples with any satisfying degree of probability.

36. SAINT JÉRÔME LISANT.
St Jerome Reading.

Original lost.
Copy: oil on canvas, 122 x 93 cm.
Musée du Louvre, Paris [Or. 43]

This is an imposing composition, marked by the pronounced contrasts we find in the night canvases, although there are direct links with early works such as the Albi series (nos. 3 and 6) and the Hampton Court version of *St. Jerome Reading* (no. 15), for example, the relatively poor organization of the still life. The painting now in the Louvre, discovered in the Delclève Collection in Nice in 1934 and acquired in 1935, was thought at first to be the original. The quality of the execution soon raised doubts, however (Sterling, 1951;

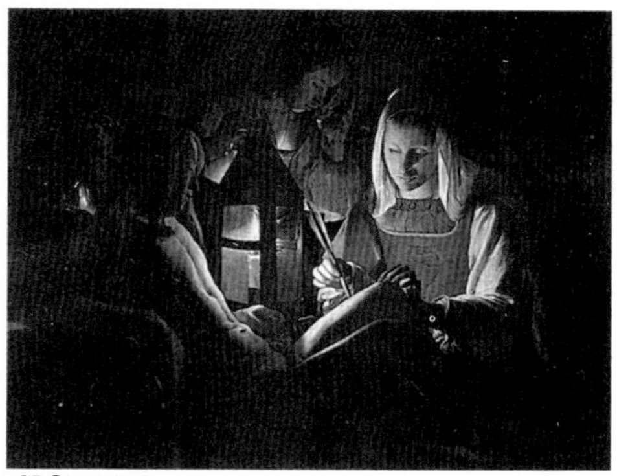
37 Rouen copy

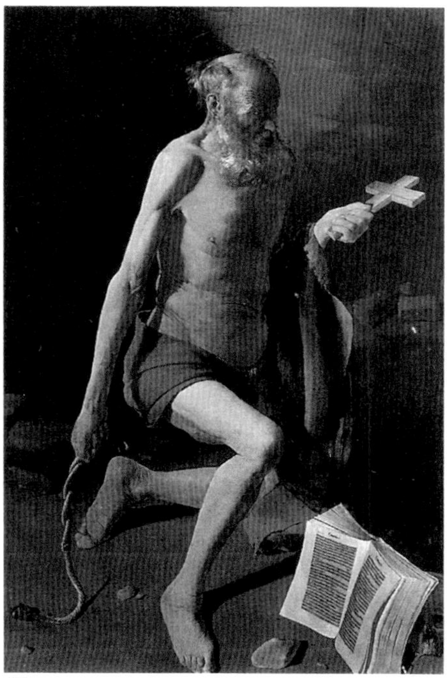
32

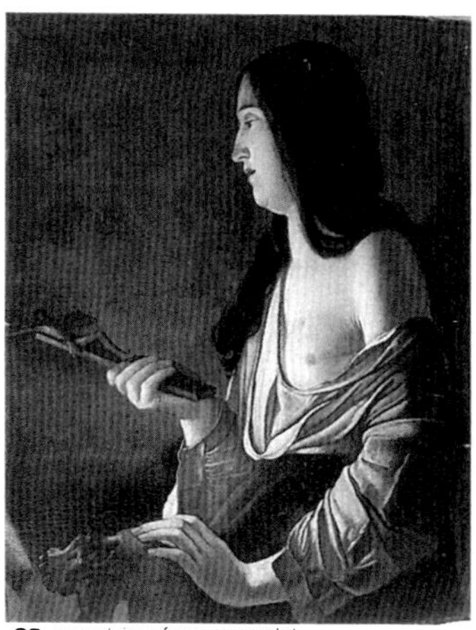
33 copy (view from an angle)

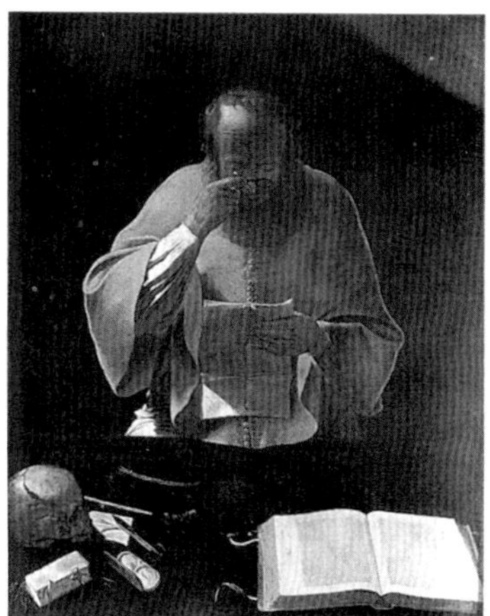
36 copy

Malraux, 1951, etc.), and these were to be confirmed when the work was studied at the time of the 1972 exhibition.
Another copy of the painting with the figure cut off at the waist is located in a private collection in Paris. It confirms the fame enjoyed by this composition, which is perhaps one of the paintings of *St. Jerome* mentioned in Paris in the seventeenth century (cf. no. A6).

37. SAINT SÉBASTIEN SOIGNÉ PAR IRÈNE (à la lanterne).
St. Sebastian Tended by Irene (with the Lantern).

Original lost.
Numerous surviving copies, notably:
Copy A: oil on canvas, 105 x 139 cm.
Musée des Beaux-Arts, Orléans [Or. 47]
Copy B: oil on canvas, 109 x 131 cm.
Musée des Beaux-Arts, Rouen.
Copy C: oil on canvas, 104 x 131 cm.
William Rockhill Nelson Gallery of Art, Kansas City.

This was undoubtedly the most famous of all La Tour's compositions, and although the original may still elude us, at least ten copies are known today.
The best of these are the three listed above. The Orléans version appears in a post-Revolutionary inventory of paintings seized from religious establishments in Orléans as "German School, in the manner of Scalf [*sic*]." It was reported by Longhi as early as 1927 and subsequently rediscovered and published by Pruvost-Auzas in 1963. It is of reasonable quality, but the colors appear to have darkened. The Rouen version similarly came into the museum's possession during the Revolution along with other confiscated works. It was recognized by Longhi and reported by Demonts as early as 1922. The drawing is more readable than in the Orléans version, but rather heavy-handed. The Kansas City painting was acquired on the market in Amsterdam in 1950 and has sometimes been posited as an original (Nicolson, 1969; Isarlo, 1972; Cleveland exhibition catalogue, 1971, with reservations). It is in fact an obvious copy, but undoubtedly the truest in terms of color. There are other copies of lesser quality in the Detroit Institute of Arts (published as an original by Richardson in 1949), the museum in Evreux (published by Lamiray in 1935), and the Chapelle Notre-Dame-de-Grâce in Honfleur (published by de Champris in 1945), as well as in a number of private collections in France and elsewhere.

This composition has been assigned widely different dates. Some have seen it as a late work (among them Sterling, 1934 and Bloch, 1960), while others believe it to be very early (Pariset, in 1948, places it around 1632-1633). In my view, it could be very conveniently placed around 1638-1639. In this case, it could be the *St. Sebastian* recorded by Dom Calmet as having been presented by La Tour to Louis XIII with the hope, it seems to me, that it would secure him the title of *"peintre ordinaire du roi"* (which he is known to have held in 1639; see entry for no. A8 below).

The subject had been a common one since the Middle Ages but was particularly popular with the Caravaggisti and their followers, Borgianni and Terbrughghen, for instance, and northern painters such as Bigot, Brébiette, and Perrier. This interest can undoubtedly be explained by the terrible outbreaks of the plague at the time (St. Sebastian was revered as protector against the plague), but also by the ambiguity of the scene: loosely interpreted, the *Passio Sebastiani* could provide a dialogue redolent at once of love and devotion, as is the case here. Also worth noting is the very hazy suggestion of a landscape on the right of the composition: this is the only place in La Tour's work where there is even a hint of an outdoor space.

38. SAINT JÉRÔME PÉNITENT (au chapeau cardinalice).
St. Jerome.
Nationalmuseum, Stockholm.

Oil on canvas, 153 x 106 cm. [Or. 11]

The painting's early history remains obscure, but it is known to have passed through several Swedish collections before entering the museum in 1917, when it was catalogued as a Mayno. It was attributed to La Tour by Voss in 1931 and is now universally regarded as an original. This is demonstrated by a number of significant pentimenti (the drapery around the wrist, for instance) and by the remarkable quality of the surface and the brushwork even though it is distinctly worn in parts. The dating, on the other hand, remains controversial: some, such as Pariset (1948), argue that the painting is earlier than the Grenoble version (no. 36), others that it is later (Grate, 1969). The greater discipline of the composition leads me to favor the second hypothesis. The importance given here to the cardinal's hat suggests that this is the *St. Jerome* owned by Richelieu (cf. no. A5).

39. LE TRICHEUR (à l'as de carreau).
The Cheat with the Ace of Diamonds.
Musée du Louvre, Paris.

Oil on canvas, 106 x 146 cm. Signed. [Or. 14]

This famous painting, signed *Georgius De La Tour fecit*, was discovered in 1926 by Landry, published by Voss in 1931, and bought by the Louvre in 1972 for what was then the exceptional sum of ten million francs. It prompted a rediscovery of La Tour's daylight work, and remains one of its highest points. The dating has varied widely. It has often been considered as one of La Tour's earliest surviving works (Pariset, for instance, in 1963, dated it about 1625; similarly Nicolson), and has sometimes been situated just before the Fort Worth version (no. 30) (a view expressed verbally by Nicolson and Landry). In my view, however, it must be dated later than the Texas painting: it is more mature, more masterly in expression, with a very different tonal range and a rather more solemn poetry. This hypothesis is supported by the conscious choice of variations and the absence of the pentimenti that are so numerous in the other version. Furthermore, the forms here are more stylized, the tonal contrasts more accentuated, and the palette cooler, all of which suggests that this version could be some time later than the first, and that, far from being a youthful work, it may in fact be contemporary with the first great surviving nocturnes.

40. SAINT FRANÇOIS MÉDITANT.
St. Francis Meditating (also wrongly called **St. Francis in Ecstasy** or **The Two Monks**).

Original lost.
Engraved during the seventeenth century.

This is clearly the earliest of the different known versions of this subject. The elegance of the composition suggests that it is close in date to the similarly engraved version of *The Magdalen* (no. 42). The theme has baffled some critics, but it was a common one in the seventeenth century, when the Franciscans had a large following. St. Francis is generally shown in ecstasy supported by an angel (Caravaggio) or shown in delight before a choir of angels (Saraceni, Guercino). El Greco, however, painted a well-known image of the saint (Prado, National Gallery of Canada, etc.) engraved before 1606 in which St. Francis is seen meditating on death with Brother Leo. It provides the key, if one were needed, to the often misunderstood iconography of La Tour's composition. The original was perhaps the painting in the collection of the Parisian "curieux" Jean Baptiste de Bretagne during La Tour's own lifetime (see no. A3).

41. LE NOUVEAU-NÉ, also known as Les Veilleuses.
The Newborn Child (Madonna and Child with St. Anne).

Original lost.
Engraved in the seventeenth century.
The engraving, by an unknown hand, is inscribed *Jac. Callot in. fran^s vanden Mijngaerde ex.*

Attributed to Callot by the publisher of the engraving and restored to La Tour by Voss as early as 1915, this work represents one of La Tour's most important compositions. It is the earliest known version of a subject that La Tour was to paint several times, and always with an eye to the inherent ambiguity of an image that is at once profane (motherhood) and sacred (the Virgin and St. Anne watching over the sleeping child, see no. 63). It should be dated around 1638-1642.

42. LA MADELEINE PÉNITENTE (Madeleine au miroir).
The Repentant Magdalen (also called **The Repentant Magdalen with the Mirror**).

Original lost.
Engraved in the seventeenth century.
Several copies survive, notably:
Copy A: oil on canvas, formerly Terff Collection, Paris.
Copy B: oil on canvas, Private collection, United States.
Engraving.

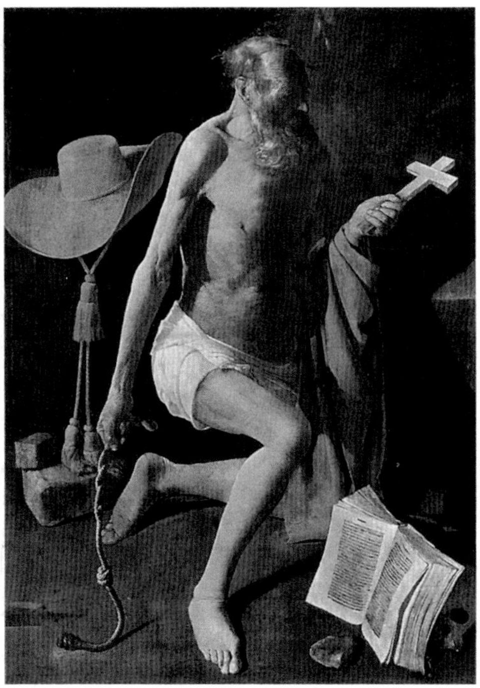
38

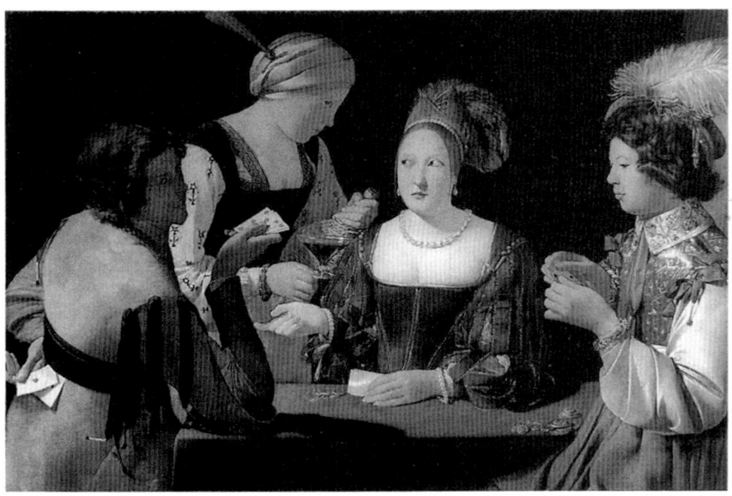
39

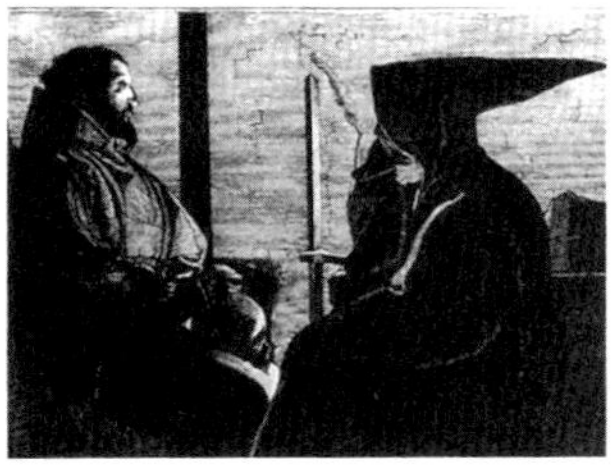

40 engraving

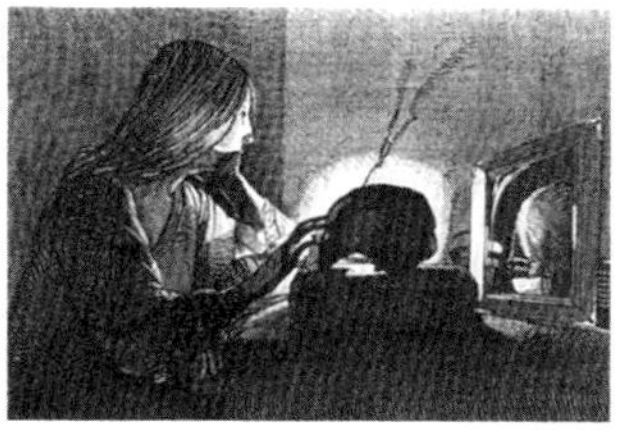

42 engraving

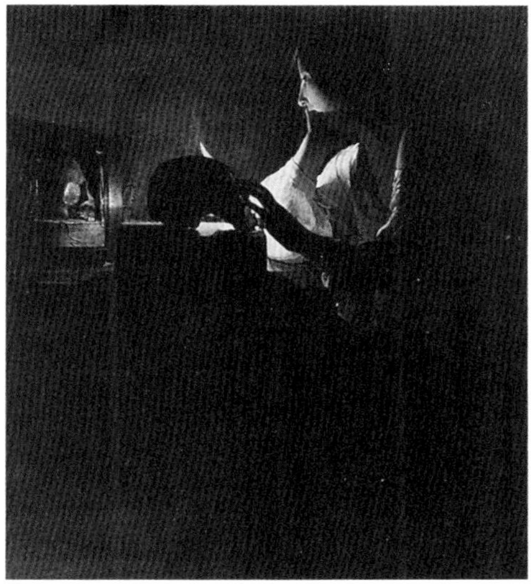

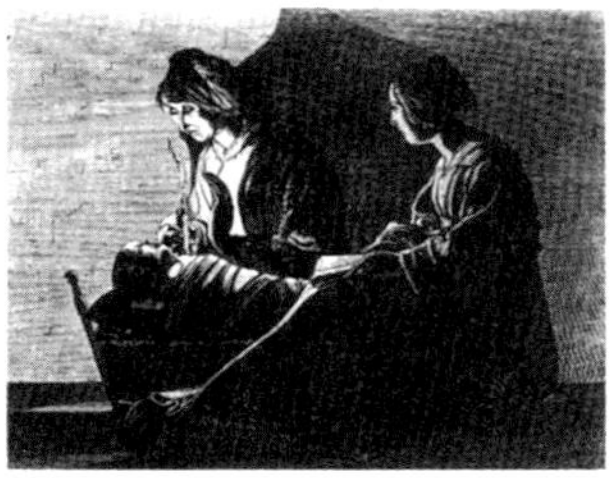

41 engraving

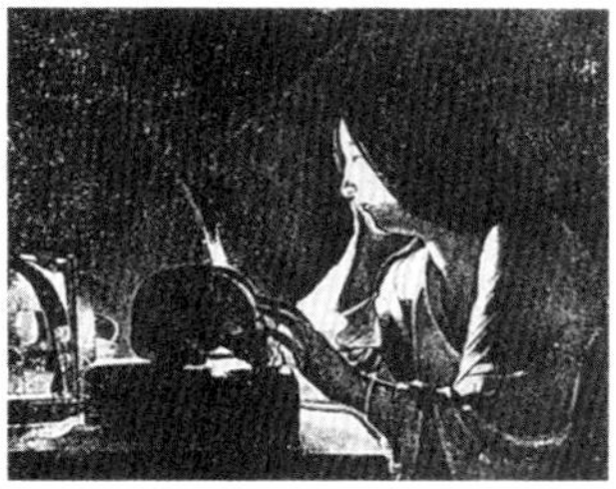

42 Terff copy

43

Several copies other than the two listed above are known. The copy formerly in the Terff Collection was reproduced in Pariset (1948); the one in the United States was exhibited in New York in 1962 and in Jacksonville and Saint Petersburg, Florida, in 1970.

Both the engraving and the two copies listed above show minor variations with regard to the *Fabius Magdalen* (no. 43)—the hair, the sleeves, the handle of the basket, the flame, the reflection of the light—which are not found in other copies such as the one now in Besançon (no. 44). This would seem to suggest (contrary to my earlier belief, as expressed in the catalogue of the Orangerie exhibition) that La Tour painted several similar versions of this kind of Magdalen (as he did for the Los Angeles and Louvre compositions), and that what we see represented here is one of the half-length versions. Even though we do not have the benefit of the original, certain details, such as the drawing of the flame and the black outline used to define the shapes in the illuminated parts (as in *The Repentant Magdalen with the Night Light*, no. 48), suggest that this version is slightly earlier than the *Fabius Magdalen*.

43. LA MADELEINE PÉNITENTE.

The Repentant Magdalen (known as the **Fabius Magdalen**)

The National Gallery of Art, Washington, D.C.

Oil on canvas, 113 x 93 cm. [Or. 15]

This painting is known to have belonged to the marquise de Caulaincourt in the second half of the nineteenth century. It was acquired by A. Fabius in 1936, and then by the museum in Washington in 1974. Universally accepted as an original La Tour, it is regarded as one of his most lyrical works. Pariset dated it first around 1628 (1948) and subsequently (1963) followed Sterling (1951) in dating it around 1645. In fact, this canvas appears to be a repetition of an earlier composition (no. 42) with a few variations, thus complicating the problem of dating even further.

44. LA MADELEINE PÉNITENTE.

The Repentant Magdalen.

Original lost.
Copy: oil on canvas, 66 x 80 cm.

Musée des Beaux-Arts, Besançon.

This copy was rediscovered in the reserves of the museum in 1947, and despite its mediocre quality, it reveals a number of small departures from the *Fabius Magdalen* (the way the hair falls, the contrast between light and shade, the folds of her dress) suggesting that it was not a direct copy of this version. It seems likely that in addition to no. 42 La Tour produced two other similar versions of the subject, one full-length (the *Fabius Magdalen*, no. 43), and the other half-length, of which this is an echo. Without the original it is obviously very difficult to situate this third version chronologically.

45. L'EXTASE DE SAINT FRANÇOIS.

St. Francis in Ecstasy.

Original lost.
Copy A: oil on canvas, 154 x 163 cm.
Musée Tessé, Le Mans [Or. 51].
Copy B: oil on canvas.
Private collection, Lyon.

This is the largest of La Tour's works known to us, and the original must have been one of the greatest in the first major series of nocturnes. The Le Mans version was published in 1938 by Sterling, but although it has often been accepted as an original (Jamot, 1939; Huyghe, 1945, etc.), doubts were soon expressed (Sterling himself, writing in 1951, suggested that it might be a studio replica). The execution is generally mediocre, and nowhere does it achieve the true quality of a La Tour. Thus, it appears to be simply a good old copy of a first-rate original. The second copy is slightly weaker but confirms that the Le Mans version is faithful to the lost original.

46. L'EXTASE DE SAINT FRANÇOIS.

St. Francis in Ecstasy.

Original lost.
Copy: oil on canvas, 66 x 78.8 cm.
Wadsworth Atheneum, Hartford, Connecticut.

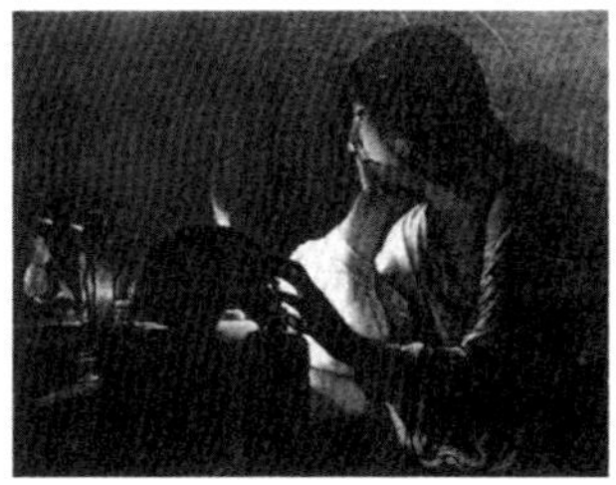

44 copy

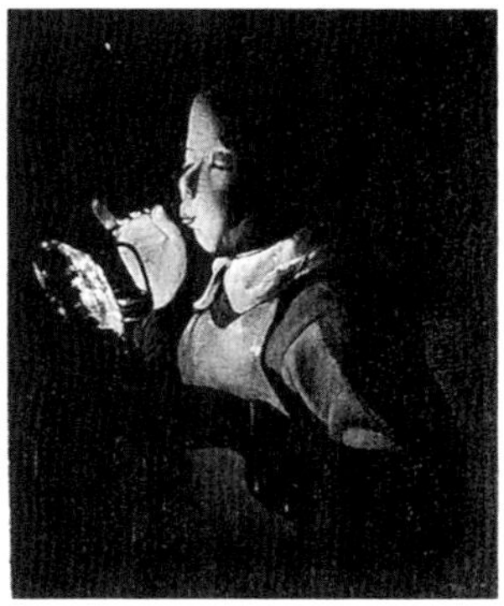

47

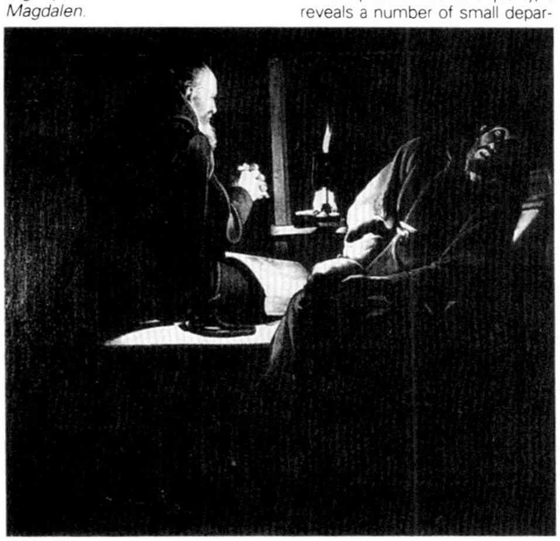

45 Le Mans copy

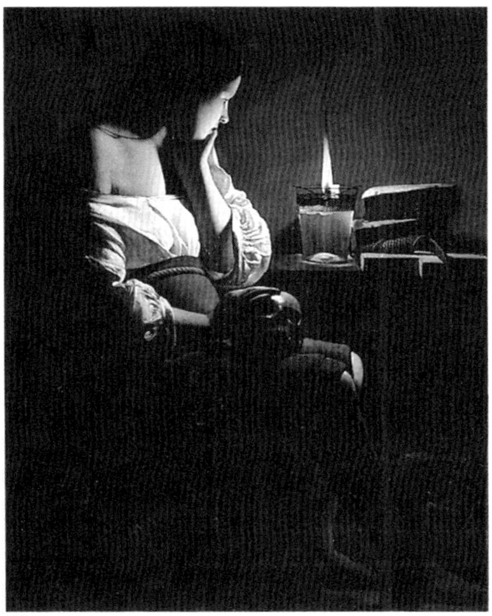

48

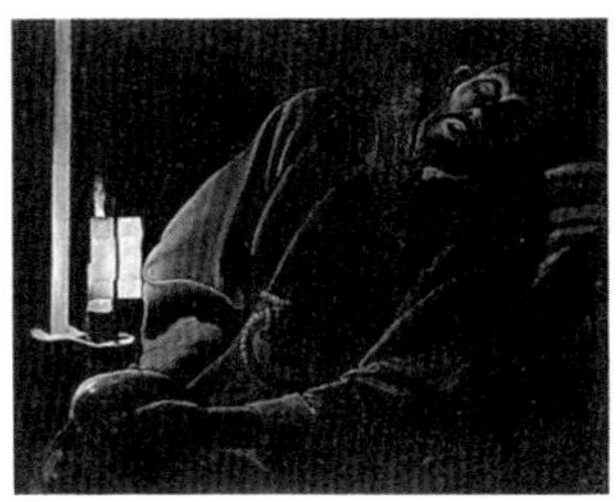

46 copy

The Hartford painting (commonly referred to as *Monk in Ecstasy*) was acquired on the American art market and published in 1940. The differences (the candlestick, for instance) between this and the composition known through the Le Mans copy (no. 45) seem to indicate the existence of at least two versions of this subject. This is hardly surprising given the following the Franciscans had in La Tour's day. Indeed, there is a reference as early as 1650 to a *Monk Asleep* in the inventory of Jean-Baptiste de Bretagne's effects carried out after his death, and this work sems to have depicted only one figure (cf. no. A4). The Hartford painting is too weak to be an original, but it could be an old copy of this composition, repainted in part.

47. LE SOUFFLEUR À LA LAMPE.
A Boy Blowing on a Charcoal Stick.
Musée des Beaux-Arts, Dijon (Granville Bequest).

Oil on canvas, 61 x 51 cm. Signed. [Or. 16]

The painting is signed top right *De La Tour f.* It was discovered in a private collection in Semur in 1960 and had been in the owner's family since at least the end of the nineteenth century. Authenticated by Hermann Voss in 1968, it was purchased by Pierre and Kathleen Granville in 1972, and shown to the public the same year at the Orangerie exhibition. It represents something of a rarity in La Tour's oeuvre as we know it: a painting aimed at a private market similar to the merchant-class clientele of the northern painters. In fact there are several references to paintings of "souffleurs," or blowing figures, in the inventories of collections in Lorraine, and more particularly one in 1649 to a "*souffleur* in the manner of La Tour." The painting takes up a theme popular with the Bassano family and frequently treated by Caravaggio's northern followers (such as Lievens, Terbrugghen, and Stomer) with the same kind of small compositions and half-length figures that were suited to private homes. La Tour's rendition is uncompromisingly solemn, however, with no hint of the picturesque. The sensitivity of the execution and the overall tonality point to more or less the same period as *Christ with St. Joseph in the Carpenter's Shop* (no. 49).

48 LA MADELEINE PÉNITENTE.
The Repentant Magdalen with the Night Light.
Los Angeles County Museum of Art.

Oil on canvas, 118 x 90 cm. Signed.

This painting was discovered at the time of the Orangerie exhibition in 1972 and bought by the museum in Los Angeles several years later. Restoration work has shown it to be a signed original in excellent condition. The composition is similar to that of the famous *Magdalen* (also signed) in the Louvre (no. 52), but differs from it in spirit as well as in a number of details (the still life, position of the legs, etc.). A less austere style, coupled with devices such as the black line around the illuminated parts and the double wisp of smoke that rises from the flame, seems to indicate that this is earlier than the Louvre version and links it to the first great series of nocturnes.

49. SAINT JOSEPH CHARPENTIER.
Christ with St. Joseph in the Carpenter's Shop.
Musée du Louvre, Paris (Percy Moore Turner Bequest).

Oil on canvas, 137 x 101 cm. [Or. 17]

This work was discovered in England (?) by Percy Moore Turner around 1938 and bequeathed to the Louvre in 1948 in memory of Paul Jamot. It is unanimously accepted as a major, albeit unsigned, original. (A good old copy, mistakenly believed to be a studio replica, is now in Besançon [Or. 52].) The uncompromising realism of the painting, its concern with three-dimensional form, its decisive and generous brushstrokes (clearly shown up by the impressive X-ray), and its use of predominantly "plum" colors unbroken by any great expanse of red, all define a very precise stylistic period (cf. nos. 47 and 50, which are directly related to it). The early 1640s would seem to coincide reasonably well with the main dates proposed so far (by Pariset and Sterling). The picture brings together in a single devout image three separate elements often united in religious writing at the time—St Joseph, the young Jesus, and the Cross—here vividly conjured up by the beam the carpenter is shaping.

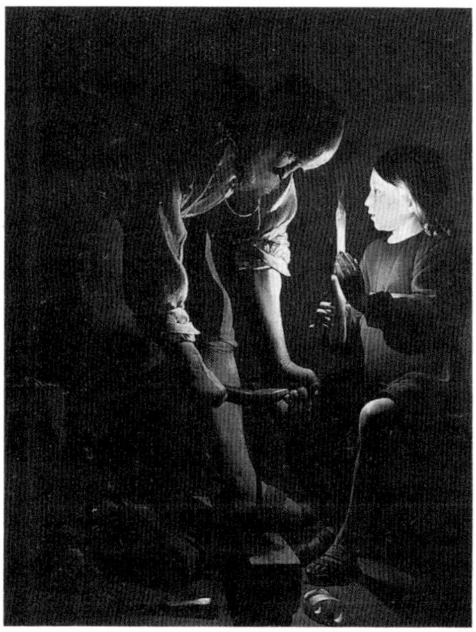

49 copy

50. L'ANGE APPARAISSANT À SAINT JOSEPH.
The Dream of St. Joseph.
Musée des Beaux-Arts, Nantes.

Oil on canvas, 93 x 81 cm. Signed [Or. 18]

The work is signed *G De La Tour.* . . . It was acquired by the museum in 1810 with the entire Cacault collection (cf. nos. 20, 76), but the provenance is unknown. It has undoubtedly been trimmed to some extent on the right, as is evident from the truncated signature. This signature was initially overlooked and subsequently interpreted after its discovery (documented in the 1833 catalogue) first as that of Quentin de La Tour (1854 catalogue) and then as that of Le Blond de La Tour (Clément de Ris, 1872), before being finally recognized as that of Georges de La Tour (Voss, 1915). It was this identification of the signature, together with that on *The Denial of St. Peter* (no. 73), that instigated the rehabilitation of La Tour's work. The quality of the painting is exceptional (the "impressionistic" technique used in the child's scarf, for example, recalls both Velásquez and Vermeer), although profoundly different from that of the great daylight pictures (nos. 31 or 32, for instance). The color is generally agreed to be closely related to that of the Louvre's *Christ with St. Joseph in the Carpenter's Shop* (no. 49). Its subject matter, on the other hand, has provoked a great deal of debate, and it has been variously identified as St. Peter delivered by the angel, St. Matthew, Elijah and Samuel, and so on. A more convincing interpretation, however, would seem to be one of the two angel's apparition to Joseph (The Dream of St. Joseph).

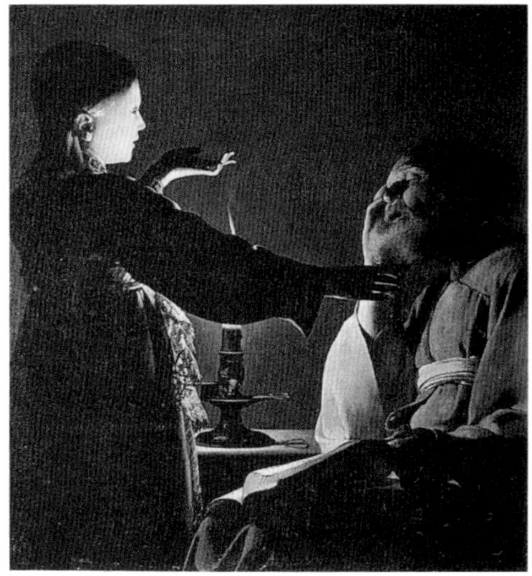

50

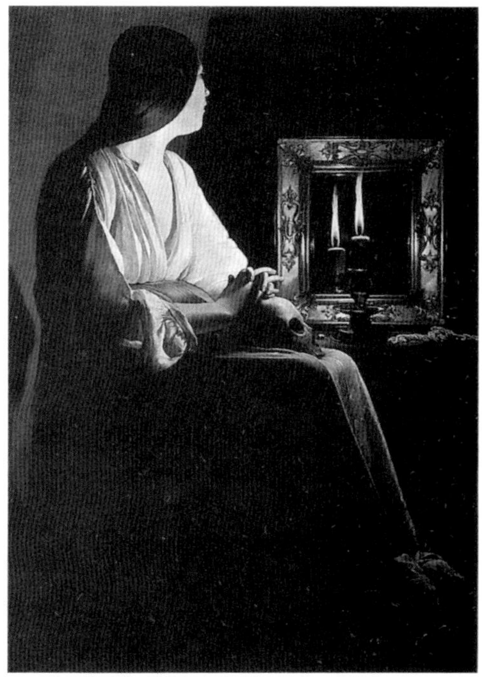

51

51. LA MADELEINE PÉNITENTE (Madeleine Wrightsman, Madeleine aux deux flammes).
The Repentant Magdalen with the Mirror (called the **Wrightsman Magdalen** or **The Magdalen with the two Flames**).
Metropolitan Museum of Art, New York.

Oil on canvas, 134 x 92 cm. [Or. 19]

Discovered in 1961 in the Côte d'Or [Burgundy], this painting had been in the collection of a French family since the middle of the nineteenth century, and it was subsequently published by Pariset. It passed through the Heim Gallery to the Wrightsman Collection in 1963. There was initial unease over the work, largely because of the gilded frame around the mirror that was wrongly thought to belong to a later period. The painting had suffered badly over the years in places, with deep cracks marring whole areas of the Magdalen's face, chest, and bodice, as well as the frame, and it underwent two extensive restorations. Its lyricism nevertheless made it stand out at the 1972 exhibition, where it met with universal acceptance and admiration. The unusual palette seems to relate it to *Christ with St. Joseph in the Carpenter's Shop* and *The Dream of St. Joseph* (nos. 49 and 50).

52. LA MADELEINE PÉNITENTE.
The Repentant Magdalen with the Night Light (known as the **Terff Magdalen**).
Musée du Louvre, Paris.

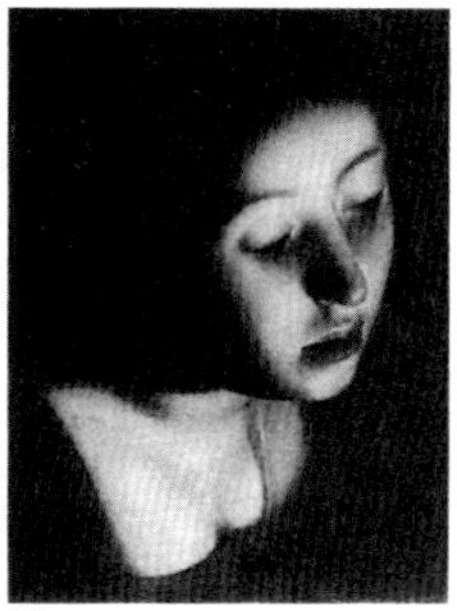

53

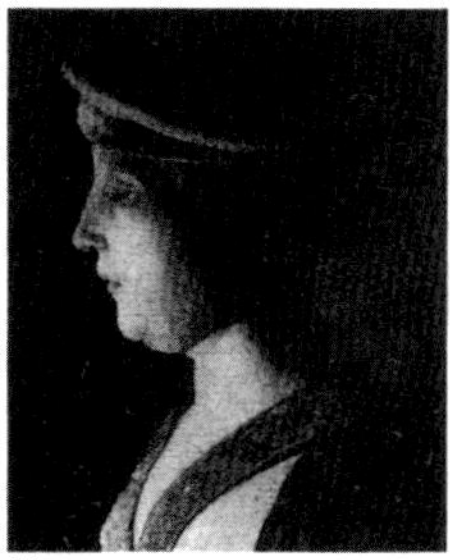

56

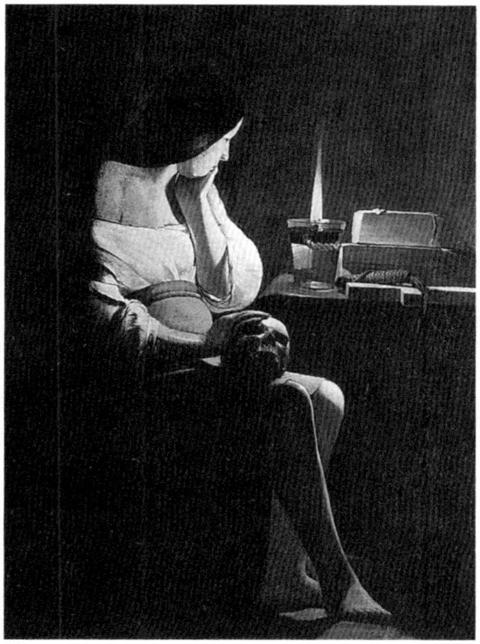

52

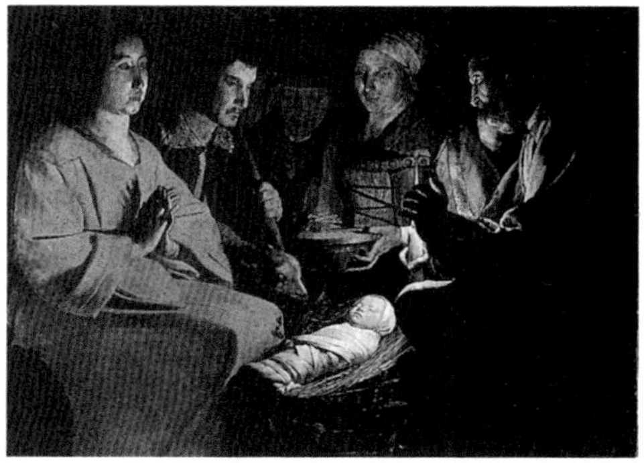

55

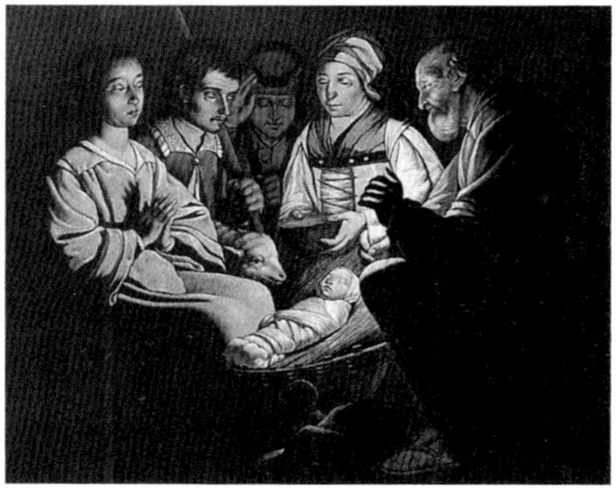

55 a copie

Oil on canvas, 128 x 94 cm
Signed [Or. 21]

The painting is signed . . . *La Tour fect.* It was acquired in Paris by Camille Terff around 1914 and finally entered the Louvre in 1949 after a certain amount of legal wrangling. The most polished of all the surviving versions of the subject, it is a reworking of another signed composition (no. 48) but with a number of slight differences. The result is considerably more austere both in style and in feel, and this stylization, coupled with a very different tonality, suggests that it is distinctly later in date. The painting seems to anticipate the change of style that was to lead to *The Adoration of the Shepherds* (no. 55) and the works of the last years. An excellent small old copy on its original canvas has been discovered in the south of France.

53. TÊTE DE FEMME.
Head of a Woman.
Schloss Fasanerie, Adolphseck (near Fulda).

Fragment of an original?
Oil on canvas.

Catalogued initially as a Caravaggio and somewhat reminiscent of his celebrated *Madonna with a Serpent,* this painting, reproduced by Nicolson in 1979 as an uncertain attribution, has never been exhibited or discussed by the specialists. It is obviously a fragment or a study of a figure from a larger composition, possibly a Nativity or a St. Sebastian.

54. LA NATIVITÉ.
Nativity.

Oil on canvas. 1644.

Presented by the town of Lunéville to the governor of Lorraine, Maréchal de La Ferté, as a New Year's gift in 1644, this work is described as a "Nativity of Our Lord in a night scene" in the town's bookkeeping records (for late 1644-early 1645) and in the inventory of the marechal's collection (made in October 1653). La Tour was paid seven hundred francs for the painting, a considerable sum in those days. Several authors have identified this work with *The Adoration of the Shepherds* now in the Louvre (cf. the entry for no. 55).

55. L'ADORATION DES BERGERS.
The Adoration of the Shepherds.
Musée du Louvre, Paris.

Oil on canvas, 107 x 137 cm.
[Or. 22]

Discovered in Amsterdam in 1926, this painting was immediately attributed to La Tour by Voss and acquired by the Louvre the same year. It has clearly been trimmed on the right-hand side and especially along the bottom, where Joseph's feet and the lower part of the crib should appear (cf. the very mediocre copy in Albi [Or. 53] that seems to render the original composition in its entirety). Although fairly worn in parts, the painting remains of a high quality and has always been regarded as a secure original. It has often been identified (Sterling, 1934; Nicolson, 1971, etc.) with the *Nativity of Our Lord* painted toward the end of 1644 and presented by the town of Lunéville to the governor of Lorraine. Stylistically, the painting would fit reasonably well with that date, but there is always the possiblity that it is a slightly later reworking of the composition.

56. TÊTE DE FEMME.
Head of a Woman.
Formerly Pierre Landry Private collection, Paris.

Fragment of an original.
Oil on canvas, 38 x 30 cm
[Or. 24].

This fragment surfaced in Munich (Fischmann Collection) around 1930, when it was published by Vitale Bloch, and was acquired by Pierre Landry around 1942. It is obviously a worn section cut from a larger composition, now destroyed (possibly a *Newborn Child* or an *Adoration of the Shepherds,* although a subject like *The Education of the Virgin* cannot be excluded). Although substantially repainted, the work has been widely accepted as an original (Bloch, 1930; Pariset, 1948) on the strength of the profile, which survives in reasonably good condition. It is undoubtedly close in date to *The Adoration of the Shepherds* (no. 55) in the Louvre.

57. L'ÉDUCATION DE LA VIERGE (à la broderie).
The Sewing Lesson.

Original destroyed.

Fragment preserved, known variously as **The Girl with the Taper** and **The Child with the Candle**.
Detroit Institute of Arts.
Oil on canvas, 57 x 44 cm
[Or. 25]

Copy of the complete composition.
Oil on canvas, 82 x 95 cm.
Del Carretto Collection, Cisano sul Neva, Savona [Or. 55]

Discovered in Lorraine by the scholar and collector Charles Friry (cf. no. 18) toward the middle of the nineteenth century, this fragment arrived in North America some time after 1934 and was acquired by the museum in Detroit in 1938. It is badly worn and has been heavily restored in places, notably the girl's dress, the background, and a large part of the face (which was slashed in 1945). The most recent restoration clearly revealed traces of the cushion and part of the Virgin's hand, proving that the picture of the child had been cut out of a larger composition, probably the original. The copy, uncovered in Italy in 1971 and presented at the 1972 exhibition, shows the composition in

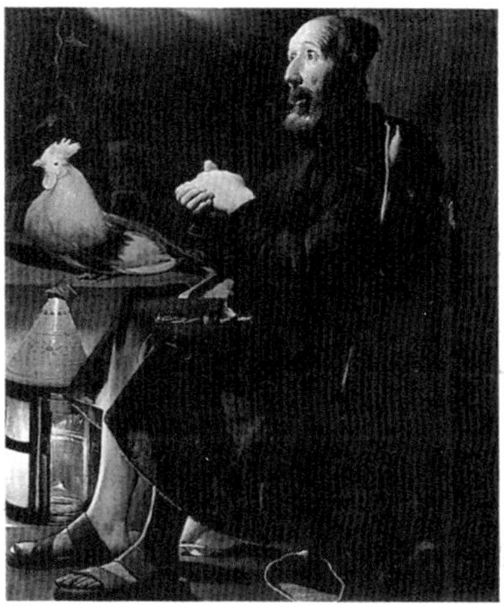

58

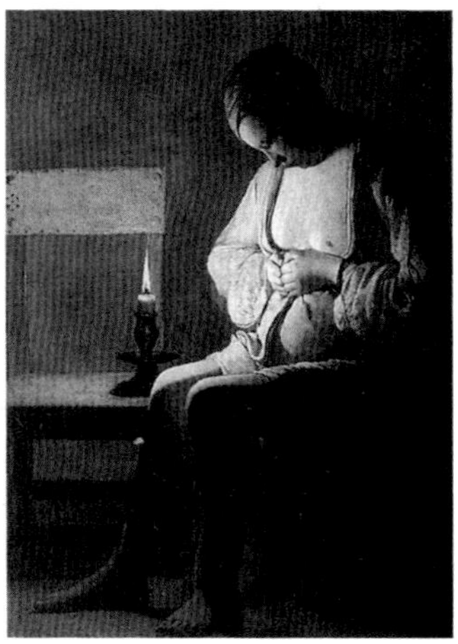

59

its entirety, indicating perhaps a date prior to the better-known *Education of the Virgin*, which would be a more developed variation on the same theme.

58. LES LARMES DE SAINT PIERRE.
The Penitent St. Peter.
Cleveland Museum of Art.

Oil on canvas, 114 x 95 cm. Signed and dated 1645 [Or. 23]

The painting is signed and dated top right "*Georg^s de La Tour Inve et Pinx . . . 1645*. It appeared on the London art market in 1950 and was declared, without documentary evidence, to have been among a group of pictures said to have belonged to Dulwich College until the mid-nineteenth century. It was acquired by the Cleveland Museum in 1951. The subject was very popular in the seventeenth century and one that La Tour himself had earlier tackled in a daylight mode (cf. nos. 27 and 28). The work seemed disconcerting, with its expressionist effect and almost baroque note that were considered uncharacteristic of La Tour. Now, by contrast, it is tempting to see it as a transition from the naturalist approach of the earlier years to the stylized manner that was to become increasingly pronounced.

59. LA FEMME À LA PUCE.
A Flea Catcher.
Musée Historique Lorrain, Nancy.

Oil on canvas, 120 x 90 cm. [Or. 20]

This painting's early history is unclear, but it was discovered by Mlle Berhaut in 1955 in a private collection in Rennes, subsequently published by Pariset, and promptly acquired by the Musée Lorrain. Although unsigned, it is universally accepted as being by La Tour's hand and is regarded as one of his most important works. The subject matter was once the focus of much debate (suggestions ranged from a religious theme, to the regret after the sin of the flesh, to the onset of labor). The picture is now generally agreed to be of a woman ridding herself of fleas—she is clearly crushing one flea between her nails, and another is discernible in the bright light shining on her belly. This was a popular theme in the seventeenth century, especially among the northern painters, but also in Rome, where it was treated in similarly sober vein by Bigot (Galleria Doria). The dating, on the other hand, has led to disagreement: some have seen it as a very early work (Pariset, 1963), others as marking the transition from daylight to night pictures (Nicolson), still others as a late work. The 1972 exhibition highlighted its similarity with *Job Mocked by His Wife* (no. 72): here were two paintings of equally unusual subjects that both made use of great expanses of flat red, and which might therefore be similarly late in date. In technique, however, *A Flea Catcher* has much in common with the more labored productions of the middle years. Like the *Terff Magdalen*, this could well be a reworking of a relatively early composition in a later and rather different style, combining a new emphasis on geometry with vestiges of the first approach, such as the rounded modeling of the head and the shape of the hands.

60. L'ÉDUCATION DE LA VIERGE (au livre).
The Education of the Virgin.
Frick Collection, New York.

Oil on canvas, 83.8 x 100.4 cm. Signed.

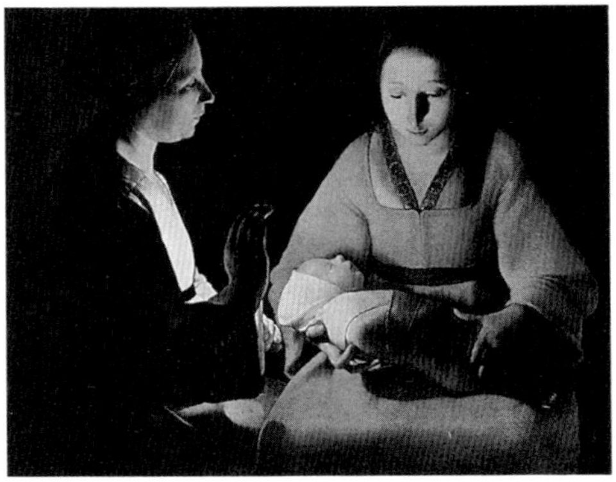

64

The painting is signed *de La Tour f.* Discovered in the south of France, it was first mentioned by Isarlo in 1947 and acquired by the Frick Collection in 1948. The composition was already known through an excellent old copy (Paris, private collection [Or. 54]), and there has never been any doubt that it was the work of La Tour. The Frick version, however, with its crude coloring and dry execution, has come under harsh judgments despite its signature. It has been variously rated as questionable (Pariset, 1948; Bloch, 1950), a copy (Sterling, 1951; Pariset, 1964), a studio production (Nicolson, 1969, and even the author of the Frick catalogue, 1968), and an old copy with a later signature (Rosenberg, 1972). My position, by contrast, is that this is an original, duly signed by La Tour, but decimated by a merciless cleaning that removed almost every trace of glaze and left only a handful of tiny details more or less unscathed. Backed with

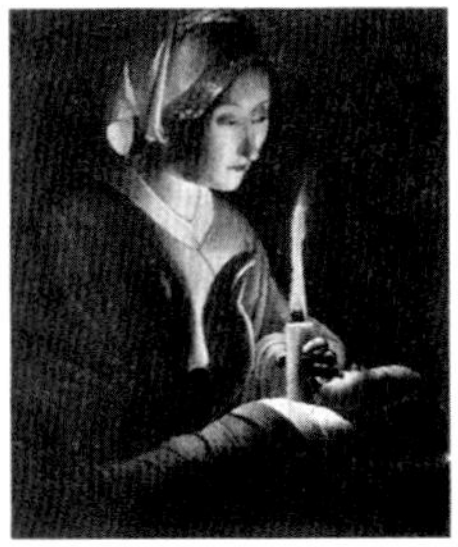

63 copy?

new canvas and restored before it entered the museum, it had been ruined beyond repair and for the most part repainted.

61. L'ÉDUCATION DE LA VIERGE (au livre).
The Education of the Virgin.

Original lost.
Copy: oil on canvas, 126 x 88 cm.
Heinz Kisters Collection, Kreuzlingen [Or. 54b]

This copy was published only in 1972 (in the second edition of the catalogue to the Orangerie exhibition, p. 255 and reprod.), although its existence had been known for some years. The composition is the same as in no. 60, but this time figures are full-length. It has enough of the character of a La Tour to make one think that it harks back to a lost vertical version painted by La Tour himself at about the same time.

62. L'ÉDUCATION DE LA VIERGE (au livre).
The Education of the Virgin.

Original lost.
Copy: oil on canvas, 74 x 85 cm.
Musée des Beaux-Arts, Dijon.

Bequeathed to the museum as part of the Devosges Collection, this painting was published by Quarré in 1943. At first sight, it looks like a simple copy of no. 60 by a rather incompetent artist who has contrived to turn St. Anne into an older woman. As Pariset rightly observed (1948), however, certain details, such as the embroidery on the headdress or that of the collar, with its large round motifs, cannot be attributed to a mere copyist. Indeed these represent some of La Tour's most distinctive hallmarks: we first meet this type of collar in the Nantes *Dream of St. Joseph* (no. 50) and the Louvre *Adoration of the Shepherds* (no. 55), and it appears more and more often thereafter, as in *The Newborn Child* in Rennes (no. 64) and *Job Mocked by His Wife* in Épinal (no. 72), for example. This work would seem, therefore, to be based on a third version of *The Education of the Virgin (with Book)*, in a half-length format like no. 60, but with altered faces and a number of variations that would point to a somewhat later date.

63. LE NOUVEAU-NÉ (St. Anne et la Vierge au Maillot).
The Newborn Child (St. Anne with the Virgin in Swaddling Clothes).

Copy (?), 66 x 54.6 cm.
Art Gallery of Ontario, Toronto.

This painting first came to light on the New York art market in 1943. Its previous history is unknown. It is very similar to the right-hand part of no. 41, *The Newborn Child*, but the differences are significant enough to suggest the existence of another, later version. Artists are known to have depicted the theme of the Nativity of the Virgin in the seventeenth century (a painting on this subject is recorded, for example, in the inventory of Claude Deruet's effects), and La Tour appears to have been no exception, for this is surely how we should interpret the "nurse and child" listed in the collection of Jean-Baptiste de Bretagne (see no. A11) in 1650.

The present version has been shown many times as an original, notably in New York in 1943 and 1946, and in Montreal in 1960 and 1965.

It has clearly undergone heavy repainting, but without examining it directly, we cannot say whether it is a repainted original or, more likely, a copy and a fragment of a larger, destroyed composition, or a complete painting that corresponds more or less closely to the composition recorded in the Bretagne collection.

64. LE NOUVEAU-NÉ.
The Newborn Child.
Musée des Beaux-Arts, Rennes.

Oil on canvas, 76 x 91 cm. [Or. 26]

This is perhaps the most famous of all La Tour's paintings. It came to the museum in 1794 with other works seized during the Revolution, although it is not known from whom it was confiscated. It has always been considered a work of outstanding quality and has been admired by, among others, Clément de Ris (1861), Taine (1863), and Gonse (1900). Maurice Denis even made a sketch of it. It was the first unsigned painting to be credited to La Tour (by Voss in 1915), and though lacking a signature to substantiate it, the attribution has never been questioned. There is a old, small copy of it in a collection in The Hague (25 x 27 cm), mentioned by Sterling as early as 1934, and another, reputed to have come from Brittany, in a private collection in northern France.

This work has always been

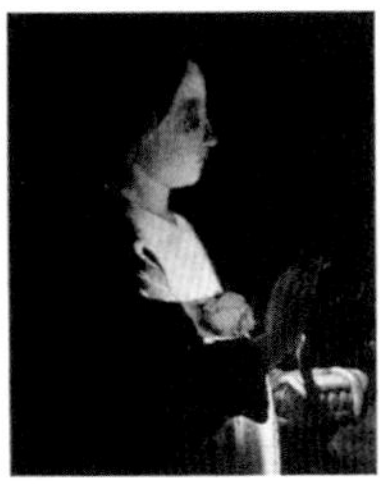

57

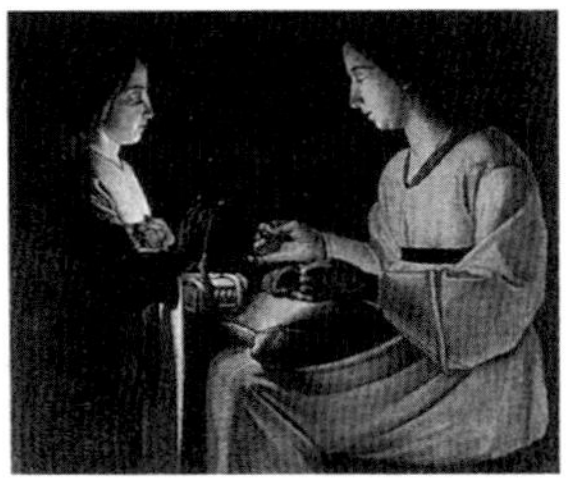

57 copy

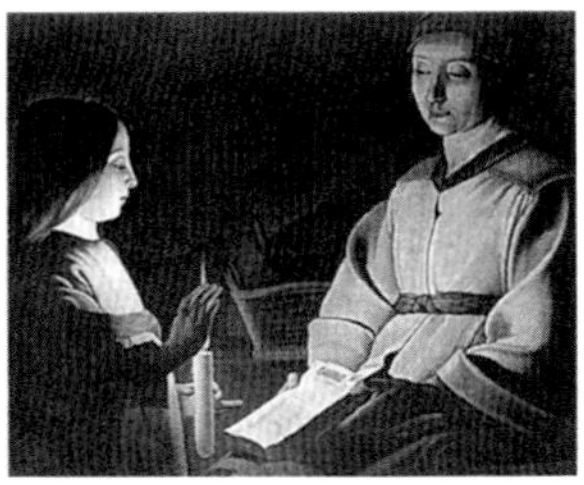

62 copy

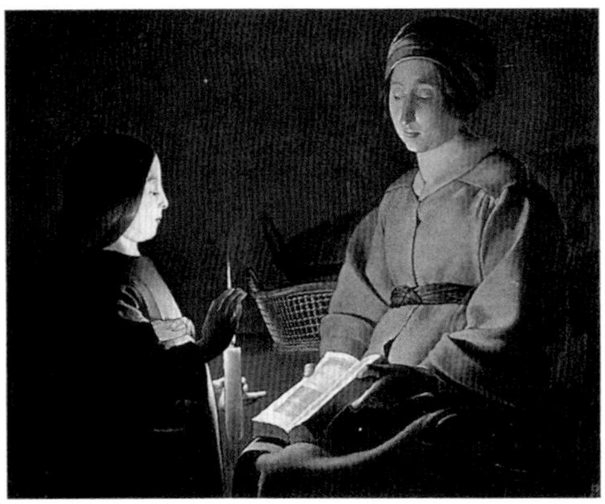

60

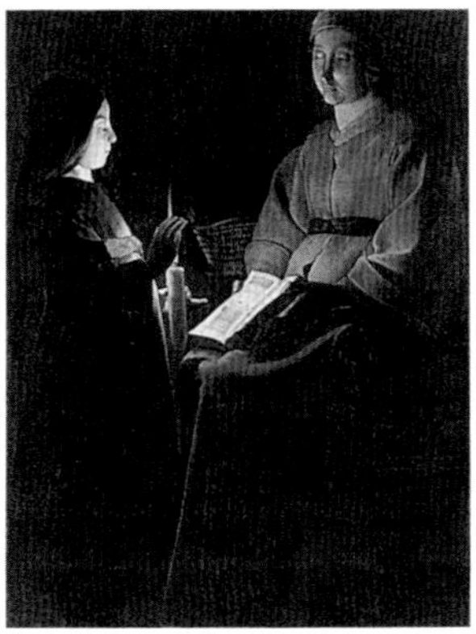

61 copy

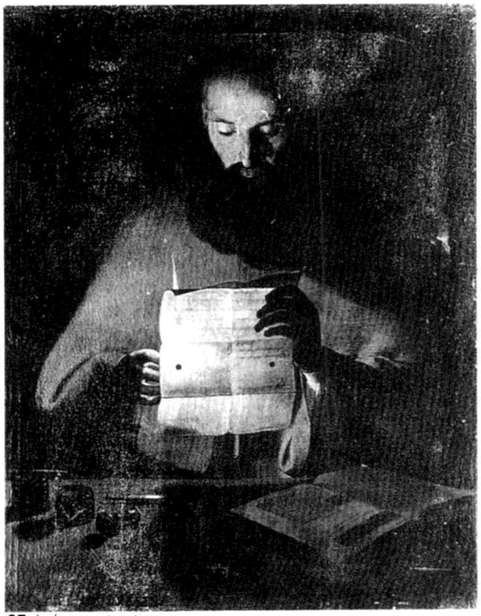

65 before restoration

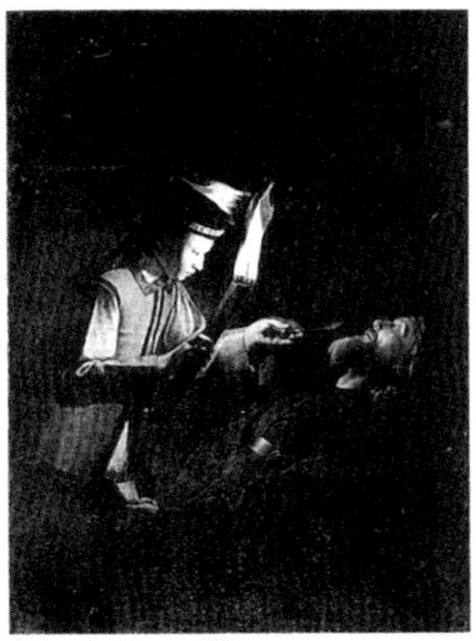

67 with later additions

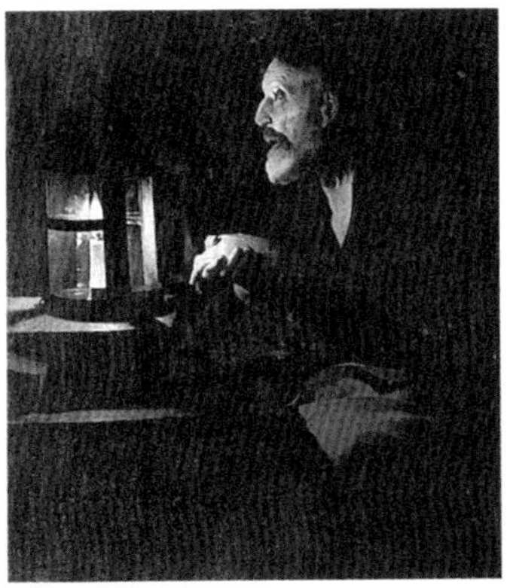

68 copy (?)

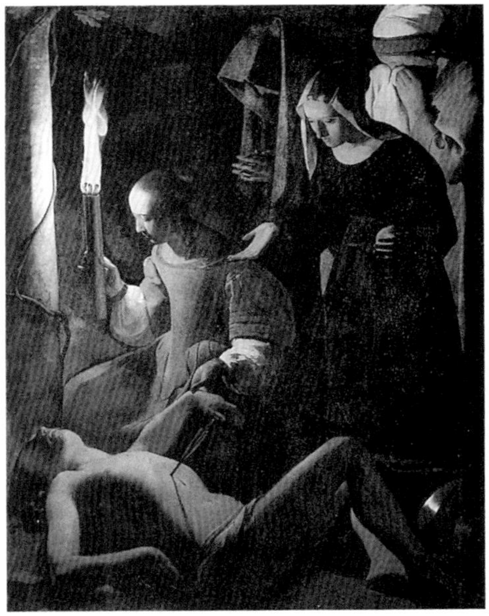

70

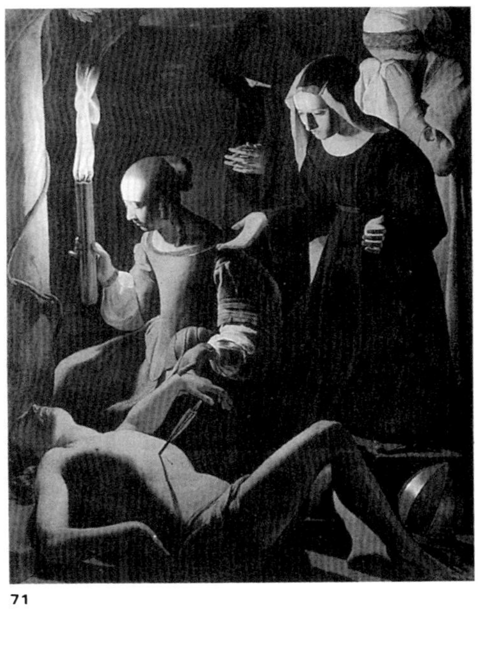

71

extraordinarily striking because of its paradoxical blend of sensitivity and style. The subject is the same as *The Newborn Child* (no. 41), but the figures are half-length, the composition is more compressed, pared down in almost "cubist" fashion, and the effect far more arresting as a result. It has been seen as an early work (Pariset in 1963, put it around 1630), but this is not really plausible. In terms of color, the painting is closely related to the *Education of the Virgin* series, and would therefore seem to be situated between 1645 and 1648. X-rays, however, reveal it to have a paint surface even thinner than that of the 1649 version of *St. Sebastian Tended by Irene* (no. 71), and far more like that of *Job Mocked by His Wife* (no. 72). It is not entirely impossible that there was a first version, now lost, that went back to around 1640 (cf. no. 38), followed by a much later one (around 1648-1651).

65. SAINT JÉRÔME LISANT.
St. Jerome Reading.
Musée Historique Lorrain, Nancy.

Oil on canvas, 92 x 72.5 cm. Signed.

This is a new reworking of the St. Jerome in his study and certainly the latest one to come down to us. The work directly evokes the early versions in Hampton Court (no. 15) and the Louvre (no. 36), but this time the composition is transposed into a "night picture," and the geometry of the volumes is pushed to its limit, as in *The Newborn Child* (no. 64). The color range, completely dominated by the red of the cardinal's robe, seems to indicate a date after 1647.
The painting is signed *la tour f.* at the lower left. Owned by an old French family and completely unknown to the specialists, it went up for auction in Poitiers on 17 June 1992 and its sale was preempted by the Musée Historique Lorrain. Its technique, simple and firm, does not have the subtleties of the brushwork that we expect from Georges de La Tour. The subject was popular, and this version was repeated several times. We cannot help but imagine that this copy was essentially the work of Étienne, which seems to be confirmed by the reduced form of the signature (cf. no. 74) and the X-ray, which shows no hesitation but rather, a great economy of means.

66. SAINT ALEXIS.
St. Alexis.

Oil on canvas, 1648.

The work is recorded in Lunéville's accounts for January 1649 as "a painting depicting the image [of] St. Alexis, purchased [from Sieur George de La Tour] as a gift for Monsieur the Marquis de la Ferté, Governor of Nancy, for the benefit and relief afforded the Community by his protection." It was bought from the artist for the sum of five hundred francs. The governor presumably passed it on fairly quickly to some person or group, because there is no mention of it in the 1653 inventory of his collection. It is generally accepted to be the same composition as no. 67.

67. LA DÉCOUVERTE DU CORPS DE SAINT ALEXIS.
St. Alexis.
Musée Historique Lorrain, Nancy.

Oil on canvas, 158 x 115 cm. [Or. 59]

This is one of the most moving of all La Tour's works. Undoubtedly the "image [of] St Alexis" (cf. no. 66) painted for La Ferté at the end of 1648—a date that is certainly very much in keeping with its style.
A version of the subject discovered in Belgium in about 1952 and acquired by the Dublin Museum in 1968 was hailed as an original when it first appeared (Pariset, 1955; Colemans, 1958), but it is probably no more than an old copy. Its virtue lies in the fact that it shows the composition in its original form. The Nancy version was discovered in an attic in the town as early as 1938, but in an altered state. It had been cut at the bottom, and a large strip had been added at the top, which gave it a more Rembrandtesque feel. It was at first universally accepted as an original (Pariset, 1938; Jamot, 1942; Furness, 1949; Sterling, 1951; Bloch, 1950 and 1953, etc.) but demoted to the rank of copy on the discovery of the other version, which is nontheless quite inferior. The fact remains that it is of a patently high standard, however. At this date, Étienne's participation was no longer negligible. It might be asked whether this is not an original that, on the one hand, reflects the considerable participation of Étienne, and on the other, has been somewhat coarsened through cleaning and restoration.

68. LES LARMES DE SAINT PIERRE.
The Penitent St. Peter (also wrongly called **Hermit Praying in a Grotto**).

Original lost.
Copy ?
Oil on canvas, 107 x 85 cm.
Private collection, France [Or. 61]

This painting was discovered by René Crozet in 1966 in a private collection in France where it had been for many years and was published by Pariset in 1967. It has been universally regarded as an excellent old copy (Pariset, 1967; Tanaka, 1969, etc.). The composition is very close in style and character to the *St. Alexis* of 1648 (no. 67), and the original must therefore have been similar in date. As a result, the hypothesis of a copy by Étienne cannot be excluded.

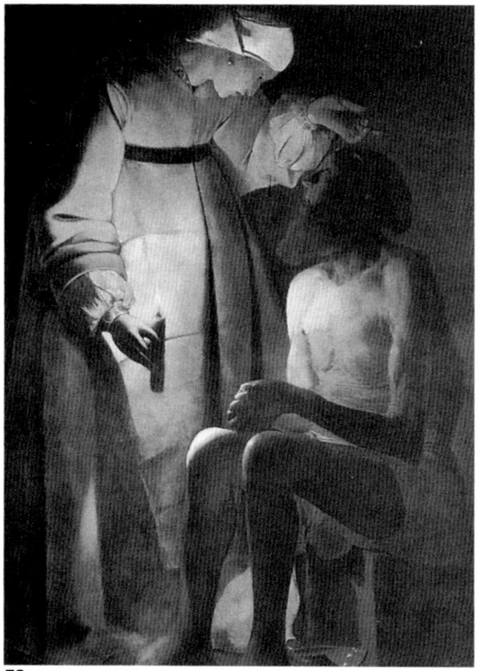

72

69. SAINT SÉBASTIEN DANS UNE NUIT.
St. Sebastian.

Oil on canvas, 1649.

This painting was commissioned by the town of Lunéville as a year-end present for the governor of Lorraine, La Ferté, and brought to Nancy in December. The town paid La Tour seven hundred francs (not including the six francs given to his daughter). It is listed in the 1653 inventory of La Ferté's collection (the document specifies that it is a night scene—a *St. Sebastian* "en nuict"). Today, it is generally agreed that this work must be either no. 70 or no. 71.

70. SAINT SÉBASTIEN SOIGNÉ PAR IRÈNE (à la torche).
St. Sebastian Tended by Irene (with the Torch).
Musée du Louvre, Paris.

Oil on canvas, 167 x 130 cm. [Or. 28]

The painting was discovered in 1945 in the little church of Bois-Anzeray, but its previous history is unknown. It was restored and temporarily exhibited in the Denon room of the Louvre in 1948. Reproduced and defended at the time by Bertin-Mourot (*Arts*, 8 August 1948), it was initially considered as perhaps no more than a studio work (Bloch, 1950) or even a mere copy (Charmet, 1958, et al.), before being more and more widely accepted as an original (Nicolson, 1958) and rated above the Berlin version. Its superior quality was emphasized by the 1972 exhibition and confirmed by the X-ray, which reveal a number of significant pentimenti (there was even a piece of sky in the upper portion) and highlight the beauty of the execution. The work was definitively acquired by the Louvre in 1981. Any lingering doubts about whether or not it is an original are swept away by the delicate quality of the atmosphere it evokes, the subtle balance of colors, and the stunning touch of lapis blue for the veil (scarcely noticeable in the Berlin version, where a less expensive pigment has been used). The subject is the same as that of the earlier St. Sebastian (no. 37), but here the composition echoes that of Caravaggio's *Entombment of Christ*, and the mood is one of a Lamentation. The work is striking in its restraint and in its stylized, almost cubist approach to form. It has often been associated with the *St. Sebastian* (no. 69) presented by the town of Lunéville to La Ferté at the end of 1649 (Jamot, 1939; Pariset, 1948), and this connection is now unanimously accepted.

71. SAINT SÉBASTIEN SOIGNÉ PAR IRÈNE (à la torche).
St. Sebastian Tended by Irene (with the Torch).
Staatliche Museen, Berlin.

Oil on canvas, 162 x 129 cm. [Or. 27]

Reputed to have been bought in Brussels, this painting entered the Stillwell Collection in New York in 1906. It was then put up for sale in 1927 and puchased by the Matthiesen Gallery in Berlin, which gave it to the Kaiser-Friedrich Museum. Even after the discovery of the Bois-Anzeray version, it was universally regarded as an original, but its authenticity has since been questioned by a great many critics who would see it as a fine old copy (particularly since the two versions were brought together at the 1972 exhibition). The painting is certainly colder in its technique; the figures are plunged in a denser atmosphere and the blue veil is unrelieved by any dash of lapis. There does not appear to be any evidence of pentimenti in the X-rays. The quality remains exceptional, nevertheless, and of a quite different order from all known copies (e.g., the Chambéry copy of no. 14; the Besançon version of no. 49). It is worth remembering that La Tour had a habit of repeating his compositions, and this would be a particularly understandable case because, with its five full-length figures, this painting is, after all, the most ambitious of all his surviving compositions. To be sure, he generally introduced a number of variations, but with the advent of a collaborator—Étienne—in the closing years of his career, La Tour's pattern of work changed completely. It seems likely then that this is a replica, doubtless prepared by Étienne but finished by Georges, and which deserves to retain its status as an original.

72. JOB ET SA FEMME.
Job Mocked by His Wife.
Musée Départemental des Vosges, Épinal.

Oil on canvas, 145 x 97 cm. Signed [Or. 29]

The painting was acquired by the museum in 1825 with the collection of the painter Krantz, a native of Nancy. Although at that time it was labeled "Italian School," by 1900 Gonse had compared it with the Rennes version of *The Newborn Child* (no. 62), and in 1922 Desmonts attributed it to La Tour. Finally, in 1972, painstaking restoration disclosed the remains of a signature: ". . . *De La Tour*. . . ." The painting has always been regarded as one of La Tour's most important works, but its subject has remained a focus of debate. Among the diverse interpretations proposed are a "prisoner" (Philippe, 1929), St. Peter delivered by the angel (Sterling, 1934; Jamot, 1939), the Virgin Mary with a supplicant (Longhi, 1935), and St. Alexis (Jamati, 1950). The general consensus now seems to be that it is Job mocked by his wife (first proposed by Lafond and Ronot in 1935 and taken further by Weisbach in 1936). The dating is no less problematic. The painting has been seen as an early work (Sterling, 1934), as a transitional one (Blunt, 1953 and 1970), and as a late one (Pariset, 1963). The extraordinary stylization and the powerful originality of the interpretation would seem to argue in favor of the last option. In my view, this must be the last known work entirely by La Tour's hand.

73. LA FILLETTE AU BRAISIER.
A Girl Blowing on a Brazier.
Private collection, United States.

Oil on canvas, 67 x 55 cm. Signed.

The signature is almost illegible. The painting is reputed to have been discovered in Toulouse around 1940 and was subsequently acquired in Nice by Jean Neger around 1947. It then passed through the saleroom several times, first at Sotheby's (28 June 1957 and 10 July 1968) and then Christie's (28 November 1975). There are several other examples that are quite clearly copies: one owned by Guy Stein around 1936; another in the Henri Cuvet Collection, exhibited in Paris in 1972 [Or. 58]; and a third, painted as a pendant to one of the copies of *A Smoker* and sold at auction with it a number of times in quick succession (see entry for no. 58). The authenticity of the present work was initially questioned (Isarlo, 1941), then generally accepted following the discovery of the signature (Arland-Marsan, 1953, etc.), only to be doubted once more as the result of a misreading (catalogue of the 1972 exhibition, entry no. 74). Restoration seems to have uncovered a more usual style of signature and has revealed a picture of sufficient quality, despite its obvious wear, to warrant being considered an original. I would place the work near *Le Souffleur à la Pipe (no. 74)*, without hiding the fact that, like the latter, it is probably a case of a subject invented relatively early and repeated over and over, in all likelihood with Étienne's help.

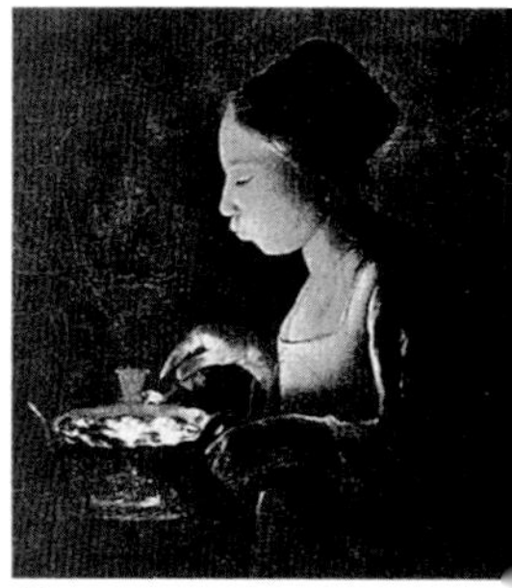

73

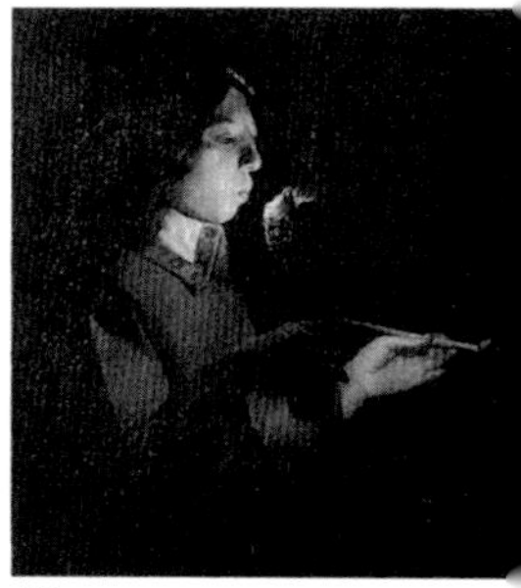

74

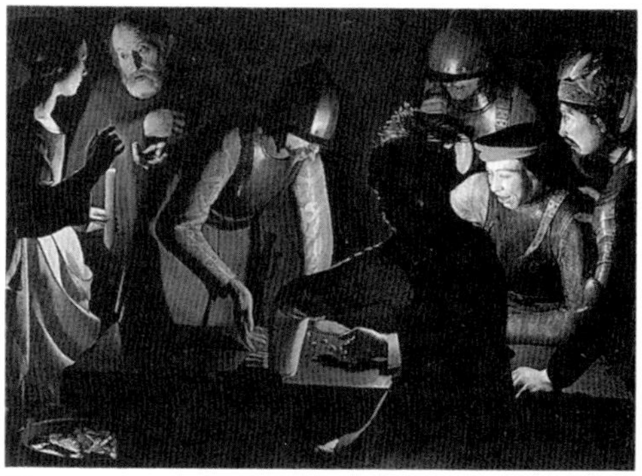

76

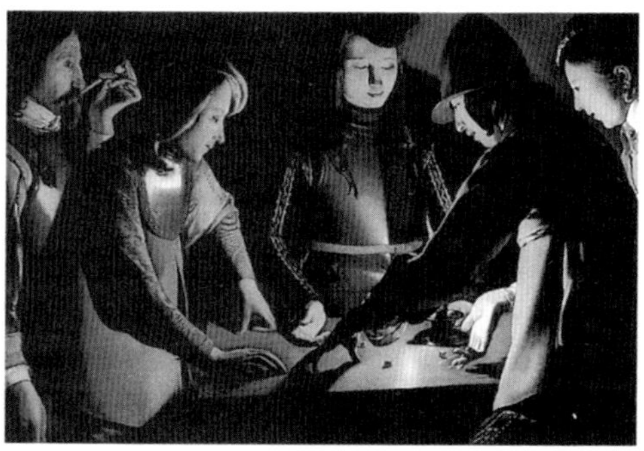

78

74. LE SOUFFLEUR À LA PIPE.
A Smoker.
Private collection, France.

Oil on canvas, 70.5 x 62.5 cm. Signed.

This is another of those small compositions specifically intended to decorate modest bourgeois interiors, and it appears to have been hugely successful: there are no fewer than nine known examples of it. The copy now in the City Art Museum of Saint Louis was published by Philippe in 1935 while it was still in the Tulpain collection in Vaudoncourt (in the Vosges), it was acquired by the museum in 1956. Often taken for the original (Pariset, 1948) it is now generally rejected. Another copy, now in the Musée Lorrain in Nancy, was also published in 1935, this time by Bloch; it was then owned by the Dorr family in Versailles, and was later acquired by Goering. There is a third copy in

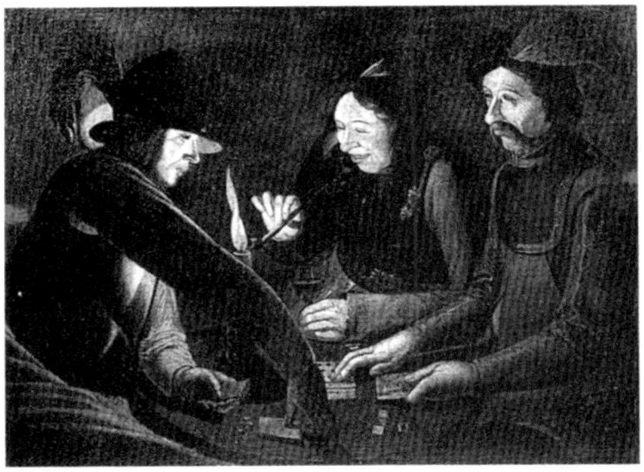

77 Paris copy

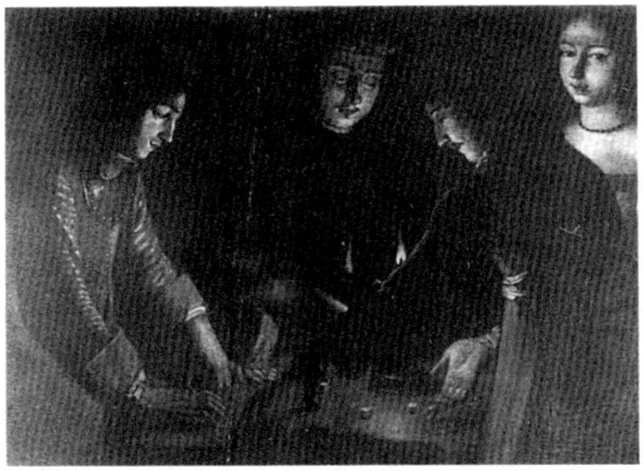

79 copy

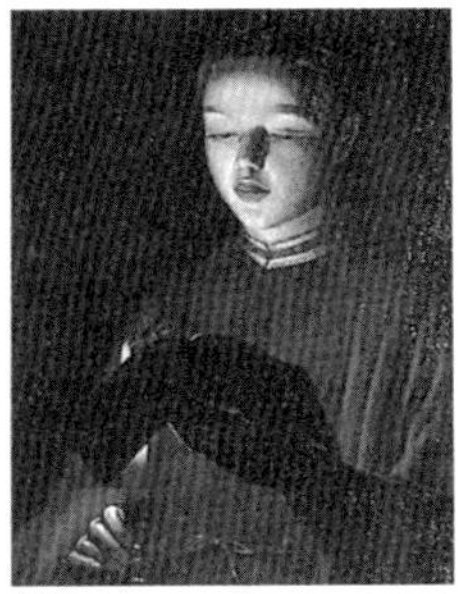

80

the Musée des Beaux-Arts in Besançon, which was discovered in the reserves of the museum under the title "Dutch School." A fourth copy has passed through the saleroom several times, as a pendant to one of the copies of *A Girl Blowing on a Brazier* (Paris, Galerie Charpentier, 5-6 December 1957, and again 8-9 June 1959). Four other copies, of lesser quality, remain in private hands. Finally, a ninth version of the picture, signed *La Tour fec* was discovered in the south of France in 1973 and was sold at the Hôtel Drouot in Paris on 3 December 1985. It had been published as an original by Rosenberg in 1973 (pp. 174-175, no. 53); Nicolson, however, saw it as no more than a studio work. It does seem quite likely that Étienne often helped his father with these small works that, as we know from their appearance in the inventories of countless Lorraine households, must have been turned out in considerable numbers. It is possible that there were other, better versions, among them the "man blowing on a brand to light a pipe" recorded in Cadiz at the beginning of the nineteenth century and probably signed in full (cf. A 19). As far as we can see from the copy we have, the style and technique go back to the period of *St. Alexis* (no. 67).

75. LE RENIEMENT DE SAINT PIERRE.
The Denial of St. Peter.

Oil on canvas, 1650.

Recorded in the Lunéville accounts as having been commissioned, in all probability at the end of 1650, as a year-end gift for the governor, at a cost of 650 francs, the painting was not given to Maréchal de la Ferté until the following March. The 1653 inventory of his collection clearly records it as a night painting: "en nuict." It is generally identified with the next entry (no. 76), which is appropriately dated 1650, but which could also be a replica or a variant.

76. LE RENIEMENT DE SAINT PIERRE.
The Denial of St. Peter.
Musée des Beaux-Arts, Nantes.

Oil on canvas, 120 x 160 cm.
Signed and dated 1650 [Or. 30]

The painting is signed *G. de la Tour in et fec MDCL*. It was acquired by the city of Nantes in 1810 as part of the Cacault Collection (cf. nos. 20 and 50), but its previous history is unknown. First listed as Seghers (1833 catalogue), then as "Flemish School" (1843 catalogue), it was finally attributed to La Tour with the discovery of the signature (1861). It was on the strength of this work, together with no. 50, that Voss in 1915 conclusively identified La Tour with the painter of night scenes of that name referred to in Lorrainese documents. The painting is generally accepted to be *The Denial of St. Peter* recorded in the Lunéville accounts as a gift to the govenor at the beginning of 1651. Several art historians have expressed reservations, sometimes exaggerated, about the quality of the work, and have even gone so far as to suggest that it is in fact by Étienne (Wright, 1969). This hypothesis does not seem likely. The composition is obviously the work of Georges, but father and son are known to have worked together at this date. Critics have also been surprised to find the man who painted *St. Sebastian* reverting late in his career to a specifically Caravaggesque theme (Manfredi, Valentin, Rombouts, et al.) and not seeking to rework the traditional schema. The composition has been linked to one by Seghers engraved by Bolswert (Pariset, 1949), but the connection remains very distant. No one but La Tour could achieve the effects the artist does here with his skillful use of light (the concealed double light source) and extreme stylization of volumes. Oddly enough, however, this economy is coupled with a vivid sense of drama reminiscent of much earlier works. It is possible that La Tour went back to a very old composition for this commission (see no. A7), adapting it fairly freely and recreating it in the colors and stylized forms of the later years, and that he got his son to do all the preparatory work before coming in with the finishing touches. This would explain the surprisingly archaic quality of the composition, the difference in style between this and an almost contemporary work like *St. Sebastian Tended by Irene* (no. 70), and the unusual character of the X-ray itself.

77. SOLDATS JOUANT AUX CARTES.
Group of Soldiers Playing Cards.

Original lost.
Copy A: oil on canvas, 89 x 110 cm.
Regional Gallery, Kursk, Russia.
Copy B: 93 x 123 cm.
Private collection, Paris [Or. 62]

The composition is known only through these two old copies. Although sketchy and clumsy, they clearly derive from an original La Tour. The quality is too poor to provide any solid ground for dating. It seems prudent, therefore, to place this work next to *The Denial of St. Peter* (no. 76), with which it has obvious parallels. See also nos. A16 and A18 below.

78. LES JOUEURS DE DÉS (cinq figures).
Dice Players (Five Figures).
Preston Hall Museum, Stockton-on-Tees.

Oil on canvas, 92.5 x 130.5 cm.
Signed (?) [Or. 30]

This work was part of a bequest to the borough of Stockton-on-Tees (County Durham) in 1930. Although it was correctly attributed in the 1934 inventory, it was not discovered until the beginning of 1972 and was shown to the public for the first time at the Orangerie exhibition. Its reappearance was headline news in England, France, and elsewhere.
There are question marks over the picture, however. The signature, *Georges De La Tour Inve' et Pinx,*. seems more than a little doubtful, but could well be a copy of, or even superimposed onto an authentic signature conceivably erased by overvigorous cleaning in the past. The execution has also raised doubts, and in some places has the look of a copy. X-rays have further highlighted the thinness of the pigment. In other respects the painting is close enough to *The Denial of St. Peter* (no. 76), notably in the color, for it to be dated around the same time (c. 1649-1651). The possiblity that this is a work of Étienne fraudulently signed in his father's name does not seem likely. Another hypothesis is that it was started by Georges and completed after his death by Étienne, but if that were so, the evidence from the X-ray image would be different. It seems far more likely to be a recasting of an earlier, perhaps famous composition—the theme is similar, for instance to that of *The Cheat* (see below), and there are stylistic parallels with the first version of *St. Sebastian Tended by Irene* (no. 37)—in the palette and stylized manner characteristic of the last years. Prepared and painted in large part by Étienne (hence the image we get from the X-ray), it would have received the finishing touches from Georges (hence the signature, and the masterly subtlety still evident in some parts—the head on the right, the fleshing out of the figures—but eliminated from others by cleaning).
Whatever the truth of the matter, the invention of the subject seems to come from Georges. Two themes are combined, the dice players and the guardroom, as was common in the seventeenth century. What is unusual is that the youngest player is not only being duped by his partners but is also being relieved of his purse by the older figure of the smoker on the left. The painting thus has direct links with both *The Fortune Teller* (no. 33) and the two versions of *The Cheat* (nos. 32 and 35), all of them illustrating the same cruel cautionary tale.

79. LES JOUEURS DE DÈS.
The Dice Players.

Original lost.
Copy, oil on canvas.
Private collection, Great Britain.

Contrary to first impressions, rather than being an adaptation by a very second-rate artist (Étienne after 1652?) of no. 78, this could in fact be a copy of a different lost original by Georges de La Tour, in yet another instance of a "double." The copy is clumsy; it has none of La Tour's poetry, and is too far removed from the original to date it with any precision or certainty. Although it could well have preceded no. 78, we shall simply leave the two next to each other.

80. JEUNE CHANTEUR.
A Young Singer.
Leicester Museum and Art Gallery, England.

Oil on canvas, 66.7 x 50.2 cm.

This painting was discovered in England in about 1980 and was acquired by the Leicester Museum and Art Gallery in 1983 and published by Wright in 1984 (*The Burlington Magazine*, June 1984, p. 351). The subject was a common one at the time, and the Nancy archives would suggest that La Tour dealt with it. It is quite likely, moreover, that he painted it several times, as he did the young smoker, to meet the demands of a modest market. We only know the work through a photograph, but it would seem to fit with the closing years of the artist's career and may even be the work of Étienne rather than Georges.

Works cited in documentary sources before 1915

Given here are the principal paintings specifically ascribed to La Tour before his rediscovery but neither dated, as were the paintings commissioned for La Ferté, nor known through reproductions, as is the picture in the collection of the archduke Leopold William described in 1659 but engraved in 1731 (see no. 28).

Most of the attributions appear in inventories drawn up during La Tour's own lifetime or very shortly after his death. The very few that are later are manifestly based on the presence of a very clear signature.

Several references can be linked with works that have come down to us or at least with compositions that we know through old copies. Others, however, clearly represent unknown compositions that may turn up one day.

A 1. LA DÉRISION DU CHRIST.
The Mocking of Christ.

Oil on canvas.

This work is recorded as early as 1653 in the collection of Maréchal de La Ferté, where it is described as a "night" picture representing a *"Blindfolded Christ being struck by a Jew"* and valued at eighty livres. It was probably presented by the town of Lunéville to the governor of Lorraine as a New Year's gift in 1645, 1646, or 1651, one of the years for which we have no specific information about what La Ferté was given. At all events the work is likely to have been painted between 1643 and 1652. The subject was common in the seventeenth century (cf. the certainly very similar treatments by Trophime Bigot, Prato, Galleria Communale, and Macerata, Palazzo Mareföschi).

A 2. LA VIERGE.
The Virgin.

Oil on canvas (?).

Cited as *"A Virgin by Monsieur de La Tour, original, five écus,"* this appears in an inventory of effects in Nancy dated 24 November 1686 (of the late Claude François, auditor of the Mint, and Jacqueline Claudel), which was studied by Michel Sylvestre. The subject was perhaps the most common of all in the seventeenth century, yet this is the only known mention of it in relation to La Tour.

A 3. DEUX CAPUCINS EN MÉDITATION À LA CHANDELLE (SAINT FRANÇOIS MÉDITANT).
Two Capuchins Meditating by Candlelight (St. Francis Meditating).

Oil on canvas.

This painting is recorded under no. 33 in the 1650 inventory of effects drawn up after Jean-Baptiste de Bretagne's death, which was published by Claude Mignot (1984, pp. 73-74): *"[a] large picture by La Tour painted on canvas with a gilded frame representing two capuchins meditating by candle-light,"* valued at twenty-five livres. Mignot points out that Jean-Baptiste de Bretagne, whose collection was famous among the *cognoscenti* in Paris, was superintendent of war and particularly active in Lorraine. He is recorded as being in Nancy in December 1639 and in September 1645, which may help to explain his interest in La Tour and the ownership of five of his works (cf. below). The well-known engraving of *St. Francis Meditating* (see no. 40) fits with the painting as described, and it is not impossible that the engraving was executed after the painting owned by the Parisian collector.

A 4. RELIGIEUX ENDORMI (EXTASE DE SAINT FRANÇOIS?).
Sleeping Monk (St. Francis in Ecstasy?).

Oil on canvas.

No. 12 in the 1650 inventory of Jean-Baptiste de Bretagne's effects drawn up after his death, this work is described as *"[a] picture painted on canvas depicting a sleeping monk [by La Tour, deleted] by la Tour complete with its gilded frame,"* and valued at twenty livres. For more on this collection, see no. A 3 above. The hesitation over the artist's name reinforces rather than undermines the attribution insofar as the reference is repeated. The painting may well have been a version of *St. Francis in Ecstasy*, apparently reduced to the solitary figure of the saint. The copy in the Wadsworth Atheneum (see no. 46) is perhaps a direct reflection of it.

A 5. SAINT JÉRÔME.
St. Jerome.

Oil on canvas.

In the posthumous inventory of Cardinal Richelieu's effects drawn up in 1643, this work (no. 1084) is mentioned as hanging in the cardinal's antechamber in Paris: *"[a] picture of Saint Jerome by La Tour five to six feet high by four feet wide complete with its matte gold frame"* (cf. Levi, 1985, p. 66). The work was valued—by no less than Simon Vouet—at 250 livres (as much as one by Sacchi, more than a Guercino). It was no doubt painted around 1638-1639, and may have been given to the cardinal in a bid to secure the title of *"peintre ordinaire du roi"* or been commissioned by him at the time this was granted. It cannot be ruled out that this is the Stockholm *St. Jerome*, with its prominently placed cardinal's hat. The measurements given in the inventory (approximately 165/198 x 132 cm) are more or less the same as those of the Stockholm painting (153 x 106 cm), assuming, as was most often the case, that they included the frame and that this was about 15 cm wide.

A 6. SAINT JÉRÔME.
St. Jerome.

This work figures in the 1644 inventory of effects drawn up after the death of Simon Cornu, painter to the king, cousin by marriage of Jacques Blanchard, and father of Nicolas Cornu, valet and painter to the king: *"a saint Jerome by sire Latour of Lorraine, without frame,"* valued at twenty-five livres (cf. Beresford, 1985, p. 132). It was among the most highly valued items in the inventory. The absence of further information (a daylight scene or a nocturne, St. Jerome reading or penitent, for instance) makes it impossible to identify this work with any known versions of the subject.

A 7. LE RENIEMENT DE SAINT PIERRE.
The Denial of St. Peter.

Oil on canvas, approx. 100 x 142 cm.

Mentioned in Paris in the 1641 inventory of effects drawn up after the death of the financial secretary, Claude de Bullion, as *"a . . . picture of a night scene representing saint Peter denying Our Lord, painted by Latour, complete with its stretcher and burnished gold frame, measuring four feet wide by three feet high or thereabouts,"* and valued at thirty livres by Simon Vouet, who was given the job of assessing the paintings (record discovered by Catherine Grodecki and published by Michel Antoine, 1979). The work must have been painted around 1638-1639, at the time when La Tour was trying to get established in Paris. It is interesting that the only known record for 1639 (see p. 110) should be signed by Bullion, the great art lover and patron.
The painting's horizontal format and relatively large size suggest that it was not a single-figure composition (St. Peter and the Cock), but rather a depiction of the denial scene itself, complete with soldiers and maidservant. This would make it an earlier (and unknown) version of the Nantes *Denial of St. Peter*.

A 8. SAINT SÉBASTIEN DANS UNE NUIT.
Night Picture of St. Sebastian.

Oil on canvas.

This painting was recorded in 1751 by Dom Calmet: *"[La Tour] presented King Louis XIII with a painting of his own hand, which represented a saint. Sebastian in a night scene; the piece was of such perfect taste that the King removed all other paintings from his chamber, so that this one might hang on its own"* (Dom Calmet, p. 948). The work was therefore painted before 1643 (when the king died); my belief is that it was presented to the king in about 1638-1639 to secure the title of *"Peintre ordinaire du Roy"* that La Tour was granted at the end of 1639 at the latest (record dated 22 December).
There is no trace of this *St. Sebastian* in the inventories of the royal collections (drawn up at the end of the century). It would be reasonable to assume, however, that it was the original of no. 37, which was so famous that at least ten copies of it have come to light.

A 9. SAINT SÉBASTIEN DANS UNE NUIT.
Night picture of St. Sebastian.

Oil on canvas.

This was similarly recorded in 1751 by Dom Calmet. Having told us about the *St. Sebastian* presented to the king, he goes on to say: *"La Tour had already presented a similar one to Duke Charles IV. This painting is known in the château of Houdemont near Nancy"* (Dom Calmet, p. 948). The work must therefore have been painted before 1643, or even 1639 (see entry for no. A 8); indeed, it is quite likely that it dates to the peaceful era when Charles IV was a resident in Nancy (1624 and 1634), which makes it an invaluable reference for establishing the date of the first night pictures.
Once again, there is no trace of this work in the archives. We cannot tell from Dom Calmet's reference if it was identical in composition to the painting presented to Louis XIII, or if—as seems more likely—it was a first, markedly different version.

A10. SAINT ANNE.
St. Anne.

Oil on canvas.

The 1653 inventory of Maréchal de La Ferté's effects records *"a night picture of St. Anne,"* valued at fifty livres. It may have been presented to the governor of Lorraine by the town of Lunéville as a New Year's gift in 1645, 1646, or 1651, one of the years for which we have no specific information about what La Ferté was given. It could well be one of the versions of *The Education of the Virgin*, often referred to as St. Anne (see entries for nos. 57, 60, 61 and 62).

A 11. UNE NOURRICE AVEC UNE ENFANT (SAINT ANNE ET LA VIERGE AU MAILLOT?).
A Nurse and Child (St. Anne with the Virgin in Swaddling Clothes).

Oil on canvas.

This work was recorded in the 1650 inventory of Jean-Baptiste de Bretagne's effects drawn up after his death and published by Mignot (1984, pp. 73-74) as *"[a picture] painted on canvas, without frame, representing a nurse and child, an original by La Tour,"* valued at fifteen livres. For more on this collection, see no. A 3 above. This was undoubtedly a composition very like *The Newborn Child* in Rennes (no. 64), or, more likely, *The Newborn Child* now in an American collection (no. 63).

A 12. LA MADELEINE.
The Magdalen.

Oil on canvas.

Cited as: *"a painting representing the Magdalen in the fashion of Sire de La Tour in an ebonized wood frame with gilded leaves in some places,"* this work appears in an inventory of effects in Nancy dated 22 January 1661 (of the late César Mirgodin, merchant, and Anne Polatel), which was studied by Michel Sylvestre. It would appear to be the same picture listed in the inventory drawn up on 10 November 1643, after the death of the merchant's first wife, without any mention of the artist, as *"a night picture of the Magdalen, without stretcher, valued at twenty-five francs."* In the absence of any more specific indication, it is impossible to identify this reference with any of the surviving versions of *The Magdalen*.

A 13. DISEUSES DE BONNE AVENTURE.
Fortune Tellers.

Oil on canvas.

This appeared in 1650 as no. 14 in the 1650 inventory of Jean-Baptiste de Bretagne's effects as: *"[a] large picture painted on canvas with its gilded frame representing fortune tellers, an original by La Tour,"* valued at thirty livres. For more on this collection, see no. A 3 above. It is by no means impossible that this is the painting now in the Metropolitan Museum (no. 31).

A 14. FLUTEURS À LA CHANDELLE.
Pipers Playing by Candlelight.

Oil on canvas.

No. 20 in the 1650 inventory of Jean-Baptiste de Bretagne's effects was: *"[a] picture painted on canvas complete with its frame representing pipers, by La Tour, playing by candlelight,"* valued at thirty-two livres. For more on this collection, see no. A 3 above. No known painting can be identified with this "musical nocturne."

A 15. NUIT AVEC MUSICIENS.
Night Picture with Musicians.

Oil on canvas.

Inventoried in the Petit-Luxembourg in Paris in 1675, after the death of the duchess of Aiguillon, Cardinal de Richelieu's niece, this was *"a night picture, painted on canvas, by the said artist La Tour, representing a group of musicians."* According to Boubli, who discovered this record (1983), the painting could have belonged to Richelieu himself and thus correspond to the same subject listed, without any mention of the artist, in the 1643 inventory drawn up at his château in Rueil.

A 16. DEUX JOUEURS DE CARTES.
Two Card Players.

Oil on canvas.

This work was recorded as early as 1653 in the collection of Maréchal de La Ferté, where it is described as *"Two card players with Tyr ... (?)"* and valued at two hundred livres. It may have been presented to the governor of Lorraine by the town of Lunéville as a New Year's gift in 1645, 1646, or 1651, one of the years for which we have no specific information about what La Ferté was given. It is perhaps the night scene we know through a bad copy (no. 77), but the last word in the record has not been deciphered: "smokers"? or "Egyptian"? Unfortunately, the original inventory appears to have been burned during the Second World War, which precludes any reliable hypothesis.

A 17. TABAGIE AVEC DEUX JOUEURS DE CARTES.
Smoking Den with Two Card Players.

Oil on canvas, approx. 195 x 230 cm.

Described as *"signed La Tour,"* this work appears in the two sales catalogues for the collection of Le Roy de la Faudignère, "dental surgeon to Mgr the Prince Palatine ruling Duke of les Deux-Ponts" (Paris, 1 March 1782, and Paris, 8 January 1787). The painting included *"five figures, representing soldiers, two playing cards, the others smoking"*; the figures were depicted *"full-length and life size."* It is without doubt one of La Tour's largest genre paintings (6 x 7 feet). No trace of it has yet been found.

A 18. UNE PARTIE DE CARTES.
A Game of Cards.

Oil on canvas.

"A big picture by La Tour, the game of cards" was recorded in 1894 in the château of Vigny (Val d'Oise), which then belonged to Count Vitalli (Alexis Martin, *Promenades et excursions dans les environs de Paris, Région du Nord*). This must have been a signed canvas. It could conceivably be the Louvre *Cheat* (no. 30), the provenance of which is unknown, but more likely contenders are the *Card Players* recorded in Maréchal de La Ferté's collection and the *Smoking Den*, which went up for sale at the end of the eighteenth century (see nos. A 16 and A 17).

A 19. LE SOUFFLEUR (à la pipe).
A Smoker.

Signed (?).

Recorded in Cadiz at the beginning of the nineteenth century in the collection of Don Sebastian Martinez, a friend of Goya (cf. Conde de Maule, *Viaje de España, Francia and Italia*, Cadiz, 1813, vol. 13, p. 40), this work was described as *"a man blowing on a brand to light a pipe, by Georges de La Tour."* The painting must therefore have been signed in full, first name included. No trace has yet been found, but it was probably an original version of no. 74.

A 20. UNE NUIT.
Night Scene.

This was listed in 1691 as no. 1049 in the posthumous inventory of Louvois's: *"a painting of a Night scene, an original by La Tour, without frame, valued at XX."* The painting reappears in 1715 as no. 664 in the inventory drawn up after the death of the minister's widow, Anne de Souvre, marquise de Louvois: *"a Night scene, an original by La Tour, w[ithout] f[rame],"* valued at ten livres.
It is impossible to say from the vague description we are given whether this is in fact a painting detailed in an earlier record in Paris, and whether, as seems likely, it is one of those compositions known to us through either an original or a copy.

A 21. UNE NUIT.
Night Scene.

The 1700 inventory drawn up after the death of André Le Nôtre, the famous designer of the gardens of Versailles and one of the leading *cognoscenti* in Paris, indicates that *"in the little study off the room where the said late seigneur Le Nostre died"* there was (no. 195) *"a picture painted by La Tour, representing a night scene, with its frame, valued at ... 15."*
The absence of any information about the subject makes it impossible to identify this painting with any known surviving work.

A 22. DAME AUX BIJOUX.
Lady with Jewels.

Oil on panel, approx. 35 x 27 cm.

No. 57 in the Gerrit Schimmelpenninck Collection sold in Amsterdam—on 12 July 1819 is recorded as: *"G. de La Tour, height 13 p. by 10 p., on panel. A Lady in white satin dress in front of a mirror, with a little red jacket trimmed with fur hanging over her chair. Behind her a negress holds a casket of jewels. This little painting is of the utmost fineness, echoing Van Mieris the elder in its well-judged brushwork"* (discovered by Mme de Roodenbeke and published by Rosenberg, 1973).
Everything about this description is surprising but it cannot be ignored, for any attribution to La Tour by first and last names at a date when these were buried in oblivion must be based on documentary evidence. It is quite possible that La Tour turned out secular paintings of this sort, and in a delicate, subtle manner somewhere between that of Bellange and Deruet. The colors described correspond fairly well to those of the daylight paintings from *St Jerome* to *The Fortune Teller*.

A 23. PAYSAGE VU AU CRÉPUSCULE.
Landscape Seen at Dusk.

Oil on canvas, 145 x 93 cm.

As dubious as it may seem at first glance, I believe this reference must be included here. Described also as a "marine" painting, it is attributed to "Claude du Mesnil-la-Tour" [*sic*] in the collection of the notary Noel in Nancy (catalogue of the collection, no. 5550, vol. 2, p. 729, Nancy 1851; sale catalogue, Nancy, 25 November 1884, no. 4). The work has never been found. Such an attribution looks like pure fantasy on the part of a provincial scholar. It could, however—especially at this very early date—stem from some material evidence (a label, for instance, or an inscription on the stretcher). It is not impossible that this was simply a painting that belonged to Claude de La Tour, the painter's daughter, or to another of his descendants. In any event, it would be distinctly unscholarly to dismiss the attribution without examining the work itself, which may yet be extant.

Additional catalogue entry

72b. SAINT JEAN-BAPTISTE DANS LE DÉSERT.
Saint John the Baptist in the Wilderness. Future Musée Georges de La Tour, Vic-sur-Seille.

Oil on canvas, 81 x 101 cm.

This painting hung undiscovered in a Parisian apartment until it was recognized when it appeared at a sale at the Hôtel Drouot on the 22nd October 1993, following the owner's death. It passed through several hands before it was put up for auction in Monaco and on the 2nd December 1994 was acquired, with state assistance, by the Conseil général de la Moselle, to be exhibited in Vic-sur-Seille, the artist's birthplace. There are no known copies, the subject does not appear in his works, nor is it mentioned in any of the rediscovered texts, and scientific examinations of the painting have not revealed a signature. Despite this, the authenticity of the work has not been questioned.
The theme of St. John the Baptist in the Wilderness, which became common in the fifteenth century, was often taken up by Caravaggio and his successors. La Tour treats it however with exceptional austerity of composition and of color: a monochrome brown, which is unbroken by either spots of color or by artificial light.
The work undoubtedly dates from the end of his career, very close to the time the *Saint Sebastian* was painted. As much in inspiration as in technique it represents the high point of asceticism in La Tour's work. It certainly seems to confirm the theory that we have been putting forward for the last five years of his life; i.e., two lines of production; works such as this one, in which La Tour's creative impulse becomes increasingly introspective, and the more commercial works which are left to a greater or lesser extent to Étienne.

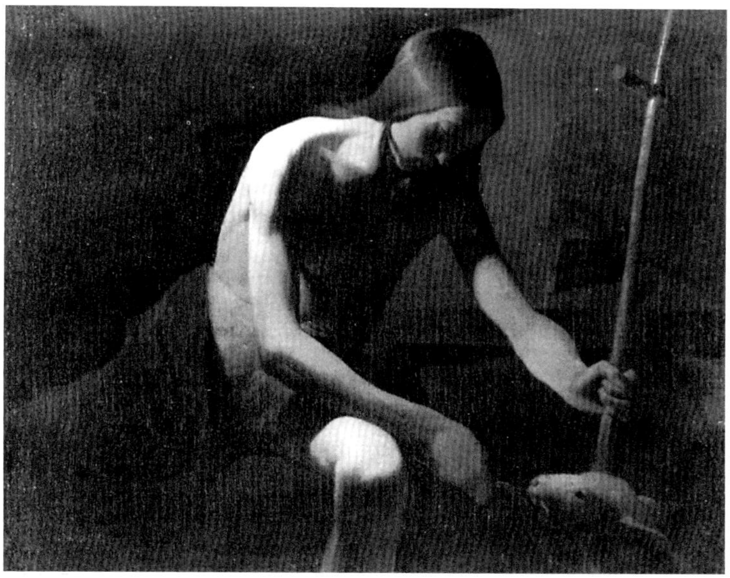

72 b

BIBLIOGRAPHY: BOOKS AND ARTICLES

I. 1600-1933 (Prior to the Exhibition "Peintres de la réalité")

1660, TENIERS
David Teniers. *Theatrum pictorium in quo exhibentur ipsius manu delineatae, ejusque cura in aes incisae picturae archetypae italicae, quas archidux in pinacothecam suam Bruxellis collegit.* Brussels.

ca. 1673, MAROLLES
Le Livre des peintres et graveurs, par Michel de Marolles, abbé de Villeloin. N.p., n.d. Repr. Georges Duplessis, 1855; 2d rev. ed., 1872. (See p. 47.)

1731, PRENNER
Anton Joseph Prenner. *Theatrum artis pictoriae in quo tabulae depictae quae in Caesarea Vindobonensi Pinacotheca servantur leviore caelatura aeri insculptae exhibentur ab Antonio Josepho de Prenner.* Vol. 3. Vienna, 1728-1733.

1735, STAMPART-PRENNER
Prodromus seu praeambulare lumen reserati portentosae magnificentiae theatri quo omnia ad aulam caesaream in augustissimae suae caesarae et regiae catholicae majestatis nostri gloriossime regnantis monarchae Caroli VI metropoli et residentia Viennae recondita artificiorum et pretiositatum decora.... Vienna.

1751, Dom CALMET
Dom Calmet. *Bibliothèque Lorraine, ou histoire des hommes illustres qui ont fleuri en Lorraine....* Nancy.

1754, CHEVRIER
Mémoires pour servir à l'histoire des hommes illustres de Lorraine, avec une réfutation de la Bibliothèque Lorraine de dom Calmet, by M. de Chevrier. Vol. 2. Brussels. (See p. 297.)

1766, EXPILLY
Dictionnaire géographique, historique et politique des Gaules et de la France, par M. l'abbé Expilly. Vol. 4. (See p. 465.)

1779, DURIVAL
Description de la Lorraine et du Barrois par M. Durival l'aîné. Vol. 2. Nancy. (See p. 79.)

1782, LE ROY DE LA FAUDIGNÈRE
Catalogue des tableaux et autres objets curieux qui composent la majeure partie de la collection de M. Le Roy de la Faudignère. Dont la vente (aura lieu le) 1er mars 1782. Paris: Imprimerie de Valleyre aîné. (See p. 8.) Another catalogue 1787, sale of 8 January.

1803, FIORILLO
J.-F. Fiorillo. *Geschichte der Künste und Wissenschaften... Achtzehnte Lieferung... enthält Geschichte der Zeichnenden Kunst I. Geschichte der Mahlerey.* Vol. 3. Göttingen.

1813, DE MAULE
Don Nicolás de la Cruz y Bahamonde, Conde de Maule. *Viaje de España, Francia y Italia.* Cadiz. (See p. 340.)

1818, GUERRIER
Guerrier. *Annales de Lunéville ou essai historique sur cette ville depuis sa fondation jusqu'à nos jours.* Lunéville: Published privately. (See p. 189.)

1829, MICHEL
Biographie historique et généalogique des hommes marquants de l'ancienne province de Lorraine, par Michel, juge de paix du canton de Vezelise. Nancy. (See p. 144.)

1836, MÉRIMÉE
Prosper Mérimée. *Notes d'un voyage dans l'Ouest de la France... Extrait d'un rapport adressé à Monsieur le Ministre de l'Intérieur.* Paris: Librairie de Fournier. (See p. 305; reprint, Paris: Pierre-Marie Auzas, 1971, p. 390.)

1838, STENDHAL
Stendhal, *Mémoires d'un touriste* (part 1; Nantes museum). Paris: A. Dupont.

1842, MAGASIN PITTORESQUE
"Musées et collections particulières des départements. Musée de Nantes. Écoles d'Italie. École espagnole." *Le Magasin pittoresque,* pp. 291-293.

1844, DASSY
L. T. Dassy. *L'Abbaye de Saint-Antoine en Dauphiné. Essai historique et descriptif.* Grenoble: N.p. (See p. 452.)

1849, NAGLER
Neues allgemeines Kunstlexikon... bearbeitet von Dr G. K. Nagler. Münich: N.p., vol. 19. (See p. 29.)

1851, NOËL
Catalogue raisonné des collections lorraines (livres, manuscrits, tableaux, gravures, etc.) de M. Noël, ancien avocat, notaire honoraire. Nancy: the author, rue de la Salpêtrière, 6, vol. 2.

1853, LEPAGE
Henri Lepage. *Les Communes de la Meurthe, Journal historique des villes, bourgs, villages, hameaux et censes de ce département.* Nancy: A. Lepage (See vol. 2, p. 33.).

1853, LEPAGE, Quelques notes...
Henri Lepage. *Quelques notes sur les peintres lorrains des 15e, 16e et 17e siècles.* Nancy: N.p. (See p. 75.)

1857, PESQUIDOUX
Léonce de Pesquidoux. *Voyage artistique en France – Études sur les Musées....* Paris: N.p. (See pp. 56-57.)

1859, Cl. de RIS
L. Clément de Ris. *Les Musées de province. Histoire et description.* Paris: Vve Jules Renouard. 2d rev. ed., Paris, 1872.

1863, JOLY
Alexandre Joly. "Du Mesnil-La-Tour, peintre." *Journal de la Société d'Archéologie Lorraine* 12, pp. 90-96.

1863, TAINE
Hippolyte Taine. *Carnets de Voyage. Notes sur la province, 1863-1865.* Paris: Hachette.

1870, LAROUSSE
"Du Ménil La Tour." *Grand Dictionnaire universel du* XIX*e siècle.* Paris: Librairie Larousse et Boyer, vol. 6, p. 1379.

1873-1891, LEPAGE
Henri Lepage. *Inventaire sommaire des archives départementales antérieures à 1790.* 6 vols. Meurthe. Nancy: N. Collin.

1883, BERGER
A. Berger. *Jahrbuch der Kunsthistorischen Sammlungen des Ah. Kaiserhauses.* (See p. CXXXIII, inventory of Archduke Leopold Wilhelm, 1659.)

1883, MERSON
Olivier Merson. "Catalogue du Musée de Nantes." *Inventaire Général des Richesses d'Art de la France, Province, Monuments civils,* vol. 2.

1883, SIRET
Adolphe Siret. *Dictionnaire historique et raisonné des peintres de toutes les écoles.* Brussels: N.p., vol. 1, p. 529.

1884, NOËL
Catalogue des tableaux anciens... composant la Collection de feu M. Noël, Notaire honoraire à Nancy... À vendre... à l'Hôtel des ventes de Nancy... par le ministère de Me Siméon... 25 November 1884. (See p. 4.)

1885, JACQUOT
Albert Jacquot. "Anoblissement d'artistes lorrains." *Réunion des Sociétés des Beaux-Arts des Départements.* Ninth session, pp. 116-132 (See p. 126 "Claude" de Latour.)

1887, AUVRAY
Louis Auvray. *Table topographique des artistes de l'école française.* Paris. 84 pp. (Table prepared for M. M. Bellier de la Chavignerie et Auvray, *Dictionnaire général des artistes de l'École française.* See p. 78.)

1894, MARTIN
Guide Alexis Martin. *Promenades et excursions dans les environs de Paris. Région Nord.* (See p. 516.)

1894, JACQUOT
Albert Jacquot. "Notes sur Claude Deruet, peintre et graveur lorrain. 1588-1660." *Réunion des Sociétés des Beaux-Arts des Départements.* Eighteenth session, pp. 763-943.

1897, HERLUISON-LEROY
"Notes artistiques sur les seigneurs de La Ferté." *Réunion des Sociétés des Beaux-Arts des Départements.* Twenty-first session, pp. 795-816.

1899, DENIS
Charles Denis. *Inventaire des registres de l'État Civil de Lunéville (1652-1792).* Nancy: Berger-Levrault.

1899, JACQUOT
Albert Jacquot. "Essai de répertoire des artistes lorrains, peintres." *Réunion des Sociétés des Beaux-Arts des Départements.* Twenty-third session, pp. 493-494.

1900, BAUMONT
H. Baumont. *Histoire de Lunéville.* Lunéville: N.p. (See pp. 77-78.)

1900, GONSE
Louis Gonse. *Les Chefs-d'œuvre des Musées de France. La peinture.* Paris: Société française d'édition d'art.

1901, SINGER
H. W. Singer. *Allgemeines Künstler-Lexikon. Leben und Werke der berühmtesten bildenden Künstler.* Frankfurt am Main, vol. 4.

1902, DIJON
Dom Hippolyte Dijon. *L'Église abbatiale de Saint-Antoine en Dauphiné. Histoire et archéologie.* Grenoble: H. Falque et F. Perrin. (See p. 212.)

1911, GUIFFREY
Jules Guiffrey. "Testament et Inventaire après décès de André le Nostre et autres documents le concernant." *Bulletin de la Société de l'Histoire de l'Art français,* pp. 217-282. (See p. 243.)

1911, MAYER
August L. Mayer. *Die Sevillaner Malerschule.* Leipzig: Klinkhardt und Biermann.

1911, NICOLLE
Marcel Nicolle. "Le 'Joueur de vielle' du Musée de Nantes." *Les Musées de France,* pp. 75-77.

1915, VOSS
Hermann Voss. "Georges du Mesnil de La Tour." *Archiv für Kunstgeschichte* 2, fasc. 3-4, plates 121, 122, 123 and text page.

1919, NICOLLE
Marcel Nicolle. *Le musée de Nantes – Peintures.* Paris: H. Laurens.

1920, MAYER
August L. Mayer. "Unbekannte Werke spanischer Meister." *Monatshefte für Wissenschaft* 13, vol. 1, pp. 88-89.

1922, DEMONTS
Louis Demonts. "Georges du Ménil de La Tour, peintre lorrain au début du XVIIe siècle." *Chronique des arts et de la curiosité*, no. 8 (30 April), pp. 60-61.

1922, JAMOT
Paul Jamot. "Sur les frères Le Nain." *Gazette des Beaux-Arts* 1, p. 308 ff. (Offprint, *Les frères Le Nain*.)

1922, MAYER
August L. Mayer. *Geschichte der spanischen Malerei*. 3d ed., Leipzig: Klinkhardt und Biermann.

1922, SAULNIER
Charles Saulnier. "Les musées de Province. Le musée de Rennes." *La Renaissance de l'Art français*, February, pp. 76-83.

1922, TORMO
Elias Tormo. "Le Père Juan Ricci, écrivain d'art et peintre de l'école de Madrid." *Congrès d'histoire de l'art, Paris*, 1921 (published 1922), pp. 188-189 (paper abstract).

1923, ELDER
Marc Elder. "Le musée de Nantes." *L'Amour de l'art*, July, pp. 617-620.

1923, NICOLLE
Marcel Nicolle. "Le 'Joueur de vielle' du Musée de Nantes." *Critique d'art ancien et moderne. Première série. Musées de Province*. Paris: Librairie académique Perrin, pp. 207-217.

1924, PHILIPPE
André Philippe. "Le musée départemental des Vosges à Épinal." *La Renaissance de l'Art français*, September, p. 507.

1926, VAUDOYER
Jean-Louis Vaudoyer. *L'Écho de Paris*, 3 December.

1926, WARNOD
André Warnod. "De nouveaux tableaux exposés au Louvre." *Comœdia*, 19 November.

1926, ZARNOWSKI
Zarnowski. *Kunstwanderer*, vol. 8. (See p. 404.)

1927, STILLWELL
The Important Art Collection of Dr. John E. Stillwell. Auction catalogue. New York (Auction of 1-3 December.) (See no. 206 p. 58 and plate.)

1927, DELORME
E. Delorme. "Un Lunévillois au Louvre." *Journal de Lunéville*, 2 January, p. 1.

1927, DELORME, Lunéville
E. Delorme. *Lunéville et son arrondissement*. Lunéville, 2 vols. (See vol. 1, pp. 118, 160-161.)

1927, LONGHI
Roberto Longhi. "Ter Brugghen e la parte nostra." *Vita artistica. Studi di Storia dell'arte* 2, no. 6, pp. 105-116.

1928, VOSS, *Art in America*
Hermann Voss. "Georges Du Mesnil de La Tour. A Forgotten French Master of the Seventeenth Century." *Art in America* 17 (December), pp. 40-48.

1928, VOSS, *Thieme-Becker*
Hermann Voss. "La Tour." In Thieme-Becker, *Künstler-Lexikon*, vol. 22.

1929, JAMOT
Paul Jamot. *Les Le Nain*. Paris: H. Laurens. (See p. 125.)

1929, MÖHLE
Hans Möhle. "Neuerwerbungen der Berliner Museen." *Belvedere* 8, no. 4, pp. 109-113.

1929, LAROUSSE
"Du Menil La Tour (Georges)." *Larousse du XXe siècle*, vol. 2.

1929, PHILIPPE
André Philippe. Entries on Georges de La Tour and the Épinal painting. In *Musée Départemental des Vosges – Catalogue de la section des Beaux-Arts*. Épinal, pp. 66-67.

1930, BLOCH
Vitale Bloch. "G. Dumesnil de La Tour. 1600-1652." *Formes*, no. 10 (December), pp. 17-19.

1930, PANDER
Arist Pander. "Georges de La Tour et bidrag til hans Kunstneriske udvikling." *Samleren*, February, pp. 23-31.

1931, GEORGE
Waldemar George. *L'esprit français et la peinture française. En marge de l'exposition d'art français à Londres*. Paris: Éditions des Quatre-Chemins, n.d., pp. 20-24.

1931, MAYER
August L. Mayer. "Tableaux de l'école espagnole conservés dans les musées français." *Gazette des Beaux-Arts* 6 (August), pp. 95-97.

1931, NICOLLE
Marcel Nicolle. "Chefs-d'œuvre des musées de province. École française, XVIIe et XVIIIe siècles." *Gazette des Beaux-Arts* 6 (August), pp. 98-124.

1931, VALENTINER
W. R. Valentiner. "An Erroneous Callot Attribution." *Art in America* 20 (April), pp. 114-121.

1931, VOSS
Hermann Voss. "Tableaux à éclairage diurne de G. de La Tour." Trans. Édouard Ciprut. *Formes*, no. 16 (June), pp. 97-100.

1932, CHAMOT
Chamot. "The Exhibition of French Art." *Apollo* 15 (January), pp. 1-6.

1932, DEZARROIS
A. Dezarrois. "L'Art français à Londres." *Revue de l'art ancien et moderne* 61 (February), pp. 73-104.

1932, FIERENS
Paul Fierens. "Le Caravage et l'Art français." *Nouvelles Littéraires*, 6 February.

1932, ISARLOV
George Isarlov. *La peinture française à l'exposition de Londres 1932*. Coll. Orbes, 4. Paris: José Corti.

1932, MÂLE
Émile Mâle. *L'art religieux de la fin du XVIe siècle, du XVIIe siècle et du XVIIIe siècle. Étude sur l'iconographie après le Concile de Trente*. Paris.

1932, PASCAL
Georges Pascal. "Le XVIIe siècle." *Art vivant*, January, p. 15.

1932, WEISBACH
Werner Weisbach. *Französische Malerei des XVII. Jahrhunderts im Rahmen von Kultur und Gesellschaft*. Berlin: Heinrich Keller.

1933, FIERENS
Paul Fierens. *Les Le Nain*. Paris: Librairie Floury. (See pp. 36-39.)

1933, SCHNEIDER
Arthur von Schneider. *Caravaggio und die Niederländer*. Reprint. Amsterdam, 1967. (See p. 126.)

II. 1934-1948 (From the Exhibition "Peintres de la réalité" to the Thesis of François-Georges Pariset)

1934, BEAUX-ARTS
"Les maîtres de la réalité." *Beaux-Arts*, 22 November, p. 1.

1934, B.A.A.M.
"L'exposition des peintres de la réalité en France au XVIIe siècle." *Bulletin de l'Art ancien et moderne*, no. 810 (December), p. 393.

1934, DIOLÉ
Philippe Diolé. "Les peintres de la réalité." *Beaux-Arts*, 30 November, p. 2.

1934, DU COLOMBIER
Pierre du Colombier. "Sur Georges de La Tour." *Beaux-Arts*, 7 December.

1934, ESCHOLIER
Raymond Escholier. "Une révélation à l'Orangerie: Georges de La Tour." *Le Journal*, 2 December, p. 6.

1934, HÉLION
Jean Hélion. "La réalité dans la peinture: à propos de l'exposition du musée de l'Orangerie." *Cahiers d'art*, nos. 9-10, pp. 253-260.

1934, LÉCUYER
Raymond Lécuyer. "Les peintres de la réalité au XVIIe siècle à l'Orangerie. Lettre à une jeune femme qui désire être avertie." *Plaisir de France* 1, no. 1 (October), p. 45.

1934, LEMOYNE
Jean-Gabriel Lemoyne. *L'Écho de Paris*, 3 December.

1934, STERLING
Charles Sterling. Entries on La Tour in the exhibition catalogue for "Les peintres de la réalité." Paris, 1934.

1935, ALFASSA
Paul Alfassa. "Les peintres de la réalité au XVIIe siècle." *Revue de Paris*, 15 January, pp. 400-411.

1935, ALPATOV
Michael Alpatov. "Probleme der französischen Malerei des 17. Jahrhunderts. Zu Werner Weisbach Französische Malerei...." In Friedrich Antal and Bruno Fürst. *Kritische Berichte zur Kunstgeschichtlichen Literatur 1927-1937*. Reprint. Georg Olms Verlag. 1972, pp. 84-85.

1935, BAZIN
Germain Bazin. "Au musée de l'Orangerie. La réalité française au XVIIe siècle." *L'Amour de l'art*, January, pp. 31-34.

1935, BEAUX-ARTS
"Rizzi ou La Tour." *Beaux-Arts*, 26 April, p. 2.

1935, BLANCHE
Jacques-Émile Blanche. "Paris and the Turning Wheel of Art." *The Studio* 2, no. 110, pp. 3-12.

1935, BLOCH, *I pittori*
Vitale Bloch. "I pittori della realtà nel Seicento." *Occidente* 10 (offprint, pp. 10-11).

1935, BLOCH, *Peintres de la réalité*
Vitale Bloch. "Peintres de la réalité." *Beaux-Arts*, 8 February, p. 2.

1935, BLUNT
Anthony Blunt. "Candlelight." *Spectator*, 1 March (Review of the Orangerie exhibit.)

1935, DU COLOMBIER
Pierre du Colombier. "Callot chez lui." *Candide*, 15 August, p. 6.

1935, FIERENS
Paul Fierens. "Autour de Callot." *Journal des débats*, 29 October.

1935, FLAMENT
Albert Flament. "Tableaux de Paris." *Revue de Paris*, 1 April, pp. 715-718.

1935, GHÉON
Henri Ghéon. "Rencontres – De Georges de La Tour à Eugène Delacroix." *Muses* no. 1 (Paris), pp. 35-39.

1935, GILLET
Louis Gillet. *La Peinture de Poussin à David*. Paris: Éd. Henri Laurens. (See pp. 32-38.)

1935, GILLET, *Les peintres*
Louis Gillet. "Les peintres de la réalité." *Revue des deux mondes*, 1 January, pp. 206-211.

1935, GOULINAT, *A.A.*
J.-G. Goulinat. "Les peintres de la réalité en France au XVIIe siècle." *L'Art et les artistes* 39, no. 153 (January), pp. 109-116.

1935, GOULINAT, *Le Dessin*
J.-G. Goulinat. "G. de La Tour." *Le Dessin*, January, p. 36.

1935, GRAPPE
Georges Grappe. "Les peintres français de la réalité au XVIIe siècle." *L'Art vivant*, no. 192 (April), n.p.

1935, HEVESY
A. de Hevesy. "Die Ausstellung der französischen Realisten des XVII. Jhts in Paris." *Pantheon* 15 (April), pp. 125-131.

1935, JAMOT
Paul Jamot. "Le réalisme dans la peinture française du XVIIe siècle.

De Louis Le Nain à Georges de La Tour. Les enseignements de deux expositions." *Revue de l'art ancien et moderne* 67 (February), pp. 69-76.

1935, LAFOND
Jean Lafond. "Le tableau de Georges de La Tour au musée d'Épinal. 'Saint Pierre délivré' ou 'Job et sa femme'?" *Bulletin de la société de l'histoire de l'art français*, pp. 11-13.

1935, LAMIRAY, *Beaux-Arts*
[Yvonne Lamiray.] "Georges de La Tour au musée d'Évreux." *Beaux-Arts*, 8 March, p. 2.

1935, LAMIRAY, *Normandie*
Yvonne Lamiray. "Georges de La Tour au musée d'Évreux." *Normandie*, 14 March.

1935, LAPRADE
Jacques de Laprade. "À propos de Georges de La Tour." *Beaux-Arts*, 4 January, pp. 1, 4.

1935, LA TOURETTE
Gilles de La Tourette. "Georges de La Tour intimiste." *L'Art et les artistes* 30, no. 156 (April), pp. 217-221.

1935, LEROY
Alfred Leroy. *Histoire de la peinture française au XVIIe siècle (1600-1700) – Son évolution et ses maîtres*. Paris: Éd. Albin Michel. (See pp. 173-175.)

1935, LONGHI
Roberto Longhi. "I pittori della réaltà in Francia ovvero i caravaggeschi francesi del Seicento." *L'Italia letteraria*, 19 January.

1935, LORD
Douglas Lord. "Les peintres de la réalité en France au XVIIe siècle." *Burlington Magazine* 66 (March), pp. 138-141.

1935, MAYER
August L. Mayer. "Notes sur quelques tableaux du musée de Grenoble." *Gazette des Beaux-Arts*, vol. 1, p. 121.

1935, PARISET, *Effets*
François-Georges Pariset. "Effets de clair-obscur dans l'école lorraine au XVIIe siècle." *Archives alsaciennes d'histoire de l'art* 14, pp. 231-248.

1935, PARISET, *Note*
François-Georges Pariset. "Note sur Georges de La Tour." *Gazette des Beaux-Arts* 14 (December), pp. 254.

1935, PARISET, *Un texte*
[François-Georges Pariset.] "Un texte sur Georges de La Tour." *Beaux-Arts*, 15 February.

1935, PETITEVILLE
François Petiteville. "Les peintres de la réalité au XVIIe siècle." *Études*, 20 February, pp. 465-504.

1935, PHILIPPE, *Beaux-Arts*
André Philippe. "Une nouvelle œuvre de Georges de La Tour." *Beaux-Arts*, 5 April, p. 2 (The Tulpain Collection *Smoker*.)

1935, PHILIPPE, *Pays lorrain*
André Philippe. "Georges de La Tour." *Le Pays lorrain*, no. 7 (July), pp. 311-320.

1935, PINEAU-CHAILLOU
Pineau-Chaillou. "Après la controverse Rizzi-La Tour. Le 'Joueur de vielle' a retrouvé sa place au Musée." *Phare de la Loire* 10, 18 April.

1935, REBATET
Lucien Rebatet. "Les peintres de la réalité." *Revue universelle*, 1 February, pp. 359-364.

1935, RONOT
Dr Henry Ronot. "De Georges de La Tour à Maurice Quentin de La Tour." *Beaux-Arts*, 8 February, p. 2.

1935, STERLING, *B.M.F.*
Charles Sterling. "Musée de l'Orangerie. L'exposition des peintres de la réalité en France au XVIIe siècle." *Bulletin des musées de France* 7, no. 1 (January), pp. 2-6.

1935, STERLING, *Espagne*
Charles Sterling. "Espagne et France au XVIIe siècle." *L'Amour de l'art*, January, pp. 7-14.

1935, STERLING, *R.A.A.M.*
Charles Sterling. "Les peintres de la réalité en France au XVIIe siècle. Les enseignements d'une exposition. I: Le mouvement caravagesque et Georges de La Tour; II: Le portrait, la scène de genre, la nature morte." *Revue de l'art ancien et moderne* 67 (January), pp. 25-40.

1935, STERLING, *Trésors*
Charles Sterling. "Georges de La Tour." In *Les Trésors de la peinture française, XVIIe siècle*. Geneva: Skira.

1935, VERGNET-RUIZ
Jean Vergnet-Ruiz. "Musée du Louvre. Peintures et dessins. Un saint Jérôme de Georges de La Tour." *Bulletin des musées de France* 7, no. 3 (March), pp. 34-35.

1936, ANSALDI
Giulio R. Ansaldi. "L'esempio del Caravaggio e gli insegnamenti dei Bolognesi nella pittura francese del Seicento." *Rassegna Italiana* (Rome), nos. 213-216 (February-May).

1936, BAZIN
Germain Bazin. "The Art of Georges de La Tour." *Apollo* 24 (November), pp. 286-290.

1936, FIERENS
Paul Fierens. "Georges de La Tour." *L'Art et la vie*, pp. 1-17.

1936, FLORISOONE
Michel Florisoone. "La jeunesse estudiante et l'art contemporain." *L'Amour de l'art*, March, pp. 97-102. (See p. 102.)

1936, GILLET
Louis Gillet. *Les Tapis enchantés*. Paris: Gallimard, pp. 241-243. (Same as 1935 text.)

1936, ISARLOV
George Isarlov. "Deux découvertes: un G. de La Tour et un A. Baugin." *Beaux-Arts*, 5 June.

1936, J.C.
J.C. "De Ribera à Georges de La Tour." *Grand Large*, no. 14.

1936, LHOTE
André Lhote. *Parlons peinture*. Paris: Denoël et Steele.

1936, PARISET, B.S.H.A.F., *Saint Sébastien*
François-Georges Pariset. "Georges de La Tour et saint Sébastien." *Bulletin de la Société de l'Histoire de l'Art français*, 1935 [1936], pp. 13-17.

1936, PARISET, B.S.H.A.F., *Textes*
François-Georges Pariset. "Textes sur Georges de La Tour à Lunéville." *Bulletin de la Société de l'Histoire de l'Art français*, 1935 [1936], pp. 118-125.

1936, PARISET, *Parnassus*
François-Georges Pariset. "Georges de La Tour, 1593-1652." *Parnassus* 8, no. 7, pp. 9-11.

1936, WEISBACH
Werner Weisbach. "L'histoire de Job dans les arts. À propos du tableau de Georges de La Tour au musée d'Épinal." *Gazette des Beaux-Arts* 16 (September), pp. 102-112.

1937, ALFASSA
Paul Alfassa. "Chefs-d'œuvre de l'art français." *La Revue de Paris*, 15 October, pp. 920-940.

1937, BÉLIARD
Octave Béliard. "Des siècles en quelques lignes." *Revue du médecin*, no. 2, n.p.

1937, CANTON
S[anchez] C[anton]. "Noticia de un cuadro de Georges de La Tour." *Archivo español de arte y arqueologia*, no. 38, p. 167.

1937, COUTELA
C. Coutela. "Le montreur de tours à l'ectropion." *Aesculape*, no. 4, pp. 166-168.

1937, COUTURIER
Père M. A. Couturier. "Greco, la mystique et les commentateurs." *Art sacré*, October, pp. 85-90.

1937, FLORISOONE
Michel Florisoone. "Le sentiment religieux et l'art de 1600 à 1900." *Art sacré*, June, pp. 187-189.

1937, FOCILLON
Henri Focillon. Introduction to catalogue, *Chefs-d'œuvre de l'art français*. Paris: Palais National des Arts, pp. XIII-XXVI.

1937, HUYGHE
René Huyghe. *Les Chefs-d'œuvre de l'art français à l'exposition internationale de 1937. La peinture française du XIVe au XVIIe siècle*. Paris: Librairie des Arts décoratifs, n.d.

1937, LANDRY
Pierre Landry. "Georges de La Tour et son atelier." *Beaux-Arts*, 8 January, p. 2.

1937, MALÉGARIE
Charles Malégarie. "Propos sur la lumière." *La Lumière*. Special issue of *La Renaissance*, May-June, pp. 7-10.

1937, MAROT
Pierre Marot. "Archéologie et histoire de l'art. C. XVIIe siècle." *Bibliographie lorraine* [1937], pp. 127-135.

1937, REY-LOCQUIN
Robert Rey and Mme Jean Locquin, eds. *Chefs-d'œuvre de l'art français*. Special issue of *La Renaissance*.

1937, SIPLE
Ella D. Siple. "An Exhibition of Georges de La Tour and the Brothers Le Nain." *Burlington Magazine* 70 (January), pp. 40-45.

1937, STERLING, *Braun*
Charles Sterling. *Peinture française. XVIe et XVIIe siècle*. Paris: Braun.

1937, STERLING, *A New Picture*
Charles Sterling. "A new Picture par Georges de La Tour." *Burlington Magazine* 71 (July), pp. 8-14, 4 figs.

1937, WALDEMAR GEORGE
Waldemar George. *L'Art français et l'esprit de suite*. Special issue of *La Renaissance*, March-April.

1937, WAT
A. Wat. "Notes from Paris." *Apollo* 25, pp. 349-351.

1938, FOCILLON
Henri Focillon. "L'autre visage de la France." *Les Nouvelles littéraires*, 19 November.

1938, GAVELLE
Robert Gavelle. "Aspects du trompe-l'œil. La réalité et son imitation suggérée." *L'Amour de l'art*, July, pp. 231-240.

1938, JEDLICKA
Gotthard Jedlicka. *Französische Malerei*. Zurich-Berlin: Atlantis-Verlag.

1938, LANE, *Apollo*
J. W. Lane. "Notes from New York." *Apollo* 28, pp. 253-256.

1938, LANE, *A.Q.*
J. W. Lane. "Recent Outstanding Acquisitions of American Museums." *Art Quarterly*, pp. 140-148.

1938, LÉCUYER
Raymond Lécuyer. "Regard sur les musées de province. Rennes." *L'Illustration* 3, no. 4991 (29 October), pp. 287-290.

1938, PARISET, *G.B.A.*
François-Georges Pariset. "L'"image saint Alexis" de Georges de La Tour." *Gazette des Beaux-Arts* 2, pp. 63-66.

1938, PARISET, *Pays lorrain*
François-Georges Pariset. *L'Image Saint Alexis de Georges de la Tour, ou Georges de La Tour au Musée historique Lorrain*. Nancy: Berger-Levrault (Previously published in *Pays lorrain*, pp. 417-430.)

1938, STERLING
Charles Sterling. "Two New Paintings by Georges de La Tour." *Burlington Magazine* 52 (May), pp. 203-208.

1938, VALENTINER
R. Valentiner. "An Unknown Painting by Georges de La Tour." *Bulletin of the Detroit Institute of Arts* 17 (March), pp. 50-51.

1939, ALBA
André Alba. *Cours d'histoire Jules Isaac. Les Temps modernes. Classe de quatrième*. Paris: Classiques Hachette, 1939.

1939, JAMOT
Paul Jamot. "Georges de La Tour. À propos de quelques tableaux nouvellement découverts." *Gazette des Beaux-Arts* 21 (April-May), pp. 243-252, 271-286.
1939, JAMOT, *New York exhibit*
Paul Jamot. "XVIIth Century." Introduction to catalogue, *Five Centuries of History Mirrored in Five Centuries of French Art*. New York World's Fair, French pavilion.
1939, LANDRY
Pierre Landry. "À propos de Georges de La Tour. Lettre ouverte à M. Paul Jamot." *Beaux-Arts*, 28 July, pp. 1-2.
1939, PARISET
François-Georges Pariset. "Georges de La Tour." *Congrès international d'histoire de l'art*, 1939, London, Section IV B, p. 40 (summary).
1941, ISARLO
George Isarlo. *Caravage et le caravagisme européen*. Vol. 2. Aix-en-Provence, pp. 165-167.
1942, DORIVAL
Bernard Dorival. *La peinture française*. Arts, styles et techniques. Paris: Librairie Larousse (Reprinted 1946).
1942, DU COLOMBIER
Pierre du Colombier. *Histoire de l'art*. Paris: Librairie Arthème Fayard. (See p. 353.)
1942, GERSON
Horst Gerson. *Ausbreitung und Nachwirkung der holländischen Malerei des 17. Jahrhunderts*. Haarlem: Deerven F. Bohn, pp. 76-77. (Reprinted 1983.)
1942, JAMOT
Paul Jamot. *Georges de La Tour*. Foreword and notes by Thérèse Bertin-Mourot. Paris: Librairie Floury. (See also 1948, Jamot – Bertin-Mourot.)
1942, LANDRY
Pierre Landry. "Georges de La Tour et le tableau des 'deux moines' du musée du Mans." *Revue historique et archéologique du Maine* 22, pp. 14-27.
1942, LHOTE
André Lhote. *Peinture d'abord*. Paris: Denoël.
1942, WILHELM
Jacques Wilhelm. "Critique d'art et roman policier. À propos de Georges de La Tour." *Beaux-Arts*, 10 November, p. 5.
1943, BROEK
Erich Broek. "G. de La Tour." *Panthéon*, pp. 152-157.
1943, JAMOT
Paul Jamot. *Introduction à l'histoire de la peinture*.
1943, *France socialiste*
"La Madeleine à la veilleuse donne lieu en correctionnelle à une curieuse contestation." *France Socialiste*, 17 April. (See also issue of 15 May 1943.)
1943, *Petit Parisien*
"La Madeleine à la veilleuse rapporte à son vendeur une belle commission… et une condamnation bien plus forte." *Le Petit Parisien*, 15 May, p. 3.
1943, QUARRÉ
Pierre Quarré. "Identification d'une peinture de la collection Devosge au musée de Dijon." *Annales de Bourgogne* 15 (June), p. 162.
1944, GUENNE
Jacques Guenne. "Le regard et l'expression dans la peinture." *Formes et couleurs*, no. 1, pp. 13-73.
1944, LAVEDAN
Pierre Lavedan. *Histoire de l'art*. Vol. 2, *Moyen Âge et Temps modernes*. Paris: Clio.
1944, TARDIEU
Jean Tardieu. *Figures*. Paris: Gallimard. (See pp. 71-77: "Georges de La Tour.")
1945, BAZIN
Germain Bazin. "Georges de La Tour." *Labyrinthe*, no. 7, 15 April, pp. 4-5.
1945, BERTIN-MOUROT
Thérèse Bertin-Mourot. "Sur un tableau de Georges de La Tour, La Madeleine à la veilleuse. Du musée de Cologne au musée du Louvre." *Arts*, 7 December, p. 3.
1945, BLUNT
Anthony Blunt. "The 'Joueur de vielle' of Georges de La Tour." *Burlington Magazine* 86 (May), pp. 108-111.
1945, FOSCA
François Fosca. "Georges de La Tour, peintre de l'école française du XVIIe siècle." *Tribune de Genève*, 28 February, p. 5.
1945, HUYGHE, *Un chef-d'œuvre*
René Huyghe. "Un chef-d'œuvre de Georges de La Tour… Le Saint François de Georges de La Tour." *L'Amour de l'art*, May, pp. 12-15.
1945, HUYGHE, *Nuit du monde*
René Huyghe. "Nuit du monde, Lumière de l'âme." *Quadrige*, no. 4, pp. 18-27.
1946, CHAMPRIS
Pierre de Champris. "S'agit-il de deux tableaux inconnus de Georges de La Tour ?" *Arts*, 27 December, pp. 1, 4.
1946, CHAMSON-DEVINOY
André Chamson. *Dans l'univers des chefs-d'œuvre. 32 photographies de Pierre Devinoy*. Paris: Paul Hartmann.
1946, CHAR
René Char. *Feuillets d'Hypnos*. Paris.
1946, COMSTOCK
Helen Comstock. "The Connoisseur in America." *The Connoisseur*, December.
1946, DORIVAL
Bernard Dorival. *Les étapes de la peinture contemporaine*. Vol. 3. Paris: Gallimard.
1946, ERLANGER
Philippe Erlanger. *Les peintres de la réalité*. Paris: Éd. de la Galerie Charpentier.
1946, GUÉHENNO
Jean Guéhenno. "L'horizon de l'Éternité." *Art et style*, no. 6 (December), n.p.
1946, HULFTEGGER
Adeline Hulftegger. "Sur une 'vanité' française du XVIIe siècle." *Bulletin des musées de France*, July, pp. 3-7.
1946, HUYGHE
René Huyghe. "L'influence de La Tour. Une œuvre perdue de Georges de La Tour." *L'Amour de l'art*, no. 9, pp. 255-258. (The Albi series.)
1946, JARDOT
M. Jardot. "Le Christ aux outrages de La Tour." *L'Amour de l'art*, no. 3 (March), pp. 74-77.
1946, MAURICHEAU-BEAUPRÉ
Mauricheau-Beaupré. *L'Art du XVIIe siècle*. Première période 1594-1661.
1946, *Réforme*
"Adoration des bergers." *Réforme*, 21 December, p. 7.
1946, T.C.H.
T.C.H. Jr. "Georges de La Tour." *Bulletin of the California Palace of the Legion of Honor* (San Francisco), September, pp. 35-43.
1946, WILHELM
Jacques Wilhelm. "Tableaux des églises de Paris." *L'Amour de l'art*, pp. 131-134.
1947, BERTIN-MOUROT
Thérèse Bertin-Mourot. "Chefs-d'œuvre de nos églises de France." *La Croix*, 29-30 August.
1947, BLOCH
Vitale Bloch. "Georges de La Tour, twee nieuwe werken." *Nederlandsch Kunsthistorisch Jaarboek*. Gravenhague, pp. 137-143.
1947, ISARLO
George Isarlo. "À la Sorbonne. G. de La Tour." *Arts*, 4 July, pp. 1, 4.
1947, MALRAUX
André Malraux. *Psychologie de l'art*. Vol. 1. *Le musée imaginaire*. Geneva: Skira.
1947, SUTTON
Denys Sutton. "À Londres – La peinture française du XVIIe siècle." *Arts*, 20 June, p. 1.
1947, TRANCHANT
Joseph Tranchant. "L'extase de saint François de Georges de La Tour." *Les Amis de saint François*, no. 44 (June-August), pp. 1-3.
1948, BERTIN-MOUROT, *Arts*
Thérèse Bertin-Mourot. "Cinq nouveaux Georges de La Tour exposés au Louvre." *Arts*, 6 August, pp. 1, 4.
1948, BERTIN-MOUROT, *Combat*
Thérèse Bertin-Mourot. "L'inspiration de Georges de La Tour." *Combat*, 1 September.
1948, BERTIN-MOUROT, *Rev. fr.*
Thérèse Bertin-Mourot. "Georges de La Tour Lorrain." *La Revue française de l'Élite*, November, pp. 56-61.
1948, BLOCH
Vitale Bloch. "Een verrassend museum." *Maanblad voor beeldende Kunsten* (Amsterdam), March, pp. 61-66.
1948, DORIVAL
Bernard Dorival. "Georges de La Tour." *Nouvelles littéraires*, 9 September, p. 5.
1948, DU COLOMBIER
Pierre du Colombier. "Les expositions. Alsace et Lorraine." *La Revue française*, Christmas, pp. 148-149.
1948, GREINDL
Edith Greindl. "Une nouvelle version du 'Joueur à la vielle' de Georges de La Tour." *Phoebus* 2 (1943-1949), pp. 21-22.
1948, JAMOT – BERTIN-MOUROT
Paul Jamot. *Georges de La Tour*. Foreword and notes by Thérèse Bertin-Mourot, 2d ed. enlarged with three recently identified paintings. Paris: Librairie Floury.
1948, PARISET, *La Tour élève du Guide*
François-Georges Pariset. "La Tour, élève du Guide." *Arts*, 3 September, p. 8.
1948, PARISET, *La Tour copiste?*
François-Georges Pariset. "Georges de La Tour copiste?" *Arts*, 5 November, pp. 1, 8.
1948, PARISET, *Peintres célèbres*
François-Georges Pariset. "La Tour." In *Les Peintres célèbres*. Paris: Mazenod, pp. 218-224.
1948, ROGER-MARX
Claude Roger-Marx. "Le Saint Joseph de Georges de La Tour entre au musée du Louvre." *Arts*, 25 June, p. 1.
1948, SUTTON
Denys Sutton. "À propos de Georges de La Tour, dont l'art opéra la synthèse de la grâce et de la connaissance." *Combat*, 25 August, p. 4.

III. 1949-1972 (From the Thesis of François-Georges Pariset to the Orangerie Exhibit)

1949, BLOCH
Vitale Bloch. "Beschouwingen over Georges de La Tour." *L'Art français, Maanblad voor beeldende Kunsten* 25, nos. 4-5 (April-May), pp. 84-99.
1949, BLUNT
Anthony Blunt. "Georges de La Tour of Lorraine, 1593-1652. By S. M. M. Furness" (review). *Burlington Magazine* 91 (October), p. 297.
1949, CHAMPIGNEULLE
Bernard Champigneulle. *Le Règne de Louis XIII*. Paris: Documents d'art et d'histoire, arts et métiers graphiques.
1949, FIERENS, *Arts*
Paul Fierens. "Georges de La Tour au musée de Bruxelles." *Arts*, 5 August, p. 3.
1949, FIERENS, *Les Arts plastiques*
Paul Fierens. "Nouvelles de Belgique. Georges de La Tour au musée de Bruxelles." *Les Arts plastiques*, summer, pp. 313-314.
1949, FURNESS
S. M. M. Furness. *Georges de La Tour of Lorraine, 1593-1652*. London: Routledge & Kegan Ltd.

1949, JEAN
René Jean. "Un maître retrouvé: Georges de La Tour." *Le Monde*, 23 September.
1949, MALRAUX
André Malraux. *Psychologie de l'art*. Vol. 3, *La Monnaie de l'Absolu*. Geneva: Skira.
1949, PARISET
François-Georges Pariset. *Georges de La Tour*. Paris: Henri Laurens.
1949, RICHARDSON, *Bull. Detr.*
E. P. Richardson. "Georges de La Tour's St. Sebastian Nursed by St. Irene." *Bulletin of the Detroit Institute of Arts* 28, no. 2, pp. 26-29.
1949, RICHARDSON, *Art Quarterly*
E. P. Richardson. "Georges de la Tour's 'St. Sebastian Nursed by St. Irene'." *Art Quarterly* 12, no. 1, pp. 81-89.
1949, WEIGERT
Roger-Armand Weigert. "La réalité dans l'art français du XVIIe siècle: les graveurs de la vie populaire." *L'Art français. Maanblad voor beeldende Kunsten* 25 (April-May), pp. 100-105.
1950, A. F.
A. F. "Quelques aspects du réalisme français." *Arts de France*, no. 32, pp. 42-47.
1950, BAGUENIER DESORMEAUX
Louis Baguenier Desormeaux. *Considérations sur les apnées volontaires: la saturation en oxygène du sang*. Dijon.
1950, BLOCH
Vitale Bloch. *Georges de La Tour*. Amsterdam: J. H. de Bussy.
1950, BLUNT
Anthony Blunt. "Georges de La Tour." *Burlington Magazine* 92 (May), pp. 144-145. (Review of book by François-Georges Pariset.)
1950, CHASTEL
André Chastel. "Nouveautés sur le XVIIe siècle." *Le Monde*, 9 May, p. 5.
1950, DU COLOMBIER
Pierre Du Colombier. "Le Saint Sébastien de Georges de La Tour et les nocturnes du XVIIe siècle." *Médecine de France*, pp. 17-20.
1950, DUPONT
Jacques Dupont. "Une petite exposition La Tour au Louvre." *Chefs-d'œuvre perdus et retrouvés, Société Poussin*, no. 3 (May), pp. 8-19.
1950, FEBVRE
Lucien Febvre. "Résurrection de peintre. À propos de La Tour." *Annales. Économies. Sociétés. Civilisations* 5, no. 1 (January-March), pp. 129-134.
1950, HOURS
Madeleine Hours. "La découverte de la vérité...." *France-Illustration*, 2 December.
1950, JAMATI
Georges Jamati. "La transposition dramatique dans l'œuvre de Georges de La Tour." *Chefs-d'œuvre perdus et retrouvés, Société Poussin*, no. 3 (May), pp. 20-22.
1950, LHOTE
André Lhote. *Traité de la figure*. Paris: Floury.
1950, PRÉ
Madeleine Pré. "Un nouveau Georges de La Tour." *Arts*, 14 July, pp. 1, 8.
1950, PRUVOST
Jacqueline Pruvost. "Un tableau de Georges de La Tour au musée des Beaux-Arts d'Orléans." *Musées de France*, no. 7 (September), p. 188.
1950, SALLES
Georges Salles. "Allocution prononcée à l'occasion de la Donation Percy Moore Turner au musée du Louvre." *Chefs d'œuvre perdus et retrouvés, Société Poussin*, no. 3 (May), pp. 4-8.
1950, TRANCHANT
Joseph Tranchant. "Note sur l'histoire de la peinture d'origine franciscaine au début du XVIIe siècle." *Les Amis de saint François*, July, pp. 6-9.
1950, VICKERS
Elisabeth Vickers. "The Iconography of Georges de La Tour." *Marsyas, Studies in the History of Art* (New York) 5 (1947-1949; publ. 1950), pp. 105-117.
1951, CHASTEL
André Chastel. "La chirurgie dans l'art." *Médecine de France*, no. 26, pp. 19-31.
1951, DUPONT – MATHEY
Jacques Dupont, François Mathey. *Les Grands siècles de la peinture: le XVIIe siècle. Les tendances nouvelles en Europe: de Caravage à Vermeer*. Geneva: Skira.
1951, HUYGHE
René Huyghe. "Vers une psychologie de l'art. II: Le sens humain de l'œuvre d'art." *La Revue des arts* 1 (December). (See p. 235.)
1951, MALRAUX
André Malraux. *Les Voix du silence*. Paris: La Galerie de la Pléiade.
1951, MORISSET
M. Morisset. "Six villes se disputent le Saint Sébastien de Georges de La Tour offert au roi Louis XIII." *Paris-Normandie*, 7 September.
1951, PARISET
François-Georges Pariset. "Le Saint Pierre repentant de Georges de La Tour." *Arts*, 20 March, pp. 1, 4.
1951, STERLING
Charles Sterling. "Observations sur Georges de La Tour à propos d'un livre récent." *La Revue des arts*, September, pp. 147-158.
1952, *Connaissance des arts*
"Joueurs de cartes." *Connaissance des arts*, no. 10, 15 December, p. 57.
1952, DIAZ
Emilio Orozco Diaz. "Un importante antecedente a los Nocturnos de G. de La Tour." *Arte español*, p. 69.
1952, FRANCIS
Henry S. Francis. "The Repentant St. Peter by Georges de La Tour." *Bulletin of the Cleveland Museum of Art* 39 (September), pp. 174-177.
1952, J.C.
J.C. "Deux 'De La Tour' à la chapelle de Grâce?" *L'Indépendant honfleurais*, 4 January, p. 2.
1952, MANNING
Bertina Suida Manning. "The Nocturnes of Luca Cambiaso." *Art Quarterly* 15, no. 3, pp. 197-220.
1952, PARISET
François-Georges Pariset. "Le Caravage et saint François." *Annales. Économies. Sociétés. Civilisations*, pp. 39-48.
1952, RENAUD
Jean-Claude Renaud. "Le problème du spectateur devant l'œuvre de Georges de La Tour. Saint Sébastien pleuré par sainte Irène." *Revue d'esthétique* 5, pp. 47-52.
1952, STERLING
Charles Sterling. *La Nature morte de l'Antiquité à nos jours*. Paris: Pierre Tisné.
1952, TOUBLET
François Toublet. "À propos de deux tableaux découverts à la chapelle de Grâce." *L'indépendant honfleurais*, 11 January, pp. 1-2.
1952, TRANCHANT
Joseph Tranchant. "Georges de La Tour. Le peintre perdu et retrouvé." *Études* 272 (February), pp. 203-216.
1953, ARLAND – MARSAN
Marcel Arland and Anna Marsan. *Georges de La Tour*. Paris: Éd. du Dimanche.
1953, *Art et style*
L'Art sacré. Cahier no. 26, *Art et style*.
1953, *Arts plastiques*
"La femme dans l'art français." *Les Arts plastiques*, no. 2 (March-April), pp. 91-106.
1953, BLOCH
Vitale Bloch. *Georges de La Tour*. Preface by Robert Longhi. Milan: Milione.
1953, BLUNT
Anthony Blunt. *Art and Architecture in France 1500-1700*. Pelican History of Art. London: Penguin.
1954, BLOCH
Vitale Bloch. "Georges de La Tour Once Again." *Burlington Magazine* 96 (March), pp. 81-82.
1954, CROZET
René Crozet. *La Vie artistique en France au XVIIe siècle (1598-1661)*. Paris: Presses Universitaires de France.
1954, FIOCCO
Giuseppe Fiocco. "Due quadri di Georges de La Tour." *Paragone* 5, no. 55, pp. 38-40.
1954, HUYGHE
René Huyghe. "Georges de La Tour." *Art News Annual* 24, pp. 125-132, 178.
1954, MARTZ
Louis L. Martz. *The Poetry of Meditation*. New Haven: Yale University Press.
1954, SCHÖNE
Wolfgang Schöne. *Über das Licht in der Malerei*. Berlin. (See pp. 145-148.)
1954, TREVES
André Treves. "Héritiers du Caravage." *Le Peintre*, no. 84 (1 May), pp. 10-11.
1955, BOUGIER, *Le message*
Annette-Marie Bougier. "Le message du Lorrain Georges de La Tour." *Message des arts*. Bloud et Gay.
1955, BOUGIER, *La résurrection*
Annette-Marie Bougier. "La résurrection de Georges de La Tour." *Enseignement chrétien*.
1955, *London News*
"A U.S. Gallery Enters Its Third Decade." *London News* 2, p. 451.
1955, MACDONALD
Robert MacDonald. "Georges de La Tour, Out of the Shadows, a Chiaroscurist." *Apollo* 42 (December), pp. 213-215.
1955, PARISET, *L'art à la cour ducale*
François-Georges Pariset. "L'art à la cour ducale de Nancy vers 1600." *Médecine de France*, no. 68, pp. 17-26.
1955, PARISET, *Mise au point*
François-Georges Pariset. "Mise au point – provisoire – sur Georges de La Tour." *Cahiers de Bordeaux, Journées internationales d'études d'art*, pp. 79-89.
1955, PARISET, *La Servante à la puce*
François-Georges Pariset. "La Servante à la puce par Georges de La Tour." *La Revue des arts* 5, no. 2, pp. 91-94.
1955, SANDOZ
Marc Sandoz. "Ribera et le thème de 'Saint Sébastien soigné par sainte Irène'." *Cahiers de Bordeaux, Journées internationales d'études d'art*, pp. 65-78.
1955, TRIBOUT DE MOREMBERT
H. Tribout de Morembert. "Du nouveau sur le peintre des nuits. Georges de La Tour et ses familiers." *Le Figaro littéraire*, 6 August, p. 11.
1956, EISENDRATH
William N. Eisendrath Jr. "Young Man with a Pipe by Georges de La Tour." *Bulletin of the City Art Museum of Saint Louis* 41, no. 3, pp. 29-36.
1956, ISARLO
George Isarlo. *Les Indépendants dans la peinture ancienne*. Paris: La Bibliothèque des Arts.
1956, JOUFFROY
Alain Jouffroy. "Une œuvre peu connue de Georges de La Tour entre au Musée de Saint-Louis." *Combat*, April.
1956, LEYMARIE
Jean Leymarie. *La Peinture hollandaise*. Geneva: Skira. (See p. 69.)

1956, PARISET, *Musée Historique*
François-Georges Pariset. "Les artistes." *Musée Historique Lorrain. Les Peintres et graveurs lorrains du XVIIe siècle*. Nancy: Palais ducal, n.d. (See pp. 16-18.)

1956, PARISET, *Atti*
François-Georges Pariset. "Jean Le Clerc et Venise." *Atti del XVIIe Congresso internazionale di Storia dell'Arte, 1955*, pp. 322-323.

1956, VERDIER
Philippe Verdier. *L'art religieux*. Formes de l'Art. Paris: Club Français de l'Art.

1957, BAZIN
Germain Bazin. *Trésors de la peinture au Louvre*. Paris: Somogy, n.d.

1957, BERHAUT
Marie Berhaut. "Les collections du musée de Rennes." *La Revue française*, no. 95 (November), pp. 21-28.

1957, CHASTEL
André Chastel. "L'art et le sentiment de la mort au XVIIe siècle." *XVIIe siècle. Bulletin de la Société d'Étude du XVIIe siècle*. Special issue: *Étude sur l'art en France au XVIIe siècle*, nos. 36-37 (July-October), pp. 287-293.

1957, COMSTOCK
Helen Comstock. "Connoisseur in America." *The Connoisseur* 140 (September), pp. 70-71.

1957, FOCILLON
Henri Focillon. *De Callot à Lautrec*. Paris: La Bibliothèque des Arts.

1957, HONOUR
Hugh Honour. "17th-Century Art in Europe." *The Connoisseur* 139, (March), p. 34.

1957, HOURS
Madeleine Hours-Miédan. *À la Découverte de la peinture par les méthodes physiques*. Paris: Arts et Métiers graphiques.

1957, ISARLO
George Isarlo. "À Rome: l'exposition du XVIIe siècle." *Combat-Art* no. 35 (4 February), p. 2.

1957, MATHEY
François Mathey. "L'Esprit des collections bisontines." *Jardin des Arts*, April, pp. 369-375.

1957, PARISET
François-Georges Pariset. "Georges de la Tour." *Enciclopedia italiana dell'arte*, vol. 8.

1957, WEHLE
Harry B. Wehle. "Realism in French Painting." *The Metropolitan Museum of Art Miniatures*. New York.

1957, VERGNET-RUIZ
Jean Vergnet-Ruiz. "L'art français du XVIIe siècle à la Royal Academy." *Revue des arts*, no. 6 (November-December), pp. 257-260.

1958, *Art News*
"The Spirit of St. Louis." *Art News* 57, November, pp. 40-41.

1958, BAZIN
Germain Bazin. *The Louvre*. New York: Harry N. Abrams.

1958, BOUGIER
Annette-Marie Bougier. "Entre Vic-sur-Seille et Mattaincourt, Georges de La Tour et Saint Pierre Fourier." *Gazette des Beaux-Arts* 52 (July-August), pp. 51-62.

1958, CHARMET
Raymond Charmet. "Apothéose de la peinture française du XVIIe siècle." *Arts, Lettres, Spectacles*, no. 652 (8-14 January), p. 20.

1958, CHARMET – HUISMAN
Raymond Charmet and Philippe Huisman. "L'Art français au XVIIe siècle." *Arts, Lettres, Spectacles*, no. 664 (2-8 April), pp. 1, 16.

1958, COLMAN
Pierre Colman. "Une nouvelle 'Image Saint Alexis' de Georges de La Tour." *Institut Royal du Patrimoine artistique*, Bulletin, 1, pp. 103-110.

1958, *Connaissance des Arts*
Le XVIIe siècle français. Connaissance des Arts. Paris: Hachette.

1958, ETTLINGER
L. D. Ettlinger. "Naturalism and Rhetoric." *The Listener*, no. 1505 (30 January), pp. 193-195. (Review of exhibition "The Age of Louis XIV.")

1958, GAYA NUÑO
Juan Antonio Gaya Nuño. *La Pintura española fuera de España*. Madrid.

1958, GROSSMANN
F. Grossmann. "A Painting by Georges de La Tour in the Collection of Archduke Leopold Wilhelm." *Burlington Magazine* 100 (March), pp. 86-91.

1958, ISARLO, *L'exposition*
George Isarlo. "L'exposition 'Le siècle de Louis XIV' à Londres." *Combat-Art* no. 45 (15 February).

1958, ISARLO, *Le prétendu*
George Isarlo. "Le prétendu 'Siècle de Louis XIV'." *Combat-Art* no. 46, 3 May.

1958, ISARLO, *La vérité*
George Isarlo. "La vérité sur le XVIIe français." *Combat-Art* no. 48, 12 May.

1958, KAUFFMANN
Georg Kauffmann. "The 'Age of Louis XIV' in London." *Kunstchronik*, June, p. 155.

1958, LACLOTTE
Michel Laclotte. "La Peinture du Grand Siècle." *L'Œil*, Christmas, pp. 46-48.

1958, NICOLSON
Benedict Nicolson. "In the Margin of the Catalogue." *Burlington Magazine* 100 (March), pp. 97-101.

1958, NICOLSON, *Terbrugghen*
Benedict Nicolson. *Hendrick Terbrugghen*. The Hague: Martinus Nijhoff.

1958, NOIRIEL
Noiriel. "Pour ou contre Georges de La Tour." *Arts, Lettres, Spectacles*, no. 664 (2-8 April).

1958, PARISET, *Note sur J. Le Clerc*
François-Georges Pariset. "Note sur Jean Le Clerc." *La Revue des arts* 8 (March), pp. 67-71.

1958, PARISET, *La Servante à la puce*
François-Georges Pariset. "La Servante à la puce." *Pays lorrain*, no. 3, pp. 100-108. (Reprinted in *Musée lorrain. Quelques enrichissements récents*. Édition du Pays lorrain, 1958, pp. 32-40.)

1958, SPIELMANN
Heinz Spielmann. "Georges de La Tour." *Das Kunstwerk* 12, no. 3 (September), pp. 13-22.

1959, BOUGIER
Annette-Marie Bougier. "Au berceau de Georges de La Tour." *Revue d'esthétique*.

1959, CHARMET
Raymond Charmet. "Exposition Festival de Bordeaux. 250 tableaux racontent la découverte de la lumière." *Arts, Lettres, Spectacles*, no. 721 (27 May-2 June).

1959, GRATE
Pontus Grate. "Quelques observations sur les Saint Jérôme de Georges de La Tour." *La Revue des arts* 9, no. 1, pp. 15-24.

1959, IVANOFF
Nicolas Ivanoff. "Jean Le Clerc et Venise." *Actes du XIXe Congrès international d'histoire de l'art*. Paris, 8-13 September 1958, pp. 390-394.

1959, JUDSON
J. Richard Judson. *Gerrit van Honthorst. A Discussion of his Position in Dutch Art*. The Hague: Martinus Nijhoff.

1959, PARISET
François-Georges Pariset. "L'exposition du XVIIe siècle français." *Annales*, April-June, pp. 337-342.

1959, PINCHERLE
Marc Pincherle. *Histoire illustrée de la musique*. L'Œil, Paris: Gallimard, NRF.

1959, TODD
Ruthven Todd. "A Sestina for Georges de La Tour." *Art News* 58 (March), p. 45.

1960, HUYGHE
René Huyghe. *L'Art et l'âme*. Paris: Flammarion.

1960, ISARLO
George Isarlo. *La Peinture en France au XVIIe siècle*. Paris: La Bibliothèque des Arts.

1960, ISARLO
George Isarlo. *L'éducation de la Vierge* (reprod.) *Combat-Art* no. 71 (17 October).

1960, NICOLSON
Benedict Nicolson. "The 'Candlelight Master' – A Follower of Honthorst in Rome." *Het Nederlands Kunsthistorisch Jaarboek*, pp. 121-164.

The *Fortune Teller* "Affair"

1960, *Art News*
"Spectacular Buy for the Metropolitan Museum." *Art News* 59 (summer).

1960, *Bull. Met. Mus.*
Acquisition notice. *Metropolitan Museum of Art Bulletin*, p. 340.

1960, *Combat*
"Le Metropolitan Museum de New York achète 'La Diseuse de bonne aventure' de Georges de La Tour." *Combat*, 13 June.

1960, *Connaissance des arts*
"Ce La Tour vient d'entrer au Metropolitan Museum." *Connaissance des arts*, no. 102 (August), pp. 50-51.

1960, *Le Figaro littéraire*, 3 September
G. V. "Comment ce La Tour a-t-il quitté la France?" *Le Figaro littéraire*, 3 September, pp. 1, 11.

1960, *Le Figaro littéraire*, 10 September
"La Bonne Aventure." *Le Figaro littéraire*, 10 September.

1960, *France-Soir*
Jean-Pierre Crespelle. "Polémique entre New York et Paris après la vente d'un tableau de La Tour au Metropolitan Museum." *France-Soir*, 14 June.

1960, *Journal Officiel, Dalbos-Malraux*
"Assemblée Nationale – Séance du vendredi 2 décembre 1960. Exportation de la toile "La bonne aventure" (Question posed by Jean-Claude Dalbos, deputy; reply of André Malraux, Minister of State.) *Journal Officiel de la République française*, 3 December, pp. 4260-4261.

1960, *Journal du Parlement*
Marcel Espiau. "La vérité sur le scandale du tableau de Georges de La Tour." *Journal du Parlement*. 4-7 October, n.p.

1960, *Life*
"Collecting Coups by U.S. Museums. Metropolitan Gets High-Priced Rarity." *Life International*, 26 September, p. 82.

1960, *Le Monde*, 11 June
"Un chef-d'œuvre de Georges de La Tour entre au Musée de New York." *Le Monde*, 11 June, p. 16.

1960, *Le Monde*, 16 June
Alfred Daber. "La trop belle aventure d'un chef-d'œuvre de Georges de La Tour." *Le Monde*, 16 June, p. 8.

1960, *Le Monde*, 19 June
René Huyghe. "Le départ pour les États-Unis de 'La Bonne Aventure.'" *Le Monde*, 19 June, p. 13.

1960, *Le Monde*, 9 July
André Chênebenoît. "Silence sur 'La Bonne Aventure.'" *Le Monde*, 9 July, p. 9.

1960, *Le Monde*, 10 July
"Un député s'inquiète de l'expatriation de La Bonne Aventure." *Le Monde*, 10 July, p. 11.

1960, *Le Monde*, 19 July
"Dans une question écrite, M. Jacques Duclos s'indigne de la vente aux États-Unis du tableau de Georges de La Tour 'La Bonne Aventure.'" *Le Monde*, 19 July, p. 9.

1960, *Le Monde*, 28 July

"L'affaire de 'La Bonne Aventure.' L'enquête sera terminée avant octobre, déclare M. André Malraux." *Le Monde*, 28 July, p. 7.
1960, *Le Monde*, 13 August
"La vente de 'La Bonne Aventure' fait l'objet d'une question écrite." *Le Monde*, 13 August, p. 7.
1960, *Le Monde*, 10 September
André Chênebenoît. "Quelques lumières sur 'La Bonne Aventure.'" *Le Monde*, 10 September, p. 9.
1960, *Le Monde*, 4-5 December
"L'affaire de 'La Bonne Aventure.' Les demandes d'exportation de chefs-d'œuvre seront désormais soumises au conseil des musées nationaux." *Le Monde*, 4-5 December, p. 11.
1960, *New York Times*, 8 June.
1960, *New York Times*, 12 June.
1960, *Noir et Blanc*
"France, tes chefs-d'œuvre f... le camp! Les députés tireront-ils au clair l'étrange aventure de 'La Bonne Aventure'?" *Noir et Blanc*, 21 October.
1960, *Time*
"Timeless Master." *Time*, 1 August, pp. 42-43.
1960, *Weltkunst*
Dr. Fritz Neugass, "Sturm der Entrüstung über eine Neuerwerbung des Metropolitan Museum." *Die Weltkunst*, 1 July, pp. 7-8.
1961, BENOIST
Luc Benoist. "G. de La Tour et les caravagesques au musée des Beaux-Arts de Nantes." *La Revue française de l'élite européenne*, August, pp. 39-50.
1961, *Chronique des arts*
"La Chronique des Arts." Supplement to *Gazette des Beaux-Arts* (February).
1961, CRESPELLE
Jean-Pierre Crespelle. "À la veille de sa réception à l'Académie française René Huyghe s'interroge sur 'La Bonne Aventure.'" *France-Soir*, 22 April.
1961, DORIVAL
Bernard Dorival. "La résurrection de Georges de La Tour." *Réalités*, February, pp. 62-71.
1961, HENRIOT
Émile Henriot. "Réponse au discours de réception à l'Académie française de René Huyghe." *Le Monde*, 26 April, p. 7.
1961, ORCIBAL
Jean Orcibal. *Saint-Cyran et le Jansénisme*. Paris: Maîtres spirituels.
1961, PARISET, *A Newly Discovered La Tour*
François-Georges Pariset. "A Newly Discovered La Tour: The Fortune Teller." *Metropolitan Museum of Art Bulletin*, n.s. 19 (March), pp. 198-205.
1961, PARISET, *La Madeleine*
François-Georges Pariset. "La Madeleine aux deux flammes: Un nouveau Georges de La Tour?" *Bulletin de la Société de l'Histoire de l'Art Français*, p. 39.
1962, BERGOT
François Bergot. "Note sur la collection de tableaux du Président de Robien au Musée de Rennes." *Annales de Bretagne* 69, fasc. 1, pp. 153-159.
1962, BOBER
Phyllis Bober. "A Painting by Georges de La Tour." *Art Journal* 22, no. 1, pp. 28-32.
1962, *Chronique des Arts*
"La Chronique des Arts." Supplement to *Gazette des Beaux-Arts* (February).
1962, FARÉ
Michel Faré. *La Nature morte en France. Son histoire et son évolution du XVIIe au XXe siècle*. 2 vols. Geneva: Pierre Cailler.
1962, HUYGHE
René Huyghe. *La Peinture française des XVIIe et XVIIIe siècles*. Paris: Flammarion.
1962, IVANOFF
Nicolas Ivanoff. "Giovanni Le Clerc." *Critica d'Arte* 9, nos. 53-54 (September-December), pp. 62-76.
1962, LACLOTTE
Michel Laclotte. "Peintures inédites ou peu connues des musées de province. Fausses attributions espagnoles." *Revue du Louvre* 12, no. 6, pp. 258-266.
1962, PARISET, *Les Bohémiens*
François-Georges Pariset. "Les Bohémiens et la découverte du monde, à propos d'un tableau de Georges de La Tour." *Cahiers de Bordeaux, Journées Internationales d'études d'art 7-9 juillet 1960*, pp. 33-37.
1962, PARISET, *La Madeleine*
François-Georges Pariset. "La Madeleine aux deux flammes." *Le Pays Lorrain*, no. 4, pp. 162-166.
1962, PARISET, *Un vielleur*
François-Georges Pariset. "Acquisitions récentes au Musée Lorrain. I. Un vielleur de l'École de Georges de La Tour." *Le Pays Lorrain*, no. 4, pp. 145-149.
1962, TERNOIS
Daniel Ternois. *L'Art de Jacques Callot*. Paris: F. de Nobele.
1962, VERGNET-RUIZ – LACLOTTE
Jean Vergnet-Ruiz and Michel Laclotte. *Petits et Grands Musées de France*. Paris: Cercle d'art.
1963, ALPATOV
Michael Alpatov. *Studies in the History of the Art of Western Europe* (in Russian). Moscow. (See pp. 279-280.)
1963, BERTIN-MOUROT
Thérèse Bertin-Mourot. "L'évangéliste à la lampe de tisseur." *Bulletin de la Société Poussin* 4, fasc. 1 (February).
1963, BOUGIER
Annette-Marie Bougier. *Georges de La Tour, Peintre du Roy*. Paris: Desclée de Brouwer.
1963, *Le Monde*, 11 January
"Le Louvre enverrait un La Tour et un Whistler aux États-Unis." *Le Monde*, 11 January, p. 9.
1963, PARISET, *Colloque*
François-Georges Pariset. "Y a-t-il affinité entre l'art espagnol et Georges de La Tour ?" In *Vélasquez, son temps, son influence. Actes du Colloque tenu à la Casa de Vélasquez (7-10 décembre 1960)*, pp. 53-64. Paris: Arts et Métiers graphiques.
1963, PARISET, *E. U. A.*
François-Georges Pariset. "La Tour." *Enciclopedia Universale dell'Arte*. Venise-Rome, Instituto per la collaborazione culturale, vol. 8, cols. 542-545.
1963, PRUVOST-AUZAS
Jacqueline Pruvost-Auzas. "Les collections du Musée des Beaux-Arts d'Orléans. Restaurations, étude et enrichissement. 1949-1951." *Revue du Louvre et des Musées de France* 13, nos. 4-5, pp. 239-244.
1963, STERLING
Charles Sterling. "La peinture française et la peinture espagnole au XVIIe siècle: affinités et échanges." In *Vélasquez, son temps, son influence. Actes du Colloque tenu à la Casa de Vélasquez (7-10 décembre 1960)*, pp. 111-119. Paris: Arts et Métiers graphiques.
1963, THUILLIER
Jacques Thuillier. "Georges de La Tour." In Albert Châtelet and Jacques Thuillier, *La peinture française*. Vol. 1: *De Fouquet à Poussin*, pp. 177-189. Geneva: Skira.
1963, *Time*
"The Show's the Thing." *Time*, 15 February, p. 46 (the Louvre *Magdalen* sent to Atlanta).
1963, VERGNET-RUIZ
Jean Vergnet-Ruiz. *La peinture française au XVIIe siècle*. Vol. 1: *Le début du siècle. Maniéristes, Baroques et Réalistes*. Publications Filmées d'Art et d'Histoire (volume illustrated with slides).
1964, ARGAN
Giulio Carlo Argan. *L'Europe des capitales, 1600-1700*. Art, Idées, Histoire. Geneva: Skira.
1964, CHAR
René Char. *Commune Présence*. Paris: Gallimard. (See p. 234.)
1964, *Connaissance des Arts*
"Nouveau chef-d'œuvre autour d'un La Tour" [*sic*]. *Connaissance des Arts*, no. 152 (October), p. 57. (Saint-Séverin *St. Luke*.)
1964, HOOG
Michel Hoog. "Georges de La Tour, 'peintre honorable' et... odieux homme." In *La Vie des Grands Peintres Français*, edited by Pierre Waleffe, pp. 39-49, Paris: Éditions du Sud.
1964, NICOLSON
Benedict Nicolson. "Un caravagiste aixois: le Maître à la chandelle." *Art de France* 4, pp. 116-139.
1964, RAMBAUD
Mireille Rambaud. *Documents du Minutier Central concernant l'histoire de l'Art (1700-1750)*. Vol. 1. Paris: Imprimerie Nationale.
1964, SJOBERG
Yves Sjoberg. "Saint François et Georges de La Tour." *Les Amis de saint François*, October-December, pp. 133-140.
1964, THUILLIER
Jacques Thuillier – Albert Châtelet. *La Peinture française*. Vol. 2: *De Le Nain à Fragonard*. Geneva: Skira. (See ch. 1, "Les Peintres français devant la réalité.")
1965, ARLAND
Marcel Arland. "Georges de La Tour peintre de Lorraine." *Jardin des Arts*, nos. 128-129 (July-August), pp. 16-25.
1965, *Chefs-d'œuvre*
"La Tour méconnu et retrouvé." *Chefs-d'œuvre de l'art* (10 February), no. 100, pp. 1600-1603.
1965, CHOUX
Abbé Jacques Choux. "A. M. Bougier: Georges de La Tour." *Annales de l'Est* 17, pp. 182-184. (Critical Review.)
1965, JANNEAU
Guillaume Janneau. *La Peinture française au XVIIe siècle*. Geneva: Pierre Cailler.
1965, PARISET, *Art classique*
François-Georges Pariset. *L'Art classique*. Les Neuf Muses. Paris: Presses Universitaires de France.
1965, PARISET, *B. S. H. A. F.*
François-Georges Pariset. "De Bellange à Deruet." *Bulletin de la Société de l'Histoire de l'Art Français*, pp. 61-73.
1965, TRIBOUT DE MOREMBERT
Henri Tribout de Morembert. "Le testament d'Alphonse de Rambervillers (1633)." *Annales de l'Est*, no. 2, pp. 149-162.
1965, VAN THIEL
P. J.-J. Van Thiel. "Rembrandts Heilige Familie bij avond." *Bulletin van het Rijksmuseum* 13, p. 159.
1965, VOSS
Hermann Voss. "Die Darstellungen des hl. Franziskus im Werk von Georges de La Tour." *Pantheon* 23, pp. 402-404.
1966, ARCANGELI
Francesco Arcangeli. "Un nuovo Saraceni." *Paragone*, no. 199, pp. 46-54.
1966, BIALOSTOCKI
Jan Bialostocki. "Puer sufflans ignes". In *Arte in Europa. Scritti di Storia dell'Arte in onore di Edoardo Arslan*, pp. 591-595. Milan.
1966, DUSSAUX
C. Dussaux. "Un érudit du XIXe siècle, Charles Friry. 1802-1883." *Pays lorrain*, pp. 12-26.
1966, GAILLARD
Yann Gaillard. *Collection particulière. Essai en forme de tableaux*. Paris: Julliard (See pp. 81-82.)
1966, *Hommages Voss*
G. Giocco, R. Longhi, H. Haug, E. Huttinger, V. Bloch, G. Ewald. *Hommage à Hermann Voss*. Strasbourg.

1966, OTTANI CAVINA
Anna Ottani Cavina. *La Tour*. I Maestri del Colore. Milan: Fratelli Fabbri.
1966, ROSENBERG
Pierre Rosenberg. *Inventaire des collections publiques françaises. Rouen, Musée des Beaux-Arts. Tableaux français du XVIIe siècle et italiens des XVIIe et XVIIIe siècles.* Paris: Éd. des musées nationaux.
1967, BAZIN
Germain Bazin. *Kindlers Malerei Lexicon*. Zurich: Kindler Verlag.
1967, LACLOTTE
Michel Laclotte. "Vingt ans d'acquisitions au Musée du Louvre; 1947-1967. Département des peintures." *Revue du Louvre et des Musées de France* 17, no. 6, pp. 327-336.
1967, MOIR
Alfred Moir. *The Italian Followers of Caravaggio*. Cambridge, Mass.: Harvard University Press.
1967, OTTANI CAVINA
Anna Ottani Cavina. *La Tour*. Chefs-d'œuvre de l'art. Grands peintres. Paris: Hachette (French edition of 1966, OTTANI CAVINA, with an additional text by F. Grouvel, "Georges de La Tour, éternel mystère," and several photographs in black and white.)
1967, PARISET
François-Georges Pariset. "L'Ermite à la lanterne et Georges de La Tour." *Hommage à Hans Haug. Cahiers Alsaciens d'Archéologie, d'Art et d'Histoire* 11, pp. 241-246.
1967, TANAKA
Hidemichi Tanaka. "Étude sur l'évolution stylistique des œuvres de Georges de La Tour" (in Japanese). *Bijutsu-shi (Journal of the Japanese Art History Society)* 16, no. 4 (March), pp. 129-143 (French summary, pp. 148-149.)
1967, TERNOIS
Daniel Ternois. "Jacques Callot et la gravure en Lorraine au XVIIe siècle." *Médecine de France*, November, pp. 17-32.
1968, CHAR
René Char. "Justesse de Georges de La Tour." In *Dans la pluie giboyeuse*. Paris: Gallimard.
1968, OTTANI CAVINA
Anna Ottani Cavina. *Carlo Saraceni*. Milan: Mario Spagnol.
1968, Frick Collection
The Frick Collection. An Illustrated Catalogue. Vol. 2: *Paintings*. New York: The Frick Collection; distributed by Princeton University Press.
1968, McLUHAN – PARKER
Marshall McLuhan – Harley Parker. *Through the Vanishing Point: Space in Poetry and Painting*. World Perspectives, vol. 37. New York: Harper & Row.
1968, WILLOCH
Sigurd Willoch. "Et mesterwerk av Georges de La Tour." *Kunst og Kultur* (Oslo) 51, pp. 105-112.
1969, *Chronique des arts*
"La Chronique des arts." Supplement to *Gazette des Beaux-Arts*, no. 425 (February), p. 104 (reprod. of St. Alexis).
1969, GEBELIN
François Gebelin. *L'Époque Henri IV et Louis XIII*. Paris: Presses Universitaires de France, pp. 162-167.
1969, LURIE
Ann Tzeutschler Lurie. "Gerard van Honthorst's Samson and Delilah." *Bulletin of the Cleveland Museum of Art* 56 (November), p. 332-344.
1969, NICOLSON
Benedict Nicolson. "A New 'Image St. Alexis'." *Burlington Magazine* 111 (February), pp. 86-88.
1969, TANAKA
Hidemichi Tanaka. "L'Œuvre de Georges de La Tour." Ph. D. diss., University of Strasbourg.
1969-1970, TANAKA
Hidemichi Tanaka. "Georges de La Tour Seen by an Oriental, 1-6" (in Japanese). *Kikan-Geijutsu*, nos. 10-15 (summer 1969-autumn 1970).
1969, WRIGHT
Christopher Wright. "A Suggestion for Étienne de La Tour." *Burlington Magazine* 111 (February), pp. 295-296.
1970, BLUNT
Anthony Blunt. *Art and Architecture in France. 1500-1700*. 2d ed., rev. Pelican History of Art. Harmondsworth: Penguin.
1970, KING – MARLY
"The Metropolitan 'Fortune Teller.'" *Burlington Magazine* 112 (October), pp. 700-701. (Letter from D. King, Deputy Keeper, Department of Textiles, Victoria and Albert Museum; reply from Diana de Marly.)
1970, LACLOTTE
Michel Laclotte. *Musée du Louvre – Peintures*. Paris: Flammarion.
1970, MARLY
Diana de Marly. "A Note on the Metropolitan 'Fortune Teller.'" *Burlington Magazine* 112 (June), pp. 388-390.
1970, TANAKA
Hidemichi Tanaka. "Georges de La Tour dans ses rapports avec Le Clerc, Callot et Rembrandt." *L'Information d'Histoire de l'art*, no. 2 (March-April), pp. 55-60.
1970, TCHERBATCHOVA
M. Tcherbatchova. "An Unknown Painting by Georges de La Tour." In *The Art of Western Europe* (in Russian), pp. 108-114. Essays in honor of Levinson-Lessing on his seventieth birthday. Leningrad. (On the Lvov Painting.)
1970, WRIGHT
Christopher Wright. "Georges de La Tour – A Note on His Early Career." *Burlington Magazine* 112 (June), p. 387.
1971, BLOCH
Vitale Bloch. "A Picture by Georges de La Tour in Russia." *Apollo* 94 (October), p. 292.
1971, NICOLSON – WRIGHT
Benedict Nicolson and Christopher Wright. "A New Painting by Georges de La Tour." *Burlington Magazine* 113 (November), pp. 669-671.
1971, SPINNER
Kaspar H. Spinner. "Helldunkel und Zeitlichkeit: Caravaggio, Ribera, Zurbaran, G. de La Tour, Rembrandt." *Zeitschrift für Kunstsgeschichte* 34, no. 3, pp. 169-183. (See pp. 177-178.)
1971, SZIGETHI
Agnès Szigethi. *Georges de La Tour* (in Hungarian), Budapest: Corvina Kiado.
1971, TANAKA
Hidemichi Tanaka. "The Works of Étienne de La Tour. True and False La Tours" (in Japanese). *Geiju-tsu-shinchô*, October, pp. 108-115.

IV. 1972-1974 (The Orangerie Exhibit and its Repercussions)

The Discovery of the *Dice Players*

1972, A. F. P.
Agence France-Presse dispatch announcing the discovery of the *Dice Players*. Variously reprinted 11 February in *Sud-Ouest, Les Dernières Nouvelles d'Alsace, La Haute-Marne libérée, l'Est Républicain* (14 February), *Le Havre Libre, La Charente Libre, Paris-Normandie, La Dépêche du Midi, L'Alsace, Le Républicain Lorrain*, etc.
1972, *L'Aurore*, 11 February
"Un trésor dans le petit musée." *L'Aurore*, 11 February.
1972, *Centre-France*, 20 February
Jean Berger. "L'impensable trouvaille du grenier." *Centre-France*, 20 February, p. 10.
1972, *Daily Express*
Norman Dowdy. "Old Master Painting Found Beneath the Dust." *Daily Express*, 10 February.
1972, *Le Figaro*, 13 March
D. N. "Ces 'Joueurs de dés' avaient disparu depuis un demi-siècle." *Le Figaro*, 13 March, p. 30.
1972, *Le Monde*, 11 February
"Un chef-d'œuvre de Georges de La Tour découvert dans le grenier d'un musée de province." *Le Monde*, 11 February, p. 27.
1972, NICOLSON
Benedict Nicolson. "Quest for La Tour. Teeside's Georges de La Tour, 'The Dice Players.'" *Encounter*, June. Also offprint (n.p., n.d.). French translation in *Lectures pour tous*, no. 233 (August 1972), pp. 66-70.
1972, *República*, 10 February
"Descoberta num sótão uma tela de La Tour." *República* (Lisbon), 10 February.
1972, *The Times*, 10 February
Peter Hopkirk. "Masterpiece Found in Northern Attic." *The Times*, 10 February, pp. 1, 2.
1972, ADHÉMAR
Hélène Adhémar. "La Tour et les couvents lorrains." *Gazette des Beaux-Arts* 80, October, pp. 219-222.
1972, ANDRÉ
Robert André. "Le Nouveau-né de La Tour." *Nouvelle Revue Française*, no. 236 (August), pp. 72-74.
1972, ARLAND
Marcel Arland. "Georges de La Tour." *Nouvelle Revue Française*, no. 236 (August), pp. 64-65.
1972, BLANCHET
André Blanchet. "Georges de La Tour, ou du merveilleux au mystère." *Études* 337 (July), pp. 57-63.
1972, BLOCH
Vitale Bloch. "Georges de La Tour (1593-1652). Zur Ausstellung in Paris, Orangerie des Tuileries." *Kunstchronik*, August, pp. 222-224.
1972, BLUNT
Anthony Blunt. "Georges de La Tour at the Orangerie." *Burlington Magazine* 114 (August), pp. 516-525.
1972, BORIAS-LACOSTE
Borias and Lacoste. *Georges de La Tour*. Paris: Office français des techniques modernes d'éducation. (Manual and 24 slides.)
1972, J. B.
J. B. "Le Georges de La Tour du musée départemental est désormais authentifié: il est signé." *La Liberté de l'Est*, 3 March.
1972, CAILLEUX
Jean Cailleux. "Notre Vermeer." *Art et Curiosité*, no. 41 (April-May), pp. 24-28.
1972, *Le Canard enchaîné*
Le Petit Lettré. "Georges de La Tour" ("poem"). *Le Canard enchaîné*, 17 May.
1972, CHABANON
J[ean] C[habanon]. "Coups d'épingle." *Le Peintre*, no. 450 (October), p. 8. (On the Louvre's purchase of the Landry *Cheat*.)
1972, CHARMET
Raymond Charmet. "Georges de La Tour. Mystères et splendeurs." *Le Nouveau Journal*, 29 July, p. 11.
1972, CHASTEL, *Médecine de France*
André Chastel. "La Tour perdu et retrouvé." *Médecine de France*, no. 233 (June), pp. 52-53.
1972, CHASTEL, *Le Monde*
André Chastel. "À l'Orangerie, le mystérieux Georges de La Tour." *Le Monde*, 10 May, pp. 1, 17.
1972, CLAY
Jean Clay. "La flamme qui brûle chez Georges de La Tour." *Réalités*, no. 317, pp. 90-97.
1972, CONIL LACOSTE
Michel Conil Lacoste. "Georges de La Tour et l'Orangerie. His-

toire et préhistoire d'une exposition." *Le Monde*, 3 May, p. 17.
1972, CORDONNIER
Paul Cordonnier. "L'exposition Georges de La Tour." *Revue historique et archéologique du Maine*, 2d ser., 52, no. 339, pp. 120-125 (on the *Fortune Teller*).
1972, CRESPELLE
Jean-Pierre Crespelle. "Georges de La Tour, redécouvert après trois siècles d'oubli, vedette de l'Orangerie." *France-Soir*, 12 May. p. 5.
1972, CREUZEAU
Jean-Marie Creuzeau. "Georges de La Tour en sa lumière ressuscité." *France catholique*, 26 May, p. 6.
1972, DALEVÈZE
Jean Dalevèze. "L'ombre et le mystère." *Les Nouvelles littéraires*, 14-21 May, pp. 15-16.
1972, DESCARGUES
Pierre Descargues. "Une troublante lumière." *Connaissance des arts*, no. 243 (May), pp. 88-96 and cover.
1972, DEROUDILLE
René Deroudille. "À l'Orangerie des Tuileries: Georges de La Tour." *Le Pharmacien de France*, no. 15 (September), pp. 636-643.
1972, DOLLFUS
Marc-Adrien Dollfus. "L'ophtalmologie et l'optique dans l'œuvre de Georges de La Tour exposée à l'Orangerie des Tuileries." *Bulletin de la Société nationale des Antiquités de France*, pp. 107-111.
1972, ELGAR
Frank Elgar. "Un peintre de génie enfin tiré de trois siècles d'oubli: Georges de La Tour." *Carrefour*, 17 May, p. 17.
1972, FERMIGIER
André Fermigier. "Un dieu de la peinture pure." *Le Nouvel Observateur*, 15-21 May, pp. 60-61.
1972, FRANÇA
José-Augusto França. "La Tour, uma exposição modelo." *Diário de Lisboa*, 2 June, pp. 4-5.
1972, GALLEGO
Julián Gállego. "La Tour, iluminado." *Goya*, no. 109 (July), pp. 35-38.
1972, GRANVILLE
Chantelou [Pierre Granville]. "Un Georges de La Tour à Londres: Rixe d'enchères pour la 'Rixe de musiciens.'" *Le Monde*, 10-11 December, p. 19.
1972, GROSJEAN
Jean Grosjean. "Ce Saint-Sépulcre." *Nouvelle Revue Française*, no. 236 (August), pp. 75-76.
1972, HILAIRE
Georges Hilaire. "La belle aventure de Georges de La Tour." *Le Spectacle du monde*, August, pp. 92-96.
1972, HUGHES
Robert Hughes. "An Analytic Stillness." *Time*, 3 July, p. 47.
1972, HÜTTINGER
E. Hüttinger. "Georges de La Tour." *Neue Zürcher Zeitung*, 16 July, p. 43.
1972, ISARLO
George Isarlo. Columns in *Combat-Art*. "Exposition Georges de La Tour," 22 May, 17 July: "À l'exposition de l'Orangerie, Georges de La Tour, peintre de mœurs et de clandestinités," no. 141 (11 September).
1972, IVANOFF
Nicolas Ivanoff. "Georges de La Tour, Carlo Saraceni e Pietro Bellotti." *Arte Veneta* 26, pp. 299-301.
1972, LAGET-MACÉ DE LÉPINAY
Elisabeth Laget and François Macé de Lépinay. *Georges de La Tour*. Le Petit journal des grandes expositions. Paris: Réunion des musées nationaux.
1972, LANDRY
Pierre Landry. "Georges de La Tour et notre temps." *Foreword to the exhibition catalogue*, Paris, 1972, pp. 1-26.
1972, LEM, *Le Vrai visage*
F.-H. Lem. "Le vrai visage de Georges de La Tour." *Le Peintre*, no. 446 (June), pp. 4-9.
1972, LEM, Salve
F.-H. Lem. "Salve après clôture, tirée en l'honneur de Georges de La Tour et de quelques autres." *Le Peintre*, no. 450 (October), pp. 4-7.
1972, LÉONARD
Pierre Léonard. "Georges de La Tour trois siècles après." *Gazette médicale de France* 79, no. 24 (23 June), pp. 4224-4230.
1972, MACÉ DE LÉPINAY
François Macé de Lépinay. "Georges de La Tour en 1972." *Colóquio Artes*, December, pp. 30-35.
1972, MARTEAU
Robert Marteau. "Georges de La Tour à l'Orangerie." *Esprit*, nos. 7-8 (July-August), pp. 118-120.
1972, MAZARS
Pierre Mazars. "Le Mythe La Tour." *Jardin des Arts*, nos. 212-213, July-August, p. 10.
1972, MÉGRET
Frédéric Mégret. "Tout l'œuvre connu de Georges de La Tour." *Le Figaro littéraire*, 29 April, pp. 13, 17.
1972, METKEN
Günter Metken. "Der französische Vermeer." *Weltkunst* 42, no. 11 (1 June), pp. 840-841.
1972, MOISY
Pierre Moisy. "Sur l'exposition Georges de La Tour." *La Revue du Bas-Poitou*, nos. 4-5 (July-October), pp. 275-278.
1972, *Le Monde*, 7 August
"'Le Tricheur' de La Tour acquis par le Louvre pour la somme de 10 millions de francs." *Le Monde*, 7 August.
1972, MOUSSALI
Ulysse Moussali. *À la recherche de Georges de La Tour*. Paris: Le Grenier aux livres.
1972, NICOLSON, *B. M.*
B[enedict] N[icolson]. "Current and Forthcoming Exhibitions." *Burlington Magazine* 114 (March), p. 189 and figs. 53-45.
1972, NICOLSON – WRIGHT
Benedict Nicolson and Christopher Wright. "Georges de La Tour et la Grande-Bretagne." *La Revue du Louvre et des musées de France*, no. 2, pp. 135-142.
1972, D'ORMESSON
Jean d'Ormesson. "Un interprète privilégié du mythe d'Alexis: Georges de La Tour." *La Nouvelle Revue Française*, no. 238 (October), pp. 78-98.
1972, OCHSÉ
Madeleine Ochsé. "Georges de La Tour. 1593-1652." *Jardin des Arts*, April, pp. 38-44.
1972, OTTANI CAVINA
Anna Ottani Cavina. "La Tour all'Orangerie e il suo primo tempo caravaggesco." *Paragone*, no. 273 (November), pp. 3-24 and pls. 1-11.
1972, PARISET, *G. B. A.*
François-Georges Pariset. "L'exposition de Georges de La Tour à l'Orangerie. Paris." *Gazette des Beaux-Arts* 80 (October), pp. 207-212.
1972, PARISET, *Plaisir de France*
François-Georges Pariset. "Consécration d'un grand peintre: Georges de La Tour." *Plaisir de France*, no. 399 (May), pp. 2-9.
1972, PICARD
Raymond Picard. "L'unité spirituelle de Georges de La Tour." *Gazette des Beaux-Arts* 80 (October), pp. 213-218.
1972, ROHOU
Guy Rohou. "Le souffleur de braise." *Nouvelle Revue Française*, no. 236 (August), pp. 69-71.
1972, ROSENBERG
Pierre Rosenberg. "Découvrons Georges de La Tour." *Jardin des Arts*, May, p. 8.
1972, ROSENBERG – THUILLIER
Pierre Rosenberg and Jacques Thuillier. *Catalogue entries*. Paris, 1972, pp. 115-264.
1972, SANI
Bernardina Sani. "Georges de La Tour, Paris, Orangerie." *Annali della Scuola Normale Superiore di Pisa*, ser. 3. 2, no. 2, pp. 1061-1068.
1972, SCHNEIDER
Pierre Schneider. "Le mystérieux Georges de La Tour." *L'Express*, 29 May-4 June, pp. 82-83.
1972, SCHNUR
Roman Schnur. "Das Letzte ist die Leichtigkeit. Die Wiederentdeckung des lothringischen Malers Georges de La Tour." *Die Welt*, 10 June, pp. III-IV.
1972, SCOTT
Barbara Scott. "Georges de La Tour at the Orangerie." *Apollo* 96 (August), pp. 159-162.
1972, SERRES
Michel Serres. "Les pensées d'un provincial: Georges de La Tour." *Critique* 28, no. 302, pp. 643-668.
1972, SILVANO
Franco Silvano. "Riscoperta di La Tour." *Le Arti* 22, nos. 9-10 (September-October), pp. 22-29.
1972, SLATKES
Leonard J. Slatkes. "Additions to Dirk van Baburen." *Album Amicorum J. G. van Gelder*. The Hague: Martinus Nijhoff, pp. 267-273. (See p. 272.)
1972, SPEAR
Richard E. Spear. "Unknown Pictures by the Caravaggisti (with Notes on "Caravaggio and His Followers")." *Storia dell'Arte*, pp. 150-161. (See p. 158.)
1972, SUTTON
Denys Sutton. "La Tour: the 300-Year Comeback." *New York Times*, 4 June.
1972, TANAKA
Hidemichi Tanaka. *The Works of Georges de La Tour* (in Japanese with French summary). Tokyo.
1972, TANAKA, *Observations*
Hidemichi Tanaka. "Observations sur l'évolution stylistique de Georges de La Tour." *Actes du XXIIe Congrès International d'Histoire de l'Art*, Budapest. 1969, vol. 2, pp. 45-50.
1972, TANAKA, *Mizué*
Hidemichi Tanaka. "The Georges de La Tour Exhibition in Paris" (in Japanese). *Mizué* (Tokyo), no. 813 (November), pp. 80-84.
1972, TERRASSE
Antoine Terrasse. "Une certitude absolue." *Nouvelle Revue Française*, no. 236 (August), pp. 66-68.
1972, THUILLIER, *Art News*
Jacques Thuillier. "La Tour, Between Yesterday and Tomorrow." *Art New* 71 (summer), pp. 24-27.
1972, THUILLIER, *Biographie*
Jacques Thuillier. "[La Tour], biographie et fortune critique." Catalogue. *Paris, 1972*, p. 55-103.
1972, THUILLIER, ***Chronologie***
Jacques Thuillier. "La Tour. Catalogue et chronologie." Catalogue. *Paris, 1972*, pp. 107-113.
1972, THUILLIER, *Énigmes*
Jacques Thuillier. "La Tour, énigmes et hypothèses." Catalogue introduction. *Paris, 1972*, pp. 27-54.
1972, THUILLIER, *Les "Nuits"*
Jacques Thuillier. "Georges de La Tour et le choix des nuits." *Bulletin de la Société des Amis du Musée de Dijon*, 1970-1972, pp. 59-66.
1972, THUILLIER, *Paradoxes*
Jacques Thuillier. "Georges de La Tour: trois paradoxes." *L'Œil*, April, pp. 2-11.
1972, TRIBOUT DE MOREMBERT, *Archivum*
Henri Tribout de Morembert. "Le peintre Georges de La Tour et l'Ordre de Saint François." *Archivum Franciscanum Historicum* 85, nos. 1-2, pp. 286-299.
1972, TRIBOUT DE MOREMBERT, *G. B. A.*
Henri Tribout de Morembert.

"Sibylle de Cropsaux, mère de La Tour." *Gazette des Beaux-Arts* 80 (October), pp. 223-224.
1972, VOLBOUDT
Pierre Volboudt. "Georges de La Tour à l'Orangerie." *xxe siècle* 34, no. 39, pp. 53, 59.
1972, VOLPE
Carlo Volpe. "Annotazioni sulla Mostra Caravaggesca di Cleveland." *Paragone*, no. 263 (January), pp. 50-76. (See pp. 54-55, 69-70.)
1972, WILDENSTEIN
Daniel Wildenstein. "À propos de l'exposition La Tour." *Gazette des Beaux-Arts*, 80 (October), pp. 205-206.
1973, ANTOINE
Michel Antoine. "Georges de La Tour et l'École lorraine." *Annales de l'Est* 25, no. 2, pp. 141-144.
1973, CAUQUELIN
Anne Cauquelin. "Deux Madeleines, Jérôme et la puce." *Revue d'esthétique* 26, no. 1, pp. 39-56.
1973, CHARPENTIER
F. Thérèse Charpentier. "Peut-on toujours parler de 'La servante à la puce'?" *Le Pays lorrain* 54, no. 2, pp. 101-108.
1973, CHOUX
Abbé Jacques Choux. "Le miroir de la Madeleine chez Georges de La Tour." *Le Pays lorrain* 54, no. 2, pp. 109-112.
1973, CONTI
Alessandro Conti. "De La Tour, osservazioni su una mostra." *Annali della Scuola Normale Superiore di Pisa*, ser. 3. 3, no. 2, pp. 593-603.
1973, DOLLFUS
Marc-Adrien Dollfus. "L'ophtalmologie et l'optique dans l'œuvre de Georges de La Tour." *Le Pays lorrain* 54, no. 2, pp. 95-100.
1973, GÁLLEGO
Julián Gállego. "Actualidad de Georges de La Tour." *Goya*, no. 112 (January-February), pp. 200-207.
1973, GROSSMANN
F. Grossmann. "Some Observations on Georges de La Tour and the Netherlandish Tradition." *Burlington Magazine* 115 (September), pp. 576-583.
1973, HELD
Julius S. Held. "The Emergence of Georges de La Tour." *Art in America* (July-August), pp. 82-87.
1973, MAROT
Pierre Marot. "La résurrection de La Tour en Lorraine." *Le Pays lorrain* 54, no. 2, pp. 53-58.
1973, PARISET
François-Georges Pariset. "L'exposition de Georges de La Tour." *Le Pays lorrain* 54, no. 2, pp. 59-86.
1973, ROSENBERG – MACÉ DE LÉPINAY
Pierre Rosenberg and François Macé de Lépinay. *Georges de La Tour. Vie et œuvre*. Fribourg: Office du Livre. German edition: *Georges de La Tour. Leben und Werk*. Berlin: Gebr. Mann, 1974.
1973, SOLESMES
François Solesmes. *Georges de La Tour*. Lausanne: La Guilde du Livre. 2d ed., 1982.
1973, THUILLIER
Jacques Thuillier. *Tout l'œuvre peint de Georges de La Tour*. Paris: Flammarion. Italian edition: *L'opera completa di Georges de La Tour*. Milan: Rizzoli, 1973. German edition: *Das Gesamtwerk des Georges de La Tour*. Lucerne: 1973.
1973, THUILLIER, *Revue de l'Art*
Jacques Thuillier. "Georges de La Tour: un an après." *Revue de l'Art*, no. 20, pp. 92-100.
1973, TRIBOUT DE MOREMBERT, *Les Carmes*
Henri Tribout de Morembert. "Un tableau de La Tour pour les Carmes de Metz." *Le Pays lorrain* 54, no. 2, pp. 87-90.
1973, TRIBOUT DE MOREMBERT, *La famille*
Henri Tribout de Morembert. "La famille de Georges de La Tour à Vic, Moyenvic et Marsal." *Le Pays lorrain* 54, no. 2, pp. 113-115.
1973, TRIBOUT DE MOREMBERT, *Réponse*
Henri Tribout de Morembert. "Georges de La Tour, homosexuel et hérétique?" *Le Pays lorrain* 54, no. 2, pp. 115-117.
1973, VAUX DE FOLETIER
François de Vaux de Foletier. "Georges de La Tour et le thème de la bonne aventure." *Le Pays lorrain* 54, no. 2, pp. 91-94.
1974, BLOCH
Vitale Bloch. "Revoyant Georges de La Tour." *Liber Amicorum Karel G. Boon*. Amsterdam: Swets & Zeitlinger, pp. 52-59.
1974, CRESPELLE
J.-P. C. [Jean-Pierre Crespelle]. "Adieu Madeleine!" *Journal du dimanche*, 29 September. (On the purchase of the Fabius *Magdalen* by the National Gallery in Washington.)
1974, DORIVAL
Bernard Dorival. *La peinture française du xviie au Musée de Grenoble*. Grenoble: (See *St. Jerome*, pp. 6-7.)
1974, *Le Monde*, 27 September
A.Fr. "La National Gallery de Washington a acheté 'La Madeleine au miroir' de Georges de La Tour." *Le Monde*, 27 September.
1974, NICOLSON – WRIGHT
Benedict Nicolson and Christopher Wright. *Georges de La Tour*. London: Phaidon. French edition: Brussels: Arcades, 1975.
1974, NOUVEAU
R. Nouveau. "Georges de La Tour, peintre lorrain." *Études touloises*, no. 2, pp. 27-29.
1974, OVSIJCUK
V. Ovsijcuk. "The Lvov Painting by Georges de La Tour" (in Russian). *Obrazotvorce Mystectvo* 41, no. 4, pp. 27-28.
1974, *Le Quotidien*, 28-29 September
"Un de La Tour pour aider Giscard?" *Le Quotidien de Paris*, 28-29 September.
1974, TANAKA
Hidemichi Tanaka. "Le problème des tableaux doubles de Georges de La Tour." *Acts of Congrès International de Grenade*.
1974, TRIBOUT DE MOREMBERT
Henri Tribout de Morembert. "Georges de La Tour, son milieu, sa famille, ses œuvres." *Gazette des Beaux-Arts* 83 (April), pp. 205-234.
1974, ZOLOTOV, *Tableau de Lvov*
Yuri Zolotov. "New Information on La Tour" (in Russian). *Tvortchestvo*, no. 208, no. 4. (Color photograph of the Lvov painting and signature.)
1974, ZOLOTOV, *L'œuvre peint*
Yuri Zolotov. "On the Paintings of Georges de La Tour" (in Russian). *Iskusstvo* 37, no. 12, pp. 62-68.
1974, ZOLOTOV, *Le caravagisme néerlandais*
Yuri Zolotov. "Georges de La Tour et le caravagisme néerlandais." *Revue de l'Art*, no. 26, pp. 57-63.

V. 1975-1991 (Recent Research)

1975, BOLOGNA
Ferdinando Bologna. "A New Work from the Youth of La Tour." *Burlington Magazine* 117 (July), pp. 434-441.
1975, BORDEAUX
Jean-Luc Bordeaux. "The J. Paul Getty Museum: la peinture française." *Connaissance des arts*, no. 278 (April), pp. 80-87.
1975, FAHY
Everett Fahy. "Georges de La Tour No Longer Unknown." *Art News* 74, pp. 46-47. (*The Fortune Teller*.)
1975, MARTIN
Gregory Martin. "La Tour by Candlelight." *Apollo*, no. 102 (August), pp. 141-142. (Review of Nicolson-Wright book.)
1975, *Le Monde*, 13 February
"Exposé en 1972 à l'Orangerie. Un Georges de La Tour acquis par un musée américain." *Le Monde*, 13 February. (*St. Philip*.)
1975, RZEPINSKA
M. Rzepinska. "Obraz Georges de La Tour, a: Sw. Sebastian ze sw. Irena." *Sprawozadania z Posiedzen Komisji Naukowych P.A.N.* 19, no. 1, pp. 115-1016.
1975, SPEAR
Richard E. Spear. *Caravaggio and His Followers*. New York: Harper and Row.
1975, VSEVOLOZHSKAYA – LINNIK
S. Vsevolozhskaya and L. Linnik. *Caravaggio and His Followers*. Paintings in Soviet Museums. Leningrad: Aurora. (See pp. 56-59, the Lvov *Payment of Dues*, commentary and color reproductions.)
1976, AUBRY – CHOUX
Marie-Thérèse Aubry and Abbot Jacques Choux. "Documents nouveaux sur la vie et l'œuvre de Georges de La Tour." *Le Pays lorrain* 57, no. 3, pp. 155-158.
1976, BOCK
Henning Bock. "Georges de La Tour essendes Bauernpaar. Neuerwerbung der Gemäldegalerie." *Berliner Museen*, September, pp. 3-4.
1976, LARCAN
Alain Larcan. "À propos du tableau de Georges de La Tour du Musée Lorrain dit 'La Femme à la puce.'" *Le Pays lorrain* 57, no. 3, pp. 159-164.
1976, PARISET
François-Georges Pariset. "Georges de La Tour. Réflexions sur l'artiste et son œuvre." *Le Pays lorrain* 57, no. 3, pp. 136-154.
1976, PUTON
Francis Puton. "Le 'La Tour' du Musée Départemental des Vosges et son donateur le duc de Choiseul-Stainville." *Bulletin de la Société Philomatique Vosgienne* 79, pp. 141-145.
1976, ROSENBERG
Pierre Rosenberg. "Benedict Nicolson and Christopher Wright 'Georges de La Tour.'" *Art Bulletin* 58 (September), pp. 452-454. (Review.)
1976, SCHLEIER
Erich Schleier. "Georges de La Tour: Essendes Bauerspaar. Zu einer Neuerwerbung der Gemäldegalerie." *Jahrbuch der Stiftung Preussischer Kulturbesitz* 13, pp. 231-241.
1976, SPEAR
Richard E. Spear. "A New Book on La Tour." *Burlington Magazine* 118 (April), pp. 223-225. (Review of Nicolson and Wright.)
1976, TRIBOUT DE MOREMBERT
Henri Tribout de Morembert. "Benedict Nicolson et Christopher Wright, 'Georges de La Tour.'" *Le Pays lorrain* 57, no. 3, pp. 170-171. (Review.)
1976, ZOLOTOV
Yuri Zolotov. [Date of Lvov painting and chronology of La Tour's work, in Russian.] *Iskusstvo* 39, no. 1, p. 67.
1977, BORDEAUX
Jean-Luc Bordeaux. "Un musée français en Californie." *Connaissance des arts*, no. 299 (January), pp. 32-41.
1977, REINBOLD
Anne Reinbold. "Le sablier de Georges de La Tour." *Annales de l'Est* 29, no. 2, pp. 95-126.
1977, WRIGHT
Christopher Wright. *Georges de La Tour*. Oxford and New York.
1977, ZOLOTOV
Yuri Zolotov. "Georges de La Tour: sur la chronologie de

l'œuvre." *Revue de l'Art*, no. 38, p. 75.

1978, FOUCART
Jacques Foucart. "Une fausse énigme: le pseudo et le véritable Van de Venne." *Revue de l'Art*, no. 42, pp. 53-62.

1978, GRODECKI
Catherine Grodecki. "La construction du château de Wideville et sa place dans l'architecture française du dernier quart du XVIe siècle." *Bulletin Monumental*, no. 2, pp. 135-175. (See inventory of Claude de Bullion.)

1978, RZEPINSKA
M. Rzepinska. "The Georges de La Tour Painting in the Berlin Museum: A footnote on the Iconography of St. Sebastian" (in Polish). *Folia Historiae Artium* (Kraków) 14, pp. 23-48.

1978, WIND
Barry Wind. "Close Encounters of the Baroque Kind: Amatory Paintings by Terbrugghen, Baburen, and La Tour." *Studies in Iconography*, vol. 4, pp. 115-124.

1979, ANTOINE
Michel Antoine. "Un séjour en France de Georges de La Tour en 1639." *Annales de l'Est* 31, no. 1, pp. 17-26.

1979, DORIVAL
Bernard Dorival. "La peinture française au XVIIe siècle (1610-1715)." In *Baroque et classicisme au XVIIe siècle en Italie et en France*, edited by Arnauld Brejon de Lavergnée and Bernard Dorival. Histoire universelle de la peinture. Geneva: Famot. (See "La Lorraine: Georges de La Tour," pp. 236-249.)

1979, NICOLSON
Benedict Nicolson. *The International Caravaggesque Movement. Lists of Pictures by Caravaggio and His Followers Throughout Europe from 1590 to 1650*. Oxford: Phaidon. (See pp. 63-66.)

1979, SAMOYAULT
Jean-Pierre Samoyault. *André-Charles Boulle et sa famille*. Geneva: Librairie Droz. (See p. 152.)

1979, SMITH
Martha Kellogg Smith. "Georges de La Tour 'Old Man' and 'Old Woman' in San Francisco." *Burlington Magazine* 121 (May), pp. 288-294.

1979, TANAKA
Hidemichi Tanaka. "Problème de l'école de Georges de La Tour. À propos d'une nouvelle 'Fillette au braisier'" (text in Japanese and French). *Histoire de l'art* (University of Tokyo), no. 2.

1979, ZOLOTOV
Yuri Zolotov. *Georges de La Tour* (in Russian; French summary). Moscow.

1980, ABRAHAM
Elga Abraham. "Trois spécialistes anglais affirment: ces deux La Tour sont faux." *Journal du Dimanche*, 16 November, pp. 1, 6.

1980, CUZIN
Jean-Pierre Cuzin. "Manfredi's Fortune Teller and Some Problems of Manfrediana Methodus." *Bulletin of the Detroit Institute of Arts* 58, no. 1, p. 15 ff.

1980, DUPONT
Jacques Dupont. "Acquisitions. 'Saint Sébastien pleuré par sainte Irène' by Georges de La Tour." *Revue du Louvre et des Musées de France* 30, no. 2, p. 122.

1980, LEE
Thomas P. Lee. "Recently Acquired French Paintings. Reflections on the Past." *Apollo* 111 (March), pp. 212-223.

1980, MARKOVA
V. Markova. [Review of Zolotov *Georges de La Tour*.] *Sovetskoe Iskusstvoznanie Moskva*, no. 2, pp. 377-383.

1980, STOICHITA
V. I. Stoichita. "Melancolia II. Eseu despre Georges de La Tour sù migratia simbolurilor in secolul al 17-lea." *Studii si Cercetari de Istoria Artei. Seria Arta Plastica Bucaresti* 27, pp. 95-131.

1980, WRIGHT
Christopher Wright. "Cheat?" *The Connoisseur* 205 (December), pp. 230-231.

1980, WRIGHT – MARLY
Christopher Wright and Diana de Marly. "Fake?" *The Connoisseur* 205 (September), pp. 22-24.

1981, BREALEY – MEYERS
John M. Brealey and Pieter Meyers. "The Fortune Teller by Georges de La Tour." *Burlington Magazine* 123 (July), pp. 422-425.

1981, LACAU ST GUILY
Agnès Lacau St Guily. "Images de la femme dans l'œuvre de Georges de La Tour." *Colóquio Artes*, no. 49 (June), pp. 18-25.

1981, ROSENBERG
Pierre Rosenberg. "The Fortune Teller by Georges de La Tour." *Burlington Magazine* 123 (August), pp. 487-488.

1981, SEWELL
"The 'Fortune Teller' by Georges de La Tour." *Burlington Magazine* 123 (September), pp. 549-550.

1982, BLUNT
Anthony Blunt. "French Seventeenth-Century Painting: the Literature of the Last Ten Years." *Burlington Magazine* 124, no. 956, pp. 705-711.

1982, BRIGSTOCKE
Hugh Brigstocke. "France in the Golden Age." *Apollo* 116 (July), pp. 8-14. (See pp. 9-10.)

1982, CÉLIER
Jacques Célier. "La diseuse de bonne aventure." *Revue historique et archéologique du Maine*, series 3, 2, pp. 160-178.

1982, CUZIN
Jean-Pierre Cuzin. "New York, French Seventeenth-Century Paintings from American Collections." *Burlington Magazine* 124, no. 953, pp. 526-530. (Review.)

1982, HACHETTE
De La Tour aux frères Le Nain. Le monde de la peinture, Chefs-d'œuvre de l'art. Paris: Hachette.

1982, MAI
Ekkehard Mai. "Ausstellung: La peinture française du XVIIe siècle dans les collections américaines." *Pantheon* 40 (April-June), pp. 153.

1982, NEXON
Yannick Nexon. "La collection de tableaux du chancelier Séguier." *Bibliothèque de l'École des Chartes* 140, pp. 189-214.

1982, REINBOLD
Anne Reinbold. "Les peintres du 17e siècle et leurs diverses perceptions de la lumière." *Dix-septième siècle*, no. 136, pp. 331-339.

1982, ROSENBERG, *Introduction*
Pierre Rosenberg. "Georges de La Tour." Introduction to exhibition catalogue, *Paris-New York-Chicago 1982-1983*, pp. 74-85.

1982, ROSENBERG, *Entries*
Pierre Rosenberg. Entries for paintings of Georges de La Tour in exhibition catalogue, *Paris-New York-Chicago 1982-1983*, pp. 253-259.

1983, MAKSIMOVA
T. V. Maksimova. [Catalogue of Western European paintings in the painting collection in Kursk.] Moscow: Muzei Hugozestvennye sobranija SSSR, Muzei USSR, vol. 4, pp. 179-204, 69 figs. (English summaries.)

1983, QUINGER
Heinz Quinger. *Georges de La Tour*. Maler und Werk. Dresden: Verlag der Kunst.

1983, SCHLEIER
Erich Schleier. "La peinture française du XVIIe siècle dans les collections américaines / France in the Golden Age." *Kunstchronik* 36 (April), pp. 184-197. (Review, see pp. 196-197.)

1984, COLLIN
Hubert Collin. "Un document nouveau concernant Georges de La Tour, 14 septembre 1639." *Le Pays lorrain* 65, no. 2, pp. 131-132.

1984, EKSERDJIAN
D. Ekserdjian. "Wright and Wrong." *Spectacle*, 6 October. (Review of Wright, 1984.)

1984, KLANGE
Else Klange. "Omkring en Jobfigur." *Iconographiske Post*, no. 1, pp. 20-24.

1984, MIGNOT
Claude Mignot. "Le cabinet de Jean-Baptiste de Bretagne: un 'curieux' parisien oublié (1650)." *Archives de l'art français*, n.s. 27, pp. 71-87.

1984, REINBOLD
Anne Reinbold. "Un document inédit: la prestation du serment à Louis XIII par Georges de La Tour à Lunéville en 1634." *Le Pays lorrain* 65, no. 2, pp. 125-130.

1984, RIBAULT
Jean-Yves Ribault. "Réalisme plastique et réalité sociale: à propos des aveugles musiciens de Georges de La Tour." *Gazette des Beaux-Arts* 104 (July-August), pp. 1-4.

1984, ROSENBERG
Pierre Rosenberg. "France in the Golden Age: A Postscript." *Metropolitan Museum of Art Journal* 17, pp. 23-46. (See p. 29.)

1984, WRIGHT
Christopher Wright. *The Art of the Forger*. London: Fraser.

1984, WRIGHT, *Burl. Mag.*
Christopher Wright. "The 'Choirboy' by Georges de La Tour." *Burlington Magazine* 126 (June), p. 351.

1985, BAJOU
Thierry Bajou. *De La Tour*. Introduction by Pierre Rosenberg. Paris: Hazan.

1985, BERESFORD
Richard Beresford. "Deux inventaires de Jacques Blanchard." *Archives de l'Art français*, n.s. 27 ("L'art à l'époque du cardinal de Richelieu"), pp. 107-134.

1985, BOUBLI
Lizzie Boubli. "Les collections parisiennes de peintures de Richelieu." *Richelieu et le monde de l'esprit*. (Catalogue of the exhibition held at the Sorbonne in November 1985, pp. 102-113. See pp. 109-110.)

1985, BOYER
Jean-Claude Boyer. "Les représentations guerrières et l'évolution des arts plastiques en France au XVIIe siècle." *Dix-septième siècle* 37, no. 148, pp. 291-305.

1985, DEL BRAVO
Carlo Del Bravo. "Quadri a lume di notte. Georges de La Tour e Sant' Agostino." *Artibus et Historiae*, no. 11 (VI), pp. 9-22.

1985, LEVI
Honor Levi. "L'Inventaire après décès du cardinal de Richelieu." *Archives de l'Art français*, n.s. 27 ("L'art à l'époque du cardinal de Richelieu"), pp. 9-83. (See p. 66.)

1985, REINBOLD
Anne Reinbold. "Une disposition testamentaire inédite de Georges de La Tour." *Le Pays lorrain*, 66, no. 4, pp. 239-241.

1985, SECOMSKA
K. Secomska. *Malarstwo francuskié* 17 w. Warsaw.

1985, SYLVESTRE
Michel Sylvestre. "Georges de La Tour. Nouveaux documents." *Bulletin de la Société de l'Histoire de l'Art français*, 1983, pp. 47-55.

1985, THUILLIER
Jacques Thuillier. *Tout l'œuvre peint de Georges de La Tour*. Rev. ed. Paris: Flammarion.

1985, WRIGHT
Christopher Wright. *The French Painters of the Seventeenth Century*. London: Orbis. (See pp. 42-51, 195-203.)

1985, WRIGHT
Christopher Wright. Entries for paintings of Georges de La Tour in exhibition catalogue, *Leicester, 1985-1986*, pp. 113-114, 146-147.
1986, LAVEISSIÈRE
Sylvain Laveissière. Entry for *St. Jerome Reading* in exhibition catalogue, *Frankfurt, 1986-1987*.
1986, MELNOTTE
Colette Melnotte. Entry for *The Repentant Magdalen (with the Mirror)* in exhibition catalogue, *Florence, 1986*, pp. 199-202.
1987, CHONÉ
Paulette Choné. "Georges de La Tour: à Lunéville, 15 August 1641." *Le Pays lorrain* 68, no. 1, pp. 32-33.
1987, CLAUDE
Henri Claude. "Georges de La Tour." In *La Vie artistique*, edited by Hubert Collin. *Encyclopédie illustrée de la Lorraine*. Nancy: pp. 140-143.
1987, MOFFIT
J. F. Moffit. "La femme à la puce: the Textual Background of Seventeenth Century Painted Flea-Hunt." *Gazette des Beaux-Arts* 110 (October), pp. 99-103.
1987, PROHASKA
Wolfgang Prohaska. *Georges de La Tour bei der Wahrsagerin*. Das Meisterwerk, no. 6, Vienna: Kunsthistorisches Museum.
1987, ROSENBERG – STEWART
Pierre Rosenberg and Marion C. Stewart. *The Fine Arts Museums of San Francisco. French Paintings 1500-1825* (critical catalogue). San Francisco. (See entry on La Tour, pp. 60-64.)
1988, BOYER
Guy Boyer. "Achetez un bout de La Tour." *Beaux-Arts*, no. 56 (April), p. 10.
1988, CHASTEL, *Le Monde*
André Chastel. "La fascination de Georges de La Tour." *Le Monde*, 19 March, pp. 1, 21.
1988, CHASTEL, *Giornale dell'Arte*
André Chastel. "I francesi si autotassano per non cedere un de La Tour agli americani." *Il Giornale dell'Arte*, no. 55 (April), p. 86.
1988, DELENDA
Odile Delenda. Entry on Georges de La Tour in exhibition catalogue, *Fontaine-de-Vaucluse 1988*, p. 70.
1988, DIEUDONNÉ
Serge Dieudonné. "Georges de La Tour." *Études* 39, pp. 639-651.
1988, DUAULT
Nicole Duault. "Le Louvre aux Français. 'Achetez ce chef-d'œuvre.'" *France-Soir*, 17 March, p. 2.
1988, ERGMANN
Raoul Ergmann. "La part des Amis du Louvre dans l'acquisition du 'Saint Thomas.'" *La Revue du Louvre et des Musées de France* 38, no. 3, p. 1.
1988, FABBRI
La Tour. Regards sur la peinture, no. 46, Milan: Fabbri.
1988, FOUCART
Bruno Foucart. "L'OPA du culte." *Le Quotidien de Paris*, 18 March, p. 27.
1988, GRATE
Pontus Grate. Entry for *St. Jerome*. In *Swedish National Art Museums French Paintings*. Vol. 1. *Seventeenth Century*. Stockholm: pp. 43-45.
1988, PERNOT
Michel Pernot. "L'apogée de la réforme catholique". In *La Vie religieuse*, edited by René Taveneaux. *Encyclopédie illustrée de la Lorraine*. Nancy-Metz: pp. 111-150.
1988, ROSENBERG
Pierre Rosenberg. "Pourquoi le Saint Thomas de La Tour aurait-il manqué sur les cimaises du Louvre?" *La Revue du Louvre et des Musées de France* 38, no. 4, pp. 325-330.
1988, TASSET
Jean-Marie Tasset. "Morale." *Le Figaro*, 22 March, p. 35.
1988, THUILLIER
Jacques Thuillier. "La certitude spirituelle." *Le Figaro*, 22 March, p. 35.
1989, COMER
Christopher D. Comer. Entry for drawing of St. Peter attributed to La Tour in exhibition catalogue, *Paris, 1989*, pp. 72-75.
1989, RODIS-LEWIS
Geneviève Rodis-Lewis. "Les Madeleine de Georges de La Tour." In *Marie Madeleine dans la mystique, les arts et les lettres*. Avignon, 1988, pp. 211-223.
1989, TOSCANO
Bruno Toscano. Entry for *St. Joseph's Workshop* by the "Serrone Master" in exhibition catalogue, *Pittura del Seicento. Ricerche in Umbria*. Spoleto, Rocca Albornoziana, July-September, pp. 165-170.
1990, PRAT
Véronique Prat. "Georges de La Tour: *Le tricheur*." *Le Figaro Magazine*, 13 October, pp. 107-123. (Contains important photodocumentation.)
1990, ROSENBERG
Pierre Rosenberg. "Un nouveau La Tour." *In Scritti in onore di Giuliano Briganti*. Milan: Longanesi & C, pp. 169-178.
1991, CHONÉ
Paulette Choné. *Emblèmes et pensée symbolique en Lorraine (1525-1633)*. Paris: Klincksieck. (See especially book 3, chapter 3, part 5, "L'empreinte emblématique dans la réforme des arts.")
1991, QUIGNARD
Pascal Quignard. *Georges de La Tour et Pascal Quignard*. Paris: Flohic.
1991, REINBOLD
Anne Reinbold. *Georges de La Tour*. Paris: Fayard.
1991, ROSENBERG, *Burl. Mag.*
Pierre Rosenberg. "An Unpublished Composition by Georges de La Tour." *Burlington Magazine* 117 (October), pp. 703-705.
1991, ROSENBERG, *Nouvelles acquisitions*
Pierre Rosenberg. Entry for *St. Thomas* in exhibition catalogue. *Paris 1991*.
1992, CARTER
Angela Carter. "L'ombre du silence. La Madeleine Wrightsman." *F. M. R.*, no. 36 (February), pp. 17-22.
1992, CHONÉ
Paulette Choné, *L'Atelier des nuits*. Nancy: Presses universitaires de Nancy.
1992, LACAU ST GUILY
Agnès Lacau St Guily. *La Tour, une lumière dans la nuit*. Mame.
1992, OTTANI CAVINA
Anna Ottani Cavina. "Donne e pulci." *La Repubblica*, 15 July, pp. 30-31. (Review of Nancy exhibition.)
1992, REINBOLD
Anne Reinbold. "Le peintre des nuits." *Beaux-Arts*, special issue, June, pp. 24-39.
1992, ROSENBERG
Pierre Rosenberg. "Georges de La Tour a-t-il livré son secret?" *Dossiers de l'Art*, no. 8, June-July, pp. 14-25. (See also *L'Objet d'art*, no. 260, July-August, pp. 30-41.)
1992, ROSENBERG
Pierre Rosenberg. Entries for La Tour in exhibition catalogue. *Nancy*, 1992.
1992, ROSENBERG-MOJANA
Pierre Rosenberg and Marina Mojana. *Georges de La Tour*. Paris: Bordas. Italian edition: Florence: Cantini.
1992, ROSENBERG-MOJANA
Pierre Rosenberg and Marina Mojana. *Georges de La Tour: catalogue complet des peintures*. Paris: Bordas.
1992, SYLVESTRE
Michel Sylvestre. "La vie quotidienne des artistes lorrains au XVIIe siècle." *Dossiers de l'Art*, no. 8, June-July, pp. 6-11.
1992, TRIBOUT DE MOREMBERT
Henri Tribout de Morembert. "Nouvelles Recherches sur Georges de La Tour." *Cahiers Lorrains*, n° 3-4, p. 475-487.
1993, BLANC
Caroline Blanc. *Regarde avec Georges La Tour* (sic). Tournai: Gamma Jeunesse (for children).
1993, CHONÉ
Paulette Choné. "À propos d'interprétations récentes des *Nuits* de Georges de La Tour." *Actes du colloque de Vic-sur-Seille*, 1989, p. 13-20.
1993, CONISBEE
Philip Conisbee. *Georges de La Tour's Repentant Magdalene*. Washington exhibition document, 1993.
1993, OKUYAMA
Catherine and Kimihito Okuyama. *Georges de La Tour*. Paris: Hazan.
1993, RAMADE
Patrick Ramade. "La Tour" catalogue entries, *Grand Siècle*. Montréal-Rennes-Montpellier, 1993, p. 106-107 and 198-205.
1993, REINBOLD, *colloque*
Conference directed by Anne Reinbold, *À la rencontre de Georges de La Tour; Actes du colloque de Vic-sur-Seille, 27 May 1989*. Conseil Général du Département de la Moselle, 1993.
1993, REINBOLD
Anne Reinbold. "La biographie de Georges de La Tour. Le fil d'une recherche." *Actes du colloque de Vic-sur-Seille, 1989*, p. 101-108.
1993, REINBOLD – RIOUX – MARTIN
Anne Reinbold, Jean-Paul Rioux and Elisabeth Martin. *Georges de La Tour ou Les chefs-d'œuvre révélés: les dossiers du Laboratoire de recherche des musées de France*. Exhibition catalogue. Metz: Serpenoise / Département de la Moselle.
1993, RODIS-LEWIS
Geneviève Rodis-Lewis. "Les Madeleines de Georges de La Tour." *Regards sur l'art*. Paris: Beauchesne, p. 70-84.
1993, ROSENBERG, *Nancy*
Pierre Rosenberg. "Notes sur l'art lorrain au XVIIe siècle (de Callot à Watteau, de La Tour à Saint-Aubin)." *Jacques Callot (1592-1635). Actes du colloque Jacques Callot*. Nancy-Paris, 25-27 June 1992; Paris, Klincksieck, p. 399-422.
1993, ROSENBERG, *Vic*
Pierre Rosenberg. "Un nouveau La Tour." *Actes du colloque de Vic-sur-Seille, 1989*, p. 7-12.
1993, SAUTER
Philippe Sauter. "*Saint Jérôme priant:* un vrai la Tour?" *L'Est républicain*, 11 September 1993.
1993, STILLER
Gabriel Stiller. "Un métier sévèrement contrôlé, dans le cadre de l'institution municipale à Vic, à la fin du XVIe siècle: les boulangers." *Actes du colloque de Vic-sur-Seille, 1989*, p. 77-96.
1993, SYLVESTRE
Michel Sylvestre. "La Tour de Vic à Lunéville." *Actes du colloque de Vic-sur-Seille, 1989*, p. 63-76.
1993, TAVENAUX
René Tavenaux. "La société vicoise au temps de Georges de La Tour." *Actes du colloque de Vic-sur-Seille, 1989*, p. 21-29.
1994, BAJOU
Thierry Bajou. "Hypothèses sur le séjour parisien de Georges de La Tour." *Georges de La Tour ou la nuit traversée. Actes du colloque de Vic-sur-Seille, 9-11 septembre 1993*, p. 71-82.
1994, BOYER
Jean-Claude Boyer. "Les Apôtres de Georges de La Tour de Paris à Albi." *Georges de La Tour ou la nuit traversée, Actes du colloque*

de Vic-sur-Seille, 9-11 septembre 1993, p. 59-69.
1994, BURY – BALTHAZAR
Pol Bury and André Balthazar. *Georges de La Tour: Le Tricheur.* Neuchâtel: Ides & Calendes.
1994, CHONÉ
Paulette Choné. "La lanterne et le flambeau." *Actes du colloque de Vic-sur-Seille, 9-11 septembre 1993*, p. 145-158.
1994, GALLEGO, *Iconografia*
Julián Gallego. "Sobre la iconografia de Georges de La Tour." Exhibition catalogue, *Madrid, 1994*, p. 33-45.
1994, GALLEGO, *Musicos...*
Julián Gallego. "Las zanfonas de La Tour." Exhibition catalogue, *Madrid, 1994*, p. 59-67.
1994, GRILLI
Cecilia Grilli. "Étude comparée entre l'*Atelier de saint Joseph* d'Everard Quirjinz Van der Maes, et l'*Atelier de saint Joseph* du Maître de Serrone." *Actes du Colloque de Vic-sur-Seille, 9-11 septembre 1993*, p. 99-102.
1994, LUNA
Juan J. Luna. "Georges de La Tour." Exhibition catalogue, *Madrid, 1994*, p. 15-31.
1994, MARTIN
Élisabeth Martin. "Dossiers scientifiques et repères chronologiques." *Actes du colloque de Vic-sur-Seille, 9-11 septembre 1993*, p. 17-27.
1994, MARTIN-REINBOLD
Élisabeth Martin and Anne Reinbold. "Hypothèse inédite à propos d'un *Vielleur* de La Tour." *Techné*, n° 1, p. 79-84.
1994, MÉROT
Alain Mérot. *La Peinture française au XVIIe siècle*, Paris, Gallimard-Electa (see especially p. 163-171).
1994, MORACCHINI
Pierre Moracchini. "Les cousins franciscains de Georges de La Tour." *Actes du colloque de Vic-sur-Seille, 9-11 septembre 1993*, p. 41-58.
1994, RAMADE
Patrick Ramade. "Le Nouveau-né de Rennes: mémoires d'une œuvre." *Actes du colloque de Vic-sur-Seille, 9-11 septembre 1993*, p. 121-132.
1994, REINBOLD, *colloque*
Conference directed by Anne Reinbold. *Georges de La Tour ou la nuit traversée, Actes du colloque de Vic-sur-Seille, 9-11 septembre 1993*, Conseil général de la Moselle. Metz: Serpenoise.
1994, REINBOLD
Anne Reinbold. "Examens en laboratoire et histoire de l'art." *Actes du colloque de Vic-sur-Seille, 9-11 septembre 1993*, p. 29-40.
1994, ROZE
Francine Roze. "Présentation d'une œuvre nouvelle du Musée Historique Lorrain: *Saint Jérôme lisant*." *Actes du colloque de Vic-sur-Seille, 9-11 septembre 1993*, p. 103-120.
1994, SYLVESTRE
Michel Sylvestre. "Arte, religión y cultura en Lorena en tiempos de Georges de La Tour." Exhibition catalogue, *Madrid, 1994*, p. 47-57.
1994, SYLVESTRE
Michel Sylvestre. "Le *Saint Jérôme lisant* du Musée Historique Lorrain et le duc Nicolas-François de Lorraine." *Pays Lorrain*, vol. 91, n° 3, p. 217-228.
1994, TOSCANO
Bruno Toscano. "*L'Atelier de saint Joseph* du Maître de Serrone." *Actes du colloque de Vic-sur-Seille, 9-11 septembre 1993*, p. 83-97.
1994, ZOLOTOV
Yuri Zolotov. "Le style de Georges de La Tour." *Actes du colloque de Vic-sur-Seille, 9-11 septembre 1993*, p. 159-171.

The discovery of "Saint John the Baptist in the Wilderness" (late 1993-early 1995)

1993, *Le Figaro*
Béatrice de Rochebouët. "La Tour ou pas La Tour." *Le Figaro*, 12 November 1993, p. 27.
1994, *Sotheby's Preview*
[Hugh Brigstocke]. "Saint John the Baptist". Entry in *Sotheby's Preview*, December 1994, p. 46-47.
1994, *Le Monde*
"Un trente-sixième 'de La Tour'?" *Le Monde*, 5 October 1994, p. 18.
1994, *Le Figaro*
Béatrice de Rochebouët. "Le marché français laisse échapper un La Tour." *Le Figaro*, 6 October 1994, p. 21.
1994, *Libération*
Vincent Noce. "Un 'Trésor national' vendu à Monaco." *Libération*, 7 October 1994, p. 34.
1994, BRIGSTOCKE
[Hugh Brigstocke]. "Saint Jean-Baptiste dans le désert." Catalogue entry for Sotheby's auction on 2 December 1994 in Monaco, *Importants Tableaux anciens et du XIXe siècle*, entry 39, p. 46-48.
1994, *Le Monde*
Catherine Bedel. "Un La Tour inédit." *Le Monde*, Saturday 26 November 1994.
1994, *Le Journal du dimanche*
Gilles Delafon. "Sotheby's et Christie's contre les Français." *Le Journal du dimanche*, 27 November 1994, p. 20.
1994, *Le Monde*
Harry Bellet. "La traversée du désert de saint Jean-Baptiste." *Le Monde*, 4-5 December 1994, p. 13.
1994, *Libération*
"Un tableau de Georges de La Tour en Moselle." *Libération*, 10-11 December 1994, p. 35.
1995, BRIGSTOCKE
Hugh Brigstocke. "George de La Tour's Saint John the Baptist". In Shop Talk: Studies in Honour of Seymour Slive. Cambridge, MA.
1995, CUZIN
Jean-Pierre Cuzin. "Un Georges de La Tour pour la Lorraine." *Revue du Louvre et des Musées de France*, vol. 43, n° 2, p. 5-6.
1995, LACAU St GUILY
Agnès Lacau St Guily. "*Saint Jean-Baptiste dans le désert*: le chef-d'œuvre inconnu de Georges de La Tour." *Le Pays lorrain*, vol. 76, n° 2, April-June 1995, p. 79-90.
1995, *Valeurs de l'art*
Armel Crex. "Mieux que le loto: l'expertise en tableaux." *Valeurs de l'art*, n° 29, February 1995, p. 35.
1995, LE FLOCH
Jean-Claude Le Floch. *Le signe de contradiction: essai sur Georges de La Tour et son œuvre.* Rennes: Presses universitaire de Rennes.
1995, *L'Objet d'art*
Laurent Thevenot, "Charade." *L'Objet d'art*, February 1995, p. 21.
1995, QUIGNARD
Pascal Quignard. *La nuit et le silence: Georges de La Tour.* Paris: Flohic.
1995, THUILLIER
Jacques Thuillier. *Saint Jean-Baptiste dans le désert*, with documentary appendix by Elisabeth Martin and Christiane Naffah, Metz, Serpenoise.
1995, WRIGHT
Christopher Wright. *The Masters of Candlelight: An Anthology of Great Masters Including Georges de La Tour, Godfried Schalcken, Joseph Wright of Derby.* Landshut: Arcos Verlag.
1996, CHONÉ
Paulette Choné. *Georges de La Tour: un peintre lorrain au XVIIe siècle.* Paris: Casterman.
1996, CONISBEE
Philip Conisbee. "An Introduction to the Life and Art of Georges de La Tour." Exhibition catalogue, *Washington-Fort Worth, 1996-1997*, p. 12-148.
1996, CONISBEE – CUZIN – BARRY
Philip Conisbee, Jean-Pierre Cuzin, Claire Barry, et al. *Georges de La Tour and his world*, catalogue d'exposition, Washington, National Gallery of Art.
1996, CUZIN
Jean-Pierre Cuzin. "La Tour Seen from the North: Observations on La Tour's Style and the Chronology of his Works." Exhibition catalogue, *Washington-Fort Worth, 1996-1997*, p. 182-197.
1996, FEIGENBAUM
Gail Feigenbaum. "Gamblers, Cheats and Fortune-Tellers." Exhibition catalogue, *Washington-Fort Worth, 1996-1997*, p. 149-181.
1996, GIFFORD – BARRY – BERRIE – PALMER
Melanie Gifford, Claire Barry, Barbara Berrie, Michael Palmer. "Some Observations on Georges de La Tour's Painting Practice." Exhibition catalogue, *Washington-Fort Worth, 1996-1997*, p. 238-257.
1996, GOODE
S. Goode. "An overdue exhibition of paintings by Georges de la Tour." *The Washington Times* 12, no. 40, pp. 36-37.
1996, MILLER
C. Miller. "The Changing Fortunes of Georges de La Tour." *Art & Antiques* 19, no. 11, pp. 48-57.
1996, BEHRE MISKIMIN
Patricia Behre Miskimin. "Lorraine in the Time of Georges de La Tour". Exhibition catalogue, *Washington-Fort Worth, 1996-1997*, p. 219-232.
1996, PILLSBURY
Edmund P. Pillsbury. "Condition and Quality." Exhibition catalogue, *Washington-Fort Worth, 1996-1997*, p. 232-237.
1996, SLATKES
Leonard J. Slatkes. "Georges de La Tour and the Netherlandish Followers of Caravaggio." Exhibition catalogue, *Washington-Fort Worth, 1996-1997*, p. 201-218.
1997, BEAUX-ARTS
"Georges de La Tour." Special issue, *Beaux arts magazine* (October), no. 161.
1997, BRÊME
Dominique Brême. *Georges de La Tour.* Paris: Somogy.
1997, BONFAIT – REINBOLD – SARRAZIN
Olivier Bonfait, Anne Reinbold and Béatrice Sarrazin. *L'ABCdaire de Georges de la Tour.* Paris: Flammarion.
1997, CUZIN – ROSENBERG
Jean-Pierre Cuzin and Pierre Rosenberg. *Georges de La Tour.* Exhibition catalogue. Paris: Réunion des musées nationaux.
1997, CUZIN – ROSENBERG – CHONÉ
Jean-Pierre Cuzin, Pierre Rosenberg, Paulette Choné, et al. "Georges de la Tour." Special issue, *Connaissance des arts* 112.
1997, CUZIN – SALMON
Jean-Pierre Cuzin and Dimitri Salmon. *Georges de La Tour, histoire d'une redécouverte.* Paris: Gallimard / Réunion des musées nationaux.
1997, FOHR
Robert Fohr. *Georges de La Tour: le maître des nuits.* Paris: Adam Biro / Metz: Serpenoise.
1997, GERMAIN
Sylvie Germain. "Solitudes de Madeleine: À l'occasion du rassemblement des cinq Madeleine de Georges de La Tour au Grand Palais, la romancière s'interroge sur le sens caché de ces images sublimes." *L'Œil* (Paris), no. 489, pp. 80-88.
1997, JOVER
M. Jover. "Beaux-arts: Mystère et silence Georges de La Tour," *Le Français dans le monde* (Paris: EDICEF), no. 292, p. 22.

1997, PÉTRY
Claude Pétry. *Georges de La Tour et les femmes*. Paris: Flammarion.
1997, RAILLARD
Georges Raillard. "Les visages de La Tour." *La Quinzaine littéraire* (Paris), October, no. 725.
1997, REINBOLD
Anne Reinbold. *Georges de La Tour*. Paris: Le Grand livre du mois.
1997, SCOTT
B. Scott. "Exhibitions, Rouen and Paris: Views of the work of two French painters, Jacques-Emile Blanche and Georges de La Tour." *Country life*, no. 51 and 52, pp. 56-57.
1997, WOLF
Laurent Wolf. "Georges de La Tour." *Études* 387, no. 7-12, pp. 549-552.
1998, CHONÉ
Paulette Choné. "La Tour, ancien peintre de Lorraine." *Le Pays Lorrain* (April-June), p. 104.
1998, CONISBEE
Philip Conisbee. "Georges de La Tour: the exhibition in Paris and other matters." *The Burlington magazine* 140 (March), pp. 201-205.
1998, CUZIN
Jean-Pierre Cuzin. "Après l'exposition La Tour." *La Revue du Louvre*, June 1998, pp. 54-60.
1998, DELPIERRE
Under the direction of Jean-Christophe Delpierre. *La Tour*. Beaux Arts special edition (Paris).
1998, MESNIL DE LA TOUR – CUZIN – MOINET
Georges du Mesnil de La Tour, Jean Pierre Cuzin, and Eric Moinet. *Le Saint-Sébastien soigné par Irène de Georges de La Tour*. Orléans: Musée des Beaux-Arts.
1999, CONISBEE, *Burl. Mag.*
Philip Conisbee. [*Le Saint Sébastien soigné par Irène*], *Burlington Magazine*, May 1999.
1999, FISCHER
C.O. Fischer, M. Gallagher, C. Laurenze, C. Schmidt, and K. Slusallek. "Digital imaging of autoradiographs from paintings by Georges de La Tour (1593-1652)." Lucerne, *Nuclear instruments & methods in physics research Section A* 424 (March), pp. 258-262.
1999, ROSENBERG
Under the direction of Pierre Rosenberg, text by Bruno Ferté. *Georges de La Tour*. Paris: Gallimard.
2000, CHOMER
Gilles Chomer. *Peintres français avant 1815: la collection du Musée de Grenoble*, Paris: RMN. Preface by Jacques Thuillier, pp. 13-17.
2000, HENRION
Jean Henrion. *Moi, Georges de La Tour, peintre fameux*. Paris: Apolline.
2000, BONFAIT – MACGREGOR
Olivier Bonfait and Neil MacGregor. *Le Dieu caché: les peintres du Grand Siècle et la vision de Dieu*. Exhibition catalogue. Rome: Académie de France.
2000, MALGOUYRES
Philippe Malgouyres. *Peintures françaises du XVIIe siècle: la collection du musée des Beaux-Arts de Rouen*, Musée des beaux-arts de Rouen and Somogy.
2000, LAVIN – SEIDEL
Irving Lavin. "Georges de La Tour. The Tears of St. Peter and the 'Occult' Light of Penitence," in *L'Europa e l'arte italiana*, ed. Max Seidel. Venice: Marsilio Editori, pp. 352-75.
2001, JUDOVITZ
Dalia Judovitz. "Spiritual Passion and the Betrayal of Painting in Georges de la Tour." *Representing Emotions: new connections in the histories of art, music and medicine*, *Congress Representing Emotions: evidence, arousal, analysis*, University of Manchester. Aldershot: Ashgate, May 2001, pp. 109-122.
2003, ASTRUA – BAVA – SPANTIGATI
Paola Astrua, Anna Maria Bava, and Carla Enrica Spantigati. *La buona ventura di Georges de la Tour e aspetti del caravaggismo nordico in Piemonte*. Milan: Electa.
2003, MCCLINTOCK
Stuart McClintock. "The iconography and iconology of Georges de la Tour's religious paintings, 1624-1650." *Studies in Art and Religious Interpretation* 31.
2004, CUZIN – SALMON
Jean-Pierre Cuzin and Dimitri Salmon. *Georges de La Tour: histoire d'une redécouverte*. Paris: Réunion des musées nationaux / Gallimard.
2004, GERMAIN
Sylvie Germain. *Ateliers de lumière: Piero della Francesca, Johannes Vermeer, Georges de La Tour*. Paris: Desclée de Brouwer.
2004, MARCADÉ
Isabelle Marcadé. *Le Nouveau-né de Georges de La Tour*. Paris: Scala / SCÉRÉN-CNDP.
2004, REINBOLD – BOYER – MARTIN
Anne Reinbold, Jean-Claude Boyer, Élisabeth Martin, et al. *Les Apôtres de Georges de La Tour: réalités et virtualités*. Paris: Hermann / Albi: musée Toulouse-Lautrec.
2005, AITKEN
Geneviève Aitken, et al. "Multimedia franco-japonais. *Les Apôtres* de Georges de La Tour", *14e rencontre triennale de l'ICOM à La Hague, 12-16 septembre*, London: James & James / Earthscan.
2005, CUZIN – TAKAHASHI
Jean-Pierre Cuzin and Akiya Takahashi. *Georges de La Tour*. Tokyo: The National Museum of Western Art / Yomiuri Shimbun.
2005, MARCHETTI – GIORGI – ZUFFI
Francesca Castria Marchetti, Rosa Giorgi, and Stefano Zuffi. *L'Art classique et baroque: 1600-1770, l'art en Europe de Caravage à Tiepolo*. Paris: Gründ.
2005, QUIGNARD
Pascal Quignard. *Georges de La Tour*. Paris: Galilée.
2005, STORK – SAID – APOSTOLOPOULOS
David G. Stork, Amir Said, and John G. Apostolopoulos. "Did Georges de la Tour use optical projections while painting Christ in the Carpenter's Studio?" *Proceeding of SPIE* (San Jose) 5685, part. 1, pp. 214-219.
2007, WRIGHT
Christopher Wright. *Georges de La Tour: master of candlelight*. Warwickshire: Compton Verney.
2008, STORK – FURUICHI
David G. Stork and Yasuo Furuichi. "Image analysis of paintings by computer graphics synthesis: An investigation of the illumination in Georges de la Tour's *Christ in the Carpenter's Studio*." *SPIE Electronic imaging: Computer image analysis in the study of art*, Bellingham: IS&T / Springfield: SPIE, January, vol. 6810 0J.
2009, BUSSAGLI – REICHE
Marco Bussagli and Mattia Reiche. *Baroque & Rococo*. New York: Sterling Publishing.
2009, CONISBEE – RAND – BAILLIO
Philip Conisbee, Richard Rand, Joseph Baillio, et al. *French paintings of the fifteenth through the eighteenth century*. Washington: National Gallery of Art / Princeton: Princeton University Press.
2010, CUZIN
Jean-Pierre Cuzin. *Figures de la réalité: caravagesques français, Georges de La Tour, les frères Le Nain*. Paris: Hazan / Institut national d'histoire de l'art.
2011, BEAUSSANT
Philippe Beaussant. *Georges de La Tour: Le Vielleur au chien*. Ennetières-en-Weppes: Invenit.
2011, MERLINI – SALMON – STORTI
Under the direction of Valeria Merlini, Dimitri Salmon and Daniela Storti. *Georges de La Tour: The Adoration of the Shepherds Christ with St. Joseph in the Carpenter's Shop*. Milan: Skira.

BIBLIOGRAPHY: EXHIBITION CATALOGUES

1931, PARIS
Exposition des chefs-d'œuvre des musées de province. École française. XVIIe et XVIIIe siècles. Musée de l'Orangerie. April-May.

1932, LONDON
Exhibition of French Art 1200-1900. Royal Academy of Arts. Introductions by Paul Léon and W. G. Constable.

1933, PARIS
Les achats du musée du Louvre et les dons de la Société des Amis du Louvre. 1922-1932. Musée de l'Orangerie. Introduction by Henri Verne.

1934, PARIS, Orangerie
Les peintres de la réalité en France au XVIIe siècle. Musée de l'Orangerie. November 1934-February 1935. Éd. des musées nationaux. Preface by Paul Jamot. Introduction by Charles Sterling. Entries by Charles Sterling. (See also 3d revised edition.)

1935, BRUSSELS
Cinq siècles d'art. Mémorial de l'Exposition. Vol. 2.

1935, PARIS
Les chefs-d'œuvre du musée de Grenoble. Petit Palais. Preface by Jean Robiquet. Catalogue by Germaine Barnaud.

1936, NEW YORK
Loan Exhibition of Paintings by G. de La Tour, Antoine, Louis, Mathieu Le Nain. Held for the benefit of the Musée de Blérancourt, France, and the Lycée Français de New York. Gallery Knœdler. Entries by L. Carré. Introduction by P. Jamot.

1936, PARIS
Portrait Français de 1400 à 1900. Res. André J. Seligmann. 9 June-1 July. Preface by Claude Roger-Marx.

1938, TORONTO
Portraits of Women. Toronto Art Gallery.

1939, SAN FRANCISCO, International Exposition
Masterworks of Five Centuries. Golden Gate International Exposition.

1939, SAN FRANCISCO, Seven Centuries
Seven Centuries of Painting. A Loan Exhibition of Old and Modern Masters. California Palace of the Legion of Honor and M. H. de Young Memorial Museum. 29 December 1939-28 January 1940.

1940, HARTFORD
Night Scenes. Wadworth Atheneum. 15 February-7 March.

1941, DETROIT
Masterpieces of Art from European and American Collections. Detroit Institute of Arts. 1 April-31 May. Entries by Francis Waring Robinson and E. P. Richardson.

1944, RIMSWELL
Exhibition of Pictures. Bishopton Road, Fairfield, 19-26 August.

1946, LONDON
The King's Pictures. Royal Academy of Arts. Preface by Alfred J. Munnings. Entries for French paintings by Anthony Blunt.

1946, NEW YORK
A Loan Exhibition of French Paintings of the Time of Louis XIII and Louis XIV. For the benefit of the Caen Library Fund. Wildenstein Gallery. 9 May-1 June. Preface, "French Painting of the Time of Louis XIII," by Charles Sterling. Discourse on the "Grande Manière," by Walter Friedlaender.

1946, PARIS, Galliera
Peintures méconnues des églises de Paris retour d'évacuation. Musée Galliera. Preface by Y. Bizardel. Introduction by Jean Verrier.

1946, PARIS, Petit Palais
Chefs-d'œuvre de la peinture française au Louvre. Des primitifs à Manet. Petit Palais.

1946, ZURICH
Le Musée et la Bibliothèque de Grenoble. Kunsthaus.

1947, LONDON
A Loan Exhibition of French Paintings of the 16th Century, in aid of the Merchant Navy Comforts Services. Wildenstein & Co, 20 June-31 July. Preface and entries by Denys Sutton.

1948, PARIS
Chefs-d'œuvre de l'art alsacien et de l'art lorrain. Musée des Arts Décoratifs. Pavillon de Marsan. October-November.

1949, GENEVA
Trois siècles de peinture française: XVIe-XVIIIe siècles. Choix d'œuvres des musées de France. Musée Rath. 11 July-16 October. Entries for seventeenth century by Clément-Paul Duprat.

1950, HOUSTON
Seventeenth-Century Masters of Painting. Museum of Fine Arts.

1950, PARIS, Charpentier
Cent portraits de femmes, du XVe siècle à nos jours. Galerie Charpentier. Preface by Henry de Montherlant.

1950, PARIS, Petit Palais
La Vierge dans l'art français. Petit Palais. Prefaces by Pierre de Gaulle, André Chamson, Jean Verrier, Jacques Dupont.

1950, RENNES
Les chefs-d'œuvre du musée des Beaux-Arts de Rennes. Hôtel de Ville.

1951, MILAN
Mostra del Caravaggio e dei Caravaggeschi. Palazzo Reale. April-June. Introduction by Roberto Longhi.

1951, PARIS, Galliera
La chirurgie dans l'art français. Palais Galliera. No catalogue.

1951, PARIS, Petit Palais
Chefs-d'œuvre des musées de Berlin. Petit Palais. Exhibition of Berlin collections, traveling since 1948; previously shown in Washington, New York, Philadelphia, Chicago, Boston, Munich, Wiesbaden, Amsterdam (catalogue in Dutch), and Brussels.

1951, PITTSBURGH
French Painting 1100-1900. Carnegie Institute, Department of Fine Arts. 18 October-2 December.

1952, HAMBURG – MUNICH
Französische Malerei von Poussin bis Ingres. Hamburg. October-December 1952; Munich, December 1952-February 1953.

1952, PARIS
Cent tableaux d'art religieux du XIVe siècle à nos jours. Galerie Charpentier. 1952-1953. Preface by Paul Claudel.

1952, SAÕ PAULO
O Retrato na França. Museu de Arte.

1953, BRUSSELS
La femme dans l'art français. Palais des Beaux-Arts. March-May.

1953, LONDON
17th- and 18th-Century French Masters. University of Western Ontario. 14 February-14 March.

1953, NEW ORLEANS
A Loan Exhibition of Masterpieces of French Painting through Five Centuries. 1400-1900. In Honor of the 15th Anniversary of the Louisiana Purchase. Isaac Delgado Museum of Art. 14 October 1953-10 January 1954.

1954, TOKYO
Exposition d'art français au Japon. 1954-1955. (Catalogue in Japanese.)

1954, PITTSBURGH
Pictures of Everyday Life Genre Painting in Europe. 1500-1900. Department of Fine Arts, Carnegie Institute. 14 October-12 December. Introduction by Gordon Bailey Washburn.

1955, BORDEAUX
L'âge d'or espagnol. La peinture en Espagne et en France autour du Caravagisme. 16 May-31 July. Catalogue by Gilberte Martin-Méry.

1955, PARIS, Heim
Caravage et les peintres français du XVIIe siècle. Exhibition organized for the *Société des Amis du Louvre.* Galerie Heim.

1956, PORTLAND
Painting from the Collection of Walter P. Chrysler, Jr. Exhibition organized by the Portland Art Museum. Also presented in Seattle, San Francisco, Los Angeles, Minneapolis, Saint Louis, Kansas City, Detroit, and Boston.

1956, ROME
Il Seicento Europeo – Realismo. Classicismo. Barocco. Palazzo delle Esposizioni. December 1956-January 1957. De Luca ed. Texts by Lionello Venturi, Luigi Salerno, Gerard Knuttel, Paul Fierens, Charles Sterling (*"La pittura francese del XVII secolo"*), Valentino Martinelli. Entries on French paintings by Charles Sterling.

1956, ZURICH
Unbekannte Schönheit. Bedeutende Werke aus fünf Jahrhunderten. Kunsthaus. 9 June-end July.

1957, GENEVA
Art et travail. Exhibition organized by the International Labor Organization and the City of Geneva in commemoration of the 25th anniversary of the death of Albert Thomas: Musée d'Art et d'Histoire. 14-22 September.

1957, PARIS
Besançon, le plus ancien musée de France. Musée des Arts décoratifs. February-April. Catalogue by M.-L. Cornillot.

1958, CHARLEROI
Art et travail. Palais des Beaux-Arts.

1958, LONDON
The Age of Louis XIV. Winter Exhibition, Royal Academy of Arts. Foreword by J. Vergnet-Ruiz. Introduction by Anthony Blunt. Catalogue by Michel Laclotte.

1958, PARIS
Le XVIIe siècle français. Chefs-d'œuvre des musées de province. Petit Palais. March. Preface by André Chamson. Introduction by Jean Vergnet-Ruiz. Catalogue by Michel Laclotte.

1958, STOCKHOLM
Fem Sekler Fransk Konst. Miniatyrer. Malningar. Teckningar. 1400-1900. National-museum.

15 August-9 November. Entries by Pontus Grate and Per Bjurström. Separate album of reproductions.

1959, BERN
Das 17. Jahrhundert in der französischen Malerei. Kunstmuseum. February-March. Introduction and catalogue by Boris Lossky, with the assistance of J. M. Girard and E. Althaus.

1959, BORDEAUX
La découverte de la lumière des Primitifs aux Impressionnistes. 20 May-31 July. Catalogue by Gilberte Martin-Méry.

1960, WASHINGTON – TOLEDO – NEW YORK
The Splendid Century, French Art: 1600-1715. National Gallery of Art, Washington; Toledo Museum of Art, Metropolitan Museum of Art. 1960-1961. Introduction by Theodore Rousseau Jr.; catalogue by Michel Laclotte.

1961-1962, CANADA
Héritage de France. French Paintings 1610-1760. Montreal Museum of Fine Arts, 6 October-6 November; Musée de la province de Québec, 16 November-16 December 1961; National Gallery of Canada, 4 January-4 February 1962; Art Gallery of Toronto, 16 February-18 March. Preface by Linda Murray.

1962, FORT WORTH
1550-1650. A Century of Masters from the Collection of Walter P. Chrysler Jr. Fort Worth Art Center. Catalogue by Bertina Suida Manning.

1962, NEW YORK, Wildenstein, Masters
Loan Exhibition. Masters of Seven Centuries. Paintings and Drawings from the 14th to the 20th Century. 1-31 March. Wildenstein Gallery.

1962, NEW YORK, Wildenstein, The Painter
The Painter as Historian. Mythological, Religious, Secular Paintings of the 15th to 19th Century. 15 November-31 December. Wildenstein Gallery.

1964, MUSÉES NATIONAUX
La société française du XVIIe et du XVIIIe siècle vue par les peintres et les graveurs. Traveling exhibition organized by Service éducatif des musées. Catalogue, Paris: Éd. des musées nationaux. Entries by S. Savanne and M.-Th. Zuber.

1964, SAN FRANCISCO
Man: Glory, Jest and Riddle. A Survey of the Human Form through the Ages. California Palace of the Legion of Honor. 10 November 1964-3 January 1965.

1965, MONTRÉAL
L'art et les saints. Images of the Saints. Musée des Beaux-Arts de Montréal. 5 March-4 April. Catalogue by Edward P. Lawson.

1966, TOKYO
The "Great Century" in the French Collections in Tokyo (in Japanese).

1966, PARIS
Dans la lumière de Vermeer. Cinq siècles de peinture. 24 September-28 November. Preface by René Huyghe. Introduction by A. B. de Vries.

1967, CARACAS
Grandes Maestros. Museo de Bellas Artes de Caracas. 5 November-17 December.

1967, MONTRÉAL
Terre des Hommes. Exposition internationale des Beaux-Arts. Expo 67.

1967, NEW YORK
A Loan Exhibition. Vouet to Rigaud. French Masters of the Seventeenth Century. Finch College Museum of Art. 20 April-18 June.

1967, PARIS, Archives
Lorraine, marche de France. Archives de France. Hôtel de Rohan, January-March.

1967, PARIS, Orangerie
Vingt ans d'acquisitions au musée du Louvre 1947-1967. Orangerie des Tuileries. December 1967-May 1968.

1967-1968, CALIFORNIA
French Paintings from French Museums XVIIth-XVIIIth Centuries. Fine Arts Gallery of San Diego, 29 September-5 November 1967; California Palace of the Legion of Honor, 17 November-1 January 1968; E. B. Crocker Art Gallery, 19 January-25 February 1968; Santa Barbara Museum of Art, 15 March-28 April 1968. Preface by Michel Laclotte.

1968, MONTRÉAL
Trésors du musée de Besançon. July-September.

1968, VIENNA
Jacques Callot und sein Kreis. Graphische Sammlung Albertina, 211. 17 December 1968-2 March 1969. Introduction and catalogue by Eckhart Knab.

1969-1970, FLORIDA
The Age of Louis XIII. Cummer Gallery of Art, Jacksonville, 29 October-7 December 1969; Museum of Fine Arts, Saint Petersburg, 5 January-8 February 1970.

1971, CLEVELAND
Caravaggio and His Followers. Cleveland Museum of Art, autumn 1971. Preface, introduction, and catalogue by Richard E. Spear.

1971, NEW YORK
The Painter's Light. Metropolitan Museum of Art, 5 October-10 November. Catalogue by John Walsh Jr.

1971, VENCE – PARIS
Exhibition René Char. Fondation Maeght, Vence; Musée d'Art Moderne de la Ville de Paris. Foreword by Jacques Dupin. Texts by Pierre Granville, Jacques Dupin, Georges Blin, Dora Vallier.

1972, PARIS
Georges de La Tour. Orangerie des Tuileries. May-September. Foreword by Pierre Landry, catalogue by Pierre Rosenberg and Jacques Thuillier. (See also 2d revised edition.)

1973, LONDON
Treasures from the European Community. Victoria and Albert Museum. January-February.

1976 TOKYO – KYOTO
Masterpieces of World Art from American Museums. National Museum of Western Art, Tokyo; Kyoto National Museum.

1976-1977, NICE – RENNES
30 peintres du XVIIe siècle français. Tableaux d'inspiration religieuse des musées de province. Musée National Message Biblique Marc Chagall, Nice, July-September 1976; Musée des Beaux-Arts, Rennes, October 1976-January 1977. Catalogue by François Bergot, Pierre Provoyeur, and Jacques Vilain. Preface by Jacques Thuillier.

1978-1979, DENVER – NEW YORK – MINNEAPOLIS
Masterpieces of French Art, The Fine Arts Museums of San Francisco (checklist); Denver Art Museum; Wildenstein Gallery, New York; Minneapolis Institute of Arts.

1980, BERLIN
Bilder vom Menschen in der Kunst des Abendlandes. Staatliche Museen Preussicher Kulturbesitz.

1980-1981, PARIS
L'instrument de musique populaire. Usages et symboles. Musée des Arts et Traditions Populaires.

1982, PARIS – NEW YORK – CHICAGO
La peinture française du XVIIe siècle dans les collections américaines. Grand Palais, Paris, January-April 1982; Metropolitan Museum of Art, New York, May-August 1982; Chicago Art Institute, September-November 1982. Catalogue by Pierre Rosenberg. Introduction by Marc Fumaroli.

1985, BOURG-EN-BRESSE
La vielle en Bresse. Musée de l'Ain.

1985-1986, LEICESTER
Masterpieces of Reality. French 17th Century Painting. Leicestershire Museum and Art Gallery. October 1985-February 1986. Catalogue by Christopher Wright.

1986, FLORENCE
La Maddalena tra Sacro e Profano. Da Giotto a Chirico. Centro Mostre, Palazzo Pitti. May-September 1986.

1986-1987, FRANKFURT
Französische Malerei des 17. und 18. Jahrhunderts aus dem Louvre. Städelsches Kunstinstitut. October 1986-March 1987. Catalogue by Sylvain Laveissière, Catherine Sahut, and Stéphane Loire.

1987, VIENNA
Georges de La Tour bei der Wahrsagerin. Kunsthistorisches Museum. February-May. Das Meisterwerk, no. 6, special issue. Text by Wolfgang Prohaska.

1988, FONTAINE-DE-VAUCLUSE
Marie Madeleine. Musée Pétrarque. Summer. Text by Odile Delenda.

1989, PARIS
Maîtres français 1550-1800. Dessins de la donation Mathias Polakovits à l'École des Beaux-Arts. École Nationale Supérieure des Beaux-Arts. Entry on La Tour by Christopher Comer.

1991, PARIS
Musée du Louvre. Nouvelles acquisitions du département des peintures (1987-1990). Musée du Louvre. Entry on St. Thomas by Pierre Rosenberg.

1992, NANCY
L'art en Lorraine au temps de Jacques Callot. Musée des Beaux-Arts. June-September. Entries on La Tour by Pierre Rosenberg.

1992, PARIS
Hommage à Charles Sterling. Des primitifs à Matisse. Musée du Louvre. Dossiers du Département des peintures, no. 40, April-June. (See in particular the interviews with Charles Sterling by Michel Laclotte, p. 52 ff.)

1993, LUNÉVILLE
Un saint Sébastien dans une nuit, Lunéville, musée du Château, 26 June-27 September 1993. Exhibition organised by Pierre Chanel. *Petit Journal* with entries by Pierre Chanel, Paulette Choné, Brigitte Heckel, René Taveneaux, Jacques Thuillier.

1993, MONTRÉAL – RENNES – MONTPELLIER
Grand Siècle. Peintures françaises du XVIIe siècle dans les collections publiques françaises, Montréal, musée des Beaux-Arts, 21 January-28 March 1993; Rennes, musée des Beaux-Arts, 14 April-20 June 1993; Montpellier, musée Fabre, 1 July-5 September 1993. Catalogue by Michel Hilaire and Patrick Ramade.

1993, VIC-SUR-SEILLE
Georges de La Tour ou les chefs-d'œuvre révélés, Vic-sur-Seille, 3 September-14 November 1993. Catalogue with entries by Élisabeth Martin, Anne Reinbold and Jean-Paul Rioux, with documentary appendix by

the Laboratoire de recherche des musées de France.
1993, WASHINGTON
Georges de La Tour's Repentant Magdalene, Washington, National Gallery of Art, 25 April-6 September 1993. Catalogue by Philip Conisbee.
1994, MADRID
Los músicos de Georges de La Tour (1593-1652), Madrid, Museo del Prado, 8 June-7 August 1994. Catalogue by Juan J. Luna.
1996, METZ
Pietà de Lorraine: autour de Georges de La Tour: les Vierges de pitié du XVe au XVIIIe siècle. Exhibition catalogue. Metz: Serpenoise.
1996-1997, WASHINGTON – FORT WORTH
Georges de La Tour and his World. Washington, National Gallery of Art, 6 October 1996-5 January 1997; Fort Worth, Kimbell Art Museum, 2 February-11 May 1997. Catalogue by Philip Conisbee.
1997-1998, PARIS
Georges de La Tour. Paris, Galeries nationales du Grand Palais. 3 October 1997-26 January 1998. Catalogue by Jean-Pierre Cuzin and Pierre Rosenberg. Introduction by Jacques Thuillier.
1998, ORLÉANS
Le Saint Sébastien soigné par Irène de Georges de La Tour. Orléans, musée des Beaux-Arts, March-April 1998. Catalogue with essays by Éric Moinet, Jean Pierre Cuzin, Élisabeth Martin and Claire Barry.
2000, BERGAMO
La luce del vero: Caravaggio, La Tour, Rembrandt, Zurbaran. Galleria d'Arte Moderna e contemporanea. 10 September-17 December.
2000–2001, ROME
Le Dieu caché: les peintres du Grand Siècle et la vision de Dieu. Rome, Académie de France. Catalogue by Olivier Bonfait et Neil MacGregor.
2004, ALBI
Les Apôtres de Georges de La Tour: réalités et virtualités. Albi, Musée Toulouse-Lautrec. 24 April–20 June. Catalogue by Anne Reinbold, Jean-Claude Boyer, Élisabeth Martin, et al.
2005, TOKYO
Georges de La Tour. Tokyo, National Museum of Western Art. 8 March-29 May. Catalogue by Jean-Pierre Cuzin and Akiya Takahashi.
2011–2012, MILAN
Georges de La Tour: The Adoration of the Shepherds and Christ with St. Joseph in the Carpenter's Shop. Milan, Palazzo Marino. 26 November 2011-8 January 2012. Catalogue by Valeria Merlini, Dimitri Salmon, and Daniela Storti.

INDEX OF PROPER NAMES

Numbers in italics refer to pages where illustrations appear.

INDEX OF LA TOUR'S WORKS

Numbers in italics refer to pages where illustrations appear.

PHOTOGRAPHIC CREDITS

ALBI, Jean-Marie Bruneau: 34, 47, 52, 53, 56, 57, 205.

AMSTERDAM, Rijksmuseum-Stichting: 76.

ANTELLA (Florence), Scala: 72, 118, 119, 132, 152, 172, 174, 175, 188, 196, 204, 210, 228.

BASEL, Offentliche Kunstsammlung, Kunstmuseum: 64, 65.

BERLIN, Jörg P.Anders: 225; Staatliche Museen: 73, 74, 75, 225.

BESANÇON, Musée des Beaux-Arts: 134.

BRUSSELS, Musée des Beaux-Arts: 62.

CHATSWORTH, The Trustees of the Chatsworth Settlement: 36, 37, 78.

CISANO SUL NEVA (Savona), coll. Marquis R. del Carretto: 216.

CLEVELAND, Museum of Art (Hanna Fund): 201.

COLOGNE, Wallraf Richartz Museum: 204.

DETROIT, Institute of Arts: 217.

DIJON, Déclic/Thierry de Girval: 173.

DRESDEN, Gemäldegalerie: 135, 172.

DUBLIN, National Gallery of Ireland: 218.

ÉPINAL, Musée Départemental: 227.

FORT WORTH, Texas, Michael Bodycomb: 77, 134.

GRENOBLE, André Morin: 124, 125, 126, 127.

HAARLEM, Teyler Museum: 11. HARTFORD (Conn.), Wadworth Atheneum: 168.

KANSAS CITY, William Rockhill Nelson Gallery of Arts: 176.

KRAKOW, Wawel Castle: 64

LEICESTER, Leicestershire Museums: 237.

LE MANS, Musée Tessé: 168.

LONDON, British Museum: 96, 97; Hampton Court Palace, collection of Her Majesty, the Queen: 59; Matthiesen Gallery: 190; National Gallery: 118. Walpole Gallery: 54.

MADRID, Prado Museum: 82.

MALIBU, Cal., The J. Paul Getty Museum: 65, 67, 68, 69, 70, 71.

MELBOURNE, National Gallery of Victoria: 176.

MIDDLESBROUGH, (England) Museum and Art Gallery: 236.

MUNICH, Blauel/Gnamm-Artothek: 10, 154.

NANCY, Municipal Archives: 43, 219; Gilbert Mangin: 48, 49, 197, 198, 199, 220; Musée Lorrain: 86.

NANTES, A.Guillard: 89, 90, 91, 92, 93, 192, 195, 230, 232, 233; H. Maertens: 191, 229: Musée des Beaux-Arts: 88.

NEW YORK, Frick Collection: 39: The Metropolitan Museum of Art (Rogers Fund): 137, 142-147, 159, 160, 161.

NORFOLK, Va., Chrysler Museum: 47, 55.

OBERLIN, Ohio, John Seyfried: 174.

OXFORD, Ashmolean Museum: 82.

PARIS, Alinari-Giraudon: 116; Artephot/A. Held: 117; Bibliothèque Nationale: 24, 25, 58, 60, 96, 99, 101, 124, 132, 133, 136, 153, 169, 171; Bulloz: 152; Collège de France: 45, 48, 49, 58, 64, 76, 88, 97, 98, 110, 111, 117, 124, 134, 136, 158, 174, 188, 203, 211, 218, 223, 224; Giraudon: 17, 24, 25, 78; Giraudon-Flammarion: 84, 85; RMN: 25, 39, 61, 78, 94, 121, 122, 123, 135, 148, 149, 150, 151, 205, 223. RMN-M. Bellot: 12, 13; RMN-H Lewandoswski: 163, 166, 167, 189, 192, 194, 205, 206, 207, 208, 297.

REMIREMONT, Musée Charles Friry: 86.

RENNES, Musée des Beaux-Arts: 211, 229.

ROUEN, Musée des Beaux-Arts: 175.

ST. PETERSBURG, Hermitage Museum: 124.

SALZBOURG, Residenzgalerie: 175.

SAN FRANCISCO, The Fine Arts Museum: 79, 80, 134, 135: De Young Memorial Oakes: 76, 77, 79, 80, 81.

SPOLETE, Archivio Coo.be.c: 29, 31, 33.

STOCKHOLM, National Museum: 120, 130, 131.

UTRECHT, Centraal Museum: 116.

VIENNA, Kunsthistorisches Museum: 60.

WARSAW, National Museum: 72, 172, 226, 234.

WASHINGTON, National Gallery of Art (Alison Mellon Bruce Fund): 39, 155, 157.

WELLESLEY, Mass., Jewett Arts Center, Herbert P. Vose: 124.

VIC-SUR-SEILLE, Municipal Archives: 15.

JACKET: New York, The Metropolitan Museum of Art (Rogers Fund), Albi. Jean-Marie Bruneau.

MAPS: Philippe Rekacewicz.